1998 EDITION

INTERNATIONAL AWARD WINNING
HARRIS REFERENCE
CATALOG

POSTAGE STAMP PRICES

of the

UNITED STATES
UNITED NATIONS
CANADA & PROVINCES

Plus: Confederate States, U.S. Possessions, U.S. Trust Territories, Albums and Accessories, Comprehensive U.S. Stamp Identifier

H.E. Harris & Co.®

Founded in 1916
Florence, AL 35631

Stock No. 1HRS71
ISBN 0-937458-62-7

ABOUT OUR CATALOG PRICES

The prices quoted in this catalog are the prices for which H.E. Harris offers stamps for retail sale at the time of publication.

These prices are based on current market values as researched by our staff, but, more importantly, on our day-to-day buying and selling activities in the stamp market.

Although you may certainly use this catalog as a guide to current market prices, you must keep in mind the fact that prices can change in response to varying levels of collector demand, or dealer promotions, special purchases, etc. We are not responsible for typographical errors.

You should also remember that condition is always the key factor in determining the value and price of a given stamp or set of stamps. Unlike some other stamp catalogs, we price U.S. stamps issued up to 1935 in three different condition grades for mint stamps, and three grades for used copies. For these earlier issues, we have also shown the percentage premium that would apply to Never Hinged Mint copies.

Our illustrated definitions of condition grades are presented on pages C1-C7.

We have not found it possible to keep every stamp in stock that is listed in this catalog, and we cannot guarantee that we can supply all of the stamps in all conditions that are listed.

However, we will search for any stamp in any condition that a customer may want if that stamp is not in our stock at the time the customer places an order for it.

INDEX

UNITED STATES STAMPS

UNITED STATES RELATED AREAS

UNITED NATIONS

CANADA & PROVINCES

OTHER FEATURES

A GUIDE FOR COLLECTORS

In this section we will attempt to define and explain some of the terms commonly used by stamp collectors. Instead of listing the terms in an alphabetical dictionary or glossary format, we have integrated them. In this way, you can see how an individual term fits within the total picture.

PRODUCTION

The manufacture of stamps involves a number of procedures. We will discuss the major steps here, with emphasis on their implications for stamp collectors. Although we present them separately, modern printing presses may combine one or more operations so that the steps tend to blend together. There also are steps in the process that we do not cover here. While they may be important to the production process, their direct implications for most collectors are minimal.

PLATE MAKING

Before anything can be printed, a printing plate must be made. Using the intaglio printing process (which is explained under **printing**) as an example, the steps involved in plate production are as follows:

- A **master die** is made. The design is recess engraved in a reverse mirror-image. Most master dies consist of only one impression of the design.
- The next step is to prepare a **transfer roll**. The soft steel of the transfer roll is rocked back and forth under pressure against the hardened master die and a series of multiple impressions, called **reliefs**, are created in the transfer roll. Note that the impression on the transfer roll will be raised above the surface, since the roll was pressed into the recesses of the master die.
- Once the transfer roll has been made and hardened, it is used to impress designs in to the soft steel of a **printing plate** that can fit up to 400 impressions of small, definitive-sized stamps or 200 impressions of large, commemorative-sized stamps. This time, the raised design on the transfer roll impresses a recessed design into the plate.

The process is much more complex than this, but these are the basics. Once the printing plate is hardened, it is almost ready to be used to create printed sheets of stamps. Depending on the printing equipment to be used, the printing plate will be shaped to fit around a cylinder for rotary press printing or remain flat for flat-bed press printing. In either form, the plate is then hardened and is ready for use in printing.

DESIGN VARIETIES

The complexity of the platemaking process can result in major or minor flaws. The inspection process will catch most of these flaws, but those that escape detection will result in **plate varieties**.

The early United States Classic issues have been examined in minute detail over the decades. Through **plating** studies, minor differences in individual stamps have been used to identify the position on the printing plate of each design variety. Sometimes called **"flyspeck philately"** because it involves the detection of minute "flyspeck" differences, such plating work has resulted in the identification of some of our greatest rarities. Compare the prices for the one cent blue issues of 1851 and 1857 (#s 5-9 and 18-24) and you will see the tremendous dollar difference that can result from minute design variations. (The Harris Stamp Identifier in this catalog explains the design differences.)

During the plate making or subsequent printing process, plate flaws that are detected will be corrected, sometimes incompletely or incorrectly. Corrections or revisions in an individual die impression or in all plate impressions include the following:

- **Retouching**—minor corrections made in a plate to repair damage or wear.
- **Recutting** or **re-engraving**—similar to, but more extensive than, retouching. Recutting usually applies to changes made before a plate has been hardened, while re-engraving is performed on a plate that has had to be tempered (softened) after hardening.
- **Redrawing**—the intentional creation of a slightly different design. The insertion of secret marks on the National Bank Notes plates when they were turned over to the Continental Bank Note Company in 1873 can be considered redrawings.
- **Reentry**—the reapplication of a design from a transfer roll to the plate, usually to improve a worn plate. If the reentry is not done completely, or if it is not done precisely on top of the previous design, a double transfer will result. Such double transfers will show on the printed stamp as an extra line at one or more points on the stamp.

Other design varieties may result from undetected plate flaws. A **plate crack** (caused by the hardened plate cracking under wear or pressure) or a **plate scratch** (caused by an object cutting into the plate) will show as an ink line on the printed stamp.

One other group that can be covered here to avoid possible confusion includes **reissues, reprints, special printings** and **reproductions**. None of these are design varieties that result from plate flaws, corrections or revisions. In fact, reissues, reprints and special printings are made from the same, unchanged plates as the originals. They show no differences in design and usually can be identified only by variations in paper, color or gum.

Reproductions (such as U.S. #3 and #4), on the other hand, are made from entirely new plates and, therefore, can be expected to show some variation from the originals.

ERRORS, FREAKS, ODDITIES

"EFOs", as they are called, are printed varieties that result from abnormalities in the production process. They are design varieties, but of a special nature because the result looks different from the norm. When you see them, you know something went wrong.

Basically, freaks and oddities can be loosely defined as minor errors. They include the following:

- **Misperforations**, that is, the placement of the perforations within the design rather than at the margins.
- **Foldovers**, caused be a sheet being turned, usually at a corner, before printing and /or perforating. The result is part of a design printed on the reverse of the sheet or placement of perforations at odd angles. Such freaks and oddities may be of relatively minor value, but they do make attractive additions to a collection. Truly major errors, on the other hand, can be of tremendous value. It would not be overstating the case to argue that many collectors are initially drawn to the hobby by the publicity surrounding discoveries of valuable errors and the hope that they might someday do the same. Major errors include the following:
- **Inverts.** These are the most dramatic and most valuable of all major errors and almost always result from printing processes that require more than on pass of a sheet through the presses. If the sheet inadvertently gets "flipped" between passes, the portion printed on the second pass will emerge inverted.

Two definitions we should introduce here are **"frame"** and **"vignette"**. The vignette is the central design of the stamp; the frame encloses the vignette and, at its outer edges, marks the end of the printed stamp design. Oftentimes, stamps described as inverted centers (vignettes) actually are inverted frames. The center was properly printed in the first pass and the frame was inverted in the second pass.

- **Color errors.** The most noticeable color errors usually involve one or more omitted colors. The sheet may not have made it through the second pass in a two-step printing process. In the past such errors were extremely rare because they were obvious enough to be noticed by inspectors. In modern multi-color printings, the chances of such errors escaping detection have increased. Nonetheless, they still qualify as major errors and carry a significant premium.

*Other color errors involve the use of an incorrect color. They may not seem as dramatic as missing colors, but the early issues of many countries include some very rare and valuable examples of these color errors.

Although technically not a color error, we can include here one of the most unusual of all errors, the United States 1917 5-cent stamps that are supposed to be blue, but are found in the carmine or rose color of the 2-cent stamps. The error was not caused by a sheet of the 5-centers being printed in the wrong color, as you might expect. Rather, because a few impressions on a 2-cent plate needed reentry, they were removed. But an error was made and the 5-cent design was entered. Thus it is a reentry error, but is described in most catalogs as a color error because that is the apparent result. Whatever the description, the 5-cent denomination surrounded by 2-cent stamps is a real showpiece.

- **Imperfs.** A distinction should be drawn here between imperforate errors and intentionally imperforate stamps. When the latter carry a premium value over their perforated counterparts, it is because they were printed in smaller quantities for specialized usages. They might have been intended, for example, for sale to vending machine manufacturers who would privately perforate the imperforate sheets

On the other hand, errors in which there is absolutely no trace of a perforation between two stamps that were supposed to be perforated carry a premium based on the rarity of the error. Some modern United States coil imperforate errors have been found in such large quantities that they carry little premium value. But imperforate errors found in small quantities represent tremendous rarities.

Be they intentional or errors, imperforate stamps are commonly collected in pairs or larger multiples because it can be extremely difficult—often impossible, to distinguish them from stamps that have had their perforations trimmed away in an attempt to pass them off as more valuable imperfs. Margin singles that show the stamp and a wide, imperforate selvage at one of the edges of the sheet are another collecting option.

PRINTING

There are three basic printing methods:

1. **Intaglio,** also known as **recess** printing. Line engraved below the surface of the printing plate (that is, in recess) accept the ink and apply it to damp paper that is forced into the recesses of the plate. Intaglio methods include **engraved** and **photogravure** (or **rotogravure**). Photogravure is regarded by some as separate from intaglio because the engraving is done by chemical etching and the finished product can be distinguished from hand or machine engraving.
2. **Typography.** This is similar to intaglio, in that it involves engraving, but the action is in reverse, with the design left at the surface of the plate and the portions to be unprinted cut away. Ink is then applied to the surface design, which is imprinted onto paper. **Typeset** letterpress printing is the most common form of typography.

3. **Lithography.** This method differs from the previous two in that it involves **surface printing**, rather than engraving. Based on the principle that oil and water do not mix, the design to be printed is applied with a greasy ink onto a plate that is then wet with a watery fluid. Printing ink run across the plate is accepted only at the greased (oiled) points. The ink applies the design to paper that is brought in contact with the plate. **Offset** printing, a modern lithographic method, involves a similar approach, but uses a rubber blanket to transfer the inked design to paper.

The printing method that was used to produce a given stamp can be determined by close inspection of that stamp.

1. Because the paper is pressed into the grooves of an intaglio plate, when viewed from the surface the design appears to be slightly raised. Running a fingernail lightly across the surface also will reveal this raised effect. When viewed from the back, the design will appear to be recessed (or pressed out toward the surface). Photogravure stamps have a similar appearance and feel, but when viewed under a magnifier, they reveal a series of dots, rather than line engravings.
2. Because the raised design on a plate is pressed into the paper when the typograph process is used, when viewed from the surface, the printing on the stamp does not have the raised effect of an intaglio product. On the other hand, when viewed from the reverse, a raised impression will be evident where the design was imprinted. Overprints often are applied by typography and usually show the raised effect on the back of the stamp.
3. Unlike either of the previous two methods, lithographed stamps look and feel flat. This dull, flat effect can be noticed on any of the United States 1918-20 offset printings, #s 525-536.

Overprints and **surcharges** are inscriptions or other markings added to printed stamps to adapt them to other uses. A **surcharge** is an overprint that changes or restates the value of the stamp. The United States Offices in China (K1-18) issues carry surcharges.

Some foreign semi-postal issues are stamps with a printed denomination that is applied to the postage fee and an overprinted surcharge that is applied to a specified charity.

Overprints can be applied for reasons other than to change their value. Examples would be for commemorative purposes (#s 646-648), to hinder the use of stolen stamps (#s 658-679 the Kansas-Nebraska issues), to change or designate the usage of the stamp (modern precancels), or to indicate usage in a distinct political unit (Canal Zone, Guam and Philippines overprints on United States stamps used during the early period of U.S. administration until new stamps could be printed).

Overprints can be applied by handstamp or even typewriter, but the most efficient and commonly used technique seen on stamps is typeset press printing.

WATERMARKS

This actually is one of the first steps in the stamp production process because it is part of paper manufacturing. A **watermark** is a slight thinning of the paper pulp, usually in the form of a relevant design. It is applied by devices attached to the rolls on papermaking machines. Without getting involved in the technical aspects, the result in a watermark that can sometimes be seen when held to the light, but more often requires watermark detector fluid.

A word of caution here. Such detector fluids may contain substances that can be harmful when inhaled. This is particularly true of lighter fluids that often are used by collectors in lieu of specially made stamp watermark detector fluids.

Watermarks are used to help detect counterfeits. Although it is possible to reproduce the appearance of a watermark, it is extremely difficult. The authorities have at times been able to identify a counterfeit by the lack of a watermark that should be present or by the presence of an incorrect watermark.

On the other hand, there are occasions when the incorrect or absent watermark did not indicate a counterfeit, but a printing error. The wrong paper may have been used or the paper may have been inserted incorrectly (resulting in an inverted or sideways watermark). The United States 30 cent orange red that is listed among the 1914-17 issues on unwatermarked paper (#467A) is an example of a printing error. It was produced on watermarked paper as part of the 1914-15 series, but a few sheets were discovered without watermarks.

Unfortunately, the difficulty encountered in detecting watermarks on light shades, such as orange or yellow, makes experts very reluctant to identify single copies of #476A. Although not visible, the watermark just might be there.

Because an examination of a full sheet allows the expert to examine the unprinted selvage and all stamps on that sheet at one time, positive identification is possible and most of the stamps that come down to us today as #476A trace back to such full sheets.

GUMMING

Gumming once was almost always applied after printing and before perforating and cutting of sheets into panes. Today, pregummed paper may be used, so the placement of this step in the process cannot be assured—nor is it the sequence of much significance.

The subject of gum will be treated more fully in the **Condition** section of this catalog. At this point, we will only note that certain stamps can be identified by their gum characteristics. Examples include the identification of rotary press stamps by the presence of gum breaker ridges or lines and the detection of the presence of original gum on certain stamps that indicates they can not be a rarer issue that was issued without gum, such as #s 40-

47. Others, such as #s 102-111 can be identified in part by their distinctive white, crackly original gum.

PERFORATING

We have already discussed the absence of perforations in the **Errors** section. Here we will concentrate on the perforating process itself.

All perforating machines use devices to punch holes into the printed stamp paper. The holes usually are round and are known as perforations. When two adjacent stamps are separated, the semicircular cutouts are the **perforations**; the remaining paper between the perforations forms **perf tips**, or **"teeth"**.

Most perforations are applied by perforators that contain a full row of punches that are driven through the paper as it is fed through the perforating equipment. **Line Perforators** drive the punches up and down; **rotary perforators** are mounted on cylinders that revolve. There are other techniques, but these are the most common.

To clear up one point of confusion, the **perforation size** (for example, "perf 11") is not the size of the hole or the number of perforations on the side of a given stamp. Rather, it describes the number of perforations that could be fit within two centimeters.

A perf 8 stamp will have visibly fewer perforations than a perf 12 stamp, but it is much harder to distinguish between perf 11 and perf 10-1/2. **Perforation gauges** enable collectors to make these distinctions with relative ease.

TAGGING

Modern, high-speed, mechanical processing of mail has created the need for "tagging" stamps by coating them with a luminescent substance that could be detected under ultraviolet (U.V.) light or by printing them on paper that included such substances. When passed under a machine capable of detecting these substances, an envelope can be positioned and the stamp automatically cancelled, thereby eliminating time-consuming and tedious manual operations. The tagged varieties of certain predominantly untagged stamps, such as #s 1036 and C67, do carry modest premiums. There also are technical differences between phosphorescent and fluorescent types of luminescent substances. But these details are primarily of interest to specialists and will not be discussed in this general work.

PAPER

The fact that we have not devoted more attention to paper should not be an indication of any lack of interest or significance. Books have been written on this one subject alone, and a lack of at least a rudimentary knowledge of the subject can lead to mis-identification of important varieties and resultant financial loss.

The three most common categories of paper on which stamps are printed are **wove**, **laid**, and **India**. The most frequently used is machine-made **wove paper**, similar to that used for most books. The semiliquid pulp for wove paper is fed onto a fine wire screen and is processed much the same as cloth would be woven. Almost all United States postage stamps are printed on wove paper.

Laid paper is formed in a process that uses parallel wires rather than a uniform screen. As a result, the paper will be thinner where the pulp was in contact with the wires. When held to the light, alternating light and dark lines can be seen. Laid paper varieties have been found on some early United States stamps.

India paper is very thin and tough, without any visible texture. It is, therefore, more suited to obtaining the sharp impressions that are needed for printers' pre-production proofs, rather than to the high-volume printing of stamps.

Other varieties include **bluish** paper, so described because of the tone created by certain substances added to the paper, and silk paper, which contains threads or fibers of silk that usually can be seen on the back of the stamp. Many United States revenue stamps were printed on silk paper.

COLLECTING FORMATS

Whatever the production method, stamps reach the collector in a variety of forms. The most common is in sheet, or more correctly, pane form.

Sheets are the full, uncut units as they come from a press. Before distribution to post offices, these sheets are cut into **panes**. For United States stamps, most regular issues are printed in sheets of 400 and cut into panes of 100; most commemoratives are printed in sheets of 200 and cut into panes of 50. There are numerous exceptions to this general rule, and they are indicated in the mint sheet listings in this catalog.

Sheets also are cut in **booklet panes** for only a few stamps—usually four to ten stamps per pane. These panes are assembled in complete booklets that might contain one to five panes, usually stapled together between two covers. An intact booklet is described as **unexploded**; when broken apart it is described as exploded.

Coils are another basic form in which stamps reach post offices. Such stamps are wound into continuous coil rolls, usually containing from 100 to 5,000 stamps, the size depending on the volume needs of the expected customer. Almost all coils are produced with perforations on two opposite sides and straight edges on the remaining two sides.

Some serious collectors prefer collecting coils in pairs or strips—two or more adjacent stamps—as further assurance of genuineness. It is much easier to fake a coil single that shows only portions of each perforation hole than a larger unit that shows the complete perf hole.

A variation on this theme is the **coil line pair**—adjacent stamps that show a printed vertical line between. On rotary press stamps the line appears where the two ends of a printing plate meet on a rotary press cylinder. The joint is not complete, so ink falls between the plate ends and is transferred onto the printed coil. On flat plate stamps the guideline is the same as that created for sheet stamps, as described below.

Paste-up coil pairs are not as popular as line pairs. They were a necessary by-product of flat plate printings in which the coil strips cut from separate sheets had to be pasted together for continuous winding into roll form.

The modern collecting counterpart to coil line pairs is the plate **number strip**—three or five adjacent coil stamps with the plate number displayed on the middle stamp. Transportation coil plate strips have become particularly sought after. On most early coil rolls, the plate numbers were supposed to be trimmed off. Freaks in which the number remains are interesting, but do not carry large premiums since they are regarded as examples of miscut oddities rather than printing errors.

Miniature sheets and **souvenir sheets** are variations on one theme—small units that may contain only one or at most a much smaller quantity of stamps than would be found on the standard postal panes. Stamps may be issued in miniature sheet format for purposes of expedience, as for example the Bret Harte $5 issue (#2196), which was released in panes of 20 to accommodate the proportionately large demand by collectors for plate blocks rather than single stamps.

As the name implies, a souvenir sheet is a miniature sheet that was released as a souvenir to be saved, rather than postally used—although such sheets or the stamps cut out from them can be used as postage. Note: **souvenir cards** are created strictly for promotional and souvenir purposes. They contain stamp reproductions that may vary in size, color or design from the originals and are not valid for postal use.

Often, a common design may be produced in sheet, coil and booklet pane form. The common design is designated by collectors as one **type**, even though it may be assigned many different catalog numbers because of variations in color, size, perforations, printing method, denomination, etc. On the other hand, even minor changes in a basic design represent a new type.

Sheet stamps offer the greatest opportunity for format variation and collecting specialization. Using the following illustration for reference, the varieties that can be derived include the following:

Block (a)—this may be any unit of four stamps or more in at least 2 by 2 format. Unless designated as a different size, blocks are assumed to be blocks of four.

Specialized forms of blocks include:

Arrow block (b)—adjacent stamps at the margin of a sheet, showing the arrow printed in the margin for registration in the printing process, as, for example, in two-color printings. When the arrow designates the point at which a sheet is cut into panes, the result will appear as one leg of the arrow, or V, on each pane.

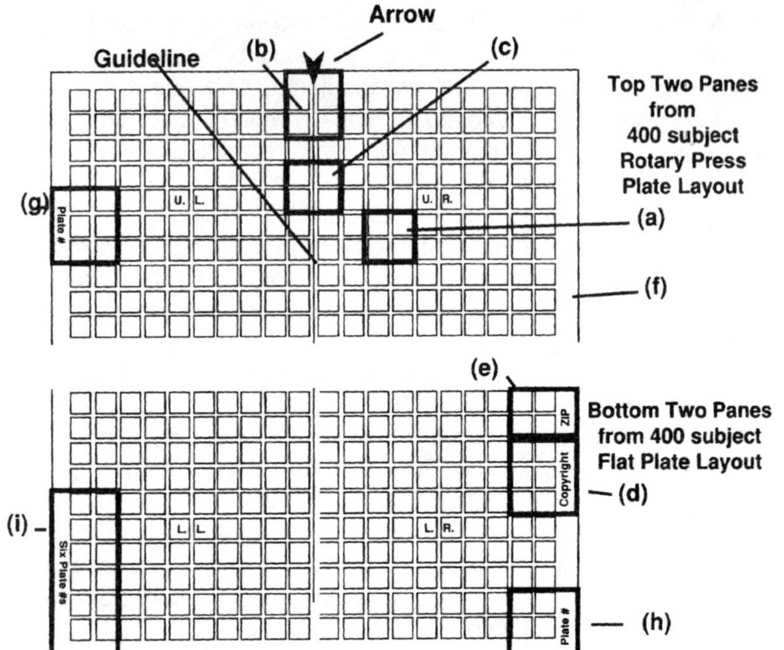

(This diagram is for placement purposes only, and is not an exact reproduction of margin markings)

Guideline block (c)—similar to arrow block, except that it can be any block that shows the registration line between two rows of two stamps each.

Gutter block—similar to guideline block, except that an uncolored gutter is used instead of a printed line. The best known United States gutter blocks are those cut from full-sheet "Farley printings". Pairs of stamps from adjacent panes on each side of the gutter form the gutter block.

Imprint, or **inscription blocks (d)** include **copyright, mail early** and **ZIP (e)** blocks. On most modern United States sheets, the **selvage**, that is, the margin that borders the outer rows of stamps **(f)**, includes one or more inscriptions in addition to the plate numbers. It may be a copyright protection notice or an inscription that encourages mail users to post their mail early or to use the ZIP code on their mail.

Because the inscription appears along the margin, rather than in one of the corners, it is customary to collect copyright blocks and mail early blocks in two rows of three stamps each, with the inscription centered in the margin. The ZIP inscription appears in one of the corners of each pane, so it is collected in corner margin blocks of four.

Plate number block—this is by far the most popular form of block collecting. On each sheet of stamps, a plate number (or numbers) is printed to identify the printing plate(s) used. Should a damage be discovered, the plate can easily be identified.

On flat plate sheets, where the plate number appeared along the margin, the format usually is plate blocks of six, with the plate number centered in the margin **(g)**.

On rotary press and other sheets where a single plate number appears in one of the four corners of the margin, the customary collecting format is a corner margin block of four **(h)**. This also is true for plate blocks with two plate numbers in two adjacent corner stamps and for modern plates where single digits are used to designate each plate number and the complete series (containing one digit for each printing color) appears in the corner.

Before single digits were adopted for modern multi-color printings, the five-digit numbers assigned to each plate might run down a substantial portion of the sheet margin. **Plate strips** are collected in such instances. Their size is two rows times as many stamps as are attached to the margin area that shows all plate numbers **(i)**.

Because a sheet of stamps is cut into separate panes, printing plates include plate numbers that can be seen on each of the cut panes. On modern sheets the plate numbers would be located in each of the four corners of the uncut sheet. Once cut, each of the four panes would show the same plate number in one of its corners. The position of the plate number, which matches the position of the pane on the uncut sheet, is designated as upper left or right and lower left or right. Some specialists seek matched sets. A **matched set** is one of each of the four positions for a given plate number. A **complete matched set** is all positions of all plate numbers for a given issue.

Other definitions that relate in one way or another to the format in which stamps are produced include:

Se-tenant—from the French, meaning joined together. A pair, block or larger multiple that contains different designs. The 1967 Space Twins issue is an example of a se-tenant pair in which the two different stamps are part of an integral design. The 1968 Historic Flags se-tenant strip contains ten separate designs, each of which can stand alone.

Tete-beche pair—from the French, meaning head-to-tail. Such pairs show adjacent stamps, one of which is upside down in relation to the other.

Proof—any trial impression used in the evaluation of prospective or final designs. **Final die proofs**—that is, those made from a completed die preparatory to its being used in the production of printing plates—are the standard proof collecting form.

Essay—a partial or complete illustration of a proposed design. In the strict philatelic sense, essays are printed in proof form.

Color trials—a preliminary proof of a stamp design in one or more colors. Trial color proofs are used to select the color in which the stamp will be printed.

Grill—a pattern of embossed cuts that break the stamp paper. See the information at the head of the 1861-67 Issue listings and the section of grills in the Harris Stamp Identifier.

POSTAL MARKINGS

The extensive subject of cancellations and postal markings on stamps and covers is too specialized to present in detail here. Volumes have been written on individual categories of markings—straight line markings, ship cancels, foreign mail cancels, flight covers, etc. In this section we will limit ourselves to the basic definitions related to the stamp and the manner in which it is cancelled, rather than the specialized usage of the envelope to which the stamp is affixed.

- **Manuscript**, or **pen cancels** were the earliest form of "killing" a stamp—that is, marking it to indicate it had been postally used.
- **Handstamps** were created shortly after the first stamps were issued. The early devices might only show a pattern such as a grid and often were carved from cork.
- **Fancy cancels** were an extension of the handstamp. Local postmasters carved cork cancelers that depicted bees, kicking mules, flowers and hundreds of other figures. Stamps with clear strikes of such fancy cancels usually carry hefty premiums over those with standard cancels.
- **Machine cancels** are applied by mechanical rather than manual means.
- A stamp is **tied** to a cover (or piece) when the cancellation, whatever its form, extends beyond the margins of the stamp onto the cover. Such a tie is one indication of the authenticity of the cover.

Specialized cancellations include the following:

- **Cut cancel**—as the name implies, a cancel that actually cuts the stamp, usually in the form of a thin, straight incision. The most common usage of cut cancels on United States stamps is on Revenue issues.
- **Perfin**, or perforated initial—usually not a cancellation as such, but rather a privately administered punching into the stamp of one or more initials. Most often, the initials were those of a large firm that wished to prevent personal use of their stamps by employees.
- **Precancel**—a cancellation printed on stamps in advance of their sale. The primary purpose of precancels is for sale to large volume mailers, whose mail is delivered to post offices and processed in bulk without necessarily receiving further cancellation.
- **Non-contemporary cancel**—a cancellation applied to a stamp long after the normal period of use for that stamp. A stamp that is worth more used than unused or a damaged unused stamp that would be worth more on cover are examples of candidates for non-contemporary markings.
- **Cancel-to-order**, or **C.T.O.**—a cancel that is printed on a stamp by an issuing country to give it the appearance of having been used, or to render it invalid for postage in that country. Special fancy cancels or "favor cancels" have been applied at various times in the countries for philatelic reasons.

CATEGORIES

The number of specialized categories into which stamps can be slotted is limited only by the imagination of the individual collector. Some collectors have attempted to collect one of each and every stamp ever issued by every nation that ever existed. Other collectors have concentrated on all the possible varieties and usages of only one stamp. Between these two extremes, stamps can be divided into certain generally accepted categories, whether or not they are used as boundaries for a collection. These categories are as follows:

- **Definitives**, or **regulars**—stamps that are issued for normal, everyday postage needs. In the United States, they are put on sale for a period limited only by changing rate needs or infrequent issuance of a new definitive series. Post offices can requisition additional stocks of definitives as needed.
- **Commemoratives**—stamps issued to honor a specific event, anniversary, individual or group. They are printed in a predetermined quantity and are intended for sale during a limited period. Although they can be used indefinitely, once stocks are sold out at a local post office, commemoratives usually are not replenished unless the issue has local significance.
- **Pictorials**—stamps that depict a design other than the portrait of an individual or a static design such as a coat of arms or a flag. While some collectors think of these strictly as commemoratives (because most commemoratives are pictorials), some definitives also can be pictorials. Any number of definitives that depict the White House are examples.
- **Airmails**, or **air posts**—stamps issued specifically for airmail use. Although they do not have to bear a legend, such as "airmail", they usually do. Airmail stamps usually can be used to pay other postage fees.

When air flights were a novelty, airmail stamp collecting was an extremely popular specialty. Part of this popularity also can be ascribed to the fact that the first airmail stamps usually were given special attention by issuing postal administrations. Produced using relatively modern technology, they often were among the most attractive of a nation's issues.

- **Zeppelin stamps**—although these do not rate as a major category, they deserve special mention. Zeppelin issues were primarily released for specific use on Zeppelin flights during the 1920s and 1930s. They carried high face values and were issued during the Great Depression period, when most collectors could not afford to purchase them. As a result, most Zeppelin issues are scarce and command substantial premiums. United States "Zepps" are the Graf Zeppelins (C13-C15) and the Century of Progress issue (C18).

- **Back-of-the-book**—specialized stamps that are identified as "back-of-the-book" because of their position in catalogs following the listings of regular and commemorative postal issues. Catalogs identified them with a prefix letter.

Some collectors include airmail stamps in this category, in part because they carry a prefix letter (C) and are listed separately. Most collectors treat the airmails as part of a standard collection and begin the back-of-the-book section with semi-postals (B) or, for the United States, special deliveries (E).

Other frequently used "b-o-b" categories include postage dues (J), offices in China, or Shanghais (K), officials (O), parcel posts (Q), newspapers (PR), and revenues (R), the latter including "Duck" hunting permit stamps (RW).

Postal stationery and postal cards are the major non-stamp back-of-the-book categories. A complete envelope or card is called an **entire**; the cutout corner from such a piece, showing the embossed or otherwise printed design, is described as a **cut square**.

Some collecting categories do not relate to the intended use of the stamps. Examples include **topicals** (stamps collected by the theme of the design, such as sports, dance, paintings, space, etc.) and **first day covers**. (Modern first day covers show a stamp or stamps postmarked in a designated first day city on the official first day of issue. The cancel design will relate to the issue and the cover may bear a privately-printed cachet that further describes and honors the subject of the stamp.

One of the oddities of the hobby is that **stampless covers** are an accepted form of "stamp" collecting. Such covers display a usage without a stamp, usually during the period before stamps were required for the payment of postage. They bear manuscript or handstamps markings such as "due 5," "PAID," etc. to indicate the manner in which postage was paid.

Although they do not constitute a postal marking, we can include **bisects** here for want of a better place. A bisect is a stamp cut in half and used to pay postage in the amount of one-half of the stamp's denomination. The 1847 ten cent stamp (#2) cut in half and used to pay the five cent rate is an example.

Bisects should be collected only on cover and properly tied. They also should reflect an authorized usage, for example, from a post office that was known to lack the proper denomination, and should pay an amount called for by the usage shown on the cover.

Not discussed in detail here is the vast subject of **covers**, or postal history. Envelopes, usually but not necessarily showing a postal use, are described by collectors as covers. Early "covers" actually were single letter sheets with a message on one side and folded into the form of an enclosing wrapper when viewed from the outside. The modern aerogramme or air letter is similar in design to these early folded letters.

Quality and Condition Definitions

In determining the value of a given stamp, a number of factors have to be taken into consideration. For mint stamps, the condition of the gum, whether or not it has been hinged, and the centering are all major factors that determine value. For used stamps, the factors to consider are cancellation and centering. The following H.E. Harris guidelines will enable you to determine the quality standards you may choose from in acquiring stamps for your collection.

Mint Stamps Gum

Unused—A stamp that is not cancelled (used), yet has had all the original gum removed. On early U.S. issues this is the condition that the majority of mint stamps exist in, as early collectors often soaked the gum off their stamps to avoid the possibility of the gum drying and splitting.

Original Gum (OG)—A stamp that still retains the adhesive applied when the stamp was made, yet has been hinged or had some of the gum removed. Mint stamps from #215 to date can be supplied in this condition.

Never Hinged (NH)—A stamp that is in "post office" condition with full gum that has never been hinged. For U.S. #215 to #1241 (1963), separate pricing columns or percentages are provided for "Never Hinged" quality. From #1242 (1964) to date, all stamps are priced as Never Hinged. Hinged Stamps 1964 to date are available at 20% off the NH price.

Cancellations

The cancellations on Used stamps range from light to heavy. A lightly cancelled stamp has the main design of the stamp clearly showing through the cancel, while a heavy cancel usually substantially obliterates the design elements of the stamp. In general it should be assumed that Very fine quality stamps will have lighter cancels than average cancellation stamps.

Heavy Cancel

Light Cancel

CONDITION

Condition is an extremely important factor in the determination of a stamp's price. Damaged stamps may sell for less than 5% of a standard catalog price while "jumbo" copies have been known to sell for 20 or more times than standard price—or more than 400 times the price of the damaged copy!

Having stated the extremes, it is important to note that the average collector seeks a middle ground, paying a reasonable price for an attractive, undamaged stamp without going to excessive lengths or paying inflated prices. There are enough options within the middle ground to satisfy a collector on a limited budget as well as one who seeks superior quality.

The "Quality and Condition Definitions" section of this catalog defines, with photographs, the condition of stamps offered by H.E. Harris & Co. We incorporate those definitions in this section, but do so within a broader discussion.

Before proceeding with specific condition factors, we should point out the important difference between "price" and "value". This is particularly important for budget-minded collectors to whom a low price can be very enticing. But when a low price is accompanied by substandard quality for that price, then the stamp is said to be overvalued, even if it does appear to be a bargain.

On the other hand, a stamp that has a higher price, but which is of exceptional quality and is accompanied by the guarantee of the seller, may be a much better value than the cheap stamp. "You get what you pay for" remains as true today as it ever did.

CENTERING

One major factor in the determination of a stamp's fair value is its **centering**, the relative balance of the stamp design within its margins. Whether the stamp has perforations or is imperforate, its centering can be judged. Because the stamp trade does not have an established system for grading or measuring centering, "eyeballing" has become the standard practice. As a result, one collector's definition may vary from another's. This can create some confusion, but the system seems to work, so it has remained in force.

Centering can range from poor to superb, as follows:

- **Poor**—so far off center that a significant portion of the design is lost because of bad centering. On a poorly centered perforated stamp, the perforations cut in so badly that even the perf tips may penetrate the design.
- **Average**—a stamp whose frame or design is cut slightly by the lack of margins on one or two sides. On a perforated stamp, the perf holes might penetrate the stamp, but some margin white space will show on the teeth. Average stamps are accepted by the majority of collectors for 19th century stamps and early 20th century stamps, as well as for the more difficult later issues.

H.E. Harris Pictorial Guide to Centering

Cat #	Very Fine	Fine	Average
1 to 293 1847 to 1898	 Perfs clear of design on all four sides. Margins may not be even.	 Perfs well clear of design on at least three sides. But may almost touch design on one side.	 Perfs cut into design on at least one side.
294 to 749 1901 to 1934	 Perfs clear of design. Margins relatively even on all four sides.	 Perfs clear of design. Margins not even on all four sides.	 Perfs touch design on at least one side.
750 to Date 1935 to Present	 Perfs clear of design. Centered with margins even on all four sides.	 Perfs clear of design. Margins may be uneven.	 Perfs may touch design on at least one side.

Note: Margins are area from edges of stamp to the design. Perfs are the serrations between stamps to aid in separating them.

- **Fine**—the perforations are clear of the design, except for those issues that are known to be extremely poorly centered, but the margins on opposite sides will not be balanced, that is, equal to each other. (Note: a stamp whose top and bottom margins are perfectly balanced may still be called fine if the left and right margins differ substantially from each other.)
- **Very fine**—the opposite margins may still appear to differ somewhat, but the stamp is closer to being perfectly centered than it is to being fine centered. Very fine stamps are sought by collectors who are particularly interested in high quality and who are willing to pay the premiums such stamps command.
- **Superb**— perfect centering. They are so scarce that no comprehensive price list could attempt to include a superb category. Superb stamps, when they are available, command very high premiums.
- **"Jumbo"**—an abnormal condition, in which the stamp's margins are oversized compared to those of the average stamp in a given issue. Such jumbos can occur in the plate making process when a design is cut into the printing plate and excessive space is allowed between that design and the adjacent stamps.

Note: Some collectors also define a "fine to very fine" condition, in which the margin balance falls into a mid-range between fine and very fine. In theory it may be an attractive compromise, but in practice the range between fine and very fine is too narrow to warrant a separate intermediate category.

GUM

The impact of the condition of the back of an unused stamp (i.e., the gum) upon that stamp's value in today's market needs careful consideration. The prices for 19th century stamps vary widely based on this element of condition.

Some traditional collectors feel that modern collectors pay too much attention to gum condition. Around the turn of the century, some collectors washed the gum off the stamps to prevent it from cracking and damaging the stamp themselves. But that generation is past and the practice not only is no longer popular, it is almost unheard of.

To some extent the washing of gum is no longer necessary, since modern gums are not as susceptible to cracking. A more important development, however, has been the advent of various mounts that allow the collector to place a stamp in an album without the use of a hinge. With that development, "never hinged" became a premium condition that could be obtained on stamps issued from the 1930s to date. As a result, gum took on added significance and its absence on 20th century stamps became unacceptable.

The standard definitions that pertain to gum condition are as follows:

- **Original gum**, or **o.g.**—the gum that was applied when the stamp was produced. There are gradations, from "full" original gum, through "partial" o.g. down to "traces". For all intents and purposes, however, a stamp must have most of its original gum to be described as "o.g."

- **Regummed**— the stamp has gum, but it is not that which would have been applied when the stamp was produced. Many collectors will avoid regummed stamps because the gum may hide some repair work. At best, regumming may give the stamp an appearance of completeness, but a premium should not be paid for a stamp that lacks its original gum.
- **Unused**—while many collectors think of this as any stamp that is not used, the narrow philatelic definition indicates a stamp that has no gum or is regummed.
- **Unhinged**—as with "unused", the term has a specific meaning to collectors: a regumming that shows no traces of a hinge mark. Unfortunately, in their confusion some collectors purchase stamps described as "unused" and "unhinged" as if they bore original gum.
- **No gum**—the stamp lacks its gum, either because it was intentionally produced without gum (also described as **ungummed**) or had the gum removed at a later date. It is customary to find 19th century stamps without gum, and the condition is acceptable to all but the most fastidious collectors. On 20th century stamps, original gum is to be expected.
- **Hinged**—the gum shows traces of having been mounted with a hinge. This can range from **lightly hinged** (the gum shows traces, but none of the hinge remains) to **heavily hinged** (a substantial portion of one or more hinge remnants is stuck to the stamp, or a significant portion of the gum has been lost in the removal of a hinge).
- **Thinned**— not only has the gum been removed, but a portion of the stamp paper has been pulled away. A thin usually will show when the stamp is held to a light. One of the faults that may be covered over on regummed stamps is a thin that has been filled in.
- **Never hinged**—as the name implies, the stamp has its original gum in post office condition and has never been hinged. Although some collectors think of **"mint"** stamps as any form of unused, o.g. stamps, the more accepted "mint" definition is never hinged.

USED STAMPS

For used stamps, the presence of gum would be the exception, since it would have been removed when the stamp was washed from the envelope, so gum is not a factor on used stamps.

The centering definitions, on the other hand, would be the same as for unused issues. In addition, the cancellation would be a factor.

We should point out here that we are not referring to the type of cancellation, such as a fancy cancel that might add considerably to the value of a stamp or a manuscript cancel that reduces its value. Rather, we are referring to the degree to which the cancellation covers the stamp.

A **lightly cancelled** used stamp, with all of the main design elements showing and the usage evidenced by an unobtrusive cancel, is the premier condition sought by collectors of used stamps. On the other hand, a stamp whose design has been substantially obliterated by a **heavy cancel** is at best a space filler that should be replaced by a moderate to lightly cancelled example.

PERFORATIONS

The condition of a stamp's perforations can be determined easily by visual examination. While not necessarily perfect, all perforations should have full teeth and clean perforation holes. A **blunt perf** is one that is shorter than it should be, while a **pulled perf** actually shows a portion of the margin or design having been pulled away. **Blind perfs** are the opposite: paper remains where the perforation hole should have been punched out.

One irony of the demand for perforation is that **straight edges**, that is, the normal sheet margin straight edge that was produced when flat-plate sheets were cut into panes, are not acceptable to many collectors. In fact, many collectors will prefer a reperforated stamp to a straight edge. (Technically, **"re"perforated** can only apply to a stamp that is being perforated again, as when a damaged or excessive margin has been cut away and new perforations are applied, but we will follow the common practice of including the perforation of normal straight edges in this category).

As a result of this preference, many straight edges no longer exist as such. When one considers that they were in the minority to start with (a pane of 100 flat plate stamps would include 19 straight edges) and that even fewer come down to us today, an argument could be made that they may someday be rarities...although it is hard to conceive of anyone paying a premium for straight edges.

FAKES, FAULTS, AND EXPERTIZING

Below the first quality level—stamps free of defects—a range of stamps can be found from attractive **"seconds"** that have barely noticeable flaws to **space fillers** that may have a piece missing and which ought to be replaced by a better copy— unless we are talking about great rarities which would otherwise be beyond the budget of most collectors.

The more common flaws include **thins**, **tears**, **creases**, **stains**, **pulled perfs**, **pinholes** (some dealers and collectors used to display their stamps pinned to boards), **face scuffs** or erasures, and **fading**.

Stamps with faults sometimes are **repaired**, either to protect them from further damage or to deceive collectors.

While the terms that are applied to stamps that are not genuine often are used interchangeably, they do have specific meaning, as follows:

- **fakes** —(in French, faux; in German, falsch)—stamps that appear to be valuable varieties, but which were made from cheaper genuine stamps. Trimming away the perforations to create an imperforate is a common example of a fake.
- **bogus** stamps, **phantoms**, **labels** —outright fantasies, usually the product of someone's imagination, produced for amusement rather than deception.

While most stamps are genuine, and the average collector need not be concerned about the possibility of repairs, **expertizing** services do exist for collectors who are willing to pay a fee to obtain an independent opinion on their more valuable stamps.

The UNITED STATES STAMP IDENTIFIER

Shows you how to distinguish between the rare and common U.S. stamps that look alike.

Types of 1¢ Franklin Design of 1851-60

TYPE I —has the most complete design of the various types of stamps. At top and bottom there is an unbroken curved line running outside the bands reading "U.S. POSTAGE" and "ONE CENT". The scrolls at bottom are turned under, forming curls. The scrolls and outer line at top are complete.

TYPE Ia — is like Type I at bottom but ornaments and curved line at top are partly cut away.

TYPE Ib —(not illustrated) is like Type I at top but little curls at bottom are not quite so complete nor clear and scroll work is partly cut away.

TYPE II —has the outside bottom line complete, but the little curls of the bottom scrolls and the lower part of the plume ornament are missing. Side ornaments are complete.

TYPE III —has the outside lines at both top and bottom partly cut away in the middle. The side ornaments are complete.

TYPE IIIa—(not illustrated) is similar to Type III with the outer line cut away at top or bottom, but not both.

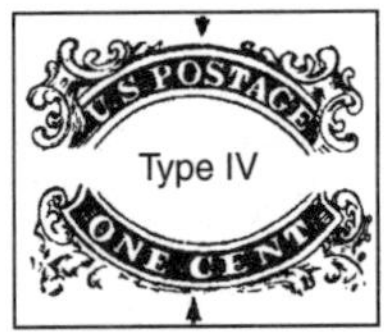

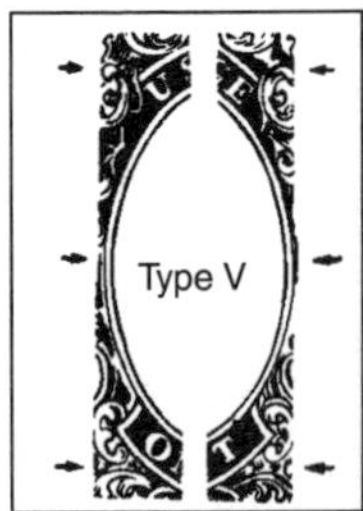

TYPE IV — is similar to Type II but the curved lines at top or bottom (or both) have been recut in several different ways, and usually appear thicker than Type IIs.

TYPE V — is similar to Type III but has the side ornaments partly cut away. Type V occurs only on perforated stamps.

The UNITED STATES STAMP IDENTIFIER

Shows you how to distinguish between the rare and common U.S. stamps that look alike.

Types of 3¢ Washington & 5¢ Jefferson Designs of 1851-60

Type I

Type II

Type IIa

Type I

Type II

3¢ WASHINGTON

Type I — has a frame line around the top, bottom and sides.

Type II — has the frame line removed at top and bottom, while the side frame lines are continuous from the top to bottom of the plate.

Type IIa— is similar to Type II, but the side frame lines were recut individually, and therefore are broken between stamps.

5¢ JEFFERSON

Type I — is a complete design with projections (arrow) at the top and bottom as well as at the sides.

Type II — has the projections at the top or bottom partly or completely cut away.

Types of the 10¢ Washington Design of 1851-60

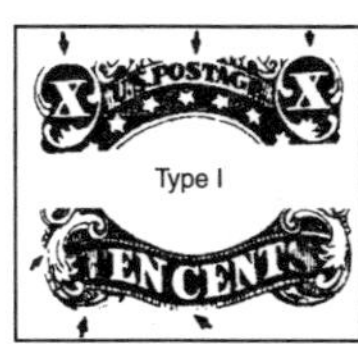

Type I

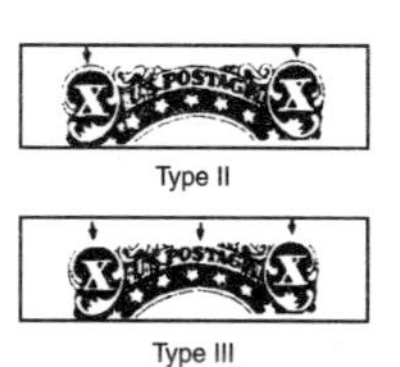
Type II

Type III

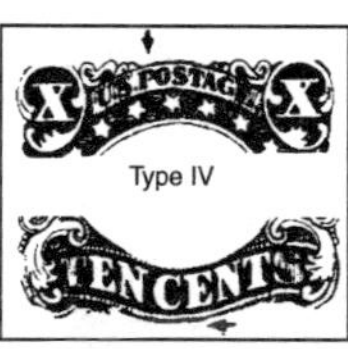

Type IV

Type I — has the "shells" at the lower corners practically complete, while the outer line below "TEN CENTS" is very nearly complete. At the top, the outer lines above "U.S. POSTAGE" above the "X" in each corner are broken.

Type II — has the design complete at the top, but the outer line at the bottom is broken in the middle and the "shells" are partially cut away.

Type III — has both top and bottom outer lines cut away; similar to Type I at the top and Type II at the bottom.

Type IV — has the outer lines at the top or bottom of the stamp, or at both places, recut to show more strongly and heavily.

Types I, II, III and IV have complete ornaments at the sides and three small circles or pearls (arrow) at the outer edges of the bottom panel.

Type V — has the side ornaments, including one or two of the small "pearls" partly cut away. Also, the outside line, over the "X" at the right top, has been partly cut away.

Types of the 12¢ Washington issues of 1851-60

Plate 1 has stronger, more complete outer frame lines than does Plate 3. Comes imperforate (#17 or perf #36).

Plate 3 has uneven or broken outer frame lines that are particularly noticeable in the corners. The stamps are perf 15. (#36b)

The REPRINT plate is similar to plate 1, but the Reprint stamps are greenish black and slightly taller than plate 1 stamps (25 mm. from top to bottom frame lines vs. 24.5 mm.). The paper is whiter and the perforations are 12 gauge.

The UNITED STATES STAMP IDENTIFIER

Shows you how to distinguish between the rare and common U.S. stamps that look alike.

Types of the 1861 Issue, Grills & Re-Issues

Shortly after the outbreak of the Civil War in 1861, the Post Office demonitized all stamps issued up to that time in order to prevent their use by the Confederacy. Two new sets of designs, consisting of six stamps shown below plus 24¢ and 30¢ demonitized, were prepared by the American Bank Note Company. The first designs, except for the 10¢ and 24¢ values, were not regularly issued and are extremely rare and valuable. The second designs became the regular issue of 1861. The illustrations in the left column show the first (or unissued) designs, which were all printed on thin, semi-transparent paper. The second (or regular) designs are shown at the right.

Types of the 1861 Issues

1st

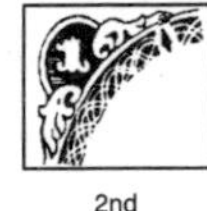

2nd

SECOND DESIGN shows a small dash (arrow) under the tip of the ornaments at the right of the figure "1" in the upper left-hand corner of the stamp.

1st

2nd

1st

2nd

SECOND DESIGN, 3¢ value, shows a small ball (arrow) at each corner of the design. Also, the ornaments at the corners are larger than in the 1st design.

SECOND DESIGN, 5¢ value has a leaflet (arrow) projecting from the scrolled ornaments at each corner of the stamp.

1st

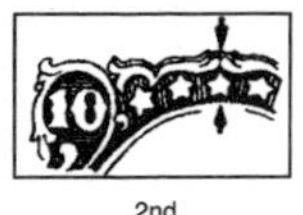

2nd

FIRST DESIGN has no curved line below the row of stars and there is only one outer line of the ornaments above them.

SECOND DESIGN has a heavy curved line below the row of stars (arrow); ornaments above the stars have double outer line.

1st 2nd

FIRST DESIGN has rounded corners.

SECOND DESIGN has an oval and a scroll (arrow) in each corner of the design.

Types of the 15¢ "Landing of Columbus" Design of 1869

TYPE I has the central picture without the frame line shown in Type II.

TYPE II has a frame line (arrows) around the central picture; also a diamond shaped ornament appears below the "T" of "Postage".

TYPE III (not illustrated) is like Type I except that the fringe of brown shading lines which appears around the sides and bottom of the picture on Types I and II has been removed.

The UNITED STATES STAMP IDENTIFIER

Shows you how to distinguish between the rare and common U.S. stamps that look alike.

IDENTIFIER CHART
1861-1867 Bank Notes

Description and Identifying Features	Pts. as seen from stamp face	Area covered Horiz. x Vert.	# of rows of Pts.	1¢	2¢	3¢	5¢	10¢	12¢	15¢	24¢	30¢	90¢
1861. National. First designs. Thin, semi-transparent paper. No grill.				55		56	57	58[1] 62B	59		60	61	62
1861-62, National. Modified designs[3]. Thicker, opaque paper. No grill.				63		64[2] 65[2] 66[2]	67	68	69		70[2]	71	72
1861-66, National. Thicker, opaque paper. No grill a. New designs					73					77			
b. Same designs, new shades						74[2]	75[2] 76[2]				78[2]		
1867, National. Grills. All on thick, opaque paper.													
Grills	Pts. as seen from stamp face	Area of covered Horiz. x Vert.	# of rows of Pts.										
A	Up	All over	—			79	80					81	
B	Up	18x15 mm	22x18			82							
C	Up	c.13x16 mm	16-17x 18-21			83							
D	Down	c.12x14 mm	15x17-18		84	85							
Z	Down	c.11x14 mm	13-14x 17-18	85A	85B	85C		85D	85E	85F			
E	Down	c.11x13 mm	14x15-17	86	87	88		89	90	91			
F	Down	c.9x13 mm	11-12x 15-17	92	93	94	95	96	97	98	99	100	101
1875, National. Re-issues. Hard, white paper. White crackly gum. No grill.				102	103	104	105	106	107	108	109	110	111

FOOTNOTES:

1. #58 does not exist used. Unused, it cannot be distinguished from #62B.
2. Different from corresponding 1861-66 issues only in color.
3. See diagrams for design modification.

The UNITED STATES STAMP IDENTIFIER

Shows you how to distinguish between the rare and common U.S. stamps that look alike.

Types of the 1870-71 Through 1887 Bank Notes

The stamps of the 1870-71 issue were printed by the National Bank Note Company. The similar issue of 1873 was printed by the Continental Bank Note Company. When Continental took over the plates previously used by National, they applied the so-called "secret marks" to the designs of the 1¢ through 15$ denominations by which the two issues can be distinguished as shown below. The illustrations at the left show the original designs of 1870-71; those at the right show secret marks applied to the issue of 1873.

1¢ Secret mark is a small curved mark in the pearl at the left of the figure "1".

3¢ Secret mark is the heavily shaded ribbon under the letters "RE".

7¢ Secret mark is two tiny semicircles drawn around the end of the lines which outline the ball in the lower right-hand corner.

12¢ Secret mark shows the "balls" at the top and bottom of the figure "2" crescent-shaped (right) instead of nearly round as at the left.

2¢ 1870-71 are red brown. The 1873 issue is brown and in some copies has a small diagonal line under the scroll at the left of the "U.S." (arrow).

6¢ Secret mark shows the first four vertical lines of shading in the lower part of the left ribbon greatly strengthened.

10¢ Secret mark is a small semicircle in the scroll at the right-hand side of the central design.

15¢ Secret mark shows as strengthened lines (arrow) in the triangle in the upper left-hand corner, forming a "V".

The UNITED STATES STAMP IDENTIFIER

Shows you how to distinguish between the rare and common U.S. stamps that look alike.

IDENTIFIER CHART
1870-1887 Bank Notes

Description and Identifying Features	1¢	2¢	3¢	5¢	6¢	7¢	10¢	12¢	15¢	21¢	30¢	90¢
1870-71, National. No secret marks, White wove paper, thin to medium thick. With grills.	134	135	136		137	138	139	140	141	142	143	144
1870-71, National. As above, except without grills.	145	146	147		148	149	150	151	152	153	154[2]	155[2]
1873, Continental. White wove paper, thin to thick. No grills.												
a. With secret marks.	156	157	158		159	160	161	162	163			
b. No secret marks.											165[2]	166[2]
1875, Continental. Special Printing. Same designs as 1873 Continental. Hard, white wove paper. No gum.	167	168	169		170	171	172	173	174	175	176	177
1875, Continental. New color or denomination. Hard, yellowish wove paper.		178		179								
1875, Continental. Printing. Same designs as 1875 Continental. Hard, white wove paper. No gum.		180		181								
1879, American. Same designs as 1873-75 Continental. Soft porous paper.	182	183[3]	184[3]	185	186[3]		187[3]		189[3]		190[3]	191[3]
a. without secret mark.							188					
1880, American. Special printing. Same as 1879 issue. Soft, porous paper. No gum.	192	193 203[3]	194[3]	204	195[3]	196	197[3]	198	199[3]	200	201[3]	202[3]
1881-82. American. Designs of 1873. Re-engraved[4]. Soft, porous paper.	206		207[5]		208		209					
1887, American. Same designs as 1881-82. New colors.		214[5]									217	218

FOOTNOTES:

1. See diagrams for secret marks.
2. Corresponding denominations differ from each other only in color.
3. Corresponding denominations differ from each other only in color and gum. The special printings are slightly deepr and richer. The lack of gum is not a positive identifier because it can be washed from the 1879 issues.
4. See diagrams for re-engravings.
5. Corresponding denominations differ from each other in color.

The UNITED STATES STAMP IDENTIFIER

Shows you how to distinguish between the rare and common U.S. stamps that look alike.

Re-Engraved Designs 1881-82

1¢ has strengthened vertical shading lines in the upper part of the stamp, making the background appear almost solid. Lines of shading have also been added to the curving ornaments in the upper corners.

3¢ has a solid shading line at the sides of the central oval (arrow) that is only about half the previous width. Also a short horizontal line has been cut below the "TS" of "CENTS".

2¢ Washington Design of 1894-98

Type I

Type II

Type III

TYPE I has horizontal lines of the same thickness within and without the triangle.

TYPE II has horizontal lines which cross the triangle but are thinner within it than without.

TYPE III has thin lines inside the triangle and these do not cross the double frame line of the triangle.

2¢ Columbian "Broken Hat" Variety of 1893

231

Broken Hat variety, 231c

As a result of a plate defect, some stamps of the 2¢ Columbian design show a noticeable white notch or gash in the hat worn by the third figure to the left of Columbus. This "broken hat" variety is somewhat less common than the regular 2¢ design.

4¢ COLUMBIAN BLUE ERROR

Collectors often mistake the many shades of the normal 4¢ ultramarine for the rare and valuable blue error. Actually, the "error" is not ultramarine at all, but a deep blue, similar to the deeper blue shades of the 1¢ Columbian.

6¢ has only three vertical lines between the edge of the panel and the outside left margin of the stamp. (In the preceding issues, there were four such lines.)

10¢ has only four vertical lines between the left side of the oval and the edge of the shield. (In the preceding issues there were five such lines.) Also, the lines in the background have been made much heavier so that these stamps appear more heavily inked than previous issues.

$1 Perry Design of 1894-95

Type I

Type II

TYPE I shows circles around the "$1" are broken at point where they meet the curved line below "ONE DOLLAR" (arrows).

TYPE II shows these circles complete.

10¢ Webster design of 1898

Type I

Type II

TYPE I has an unbroken white curved line below the words "TEN CENTS".

TYPE II shows white line is broken by ornaments at a point just below the "E" in "TEN" and the ""T" in "CENTS" (arrows).

2¢ Washington Issue of 1903

Die I
319, 319g,
320

Die II
319f, 320a

The rounded inner frame line below and to the left "T" in "TWO" has a dark patch of color that narrows, but remains strong across the bottom.

2¢ "cap on 2" Variety of 1890

Cap on left "2"

Cap on Right "2"

Plate defects in the printing of the 2¢ "Washington" stamp of 1890 accounts for the "Cap on left 2" and "Cap on both 2s" varieties illustrated above.

The UNITED STATES STAMP IDENTIFIER

Shows you how to distinguish between the rare and common U.S. stamps that look alike.

FRANKLIN AND WASHINGTON ISSUES OF 1908-22

Perforation	Watermark	Other Identifying Features					3¢ thru $1 denominations	8¢ thru $1 denominations
PERF. 12	USPS	White paper	331	332			333-42	422-23
		Bluish gray paper	357	358			359-66	
	USPS	White paper	374	375	405	406	376-82 407	414-21
COIL 12	USPS	Perf. Horizontal	348	349			350-51	
		Perf. Vertical	352	353			354-56	
	USPS	Perf. Horizontal	385	386				
		Perf. Vertical	387	388			389	
IMPERF.	USPS		343	344			345-47	
	USPS	Flat Plate	383	384	408	409		
		Rotary Press				459		
	Unwmkd.	Flat Plate			481	482-82A	483-85	
		Offset			531	532-34B	535	
COIL $8^1/_2$	USPS	Perf. Horizontal	390	391	410	411		
		Perf. Vertical	392	393	412	413	394-96	
PERF. 10	USPS							460
	USPS				424	425	426-30	431-40
	Unwmkd.	Flat Plate			462	463	464-69	470-78
		Rotary Press			543			
COIL 10	USPS	Perf. Horiz. Flat			441	442		
		Perf. Horiz. Rotary			448	449-50		
		Perf. Vert. Flat			443	444	445-47	
		Perf. Vert. Rotary			452	453-55	456-58	
	Unwmkd.	Perf Horizontal			486	487-88	489	
		Perf. Vertical			490	491-92	493-96	497
PERF. 11	USPS			519				
	USPS					461		
	Unwmkd.	Flat Plate			498	499-500	501-07	508-18
		Rotary Press			*544-45	546		
		Offset			525	526-28B	529-30	
Perf. $12^1/_2$	Unwmkd.	Offset			536			
11 x 10	Unwmkd.	Rotary			538	539-40	541	
10 x 11	Unwmkd.	Rotary			542			

¢Design of #544 is 19 mm. wide x $22^1/_2$ mm. high. #545 is $19^1/_2$ to 20 mm. wide x 22 mm. high

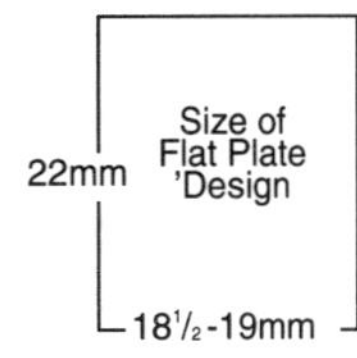

Stamps printed by rotary press are always slightly wider or taller on issues prior to 1954. Measurements do not apply to booklet singles.

HOW TO USE THIS IDENTIFICATION CHART

Numbers referred to herein are from Scott's Standard Postage Stamp Catalog. To identify any stamp in this series, first check the type by comparing it with the illustrations at the top of the chart. Then check the perforations, and whether the stamp is single or double line watermarked or unwatermarked. With this information you can quickly find out the Standard Catalog number by checking down and across the chart. For example, a 1¢ Franklin, perf. 12, single line watermark, must be Scott's #374.

The UNITED STATES STAMP IDENTIFIER

Shows you how to distinguish between the rare and common U.S. stamps that look alike.

Types of The 2¢ Washington Design of 1912-20

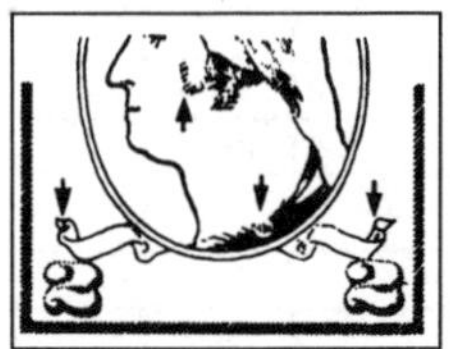
Type I

Type I where the ribbon at left above the figure "2" has one shading line in the first curve, while the ribbon at the right has one shading line in the second curve. Bottom of toga has a faint outline. Top line of toga, from bottom to front of throat, is very faint. Shading lines of the face, terminating in front of the ear, are not joined. Type I occurs on both flat and rotary press printings.

Type Ia is similar to Type I except that all of the lines are stronger. Lines of the Toga button are heavy. Occurs only of flat press printings

Type I

Type II

Type II has ribbons shaded as in Type I. Toga button and shading lines to left of it are heavy. Shading lines in front of ear are joined and end in a strong vertically curved line (arrow). Occurs only on rotary press printings.

Type III where ribbons are shaded with two lines instead of one; otherwise similar to Type II. Occurs on rotary press printings only.

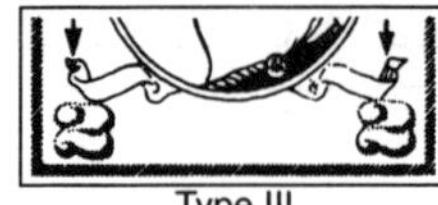
Type III

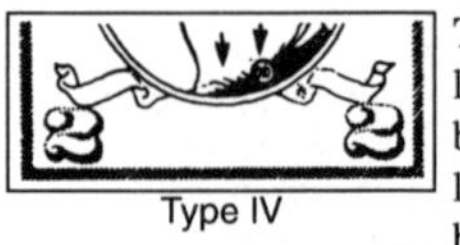
Type IV

Type IV where top line of toga is broken. Shading lines inside the toga bottom read "Did". The Line of color in the left "2" is very thin and usually broken. Occurs on offset printings only.

Type V

Type V in which top line of toga is complete. Toga button has five vertical shaded lines. Line of color in the left "2" is very thin and usually broken. Nose shaded as shown in illustration. Occurs on offset printings only.

Type Va is same as Type V except in shading dots of nose. Third row of dots from bottom has four dots instead of six. Also, the Overall height of Type Va is 1/3 millimeter less than Type V. Occurs on offset printings only.

Type Va

Type VI is same as Type V except that the line of color in left "2" is very heavy (arrow). Occurs in offset printings only.

Type VI

Type VII in which line of color in left "2" is clear and continuous and heavier than Types V or Va, but not as heavy as in Type VI. There are three rows of vertical dots (instead of two) in the shading of the upper lip, and additional dots have been added to have been added to hair at top of the head. Occurs on offset printings only.

Type VII

The UNITED STATES STAMP IDENTIFIER

Shows you how to distinguish between the rare and common U.S. stamps that look alike.

Types Of The 3¢ Washington Design Of 1908-20

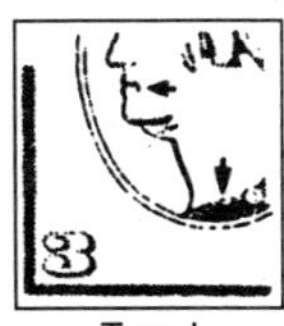
Type I

TYPE I in which the top line of the toga is weak, as are the top parts of the shading lines that join the toga line. The fifth shading line from the left (arrow) is partly cut away at the top. Also the line between the lips is thin. Occurs on flat and rotary press printings.

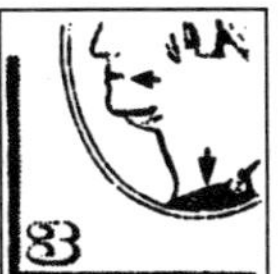
Type II

TYPE II where top line of toga is strong and the shading lines that join it are heavy and complete. The line between the lips is heavy. Occurs on flat and rotary press printings.

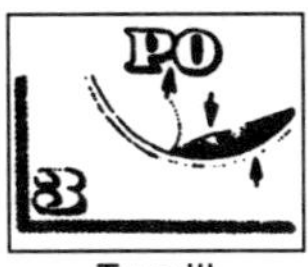
Type III

TYPE III in which top line of toga is strong, but the fifth shading line from the left (arrow) is missing. The center line of the toga button consists of two short vertical lines with a dot between them. The "P" and "O" of "POSTAGE" are separated by a small line of color. Occurs on offset printings only.

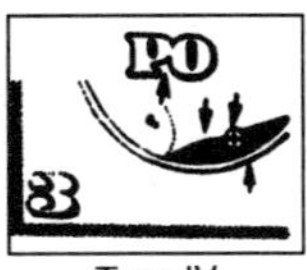
Type IV

TYPE IV in which the shading lines of the toga are complete. The center line of the toga button consists of a single unbroken vertical line running through the dot in the center. The "P" and the "O" of "POSTAGE" are joined. Type IV occurs only in offset printings.

COMMEMORATIVE IDENTIFIER

The following handy identifier is a list of commemoratives organized alphabetically by key words on the stamp which are the most prominent after "U.S. Postage" and matches the stamp with its corresponding Scott number.

- A Stamp . . . 1735-1736
- Abbott & Costello . . . 2566
- Abraham Lincoln . . . 2975j
- Abyssinian Cat . . . 2373
- Acadia National Park . . . 746, 762
- Acheson, Dean . . . 2755
- Acoma Pot . . . 1709
- Adams
  - Abigail . . . 2146
  - John . . . 806, 841, 850, 1687a, 2201, 2216b
  - John Quincy . . . 811, 846, 2201, 2216f
- Addams, Jane . . . 878
- Admiralty Head Lighthouse (WA) . . . 2470, 2474
- Adventures of Huckleberry Finn, The . . . 2787
- African
  - Americans . . . 873, 902, 953, 1085, 1233, 1290, 1361, 1372, 1486, 1490-1491, 1493, 1495, 1554, 1560, 1772, 1790, 1791, 1860, 1865, 2027, 2043, 2051, 2083, 2084, 2097, 2164, 2211, 2223, 2275, 2420, 2496, 2746, 2766, C97, C102, C103, C105
  - Elephant Herd . . . 1388
  - Violet . . . 2495
- Agave Cactus . . . 1943
- Aging Together . . . 2011
- AIDS Awareness . . . 2806
- Air
  - Air Service Emblem . . . C5
  - -Cushion Vehicle . . . C123, C126
  - Force . . . 1013, C49
  - Mail Service, US . . . C74
  - Save Our . . . 1413
  - Service Emblem . . . C5
- Aircraft Gun 90mm, Anti . . . 900
- Airlift . . . 1341
- Airliner, Hypersonic . . . C122, C126
- Alabama . . . 1654, 1953
  - Statehood . . . 1375
- Alamo, The . . . 776, 778, 1043
- Alaska . . . 1681, 1954
  - (Cook, Captain James) . . . 1732, 1733
  - Highway . . . 2635
  - Purchase . . . C70
  - Statehood . . . 2066, C53
  - Territory . . . 800
  - -Yukon Pacific Exposition . . . 370-371
- Alaskan Malamute . . . 2100
- Albania . . . 918
- Alcoholism, You Can Beat It . . . 1927
- Alcott, Louisa May . . . 862
- Alexandria . . . C40
- Alger, Horatio . . . 2010
- Allegiance, Pledge of . . . 2594
- Allen, Ethan . . . 1071
- Alliance for Progress . . . 1234
- Alliance, French . . . 1753
- Allied Nations . . . 537, 907
- Allied Victory . . . 537
- Alligator . . . 1428
- Allosaurus . . . 1390
- Alta, California, 1st Civil Settlement . . . 1725
- Amateur Radio . . . 1260
- Ambulance . . . 2128, 2231
- America, Beautification of . . . 1318, 1365, 1366
- America's Libraries . . . 2015
- America PUAS . . . 2426, 2512, C121, C127
- America/PUASP . . . C131
- American . . . 1596, 1597, 1598, 1599, 1603-1606, 1608, 1610-1615
  - Architecture . . . 1779-1782, 1838, 1839-1841, 1928-1931, 2019-2022
  - Arts . . . 1484-1487, 1553-1555
  - ATM Stamps . . .
  - Automobile Association . . . 1007
  - Bald Eagle . . . 1387
  - Bankers Association, Jan. 3 . . . 987
  - Bar Association . . . 1022
  - Bicentennial . . . 1432, 1456-1459, 1476-1479, 1480-1483, 1543-1546, 1559-1568, 1629-1631, 1633-1647, 1648-1667, 1668-1674, 1676-1682, 1686-1694, 1704, 1716-1720, 1722, 1726, 1728, 1753, 1789, 1811, 1813, 1816, 1937-1938, 2052
  - Cats . . . 2372-2373, 2374-2375
  - Chemical Society . . . 1002
  - Circus . . . 1309
  - Credo . . . 1139-1144
  - Dance . . . 1749-1752
  - Dance, Ballet . . . 1749
  - Dogs . . . 2098-2101
  - Flag . . . 1623, 2116
  - Folklore . . . 1317, 1330, 1357, 1370, 1470, 1548
  - Foxhound . . . 2101
  - Horses . . . 2155-2158
  - Indian . . . 565, 695, 1364
  - Indian Dances . . . 3072-3076
  - Institute of Architects . . . 1089
  - Kestrel . . . 2476-2477, 3044
  - Legion . . . 1369
  - Militia . . . 1568
  - Music . . . 1252, 2721-2737, 2767-2778, 2849-2861, 2982-2992
  - Owls . . . 1760-1763
  - Philatelic Society . . . 730-731, 750, 766, 770
  - Red Cross . . . 702, 967, 1910
  - Revolution . . . 551, 645, 651, 653, 657, 689, 690, 727, 734, 752, 1010, 1729, 1851, 1937-1938
  - Revolution Battles . . . 617-619, 629-630, 643-644, 646, 688, 1003, 1361, 1563-1564, 1686, 1722, 1728, 1826
  - Shoals Lighthouse (FL) . . . 2473
  - Shorthair Cat . . . 2375
  - Sign Language . . . 2784
  - Society of Civil Engineers . . . 1012
  - Sports . . . 1932-1933, 2046, 2097, 2376-2377, 2417
  - Streetcar, First . . . 2059
  - Trees . . . 1764-1767
  - Turners Society . . . 979
  - Washington . . . 1675
  - Wildlife . . . 2286-2287, 2288-2307, 2308-2316, 2322-2335
  - Woman . . . 1152

BLANK PAGES FOR U.S. AND WORLDWIDE ALBUMS

Speed-rille® Album Pages. Faint guide lines help you make neat, attractive arrangements without a lot of measuring. Use them to expand your album or create your own specialty pages. 128 pages (64 sheets) each package, printed on both sides with borders to match your worldwide albums. **$7.95 each**

3HRS17	Speed-rille® Pages for Worldwide
3HRS15	Speed-rille® Pages for U.S. and Canada

Blank Album Pages. Bordered blank pages to fit your loose-leaf worldwide albums. 128 pages (64 sheets) printed on both sides in each package. **$7.95 each**

3HRS18	Blank Worldwide Pages
3HRS16	Blank U.S. and Canada Pages

U.S. Postage #1-4

GENERAL ISSUES

1, 3, 948a
Franklin

2, 4, 948b
Washington

1847, THE FIRST ISSUE

Imperforate

"For every single letter in manuscript or paper of any kind by or upon which information shall be asked or communicated in writing or by marks or signs conveyed in the mail, for any distance under three hundred miles, five cents; and for any distance over three hundred miles, ten cents . . . and every letter or parcel not exceeding half an ounce in weight shall be deemed a single letter, and every additional weight of half ounce, shall be charged with an additional single postage."

With these words, the Act of March 3, 1845, authorized, but not required, the prepayment of postage effective July 1, 1847, and created a need for the first United States postage stamps. Benjamin Franklin, as the first Postmaster General of the United States and the man generally regarded as the "father" of the postal system, was selected for the 5 cent stamp. As the first President of the United States, George Washington was designated for the 10 cent issue.

The 1847 stamps were released July 1, 1847, but were available only in the New York City post office on that date. The earliest known usages are July 7 for the 5 cent and July 2 for the 10 cent.

The best estimates are that 4,400,000 of the 5 cent and 1,050,000 of the 10 cent stamps reached the public. The remaining stocks were destroyed when the stamps were demonetized and could no longer be used for postage as of July 1, 1851.

Like most 19th century United States stamps, the first Issue is much more difficult to find unused than used. Stamps canceled by "handstamp" marking devices—usually carved from cork—are scarcer than those with manuscript, or "pen", cancels.

Issued without gum, the Reproductions of the 1847 issue were printed from entirely new dies for display at the 1876 Centennial Exposition and were not valid for postal use. The issue also was reproduced on a souvenir sheet issued in 1947 to celebrate the centenary of the First Issue. Differences between the 1847 issue, 1875 Reproductions and 1948 stamps are described in the Stamp Identifier at the front of this catalog.

SCOTT NO.	DESCRIPTION	UNUSED VF	UNUSED F	UNUSED AVG	USED VF	USED F	USED AVG
	1847 Imperforate						
1	5¢ red brown	7950.00	5250.00	3250.00	875.00	550.00	375.00
1	— Pen cancel	....	....	....	600.00	400.00	275.00
2	10¢ black	36000.00	19000.00	10500.00	2100.00	1550.00	900.00
2	— Pen cancel	....	....	....	1350.00	800.00	600.00
	1875 Reprints of 1847 Issues, without gum						
3	5¢ red brown	1600.00	950.00	850.00	....	....	....
4	10¢ black	1950.00	1150.00	1000.00	....	....	....

U.S. Postage #5-47

5-9, 18-24, 40
Franklin

10, 11, 25, 26, 41
Washington

12, 27-30A, 42
Jefferson

13-16, 31-35, 43
Washington

1851-61. THE CLASSIC ISSUES

An act of Congress approved March 3, 1851, enacted new, reduced postage rates, introduced additional rates and made the prepayment of additional postage compulsory. Although the use of postage stamps was not required, the 1851 Act stimulated their use and paved the way for their required usage from July 1, 1855 on.

Under the Act of 1851, the basic prepaid single letter rate (defined as one-half ounce or less) was set at 3 cents. As this would be the most commonly used value, it was decided that a likeness of George Washington should grace the 3 cent stamp. Benjamin Franklin was assigned to the 1 cent stamp, which, among other usages, met the newspaper and circular rates.

Washington also appears on the 10, 12, 24 and 90 cent stamps and Franklin on the 30 cent value. Thomas Jefferson was selected for the new 5 cent stamp that was issued in 1856.

By 1857, improved production techniques and the increasing usage of stamps led to the introduction of perforated stamps that could be more easily separated. The result was the 1857-61 series whose designs are virtually identical to the 1851 set. The 1857-61 perforated stamps were set in the printing plates with very little space between each stamp. As a result, insufficient space was allowed to accommodate the perforations, which often cut into the design on these stamps. In fact, stamps with complete designs and wide margins on all four sides are the exception and command very substantial premiums.

The most fascinating—and most challenging—feature of the 1851-61 stamps is the identification of many major and minor types. An extremely slight design variation can mean a difference of thousands of dollars and collectors even today can apply their knowledge to discover rare, mis-identified types.

The various "Types", identified below by Roman numerals in parentheses, resulted from minor changes in the printing plates caused by wear or plate retouching. The 1851-57 one-cent blue stamp may be the most studied of all the United States issues and is found in seven major catalog-listed Types (14, if we count imperforate and perforated stamps separately), plus countless minor listed and unlisted varieties. A thorough explanation of the differences in the major types for all denominations of the 1857-61 series is contained in the Harris Stamp Identifier in this catalog.

Shortly after the outbreak of the Civil War, the 1851-61 stamps were demonetized to prevent Southern post offices from selling the stamps in the North to raise cash for the Confederate States. After the war, large supplies of unused 1857-61 stamps were located in Southern post offices and purchased by stamp dealers and collectors. This explains the relatively large supply of unused 1857-61 issues that still exist today. The short life and limited use of 90 cent high value, which was issued in 1860, and the 5 cent orange brown, released May 8, 1861, explains why those stamps sell for more used than unused.

U.S. Postage #5-47

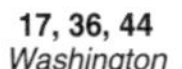

17, 36, 44
Washington

37, 45
Washington

38, 46
Franklin

39, 47
Washington

SCOTT NO.	DESCRIPTION	UNUSED VF	UNUSED F	UNUSED AVG	USED VF	USED F	USED AVG
	1851-57 Imperforate (OG + 50%)						
5	1¢ blue (I)	....	....	....	....	....	....
5A	1¢ blue (Ib)	20500.00	12000.00	8000.00	7000.00	3800.00	2500.00
6	1¢ dark blue (Ia)	35000.00	25000.00	15000.00	9000.00	5950.00	3750.00
7	1¢ blue (II)	800.00	485.00	310.00	170.00	85.00	55.00
8	1¢ blue (III)	8000.00	4800.00	3200.00	2500.00	1400.00	825.00
8A	1¢ blue (IIIa)	3500.00	2100.00	1300.00	950.00	550.00	340.00
9	1¢ blue (IV)	580.00	320.00	210.00	140.00	75.00	50.00
10	3¢ orange brown (I)	1800.00	1000.00	700.00	75.00	40.00	32.00
11	3¢ deep claret (I)	240.00	125.00	85.00	13.00	6.00	4.50
12	5¢ red brown (I)	15000.00	9000.00	6000.00	1600.00	900.00	650.00
13	10¢ green (I)	14000.00	8500.00	5500.00	1050.00	550.00	400.00
14	10¢ green (II)	2900.00	1800.00	1100.00	400.00	240.00	180.00
15	10¢ green (III)	3000.00	1850.00	1200.00	450.00	240.00	190.00
16	10¢ green (IV)	18000.00	10000.00	7000.00	1800.00	1000.00	850.00
17	12¢ black	4000.00	2400.00	1350.00	420.00	240.00	170.00
	1857-61 Same design as preceding Issue, Perf. 15-1/2 (†) (OG + 50%)						
18	1¢ blue (I)	1300.00	725.00	450.00	525.00	340.00	225.00
19	1¢ blue (Ia)	18000.00	10000.00	6500.00	4000.00	2500.00	1550.00
20	1¢ blue (II)	800.00	450.00	285.00	250.00	120.00	80.00
21	1¢ blue (III)	8000.00	4500.00	2400.00	2200.00	1290.00	700.00
22	1¢ blue (IIIa)	1250.00	700.00	390.00	350.00	235.00	140.00
23	1¢ blue (IV)	3400.00	1900.00	1100.00	425.00	295.00	180.00
24	1¢ blue (V)	200.00	110.00	65.00	52.00	22.50	16.00
25	3¢ rose (I)	1100.00	600.00	395.00	55.00	27.50	18.00
26	3¢ dull red (II)	100.00	40.00	35.50	8.00	3.00	2.00
26a	3¢ dull red (IIa)	175.00	100.00	70.00	40.00	22.50	12.75
27	5¢ brick red (I)	11750.00	7600.00	4850.00	1500.00	750.00	425.00
28	5¢ red brown (I)	2500.00	1350.00	850.00	600.00	250.00	135.00
28A	5¢ Indian red (I)	16000.00	9200.00	6300.00	3400.00	1850.00	1150.00
29	5¢ brown (I)	1400.00	775.00	460.00	400.00	190.00	110.00
30	5¢ orange brown (II) ...	1200.00	725.00	475.00	1500.00	800.00	475.00
30A	5¢ brown (II)	750.00	420.00	250.00	325.00	175.00	105.00
31	10¢ green (I)	9500.00	5200.00	2950.00	900.00	500.00	290.00
32	10¢ green (II)	3200.00	1800.00	1025.00	300.00	165.00	110.00
33	10¢ green (III)	3200.00	1800.00	1025.00	300.00	165.00	110.00
34	10¢ green (IV)	25000.00	16500.00	11250.00	3000.00	1550.00	800.00
35	10¢ green (V)	325.00	190.00	110.00	115.00	50.00	30.00
36	12¢ black, Plate I	515.00	360.00	195.00	145.00	80.00	50.00
36b	12¢ black, Plate III	550.00	320.00	155.00	180.00	100.00	65.00
37	24¢ gray lilac	1050.00	575.00	350.00	380.00	215.00	135.00
38	30¢ orange	1250.00	650.00	450.00	500.00	260.00	140.00
39	90¢ blue	2150.00	1100.00	800.00	6500.00	3100.00	2000.00
	1875 Reprints of 1857-61 Issue. Perf. 12 Without Gum						
40	1¢ bright blue	950.00	650.00	425.00	....	....	....
41	3¢ scarlet	4875.00	3250.00	2150.00	....	....	....
42	5¢ orange brown	1650.00	1100.00	700.00	....	....	....
43	10¢ blue green	3750.00	2500.00	1600.00	....	....	....
44	12¢ greenish black	4500.00	3000.00	2000.00	....	....	....
45	24¢ blackish violet	4875.00	3250.00	2150.00	....	....	....
46	30¢ yellow orange	4725.00	3150.00	2100.00	....	....	....
47	90¢ deep blue	7100.00	4750.00	3200.00	....	....	....

(†) means Issue is actually very poorly centered.
Perforations may touch the design on "Fine" quality.

U.S. Postage #55-78

55, 63, 85A
86, 92, 102
Franklin

56, 64-66, 74, 79, 82,
83, 85, 85C, 88, 94, 104
Washington

57, 67, 75, 76
80, 95, 105
Jefferson

58, 62B, 68
85D, 89, 96, 106
Washington

59, 69, 85E,
90, 97, 107
Washington

60, 70, 78,
99, 109
Washington

61, 71, 81,
100, 110
Franklin

62, 72, 101, 111
Washington

73, 84, 85B
87, 93, 103
Jackson

77, 85F, 91,
98, 108
Lincoln

THE 1861-67 ISSUE

The 1861-66 Issue and its 1867 Grilled varieties are among the most interesting and controversial of all stamps. Born out of the need to demonetize previously-issued stamps in the possession of Southern post offices, they were rushed into service shortly after the outbreak of the Civil War.

The controversy begins with the "August Issues", catalog #s 55-62B. It is now generally accepted that all but the 10 and 24 cent values never were issued for use as postage. The set is more aptly described as "First Designs", because they were printed by the National Bank Note Company and submitted to the Post Office Department as fully gummed and perforated sample designs.

SCOTT NO.	DESCRIPTION	UNUSED VF	UNUSED F	UNUSED AVG	USED VF	USED F	USED AVG
	1861 First Designs (†) Perf. 12 (OG + 50%)						
55	1¢ indigo	30000.00	20000.00	10000.00	....	....	....
56	3¢ brown red	1250.00	825.00	500.00	....	....	....
57	5¢ brown	22500.00	15000.00	9000.00	....	....	....
58	10¢ dark green	10000.00	6700.00	4000.00	....	....	....
59	12¢ black	63500.00	42500.00	27500.00	....	....	....
60	24¢ dark violet	10500.00	7000.00	4250.00	....	....	....
61	30¢ red orange	27500.00	19000.00	14500.00	....	....	....
62	90¢ dark blue	33500.00	27500.00	14000.00	....	....	....
62B	10¢ dark green	10500.00	7000.00	4500.00	825.00	550.00	325.00
	1861-62 Second Design (†) Perf. 12 (OG + 50%)						
63	1¢ blue	250.00	125.00	82.00	40.00	20.00	13.00
64	3¢ pink	5280.00	3250.00	2000.00	650.00	400.00	275.00
64b	3¢ rose pink	600.00	300.00	180.00	105.00	58.00	35.00
65	3¢ rose	125.00	62.00	40.00	4.00	1.80	1.00
66	3¢ lake	2850.00	1900.00	1200.00	....	....	....
67	5¢ buff	8000.00	4800.00	3200.00	700.00	425.00	250.00
68	10¢ yellow green	520.00	260.00	150.00	60.00	33.00	19.00
69	12¢ black	950.00	500.00	325.00	120.00	65.00	30.00
70	24¢ red lilac	1100.00	600.00	375.00	160.00	95.00	55.00
71	30¢ orange	950.00	525.00	325.00	130.00	70.00	40.00
72	90¢ blue	2400.00	1300.00	710.00	450.00	265.00	160.00
	1861-66 (†) (OG + 50%)						
73	2¢ black	240.00	125.00	50.00	60.00	22.00	14.00
74	3¢ scarlet	7800.00	4350.00	2850.00	2900.00	1970.00	1125.00
75	5¢ red brown	2300.00	1300.00	750.00	370.00	225.00	140.00
76	5¢ brown	550.00	315.00	195.00	85.00	55.00	35.00
77	15¢ black	800.00	500.00	275.00	105.00	65.00	40.00
78	24¢ lilac	525.00	275.00	145.00	95.00	48.00	33.50

U.S. Postage #79-111

From 1867 to 1870, grills were embossed into the stamp paper to break the fiber and prevent the eradication of cancellations. The first "A" grilled issues were grilled all over. When postal clerks found that the stamps were as likely to separate along the grill as on the perforations, the Post Office abandoned the "A" grill and tried other configurations, none of which proved to be effective. The Grilled Issues include some of our greatest rarities. The most notable is the 1 cent "Z", only two of which are known to exist. One realized $418,000 in a 1986 auction, making it the most valuable United States stamp. The grills are fully explained and identified in the Harris Stamp Identifier.

SCOTT NO.	DESCRIPTION	UNUSED VF	UNUSED F	UNUSED AVG	USED VF	USED F	USED AVG
	1867 Grill with Points Up A. Grill Covering Entire Stamp (†) (OG + 50%)						
79	3¢ rose	3600.00	1850.00	1100.00	710.00	375.00	250.00
80	5¢ brown	75000.00	50000.00	30000.00	70000.00	47000.00	28000.00
81	30¢ orange	....	....	....	54000.00	30000.00	21500.00
	B. Grill about 18 x 15 mm. (OG + 50%)						
82	3¢ rose	....	....	....	75000.00	42000.00	30000.00
	C. Grill About 13 x 16 mm. (†) (OG + 50%)						
83	3¢ rose	3300.00	1800.00	1100.00	700.00	375.00	240.00
	1867 Grill with Points Down D. Grill About 12 x 14 mm. (†) (OG + 50%)						
84	2¢ black	6100.00	3950.00	2050.00	1800.00	1000.00	625.00
85	3¢ rose	2800.00	1500.00	890.00	775.00	435.00	275.00
	Z. Grill About 11 x 14 mm. (†) (OG + 50%)						
85A	1¢ blue	....	....	....	....	....	....
85B	2¢ black	2500.00	1350.00	725.00	650.00	360.00	205.00
85C	3¢ rose	7000.00	4100.00	2150.00	1400.00	900.00	550.00
85E	12¢ black	3200.00	1800.00	980.00	900.00	525.00	325.00
85F	15¢ black	....	....	....	....	....	....
	E. Grill About 11 x 13 mm. (†) (OG + 50%)						
86	1¢ blue	1400.00	800.00	435.00	420.00	225.00	140.00
87	2¢ black	600.00	365.00	215.00	140.00	70.00	38.00
88	3¢ rose	480.00	260.00	155.00	18.00	10.00	6.00
89	10¢ green	2400.00	1400.00	800.00	290.00	160.00	100.00
90	12¢ black	3200.00	1750.00	900.00	320.00	180.00	120.00
91	15¢ black	5900.00	3200.00	1650.00	800.00	435.00	260.00
	F. Grill About 9 x 13 mm. (†) (OG + 50%)						
92	1¢ blue	700.00	425.00	250.00	165.00	100.00	60.00
93	2¢ black	210.00	140.00	75.00	55.00	25.00	18.00
94	3¢ red	150.00	95.00	55.00	6.00	3.00	1.50
95	5¢ brown	1500.00	850.00	495.00	400.00	225.00	135.00
96	10¢ yellow green	1200.00	725.00	370.00	180.00	100.00	65.00
97	12¢ black	1200.00	750.00	370.00	210.00	120.00	70.00
98	15¢ black	1450.00	750.00	375.00	200.00	125.00	75.00
99	24¢ gray lilac	2500.00	1450.00	825.00	800.00	425.00	275.00
100	30¢ orange	3200.00	1750.00	850.00	600.00	340.00	225.00
101	90¢ blue	7000.00	4200.00	2450.00	1300.00	750.00	525.00

The Re-Issues of the 1861-66 Issue were issued with gum and, while scarce, are found used. They can be distinguished by their bright colors, sharp printing impressions, hard paper and white, crackly original gum.

SCOTT NO.	DESCRIPTION	UNUSED VF	UNUSED F	UNUSED AVG	USED VF	USED F	USED AVG
	1875. Re-Issue of 1861-66 Issue. Hard White Paper (OG + 50%)						
102	1¢ blue	800.00	575.00	385.00	1250.00	900.00	600.00
103	2¢ black	4000.00	2850.00	1900.00	5950.00	4250.00	2850.00
104	3¢ brown red	5250.00	3750.00	2500.00	6750.00	4850.00	3250.00
105	5¢ brown	2800.00	2000.00	1300.00	3500.00	2500.00	1700.00
106	10¢ green	3200.00	2350.00	1500.00	5600.00	4000.00	2700.00
107	12¢ black	4550.00	3250.00	2150.00	6300.00	4500.00	2950.00
108	15¢ black	4550.00	3250.00	2150.00	7000.00	5000.00	3350.00
109	24¢ deep violet	6300.00	4500.00	3000.00	8400.00	6000.00	4000.00
110	30¢ brownish orange	6500.00	4650.00	3100.00	9800.00	7000.00	4500.00
111	90¢ blue	8750.00	6250.00	4150.00	28000.00	20000.00	12000.00

U.S. Postage #112-133a

112, 123, 133, 133a
Franklin

113, 124
Pony Express Rider

114, 125
Locomotive

115, 126
Washington

116, 127
Shield & Eagle

117, 128
S.S. Adriatic

118, 119, 129
Landing of Columbus

120, 130
Signing of Declaration

121, 131
Shield, Eagle & Flags

122, 132
Lincoln

THE 1869 PICTORIALS

As the first United States series to include pictorial designs, the 1869 issue is one of the most popular today. They were so unpopular that they were removed from sale less than a year after issue. Most protests were directed toward their odd size and the tradition-breaking pictorial designs.

The 1869 issue broke important new ground in the use of two color designs. Not only does this add to their attractiveness; it also is the source for the first United States "Inverted Centers". These inverted errors appear on the bi-colored 15, 24 and 30 cent values. The printing technology of the time required a separate printing pass for each color. On the first pass, the central designs, or vignettes, were printed. The second pass applied the frames.

In a very few instances, the sheets with their central designs already printed were passed upside down through the printing press. As a result, the frames were printed upside down. So the description "inverted center" for the 15 and 24 cent errors is technically incorrect, but the form in which these errors are photographed and displayed is with the center, rather than the frame, inverted.

Used copies of the 1869 Pictorials are not as scarce as might be expected. Any of the stamps above the 3 cent denomination were used on mail to Europe and were saved by collectors overseas. When stamp collecting became popular in the United States and Americans were able to purchase stamps abroad at relatively low prices, many of these used 1869 Pictorials found their way back to this country. On the other hand, because of the short life of the issue in post offices and their sudden withdrawal, unused stamps—particularly the high values—are quite rare.

All values of the 1869 Pictorials are found with the "G" grill. Ungrilled varieties are known on all values except the 6, 10, 12 and type II 15 cent stamps. (The Harris Stamp Identifier describes the difference in the three 15 cent types.)

The 1869 Pictorials were re-issued in 1875 in anticipation of the 1876 Centennial Exposition. Most collectors who had missed the original 1869 issue were delighted to have a second chance to purchase the stamps, which explains why the high value re-issues carry lower prices today than do the original 1869 pictorials. At the time, most collectors did not realize they were buying entirely different stamps. The same designs were used, but the re-issues were issued on a distinctive hard, white paper without grills.

The 1 cent stamp was re-issued a second time, in 1880. This re-issue can be distinguished by the lack of a grill and by the soft, porous paper used by the American Bank Note Company.

U.S. Postage #112-133a

SCOTT NO.	DESCRIPTION	UNUSED VF	UNUSED F	UNUSED AVG	USED VF	USED F	USED AVG
	1869 G. Grill measuring 9-1/2 x 9-1/2 mm. (†) (OG + 40%)						
112	1¢ buff	400.00	225.00	125.00	110.00	65.00	41.50
113	2¢ brown	300.00	175.00	105.00	45.00	30.00	18.50
114	3¢ ultramarine	275.00	150.00	85.00	10.00	7.50	4.50
115	6¢ ultramarine	1200.00	700.00	400.00	140.00	100.00	65.00
116	10¢ yellow	1400.00	810.00	410.00	140.00	95.00	62.50
117	12¢ green	1200.00	725.00	425.00	145.00	105.00	57.50
118	15¢ brown & blue (I)	3000.00	1800.00	1075.00	600.00	425.00	200.00
119	15¢ brown & blue (II)	1600.00	900.00	500.00	275.00	160.00	85.00
120	24¢ green & violet	3500.00	2000.00	1100.00	700.00	500.00	310.00
121	30¢ blue & carmine	3800.00	2100.00	1200.00	375.00	260.00	165.00
122	90¢ carmine & black	9850.00	6000.00	3500.00	1750.00	1275.00	775.00
	1875 Re-Issue of 1869 Issue. Hard White Paper. Without Grill (OG + 30%)						
123	1¢ buff	550.00	300.00	210.00	350.00	200.00	125.00
124	2¢ brown	650.00	350.00	235.00	600.00	350.00	205.00
125	3¢ blue	5000.00	3000.00	2150.00	....	....	....
126	6¢ blue	1400.00	800.00	550.00	900.00	500.00	375.00
127	10¢ yellow	2400.00	1300.00	890.00	2000.00	1250.00	875.00
128	12¢ green	2800.00	1500.00	900.00	2400.00	1300.00	875.00
129	15¢ brown & blue (III)	2200.00	1250.00	800.00	1100.00	600.00	400.00
130	24¢ green & violet	2000.00	1200.00	750.00	1000.00	575.00	385.00
131	30¢ blue & carmine	3000.00	1600.00	1100.00	1800.00	1100.00	750.00
132	90¢ carmine & black	9000.00	5000.00	3500.00	11500.00	6000.00	4500.00
	1880 Re-Issue. Soft Porous Paper, Issued Without Grill (†) (#133 OG +30%)						
133	1¢ buff	350.00	200.00	130.00	250.00	135.00	80.00
133a	1¢ brown orange (issued w/o gum)	325.00	175.00	120.00	190.00	110.00	65.00

1870 Bank Note Issues

134, 145, 156, 167, 182, 192, 206 *Franklin*	**135, 146, 157, 168, 178, 180, 183, 193, 203** *Jackson*	**136, 147, 158, 169, 184, 194, 207, 214** *Washington*	**137, 148, 159, 170, 186, 195, 208** *Lincoln*	**138, 149, 160, 171, 196** *Stanton*	**139, 150, 161, 172, 187, 188, 197, 209** *Jefferson*

THE 1870-88 BANK NOTE ISSUES

The "Bank Notes" are stamps that were issued between 1870 and 1888 by the National, Continental and American Bank Note Companies.

The myriad of varieties, secret marks, papers, grills, re-engravings and special printings produced by the three companies resulted in no less than 87 major catalog listings for what basically amounts to 16 different designs. For collectors, what seems to be the very difficult task of properly identifying all these varieties can be eased by following these guidelines:

1. The chronological order in which the three Bank Note companies produced stamps is their reverse alphabetical order: National, Continental, American.

2. "3, 6, 9" identifies the number of years each of the companies printed stamps within the 18-year Bank Note period. Starting in 1870, National continued its work for 3 more years, until 1873, when the Continental Company began printing stamps. That company served for the next 6 years, until 1879, when American took over the Continental company. Although American printed some later issues, the "Bank Note" period ended 9 years later, in 1888.

3. The first Bank Note issue, the Nationals of 1870-71, continued the practice of grilling stamps. Although some specialists contend there are grilled Continental stamps, for all intents and purposes, if a Bank Note stamp bears a genuine grill, it must be from the 1870-71 National issue.

4. The secret marks on values through the 12 cent, and possibly the 15 cent value, were added when the Continental Company took over. They enabled the government to distinguish between National's work and that of its successor. If a Bank Note stamp did not show a secret mark, the Post Office could identify it as the work of the National Bank Note Company. You can do the same.

5. The paper used by the National and Continental companies is similar, but that of the American Bank Note company is noticably different from the first two. When held to the light, the thick, soft American paper shows its coarse, uneven texture, while that of its two predecessors is more even and translucent. The American Bank Note paper also reveals a yellowish hue when held to the light, whereas the National and Continental papers are whiter.

6. Experienced collectors also apply a "snap test" to identify American Bank Note paper by gently flexing a Bank Note stamp at one of its corners. The American Bank Note paper will not "snap" back into place. The National and Continental stamps, on the other hand, often give off a noticeable sound when the flex is released.

U.S. Postage #134-166

140, 151, 162, 173, 198
Clay

141, 152, 163, 174, 189, 199
Webster

142, 153, 164, 175, 200
Scott

143, 154, 165, 176, 190, 201, 217
Hamilton

144, 155, 166, 177, 191, 202, 218
Perry

7. By purchasing one Bank Note design put into use after 1882 (which can only be an American) and one early Bank Note stamp without the secret mark, (which can only be a National), the collector has a reference point against which to compare any other Bank Note stamp. If it is a soft paper, it is an American Bank Note issue; if a harder paper, it is either a National or a Continental—and these two can be classified by the absence (National) or presence (Continental) of the secret marks or other distinguishing features or colors. The Harris Stamp Identifier in this catalog provides illustrations of the secret marks and further information on the distinguishing features of the various Bank Notes. With two reference stamps, some practice and the use of the information in this catalog, collectors can turn the "job" of understanding the Bank Notes into a pleasant adventure.

1870 National Bank Note Co., without Secret Marks.
With H Grill about (10x 12mm. or 8-1/2x 10 mm.) Perf 12. (†)
(OG + 40%)

SCOTT NO.	DESCRIPTION	UNUSED VF	UNUSED F	UNUSED AVG	USED VF	USED F	USED AVG
134	1¢ ultramarine	900.00	540.00	265.00	100.00	56.00	33.50
135	2¢ red brown	700.00	390.00	195.00	60.00	35.00	22.50
136	3¢ green	575.00	300.00	150.00	18.00	10.00	7.50
137	6¢ carmine	3000.00	1650.00	825.00	400.00	235.00	140.00
138	7¢ vermillion	2100.00	1150.00	595.00	390.00	225.00	130.00
139	10¢ brown	2500.00	1400.00	750.00	700.00	390.00	235.00
140	12¢ dull violet	25000.00	13000.00	8000.00	2500.00	1400.00	850.00
141	15¢ orange	3750.00	2000.00	960.00	1200.00	680.00	375.00
142	24¢ purple	....	....	....	18000.00	9500.00	6000.00
143	30¢ black	8000.00	4500.00	2400.00	1500.00	800.00	475.00
144	90¢ carmine	9800.00	6000.00	3100.00	1350.00	725.00	400.00

1870-71. National Bank Note Co., without Secret Marks.
Without Grill. Perf 12. (†)
(OG + 40%)

SCOTT NO.	DESCRIPTION	UNUSED VF	UNUSED F	UNUSED AVG	USED VF	USED F	USED AVG
145	1¢ ultramarine	320.00	175.00	95.00	14.00	7.00	5.00
146	2¢ red brown	120.00	65.00	40.00	10.00	5.00	3.00
147	3¢ green	200.00	125.00	75.00	2.00	.50	.25
148	6¢ carmine	400.00	220.00	120.00	18.00	10.00	7.00
149	7¢ vermillion	600.00	340.00	180.00	80.00	45.00	28.00
150	10¢ brown	400.00	240.00	115.00	20.00	10.00	7.00
151	12¢ dull violet	950.00	525.00	280.00	120.00	60.00	36.00
152	15¢ bright orange	950.00	500.00	270.00	120.00	60.00	35.00
153	24¢ purple	1050.00	600.00	325.00	150.00	75.00	46.00
154	30¢ black	1800.00	1050.00	525.00	160.00	90.00	52.00
155	90¢ carmine	2500.00	1400.00	750.00	300.00	170.00	100.00

1873. Continental Bank Note Co. Same designs as 1870-71, with Secret Marks, on thin hard grayish white paper. Perf 12 (†)
(OG + 30%)

SCOTT NO.	DESCRIPTION	UNUSED VF	UNUSED F	UNUSED AVG	USED VF	USED F	USED AVG
156	1¢ ultramarine	100.00	55.00	30.00	4.00	2.00	1.50
157	2¢ brown	300.00	155.00	80.00	13.00	7,50	4.00
158	3¢ green	85.00	45.00	25.00	.40	.15	.15
159	6¢ dull pink	360.00	200.00	110.00	18.00	9.50	5.75
160	7¢ orange vermillion ...	760.00	420.00	245.00	90.00	50.00	28.00
161	10¢ brown	410.00	230.00	125.00	17.00	9.00	5.50
162	12¢ black violet	1000.00	610.00	315.00	125.00	70.00	35.00
163	15¢ yellow orange	1000.00	600.00	310.00	110.00	60.00	36.00
165	30¢ gray black	1100.00	650.00	390.00	110.00	60.00	36.00
166	90¢ rose carmine	2200.00	1350.00	710.00	340.00	195.00	110.00

U.S. Postage #167-204

1875 Special Printing—On Hard White Wove Paper—Without Gum
Perf 12

SCOTT NO.	DESCRIPTION	UNUSED VF	UNUSED F	UNUSED AVG	USED VF	USED F	USED AVG
167	1¢ ultramarine	13500.00	8500.00	5250.00	....	....	....
168	2¢ dark brown	6350.00	4000.00	2650.00	....	....	....
169	3¢ blue green	16750.00	10500.00	6500.00	....	....	....
170	6¢ dull rose	15250.00	9500.00	5750.00	....	....	....
171	7¢ reddish vermillion	3600.00	2250.00	1350.00	....	....	....
172	10¢ pale brown	13750.00	8750.00	5500.00	....	....	....
173	12¢ dark violet	5200.00	3250.00	2000.00	....	....	....
174	15¢ bright orange	14350.00	9000.00	5350.00	....	....	....
175	24¢ dull purple	3200.00	2000.00	1250.00	....	....	....
176	30¢ greenish black	12750.00	8000.00	5000.00	....	....	....
177	90¢ violet carmine	12750.00	8000.00	5000.00	....	....	....

179, 181, 185, 204
Taylor

205, 205C, 216
Garfield

210, 211B, 213
Washington

211, 211D, 215
Jackson

212
Franklin

1875 Continental Bank Note Co.

Hard yellowish paper, Perf 12. (†)
(OG + 30%)

SCOTT NO.	DESCRIPTION	UNUSED VF	UNUSED F	UNUSED AVG	USED VF	USED F	USED AVG
178	2¢ vermillion	300.00	160.00	95.00	10.00	5.00	3.00
179	5¢ blue	325.00	190.00	100.00	15.00	8.00	5.00

1875 Continental Bank Note Co., Special Printings.
Same as 1875, on hard white paper, without gum. Perf 12.

SCOTT NO.	DESCRIPTION	UNUSED VF	UNUSED F	UNUSED AVG	USED VF	USED F	USED AVG
180	2¢ carmine vermillion	27500.00	20000.00	12000.00	....	....	....
181	5¢ bright blue	50000.00	35500.00	22500.00	....	....	....

1879 American Bank Note Co.

Same designs as 1870-71 Issue (with Secret Marks) and 1875 Issue on soft, porous, coarse, yellowish paper. Perf 12. (†)
(OG + 30%)

SCOTT NO.	DESCRIPTION	UNUSED VF	UNUSED F	UNUSED AVG	USED VF	USED F	USED AVG
182	1¢ dark ultramarine	200.00	135.00	75.00	2.50	1.50	1.00
183	2¢ vermilion	100.00	60.00	30.00	2.50	1.50	1.00
184	3¢ green	80.00	45.00	28.00	.35	.25	.15
185	5¢ blue	410.00	240.00	120.00	13.50	8.00	5.00
186	6¢ pink	800.00	460.00	245.00	20.00	11.00	7.00
187	10¢ brown (no secret mark)	1400.00	775.00	395.00	24.00	13.00	8.50
188	10¢ brown (secret mark)	850.00	465.00	250.00	28.00	15.00	9.50
189	15¢ red orange	300.00	165.00	95.00	28.00	15.00	10.00
190	30¢ full black	800.00	465.00	240.00	50.00	30.00	17.00
191	90¢ carmine	1800.00	1000.00	595.00	260.00	145.00	90.00

1880 American Bank Note Co., Special Printings.
Same as 1879 Issue, on soft, porous paper, without gum. Perf 12.

SCOTT NO.	DESCRIPTION	UNUSED VF	UNUSED F	UNUSED AVG	USED VF	USED F	USED AVG
192	1¢ dark ultramarine	16000.00	10000.00	6000.00	....	....	....
193	2¢ black brown	10350.00	6500.00	3850.00	....	....	....
194	3¢ blue green	23500.00	15000.00	9500.00	....	....	....
195	6¢ dull rose	17500.00	11000.00	6750.00	....	....	....
196	7¢ scarlet vermillion	4000.00	2500.00	1500.00	....	....	....
197	10¢ deep brown	15500.00	10000.00	6000.00	....	....	....
198	12¢ black purple	7250.00	4500.00	2750.00	....	....	....
199	15¢ orange	14350.00	9000.00	5450.00	....	....	....
200	24¢ dark violet	4750.00	3000.00	1850.00	....	....	....
201	30¢ greenish black	12750.00	8000.00	4850.00	....	....	....
202	90¢ dull carmine	12750.00	8000.00	4850.00	....	....	....
203	2¢ scarlet vermillion	28750.00	17500.00	11250.00	....	....	....
204	5¢ deep blue	51250.00	31500.00	19250.00	....	....	....

U.S. Postage #205-218

1882 American Bank Note Company Perf 12.
(OG + 60%)

SCOTT NO.	DESCRIPTION	UNUSED VF	UNUSED F	UNUSED AVG	USED VF	USED F	USED AVG
205	5¢ yellow brown	155.00	120.00	65.00	7.50	5.00	3.00

1882 American Bank Note Co., Special Printing.
Same as in 1882 Issue, on soft, porous Paper. Perf 12.

SCOTT NO.	DESCRIPTION	UNUSED VF	UNUSED F	UNUSED AVG	USED VF	USED F	USED AVG
205C	5¢ gray brown	....	....	....	....	....	....

1881-82 American Bank Note Co.
Same designs as 1873, Re-Engraved. On soft, porous paper. Perf 12. (†)
(OG + 60%)

SCOTT NO.	DESCRIPTION	UNUSED VF	UNUSED F	UNUSED AVG	USED VF	USED F	USED AVG
206	1¢ gray blue	52.50	32.50	19.50	1.25	.85	.55
207	3¢ blue green	65.00	37.50	20.00	.35	.25	.20
208	6¢ rose	375.00	215.00	125.00	85.00	45.00	28.00
208a	6¢ brown red	300.00	195.00	110.00	100.00	55.00	34.00
209	10¢ black brown	120.00	75.00	47.50	4.00	2.75	1.75
209b	10¢ black brown	180.00	100.00	60.00	13.00	8.50	5.50
210	2¢ red brown	50.00	28.00	17.50	.25	.20	.15
211	4¢ blue green	250.00	145.00	80.00	12.00	8.00	4.85

1883 American Bank Note Co. Special Printing.
Same design as 1883 Issue, on soft porous paper, without gum. Perf 12.

SCOTT NO.	DESCRIPTION	UNUSED VF	UNUSED F	UNUSED AVG	USED VF	USED F	USED AVG
211B	2¢ pale red brown	....	850.00	550.00	....	....	....
211D	4¢ deep blue green	....	....	....	....	....	....

1887 American Bank Note Co.
New designs or colors. Perf 12.
(OG + 60%)

SCOTT NO.	DESCRIPTION	UNUSED VF	UNUSED F	UNUSED AVG	USED VF	USED F	USED AVG
212	1¢ ultramarine	100.00	52.00	32.00	1.40	.85	.60
213	2¢ green	40.00	20.00	12.00	.25	.15	.10
214	3¢ vermillion	70.00	42.00	25.00	60.00	34.00	25.00

1888 American Bank Note Company.
New Colors Perf 12.
(NH + 50%)

SCOTT NO.	DESCRIPTION	UNUSED O.G. VF	UNUSED O.G. F	UNUSED O.G. AVG	USED VF	USED F	USED AVG
215	4¢ carmine	225.00	130.00	77.50	17.50	10.00	6.50
216	5¢ indigo	225.00	125.00	77.50	10.50	7.50	4.00
217	30¢ orange brown	575.00	295.00	210.00	125.00	70.00	48.50
218	90¢ purple	1150.00	650.00	445.00	245.00	130.00	95.00

NOTE: For further detail on the various types of similar appearing stamps, please refer to our U.S. Stamp Identifier.

*** A dotted line (......) in pricing columns indicates that the stamp exists yet is extremely rare. Such stamps are usually sold only at auction or by private sale.**

U.S. Postage #219-229

219 *Franklin* — **219D, 220** *Washington* — **221** *Jackson* — **222** *Lincoln* — **223** *Grant* — **224** *Garfield*

225 *Sherman* — **226** *Webster* — **227** *Clay* — **228** *Jefferson* — **229** *Perry*

THE 1890-93 SMALL BANK NOTE ISSUES

Unlike the complex Large Bank Notes, the 1890-93 series is the simplest of the 19th century definitive issues. They were printed by the American Bank Note Company, with no paper variations, grills, secret marks or special printings and what few printing varieties there are can easily be determined by using the Harris Stamp Identifier.

The 2 cent stamp is the most common in the set, the total quantity issued exceeding 6.3 billion stamps. It also offers the only major catalog-listed color and printing varieties in the series.

The color change resulted from complaints about the lake shade originally selected and issued February 22, 1890, the main concern being that it tended to rub or wash off. A new carmine shade was selected and rushed into service on May 12, 1890. As a result, the lake stamps were in service less than three months and most were used in the normal course of business. This explains why the mint 2 cent lake stamps (#219D) are relatively scarce even though 100 million copies were issued.

The two major printing varieties are the 2 cent carmine with a “cap” on the left 2 (#219a) or both 2s (#219c).

The “cap” appears to be just that—a small flat hat just to the right of center on top of the denomination numeral 2. It was caused by a breakdown in the metal of the transfer roll that went undetected while it was being used to enter the designs into a few printing plates.

Imperforate examples of all stamps, including the 2 cent lake, also exist. Even when printed on stamp paper and gummed these were determined to be proofs that reached the public outside normal postal channels and were never issued as stamps.

SCOTT NO.	DESCRIPTION	UNUSED O.G. VF	UNUSED O.G. F (NH + 50%)	UNUSED O.G. AVG	USED VF	USED F	USED AVG
219	1¢ dull blue	28.00	16.00	10.00	.25	.20	.15
219D	2¢ lake	250.00	140.00	80.00	1.00	.30	.30
220	2¢ carmine	25.00	14.00	9.00	.25	.20	.15
220a	Cap on left “2”	60.00	39.00	25.00	2.00	1.00	.65
220c	Cap on both “2”s	180.00	105.00	70.00	12.00	7.50	4.00
221	3¢ purple	80.00	48.00	30.00	9.50	4.50	3.00
222	4¢ dark brown	80.00	48.00	30.00	3.00	1.75	1.00
223	5¢ chocolate	80.00	48.00	30.00	3.00	1.75	1.00
224	6¢ brown red	85.00	52.00	32.00	25.00	14.00	8.00
225	8¢ lilac	62.50	38.00	20.00	14.00	8.00	5.00
226	10¢ green	155.00	88.00	50.00	3.00	1.75	1.00
227	15¢ indigo	200.00	125.00	78.00	25.00	14.00	8.00
228	30¢ black	295.00	200.00	95.00	34.00	18.00	12.00
229	90¢ orange	540.00	310.00	170.00	160.00	90.00	50.00

U.S. Postage #230-245

THE COLUMBIANS

Perhaps the most glamorous of all United States issues is the 1893 Columbians set. Consisting of 16 denominations, the set was issued to celebrate the 1893 World's Columbian Exposition.

Even then, the Post Office Department was aware that stamps could be useful for more than just the prepayment of postage. We quote from an internal Post Office Department report of November 20, 1892:

"During the past summer the determination was reached by the Department to issue, during the progress of the Columbian Exposition at Chicago, a special series of adhesive postage stamps of such a character as would help to signalize the four hundredth anniversary of the discovery of America by Columbus. This course was in accordance with the practice of other great postal administrations on occasions of national rejoicing.

The collecting of stamps is deserving of encouragement, for it tends to the cultivation of artistic tastes and the study of history and geography, especially on the part of the young. The new stamps will be purchased in large quantities simply for the use of collections, without ever being presented in payment of postage; and the stamps sold in this way will, of course, prove a clear gain to the department."

As it turned out, the Columbians issue did sell well, being purchased in large quantities not only by collectors, but by speculators hoping to capitalize on the expected demand for the stamps and the fact that they were supposed to be on sale for only one year, from January 2 to December 31, 1893. (The 8 cent stamp was issued March 3,1893 to meet the new, reduced Registration fee.)

Although sales of the stamps were brisk at the Exposition site in Chicago, speculation proved less than rewarding. The hordes that showed up on the first day of sale in Chicago (January 3rd) and purchased large quantities of the issue ended up taking losses on most of the stamps.

The set was the most expensive postal issue produced to date by the Post Office. The lower denominations matched those of the previous, "Small" Bank Note issue and the 50 cent Columbian replaced the 90 cent Bank Note denomination. But the $1 through $5 denominations were unheard of at that time. The reason for their release was explained in the November 20, 1892 report: "...such high denominations having heretofore been called for by some of the principal post offices".

The Columbians were an instant success. Businesses did not like the wide size, but they usually could obtain the smaller Bank Note issue. Collectors enjoyed the new stamps, although at least one complained that some of the high values purchased by him had straight edges— and was quickly authorized to exchange "the imperfect stamps" for perfect ones.

The one major variety in this set is the 4 cent blue error of color. It is similar to, but richer in color than, the 1 cent Columbian and commands a larger premium over the normal 4 cent ultramarine color.

The imperforates that are known to exist for all values are proofs which were distributed as gifts and are not listed as postage stamps. The only exception, the 2 cent imperforate, is believed to be printers' waste that was saved from destruction.

U. S. Columbian Issue #230-245

230
In Sight of Land

231
Landing of Columbus

232
Flagship

233
Fleet of Columbus

234
Soliciting Aid

235
At Barcelona

236
Restored To Favor

237
Presenting Natives

238
Discovery

239
At La Rábida

240
Recall of Columbus

241
Pledging Jewels

242
Columbus in Chains

243
Describing Third Voyage

244
Isabella & Columbus

245
Portrait of Columbus

1893 COLUMBIAN ISSUE
(NH + 40%)

SCOTT NO.	DESCRIPTION	UNUSED O.G. VF	F	AVG	USED VF	F	AVG
230	1¢ deep blue	36.00	20.50	12.50	.60	.40	.30
231	2¢ brown violet	35.50	20.00	12.00	.25	.20	.15
231C	2¢ "broken hat"	105.00	52.50	38.50	.80	.50	.30
232	3¢ green	72.00	40.00	27.50	28.00	15.00	9.00
233	4¢ ultramarine	100.00	56.00	36.50	11.00	6.75	3.95
234	5¢ chocolate	110.00	65.00	42.50	14.00	7.50	5.50
235	6¢ purple	100.00	58.00	38.50	30.00	18.50	12.50
236	8¢ magenta	100.00	60.00	35.00	16.00	9.00	5.50
237	10¢ black brown	195.00	110.00	70.00	12.50	7.00	4.50
238	15¢ dark green	375.00	200.00	125.00	140.00	70.00	47.00
239	30¢ orange brown	550.00	300.00	175.00	170.00	85.00	57.50
240	50¢ slate blue	690.00	375.00	205.00	240.00	130.00	80.00
241	$1 salmon	1900.00	1075.00	665.00	1000.00	550.00	325.00
242	$2 brown red	2000.00	1150.00	700.00	900.00	500.00	315.00
243	$3 yellow green	3350.00	2250.00	1450.00	1800.00	950.00	625.00
244	$4 crimson lake	4650.00	2950.00	1800.00	2400.00	1350.00	825.00
245	$5 black	5400.00	3100.00	2000.00	2900.00	1500.00	1000.00

U. S. Postage #246-284

246, 247
264, 279
Franklin

248-252, 265-
267, 279B
Washington

253, 268
Jackson

254, 269, 280
Lincoln

255, 270, 281
Grant

256, 271, 282
Garfield

1894-98 THE FIRST BUREAU ISSUES

In 1894, the United States Bureau of Engraving and Printing replaced the American Bank Note Company as the contractor for all United States postage stamps. The "First" Bureau issues, as they are commonly known, actually consist of three series, as follows:

The 1984 Series. In order to expedite the transfer of production to the Bureau, the plates then being used by the American Bank Note Company for the 1890-93 Small Bank Notes were modified, small triangles being added in the upper corners. The 1 cent through 15 cent stamps are otherwise essentially the same as the 1890-93 issue although minor variations have been noted on some values. The 30 cent and 90 cent 1890-93 denominations were changed to 50 cents and $1, respectively, and new $2 and $5 denominations were added.

The 1895 Series. To protect against counterfeiting of United States stamps, the Bureau adopted the use of watermarked paper. (A scheme for counterfeiting 2 cent stamps had been uncovered around the same time the watermarked paper was being adopted. Some of these counterfeits are known postally used.) This series is almost exactly the same as the 1984 series except for the presence of watermarks. The watermarks can be difficult to detect on this series, particularly on the light-colored stamps, such as the 50 cent, and on used stamps. Since the 1894 unwatermarked stamps (with the exception of the 2 cent carmine type I) are worth more than the 1895 watermarked stamps, collectors will want to examine their 1894 stamps carefully. (Some collectors feel they can recognize the 1894 stamps by their ragged perforations, caused by difficulties the Bureau encountered when it first took over the production of postage stamps. This is not a reliable method.)

The 1898 "Color Changes". With the adoption of a Universal Postal Union code that recommended standard colors for international mail, the United States changed the colors for the lower values in the 1895 Series. The stamps were printed on the same watermarked paper as that used for the 1895 Series. Except for the 2 cent, which was changed from carmine to red, the colors of the 1898 Series are easily differentiated from the 1895 set. The 2 cent value is the most complicated of the First Bureau Issues. In addition to the color changes that took place, three different triangle types are known. The differences are attributed to the possibility that the work of engraving the triangles into the American Bank Note plates was performed by several Bureau engravers.

The 10 cent and $1 types I and II can be distinguished by the circles surrounding the numeral denominations. The Type IIs are identical to the circles of the 1890-93 Small Bank Notes.

All stamps in these series are perf 12. The Harris Stamp Identifier at the front of this catalog provides additional information on the major types and watermarks of all three series.

U.S. Postage #246-284

257, 272
Sherman

258, 273, 282C, 283
Webster

259, 274, 284
Clay

260, 275
Jefferson

261, 261A, 276, 276A
Perry

262, 277
Madison

263, 278
Marshall

1894 Unwatermarked (†)
(NH + 50%)

SCOTT NO.	DESCRIPTION	UNUSED O.G. VF	UNUSED O.G. F	UNUSED O.G. AVG	USED VF	USED F	USED AVG
246	1¢ ultramarine	28.00	18.00	13.50	4.50	3.00	2.00
247	1¢ blue	75.00	45.00	30.00	2.75	1.60	1.00
248	2¢ pink (I)	26.00	15.00	10.50	3.30	2.00	1.20
249	2¢ carmine lake (I)	150.00	90.00	70.00	2.50	1.40	.80
250	2¢ carmine (I)	26.00	17.00	12.00	.50	.25	.15
251	2¢ carmine (II)	225.00	140.00	90.00	3.75	2.00	1.00
252	2¢ carmine (III)	135.00	80.00	52.00	5.00	3.00	2.00
253	3¢ purple	95.00	60.00	45.00	11.50	7.00	4.00
254	4¢ dark brown	125.00	75.00	40.00	4.50	3.00	1.95
255	5¢ chocolate	95.00	60.00	42.00	6.50	4.00	2.75
256	6¢ dull brown	175.00	115.00	80.00	24.00	15.00	9.00
257	8¢ violet brown	160.00	95.00	62.50	18.00	11.00	7.25
258	10¢ dark green	240.00	150.00	95.00	10.00	6.00	3.50
259	15¢ dark blue	320.00	200.00	140.00	60.00	38.00	25.00
260	50¢ orange	400.00	250.00	175.00	125.00	70.00	42.00
261	$1 black (I)	900.00	600.00	380.00	365.00	210.00	140.00
261A	$1 black (II)	2200.00	1400.00	900.00	725.00	425.00	240.00
262	$2 bright blue	3000.00	1800.00	1200.00	800.00	500.00	360.00
263	$5 dark green	4200.00	2600.00	1600.00	1800.00	1000.00	590.00

1895 Double Line Watermark
"USPS" (†) (NH + 50%)

SCOTT NO.	DESCRIPTION	UNUSED O.G. VF	UNUSED O.G. F	UNUSED O.G. AVG	USED VF	USED F	USED AVG
264	1¢ blue	6.00	4.00	2.75	.25	.20	.15
265	2¢ carmine (I)	32.00	19.00	13.00	1.20	.60	.50
266	2¢ carmine (II)	28.00	17.00	12.00	3.75	2.50	1.50
267	2¢ carmine (III)	5.00	3.00	2.00	.25	.20	.15
268	3¢ purple	45.00	28.00	20.00	1.85	1.25	.70
269	4¢ dark brown	50.00	30.00	20.00	2.25	1.40	.85
270	5¢ chocolate	50.00	30.00	20.00	2.95	1.95	1.10
271	6¢ dull brown	80.00	50.00	37.50	6.00	4.00	2.50
272	8¢ violet brown	60.00	35.00	24.00	2.00	1.25	.75
273	10¢ dark green	80.00	50.00	30.00	2.00	1.25	.75
274	15¢ dark blue	200.00	130.00	80.00	15.00	10.00	5.00
275	50¢ orange	325.00	200.00	135.00	33.00	21.50	12.00
276	$1 black (I)	750.00	425.00	300.00	90.00	60.00	38.00
276A	$1 black (II)	1550.00	1000.00	680.00	190.00	125.00	74.00
277	$2 bright blue	1350.00	800.00	525.00	400.00	295.00	160.00
278	$5 dark green	3000.00	1800.00	1050.00	625.00	400.00	240.00

1898 New Colors
(NH + 50%)

SCOTT NO.	DESCRIPTION	UNUSED O.G. VF	UNUSED O.G. F	UNUSED O.G. AVG	USED VF	USED F	USED AVG
279	1¢ deep green	13.00	8.00	5.50	.30	.20	.15
279B	2¢ red (III)	13.00	7.50	5.00	.30	.20	.15
279Bc	2¢ rose carmine (III)	240.00	140.00	85.00	52.00	36.50	22.00
279Bd	2¢ orange red (III) .	17.50	10.00	7.00	.25	.20	.15
280	4¢ rose brown	40.00	27.00	18.00	1.50	.80	.50
281	5¢ dark blue	48.00	29.00	18.00	1.50	.80	.50
282	6¢ lake	60.00	40.00	30.00	4.00	2.25	1.50
282C	10¢ brown (I)	200.00	125.00	80.00	4.00	2.25	1.50
283	10¢ orange brown (II)	130.00	80.00	50.00	3.25	2.00	1.20
284	15¢ olive green	180.00	110.00	68.00	11.00	6.50	4.25

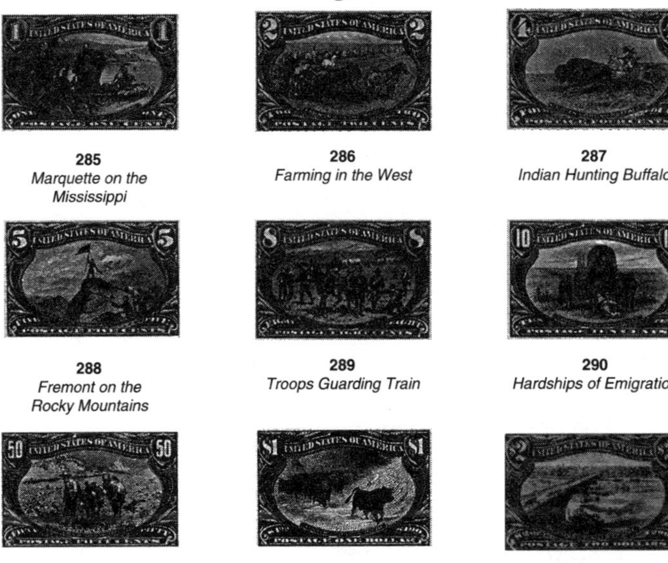

285 *Marquette on the Mississippi*

286 *Farming in the West*

287 *Indian Hunting Buffalo*

288 *Fremont on the Rocky Mountains*

289 *Troops Guarding Train*

290 *Hardships of Emigration*

291 *Western Mining Prospector*

292 *Western Cattle in Storm*

293 *Eads Bridge over Mississippi River*

1898 THE TRANS-MISSISSIPPI ISSUE

Issued for the Trans-Mississippi Exposition in Omaha, Nebraska, the "Omahas", as they also are known, did not receive the same welcome from collectors as that accorded the first commemorative set, the 1893 Columbians. Although the uproar was ascribed to the fact that collectors felt put upon by another set with $1 and $2 values, had the $1 to $5 values in the Columbian series appreciated in value, no doubt the protests would have been muted.

On the other hand, the public at large enjoyed the new issue. The Trans-Mississippi issues depict various works of art and are among the most beautiful stamps ever issued by the United States. The 8 and 10 cent values reproduce works by Frederic Remington and the $1 "Western Cattle in Storm", based on a work by J.A. MacWhirter, is regarded as one of our finest examples of the engraver's art.

As appealing as these stamps are in single colors, the set might have been even more beautiful. The original intent was to print each stamp with the vignette, or central design, in black and the frame in a distinctive second color that would be different for each denomination. That plan had to be dropped when the Bureau was called upon to produce large quantities of revenue stamps at the outbreak of the Spanish-American War.

1898 Trans-Mississippi Exposition Issue (†)
(NH + 50%)

SCOTT NO.	DESCRIPTION	UNUSED O.G. VF	F	AVG	USED VF	F	AVG
285	1¢ dark yellow green	40.00	24.50	19.50	9.75	6.00	3.50
286	2¢ copper red............	35.00	22.50	17.50	2.50	1.50	1.00
287	4¢ orange..................	190.00	120.00	85.00	37.00	22.00	14.00
288	5¢ dull blue................	180.00	115.00	80.00	34.00	20.00	12.00
289	8¢ violet brown..........	225.00	140.00	95.00	67.00	38.00	22.00
290	10¢ gray violet...........	280.00	160.00	115.00	34.00	19.00	13.00
291	50¢ sage green.........	995.00	600.00	450.00	255.00	150.00	90.00
292	$1 black.....................	2600.00	1400.00	1050.00	875.00	475.00	330.00
293	$2 orange brown.......	3800.00	2200.00	1600.00	1250.00	750.00	480.00

U.S. Postage #294-299

294, 294a
Fast Lake Navigation

295, 295a
Fast Express

296, 296a
Automobile

297
Bridge at Niagara Falls

298
Canal at Sault Ste. Marie

299
Fast Ocean Navigation

1901 THE PAN-AMERICAN ISSUE

Issued to commemorate the Pan-American Exposition in Buffalo, N.Y., this set depicts important engineering and manufacturing achievements. The beautiful engraving is showcased by the bicolored printing.

1901 Pan-American Issue
(NH + 40%)

SCOTT NO.	DESCRIPTION	UNUSED O.G. VF	F	AVG	USED VF	F	AVG
294-99	**1¢-10¢ .... (6 varieties, complete)**	**780.00**	**475.00**	**290.00**	**225.00**	**122.00**	**80.00**
294	1¢ green & black......... ..	32.50	17.00	9.00	7.50	4.00	2.00
294a	same, center inverted ...	...	12500.00	...	...	6500.00	...
295	2¢ carmine & black..... ..	30.00	16.00	9.00	2.00	1.35	.75
295a	same, center inverted ...	...	37500.00	...	...	16000.00	...
296	4¢ deep red brown & black...	130.00	80.00	50.00	32.50	17.00	11.00
296a	same, center inverted ...	...	10000.00	...	...	...	...
296aS	same, center inverted (Specimen)	...	5500.00	...	...	...	...
297	5¢ ultramarine & black ..	150.00	90.00	55.00	32.50	17.00	11.00
298	8¢ brown violet & black	180.00	115.00	75.00	115.00	62.00	42.00
299	10¢ yellow brown & black.	300.00	180.00	110.00	50.00	28.00	19.00

	PLATE BLOCKS OF 6 UNUSED NH F	AVG	UNUSED OG F	AVG	ARROW BLOCKS UNUSED NH F	AVG	UNUSED OG F	AVG
294	365.00	285.00	240.00	180.00	160.00	100.00	65.00	50.00
295	365.00	265.00	235.00	180.00	160.00	100.00	65.00	50.00
296	3750.00	2400.00	2100.00	1650.00	800.00	450.00	350.00	290.00
297	4000.00	2500.00	2600.00	2000.00	825.00	500.00	400.00	325.00
298	7500.00	4650.00	4000.00	3200.00	1050.00	650.00	500.00	375.00
299	10500.00	6500.00	6000.00	4800.00	1500.00	900.00	695.00	500.00

300, 314, 316, 318 *Franklin* · **301** *Washington* · **302** *Jackson* · **303, 314A** *Grant* · **304, 315, 317** *Lincoln* · **305** *Garfield*

306 *Martha Washington* · **307** *Webster* · **308** *Harrison* · **309** *Clay* · **310** *Jefferson*

311 *Farragut* · **312, 479** *Madison* · **313, 480** *Marshall* · **319-22** *Washington*

THE 1902-03 SERIES

The Series of 1902-03 was the first regular issue designed and produced by the United States Bureau of Engraving and Printing, most of the work on the 1894-98 series having been performed by the American Bank Note Company. (When the Bureau was awarded the contract to produce the 1894 series, they added triangles in the upper corners of the American Bank Note designs.)

The new series filled a number of gaps and was the first United States issue to feature a woman—in this case Martha Washington, on the 8 cent value.

Modern collectors consider the 1902-03 issue one of the finest regular series ever produced by the Bureau.

The intricate frame designs take us back to a period when such work still was affordable. In its time, however, the 1902-03 set was looked upon with disdain. The 2 cent Washington, with its ornate frame design and unflattering likeness of George Washington, came in for particular scorn. Yielding to the clamor, in 1903, less than one year after its release, the Post Office recalled the much criticized 2 cent stamp and replaced it with an attractive, less ornate design that cleaned up Washington's appearance, particularly in the area of the nose, and used a shield design that was less ornate.

The issue marked the first time United States stamps were issued in booklet form, the 1 and 2 cent values being printed in panes of six stamps each. Also for the first time since perforating was adopted in 1857, United States stamps were once again deliberately issued in imperforate form for postal use. The intent was to have such stamps available in sheet and coil form for use in vending machines. The manufacturers of such machines could purchase the imperforate stamps and perforate them to fit their equipment. One of these imperforate issues, the 4 cent brown of 1908 (#314A), ranks as one of the great rarities of 20th century philately. It is found only with the private perforations of the Schermack Mailing Machine Company.

Coil stamps intended for use in stamp affixing and vending machines also made their inaugural appearance with this issue. Their availability was not widely publicized and few collectors obtained copies of these coils. All genuine coils from this series are very rare and extremely valuable. We emphasize the word "genuine" because most coils that are seen actually have been faked by trimming the perforated stamps or fraudulently perforating the imperfs.

The only major design types are found on the 1903 2 cent, catalog #s 319 and 320. Identified as Die I and Die II, the differences are described in the Harris Stamp Identifier.

Please refer to the condition section (C1-C8) for premiums pertaining to gum (O.G./N.H./etc.).

U.S. Postage #300-322

1902-03 Perf. 12 (†)
(NH + 50%)

SCOTT NO.	DESCRIPTION	UNUSED O.G. VF	F	AVG	USED VF	F	AVG
300	1¢ blue green	16.00	9.00	5.00	.20	.20	.15
300b	1¢ booklet pane of 6 ...	....	550.00	375.00	....	....	....
301	2¢ carmine	18.00	10.50	6.00	.25	.20	.15
301c	2¢ booklet pane of 6 ...	....	500.00	335.00	....	....	....
302	3¢ brown violet	75.00	39.00	25.00	5.75	3.00	1.95
303	4¢ brown	75.00	39.00	25.00	2.00	1.25	.75
304	5¢ blue	90.00	48.00	30.00	2.00	1.25	.65
305	6¢ claret	90.00	50.00	30.00	5.00	2.75	1.50
306	8¢ violet black	60.00	32.00	20.00	3.75	2.00	1.25
307	10¢ pale red brown	98.00	55.00	45.00	3.00	1.60	.95
308	13¢ purple black	60.00	32.00	20.00	17.00	9.00	5.50
309	15¢ olive green	195.00	110.00	65.00	12.75	6.75	3.80
310	50¢ orange	625.00	335.00	200.00	48.00	27.50	13.00
311	$1 black	1125.00	550.00	350.00	90.00	50.00	33.00
312	$2 dark blue	1400.00	775.00	500.00	300.00	175.00	110.00
313	$5 dark green	3200.00	1850.00	1200.00	950.00	575.00	360.00

1906 Imperforate
(NH + 40%)

This and all subsequent imperforate issues can usually be priced as unused pairs at double the single price.

SCOTT NO.	DESCRIPTION	UNUSED O.G. VF	F	AVG	USED VF	F	AVG
314	1¢ blue green	35.00	22.50	18.00	25.00	19.00	12.00
314A	4¢ brown	....	....	....	....	....	....
315	5¢ blue	500.00	410.00	275.00	455.00	300.00	205.00

1908 Coil Stamps. Perf 12 Horizontally

SCOTT NO.	DESCRIPTION	UNUSED O.G. VF	F	AVG	USED VF	F	AVG
316	1¢ blue green, pair	....	50000.00	....	....	....	....
317	5¢ blue, pair	....	6000.00	....	....	....	....

1908 Coil Stamps. Perf 12 Vertically

SCOTT NO.	DESCRIPTION	UNUSED O.G. VF	F	AVG	USED VF	F	AVG
318	1¢ blue green, pair	....	5500.00	....	....	....	....

1903. Perf. 12 (†)
(NH + 40%)

SCOTT NO.	DESCRIPTION	UNUSED O.G. VF	F	AVG	USED VF	F	AVG
319	2¢ carmine, Die I	10.00	6.00	4.80	.25	.20	.15
319f	2¢ lake, Die II	12.00	7.50	5.10	.40	.30	.20
319g	2¢ carmine, Die I, booklet pane of 6	....	125.00	75.00	......	......	......

1906 Imperforate
(NH + 40%)

SCOTT NO.	DESCRIPTION	UNUSED O.G. VF	F	AVG	USED VF	F	AVG
320	2¢ carmine, Die I	30.00	21.50	13.00	28.00	16.00	9.00
320a	2¢ lake, Die I	80.00	65.00	40.00	58.00	40.00	22.00

1908 Coil Stamps. Perf 12 Horizontally

SCOTT NO.	DESCRIPTION	UNUSED O.G. VF	F	AVG	USED VF	F	AVG
321	2¢ carmine, pair	....	....	....	....	....	....

1908 Coil Stamps. Perf 12 Vertically

SCOTT NO.	DESCRIPTION	UNUSED O.G. VF	F	AVG	USED VF	F	AVG
322	2¢ carmine, pair	....	7500.00	....	....	....	....

SCOTT NO.	UNUSED NH F	AVG	UNUSED OG F	AVG
	PLATE BLOCKS OF 6			
300	280.00	160.00	175.00	110.00
301	325.00	170.00	180.00	120.00
314	365.00	235.00	195.00	195.00
319	155.00	90.00	85.00	63.50
320	415.00	290.00	260.00	185.00

SCOTT NO.	UNUSED NH F	AVG	UNUSED OG F	AVG
	CENTER LINE BLOCKS			
314	300.00	200.00	180.00	135.00
320	305.00	210.00	185.00	145.00
	ARROW BLOCKS			
314	190.00	140.00	160.00	110.00
320	190.00	140.00	160.00	110.00

U.S. Postage #323-330

323

Robert R. Livingston

324
Jefferson

325
Monroe

326
McKinley

327
Map of Louisiana Purchase

1904 THE LOUISIANA PURCHASE ISSUE

Issued to commemorate the Louisiana Purchase Exposition held in St. Louis in 1904, these stamps were not well received. Collectors at the time did not purchase large quantities of the stamps, and the series was on sale for only seven months. As a result, well centered unused stamps are extremely difficult to locate.

1904 Louisiana Purchase Issue
(NH + 40%)

SCOTT NO.	DESCRIPTION	UNUSED O.G. VF	F	AVG	USED VF	F	AVG
323-27	**1¢-10¢ (5 vars., cpl.) .**	**560.00**	**300.00**	**200.00**	**150.00**	**85.00**	**55.00**
323	1¢ green	48.00	22.00	14.00	8.80	5.00	3.00
324	2¢ carmine	45.00	20.00	12.00	2.80	2.00	1.00
325	3¢ violet	135.00	70.00	45.00	54.50	32.00	20.00
326	5¢ dark blue	140.00	75.00	50.00	36.00	19.00	14.00
327	10¢ red brown	225.00	130.00	90.00	56.00	32.00	20.00

328
Capt. John Smith

329
Founding of Jamestown

330
Pocahontas

1907 THE JAMESTOWN EXPOSITION ISSUE

This set may be the most difficult United States 20th century issue to find well centered. Issued in April, 1907 for the Jamestown Exposition at Hampton Roads, Virginia, the set was removed from sale when the Exposition closed on November 30th of that year. Very fine copies carry hefty premiums.

1907 Jamestown Exposition Issue
(NH + 40%)

SCOTT NO.	DESCRIPTION	UNUSED O.G. VF	F	AVG	USED VF	F	AVG
328-30	**1¢-5¢ (3 vars., cpl.) ...**	**285.00**	**132.00**	**77.00**	**78.50**	**34.50**	**18.00**
328	1¢ green	40.00	18.00	10.00	7.50	3.75	2.50
329	2¢ carmine	50.00	21.00	11.00	10.00	5.00	2.50
330	5¢ blue	210.00	100.00	60.00	65.00	27.50	14.00

SCOTT NO.	PLATE BLOCKS OF 6 UNUSED NH F	AVG	UNUSED OG F	AVG	ARROW BLOCK UNUSED NH F	AVG	UNUSED OG F	AVG
323	455.00	260.00	260.00	180.00	200.00	115.00	125.00	80.00
324	455.00	260.00	260.00	180.00	160.00	100.00	95.00	65.00
325	1250.00	750.00	900.00	600.00	550.00	355.00	400.00	265.00
326	1450.00	950.00	990.00	700.00	675.00	380.00	375.00	250.00
327	3000.00	1950.00	1950.00	1450.00	1100.00	715.00	650.00	530.00
328	420.00	230.00	240.00	180.00	125.00	70.00	75.00	50.00
329	590.00	320.00	350.00	240.00	170.00	95.00	90.00	65.00
330	3600.00	1900.00	2000.00	1450.00	765.00	425.00	350.00	250.00

Washington, Franklin Issues

331-392
Franklin

332-393, 519

333-541
Washington

THE WASHINGTON-FRANKLIN HEADS

The Washington-Franklin Heads—so called because all stamps in the regular series featured the busts of George Washington and Benjamin Franklin—dominated the postal scene for almost two decades. Using a variety of papers, denominations, perforation sizes and formats, watermarks, design modifications and printing processes, almost 200 different major catalog listings were created from two basic designs.

The series started modestly, with the issuance of 12 stamps (#331-342) between November 1908 and January 1909. The modest designs on the new set replaced the ornate 1902-03 series. Their relative simplicity might have relegated the set to a secondary position in 20th century United States philately had it not been for the complexity of the varieties and the years of study the Washington-Franklin Heads now present to collectors.

The first varieties came almost immediately, in the form of imperforate stamps (#343-347) and coils, the latter being offered with horizontal (#348-351) or vertical (#352-356) perforations. The imperfs were intended for the fading vending machine technology that required private perforations while the coils were useful in standardized dispensers that were just coming into their own.

Then, in 1909, the Post Office began its experimentation. In this instance, it was the paper. As noted in our introduction to the 1909 Bluish Papers which follows, the Post Office Department and the Bureau of Engraving and Printing hoped that the new paper would reduce losses due to uneven shrinkage of the white wove paper used at the time. The experimental Washington-Franklin Bluish Papers (#357-66) are now among the most valuable in the series and the 8 cent Bluish Paper (#363) is the highest priced of the major listed items.

Attention was next directed to the double line watermark as the cause of the uneven shrinkage, as well as for weakness and thinning in the paper. As a result, a narrower, single line watermark was adopted for sheet stamps (#374-82), imperforates (#383-84), and coils with horizontal perfs (#385-86) and vertical perfs (#387-89).

Even as these experiments were being conducted, the perforation size was being examined to determine if a change was in order. Up until now, the perf 12 gauge had been used on all Washington-Franklin Heads.

The first perforation change was necessitated by the development of new coil manufacturing equipment. Under the increased pressure of the new equipment, the coil strips with the closely-spaced perf 12 gauge were splitting while being rolled into coils. To add paper between the holes, a perf 8-1/2 gauge was adopted for coil stamps and two new major varieties were created: with horizontal perfs (#390-91) and vertical perfs (#392-396).

Necessity was the driving force behind still more changes in 1912, when stamps with numeral denominations were issued to replace the "ONE CENT" and "TWO CENTS" stamps. This responded to the need for numeral denominations on foreign mail and created new sheets (#410-11) and vertically perforated (#412-13) coils. At the same time, a 7 cent value (#407) was issued to meet changing rate requirements.

FRANKLIN AND WASHINGTON ISSUES OF 1908-22

FRANKLIN AND WASHINGTON ISSUES OF 1908-22

Perforation	Watermark	Other Identifying Features					3¢ thru $1 denominations	8¢ thru $1 denominations
PERF. 12	USPS	White paper	331	332			333-42	422-23
		Bluish gray paper	357	358			359-66	
	USPS	White paper	374	375	405	406	376-82 407	414-21
COIL 12	USPS	Perf. Horizontal	348	349			350-51	
		Perf. Vertical	352	353			354-56	
	USPS	Perf. Horizontal	385	386				
		Perf. Vertical	387	388			389	
IMPERF.	USPS		343	344			345-47	
	USPS	Flat Plate	383	384	408	409		
		Rotary Press				459		
	Unwmkd.	Flat Plate			481	482-82A	483-85	
		Offset			531	532-34B	535	
COIL 8½	USPS	Perf. Horizontal	390	391	410	411		
		Perf. Vertical	392	393	412	413	394-96	
PERF. 10	USPS							460
	USPS				424	425	426-30	431-40
	Unwmkd.	Flat Plate			462	463	464-69	470-78
		Rotary Press			543			
COIL 10	USPS	Perf. Horiz. Flat			441	442		
		Perf. Horiz. Rotary			448	449-50		
		Perf. Vert. Flat			443	444	445-47	
		Perf. Vert. Rotary			452	453-55	456-58	
	Unwmkd.	Perf Horizontal			486	487-88	489	
		Perf. Vertical			490	491-92	493-96	497
PERF. 11	USPS			519				
	USPS					461		
	Unwmkd.	Flat Plate			498	499-500	501-07	508-18
		Rotary Press			*544-45	546		
		Offset			525	526-28B	529-30	
Perf. 12½	Unwmkd.	Offset			536			
11 x 10	Unwmkd.	Rotary			538	539-40	541	
10 x 11	Unwmkd.	Rotary			542			

¢Design of #544 is 19 mm. wide x 22½ mm. high. #545 is 19½ to 20 mm. wide x 22 mm. high

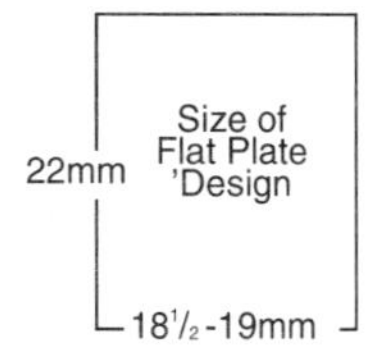

Stamps printed by rotary press are always slightly wider or taller on issues prior to 1954. Measurements do not apply to booklet singles.

HOW TO USE THIS IDENTIFICATION CHART

Numbers referred to herein are from Scott's Standard Postage Stamp Catalog. To identify any stamp in this series, first check the type by comparing it with the illustrations at the top of the chart. Then check the perforations, and whether the stamp is single or double line watermarked or unwatermarked. With this information you can quickly find out the Standard Catalog number by checking down and across the chart. For example, a 1¢ Franklin, perf. 12, single line watermark, must be Scott's #374.

Washington, Franklin Issues (continued)

In conjunction with the introduction of numerals on the 1 and 2 cent stamps, the design of the 1 cent was changed, with the bust of Washington replacing that of Franklin. Meanwhile, the bust of Franklin, which had been used only on the 1 cent stamp, was placed on all values from 8 cents to the $1 (#414-21) and a ribbon was added across their top to make the high value stamp even more noticeable to postal clerks.

As if to add just a little more variety while all the other changes were being made—but in actuality to use up a supply of old double-line watermark paper—50 cent and $1 issues with double-line watermarks (#422-23) were introduced.

The work with perforation changes on coil stamps carried over to sheet stamps in 1914 with the release of a perf 10 series (#424-40). The perf 10 size was then adapted to coils perforated horizontally (#441-42) and vertically (#443-47).

The transition to Rotary Press printing created new coils perforated 10 horizontally (#448-50) and vertically (#452-58). An imperforate Rotary coil (#459) for vending machine manufacturers also was produced.

A perf 10 double-line watermark $1 (#460) and a perf 11 two-cent sheet stamp (#461) added only slightly to the variety, but were followed by completely new runs on unwatermarked paper: perf 10 sheet stamps (#462-478) and imperforates (#481-84) were produced on the flat plate presses, while the Rotary press was used for coils perforated horizontally (#486-489) and vertically (#490-97).

While all this was taking place, the amazing 5 cent carmine error of color (#485) appeared on certain imperf 2 cent sheets. That same error (in rose, #505) was found when perf 11 sheet stamps (#498-518) were issued. The stamps turned out to be too hard to separate. Another strange issue, a 2 cent stamp on double-line watermark paper but perforated 11 (#519), came about when a small supply of old imperfs (#344) were discovered and put into the postal stream.

New $2 and $5 Franklins (#523-24), the former using an erroneous color, were released. To compensate for plate damage being caused by poor quality offset printings, perf 11 (#525-530) and imperforate (#531-535) were tried—and quickly resulted in a whole new series of "types" that had collectors spending more time with their magnifying glasses than with their families.

Odd perf sizes and printings (#538/546) came about as the Bureau cleaned out old paper stock. Then, in one final change, the Bureau corrected the color of the $2 from orange red and black to carmine and black. Almost 200 different stamps, all from two basic designs!

1909 THE BLUISH PAPERS

The Bluish Paper varieties are found on the 1 through 15 cent Washington-Franklin series of 1908-09 and on the 1909 Commemoratives. According to Post Office notices of the period, the experimental paper was a 30% rag stock that was intended to reduce paper waste. After being wet, a preliminary operation in the printing process, the standard white wove paper often would shrink so much that the perforators would cut into the designs. The rag paper did not solve the problem, the experiment was quickly abandoned and the 1909 Bluish Papers became major rarities.

The Harris Stamp Identifier provides further information on identifying the Washington-Franklin Heads.

U.S. Postage #331-356

1908-09 Double Line Watermark "USPS" Perf. 12
(NH + 40%)

SCOTT NO.	DESCRIPTION	UNUSED O.G. VF	UNUSED O.G. F	UNUSED O.G. AVG	USED VF	USED F	USED AVG
331-42	**1¢-$1 (12 varieties, cpl.)**	**1545.00**	**915.00**	**540.00**	**230.00**	**133.00**	**80.00**
331	1¢ green	11.00	6.25	4.00	.35	.20	.15
331a	1¢ booklet pane of 6	200.00	145.00	95.00	......	......	......
332	2¢ carmine	10.00	6.00	3.75	.35	.20	.15
332a	2¢ booklet pane of 6	165.00	110.00	72.50	......	......	......
333	3¢ deep violet (I)	50.00	28.00	17.00	4.80	3.25	2.00
334	4¢ orange brown	52.00	30.00	19.00	1.80	1.20	.75
335	5¢ blue	72.00	40.00	24.00	3.25	2.25	1.45
336	6¢ red orange	78.00	45.00	28.00	8.50	5.00	3.15
337	8¢ olive green	60.00	34.00	21.00	5.00	3.00	2.00
338	10¢ yellow	80.00	45.00	36.00	3.00	1.50	.90
339	13¢ blue green	52.50	27.50	20.00	40.00	24.00	14.00
340	15¢ pale ultramarine	82.00	45.00	32.00	10.00	6.50	4.00
341	50¢ violet	440.00	260.00	140.00	30.00	17.50	11.00
342	$1 violet brown	640.00	395.00	225.00	135.00	75.00	45.00

1908-09 Imperforate
(NH + 40%)

SCOTT NO.	DESCRIPTION	UNUSED O.G. VF	UNUSED O.G. F	UNUSED O.G. AVG	USED VF	USED F	USED AVG
343-47	**1¢-5¢ (5 varieties, cpl.)**	**132.00**	**100.00**	**65.00**	**105.00**	**65.00**	**47.50**
343	1¢ green	10.00	7.00	5.00	5.75	4.00	2.65
344	2¢ carmine	12.00	9.50	6.00	5.75	4.00	2.65
345	3¢ deep violet (I)	22.00	17.00	10.00	22.00	14.00	11.00
346	4¢ orange brown	36.00	27.50	18.00	28.50	18.00	13.00
347	5¢ blue	59.00	45.00	30.00	50.00	30.00	21.00

1908-10 Coil Stamps Perf. 12 Horizontally
(NH + 40%)

SCOTT NO.	DESCRIPTION	UNUSED O.G. VF	UNUSED O.G. F	UNUSED O.G. AVG	USED VF	USED F	USED AVG
348	1¢ green	38.00	23.00	15.50	20.00	12.00	8.00
349	2¢ carmine	60.00	38.00	24.00	15.00	8.00	4.00
350	4¢ orange brown	140.00	85.00	52.00	110.00	67.50	42.50
351	5¢ blue	170.00	100.00	62.00	140.00	85.00	52.00

NOTE: Counterfeits are common on #348-56 and #385-89
1909 Coil Stamps Perf. 12 Vertically
(NH + 40%)

SCOTT NO.	DESCRIPTION	UNUSED O.G. VF	UNUSED O.G. F	UNUSED O.G. AVG	USED VF	USED F	USED AVG
352	1¢ green	78.00	48.00	32.00	40.00	28.00	18.00
353	2¢ carmine	75.00	45.00	26.50	14.00	8.00	4.50
354	4¢ orange brown	180.00	100.00	70.00	90.00	50.00	32.50
355	5¢ blue	190.00	110.00	70.00	140.00	70.00	43.00
356	10¢ yellow	2500.00	1350.00	725.00	1080.00	625.00	400.00

PLATE BLOCKS OF 6

SCOTT NO.	UNUSED NH F	UNUSED NH AVG	UNUSED OG F	UNUSED OG AVG
331	90.00	60.00	65.00	48.00
332	90.00	70.00	65.00	47.50
333	450.00	325.00	290.00	210.00
334	500.00	340.00	360.00	255.00
335	850.00	635.00	575.00	465.00
337	700.00	495.00	375.00	275.00
338	950.00	750.00	700.00	450.00
339	700.00	575.00	400.00	300.00
343	110.00	90.00	75.00	50.00
344	160.00	130.00	140.00	100.00
345	300.00	225.00	240.00	190.00
346	400.00	300.00	310.00	260.00
347	525.00	425.00	450.00	325.00

CENTER LINE BLOCKS

SCOTT NO.	UNUSED NH F	UNUSED NH AVG	UNUSED OG F	UNUSED OG AVG
343	72.00	50.00	50.00	33.00
344	85.00	60.00	62.00	90.00
345	150.00	105.00	110.00	75.00
346	290.00	200.00	205.00	150.00
347	450.00	315.00	325.00	230.00

ARROW BLOCKS

SCOTT NO.	UNUSED NH F	UNUSED NH AVG	UNUSED OG F	UNUSED OG AVG
343	45.00	31.50	33.00	22.00
344	60.00	42.00	40.00	40.00
345	110.00	75.00	77.50	55.00
346	185.00	130.00	125.00	82.50
347	290.00	205.00	210.00	150.00

(NH + 40%)

	COIL LINE PAIRS UNUSED OG VF	COIL LINE PAIRS UNUSED OG F	COIL LINE PAIRS UNUSED OG AVG	COIL PAIRS UNUSED OG VF	COIL PAIRS UNUSED OG F	COIL PAIRS UNUSED OG AVG
348	240.00	200.00	105.00	80.00	50.00	35.00
349	290.00	225.00	150.00	130.00	80.00	50.00
350	1225.00	700.00	490.00	300.00	190.00	110.00
351	1295.00	700.00	490.00	375.00	210.00	130.00
352	455.00	300.00	195.00	175.00	110.00	70.00
353	455.00	300.00	195.00	160.00	100.00	60.00
354	1225.00	795.00	525.00	400.00	220.00	150.00
355	1260.00	800.00	550.00	425.00	240.00	150.00
356	13000.00	8450.00	5750.00	4950.00	2750.00	1600.00

U.S. Postage #357-384

1909 Bluish Gray paper Perf. 12 (NH + 40%)

SCOTT NO.	DESCRIPTION	UNUSED O.G. VF	F	AVG	USED VF	F	AVG
357	1¢ green	145.00	90.00	57.00	160.00	75.00	55.00
358	2¢ carmine	110.00	85.00	50.00	100.00	60.00	42.00
359	3¢ deep violet (I)	3000.00	1450.00	900.00	2000.00	1350.00	800.00
360	4¢ orange brown	......	16000.00	11000.00	......	......	......
361	5¢ blue	5000.00	2900.00	1900.00	5800.00	3500.00	2500.00
362	6¢ red orange	2000.00	1200.00	625.00	1500.00	890.00	445.00
363	8¢ olive green	......	16500.00	11500.00	......	......	......
364	10¢ yellow	2000.00	1200.00	675.00	1600.00	900.00	485.00
365	13¢ blue green	3500.00	2000.00	1300.00	2000.00	1150.00	610.00
366	15¢ pale ultramarine ...	2000.00	875.00	550.00	1200.00	700.00	455.00

367-369
Lincoln

370, 371
William H. Seward

372, 373
S.S. Clermont

THE 1909 COMMEMORATIVES

After the 16-value Columbian commemorative set, the Post Office Department began gradually reducing the number of stamps in subsequent series. The 1909 commemoratives were the first to use the single-stamp commemorative approach that is now the common practice.

The Lincoln Memorial issue was released on the 100th anniversary of the birth of America's 16th President. The Alaska-Yukon was issued for the Alaska-Yukon Exposition held in Seattle to publicize the development of the Alaska territory. The Hudson-Fulton stamp commemorated Henry Hudson's 1609 discovery of the river that bears his name, the 1807 voyage of Robert Fulton's "Clermont" steamboat and the 1909 celebration of those two events.

As noted earlier, the 1909 Commemoratives were issued on experimental "bluish" paper in addition to the white wove standard. The stamps on white wove paper also were issued in imperforate form for private perforation by vending and stamp-affixing machine manufacturers.

1909 LINCOLN MEMORIAL ISSUE (NH + 35%)

SCOTT NO.	DESCRIPTION	UNUSED O.G. VF	F	AVG	USED VF	F	AVG
367	2¢ carmine, perf.	8.00	6.00	4.00	3.50	2.00	1.40
368	2¢ carmine, imperf.	28.00	20.00	14.00	30.00	16.00	12.00
369	2¢ carmine (bluish paper)	300.00	180.00	130.00	320.00	180.00	130.00

1909 ALASKA-YUKON ISSUE

SCOTT NO.	DESCRIPTION	UNUSED O.G. VF	F	AVG	USED VF	F	AVG
370	2¢ carmine, perf.	17.50	9.50	6.00	3.00	1.75	1.00
371	2¢ carmine, imperf.	40.00	30.00	20.00	39.00	20.00	14.00

1909 HUDSON-FULTON ISSUE

SCOTT NO.	DESCRIPTION	UNUSED O.G. VF	F	AVG	USED VF	F	AVG
372	2¢ carmine, perf.	18.00	12.00	9.50	5.00	3.00	2.00
373	2¢ carmine, imperf	42.00	30.00	25.00	32.00	22.00	17.00

1910-11 Single Line Watermark "USPS" Perf. 12 (NH + 35%)

SCOTT NO.	DESCRIPTION	UNUSED O.G. VF	F	AVG	USED VF	F	AVG
374-82	**1¢-15¢ (9 vars., cpl.) ....**	**875.00**	**480.00**	**325.00**	**58.00**	**33.75**	**22.00**
374	1¢ green	11.50	6.00	4.00	.25	.20	.15
374a	1¢ booklet pane of 6 ...	190.00	130.00	80.00	......	......	......
375	2¢ carmine	10.50	6.00	4.00	.25	.20	.15
375a	2¢ booklet pane of 6 ...	150.00	105.00	65.50	......	......	......
376	3¢ deep violet (I)	30.00	17.00	11.00	3.00	1.75	1.10
377	4¢ brown	40.00	24.00	17.50	.90	.50	.30
378	5¢ blue	40.00	24.00	17.50	1.00	.50	.30
379	6¢ red orange	50.00	30.00	19.00	1.55	.90	.60
380	8¢ olive green	160.00	95.00	65.00	22.00	13.50	8.50
381	10¢ yellow	160.00	90.00	65.00	6.00	4.00	2.65
382	15¢ pale ultramarine ...	425.00	215.00	140.00	26.00	14.00	9.00

1911 Imperforate

SCOTT NO.	DESCRIPTION	UNUSED O.G. VF	F	AVG	USED VF	F	AVG
383	1¢ green	5.00	3.00	1.75	4.80	2.40	1.60
384	2¢ carmine	6.00	4.50	2.75	3.00	1.50	.90

U.S. Postage #367-396

SCOTT NO.	UNUSED NH F	UNUSED NH AVG	UNUSED OG F	UNUSED OG AVG
		PLATE BLOCKS OF 6		
367	175.00	120.00	115.00	85.00
368	300.00	210.00	200.00	150.00
370	320.00	220.00	220.00	150.00
371	390.00	275.00	280.00	190.00
372	380.00	240.00	280.00	190.00
373	415.00	300.00	290.00	200.00
374	100.00	65.00	70.00	50.00
375	105.00	65.00	75.00	50.00
376	200.00	140.00	135.00	100.00
377	240.00	170.00	170.00	120.00
378	300.00	225.00	215.00	140.00
383	80.00	55.00	50.00	36.00
384	210.00	150.00	135.00	95.00

SCOTT NO.	UNUSED NH F	UNUSED NH AVG	UNUSED OG F	UNUSED OG AVG
		CENTER LINE BLOCKS		
368	200.00	140.00	150.00	95.00
371	285.00	195.00	200.00	135.00
373	305.00	215.00	220.00	150.00
383	42.00	30.00	30.00	20.00
384	75.00	52.50	50.00	30.00
		ARROW BLOCKS		
368	170.00	120.00	110.00	75.00
371	220.00	160.00	155.00	110.00
373	250.00	175.00	175.00	120.00
383	21.00	15.00	15.00	10.00
384	31.50	23.00	23.00	15.00

COIL STAMPS

1910 Perf. 12 Horizontally
(NH + 40%)

SCOTT NO.	DESCRIPTION	UNUSED O.G. VF	UNUSED O.G. F	UNUSED O.G. AVG	USED VF	USED F	USED AVG
385	1¢ green	40.00	22.00	14.00	18.00	10.00	6.00
386	2¢ carmine	60.00	36.00	23.00	20.00	12.50	8.50
	1910-11 Perf. 12 Vertically (†)						
387	1¢ green	80.00	48.00	30.00	40.00	27.50	16.50
388	2¢ carmine	800.00	425.00	325.00	295.00	140.00	90.00
389	3¢ deep violet (I)	......	17500.00	......	......	8000.00	......
	1910 Perf. 8-1/2 Horizontally						
390	1¢ green	6.00	3.50	2.00	6.00	4.00	3.75
391	2¢ carmine	42.00	24.00	16.00	15.00	9.00	5.00
	1910-13 Perf. 8-1/2 Vertically						
392	1¢ green	24.00	15.00	10.00	26.00	15.00	13.50
393	2¢ carmine	50.00	30.00	20.00	11.00	7.00	4.50
394	3¢ deep violet (I)	55.00	35.00	24.00	65.00	40.00	30.00
395	4¢ brown	55.00	35.00	24.00	65.00	40.00	30.00
396	5¢ blue	55.00	35.00	24.00	65.00	40.00	30.00

(NH + 40%)

	COIL LINE PAIRS UNUSED OG VF	COIL LINE PAIRS UNUSED OG F	COIL LINE PAIRS UNUSED OG AVG	COIL PAIRS UNUSED OG VF	COIL PAIRS UNUSED OG F	COIL PAIRS UNUSED OG AVG
385	280.00	200.00	120.00	100.00	50.00	30.00
386	750.00	400.00	275.00	140.00	100.00	65.00
387	490.00	275.00	195.00	295.00	120.00	80.00
390	42.00	24.00	16.00	20.00	10.00	6.00
391	330.00	235.00	140.00	136.00	59.00	38.00
392	175.00	100.00	65.00	90.00	35.00	34.00
393	280.00	160.00	120.00	160.00	80.00	55.00
394	400.00	240.00	160.00	175.00	80.00	55.00
395	400.00	240.00	160.00	175.00	80.00	55.00
396	400.00	240.00	160.00	175.00	80.00	55.00

Very Fine Plate Blocks from this period command premiums.

Postage #397-409

397, 401
Balboa

398, 402
Panama Canal

399, 403
Golden Gate

400, 400A, 404
Discovery of San Francisco Bay

THE PANAMA-PACIFIC ISSUE

The Panama-Pacific stamps were issued to commemorate the discovery of the Pacific Ocean in 1513 and the opening of the 1915 Panama-Pacific Exposition that celebrated the completion of the Panama Canal. Released in perf 12 form in 1913, the set of four denominations was changed to perf 10 in 1914. Before the perf change, the 10 cent orange yellow shade was determined to be too light. It was changed to the deeper orange color that is found both perf 12 and perf 10.

Because many collectors ignored the perf 10 stamps when they were issued, these stamps are scarcer than their perf 12 predecessors. In fact, #404 is the rarest 20th century commemorative issue.

SCOTT NO.	DESCRIPTION	UNUSED O.G. VF	F	AVG	USED VF	F	AVG
			1913 Perf. 12 (NH + 40%)				
397-400A	**1¢-10¢. 5 vars., cpl.**	**660.00**	**340.00**	**230.00**	**80.00**	**44.50**	**28.00**
397	1¢ green	20.00	12.00	8.00	3.00	1.80	1.25
398	2¢ carmine	28.00	15.00	10.00	1.25	.85	.55
399	5¢ blue	100.00	60.00	40.00	18.00	10.00	6.00
400	10¢ orange yellow	200.00	100.00	65.00	32.00	18.00	12.00
400A	10¢ orange	345.00	170.00	120.00	30.00	16.00	10.00
			1914-15 Perf. 10 (NH + 40%)				
401-04	**1¢-10¢, 4 vars., cpl. ...**	**1745.00**	**995.00**	**725.00**	**142.00**	**82.00**	**54.00**
401	1¢ green	35.00	20.00	14.00	9.00	6.50	4.00
402	2¢ carmine	120.00	70.00	50.00	3.20	1.95	1.25
403	5¢ blue	255.00	135.00	95.00	28.00	18.00	12.00
404	10¢ orange	1600.00	825.00	600.00	110.00	60.00	40.00

405-545

406-546

414-518

SCOTT NO.	DESCRIPTION	UNUSED O.G. VF	F	AVG	USED VF	F	AVG
			1912-14 Single Line Watermark Perf. 12 (NH + 40%)				
405	1¢ green	10.00	5.00	2.50	.25	.20	.15
405b	1¢ booklet pane of 6 ...	80.00	48.00	36.00	......	......	......
406	2¢ carmine (I)	9.50	4.00	2.25	.25	.20	.15
406a	2¢ booklet pane of 6 ...	99.00	68.50	36.50	......	......	......
407	7¢ black	100.00	70.00	50.00	15.00	8.00	5.00
			1912 Imperforate				
408	1¢ green	1.50	1.00	.75	.80	.50	.35
409	2¢ carmine (I)	1.60	1.20	.80	.80	.50	.35

SCOTT NO.	UNUSED NH F	AVG	UNUSED OG F	AVG
	PLATE BLOCKS OF 6			
397	190.00	130.00	140.00	90.00
398	325.00	260.00	215.00	150.00
401	425.00	250.00	275.00	195.00
405	140.00	70.00	90.00	60.00
406	160.00	120.00	100.00	70.00
408	32.00	24.00	19.00	14.00
409	56.00	40.00	36.00	25.00

SCOTT NO.	UNUSED NH F	AVG	UNUSED OG F	AVG
	CENTER LINE BLOCKS			
408	15.50	11.00	11.00	8.50
409	17.00	11.95	14.50	9.50
	ARROW BLOCKS			
408	7.50	8.00	6.00	4.50
409	9.00	9.00	7.25	5.00

Postage #410-440

SCOTT NO.	DESCRIPTION	UNUSED O.G. VF	F	AVG	USED VF	F	AVG
	COIL STAMPS 1912 Perf. 8-1/2 Horizontally (NH + 40%)						
410	1¢ green	8.50	5.00	3.50	6.00	3.50	2.10
411	2¢ carmine (I)	10.00	6.50	4.50	5.00	3.25	2.00
	1912 Perf. 8-1/2 Vertically						
412	1¢ green	28.00	17.00	11.00	8.00	5.00	3.50
413	2¢ carmine (I)	48.00	28.00	18.50	1.20	.75	.50

SCOTT NO.	COIL LINE PAIRS UNUSED OG VF	F	AVG	COIL PAIRS UNUSED OG VF	F	AVG
	(NH + 40%)					
410	48.00	29.00	18.00	19.00	12.50	8.00
411	56.00	36.00	24.00	28.00	16.00	10.50
412	120.00	79.00	50.00	55.00	38.00	24.00
413	245.00	165.00	100.00	100.00	65.00	45.00

SCOTT NO.	DESCRIPTION	UNUSED O.G. VF	F	AVG	USED VF	F	AVG
	1912-14 Perf. 12 Single Line Watermark (NH + 40%)						
414	8¢ pale olive green	48.00	34.00	21.20	2.35	1.30	1.00
415	9¢ salmon red	70.00	45.00	26.50	23.50	14.00	9.00
416	10¢ orange yellow	50.00	32.00	20.00	.55	.40	.25
417	12¢ claret brown	52.00	36.00	24.50	6.50	4.25	2.85
418	15¢ gray	90.00	58.00	36.00	5.60	3.50	2.40
419	20¢ ultramarine	240.00	140.00	90.00	24.00	14.00	10.00
420	30¢ orange red	160.00	105.00	65.00	24.00	14.00	10.00
421	50¢ violet	700.00	395.00	250.00	25.00	16.00	11.00
	1912 Double Line Watermark "USPS" Perf 12						
422	50¢ violet	350.00	185.00	125.00	26.00	16.50	10.00
423	$1 violet black	725.00	400.00	275.00	100.00	60.00	38.00
	1914-15 Single Line Watermark, "USPS" Perf. 10 (NH + 30%)						
424-40	**1¢-50¢, 16 vars., cpl. .**	**2180.00**	**1260.00**	**970.00**	**115.00**	**72.50**	**48.50**
424	1¢ green	3.75	2.25	1.50	.25	.20	.15
424d	1¢ booklet pane of 6 ...	8.00	4.00	3.00	....	....	....
425	2¢ rose red	3.75	1.90	1.25	.25	.20	.15
425e	2¢ booklet pane of 6 ...	25.00	12.50	8.00	....	....	....
426	3¢ deep violet (I)	20.00	12.00	7.50	2.65	1.50	1.00
427	4¢ brown	45.00	28.00	19.75	.90	.55	.40
428	5¢ blue	36.00	25.00	16.00	.90	.55	.40
429	6¢ red orange	48.00	30.00	21.50	2.00	1.35	1.00
430	7¢ black	120.00	70.00	52.00	8.00	5.00	3.00
431	8¢ pale olive green	55.00	30.00	22.00	2.45	1.60	1.00
432	9¢ salmon red	64.00	40.00	28.50	12.50	8.00	4.80
433	10¢ orange yellow	55.00	35.00	25.00	.50	.35	.20
434	11¢ dark green	33.50	18.00	13.50	11.50	7.00	5.00
435	12¢ claret brown	34.50	22.00	15.50	7.20	4.25	2.80
437	15¢ gray	160.00	85.00	64.00	11.50	7.00	4.80
438	20¢ ultramarine	280.00	170.00	120.00	6.50	4.00	2.80
439	30¢ orange red	385.00	210.00	165.00	26.50	17.00	11.50
440	50¢ violet	950.00	550.00	450.00	28.00	18.00	12.00

PLATE BLOCKS OF 6

SCOTT NO.	UNUSED NH F	AVG	UNUSED OG F	AVG	SCOTT NO.	UNUSED NH F	AVG	UNUSED OG F	AVG
414	400.00	275.00	330.00	235.00	429	300.00	240.00	325.00	190.00
415	625.00	440.00	525.00	375.00	430	900.00	650.00	800.00	550.00
416	500.00	350.00	400.00	280.00	431	410.00	335.00	400.00	280.00
417	450.00	325.00	365.00	250.00	432	700.00	475.00	600.00	425.00
418	650.00	475.00	525.00	375.00	433	700.00	475.00	600.00	425.00
424 (6)	55.00	40.00	30.00	20.00	434	275.00	180.00	200.00	115.00
424 (10)	190.00	120.00	130.00	80.00	435	355.00	200.00	240.00	150.00
425 (6)	30.00	20.00	20.00	15.00	437	925.00	650.00	750.00	525.00
425 (10)	180.00	120.00	130.00	90.00	438	2850.00	1950.00	2000.00	1550.00
426	155.00	110.00	105.00	70.00	439	4250.00	2790.00	2950.00	2000.00
427	415.00	300.00	300.00	210.00	440	13000.00	9500.00	10000.00	7000.00
428	325.00	240.00	225.00	140.00					

VF Plate Blocks command premiums

U.S. Postage #441-484

SCOTT NO.	DESCRIPTION	UNUSED O.G. VF	F	AVG	USED VF	F	AVG
	COIL STAMPS						
	1914 Perf. 10 Horizontally (NH + 30%)						
441	1¢ green	1.75	1.00	.65	1.40	1.00	.65
442	2¢ carmine (I)	11.00	7.00	4.50	11.00	7.20	4.00
	1914 Perf.10 Vertically (NH + 30%)						
443	1¢ green	25.00	17.00	12.00	8.50	5.00	3.00
444	2¢ carmine (I)	35.00	23.00	15.00	2.00	1.45	.95
445	3¢ violet (I)	300.00	180.00	130.00	155.00	100.00	65.00
446	4¢ brown	150.00	100.00	70.00	56.00	35.00	23.00
447	5¢ blue	48.00	32.00	24.00	32.50	21.00	13.00
	ROTARY PRESS COIL STAMPS 1915-16 Perf. 10 Horizontally (NH + 30%)						
448	1¢ green	9.50	7.00	4.00	4.00	2.90	1.95
449	2¢ red (I)	......	1700.00	875.00	475.00	350.00	200.00
450	2¢ carmine (III)	16.00	11.50	8.00	4.20	3.50	1.95
	1914-16 Perf. 10 Vertically (NH + 30%)						
452	1¢ green	16.50	9.00	6.00	3.00	1.60	1.25
453	2¢ carmine rose (I)	160.00	90.00	60.00	6.00	3.75	3.00
454	2¢ red (II)	150.00	80.00	65.00	16.00	9.00	6.00
455	2¢ carmine (III)	15.50	7.00	5.00	1.60	1.00	.50
456	3¢ violet (I)	400.00	220.00	165.00	155.00	90.00	60.00
457	4¢ brown	44.00	22.50	16.00	27.00	15.00	10.00
458	5¢ blue.	44.00	22.50	16.00	27.00	15.00	10.00
	1914 Imperforate Coil (NH + 30%)						
459	2¢ carmine (I)	450.00	375.00	300.00	850.00	650.00	....
	1915 Flat Plate Printing Double Line Watermark Perf. 10 (NH + 30%)						
460	$1 violet black	1150.00	695.00	520.00	175.00	90.00	65.00
	1915 Single Line Watermark "USPS" Perf. 11 (NH + 30%)						
461	2¢ pale carmine red (I)	200.00	115.00	65.00	250.00	160.00	95.00
	1916-17 Unwatermarked Perf. 10 (NH + 30%)						
462	1¢ green	11.50	8.00	5.00	.75	.40	.25
462a	1¢ booklet pane of 6	16.00	10.00	6.00	....	....	....
463	2¢ carmine (I)	6.75	4.50	3.00	.25	.20	.15
463a	2¢ booklet pane of 6	110.00	62.00	45.00	....	....	....
464	3¢ violet (I)	120.00	65.00	48.00	21.50	14.00	9.00
465	4¢ orange brown	66.50	42.00	25.00	3.25	2.25	1.35
466	5¢ blue	120.00	65.00	40.00	3.25	2.25	1.35
467	5¢ carmine (error)	1200.00	600.00	500.00	720.00	520.00	320.00
468	6¢ red orange	140.00	75.00	45.00	12.50	7.00	4.00
469	7¢ black	180.00	100.00	68.00	20.00	12.00	7.00
470	8¢ olive green	80.00	45.00	30.00	10.50	6.00	4.00
471	9¢ salmon red	90.00	50.00	32.00	28.50	15.00	10.00
472	10¢ orange yellow	160.00	88.00	65.00	2.00	1.00	.70
473	11¢ dark green	48.00	28.00	18.00	30.00	17.00	11.50
474	12¢ claret brown	70.00	45.00	32.50	10.00	6.00	4.00
475	15¢ gray	220.00	135.00	90.00	20.00	11.00	8.00
476	20¢ light ultramarine	400.00	220.00	160.00	20.50	12.00	8.00
476A	30¢ orange red	....	....	....	....	....	....
477	50¢ light violet	1990.00	1000.00	700.00	110.00	70.00	45.00
478	$1 violet black.	1175.00	675.00	490.00	31.50	21.50	12.50
	Design of 1902-03						
479	$2 dark blue	715.00	425.00	300.00	74.50	42.00	33.50
480	$5 light green	600.00	325.00	225.00	80.00	45.00	32.00
	1916-17 Imperforate (NH + 35%)						
481	1¢ green	1.50	1.00	.50	1.50	.80	.50
482	2¢ carmine (I)	2.00	1.25	.75	2.50	1.50	1.00
483	3¢ violet (I)	16.00	13.00	9.00	10.00	8.00	6.00
484	3¢ violet (II)	13.00	10.00	6.00	6.00	4.00	3.00

U.S. Postage #441-497

SCOTT NO.	COIL LINE PAIRS UNUSED OG VF	F	AVG	(NH + 30%) COIL PAIRS UNUSED OG VF	F	AVG
441	10.00	7.00	4.00	4.50	2.50	2.00
442	90.00	48.00	30.00	30.00	16.00	10.00
443	150.00	90.00	60.50	70.00	38.00	28.00
444	260.00	150.00	100.00	100.00	52.00	38.00
445	1600.00	900.00	600.00	700.00	400.00	280.00
446	900.00	500.00	350.00	450.00	260.00	160.00
447	325.00	185.00	127.00	136.00	75.00	50.00
448	62.00	39.00	25.00	32.00	18.00	12.00
450	90.00	49.00	35.00	40.00	25.50	17.50
452	115.00	65.00	40.00	40.00	22.00	15.00
453	850.00	450.00	350.00	400.00	225.00	160.00
454	900.00	425.00	325.00	350.00	200.00	140.00
455	90.00	50.00	35.00	32.00	18.00	12.00
456	875.00	560.00	365.00	850.00	500.00	350.00
457	240.00	130.00	90.00	90.00	55.00	40.00
458	250.00	135.00	95.00	95.00	55.00	40.00
459	2800.00	1400.00	900.00	1500.00	850.00	650.00

SCOTT NO.	UNUSED NH F	AVG	UNUSED OG F	AVG
	PLATE BLOCKS OF 6			
462	160.00	110.00	110.00	70.00
463	135.00	75.00	100.00	60.00
464	1300.00	1000.00	1150.00	825.00
465	700.00	475.00	600.00	425.00
466	950.00	750.00	950.00	565.00
470	675.00	500.00	545.00	320.00
471	725.00	575.00	595.00	355.00
	CENTER LINE BLOCKS			
481	12.00	8.00	7.00	4.00
482	13.00	8.00	7.00	4.00
483	120.00	70.00	65.00	45.00
484	90.00	60.00	50.00	30.00

SCOTT NO.	UNUSED NH F	AVG	UNUSED OG F	AVG
	PLATE BLOCKS OF 6			
472	1400.00	1100.00	1200.00	800.00
473	360.00	230.00	250.00	150.00
474	600.00	400.00	400.00	250.00
481	15.00	10.00	12.00	8.00
482	28.00	20.00	20.00	16.00
483	190.00	150.00	140.00	90.00
484	140.00	90.00	115.00	80.00
	ARROW BLOCKS			
481	8.00	5.00	4.00	3.00
482	9.00	6.00	4.75	3.50
483	100.00	60.00	50.00	35.00
484	72.00	42.00	35.00	25.00

ROTARY PRESS COIL STAMPS 1916-19 Perf. 10 Horizontally
(NH + 35%)

SCOTT NO.	DESCRIPTION	UNUSED OG VF	F	AVG	USED VF	F	AVG
486	1¢ green	1.50	.80	.50	.40	.30	.20
487	2¢ carmine (II)	24.00	14.00	9.00	4.25	2.80	2.00
488	2¢ carmine (III)	4.75	2.75	1.75	2.40	1.75	1.00
489	3¢ violet (I)s	7.00	4.50	3.00	2.00	1.40	.85
	1916-22 Perf. 10 Vertically (NH + 35%)						
490	1¢ green	1.00	.60	.40	.35	.25	.15
491	2¢ carmine (II)	2100.00	1425.00	825.00	650.00	400.00	300.00
492	2¢ carmine (III)	16.00	9.00	6.00	.30	.20	.15
493	3¢ violet (I)	28.00	16.00	12.00	5.00	3.00	2.00
494	3¢ violet (II)	16.00	9.00	6.00	1.20	.80	.60
495	4¢ orange brown	18.00	10.00	7.00	6.50	3.75	7.50
496	5¢ blue	7.00	4.00	3.00	1.60	1.00	.75
497	10¢ orange yellow	35.00	20.00	15.00	12.00	7.50	4.50

SCOTT NO.	COIL LINE PAIRS UNUSED OG VF	F	AVG	(NH + 35%) COIL PAIRS UNUSED OG VF	F	AVG
486	6.00	3.75	2.50	3.00	2.00	1.25
487	160.00	105.00	75.00	45.00	32.00	20.00
488	28.00	18.00	12.00	9.00	6.50	4.00
489	40.00	30.00	24.00	18.00	11.00	7.00
490	5.00	3.75	1.90	2.80	2.00	1.20
491	......	7000.00	3950.00	4450.00	3000.00	2000.00
492	70.00	50.00	35.00	36.00	24.00	16.00
493	160.00	100.00	70.00	60.00	38.00	28.00
494	90.00	60.00	48.00	36.00	24.00	18.00
495	100.00	68.00	50.00	42.00	26.00	19.00
496	36.00	25.00	17.50	15.00	10.00	6.00
497	160.00	100.00	70.00	80.00	52.00	38.00

Postage #498-528

SCOTT NO.	DESCRIPTION	UNUSED O.G. VF	F	AVG	USED VF	F	AVG
			1917-19 Flat Plate Printing Perf. 11 (NH + 30%)				
498-518	**(498-99,501-04,506-18) 19 var.**	**695.00**	**400.00**	**265.00**	**35.00**	**22.25**	**16.95**
498	1¢ green	.80	.50	.40	.25	.20	.15
498e	1¢ booklet pane of 6	4.50	2.75	2.00	....	....	....
498f	1¢ booklet pane of 30	640.00	475.00	300.00	....	....	....
499	2¢ rose (I)	.80	.40	.30	.25	.20	.15
499e	2¢ booklet pane of 6	4.00	2.50	1.80	....	....	....
500	2¢ deep rose (Ia)	400.00	225.00	165.00	170.00	120.00	72.00
501	3¢ light violet (I)	20.00	12.00	8.00	.35	.25	.20
501b	3¢ booklet pane of 6	85.00	50.00	35.00	....	....	....
502	3¢ dark violet (II)	26.00	15.00	10.00	.60	.35	.25
502b	3¢ booklet pane of 6	80.00	45.00	30.00	....	....	....
503	4¢ brown	18.00	10.00	6.00	.35	.25	.15
504	5¢ blue	14.00	8.00	5.00	.30	.20	.15
505	5¢ rose (error)	680.00	400.00	275.00	545.00	385.00	220.00
506	6¢ red orange	22.00	13.00	8.00	.55	.40	.25
507	7¢ black	42.00	25.00	17.00	2.00	1.45	.80
508	8¢ olive bistre	17.00	10.00	6.00	1.45	1.20	.80
509	9¢ salmon red	24.00	14.00	9.00	3.65	2.30	1.65
510	10¢ orange yellow	28.00	16.00	10.00	.30	.20	.15
511	11¢ light green	14.00	8.00	3.00	5.60	3.50	2.40
512	12¢ claret brown	14.00	8.00	5.00	1.15	.65	.50
513	13¢ apple green	19.00	11.00	7.00	12.00	7.00	6.40
514	15¢ gray	64.00	38.00	26.00	1.60	1.00	.75
515	20¢ light ultramarine	85.00	46.00	34.00	.55	.35	.25
516	30¢ orange red	70.00	40.00	30.00	1.60	1.00	.85
517	50¢ red violet	100.00	75.00	50.00	1.50	.80	.75
518	$1 violet black	95.00	65.00	45.00	3.00	2.00	1.25

1917 Design of 1908-09
Double Line Watermark Perf. 11

SCOTT NO.	DESCRIPTION	UNUSED O.G. VF	F	AVG	USED VF	F	AVG
519	2¢ carmine	330.00	215.00	130.00	725.00	495.00	295.00

523, 524, 547
Franklin

537
"Victory" and Flags

1918 Unwatermarked

SCOTT NO.	DESCRIPTION	UNUSED O.G. VF	F	AVG	USED VF	F	AVG
523	$2 orange red & black	1100.00	710.00	500.00	400.00	240.00	130.00
524	$5 deep green & black	480.00	325.00	175.00	37.00	25.00	18.00

PLATE BLOCKS OF 6

SCOTT NO.	UNUSED NH F	AVG	UNUSED OG F	AVG
498	18.00	14.75	13.00	12.00
499	17.00	13.75	18.50	11.50
501	180.00	128.00	160.00	100.00
502	200.00	180.00	185.00	128.00
503	190.00	150.00	190.00	115.00
504	165.00	100.00	135.00	80.00
506	230.00	155.00	210.00	125.00
507	300.00	265.00	365.00	210.00
508	220.00	150.00	200.00	120.00
509	200.00	150.00	200.00	120.00
510	260.00	215.00	280.00	170.00
511	200.00	110.00	150.00	90.00
512	185.00	100.00	130.00	77.50
513	185.00	105.50	145.00	85.00
514	835.00	465.00	635.00	385.00
515	975.00	565.00	705.00	425.00
516	750.00	440.00	600.00	350.00
517	1875.00	1050.00	1300.00	800.00
518	1500.00	825.00	1050.00	685.00
519	3000.00	1725.00	2285.00	1350.00
	ARROW BLOCK			
518	480.00	280.00	375.00	225.00

1918-20 Offset Printing Perf. 11
(NH + 35%)

SCOTT NO.	DESCRIPTION	UNUSED O.G. VF	F	AVG	USED VF	F	AVG
525	1¢ gray green	2.75	1.80	1.00	1.25	.85	.50
526	2¢ carmine (IV)	35.00	25.00	13.00	6.00	4.25	2.75
527	2¢ carmine (V)	18.00	12.00	7.50	1.45	1.25	.70
528	2¢ carmine (Va)	11.00	7.00	4.50	.30	.25	.15

U.S. Postage #528A-550

SCOTT NO.	DESCRIPTION	UNUSED O.G. (NH + 35%) VF	F	AVG	USED VF	F	AVG
528A	2¢ carmine (VI)	50.00	40.00	29.50	2.00	1.00	.80
528B	2¢ carmine (VII)	22.00	15.00	12.00	.25	.20	.15
529	3¢ violet (III)	4.00	3.00	2.40	.25	.20	.15
530	3¢ purple (IV)	1.50	.90	.60	.25	.20	.15
	1918-20 Offset Printing Imperforate						
531	1¢ gray green	13.00	8.00	6.00	13.00	8.00	6.00
532	2¢ carmine rose (IV) ...	48.00	35.00	25.00	52.50	30.00	24.00
533	2¢ carmine (V)	250.00	190.00	150.00	100.00	60.00	48.00
534	2¢ carmine (Va)	16.00	14.00	8.00	16.50	9.00	6.00
534A	2¢ carmine (VI)	46.00	35.00	25.00	44.00	29.00	21.50
534B	2¢ carmine (VII)	1800.00	1400.00	1000.00	585.00	435.00	290.00
535	3¢ violet (IV)	20.00	8.00	5.50	10.00	6.50	4.00
	1919 Offset Printing Perf. 12-1/2						
536	1¢ gray green	20.00	12.00	8.00	24.00	13.00	8.00
	1919 VICTORY ISSUE (NH + 35%)						
537	3¢ violet	17.00	9.00	6.50	6.50	4.00	2.50
	1919-21 Rotary Press Printings—Perf. 11 x 10 (†) (NH + 35%)						
538	1¢ green	16.00	9.00	6.00	13.50	9.50	5.50
538a	Same, imperf. horizontally	80.00	50.00	35.50	....	....	....
539	2¢ carmine rose (II).....	3100.00	2250.00	1300.00	....	1950.00	1350.00
540	2¢ carmine rose (III) ...	17.50	10.00	6.00	16.00	9.50	6.50
540a	Same, imperf. horizontally	75.00	45.00	35.50	....	....	....
541	3¢ violet (II)	50.00	30.00	23.50	52.00	30.00	22.50
	Perf. 10 x 11						
542	1¢ green	13.00	9.50	5.50	1.60	1.00	.75
	Perf. 10						
543	1¢ green	1.50	.50	.55	.25	.20	.15
	Perf. 11						
544	1¢ green (19 x 22-1/2mm)	11200.00	8000.00	3900.00	2595.00	1950.00	1300.00
545	1¢ green (19-1/2 x 22mm)	190.00	125.00	75.00	175.00	120.00	80.00
546	2¢ carmine rose (III) ...	125.00	75.00	45.00	135.00	85.00	52.50
	1920 Flat Plate Printing Perf. 11						
547	$2 carmine & black	430.00	300.00	235.00	64.00	38.00	30.00

SCOTT NO.	UNUSED NH F	AVG	UNUSED OG F	AVG
PLATE BLOCKS OF 6				
525 (6)	29.00	22.50	20.00	14.00
526 (6)	260.00	200.00	185.00	140.00
527 (6)	150.00	100.00	100.00	70.00
528 (6)	70.00	52.00	50.00	30.00
528A (6)	410.00	290.00	275.00	180.00
528B (6)	150.00	120.00	120.00	80.00
529 (6)	60.00	40.00	50.00	35.00
530 (6)	14.00	9.00	10.00	6.00
531 (6)	110.00	80.00	85.00	60.00
532 (6)	340.00	220.00	240.00	190.00
534 (6)	115.00	80.00	100.00	60.00
534A (6)	380.00	250.00	280.00	220.00
CENTER LINE				
531	55.00	37.50	46.00	32.00
532	175.00	125.00	150.00	105.00
533	900.00	625.00	775.00	540.00
534	55.00	37.50	46.00	32.00
534A	165.00	115.00	140.00	98.00
535	40.00	28.00	32.00	22.00
547	1400.00	975.00	1175.00	825.00

SCOTT NO.	UNUSED NH F	AVG	UNUSED OG F	AVG
PLATE BLOCKS OF (—)				
535 (6)	80.00	60.00	60.00	50.00
536 (6)	200.00	140.00	140.00	90.00
537 (6)	150.00	105.00	100.00	75.00
538 (4)	110.00	80.00	75.00	50.00
540 (4)	110.00	80.00	80.00	50.00
541 (4)	465.00	325.00	310.00	210.00
542 (6)	195.00	135.00	135.00	90.00
543 (4)	23.00	16.00	15.00	10.00
543 (6)	45.00	32.00	30.00	20.00
545 (4)	900.00	630.00	750.00	525.00
546 (4)	700.00	500.00	550.00	395.00
547 (8)	4750.00	3500.00	3800.00	2750.00
548 (6)	55.00	39.50	40.00	30.00
549 (6)	84.00	58.75	60.00	45.00
550 (6)	725.00	525.00	475.00	330.00
ARROW BLOCKS				
531	50.00	35.00	40.00	28.00
532	230.00	170.00	155.00	120.00
533	775.00	540.00	625.00	440.00
534	65.00	45.00	45.00	37.50
534A	210.00	150.00	150.00	110.00
535	50.00	35.00	35.00	25.00
547	1175.00	830.00	975.00	695.00

U.S. Postage #548-560

548
The "Mayflower"

549
Landing of the Pilgrims

550
Signing of the Compact

1920 PILGRIM TERCENTENARY ISSUE
(NH + 35%)

SCOTT NO.	DESCRIPTION	UNUSED O.G. VF	F	AVG	USED VF	F	AVG
548-50	**1¢-5¢, 3 vars., cpl ......**	**85.00**	**48.00**	**37.00**	**34.75**	**19.00**	**16.00**
548	1¢ green	7.00	4.00	3.00	5.50	3.00	2.00
549	2¢ carmine rose	12.50	7.00	4.00	3.50	2.00	1.60
550	5¢ deep blue	70.00	40.00	32.00	27.50	15.00	13.50

THE 1922-25 ISSUE

551, 653
Nathan Hale

552, 575, 578, 581, 594, 596, 597, 604, 632
Franklin

553, 576, 582, 598, 605, 631, 633
Harding

554, 577, 579, 583, 595, 599-99A, 606, 634-34A
Washington

555, 584, 600, 635
Lincoln

556, 585 601, 636
Martha Washing

557, 586, 602, 637
Roosevelt

558, 587, 638, 723
Garfield

559, 588, 639
McKinley

560, 589, 640
Grant

561, 590, 641
Jefferson

562, 591, 603, 6
Monroe

563, 692
Hayes

564, 693
Cleveland

565, 695
American Indian

566, 696
Statue of Liberty

567, 698
Golden Gate

568, 699
Niagara Falls

569,700
Bison

570, 701
Arlington Amphitheatre

571
Lincoln Memorial

572
U.S. Capitol

573
"America"

Flat Plate Printings
1922-25 Perf. 11 (NH + 25%)

SCOTT NO.	DESCRIPTION	UNUSED O.G. VF	F	AVG	USED VF	F	AVG
551-73	**1/2¢-$5, 23 vars., cpl**	**1150.00**	**675.00**	**485.00**	**53.75**	**33.50**	**22.00**
551	1/2¢ olive brown (1925)	.30	.25	.15	.25	.20	.15
552	1¢ deep green (1923) .	2.25	1.60	1.20	.25	.20	.15
552a	1¢ booklet pane of 6 ...	8.00	5.25	3.75	....	....	....
553	1-1/2¢ yellow brown (1925)	3.75	2.40	1.80	.50	.35	.25
554	2¢ carmine (1923)	2.70	1.80	1.20	.25	.20	.15
554c	2¢ booklet pane of 6 ...	10.00	7.00	4.50	....	....	....
555	3¢ violet (1923)	24.00	17.00	11.00	1.75	1.00	.75
556	4¢ yellow brown (1923)24.00	17.00	11.00	.50	.35	.25	
557	5¢ dark blue	24.00	17.00	11.00	.30	.20	.15
558	6¢ red orange	47.00	30.00	22.00	1.30	.80	.60
559	7¢ black (1923)	12.00	8.00	6.00	1.20	.70	.50
560	8¢ olive green (1923) ..	62.00	42.00	30.00	1.20	.80	.60

U.S. Postage #561-596

SCOTT NO.	DESCRIPTION	UNUSED O.G. VF	F	AVG	USED VF	F	AVG
561	9¢ rose (1923)	20.00	12.00	8.00	2.45	1.40	1.00
562	10¢ orange (1923)	28.00	18.00	12.00	.30	.20	.15
563	11¢ light blue	2.80	2.00	1.25	.75	.50	.30
564	12¢ brown violet (1923)	13.50	7.00	4.50	.30	.20	.15
565	14¢ blue (1923)	9.00	5.00	3.00	1.20	1.00	.60
566	15¢ gray	40.00	23.00	17.50	.25	.20	.15
567	20¢ carmine rose (1923)	32.00	20.00	16.00	.25	.20	.15
568	25¢ yellow green	30.00	19.00	13.00	.90	.55	.40
569	30¢ olive brown (1923)	50.00	35.00	25.00	.80	.50	.35
570	50¢ lilac	85.00	50.00	40.00	.35	.20	.15
571	$1 violet black (1923)	60.00	40.00	30.00	.75	.50	.30
572	$2 deep blue (1923)	140.00	90.00	75.00	16.00	10.00	6.00
573	$5 carmine & blue (1923)	300.00	225.00	175.00	25.00	15.00	10.00
	1923-25 Imperforate						
575	1¢ green	11.00	8.00	6.00	4.50	3.00	2.40
576	1-1/2¢ yellow brown (1925)	2.50	1.60	1.00	3.00	1.60	1.25
577	2¢ carmine	3.00	2.00	1.20	3.00	1.75	1.25
	Rotary Press Printings 1923 Perf. 11 x 10 (†) (NH + 35%)						
578	1¢ green	110.00	65.00	42.50	140.00	75.00	42.50
579	2¢ carmine	80.00	50.00	30.00	100.00	60.00	32.50
	1923-26 Perf. 10 (†)						
581-91	**1¢-10¢, 11 vars. cpl**	**268.00**	**152.50**	**108.50**	**25.00**	**15.35**	**9.75**
581	1¢ green	12.00	7.00	4.00	1.20	.85	.60
582	1-1/2¢ brown (1925)	6.00	4.00	3.00	1.20	.85	.60
583	2¢ carmine (1924)	4.00	2.00	1.20	.25	.20	.15
583a	2¢ booklet pane of 6 (1924)	110.00	60.00	40.00	....	....	....
584	3¢ violet (1925)	40.00	24.00	16.50	2.80	2.00	1.20
585	4¢ yellow brown (1925)	24.00	13.00	9.00	.80	.60	.40
586	5¢ blue (1925)	24.00	13.00	9.00	.45	.35	.20
587	6¢ red orange (1925)	16.00	8.50	5.50	1.00	.60	.40
588	7¢ black (1926)	17.00	9.00	6.00	9.00	5.00	3.00
589	8¢ olive green (1926)	40.00	21.00	15.00	5.00	3.25	2.00
590	9¢ rose (1926)	8.00	4.00	3.00	4.50	2.25	1.50
591	10¢ orange (1925)	90.00	55.00	41.50	.25	.20	.15
	Perf. 11 (†)						
594	1¢ green	10000.00	7200.00	4500.00	4500.00	3500.00	2200.00
595	2¢ carmine	300.00	190.00	110.00	475.00	200.00	110.00
	Perf. 11						
596	1¢ green	....	....	....	21500.00	15000.00	11000.00

PLATE BLOCKS (6)

SCOTT NO.	DESCRIPTION	UNUSED NH VF	F	AVG.	UNUSED OG VF	F	AVG.
551	1/2¢ olive brown (1923)	12.00	6.50	5.00	15.50	5.00	7.20
552	1¢ deep green (1923)	52.00	30.00	25.00	56.50	20.00	24.00
553	1-1/2¢ yellow brown (1923)	80.00	52.00	40.00	60.00	30.00	28.00
554	2¢ carmine (1923)	50.00	28.00	22.00	42.50	20.00	20.50
555	3¢ violet (1923)	400.00	225.00	180.00	375.00	160.00	160.00
556	4¢ yellow brown (1923)	375.00	240.00	200.00	365.00	165.00	190.00
557	5¢ dark blue	375.00	240.00	200.00	395.00	170.00	200.00
558	6¢ red orange	750.00	450.00	400.00	715.00	350.00	340.00
559	7¢ black (1923)	175.00	100.00	70.00	130.00	65.00	60.00
560	8¢ olive green (1923)	1100.00	740.00	650.00	1300.00	500.00	520.00
561	9¢ rose (1923)	340.00	225.00	160.00	280.00	160.00	130.00
562	10¢ orange (1923)	450.00	290.00	200.00	485.00	200.00	250.00
563	11¢ light blue	55.00	38.00	32.00	67.50	28.00	27.50
564	12¢ brown violet (1923)	170.00	100.00	70.00	145.00	78.00	70.00
565	14¢ blue (1923)	120.00	80.00	57.50	100.00	49.00	47.50
566	15¢ grey	500.00	350.00	240.00	425.00	250.00	190.00
567	20¢ carmine rose (1923)	475.00	320.00	240.00	400.00	220.00	190.00
568	25¢ yellow green	420.00	260.00	200.00	460.00	190.00	225.00
569	30¢ olive brown (1923)	720.00	450.00	390.00	640.00	310.00	325.00
570	50¢ lilac	2175.00	1550.00	910.00	1650.00	1100.00	720.00
571	$1 violet black (1923)	800.00	520.00	400.00	900.00	400.00	400.00
572	$2 deep blue (1923)	3450.00	2575.00	1485.00	2750.00	1850.00	1150.00
573	$5 carmine + blue (1923)	13500.00	9350.00	5600.00	9950.00	7025.00	4500.00

U.S. Postage #571-606

SCOTT NO.		CENTER LINE BLOCKS F/NH	F/OG	AVG/OG	ARROW BLOCKS F/NH	F/OG	AVG/OG
571	$1 violet black	....	....	....	195.00	165.00	115.00
572	$2 deep blue	....	....	....	425.00	365.00	255.00
573	$5 carmine & blue	1050.00	900.00	625.00	1000.00	850.00	595.00
575	1¢ imperforate	58.00	45.00	35.00	45.00	37.50	28.00
576	1-1/2¢ imperforate	19.50	15.00	10.50	11.00	8.00	5.00
577	2¢ imperforate	22.50	17.50	12.00	12.00	9.00	7.00

SCOTT NO.		PLATE BLOCKS UNUSED NH VF	F	AVG.	UNUSED OG VF	F	AVG.
575 (6)	1¢ green	160.00	110.00	75.00	110.00	70.00	50.00
576 (6)	1-1/2¢ yellow brown (1925)	50.00	33.00	25.00	35.00	22.00	16.00
577 (6)	2¢ carmine	50.00	34.00	25.00	42.00	25.00	18.00
578	1¢ green	975.00	750.00	575.00	815.00	625.00	495.00
579	2¢ carmine	750.00	440.00	290.00	450.00	335.00	245.00
581	1¢ green	240.00	140.00	80.00	120.00	90.00	68.50
582	1-1/2¢ brown (1925)	72.00	45.00	32.00	50.00	34.00	24.00
583	2¢ carmine (1923)	60.00	35.00	28.50	40.00	24.00	18.00
584	3¢ violet (1925)	400.00	260.00	190.00	260.00	190.00	150.00
585	4¢ yellow green (1925)	275.00	190.00	150.00	170.00	145.00	105.00
586	5¢ blue (1925)	265.00	180.00	140.00	170.00	140.00	100.00
587	6¢ red orange (1925)	120.00	75.00	55.00	80.00	55.00	40.00
588	7¢ black (1926)	190.00	110.00	75.00	110.00	79.00	60.00
589	8¢ olive green (1926)	400.00	260.00	190.00	275.00	190.00	125.00
590	9¢ rose (1926)	70.00	48.00	32.00	65.00	40.00	28.00
591	10¢ orange (1925)	1200.00	750.00	520.00	700.00	525.00	380.00

SCOTT NO.	DESCRIPTION	UNUSED VF	F	AVG	USED VF	F	AVG
	1923-29 Rotary Press Coil Stamps (NH + 25%)						
597-606	**(597-99, 600-06)10 vars.**	**24.50**	**16.50**	**11.00**	**3.50**	**2.45**	**1.65**
	Perf. 10 Vertically						
597	1¢ green	.50	.30	.20	.25	.20	.15
598	1-1/2¢ deep brown (1925)	1.00	.70	.50	.30	.20	.15
599	2¢ carmine (I) (1923)	.60	.40	.30	.25	.20	.15
599A	2¢ carmine (II) (1929)	200.00	110.00	70.00	22.00	13.50	8.50
600	3¢ violet (1924)	10.00	6.50	4.00	.25	.20	.15
601	4¢ yellow brown	5.00	3.50	2.50	1.00	.50	.30
602	5¢ dark blue (1924)	2.40	1.50	1.00	.40	.25	.15
603	10¢ orange (1924)	5.00	3.50	2.40	.35	.20	.15
	Perf. 10 Horizontally						
604	1¢ yellow green (1924)	.45	.30	.20	.25	.20	.15
605	1-1/2¢ yellow brown (1925)	.45	.30	.20	.45	.30	.20
606	2¢ carmine	.50	.30	.20	.30	.20	.15

SCOTT NO.		COIL LINE PAIRS UNUSED OG VF	F	AVG.	(NH + 25%) COIL PAIRS UNUSED OG VF	F	AVG.
597	1¢ green	2.55	1.95	1.40	.95	.55	.35
598	1-1/2¢ brown (1925)	6.75	5.25	4.00	1.85	1.35	.95
599	2¢ carmine (I)	2.15	1.65	1.20	1.10	.75	.55
599A	2¢ carmine (II) (1929)	750.00	575.00	385.00	375.00	215.00	135.00
600	3¢ deep violet (1924)	34.50	26.50	20.50	19.50	12.75	7.85
601	4¢ yellow brown	35.75	27.50	22.00	9.50	6.85	4.85
602	5¢ dark blue (1924)	11.75	9.00	6.00	4.50	2.90	1.95
603	10¢ orange (1924)	28.50	22.00	16.00	9.50	6.85	4.50
604	1¢ green (1924)	3.40	2.60	1.65	.85	.55	.35
605	1-1/2¢ yellow brown (1925)	3.25	2.50	1.65	.85	.55	.35
606	2¢ carmine	2.15	1.65	1.10	.95	.55	.35

Postage #610-623

610-613
Harding

614
Ship "New Netherlands"

615
Landing at Fort Orange

616
Monument at Mayport, Fla.

SCOTT NO.	DESCRIPTION	UNUSED O.G. VF	F	AVG	USED VF	F	AVG
	1923 HARDING MEMORIAL ISSUE (NH + 25%)						
610	2¢ black, perf 11 flat ...	1.10	.60	.50	.25	.20	.15
611	2¢ black, imperf	12.00	7.00	6.00	10.00	5.50	4.00
612	2¢ black, perf 10 rotary	27.00	14.00	12.00	4.00	2.40	1.75
613	2¢ black perf 11 rotary	......	......	......	......	......	......
	1924 HUGUENOT-WALLOON ISSUE (NH + 25%)						
614-16	**1¢-5¢, 3 vars., cpl. .....**	**51.75**	**38.00**	**28.50**	**31.75**	**22.75**	**17.50**
614	1¢ dark green	4.50	3.25	2.50	5.50	3.25	2.50
615	2¢ carmine rose	10.00	6.00	4.00	4.00	2.75	2.00
616	5¢ dark blue	40.00	31.00	24.00	24.00	18.00	14.00

617
Washington at Cambridge

618
Birth of Liberty

619
The Minute Man

SCOTT NO.	DESCRIPTION	UNUSED O.G. VF	F	AVG	USED VF	F	AVG
	1925 LEXINGTON-CONCORD SESQUICENTENNIAL (NH + 25%)						
617-19	**1¢-5¢, 3 vars., cpl ......**	**49.50**	**36.50**	**27.25**	**28.50**	**20.75**	**14.50**
617	1¢ deep green	5.00	3.25	2.75	4.00	2.50	1.75
618	2¢ carmine rose	9.00	6.00	4.00	6.00	4.50	3.50
619	5¢ dark blue	38.00	29.00	22.00	20.00	15.00	10.00

620
Sloop "Restaurationen"

621
Viking Ship

622, 694
Harrison

623, 697
Wilson

SCOTT NO.	DESCRIPTION	UNUSED O.G. VF	F	AVG	USED VF	F	AVG
	1925 NORSE-AMERICAN ISSUE (NH + 25%)						
620-21	**2¢-5¢, 2 vars., cpl. .....**	**41.75**	**24.75**	**21.75**	**27.50**	**20.75**	**14.00**
620	2¢ carmine & black	9.00	5.00	5.50	7.00	5.00	3.00
621	5¢ dark blue & black ..	35.00	21.00	17.50	22.00	17.00	12.00
	1925-26 Flat Plate Printings, Perf. 11						
622	13¢ green (1926)	24.00	15.00	11.00	1.35	.75	.60
623	17¢ black	28.00	17.00	13.00	.60	.40	.30

PLATE BLOCKS

SCOTT NO.		UNUSED NH VF	F	AVG.	UNUSED OG VF	F	AVG.
610 (6)	2¢ black perf 11 flat	45.00	30.00	22.00	33.00	23.00	18.00
611 (6)	2¢ black imperf.	210.00	140.00	90.00	160.00	105.00	80.00
611 (4)	2¢ black center line block	110.00	85.00	60.00	77.50	60.00	45.00
611 (4)	2¢ black arrow block	58.00	45.00	32.50	45.00	35.00	25.00
612 (4)	2¢ black perf 10 rotary	500.00	370.00	300.00	390.00	275.00	210.00
614 (6)	1¢ dark green	80.00	54.00	40.00	60.00	39.00	25.00
615 (6)	2¢ carmine rose	150.00	90.00	65.00	110.00	75.00	55.00
616 (6)	5¢ dark blue	620.00	450.00	350.00	510.00	325.00	250.00
617 (6)	1¢ deep green	90.00	50.00	40.00	65.00	40.00	30.00
618 (6)	2¢ carmine rose	160.00	95.00	75.00	115.00	72.00	55.00
619 (6)	5¢ dark blue	510.00	395.00	300.00	410.00	315.00	220.00
620 (8)	2¢ carmine black	325.00	250.00	175.00	235.00	180.00	125.00
621 (8)	5¢ dark blue+black	1050.00	800.00	550.00	815.00	625.00	435.00
622 (6)	13¢ green (1926)	280.00	215.00	150.00	190.00	145.00	105.00
623 (6)	17¢ black	325.00	250.00	175.00	255.00	195.00	136.50

Postage #627-648

627
Liberty Bell

628
John Ericsson Statue

629
Hamilton's Battery

SCOTT NO.	DESCRIPTION	UNUSED O.G. VF	F	AVG	USED VF	F	AVG
	1926-27 COMMEMORATIVES (NH + 25%)						
627-644	**(627-29, 43-44) 5 vars., cpl.**	**20.75**	**15.75**	**11.25**	**13.45**	**10.15**	**6.85**
	1926 COMMEMORATIVES						
627	2¢ Sesquicentennial	4.00	3.00	2.25	.85	.65	.45
628	5¢ Ericsson Memorial	8.35	6.50	4.50	5.25	3.85	2.75
629	2¢ White Plains	2.95	2.25	1.55	2.55	1.95	1.25
630	White Plains Sheet of 25 .	600.00	450.00	360.00	....	....	....
630V	2¢ Dot over "S" variety	615.00	475.00	360.00	....	....	....
	Rotary Press Printings Designs of 1922-25 1926 Imperforate						
631	1-1/2¢ yellow brown	2.65	2.00	1.50	2.40	1.75	1.20
631	1-1/2¢ center line block ...	26.00	20.00	13.50	....	....	....
631	1-1/2¢ arrow block	12.25	9.50	6.50	....	....	....
	1926-28 Perf. 11 x 10 1/2						
632-42	**1¢-10¢ (632-34, 35-42) 11 vars.**	**26.75**	**20.50**	**15.25**	**2.60**	**2.10**	**1.55**
632	1¢ green (1927)	.35	.25	.20	.25	.20	.15
632a	1¢ booklet pane of 6	5.75	4.50	3.35	....	....	....
633	1-1/2¢ yellow brown (1927)	2.95	2.25	1.55	.25	.20	.15
634	2¢ carmine (I)	.35	.25	.20	.25	.20	.15
634	Electric Eye Plate	5.50	4.25	2.75	....	....	....
634d	2¢ booklet pane of 6	2.15	1.65	1.15	....	....	....
634A	2¢ carmine (II) (1928)	325.00	250.00	155.00	21.50	16.50	11.00
635	3¢ violet (1927)	.55	.45	.30	.25	.20	.15
636	4¢ yellow brown (1927) ...	3.50	2.75	2.20	.25	.20	.15
637	5¢ dark blue (1927)	2.95	2.25	1.65	25	.20	.15
638	6¢ red orange (1927)	2.95	2.25	1.65	25	.20	.15
639	7¢ black (1927)	2.95	2.25	1.65	25	.20	.15
640	8¢ olive green (1927)	2.95	2.25	1.65	25	.20	.15
641	9¢ orange red (1931)	2.95	2.25	1.65	25	.20	.15
642	10¢ orange (1927)	5.75	4.50	3.35	.25	.20	.15

643 644 645 646 647 648

SCOTT NO.	DESCRIPTION	UNUSED O.G. VF	F	AVG	USED VF	F	AVG
	1927 COMMEMORATIVES						
643	2¢ Vermont	1.75	1.35	.95	1.55	1.20	.85
644	2¢ Burgoyne	4.75	3.60	2.60	3.95	3.00	1.95
	1928 COMMEMORATIVES						
645-50	**6 varieties, cpl. ....**	**34.00**	**25.75**	**18.00**	**32.50**	**23.50**	**16.00**
645	2¢ Valley Forge	1.30	1.00	.75	.70	.55	.40
646	2¢ Molly Pitcher	1.35	1.10	.85	1.40	1.10	.75
647	2¢ Hawaii	5.75	4.50	3.00	5.35	4.15	2.50
648	5¢ Hawaii	17.75	13.75	9.50	18.25	14.00	9.50

Postage #649-679

649 650 651 654-656 657

(NH + 25%)

SCOTT NO.	DESCRIPTION	UNUSED O.G. VF	F	AVG	USED VF	F	AVG
649	2¢ Aeronautics	2.00	1.35	1.00	1.75	1.00	.70
650	5¢ Aeronautics	8.00	5.50	4.00	7.25	4.00	3.00

1929 COMMEMORATIVES
(NH + 25%)

SCOTT NO.	DESCRIPTION	UNUSED O.G. VF	F	AVG	USED VF	F	AVG
651-81	**(651, 654-55, 657, 680-81) 6 varieties ....**	**5.00**	**3.80**	**2.95**	**5.00**	**3.70**	**2.75**
651	2¢ George R. Clark	1.00	.60	.50	1.00	.60	.50
	Same, arrow block of 4	4.50	3.35	2.35	....	....	....

1929 Design of 1922-25
Rotary Press Printing Perf. 11x10-1/2

SCOTT NO.	DESCRIPTION	UNUSED O.G. VF	F	AVG	USED VF	F	AVG
653	1/2¢ olive brown	.30	.25	.20	.25	.20	.15

1929 COMMEMORATIVES

SCOTT NO.	DESCRIPTION	UNUSED O.G. VF	F	AVG	USED VF	F	AVG
654	2¢ Edison, Flat, Perf 11. .	90	.70	.55	1.15	.90	.65
655	2¢ Edison, Rotary,11x10-1/2.	.85	.65	.50	.40	.30	.20
656	2¢ Edison, Rotary Press Coil, Perf. 10 Vertically	17.50	13.50	9.00	2.95	2.25	1.35
657	2¢ Sullivan Expedition	.90	.70	.55	.85	.65	.50

1929. 632-42 Overprinted Kansas
(NH + 35%)

SCOTT NO.	DESCRIPTION	UNUSED O.G. VF	F	AVG	USED VF	F	AVG
658-68	**1¢-10¢ 11 vars., cpl. ....**	**275.00**	**180.00**	**135.00**	**205.00**	**135.00**	**110.00**
658	1¢ green	2.95	1.95	1.50	2.65	1.75	1.40
659	1-1/2¢ brown	3.75	2.50	2.00	5.00	3.35	2.75
660	2¢ carmine	3.75	2.50	2.00	1.15	.75	.60
661	3¢ violet	21.75	14.50	11.50	15.00	10.00	8.00
662	4¢ yellow brown	21.75	14.50	11.50	9.75	6.50	5.00
663	5¢ deep blue	16.50	11.00	9.00	12.00	8.00	6.25
664	6¢ red orange	37.50	25.00	20.00	22.50	15.00	12.00
665	7¢ black	33.00	22.00	18.00	27.00	18.00	14.50
666	8¢ olive green	97.50	65.00	50.00	90.00	60.00	48.00
667	9¢ light rose	16.50	11.00	9.00	14.25	9.50	7.75
668	10¢ orange yellow	27.00	18.00	14.00	13.50	9.00	7.50

1929. 632-42 Overprinted Nebraska
(NH + 35%)

SCOTT NO.	DESCRIPTION	UNUSED O.G. VF	F	AVG	USED VF	F	AVG
669-79	**1¢-10¢, 11 vars., cpl. ......**	**345.00**	**230.00**	**138.00**	**165.00**	**110.00**	**60.75**
669	1¢ green	3.25	2.15	1.40	2.40	1.60	.90
670	1-1/2¢ brown	3.30	2.20	1.55	3.50	1.95	1.10
671	2¢ carmine	2.40	1.60	1.00	1.05	.70	.40
672	3¢ violet	15.00	9.50	6.00	10.50	7.00	4.00
673	4¢ yellow brown	22.50	15.50	8.25	14.50	9.50	5.00
674	5¢ deep blue	21.00	14.00	8.00	16.50	11.00	6.00
675	6¢ red orange	51.50	34.00	20.00	24.00	16.00	9.50
676	7¢ black	27.00	18.00	11.00	19.50	13.00	7.00
677	8¢ olive green	37.50	25.00	15.50	28.50	21.00	10.50
678	9¢ light rose	44.50	29.50	18.00	31.50	21.00	11.50
679	10¢ orange yellow	135.00	90.00	54.50	22.50	15.00	8.00

U.S. Plate Blocks #627-679

SCOTT NO.		PLATE BLOCKS UNUSED NH VF	F	AVG.	UNUSED OG VF	F	AVG.
627 (6)	Sesquicentennial	65.00	50.00	35.00	49.50	38.00	26.00
628 (6)	5¢ Ericsson Memorial	145.00	110.00	77.50	110.00	85.00	60.00
629 (6)	2¢ White Plains	67.50	52.00	35.00	52.00	40.00	30.00
631	1-1/2¢ yellow brown	93.00	71.50	50.00	70.00	55.00	40.00
632	1¢ green	3.25	2.50	1.75	2.60	2.00	1.40
633	1-1/2¢ yellow brown (1927)	120.00	92.50	65.00	90.00	70.00	48.00
634	2¢ carmine (1)	2.10	1.60	1.10	1.85	1.40	1.00
635	3¢ violet	12.50	8.50	6.00	9.75	7.50	4.50
636	4¢ yellow brown (1927)	130.00	95.00	70.00	105.00	80.00	55.00
637	5¢ dark blue (1927)	29.50	22.50	15.75	22.75	17.50	12.75
638	6¢ red orange (1927)	29.50	22.50	15.75	22.75	17.50	12.75
639	7¢ black (1927)	29.50	22.50	15.75	22.75	17.50	12.75
640	8¢ olive green (1927)	29.50	22.50	15.75	22.75	17.50	12.75
641	9¢ orange red (1931)	30.00	23.00	16.00	23.00	18.00	13.00
642	10¢ orange (1927)	43.50	33.50	23.00	34.00	26.00	18.25
643 (6)	2¢ Vermont	65.00	50.00	35.00	58.00	42.00	28.00
644 (6)	2¢ Burgoyne	80.00	57.00	42.00	60.00	45.00	30.00
645 (6)	2¢ Valley Forge	58.00	40.00	28.00	41.00	30.00	19.50
646	2¢ Molly Pitcher	60.00	42.50	32.00	42.00	33.00	25.00
647	2¢ Hawaii	205.00	140.00	110.00	145.00	110.00	77.00
648	5¢ Hawaii	405.00	315.00	225.00	335.00	260.00	185.00
649 (6)	2¢ Aeronautics	24.00	18.00	12.00	19.50	14.00	10.00
650 (6)	5¢ Aeronautics	115.00	90.00	65.00	85.00	65.00	47.50
651 (6)	2¢ George R. Clark	19.50	15.00	10.00	14.50	11.00	7.50
653	1/2¢ olive brown	1.55	1.20	.85	1.30	1.00	.65
654 (6)	2¢ Edison	51.00	39.50	28.00	40.00	31.50	22.50
655	2¢ Edison	70.00	55.00	40.00	58.00	45.00	30.50
657 (6)	2¢ Sullivan Expedition	45.00	35.00	26.50	39.50	30.00	22.50

		LINE PAIR UNUSED NH			LINE PAIR UNUSED OG		
656	2¢ Edison, coil	125.00	95.00	65.00	80.00	62.50	45.00

SCOTT NO.		PLATE BLOCKS UNUSED NH VF	F	AVG.	UNUSED OG VF	F	AVG.
658	1¢ green	45.00	30.00	20.00	31.50	22.50	15.00
659	1-1/2¢ brown	67.50	45.00	30.00	52.50	35.00	22.50
660	2¢ carmine	65.00	43.00	28.00	49.50	33.00	22.50
661	3¢ violet	290.00	175.00	130.00	215.00	145.00	100.00
662	4¢ yellow brown	290.00	175.00	130.00	215.00	145.00	100.00
663	5¢ deep blue	245.00	165.00	110.00	180.00	120.00	80.00
664	6¢ red orange	675.00	425.00	300.00	495.00	330.00	220.00
665	7¢ black	615.00	425.00	295.00	475.00	325.00	210.00
666	8¢ olive green	1275.00	800.00	600.00	975.00	650.00	425.00
667	9¢ light rose	300.00	195.00	120.00	225.00	150.00	100.00
668	10¢ orange yellow	525.00	325.00	235.00	390.00	260.00	175.00
669	1¢ green	43.50	31.50	22.50	31.00	23.00	16.00
670	1-1/2¢ brown	65.00	42.50	32.50	49.50	35.00	25.00
671	2¢ carmine	42.00	30.00	21.00	42.00	30.00	21.00
672	3¢ violet	225.00	150.00	110.00	230.00	165.00	110.00
673	4¢ yellow brown	315.00	210.00	160.00	210.00	150.00	105.00
674	5¢ deep blue	330.00	225.00	160.00	225.00	160.00	110.00
675	6¢ red orange	775.00	500.00	400.00	550.00	400.00	275.00
676	7¢ black	450.00	375.00	210.00	300.00	215.00	135.00
677	8¢ olive green	625.00	395.00	290.00	435.00	315.00	225.00
678	9¢ light rose	675.00	425.00	300.00	500.00	360.00	250.00
679	10¢ orange yellow	1500.00	950.00	600.00	1100.00	800.00	550.00

U.S. Postage #680-701

680 681 682 683

SCOTT NO.	DESCRIPTION	UNUSED O.G. VF	F	AVG	USED VF	F	AVG
	1929 COMMEMORATIVES (NH + 20%)						
680	2¢ Fallen Timbers	1.05	.80	.55	1.05	.80	.55
681	2¢ Ohio River Canal	.70	.55	.40	.85	.65	.50
	1930-31 COMMEMORATIVES						
682-703	**(682-83, 688-90, 702-03) 7 varieties, complete .....**	**5.30**	**4.00**	**3.00**	**5.35**	**4.15**	**2.85**
	1930 COMMEMORATIVES						
682	2¢ Massachusetts Bay	.80	.60	.45	.65	.50	.35
683	2¢ Carolina-Charleston	1.55	1.20	.95	1.75	1.35	.95

684, 686 685, 687 688 689 690

SCOTT NO.	DESCRIPTION	UNUSED O.G. VF	F	AVG	USED VF	F	AVG
	1930 Rotary Press Printing Perf. 11 x 10-1/2 (NH + 20%)						
684	1-1/2¢ Harding	.40	.30	.25	.25	.20	.15
685	4¢ Taft	1.05	.80	.50	.25	.20	.15
	1930 Rotary Press Coil Stamps Perf. 10 Vertically						
686	1-1/2¢ Harding	2.10	1.60	1.05	.25	.20	.15
687	4¢ Taft	4.25	3.35	2.25	.70	.55	.35
	1930 COMMEMORATIVES						
688	2¢ Braddock's Field	1.30	1.00	.65	1.45	1.00	.70
689	2¢ Von Steuben	.65	.50	.40	.70	.55	.40
	1931 COMMEMORATIVES						
690	2¢ Pulaski	.35	.25	.20	.25	.20	.15
	1931 Designs of 1922-26. Rotary Press Printing. (NH + 20%)						
692-701	**11¢ to 50¢, 10 vars., cpl.**	**120.00**	**92.50**	**67.00**	**3.10**	**2.40**	**1.70**
	Perf. 11 x 10-1/2						
692	11¢ light blue	2.95	2.25	1.50	.25	.20	.15
693	12¢ brown violet	6.50	5.00	3.00	.25	.20	.15
694	13¢ yellow green	2.55	1.95	1.40	.35	.25	.15
695	14¢ dark blue	3.95	3.00	1.95	.70	.55	.35
696	15¢ gray	9.95	7.75	5.50	.25	.20	.15
	Perf. 10-1/2 x 11						
697	17¢ black	5.25	4.00	2.75	.45	.35	.25
698	20¢ carmine rose	12.50	9.50	6.00	.25	.20	.15
699	25¢ blue green	11.75	9.00	5.50	.25	.20	.15
700	30¢ brown	17.25	13.25	9.50	.25	.20	.15
701	50¢ lilac	53.50	41.50	33.50	.25	.20	.15

Note: Plate Block listings for #s 680-749 on pages 45 and 46. Pairs on page 46.

U.S. Postage #702-719

702 703

1931 COMMEMORATIVES
(NH + 20%)

SCOTT NO.	DESCRIPTION	UNUSED O.G. VF	F	AVG	USED VF	F	AVG
702	2¢ Red Cross	.35	.25	.20	.25	.20	.15
702	2¢ arrow block	1.00	.70	.55	....	....	....
703	2¢ Yorktown	.60	.40	.40	.60	.40	.30
703	2¢ center line block	3.00	2.15	1.75	....	....	....
703	2¢ arrow block	2.75	1.95	1.45	....	....	....

704 705 706 707 708 709

710 711 712 713 714 715

1932. WASHINGTON BICENTENNIAL ISSUE

Planning for this set, which celebrated the 200th anniversary of the birth of George Washington, began more than eight years before its release. Despite many suggestions that a pictorial series be created, the final set depicted 12 portraits of Washington at various stages of his life. For reasons of economy, the stamps were produced in single colors and in the same size as regular issues. Nevertheless, the set was an instant success and it was reported that more than a million covers were mailed from Washington, D.C. on January 1, 1932, the first day of issue.

(NH + 20%)

SCOTT NO.	DESCRIPTION	UNUSED O.G. VF	F	AVG	USED VF	F	AVG
704-15	**1/2¢ to 10¢ 12 vars., cpl.**	**30.95**	**23.75**	**17.00**	**4.00**	**3.05**	**2.40**
704	1/2¢ olive brown	.35	.25	.20	.25	.20	.15
705	1¢ green	.35	.25	.20	.25	.20	.15
706	1-1/2¢ brown	.60	.45	.20	.25	.20	.15
707	2¢ carmine rose	.35	.25	.20	.25	.20	.15
708	3¢ deep violet	.85	.65	.45	.25	.20	.15
709	4¢ light brown	.40	.30	.20	.25	.20	.15
710	5¢ blue	2.00	1.55	1.10	.30	.20	.15
711	6¢ red orange	4.75	3.60	2.75	.25	.20	.15
712	7¢ black	.40	.30	.20	.35	.25	.20
713	8¢ olive bistre	4.00	3.10	2.50	1.20	.85	.75
714	9¢ pale red	3.55	2.75	1.95	.40	.30	.25
715	10¢ orange yellow	15.00	11.50	8.00	.25	.20	.15

716 

717  718 719

1932 COMMEMORATIVES
(NH + 20%)

SCOTT NO.	DESCRIPTION	UNUSED O.G. VF	F	AVG	USED VF	F	AVG
716-25	**(716-19, 724-25) 6 vars.**	**7.00**	**5.30**	**4.25**	**2.10**	**1.55**	**1.25**
716	2¢ Winter Olympics	.65	.50	.35	.40	.30	.25
717	2¢ Arbor Day	.35	.25	.20	.25	.20	.15
718	3¢ Summer Olympics	2.10	1.60	1.35	.25	.20	.15
719	5¢ Summer Olympics	3.25	2.50	1.95	.40	.30	.25

U.S. Postage #720-734

720-722

724

SCOTT NO.	DESCRIPTION	UNUSED O.G. VF	F	AVG	(NH + 20%) USED VF	F	AVG
	1932 Rotary Press						
720	3¢ deep violet	.35	.25	.20	.25	.20	.15
720b	3¢ booklet pane of 6	36.50	28.00	18.00	....	....	....
721	3¢ deep violet coil perf 10 vertically	3.60	2.75	1.90	.25	.20	.15
722	3¢ deep violet coil perf 10 horizontally	1.80	1.40	.90	1.00	.80	.65
723	6¢ Garfield, coil perf 10 vertically	13.00	10.00	6.75	.30	.25	.20
	1932 COMMEMORATIVES						
724	3¢ Penn	.40	.30	.25	.35	.25	.20

725

726

727, 752

728, 730, 766

729, 731, 767

732

SCOTT NO.	DESCRIPTION	UNUSED O.G. VF	F	AVG	USED VF	F	AVG
725	3¢ Webster	.60	.45	.35	.55	.40	.30
	1933 COMMEMORATIVES (NH + 20%)						
726-34	**(726-29, 732-34) 7 vars. .**	**2.95**	**2.35**	**1.75**	**2.40**	**1.90**	**1.40**
726	3¢ Oglethorpe	.40	.30	.25	.30	.25	.15
727	3¢ Washington's Headquarters	.30	.25	.20	.25	.20	.15
728	1¢ Fort Dearborn	.30	.25	.15	.25	.20	.15
729	3¢ Federal Building	.30	.25	.15	.25	.20	.15
	Special Printing for A.P.S. Convention Imperforate: Without Gum						
730	1¢ yellow green, sheet of 25	36.75	33.50	27.50	34.00	31.00	26.00
730a	1¢ yellow green single	.85	.75	.55	.50	.45	.35
731	3¢ violet, sheet of 25	31.00	28.50	22.50	33.00	30.00	25.00
731a	3¢ violet, single	.65	.60	.45	.50	.45	.35

733, 735, 753, 768

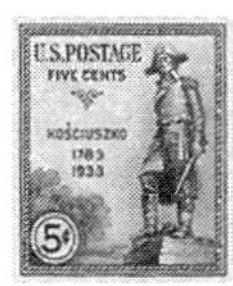

734

736

737, 738, 754

739, 755

SCOTT NO.	DESCRIPTION	UNUSED O.G. VF	F	AVG	USED VF	F	AVG
732	3¢ N.R.A	.30	.25	.20	.25	.20	.15
733	3¢ Byrd	.70	.55	.45	.80	.60	.45
734	5¢ Kosciuszko	.80	.60	.45	.45	.35	.25

Note: Plate Block listings for #s 680-749 on pages 45 and 46. Pairs on page 46.

U.S. Postage #735-751a

SCOTT NO.	DESCRIPTION	UNUSED O.G. VF	F	AVG	USED VF	F	AVG
	1934 NATIONAL PHILATELIC EXHIBITION Imperforate Without Gum (NH + 20%)						
735	3¢ dark blue, sheet of 6 ...	21.50	17.50	15.75	18.50	15.00	11.50
735a	3¢ dark blue, single	2.95	2.25	1.80	2.50	1.95	1.65
	1934 COMMEMORATIVES (NH + 20%)						
736-39	**4 varieties ....**	**1.30**	**.90**	**.75**	**.95**	**.75**	**.55**
736	3¢ Maryland	.35	.25	.20	.25	.20	.15
737	3¢ Mother's Day, rotary, perf 11 x 10-1/2	.35	.25	.20	.25	.20	.15
738	3¢ Mother's Day, flat, perf 11	.35	.25	.20	.25	.20	.15
739	3¢ Wisconsin	.35	.25	.20	.25	.20	.15

740, 751, 756, 769

741, 757

742, 750, 758, 770

744, 760

743, 759

745, 761

747, 763

746, 762

748, 764

749, 765

1934 NATIONAL PARKS ISSUE (NH + 20%)

SCOTT NO.	DESCRIPTION	UNUSED O.G. VF	F	AVG	USED VF	F	AVG
740-49	**1¢-10¢ varieties, complete**	**14.25**	**10.95**	**8.75**	**9.25**	**7.10**	**4.80**
740	1¢ Yosemite	.30	.25	.20	.25	.20	.15
741	2¢ Grand Canyon	.30	.25	.20	.25	.20	.15
742	3¢ Mt. Rainier	.35	.25	.20	.25	.20	.15
743	4¢ Mesa Verde	.60	.45	.35	.60	.45	.30
744	5¢ Yellowstone	1.15	.90	.70	.85	.65	.45
745	6¢ Crater Lake	1.55	1.20	.85	1.45	1.10	.70
746	7¢ Acadia	.95	.75	.55	1.15	.90	.60
747	8¢ Zion	2.60	2.00	1.60	2.75	2.10	1.45
748	9¢ Glacier	2.50	1.90	1.55	.85	.65	.45
749	10¢ Great Smoky Mountains	4.70	3.60	3.05	1.30	1.00	.65
	Special Printing for the A.P.S. Convention & Exhibition of Atlantic City Imperforate Souvenir Sheet (NH + 25%)						
750	3¢ deep violet, sheet of 6	....	40.00	....	....	28.00	....
750a	3¢ deep violet, single	6.00	5.00	3.75	4.10	3.75	3.00
	Special Printing for Trans-Mississippi Philatelic Exposition and Convention at Omaha Imperforate Souvenir Sheet (NH + 20%)						
751	1¢ green, sheet of 6	....	13.00	....	....	11.50	....
751a	1¢ green, single	1.80	1.60	1.40	1.80	1.60	1.40

Note: Plate Blocks for #680-749 on pages 45 and 46. Pairs on page 46.

U.S. Plate Blocks #680-739

SCOTT NO.		PLATE BLOCKS UNUSED NH VF	F	AVG.	UNUSED OG VF	F	AVG.
680 (6)	2¢ Fallen Timbers	48.00	35.00	22.50	36.00	27.50	21.00
681 (6)	2¢ Ohio River Canal	33.75	25.00	15.75	26.00	20.00	12.00
682 (6)	2¢ Massachusetts Bay	58.50	40.00	27.00	39.00	30.00	18.00
683 (6)	2¢ Carolina-Charleston	85.00	60.00	40.00	64.50	49.50	36.00
684	1-1/2¢ Harding	3.65	2.50	1.70	2.90	2.25	1.65
685	4¢ Taft	15.50	11.00	7.00	13.00	10.00	6.00
688 (6)	3¢ Braddock's Field	71.50	47.50	33.00	52.00	40.00	24.00
689 (6)	2¢ Von Steuben	40.95	31.50	18.95	32.50	25.00	15.00
690 (6)	2¢ Pulaski	23.50	17.00	10.75	18.25	14.00	8.50
			LINE PAIR				
686	1-1/2¢ Harding	11.50	9.00	5.50	8.75	6.75	4.00
687	4¢ Taft	24.75	19.00	11.50	26.00	14.00	9.00

SCOTT NO.		PLATE BLOCKS UNUSED NH VF	F	AVG.	UNUSED OG VF	F	AVG.
692	11¢ light blue	21.50	16.50	10.00	16.50	12.75	9.50
693	12¢ brown violet	36.50	27.00	16.75	27.95	21.50	16.00
694	13¢ yellow green	21.50	16.50	10.00	16.50	12.75	9.50
695	14¢ dark blue	27.95	21.00	12.95	20.00	15.50	11.50
696	15¢ grey	61.00	45.00	28.25	46.75	36.00	27.00
697	17¢ black	36.50	26.50	16.75	27.95	21.50	16.00
698	20¢ carmine rose	68.00	50.00	31.50	52.00	40.00	24.00
699	25¢ blue green	65.00	50.00	30.00	50.00	38.50	23.00
700	30¢ brown	115.00	80.00	55.00	84.50	65.00	39.00
701	50¢ lilac	335.00	250.00	155.00	250.00	195.00	115.00
702	2¢ Red Cross	3.55	2.60	1.65	2.95	2.25	1.40
703	2¢ Yorktown (6)	5.75	4.00	2.70	4.25	3.35	2.65
704-715	Washington Bicentennial	560.00	420.00	260.00	400.00	320.00	230.00
704	1/2¢ olive brown	5.75	4.25	2.70	4.70	3.60	2.25
705	1¢ green	7.00	5.00	3.30	5.85	4.50	2.75
706	1-1/2¢ brown	28.00	20.00	13.00	2.10	16.00	12.75
707	2¢ carmine rose	2.10	1.60	.95	1.80	1.40	.95
708	3¢ deep violet	22.75	17.00	10.50	18.00	14.00	9.00
709	4¢ light brown	8.45	6.00	4.00	7.15	5.50	3.60
710	5¢ blue	28.50	21.00	13.00	23.50	18.00	14.00
711	6¢ red orange	105.00	80.00	49.50	78.00	60.00	46.50
712	7¢ black	10.00	7.00	4.50	7.75	6.00	4.15
713	8¢ olive bistre	105.00	80.00	49.50	78.00	60.00	40.00
714	9¢ pale red	68.00	52.50	31.50	50.00	38.50	26.00
715	10¢ orange yellow	200.00	150.00	93.00	145.00	110.00	82.50
716 (6)	2¢ Winter Olympics	22.00	16.00	11.00	16.95	13.00	9.50
717	2¢ Arbor Day	14.00	10.50	6.50	10.75	8.25	6.00
718	3¢ Summer Olympics	26.00	19.00	12.00	19.50	15.00	11.00
719	5¢ Summer Olympics	43.50	32.50	20.00	32.50	25.00	19.50
720	3¢ deep violet	2.95	2.00	1.40	2.15	1.65	1.10
724 (6)	3¢ Penn	20.00	14.00	9.50	14.00	11.00	9.00
725 (6)	3¢ Daniel Webster	35.75	26.00	14.00	28.00	22.00	16.00
726 (6)	3¢ Oglethorpe	23.50	16.50	11.00	18.00	14.00	10.00
727	3¢ Washington Hdqrs	10.00	7.00	4.50	7.95	6.00	4.50
728	1¢ Fort Dearborn	3.55	2.75	1.65	2.95	2.25	1.65
729	3¢ Federal Building	6.00	4.00	2.75	4.25	3.35	2.25
732	3¢ N.R.A.	2.95	2.00	1.40	2.55	1.95	1.40
733 (6)	3¢ Byrd	27.50	20.00	13.00	21.00	16.00	13.00
734 (6)	5¢ Kosciuszko	60.00	45.00	28.00	42.95	33.00	25.00
736 (6)	3¢ Maryland	17.50	12.50	8.25	13.00	10.00	8.25
737	3¢ Mother's Day, rotary perf. 11 x 10-1/2	2.95	2.00	1.30	2.40	1.75	1.40
738 (6)	3¢ Mother's Day, flat, perf. 11	8.50	6.50	3.95	6.50	5.00	3.85
739 (6)	3¢ Wisconsin	7.00	5.00	3.25	5.75	4.50	3.25

U.S. Plate Blocks #740-749
And Coil Pairs #686-723

SCOTT NO.		Coil Line Pairs UNUSED OG VF	(NH + 25%) F	AVG.	Coil Pairs UNUSED OG VF	F	AVG.
686	1-1/2¢ Harding	8.50	6.50	4.50	4.50	3.00	2.00
687	4¢ Taft	18.00	14.00	9.00	8.50	6.50	4.50
721	3¢ deep violet perf 10 vertically	10.75	8.25	5.50	7.00	5.25	4.00
722	3¢ deep violet perf 10 horizontally	7.75	6.00	4.15	4.00	2.75	1.85
723	6¢ Garfield perf 10 vertically	71.50	55.00	33.00	25.00	19.25	13.25

SCOTT NO.		PLATE BLOCKS UNUSED NH VF	F	AVG.	UNUSED OG VF	F	AVG.
740-749	10 varieties complete	210.00	160.00	96.50	160.00	125.00	94.00
740 (6)	1¢ Yosemite	2.55	1.80	1.15	2.00	1.55	1.10
741 (6)	2¢ Grand Canyon	2.65	1.95	1.25	2.15	1.65	1.20
742 (6)	3¢ Mt. Rainier	3.50	2.75	1.65	3.00	2.30	1.55
743 (6)	4¢ Mesa Verde	15.50	12.00	7.25	13.00	10.00	7.00
744 (6)	5¢ Yellowstone	19.50	15.00	9.00	14.00	11.00	8.25
745 (6)	6¢ Crater Lake	33.50	26.00	15.50	26.50	20.50	15.50
746 (6)	7¢ Acadia	21.50	16.50	10.00	17.25	13.25	10.00
747 (6)	8¢ Zion	33.50	26.00	15.50	26.50	20.50	15.50
748 (6)	9¢ Glacier	33.50	26.00	15.50	26.50	20.50	15.50
749 (6)	10¢ Great Smoky Mountains	53.50	41.25	24.75	39.00	30.00	23.50

THE FARLEY PERIOD

The 1933-35 period was one of great excitement for the hobby. With a stamp collector in the White House, in the person of President Franklin Delano Roosevelt, it was a period during which special Souvenir Sheets were issued for the A.P.S. Convention in 1933 (catalog #730) and the National Philatelic Exhibition in 1934 (#735). Collectors gloried in the limelight.

But there was a darker side, in the form of rare imperforate sheets that were being released to then Postmaster General James A. Farley, President Roosevelt himself, and a few other prominent personages. The protests against the practice grew to unmanageable proportions when word got around that one of the imperforate sheets of the 1934 Mother's Day issue had been offered to a stamp dealer for $20,000. Adding insult to injury, it was learned shortly thereafter that not only were there individual sheets floating around, but full, uncut sheets also had been presented as gifts to a fortunate few.

The outcry that followed could not be stifled. Congress had become involved in the affair and the demands were mounting that the gift sheets be recalled and destroyed. This being deemed impractical or undesirable, another solution was found—one that comes down to us today in the form of "The Farleys".

The solution was to let everyone "share the wealth", so to speak. Instead of recalling the few sheets in existence, additional quantities of the imperforates were issued in the same full sheet form as the gift sheets. Naturally, this step substantially reduced the value of the original, very limited edition, but it satisfied most collectors and left as its legacy "The Farley Issues".

The Farleys were issued March 15, 1935, and consisted of reprints of 20 issues. They remained on sale for three months, a relatively short time by most standards, but more than enough time for collectors who really cared. Although purists felt then—and some still do now—that President Roosevelt would have saved collectors a considerable sum by having the first few sheets destroyed, the issue has provided us with a wondrous selection of Gutters and Lines, arrow blocks, single sheets and full panes.

The collector on a limited budget can fill the spaces in an album with single imperforates. But the Farleys are such an interesting study that owning and displaying at least one of each variety of any one issue is a must. We illustrate here one of the full sheets of the 1 cent Century of Progress Farley Issue. The full sheets consisted of nine panes of 25 stamps each. The individual panes were separated by wide horizontal **(A)** or vertical **(B)** gutters and the gutters of four adjacent sheets formed a cross gutter **(C)**.

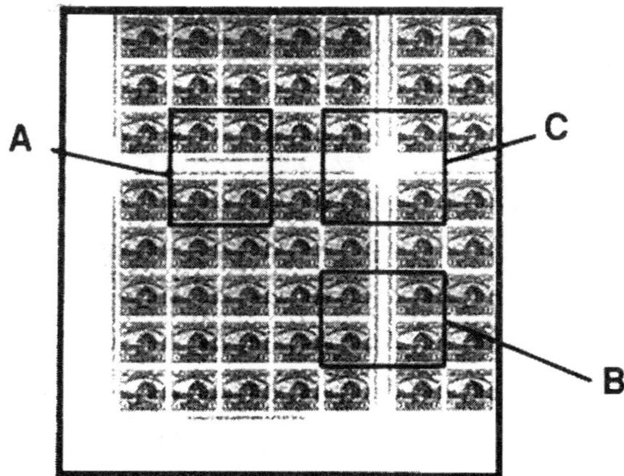

NOTE: For #s 753-765 and 771, lines separated the individual panes. The lines ended in arrows at the top, bottom and side margins.

1935 "FARLEY SPECIAL PRINTINGS"

Designs of 1933-34 Imperforate (#752, 753 Perf.) Without Gum

SCOTT NO.		PLATE BLOCK	CENTER LINE BLOCK	T OR B ARROW BLOCK	L OR R ARROW BLOCK	PAIR WITH V. LINE	PAIR WITH H. LINE	FINE UNUSED	FINE USED
752-71	**20 varieties, complete**	....	**470.00**	....	....	**135.00**	**91.50**	**26.00**	**25.50**
752	3¢ Newburgh	16.00	50.00	16.50	9.50	7.50	4.50	.20	.15
753	3¢ Byrd	(6)19.00	95.00	90.00	4.00	42.50	1.65	.60	.60
754	3¢ Mother's Day	(6)19.00	9.50	4.00	4.25	1.65	1.75	.65	.55
755	3¢ Wisconsin	(6)19.00	9.50	4.00	4.25	1.65	1.75	.65	.55
756-65	**1¢-10¢ Parks 10 varieties, complete**	**295.00**	**150.00**	**140.00**	**140.00**	**42.25**	**43.50**	**16.75**	**15.00**
756	1¢ Yosemite	(6) 5.00	4.00	1.40	1.10	.60	.50	.20	.15
757	2¢ Grand Canyon	(6) 6.50	5.50	1.55	1.45	.65	.85	.25	.20
758	3¢ Mt. Rainier	(6)16.50	6.50	3.60	4.00	1.55	1.75	.60	.55
759	4¢ Mesa Verde	(6)22.00	11.00	6.00	7.00	2.50	3.10	1.10	1.10
760	5¢ Yellowstone	(6)27.50	16.50	12.00	10.50	5.25	4.75	2.25	1.85
761	6¢ Crater Lake	(6)45.00	22.00	15.00	16.50	6.50	7.50	2.75	2.50
762	7¢ Acadia	(6)36.00	18.00	10.50	12.25	4.50	5.50	1.95	1.75
763	8¢ Zion	(6)45.00	20.00	14.50	12.00	6.25	5.35	2.25	2.00
764	9¢ Glacier	(6)50.00	22.00	13.00	5.75	5.75	6.50	2.30	2.10
765	10¢ Great Smoky Mountains ...	(6)57.50	33.00	25.00	22.00	11.00	10.00	4.10	3.75
766a-70a	**5 varieties, complete**	....	**80.00**	....	....	**40.00**	**35.50**	**9.45**	**7.75**
766a	1¢ Fort Dearborn	....	16.50	....	....	9.00	6.50	.75	.45
767a	3¢ Federal Building	....	16.50	....	....	9.00	6.50	.75	.45
768a	3¢ Byrd	....	19.00	....	....	7.75	6.50	3.00	2.75
769a	1¢ Yosemite	....	11.00	....	....	5.25	5.00	1.85	1.50
770a	3¢ Mt. Rainier	....	28.00	....	....	11.50	13.00	3.60	3.05
771	16¢ Air Post Special Delivery ...	(6)80.00	82.50	15.00	16.50	6.75	7.50	2.75	2.50

U.S. FARLEY ISSUE COMPLETE MINT SHEETS

SCOTT NO.	F/WG SHEET	SCOTT NO.	F/WG SHEET	SCOTT NO.	F/WG SHEET	SCOTT NO.	F/WG SHEET
752-71 set	7300.00	756 (200)	67.50	762 (200)	420.00	767 (225)	400.00
752 (400)	335.00	757 (200)	70.00	763 (200)	525.00	768 (150)	550.00
753 (200)	635.00	758 (200)	160.00	764 (200)	575.00	769 (120)	240.00
754 (200)	190.00	759 (200)	280.00	765 (200)	900.00	770 (120)	600.00
755 (200)	190.00	761 (200)	575.00	766 (225)	400.00	771 (200)	725.00
756-65 set	3395.00						

SELECTED U.S. COMMEMORATIVE MINT SHEETS

SCOTT NO.	F/NH SHEET	SCOTT NO.	F/NH SHEET	SCOTT NO.	F/NH SHEET	SCOTT NO.	F/NH SHEET
610 (100)	130.00	651 (50)	46.50	708 (100)	90.00	732 (100)	14.00
614 (50)	255.00	654 (100)	130.00	709 (100)	40.00	733 (50)	50.00
615 (50)	450.00	655 (100)	140.00	710 (100)	235.00	734 (100)	110.00
617 (50)	280.00	657 (100)	135.00	711 (100)	490.00	736 (100)	33.00
618 (50)	420.00	680 (100)	140.00	712 (100)	40.00	737 (50)	9.00
620 (100)	825.00	681 (100)	120.00	713 (100)	500.00	738 (50)	15.00
627 (50)	230.00	682 (100)	110.00	714 (100)	400.00	739 (50)	15.00
628 (50)	595.00	683 (100)	205.00	715 (100)	1750.00	740-49 set	665.00
629 (100)	365.00	688 (100)	155.00	716 (100)	67.50	740 (50)	6.50
643 (100)	285.00	689 (100)	82.50	717 (100)	26.00	741 (50)	9.00
644 (50)	290.00	690 (100)	45.00	718 (100)	195.00	742 (50)	13.00
645 (100)	175.00	702 (100)	20.00	719 (100)	305.00	743 (50)	33.50
646 (100)	180.00	703 (50)	28.00	724 (100)	50.00	744 (50)	55.00
647 (100)	665.00	704-15 set	3485.00	725 (100)	82.50	745 (50)	85.00
648 (100)	1850.00	704 (100)	16.50	726 (100)	55.00	746 (50)	46.50
649 (50)	85.00	705 (100)	21.50	727 (100)	22.00	747 (50)	120.00
650 (50)	420.00	706 (100)	71.50	728 (100)	15.00	748 (50)	115.00
		707 (100)	14.00	729 (100)	22.00	749 (50)	215.00

FIRST DAY COVERS: First Day Covers are envelopes cancelled on the "First Day of Issue" of the stamp used on an envelope. Usually they also contain a picture (cachet) on the left side designed to go with the theme of the stamp. From 1935 to 1949, prices listed are for cacheted, addressed covers. From 1950 to date, prices are for cacheted, unaddressed covers.

U.S. Postage #772-784

772, 778a

773, 778b

775, 778c

776, 778d

774

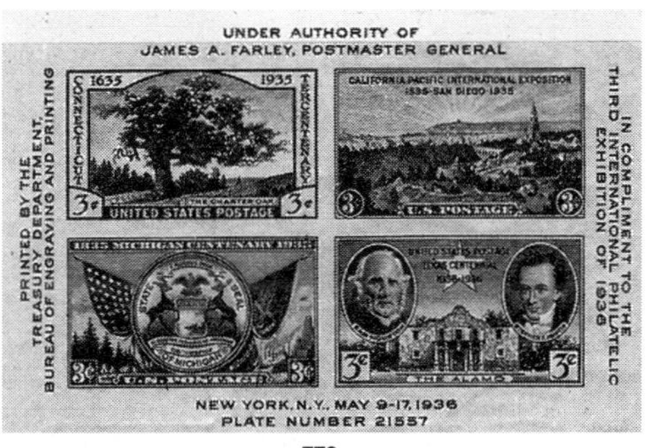

778

777

782

783

784

SCOTT NO.	DESCRIPTION	FIRST DAY COVERS SING	FIRST DAY COVERS PL. BLK.	MINT SHEET	PLATE BLOCK F/NH	UNUSED F/NH	USED F
	1935-36 COMMEMORATIVES						
772/84	**(772-77, 782-84) 9 varieties**	....	....	....	....	**1.55**	**1.15**
772	3¢ Connecticut	7.00	17.50	10.00 (50)	1.95	.20	.15
773	3¢ San Diego	7.00	17.50	6.50 (50)	1.60	.20	.15
774	3¢ Boulder Dam	7.00	17.50	7.75 (50)	(6)2.30	.20	.15
775	3¢ Michigan	7.00	17.50	6.50 (50)	1.65	.20	.15
	1936 COMMEMORATIVE						
776	3¢ Texas	11.00	25.00	7.75 (50)	1.65	.20	.15
777	3¢ Rhode Island	7.00	17.50	9.50 (50)	1.95	.20	.15
	1936 THIRD INTERNATIONAL PHILATELIC EXHIBITION "TIPEX" Imperforate Souvenir Sheet Designs of 772, 773, 775, 776						
778	red violet, sheet of 4	16.50	....	....	....	3.00	3.00
778a	3¢ Connecticut	....	....	....	....	.75	.70
778b	3¢ San Diego	....	....	....	....	.75	.70
778c	3¢ Michigan	....	....	....	....	.75	.70
778d	3¢ Texas	....	....	....	....	.75	.70
782	3¢ Arkansas Statehood	7.00	17.50	7.75 (50)	1.65	.20	.15
783	3¢ Oregon Territory	7.00	17.50	7.00 (50)	1.45	.20	.15
784	3¢ Suffrage for Women	7.00	17.50	12.50 (100)	.95	.20	.15

FOR YOUR CONVENIENCE IN ORDERING, COMPLETE SETS ARE LISTED BEFORE SINGLE STAMP LISTINGS

U.S. Postage #785-802

785

786

787

788

789

790

791

792

793

794

795

798

799

800

796

801

802

SCOTT NO.	DESCRIPTION	FIRST DAY COVERS SING.	FIRST DAY COVERS PL. BLK.	MINT SHEET	PLATE BLOCK F/NH	UNUSED F/NH	USED F
	1936-37 ARMY AND NAVY ISSUE						
785-94	**10 varieties, complete ....**	**53.50**	**......**	**......**	**56.00**	**3.80**	**1.60**
	ARMY COMMEMORATIVES						
785	1¢ green	5.00	12.00	5.25 (50)	1.20	.20	.15
786	2¢ carmine	5.00	12.00	6.50 (50)	1.20	.20	.15
787	3¢ purple	5.00	12.00	13.75 (50)	1.65	.30	.15
788	4¢ gray	6.00	14.50	33.00 (50)	12.00	.45	.20
789	5¢ ultramarine	7.00	14.50	50.00 (50)	13.50	.90	.20
	NAVY COMMEMORATIVES						
790	1¢ green	5.00	12.00	5.25 (50)	1.20	.20	.15
791	2¢ carmine	5.00	12.00	6.50 (50)	1.20	.20	.15
792	3¢ purple	5.00	12.00	9.50 (50)	1.50	.30	.15
793	4¢ gray	6.00	14.50	33.00 (50)	12.00	.45	.20
794	5¢ ultramarine	7.00	14.50	50.00 (50)	13.50	.90	.20
	1937 COMMEMORATIVES						
795/802	**(795-96, 798-802) 7 varieties**	**.......**	**.......**	**.......**	**.......**	**1.25**	**.95**
795	3¢ Northwest Ordinance	6.50	16.00	7.25 (50)	1.40	.20	.15
796	5¢ Virginia Dare	6.50	16.00	17.50 (48)	9.00(6)	.25	.20
	1937 S.P.A. CONVENTION ISSUE **Design of 749 Imperforate Souvenir Sheet**						
797	10¢ blue green	6.50	....	....	....	.85	.65
798	3¢ Constitution	6.50	16.00	8.25 (50)	1.70	.20	.15
799	3¢ Hawaii	6.50	16.00	8.25 (50)	1.65	.20	.15
800	3¢ Alaska	6.50	16.00	8.25 (50)	1.65	.20	.15
801	3¢ Puerto Rico	6.50	16.00	8.25 (50)	1.65	.20	.15
802	3¢ Virgin Islands	6.50	16.00	8.25 (50)	1.65	.20	.15

Presidential Series of 1938 #803-834

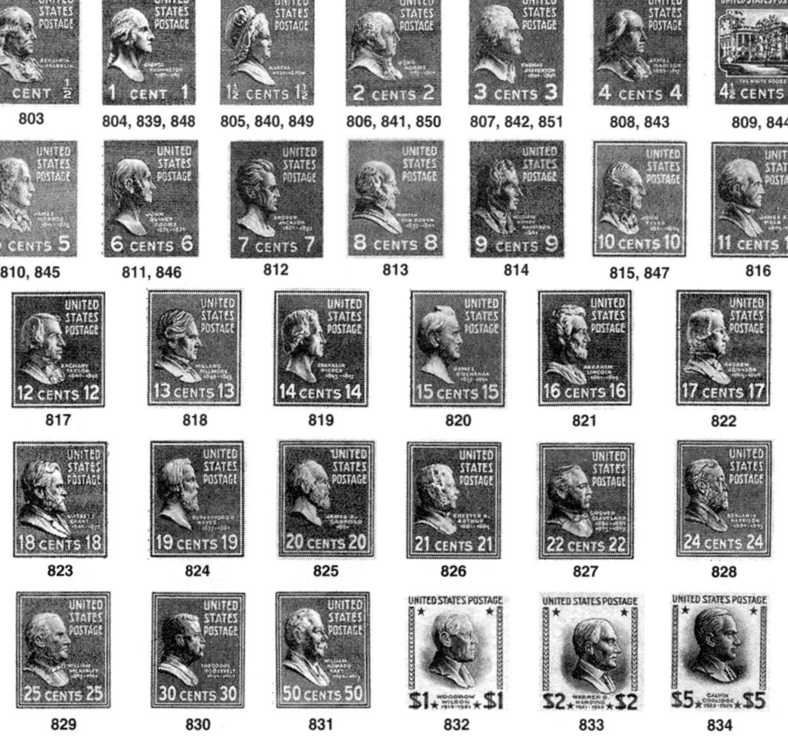

1938 Presidential Series

In 1938 a new set of definitive stamps was issued honoring the first 29 presidents, Ben Franklin, Martha Washington, and the White House. These were regular issues that effectively replaced the previous definitive issues of the 1922-25 series.

The "Presidential Series" contained 32 denominations ranging from 1/2¢-$5.00. It is an interesting series because various printing methods were employed. The 1/2¢-50¢ values were printed in single colors on rotary presses using both normal and "electric eye" plates. The $1.00 to $5.00 values were printed in two colors on flat plate presses.

The $1.00 value was reprinted twice, once in 1951 on revenue paper watermarked "USIR" (#832b) and again in 1954. The 1954 issue was "dry printed" on thick white paper, with an experimental colorless gum (832c).

This series in regular and coil form was used for 16 years until it was replaced by the new definitive issues of 1954.

U.S. Postage #803-838

SCOTT NO.	DESCRIPTION	FIRST DAY COVERS SING	FIRST DAY COVERS PL. BLK.	MINT SHEET	PLATE BLOCK F/NH	UNUSED F/NH	USED F
	1938 PRESIDENTIAL SERIES						
803-34	**1/2¢-$5, 32 varieties, cpl.**	**500.00**	....	....	**845.00**	**185.00**	**17.00**
803-31	**1/2¢-50¢, 29 varieties**	**92.75**	....	....	**180.00**	**37.50**	**5.30**
803	1/2¢ Franklin	2.25	5.50	9.50(100)	.70	.20	.15
804	1¢ G. Washington	2.25	5.50	9.50100)	.70	.20	.15
804b	1¢ booklet pane of 6	14.00	....	....	....	2.25	....
805	1-1/2¢ M. Washington	2.25	5.50	9.50(100)	.70	.20	.15
806	2¢ J. Adams	2.25	5.50	9.50(100)	.70	.20	.15
806	E.E. Plate Block of 10	....	....	....	5.00	....	....
806b	2¢ booklet pane of 6	14.00	....	....	....	4.50	....
807	3¢ Jefferson	2.25	5.50	12.00(100)	.70	.20	.15
807	E.E. Plate Block of 10	....	....	....	28.00	....	....
807a	3¢ booklet pane of 6	14.00	....	....	....	8.25	....
808	4¢ Madison	2.25	5.50	95.00(100)	4.50	.95	.15
809	4-1/2¢ White House	2.25	5.50	15.50(100)	1.40	.20	.15
810	5¢ J. Monroe	2.25	5.50	23.50(100)	1.20	.25	.15
811	6¢ J.Q. Adams	2.25	5.50	28.00(100)	1.50	.30	.15
812	7¢ A. Jackson	2.25	5.50	27.00(100)	1.80	.40	.15
813	8¢ Van Buren	2.25	5.50	38.00(100)	2.35	.45	.15
814	9¢ Harrison	2.25	5.50	42.50(100)	2.50	.45	.15
815	10¢ Tyler	2.25	5.50	31.50(100)	1.65	.35	.15
816	11¢ Polk	2.75	6.75	62.50(100)	4.50	.70	.15
817	12¢ Taylor	2.75	6.75	120.00(100)	6.25	1.30	.15
818	13¢ Fillmore	2.75	6.75	180.00(100)	8.50	1.95	.15
819	14¢ Pierce	2.75	6.75	105.00(100)	6.00	1.15	.15
820	15¢ Buchanan	2.75	6.75	57.50(100)	2.75	.60	.15
821	16¢ Lincoln	3.35	8.25	120.00(100)	6.00	1.20	.45
822	17¢ Johnson	3.35	8.25	110.00(100)	5.50	1.15	.15
823	18¢ Grant	3.35	8.25	215.00(100)	11.00	2.25	.15
824	19¢ Hayes	3.35	8.25	175.00(100)	9.00	1.85	.60
825	20¢ Garfield	4.00	11.25	85.00(100)	4.00	.90	.15
826	21¢ Arthur	4.00	11.25	220.00(100)	11.00	2.30	.15
827	22¢ Cleveland	4.50	11.25	125.00(100)	13.50	1.25	.55
828	24¢ B. Harrison	4.50	11.25	415.00(100)	20.00	4.15	.25
829	25¢ McKinley	5.50	13.75	82.50(100)	4.00	.90	.15
830	30¢ T. Roosevelt	5.50	13.75	495.00(100)	23.50	5.25	.15
831	50¢ Taft	15.00	30.00	825.00(100)	35.00	8.25	.15
	Flat Plate Printing Perf. 11						
832	$1 Wilson	70.00	150.00	1025.00(100)	45.00	9.50	.15
832	$1 center line block	....	....	....	45.00	....	....
832	$1 arrow block	....	....	....	40.00	....	....
832b	$1 Watermarked "USIR"	....	....	....	....	325.00	70.00
832c	$1 dry print thick paper (1954)	35.00	75.00	725.00(100)	32.50	7.25	.15
833	$2 Harding	135.00	275.00	....	140.00	26.00	6.50
833	$2 center line block	....	....	....	115.00	....	....
833	$2 arrow block	....	....	....	110.00	....	....
834	$5 Coolidge	225.00	400.00	....	525.00	120.00	6.00
834	$5 center line block	....	....	....	525.00	....	....
834	$5 arrow block	....	....	....	500.00	....	....

835

836

837

838

SCOTT NO.	DESCRIPTION	FIRST DAY COVERS SING	FIRST DAY COVERS PL. BLK.	MINT SHEET	PLATE BLOCK F/NH	UNUSED F/NH	USED F
	1938-39 COMMEMORATIVES						
835-58	**(835-38, 852-58) 11 vars., cpl**	....	....	....	....	**3.70**	**1.45**
835	3¢ Ratification	6.00	12.00	21.00(50)	5.00	.40	.15
836	3¢ Swedes-Finns	6.00	12.00	9.50(48)	(6)3.50	.20	.15
837	3¢ Northwest Territory	6.00	12.00	26.00(100)	11.50	.20	.15
838	3¢ Iowa Territory	6.00	12.00	16.00(50)	8.50	.20	.15

U.S. Postage #839-863

SCOTT NO.	DESCRIPTION	FIRST DAY COVERS SING.	FIRST DAY COVERS PL. BLK.	MINT SHEET	PLATE BLOCK F/NH	UNUSED F/NH	USED F
	1939 Presidentials Rotary Press Coil						
			L.PR.		**LINE PAIR**		
839-51	**13 varieties, complete ....**	**67.50**	**120.00**	....	**145.00**	**35.00**	**4.50**
	Perforated 10 Vertically						
839	1¢ G. Washington	5.00	8.50	....	1.25	.30	.15
840	1-1/2¢ M. Washington	5.00	8.50	....	1.50	.35	.15
841	2¢ J. Adams	5.00	8.50	....	1.60	.35	.15
842	3¢ T. Jefferson	5.00	8.50	....	1.50	.55	.15
843	4¢ J. Madison	5.75	10.50	....	32.50	8.00	.50
844	4-1/2¢ White House	5.75	10.50	....	5.50	.55	.50
845	5¢ J. Monroe	5.75	11.00	....	30.00	5.50	.50
846	6¢ J.Q. Adams	5.75	11.00	....	7.25	1.25	.15
847	10¢ J. Tyler	8.50	16.00	....	50.00	12.00	.75
	Perforated 10 Horizontally						
848	1¢ G. Washington	5.00	8.50	....	3.00	.80	.15
849	1-1/2¢ M. Washington	5.00	8.50	....	4.25	1.50	.50
850	2¢ J. Adams	5.00	8.50	....	7.50	3.25	.60
851	3¢ T. Jefferson	5.00	8.50	....	7.00	2.75	.50

852 853 854 857

855 856 858

1939 COMMEMORATIVES

SCOTT NO.	DESCRIPTION	FIRST DAY COVERS SING.	FIRST DAY COVERS PL. BLK.	MINT SHEET	PLATE BLOCK F/NH	UNUSED F/NH	USED F
852	3¢ Golden Gate	6.00	12.00	8.00(50)	1.75	.20	.15
853	3¢ World's Fair	6.50	12.00	9.00(50)	2.25	.20	.15
854	3¢ Inauguration	6.50	12.00	28.00(50)	(6)4.75	.55	.15
855	3¢ Baseball	35.00	50.00	82.50(50)	9.00	1.75	.20
856	3¢ Panama Canal	6.00	12.00	13.50(50)	(6)4.50	.25	.15
857	3¢ Printing	6.00	12.00	7.25(50)	1.50	.20	.15
858	3¢ Four States	6.00	12.00	7.50(50)	1.75	.20	.15

859 860 861 862 863

1940 FAMOUS AMERICANS ISSUES

SCOTT NO.	DESCRIPTION	FIRST DAY COVERS SING.	FIRST DAY COVERS PL. BLK.	MINT SHEET	PLATE BLOCK F/NH	UNUSED F/NH	USED F
859-93	**35 varieties, complete ....**	**98.00**	....	**2555.00**	**465.00**	**38.50**	**19.00**
859/91	**All 1¢, 2¢, 3¢ values, 21 vars........**		....	....	**37.50**	**4.20**	**3.00**
	American Authors						
859	1¢ Washington Irving	2.25	4.00	6.00(70)	1.50	.20	.15
860	2¢ James F. Cooper	2.25	4.00	7.00(70)	1.50	.20	.15
861	3¢ Ralph W. Emerson	2.25	4.00	8.25(70)	1.60	.20	.15
862	5¢ Louisa May Alcott	3.00	6.00	35.00(70)	13.00	.40	.35
863	10¢ Samuel L. Clemens	6.00	13.50	160.00(70)	52.50	2.40	2.00

U.S. Postage #864-883

SCOTT NO.	DESCRIPTION	FIRST DAY COVERS SING.	FIRST DAY COVERS PL. BLK.	MINT SHEET	PLATE BLOCK F/NH	UNUSED F/NH	USED F

864 865 866 867 868

American Poets

SCOTT NO.	DESCRIPTION	SING.	PL. BLK.	MINT SHEET	PLATE BLOCK F/NH	UNUSED F/NH	USED F
864	1¢ Henry W. Longfellow	2.25	4.00	8.25(70)	2.50	.20	.15
865	2¢ John Whittier	2.25	4.00	8.25(70)	2.50	.20	.15
866	3¢ James Lowell	2.25	4.00	10.50(70)	3.00	.20	.15
867	5¢ Walt Whitman	3.00	6.00	40.00(70)	13.00	.40	.35
868	10¢ James Riley	5.00	11.50	195.00(70)	50.00	2.50	2.25

869 870 871 872 873

American Educators

SCOTT NO.	DESCRIPTION	SING.	PL. BLK.	MINT SHEET	PLATE BLOCK F/NH	UNUSED F/NH	USED F
869	1¢ Horace Mann	2.25	4.00	7.25(70)	3.00	.20	.15
870	2¢ Mark Hopkins	2.25	4.00	7.50(70)	1.50	.20	.15
871	3¢ Charles W. Eliot	2.25	4.00	16.50(70)	3.50	.25	.15
872	5¢ Frances Willard	3.00	6.00	50.00(70)	15.00	.50	.35
873	10¢ Booker T. Washington .	6.00	13.50	155.00(70)	38.00	2.25	2.00

874 875 876 877 878

American Scientists

SCOTT NO.	DESCRIPTION	SING.	PL. BLK.	MINT SHEET	PLATE BLOCK F/NH	UNUSED F/NH	USED F
874	1¢ John J. Audubon	2.25	4.00	5.75(70)	1.50	.20	.15
875	2¢ Dr. Crawford Long	2.25	4.00	7.25(70)	1.25	.20	.15
876	3¢ Luther Burbank	2.25	4.00	9.50(70)	1.50	.20	.15
877	5¢ Dr. Walter Reed	3.00	6.00	29.50(70)	9.00	.35	.35
878	10¢ Jane Addams	5.00	11.50	115.00(70)	30.00	1.40	1.30

879 880 881 882 883

American Composers

SCOTT NO.	DESCRIPTION	SING.	PL. BLK.	MINT SHEET	PLATE BLOCK F/NH	UNUSED F/NH	USED F
879	1¢ Stephen Foster	2.25	4.00	5.75(70)	1.50	.20	.15
880	2¢ John Philip Sousa	2.25	4.00	11.50(70)	1.60	.20	.15
881	3¢ Victor Herbert	2.25	4.00	11.00(70)	1.60	.20	.15
882	5¢ Edward A. MacDowell	3.00	6.00	42.50(70)	14.00	.60	.35
883	10¢ Ethelbert Nevin	5.00	11.50	370.00(70)	50.00	5.00	1.80

MINT SHEETS: From 1935 to date, we list prices for standard size Mint Sheets in Fine, Never Hinged condition. The number of stamps in each sheet is noted in ( ).

FAMOUS AMERICANS: Later additions to the Famous American series include #945 Edison, #953 Carver, #960 White, #965 Stone, #975 Rogers, #980 Harris, #986 Poe, and #988 Gompers.

U.S. Postage #884-898

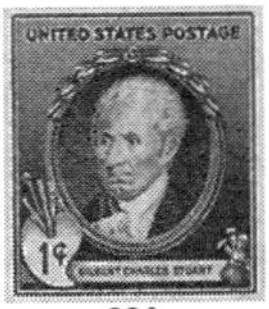

SCOTT NO.	DESCRIPTION	FIRST DAY COVERS SING.	FIRST DAY COVERS PL. BLK.	MINT SHEET	PLATE BLOCK F/NH	UNUSED F/NH	USED F
	American Artists						
884	1¢ Gilbert Stuart	2.25	4.00	6.00(70)	1.35	.20	.15
885	2¢ James Whistler	2.25	4.00	6.25(70)	1.35	.20	.15
886	3¢ A. Saint-Gaudens	2.25	4.00	8.00(70)	1.35	.20	.15
887	5¢ Daniel C. French	3.00	6.00	48.00(70)	12.50	.70	.35
888	10¢ Frederic Remington	5.00	11.50	175.00(70)	40.00	2.25	2.00
	American Inventors						
889	1¢ Eli Whitney	2.25	4.00	9.00(70)	2.50	.20	.15
890	2¢ Samuel Morse	2.25	4.00	9.00(70)	1.50	.25	.15
891	3¢ Cyrus McCormick	2.25	4.00	26.50(70)	2.00	.35	.15
892	5¢ Elias Howe	3.00	6.00	92.50(70)	18.00	1.25	.50
893	10¢ Alexander G. Bell	7.25	20.00	995.00(70)	95.00	16.00	3.00

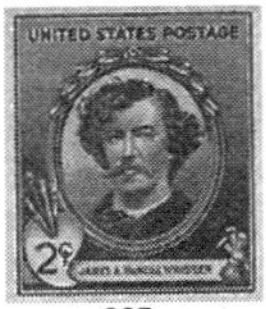

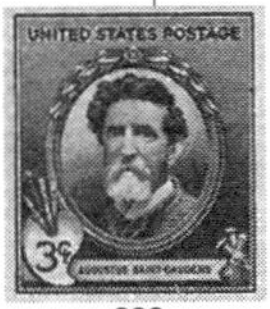

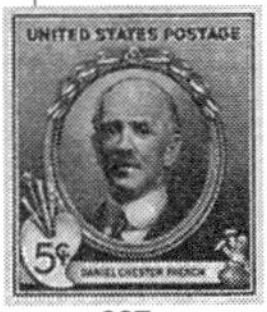

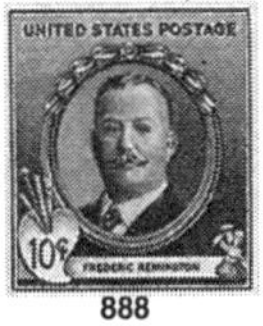

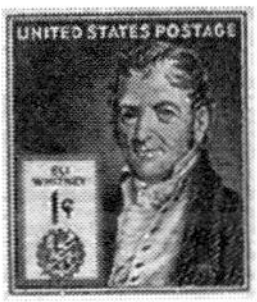

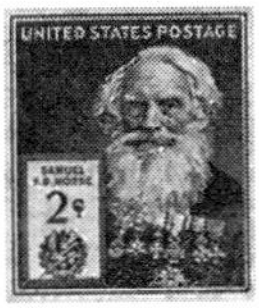

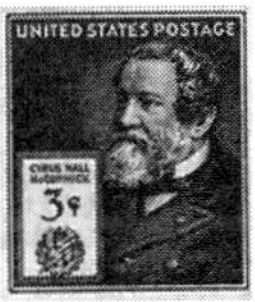

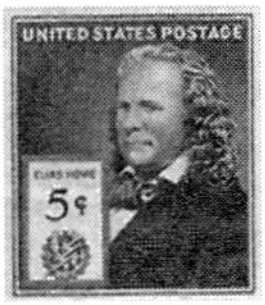

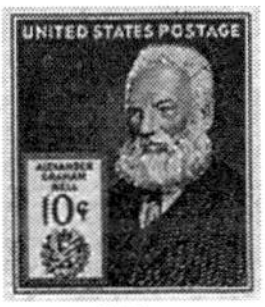

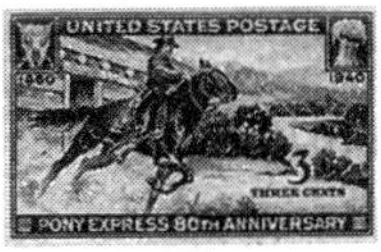

884 885 886 887 888

889 890 891 892 893

894 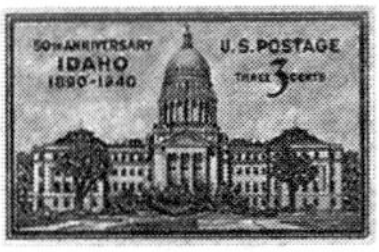 896 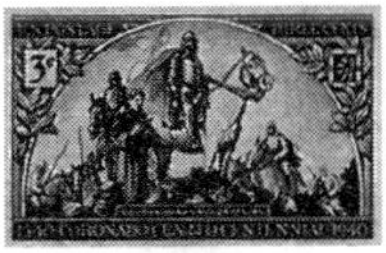 898

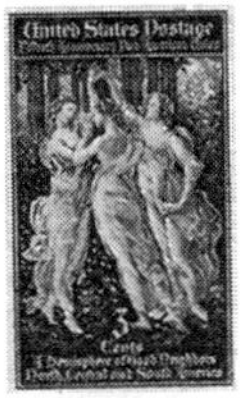

895 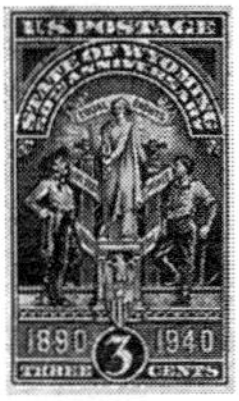 897 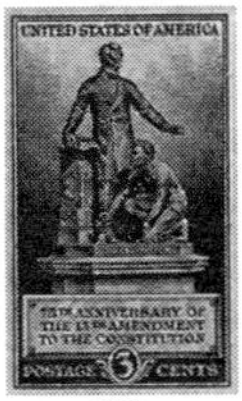 902

1940 COMMEMORATIVES

SCOTT NO.	DESCRIPTION	FIRST DAY COVERS SING.	FIRST DAY COVERS PL. BLK.	MINT SHEET	PLATE BLOCK F/NH	UNUSED F/NH	USED F
894-902	**9 varieties, complete**	....	....	....	....	**1.70**	**1.20**
894	3¢ Pony Express	5.00	11.00	18.00(50)	4.50	.25	.20
895	3¢ Pan Am Union	5.00	11.00	18.00(50)	4.50	.25	.15
896	3¢ Idaho Statehood	5.00	11.00	10.50(50)	3.00	.20	.15
897	3¢ Wyoming Statehood	5.00	11.00	9.00(50)	2.25	.20	.15
898	3¢ Coronado Expedition	5.00	11.00	9.00(52)	2.25	.20	.15

899

900

901

U.S. Postage #899-908

SCOTT NO.	DESCRIPTION	FIRST DAY COVERS SING.	FIRST DAY COVERS PL. BLK.	MINT SHEET	PLATE BLOCK F/NH	UNUSED F/NH	USED F
	NATIONAL DEFENSE ISSUE						
899	1¢ Liberty	3.00	7.00	7.00(100)	.65	.20	.15
900	2¢ Gun	3.00	7.00	7.50(100)	.65	.20	.15
901	3¢ Torch	3.00	7.00	10.00(100)	.85	.20	.15
902	3¢ Emancipation	5.00	11.00	14.75(50)	4.75	.25	.20

903  904  905  906

907  908

1941-43 COMMEMORATIVES

SCOTT NO.	DESCRIPTION	FIRST DAY COVERS SING.	FIRST DAY COVERS PL. BLK.	MINT SHEET	PLATE BLOCK F/NH	UNUSED F/NH	USED F
903-08	**3¢-5¢ six varieties**	....	....	....	....	**1.15**	**.85**
	1941 COMMEMORATIVES						
903	3¢ Vermont	5.00	10.75	10.00(50)	2.25	.20	.15
	1942 COMMEMORATIVES						
904	3¢ Kentucky	5.00	10.75	8.50(50)	1.65	.20	.15
905	3¢ Win The War	3.75	7.50	12.00(100)	.70	.20	.15
906	5¢ China Resistance	7.00	12.50	20.00(50)	12.50	.75	.25
	1943 COMMEMORATIVES						
907	2¢ Allied Nations	3.95	7.50	6.75(100)	.50	.20	.15
908	1¢ Four Freedoms	5.00	10.50	6.75(100)	.70	.20	.15

909  910  911  912

913  914  915

916  917  918

919  920  921

U.S. Postage #909-933

SCOTT NO.	DESCRIPTION	FIRST DAY COVERS SING.	FIRST DAY COVERS PL. BLK.	MINT SHEET	PLATE BLOCK F/NH	UNUSED F/NH	USED F
	1943-44 OVERRUN COUNTRIES SERIES						
909-21	**13 varieties, complete ....**	**45.00**	....	....	**70.00**	**2.90**	**2.35**
909	5¢ Poland	5.00	11.75	16.50(50)	8.00	.20	.15
910	5¢ Czechoslovakia	3.60	9.00	12.50(50)	4.00	.20	.15
911	5¢ Norway	3.60	9.00	9.00(50)	2.25	.20	.15
912	5¢ Luxembourg	3.60	9.00	9.00(50)	1.50	.20	.15
913	5¢ Netherlands	3.60	9.00	9.00(50)	1.50	.20	.15
914	5¢ Belgium	3.60	9.00	9.00(50)	1.50	.20	.15
915	5¢ France	3.60	9.00	9.00(50)	1.50	.20	.15
916	5¢ Greece	3.60	9.00	36.00(50)	17.50	.50	.40
917	5¢ Yugoslavia	3.60	9.00	20.00(50)	8.00	.35	.25
918	5¢ Albania	3.60	9.00	17.50(50)	8.00	.20	.20
919	5¢ Austria	3.60	9.00	14.00(50)	6.00	.20	.20
920	5¢ Denmark	3.60	9.00	20.00(50)	8.00	.20	.20
921	5¢ Korea (1944)	3.60	9.00	13.00(50)	7.00	.20	.20

922 923 924 925

SCOTT NO.	DESCRIPTION	FIRST DAY COVERS SING.	FIRST DAY COVERS PL. BLK.	MINT SHEET	PLATE BLOCK F/NH	UNUSED F/NH	USED F
	1944 COMMEMORATIVES						
922-26	**5 varieties ....**	....	....	....	....	**.90**	**.70**
922	3¢ Railroad	3.75	7.50	15.00(50)	2.00	.25	.15
923	3¢ Steamship	3.00	6.00	7.00(50)	2.00	.20	.15
924	3¢ Telegraph	3.00	6.00	6.50(50)	1.25	.20	.15
925	3¢ Corregidor	3.00	6.00	6.50(50)	1.40	.20	.15

926 927 928 929

SCOTT NO.	DESCRIPTION	FIRST DAY COVERS SING.	FIRST DAY COVERS PL. BLK.	MINT SHEET	PLATE BLOCK F/NH	UNUSED F/NH	USED F
926	3¢ Motion Picture	3.00	6.00	7.50(50)	1.40	.20	.15
	1945-46 COMMEMORATIVES						
927-38	**1¢-5¢, 12 varieties, complete ....**		....	....	....	**2.00**	**1.60**
927	3¢ Florida	3.00	6.00	5.50(50)	.80	.20	.15
928	5¢ Peace Conference	3.00	6.00	5.50(50)	.75	.20	.15
929	3¢ Iwo Jima	8.00	14.00	5.50(50)	.75	.20	.15

930 931 932 933

SCOTT NO.	DESCRIPTION	FIRST DAY COVERS SING.	FIRST DAY COVERS PL. BLK.	MINT SHEET	PLATE BLOCK F/NH	UNUSED F/NH	USED F
930	1¢ FDR & Hyde Park	3.00	6.00	2.50(50)	.50	.20	.15
931	2¢ FDR & "Little White House"	3.00	6.00	3.00(50)	.55	.20	.15
932	3¢ FDR & White House	3.00	6.00	5.50(50)	.75	.20	.15
933	5¢ FDR & Globe (1946)	3.00	6.00	6.00(50)	.75	.20	.15

NEVER HINGED: From 1893 to 1965, Unused OG or Unused prices are for stamps with original gum that have been hinged. If you desire Never Hinged stamps, refer to the NH listings.

U.S. Postage #934-947

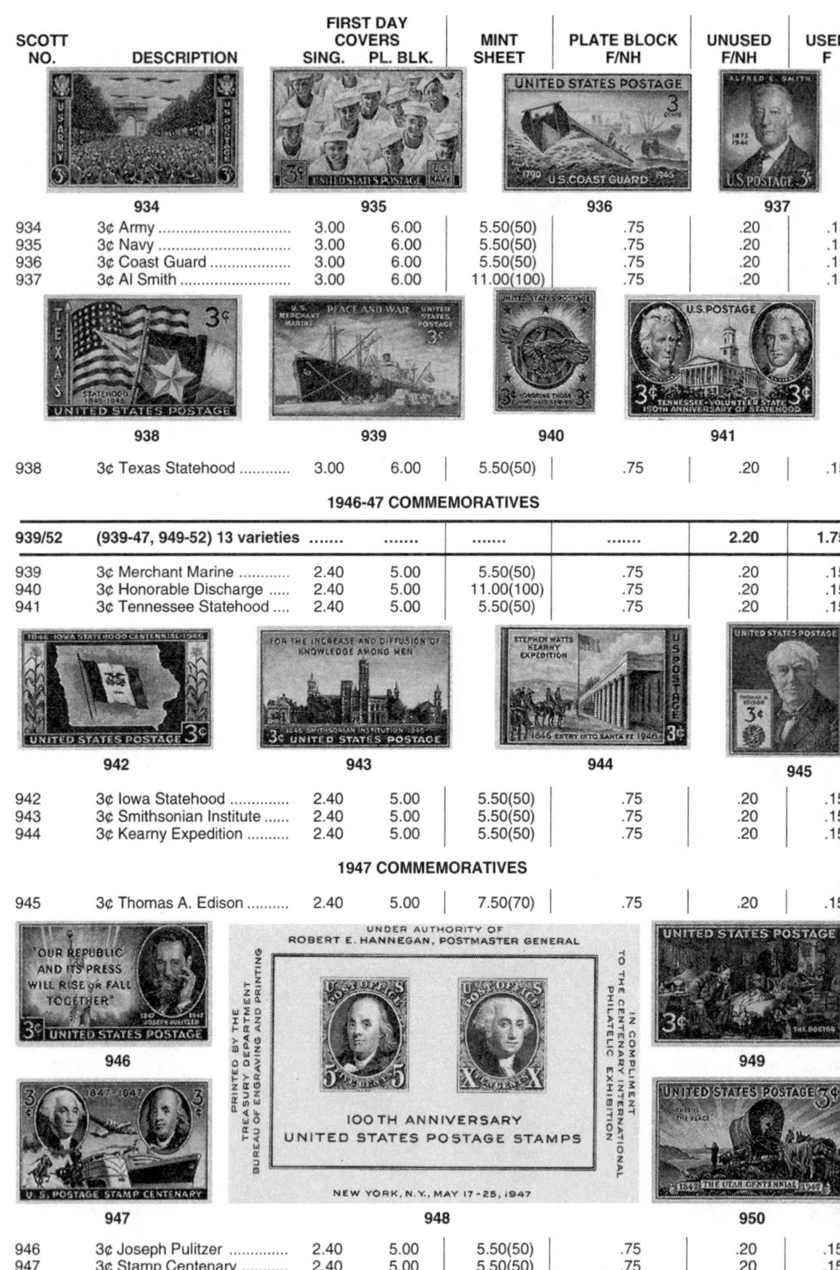

934 935 936 937 938 939 940 941 942 943 944 945 946 947 948 949 950

SCOTT NO.	DESCRIPTION	FIRST DAY COVERS SING.	FIRST DAY COVERS PL. BLK.	MINT SHEET	PLATE BLOCK F/NH	UNUSED F/NH	USED F
934	3¢ Army	3.00	6.00	5.50(50)	.75	.20	.15
935	3¢ Navy	3.00	6.00	5.50(50)	.75	.20	.15
936	3¢ Coast Guard	3.00	6.00	5.50(50)	.75	.20	.15
937	3¢ Al Smith	3.00	6.00	11.00(100)	.75	.20	.15
938	3¢ Texas Statehood	3.00	6.00	5.50(50)	.75	.20	.15
	1946-47 COMMEMORATIVES						
939/52	**(939-47, 949-52) 13 varieties**	....	....	....	....	**2.20**	**1.75**
939	3¢ Merchant Marine	2.40	5.00	5.50(50)	.75	.20	.15
940	3¢ Honorable Discharge	2.40	5.00	11.00(100)	.75	.20	.15
941	3¢ Tennessee Statehood	2.40	5.00	5.50(50)	.75	.20	.15
942	3¢ Iowa Statehood	2.40	5.00	5.50(50)	.75	.20	.15
943	3¢ Smithsonian Institute	2.40	5.00	5.50(50)	.75	.20	.15
944	3¢ Kearny Expedition	2.40	5.00	5.50(50)	.75	.20	.15
	1947 COMMEMORATIVES						
945	3¢ Thomas A. Edison	2.40	5.00	7.50(70)	.75	.20	.15
946	3¢ Joseph Pulitzer	2.40	5.00	5.50(50)	.75	.20	.15
947	3¢ Stamp Centenary	2.40	5.00	5.50(50)	.75	.20	.15

PLATE BLOCKS: are portions of a sheet of stamps adjacent to the number(s) indicating the printing plate number used to produce that sheet. Flat plate issues are usually collected in plate blocks of six (number opposite middle stamp) while rotary issues are normally corner blocks of four.

U.S. Postage #948-966

SCOTT NO.	DESCRIPTION	FIRST DAY COVERS SING.	FIRST DAY COVERS PL.BLK.	MINT SHEET	PLATE BLOCK F/NH	UNUSED F/NH	USED F
	"CIPEX" SOUVENIR SHEET						
948	5¢ & 10¢ Sheet of 2	3.90	....	....	....	.85	.75
948a	5¢ blue, single stamp	....	....	....	....	.30	.25
948b	10¢ brown orange, single stamp.......		....	....	....	.50	.35
949	3¢ Doctors	2.40	5.00	5.50(50)	.75	.20	.15
950	3¢ Utah Centennial	2.40	5.00	5.50(50)	.75	.20	.15

951 952 953 954

SCOTT NO.	DESCRIPTION	FIRST DAY COVERS SING.	FIRST DAY COVERS PL.BLK.	MINT SHEET	PLATE BLOCK F/NH	UNUSED F/NH	USED F
951	3¢ "Constitution"	2.40	5.00	5.50(50)	.75	.20	.15
952	3¢ Everglades National Park	2.40	5.00	5.50(50)	.75	.20	.15
	1948 COMMEMORATIVES						
953-80	**3¢-5¢, 28 varieties, complete ....**		**.......**	**.......**	**.......**	**4.70**	**3.60**
953	3¢ George Washington Carver	2.40	5.00	7.50(70)	.75	.20	.15
954	3¢ Gold Rush	2.40	5.00	5.50(50)	.75	.20	.15

955 956 957 958

SCOTT NO.	DESCRIPTION	FIRST DAY COVERS SING.	FIRST DAY COVERS PL.BLK.	MINT SHEET	PLATE BLOCK F/NH	UNUSED F/NH	USED F
955	3¢ Mississippi Territory	2.40	5.00	5.50(50)	.75	.20	.15
956	3¢ Chaplains	2.40	5.00	5.50(50)	.75	.20	.15
957	3¢ Wisconsin Statehood	2.40	5.00	5.50(50)	.75	.20	.15
958	5¢ Swedish Pioneer	2.40	5.00	6.50(50)	.75	.20	.15

959 960 961 962

963 964 965 966

SCOTT NO.	DESCRIPTION	FIRST DAY COVERS SING.	FIRST DAY COVERS PL.BLK.	MINT SHEET	PLATE BLOCK F/NH	UNUSED F/NH	USED F
959	3¢ Women's Progress	2.40	5.00	5.50(50)	.75	.20	.15
960	3¢ William White	2.40	5.00	7.50(70)	.75	.20	.15
961	3¢ U.S.-Canada Friendship	2.40	5.00	5.50(50)	.75	.20	.15
962	3¢ Francis S. Key	2.40	5.00	5.50(50)	.75	.20	.15
963	3¢ Salute to Youth	2.40	5.00	5.50(50)	.75	.20	.15
964	3¢ Oregon Territory	2.40	5.00	5.50(50)	.75	.20	.15
965	3¢ Harlan Stone	2.40	5.00	6.50(70)	1.00	.20	.15
966	3¢ Mt. Palomar	3.00	5.00	7.50(70)	1.50	.20	.15

U.S. Postage #967-984

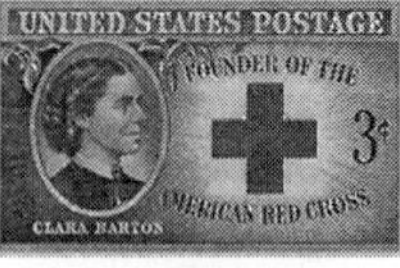

967

968

970

971

972

969

973

SCOTT NO.	DESCRIPTION	FIRST DAY COVERS SING.	FIRST DAY COVERS PL.BLK.	MINT SHEET	PLATE BLOCK F/NH	UNUSED F/NH	USED F
967	3¢ Clara Barton	2.40	5.00	5.50(50)	.75	.20	.15
968	3¢ Poultry	2.40	5.00	5.50(50)	.75	.20	.15
969	3¢ Gold Star Mothers	2.40	5.00	5.50(50)	.75	.20	.15
970	3¢ Fort Kearny	2.40	5.00	5.50(50)	.75	.20	.15
971	3¢ Volunteer Firemen	2.40	5.00	5.50(50)	.75	.20	.15
972	3¢ Indian Centennial	2.40	5.00	5.50(50)	.75	.20	.15
973	3¢ Rough Riders	2.40	5.00	5.50(50)	.75	.20	.15

974

975

976

977

978

979

980

SCOTT NO.	DESCRIPTION	FIRST DAY COVERS SING.	FIRST DAY COVERS PL.BLK.	MINT SHEET	PLATE BLOCK F/NH	UNUSED F/NH	USED F
974	3¢ Juliette Low	2.40	5.00	5.50(50)	.75	.20	.15
975	3¢ Will Rogers	2.40	5.00	5.50(50)	.85	.20	.15
976	3¢ Fort Bliss	2.40	5.00	10.00(50)	1.60	.20	.15
977	3¢ Moina Michael	2.40	5.00	7.50(50)	.75	.20	.15
978	3¢ Gettysburg Address	2.40	5.00	5.50(50)	.75	.20	.15
979	3¢ American Turners	2.40	5.00	5.50(50)	.75	.20	.15
980	3¢ Joel C. Harris	2.40	5.00	7.50(50)	.75	.20	.15

981

982

983

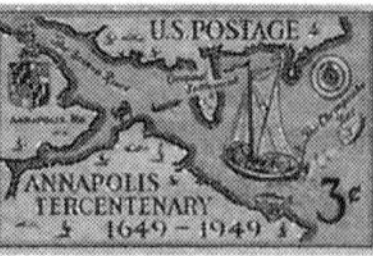

984

1949-50 COMMEMORATIVES

SCOTT NO.	DESCRIPTION	FIRST DAY COVERS SING.	FIRST DAY COVERS PL.BLK.	MINT SHEET	PLATE BLOCK F/NH	UNUSED F/NH	USED F
981-97	**17 varieties, complete**	....	....	....	....	**2.90**	**2.20**
981	3¢ Minnesota Territory	2.00	4.25	5.50(50)	.70	.20	.15
982	3¢ Washington & Lee University	2.00	4.25	5.50(50)	.70	.20	.15
983	3¢ Puerto Rico	2.00	4.25	5.50(50)	.70	.20	.15
984	3¢ Annapolis	2.00	4.25	5.50(50)	.70	.20	.15

U.S. Postage #985-1001

985 986 987 988

SCOTT NO.	DESCRIPTION	FIRST DAY COVERS SING.	FIRST DAY COVERS PL.BLK.	MINT SHEET	PLATE BLOCK F/NH	UNUSED F/NH	USED F
85	3¢ G.A.R.	2.00	4.25	5.50(50)	.70	.20	.15
86	3¢ Edgar A. Poe	2.00	4.25	7.50(70)	.70	.20	.15
	1950 COMMEMORATIVES						
87	3¢ Bankers Association	2.00	4.25	5.50(50)	.70	.20	.15
88	3¢ Samuel Gompers	2.00	4.25	7.50(70)	.70	.20	.15

990 991 992

989

SCOTT NO.	DESCRIPTION	FIRST DAY COVERS SING.	FIRST DAY COVERS PL.BLK.	MINT SHEET	PLATE BLOCK F/NH	UNUSED F/NH	USED F
89	3¢ Statue of Freedom	2.00	4.25	5.50(50)	.70	.20	.15
90	3¢ Executive Mansion	2.00	4.25	5.50(50)	.70	.20	.15
91	3¢ Supreme Court	2.00	4.25	5.50(50)	.70	.20	.15
92	3¢ United States Capitol	2.00	4.25	5.50(50)	.70	.20	.15

993 994 995 996

SCOTT NO.	DESCRIPTION	FIRST DAY COVERS SING.	FIRST DAY COVERS PL.BLK.	MINT SHEET	PLATE BLOCK F/NH	UNUSED F/NH	USED F
93	3¢ Railroad	2.00	4.25	5.50(50)	.70	.20	.15
94	3¢ Kansas City	2.00	4.25	5.50(50)	.70	.20	.15
95	3¢ Boy Scouts	3.00	5.50	5.50(50)	.70	.20	.15
96	3¢ Indiana Territory	2.00	4.25	5.50(50)	.70	.20	.15

997 998 999

SCOTT NO.	DESCRIPTION	FIRST DAY COVERS SING.	FIRST DAY COVERS PL.BLK.	MINT SHEET	PLATE BLOCK F/NH	UNUSED F/NH	USED F
97	3¢ California Statehood	2.00	4.25	5.50(50)	.70	.20	.15
	1951-52 COMMEMORATIVE						
98-1016	**19 varieties, complete**	....	....	....	....	**3.20**	**2.45**
98	3¢ Confederate Veterans	2.00	4.25	5.50(50)	.70	.20	.15
99	3¢ Nevada Settlement	2.00	4.25	5.50(50)	.70	.20	.15

1000 1001 1002 1003

SCOTT NO.	DESCRIPTION	FIRST DAY COVERS SING.	FIRST DAY COVERS PL.BLK.	MINT SHEET	PLATE BLOCK F/NH	UNUSED F/NH	USED F
000	3¢ Landing of Cadillac	2.00	4.25	5.50(50)	.70	.20	.15
001	3¢ Colorado Statehood	2.00	4.25	5.50(50)	.70	.20	.15

U.S. Postage #1002-1017

SCOTT NO.	DESCRIPTION	FIRST DAY COVERS SING.	FIRST DAY COVERS PL.BLK.	MINT SHEET	PLATE BLOCK F/NH	UNUSED F/NH	USED F
1002	3¢ Chemical Society	2.00	4.25	5.50(50)	.70	.20	.15
1003	3¢ Battle of Brooklyn	2.00	4.25	5.50(50)	.70	.20	.15

1004

1005

1006

1007

1008

1009

1952 COMMEMORATIVES

SCOTT NO.	DESCRIPTION	FIRST DAY COVERS SING.	FIRST DAY COVERS PL.BLK.	MINT SHEET	PLATE BLOCK F/NH	UNUSED F/NH	USED F
1004	3¢ Betsy Ross	2.50	5.50	5.50(50)	.70	.20	.15
1005	3¢ 4-H Club	2.00	4.25	5.50(50)	.70	.20	.15
1006	3¢ B. & O. Railroad	2.00	4.25	5.50(50)	.70	.20	.15
1007	3¢ AAA	2.00	4.25	5.50(50)	.70	.20	.15
1008	3¢ NATO	2.00	4.25	11.00(100)	.70	.20	.15
1009	3¢ Grand Coulee Dam	2.00	4.25	5.50(50)	.70	.20	.15

1010

1011

1012

1013

SCOTT NO.	DESCRIPTION	FIRST DAY COVERS SING.	FIRST DAY COVERS PL.BLK.	MINT SHEET	PLATE BLOCK F/NH	UNUSED F/NH	USED F
1010	3¢ Lafayette	2.00	4.25	5.50(50)	.70	.20	.15
1011	3¢ Mt. Rushmore	2.00	4.25	5.50(50)	.70	.20	.15
1012	3¢ Civil Engineers	2.00	4.25	5.50(50)	.70	.20	.15
1013	3¢ Service Women	2.00	4.25	5.50(50)	.70	.20	.15

1014

1015

1016

1017

SCOTT NO.	DESCRIPTION	FIRST DAY COVERS SING.	FIRST DAY COVERS PL.BLK.	MINT SHEET	PLATE BLOCK F/NH	UNUSED F/NH	USED F
1014	3¢ Gutenburg Press	2.00	4.25	5.50(50)	.70	.20	.15
1015	3¢ Newspaper Boys	2.00	4.25	5.50(50)	.70	.20	.15
1016	3¢ Red Cross	2.00	4.25	5.50(50)	.70	.20	.15

1953-54 COMMEMORATIVES

SCOTT NO.	DESCRIPTION	FIRST DAY COVERS SING.	FIRST DAY COVERS PL.BLK.	MINT SHEET	PLATE BLOCK F/NH	UNUSED F/NH	USED F
1017/63	**(1017-29, 1060-63) 17 varieties, complete..........**	....	....	....	....	**2.90**	**2.20**
1017	3¢ National Guard	2.00	4.25	6.75(50)	.70	.20	.15

NOTE: To determine the VF price on stamps issued from 1941 to date, add 20% to the F/NH or F (used) price. All VF unused stamps from 1941 to date will be NH.

U.S. Postage #1018-1035a

1018 1019 1020 1021

SCOTT NO.	DESCRIPTION	FIRST DAY COVERS SING.	FIRST DAY COVERS PL.BLK.	MINT SHEET	PLATE BLOCK F/NH	UNUSED F/NH	USED F
1018	3¢ Ohio Statehood	2.00	4.25	7.50(70)	.70	.20	.15
1019	3¢ Washington Territory . . .	2.00	4.25	5.50(50)	.70	.20	.15
1020	3¢ Louisiana Purchase	2.00	4.25	5.50(50)	.70	.20	.15
1021	5¢ Opening of Japan	2.00	4.25	7.00(50)	.95	.20	.15

1022 1023 1024 1025

SCOTT NO.	DESCRIPTION	FIRST DAY COVERS SING.	FIRST DAY COVERS PL.BLK.	MINT SHEET	PLATE BLOCK F/NH	UNUSED F/NH	USED F
1022	3¢ American Bar Association	2.00	4.25	5.50(50)	.70	.20	.15
1023	3¢ Sagamore Hill	2.00	4.25	5.50(50)	.70	.20	.15
1024	3¢ Future Farmers	2.00	4.25	5.50(50)	.70	.20	.15
1025	3¢ Trucking Industry	2.00	4.25	5.50(50)	.70	.20	.15

1026 1027 1028 1029

SCOTT NO.	DESCRIPTION	FIRST DAY COVERS SING.	FIRST DAY COVERS PL.BLK.	MINT SHEET	PLATE BLOCK F/NH	UNUSED F/NH	USED F
1026	3¢ Gen. George S. Patton . .	2.00	4.25	7.00(50)	.70	.20	.15
1027	3¢ New York City.	2.00	4.25	5.50(50)	.70	.20	.15
1028	3¢ Gadsden Purchase	2.00	4.25	5.50(50)	.70	.20	.15

1954 COMMEMORATIVE

SCOTT NO.	DESCRIPTION	FIRST DAY COVERS SING.	FIRST DAY COVERS PL.BLK.	MINT SHEET	PLATE BLOCK F/NH	UNUSED F/NH	USED F
1029	3¢ Columbia University	2.00	4.25	5.50(50)	.70	.20	.15

1030 1031, 1054 1031A, 1054A 1032 1033, 1055 1034, 1056

1035, 1057, 1075a 1036, 1058 1037, 1059 1038 1039 1040

1954-68 LIBERTY SERIES

SCOTT NO.	DESCRIPTION	FIRST DAY COVERS SING.	FIRST DAY COVERS PL.BLK.	MINT SHEET	PLATE BLOCK F/NH	UNUSED F/NH	USED F
1030-53	**1/2¢-$5, 27 varieties, cpl.. .**	**110.00**	**235.00**	**......**	**525.00**	**120.00**	**12.35**
1030-51	**1/2¢-50¢, 25 varieties. . . . .**	**55.00**	**115.00**	**......**	**57.50**	**12.95**	**3.50**
1030	1/2¢ Benjamin Franklin (1955)	2.00	4.25	6.35(100)	.70	.20	.15
1031	1¢ George Washington	2.00	4.25	5.75(100)	.70	.20	.15
1031A	1-1/4¢ Palace of Gov. (1960)	2.00	4.25	6.75(100)	.70	.20	.15
1032	1-1/2¢ Mt. Vernon	2.00	4.25	13.50(100)	3.00	.20	.15
1033	2¢ Thomas Jefferson	2.00	4.25	8.50(100)	.70	.20	.15
1034	2-1/2¢ Bunker Hill (1959) . .	2.00	4.25	13.50(100)	.70	.20	.15
1035	3¢ Statue of Liberty	2.00	4.25	13.50(100)	.70	.20	.15
1035a	3¢ booklet pane of 6	3.00	......	......	......	4.00	......

U.S. Postage #1036-1059A

SCOTT NO.	DESCRIPTION	FIRST DAY COVERS SING.	FIRST DAY COVERS PL.BLK.	MINT SHEET	PLATE BLOCK F/NH	UNUSED F/NH	USED F
1036	4¢ Abraham Lincoln	2.00	4.25	18.50(100)	.75	.20	.15
1036a	4¢ booklet pane of 6	3.00	....	....	....	3.00	....
1037	4-1/2¢ Hermitage (1959)	2.00	4.25	21.00(100)	.80	.20	.15
1038	5¢ James Monroe	2.00	4.25	25.00(100)	.75	.20	.15
1039	6¢ T. Roosevelt (1955)	2.00	4.25	70.00(100)	1.50	.35	.15
1040	7¢ Woodrow Wilson (1956) .	2.00	4.25	42.75(100)	1.60	.40	.15

1041, 1041B, 1075b

1042 (re-engraved)

1042A

1043

1044

1044A

1045

1046

1047

1048, 1059A

1049

1050

1051

1052

1053

SCOTT NO.	DESCRIPTION	FIRST DAY COVERS SING.	FIRST DAY COVERS PL.BLK.	MINT SHEET	PLATE BLOCK F/NH	UNUSED F/NH	USED F
1041	8¢ Statue of Liberty (flat plate)	2.00	4.25	40.00(100)	3.00	.25	.15
1041B	8¢ Statue of Liberty	2.00	4.25	40.00(100)	3.00	.25	.15
1042	8¢ Liberty re-engraved (1958)	2.00	4.25	50.00(100)	1.20	.25	.15
1042A	8¢ John J. Pershing (1961) .	2.25	5.00	50.00(100)	1.20	.30	.15
1043	9¢ Alamo (1956)	2.25	5.00	57.50(100)	2.25	.40	.15
1044	10¢ Independence Hall (1956)	2.25	5.00	50.00(100)	1.35	.30	.15
1044A	11¢ Statue of Liberty (1961)	2.25	5.00	50.00(100)	1.50	.40	.15
1045	12¢ Benjamin Harrison (1959)	2.25	5.00	75.00(100)	2.00	.45	.15
1046	15¢ John Jay (1958)	2.50	5.25	120.00(100)	4.95	1.10	.15
1047	20¢ Monticello (1956)	2.50	5.25	110.00(100)	2.75	.60	.15
1048	25¢ Paul Revere (1958)	2.50	5.25	375.00(100)	7.25	1.75	.15
1049	30¢ Robert E. Lee (1955) ...	3.00	6.00	240.00(100)	4.95	1.10	.15
1050	40¢ John Marshall (1955) ...	3.25	7.00	500.00(100)	10.25	2.00	.15
1051	50¢ Susan B. Anthony (1955)	4.25	8.50	425.00(100)	9.00	2.00	.15
1052	$1 Patrick Henry (1955)	8.50	17.50	....	30.00	7.00	.25
1053	$5 Alexander Hamilton (1956)	50.00	110.00	....	450.00	105.00	9.00

1954-73 COIL STAMPS
Perf. 10 Vertically or Horizontally

			L.PR		LINE PAIR		
1054-59A	**1¢-25¢ varieties, complete**	**16.00**	**29.75**	....	**30.00**	**3.50**	**2.40**
1054	1¢ George Washington	2.00	3.75	....	1.25	.25	.15
1054A	1-1/4¢ Palace of Gov. (1960)	2.00	3.75	....	2.75	.20	.15
1055	2¢ Thomas Jefferson	2.00	3.75	....	.60	.20	.15
1056	2-1/2¢ Bunker Hill Mon. (1959)	2.00	3.75	....	5.50	.35	.30
1057	3¢ Statue of Liberty	2.00	3.75	....	.75	.20	.15
1058	4¢ Abraham Lincoln (1958) .	2.00	3.75	....	.75	.20	.15
1059	4-1/2¢ Hermitage (1959)	2.00	3.75	....	18.00	1.50	1.25
1059A	25¢ Paul Revere (1965)	2.50	5.00	....	2.00	.75	.20

NOTE: Pairs of the above can be priced at two times the single price.

COIL LINE PAIRS: are two connected coil stamps with a line the same color as the stamps printed between the two stamps. This line usually appears every twenty to thirty stamps on a roll depending on the issue.

U.S. Postage #1060-1072

1060

1061

1062

1063

SCOTT NO.	DESCRIPTION	FIRST DAY COVERS SING.	FIRST DAY COVERS PL.BLK.	MINT SHEET	PLATE BLOCK F/NH	UNUSED F/NH	USED F
1060	3¢ Nebraska Territory	2.00	4.25	5.50(50)	.70	.20	.15
1061	3¢ Kansas Territory	2.00	4.25	5.50(50)	.70	.20	.15
1062	3¢ George Eastman	2.00	4.25	7.50(70)	.70	.20	.15
1063	3¢ Lewis & Clark	2.00	4.25	5.50(50)	.70	.20	.15

1064

1065

1066

1067

1068

1955 COMMEMORATIVES

SCOTT NO.	DESCRIPTION	FIRST DAY COVERS SING.	FIRST DAY COVERS PL.BLK.	MINT SHEET	PLATE BLOCK F/NH	UNUSED F/NH	USED F
1064-72	**3¢-8¢, 9 varieties, complete**	....	....	....	....	**1.50**	**1.20**
1064	3¢ Pennsylvania Academy ..	2.00	4.25	5.50(50)	.70	.20	.15
1065	3¢ Land Grant Colleges	2.00	4.25	5.50(50)	.70	.20	.15
1066	8¢ Rotary International	2.00	4.25	10.00(50)	1.25	.20	.15
1067	3¢ Armed Forces Reserve ..	2.00	4.25	5.50(50)	.70	.20	.15
1068	3¢ Great Stone Face	2.00	4.25	5.50(50)	.70	.20	.15

1069

1070

1071

1072

SCOTT NO.	DESCRIPTION	FIRST DAY COVERS SING.	FIRST DAY COVERS PL.BLK.	MINT SHEET	PLATE BLOCK F/NH	UNUSED F/NH	USED F
1069	3¢ Soo Locks	2.00	4.25	5.50(50)	.70	.20	.15
1070	3¢ Atoms for Peace	2.00	4.25	5.50(50)	.70	.20	.15
1071	3¢ Fort Ticonderoga	2.00	4.25	5.50(50)	.70	.20	.15
1072	3¢ Andrew Mellon	2.00	4.25	5.50(70)	.70	.20	.15

PLATE BLOCKS: are portions of a sheet of stamps adjacent to the number(s) indicating the printing plate number used to produce that sheet. Flat plate issues are usually collected in plate blocks of six (number opposite middle stamp) while rotary issues are normally corner blocks of four.

U.S. Postage #1073-1079

SCOTT NO.	DESCRIPTION	FIRST DAY COVERS SING.	FIRST DAY COVERS PL.BLK.	MINT SHEET	PLATE BLOCK F/NH	UNUSED F/NH	USED F

1073

1074

1956 COMMEMORATIVES

SCOTT NO.	DESCRIPTION	FIRST DAY COVERS SING.	FIRST DAY COVERS PL.BLK.	MINT SHEET	PLATE BLOCK F/NH	UNUSED F/NH	USED F
1073/85	**(1073-74, 1076-85) 12 varieties........**		**.......**	**.......**	**.......**	**2.00**	**1.50**
1073	3¢ Benjamin Franklin	2.00	4.25	5.50(50)	.70	.20	.15
1074	3¢ Booker T. Washington ...	2.00	4.25	5.50(50)	.70	.20	.15

Plate blocks will be blocks of 4 stamps unless otherwise noted.

1075

SCOTT NO.	DESCRIPTION	FIRST DAY COVERS SING.	FIRST DAY COVERS PL.BLK.	MINT SHEET	PLATE BLOCK F/NH	UNUSED F/NH	USED F
1075	3¢ & 8¢ FIPEX Sheet of 2 ...	8.00	....	....	....	2.75	2.50
1075a	3¢ deep violet, single	....	....	....	....	1.10	1.05
1075b	8¢ violet blue & carmine, single.......		....	....	....	1.40	1.25

1076

1077

1078

1079

SCOTT NO.	DESCRIPTION	FIRST DAY COVERS SING.	FIRST DAY COVERS PL.BLK.	MINT SHEET	PLATE BLOCK F/NH	UNUSED F/NH	USED F
1076	3¢ FIPEX	2.00	4.25	5.50(50)	.70	.20	.15
1077	3¢ Wild Turkey	2.00	4.25	5.50(50)	.70	.20	.15
1078	3¢ Antelope	2.00	4.25	5.50(50)	.70	.20	.15
1079	3¢ Salmon	2.00	4.25	5.50(50)	.70	.20	.15

U.S. Postage #1080-1092

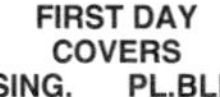

SCOTT NO.	DESCRIPTION	FIRST DAY COVERS SING.	FIRST DAY COVERS PL.BLK.	MINT SHEET	PLATE BLOCK F/NH	UNUSED F/NH	USED F

1080

1081

1082

1083

1084

SCOTT NO.	DESCRIPTION	FIRST DAY COVERS SING.	FIRST DAY COVERS PL.BLK.	MINT SHEET	PLATE BLOCK F/NH	UNUSED F/NH	USED F
1080	3¢ Pure Food & Drug Act	2.00	4.25	5.50(50)	.70	.20	.15
1081	3¢ "Wheatland"	2.00	4.25	5.50(50)	.70	.20	.15
1082	3¢ Labor Day	2.00	4.25	5.50(50)	.70	.20	.15
1083	3¢ Nassau Hall	2.00	4.25	5.50(50)	.70	.20	.15
1084	3¢ Devil's Tower	2.00	4.25	5.50(50)	.70	.20	.15

1085

1086

1087

1088

1089

1090

1091

1092

SCOTT NO.	DESCRIPTION	FIRST DAY COVERS SING.	FIRST DAY COVERS PL.BLK.	MINT SHEET	PLATE BLOCK F/NH	UNUSED F/NH	USED F
1085	3¢ Children of the World	2.00	4.25	5.50(50)	.70	.20	.15
	1957 COMMEMORATIVES						
1086-99	**14 varieties, complete ....**	**.......**	**.......**	**.......**	**.......**	**2.50**	**1.80**
1086	3¢ Alexander Hamilton	2.00	4.25	5.50(50)	.70	.20	.15
1087	3¢ Polio	2.00	4.25	5.50(50)	.70	.20	.15
1088	3¢ Coast and Geodetic Survey	2.00	4.25	5.50(50)	.70	.20	.15
1089	3¢ Architects	2.00	4.25	5.50(50)	.70	.20	.15
1090	3¢ Steel Industry	2.00	4.25	5.50(50)	.70	.20	.15
1091	3¢ International Naval Review	2.00	4.25	5.50(50)	.70	.20	.15
1092	3¢ Oklahoma Statehood	2.00	4.25	5.50(50)	.70	.20	.15

FIRST DAY COVERS: First Day Covers are envelopes cancelled on the "First Day of Issue" of the stamp used on the envelope. Usually they also contain a picture (cachet) on the left side designed to go with the theme of the stamp. From 1935 to 1949, prices listed are for cacheted, addressed covers. From 1950 to date, prices are for cacheted, unaddressed covers.

U.S. Postage #1093-1109

1093

1094

1095

1096

1097

SCOTT NO.	DESCRIPTION	FIRST DAY COVERS SING.	FIRST DAY COVERS PL.BLK.	MINT SHEET	PLATE BLOCK F/NH	UNUSED F/NH	USED F
1093	3¢ School Teachers	2.00	4.25	5.50(50)	.70	.20	.15
1094	4¢ 48-Star Flag	2.00	4.25	6.00(50)	.70	.20	.15
1095	3¢ Shipbuilding Anniversary	2.00	4.25	7.50(50)	.70	.20	.15
1096	8¢ Ramon Magsaysay	2.50	4.25	9.50(48)	1.00	.25	.15
1097	3¢ Birth of Lafayette	2.00	4.25	5.50(50)	.70	.20	.15

1098

1099

1100

1104

1105

SCOTT NO.	DESCRIPTION	FIRST DAY COVERS SING.	FIRST DAY COVERS PL.BLK.	MINT SHEET	PLATE BLOCK F/NH	UNUSED F/NH	USED F
1098	3¢ Whooping Cranes	2.00	4.25	5.50(50)	.70	.20	.15
1099	3¢ Religious Freedom	2.00	4.25	5.50(50)	.70	.20	.15

1958 COMMEMORATIVES

SCOTT NO.	DESCRIPTION	FIRST DAY COVERS SING.	FIRST DAY COVERS PL.BLK.	MINT SHEET	PLATE BLOCK F/NH	UNUSED F/NH	USED F
1100-23	**21 varieties, complete ....**	....	....	....	....	**3.70**	**2.70**
1100	3¢ Gardening & Horticulture	2.00	4.25	5.50(50)	.70	.20	.15
1104	3¢ Brussels Exhibition	2.00	4.25	5.50(50)	.70	.20	.15
1105	3¢ James Monroe	2.00	4.25	7.50(70)	.70	.20	.15

1106

1107

1108

1109

SCOTT NO.	DESCRIPTION	FIRST DAY COVERS SING.	FIRST DAY COVERS PL.BLK.	MINT SHEET	PLATE BLOCK F/NH	UNUSED F/NH	USED F
1106	3¢ Minnesota Statehood	2.00	4.25	5.50(50)	.70	.20	.15
1107	3¢ Int'l. Geophysical Year ...	2.00	4.25	5.50(50)	.70	.20	.15
1108	3¢ Gunston Hall	2.00	4.25	5.50(50)	.70	.20	.15
1109	3¢ Mackinac Bridge	2.00	4.25	5.50(50)	.70	.20	.15

U.S. Postage #1110-1128

1110, 1111

1113

1114

1117, 1118

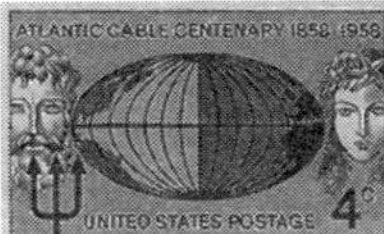

1112

1115

1116

SCOTT NO.	DESCRIPTION	FIRST DAY COVERS SING.	FIRST DAY COVERS PL.BLK.	MINT SHEET	PLATE BLOCK F/NH	UNUSED F/NH	USED F
1110	4¢ Simon Bolivar	2.00	4.25	8.00(70)	.70	.20	.15
1111	8¢ Simon Bolivar	2.00	4.50	15.50(72)	1.85	.25	.15
1112	4¢ Atlantic Cable Centenary	2.00	4.25	6.000(50)	.70	.20	.15
1113	1¢ Abraham Lincoln (1959)	2.00	4.25	2.25(50)	.55	.20	.15
1114	3¢ Bust of Lincoln (1959)	2.00	4.25	5.50(50)	.70	.20	.15
1115	4¢ Lincoln-Douglas Debates	2.00	4.25	6.00(50)	.70	.20	.15
1116	4¢ Statue of Lincoln (1959)	2.00	4.25	6.00(50)	.70	.20	.15
1117	4¢ Lajos Kossuth	2.00	4.25	8.00(70)	.70	.20	.15
1118	8¢ Lajos Kossuth	2.00	4.50	15.50(72)	1.60	.25	.15

1119

1120

1121

1122

1123

SCOTT NO.	DESCRIPTION	FIRST DAY COVERS SING.	FIRST DAY COVERS PL.BLK.	MINT SHEET	PLATE BLOCK F/NH	UNUSED F/NH	USED F
1119	4¢ Freedom of Press	2.00	4.25	6.00(50)	.70	.20	.15
1120	4¢ Overland Mail	2.00	4.25	6.00(50)	.70	.20	.15
1121	4¢ Noah Webster	2.00	4.25	8.00(70)	.70	.20	.15
1122	4¢ Forest Conservation	2.00	4.25	6.00(50)	.70	.20	.15
1123	4¢ Fort Duquesne	2.00	4.25	6.00(50)	.70	.20	.15

1124

1125, 1126

1127

1128

1959 COMMEMORATIVES

SCOTT NO.	DESCRIPTION	FIRST DAY COVERS SING.	FIRST DAY COVERS PL.BLK.	MINT SHEET	PLATE BLOCK F/NH	UNUSED F/NH	USED F
1124-38	**4¢-8¢, 15 varieties**	......	....	....	....	**2.70**	**1.95**
1124	4¢ Oregon Statehood	2.00	4.25	6.00(50)	.70	.20	.15
1125	4¢ José de San Martin	2.00	4.25	8.00(70)	.70	.20	.15
1126	8¢ José de San Martin	2.00	4.25	15.50(72)	1.25	.25	.15
1127	4¢ NATO	2.00	4.25	8.00(70)	.70	.20	.15
1128	4¢ Arctic Exploration	2.00	4.25	6.00(50)	.70	.20	.15

U.S. Postage #1129-1144

1129 1130

1131

1132

SCOTT NO.	DESCRIPTION	FIRST DAY COVERS SING.	FIRST DAY COVERS PL.BLK.	MINT SHEET	PLATE BLOCK F/NH	UNUSED F/NH	USED F
1129	8¢ World Peace & Trade	2.00	4.25	9.50(50)	1.10	.25	.15
1130	4¢ Silver Centennial	2.00	4.25	6.00(50)	.70	.20	.15
1131	4¢ St. Lawrence Seaway	2.00	4.25	6.00(50)	.70	.20	.15
1132	4¢ 49-Star Flag	2.00	4.25	6.00(50)	.70	.20	.15

1133

1134

1135

1136, 1137

1138

SCOTT NO.	DESCRIPTION	FIRST DAY COVERS SING.	FIRST DAY COVERS PL.BLK.	MINT SHEET	PLATE BLOCK F/NH	UNUSED F/NH	USED F
1133	4¢ Soil Conservation	2.00	4.25	6.00(50)	.70	.20	.15
1134	4¢ Petroleum	2.00	4.25	6.00(50)	.70	.20	.15
1135	4¢ Dental Health	2.00	4.25	6.00(50)	.70	.20	.15
1136	4¢ Ernst Reuter	2.00	4.25	8.00(70)	.70	.20	.15
1137	8¢ Ernst Reuter	2.00	4.25	15.50(72)	1.25	.25	.15
1138	4¢ Dr. Ephraim McDowell	2.00	4.25	8.00(70)	.70	.20	.15

1139

1140

1141

1142

1143

1144

1960-61 CREDO OF AMERICA SERIES

SCOTT NO.	DESCRIPTION	FIRST DAY COVERS SING.	FIRST DAY COVERS PL.BLK.	MINT SHEET	PLATE BLOCK F/NH	UNUSED F/NH	USED F
1139-44	**6 varieties, complete**	....	....	....	....	**1.10**	**.85**
1139	4¢ Credo—Washington	2.00	4.25	6.00(50)	.70	.20	.15
1140	4¢ Credo—Franklin	2.00	4.25	6.00(50)	.70	.20	.15
1141	4¢ Credo—Jefferson	2.00	4.25	6.00(50)	.70	.20	.15
1142	4¢ Credo—Key	2.00	4.25	6.00(50)	.70	.20	.15
1143	4¢ Credo—Lincoln	2.00	4.25	8.00(50)	.70	.20	.15
1144	4¢ Credo—Henry (1961)	2.00	4.25	8.00(50)	.70	.20	.15

1145

1146

1147, 1148

1149

U.S. Postage #1145-1164

SCOTT NO.	DESCRIPTION	FIRST DAY COVERS SING.	FIRST DAY COVERS PL.BLK.	MINT SHEET	PLATE BLOCK F/NH	UNUSED F/NH	USED F

1150

1151

1152

1153

1960 COMMEMORATIVES

SCOTT NO.	DESCRIPTION	FIRST DAY COVERS SING.	FIRST DAY COVERS PL.BLK.	MINT SHEET	PLATE BLOCK F/NH	UNUSED F/NH	USED F
1145-73	**4¢-8¢, 29 varieties**	....	....	....	....	**5.15**	**3.70**
1145	4¢ Boy Scouts	2.75	6.00	6.00(50)	.70	.20	.15
1146	4¢ Winter Olympics	2.00	4.25	6.00(50)	.70	.20	.15
1147	4¢ Thomas Masaryk	2.00	4.25	8.00(70)	.70	.20	.15
1148	8¢ Thomas Masaryk	2.00	4.25	15.50(72)	1.25	.25	.15
1149	4¢ World Refugee Year	2.00	4.25	6.00(50)	.70	.20	.15
1150	4¢ Water Conservation	2.00	4.25	6.00(50)	.70	.20	.15
1151	4¢ SEATO	2.00	4.25	8.00(70)	.70	.20	.15
1152	4¢ American Women	2.00	4.25	6.00(50)	.70	.20	.15
1153	4¢ 50-Star Flag	2.00	4.25	6.00(50)	.70	.20	.15

1154

1155

1156

1157

1158

SCOTT NO.	DESCRIPTION	FIRST DAY COVERS SING.	FIRST DAY COVERS PL.BLK.	MINT SHEET	PLATE BLOCK F/NH	UNUSED F/NH	USED F
1154	4¢ Pony Express	2.00	4.25	6.00(50)	.70	.20	.15
1155	4¢ Employ the Handicapped	2.00	4.25	6.00(50)	.70	.20	.15
1156	4¢ World Forestry Congress	2.00	4.25	6.00(50)	.70	.20	.15
1157	4¢ Mexican Independence ..	2.00	4.25	6.00(50)	.70	.20	.15
1158	4¢ U.S.-Japan Treaty	2.00	4.25	6.00(50)	.70	.20	.15

1159, 1160

1161

1162

1163

1164

SCOTT NO.	DESCRIPTION	FIRST DAY COVERS SING.	FIRST DAY COVERS PL.BLK.	MINT SHEET	PLATE BLOCK F/NH	UNUSED F/NH	USED F
1159	4¢ Ignacy Paderewski	2.00	4.25	8.00(70)	.70	.20	.15
1160	8¢ Ignacy Paderewski	2.00	4.25	15.50(72)	1.25	.25	.15
1161	4¢ Robert A. Taft	2.00	4.25	8.00(70)	.70	.20	.15
1162	4¢ Wheels of Freedom	2.00	4.25	6.00(50)	.70	.20	.15
1163	4¢ Boys' Club of America	2.00	4.25	6.00(50)	.70	.20	.15
1164	4¢ Automated Post Office ...	2.00	4.25	6.00(50)	.70	.20	.15

BUY COMPLETE SETS AND SAVE

NEVER HINGED: From 1893 to 1965, Unused OG or Unused prices are for stamps with original gum that have been hinged. If you desire Never Hinged stamps, refer to the NH listings.

U.S. Postage #1165-1184

SCOTT NO.	DESCRIPTION	FIRST DAY COVERS SING.	FIRST DAY COVERS PL.BLK.	MINT SHEET	PLATE BLOCK F/NH	UNUSED F/NH	USED F

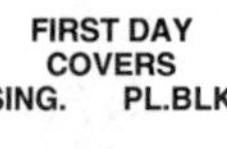

1165, 1166 — 1167 — 1168, 1169 — 1170 — 1171 — 1172

SCOTT NO.	DESCRIPTION	SING.	PL.BLK.	MINT SHEET	PLATE BLOCK F/NH	UNUSED F/NH	USED F
1165	4¢ Gustaf Mannerheim	2.00	4.25	8.00(70)	.70	.20	.15
1166	8¢ Gustaf Mannerheim	2.00	4.25	15.50(72)	1.25	.25	.15
1167	4¢ Camp Fire Girls	2.00	4.25	6.00(50)	.70	.20	.15
1168	4¢ Giuseppe Garibaldi	2.00	4.25	8.00(70)	.70	.20	.15
1169	8¢ Giuseppe Garibaldi	2.00	4.25	15.50(72)	1.25	.25	.15
1170	4¢ Walter George	2.00	4.25	8.00(70)	.70	.20	.15
1171	4¢ Andrew Carnegie	2.00	4.25	8.00(70)	.70	.20	.15
1172	4¢ John Foster Dulles	2.00	4.25	8.00(70)	.70	.20	.15

1173 — 1174, 1175 — 1176 — 1177

SCOTT NO.	DESCRIPTION	SING.	PL.BLK.	MINT SHEET	PLATE BLOCK F/NH	UNUSED F/NH	USED F
1173	4¢ "ECHO I" Satellite	3.00	6.50	11.50(50)	1.00	.25	.15

1961 COMMEMORATIVES

SCOTT NO.	DESCRIPTION	SING.	PL.BLK.	MINT SHEET	PLATE BLOCK F/NH	UNUSED F/NH	USED F
1174/90	**(1174-77, 1183-90) 12 varieties ....**	....		....	....	**2.10**	**1.40**
1174	4¢ Mahatma Gandhi	2.00	4.25	8.00(70)	.70	.20	.15
1175	8¢ Mahatma Gandhi	2.00	4.25	15.50(72)	1.25	.25	.15
1176	4¢ Range Conservation	2.00	4.25	6.00(50)	.70	.20	.15
1177	4¢ Horace Greeley	2.00	4.25	8.00(70)	.70	.20	.15

1178

1180

1183

1179

1181

1182

1184

1961-65 CIVIL WAR CENTENNIAL SERIES

SCOTT NO.	DESCRIPTION	SING.	PL.BLK.	MINT SHEET	PLATE BLOCK F/NH	UNUSED F/NH	USED F
1178-82	**4¢-5¢, 5 varieties, complete**	....	....	....	....	**1.15**	**.60**
1178	4¢ Fort Sumter	2.25	4.50	10.00(50)	1.00	.25	.15
1179	4¢ Shiloh (1962)	2.25	4.50	7.00(50)	.70	.20	.15
1180	5¢ Gettysburg (1963)	2.25	4.50	9.25(50)	.95	.20	.15
1181	5¢ Wilderness (1964)	2.25	4.50	9.25(50)	.95	.20	.15
1181	Zip Code Block	....	....	....	.90	....	....
1182	5¢ Appomattox (1965)	2.25	4.50	18.50(50)	1.75	.40	.15
1182	Zip Code Block	....	....	....	1.60	....	....

1961 COMMEMORATIVES

SCOTT NO.	DESCRIPTION	SING.	PL.BLK.	MINT SHEET	PLATE BLOCK F/NH	UNUSED F/NH	USED F
1183	4¢ Kansas Statehood	2.00	4.25	6.00(50)	.70	.20	.15
1184	4¢ George W. Norris	2.00	4.25	6.00(50)	.70	.20	.15

U.S. Postage #1185-1202

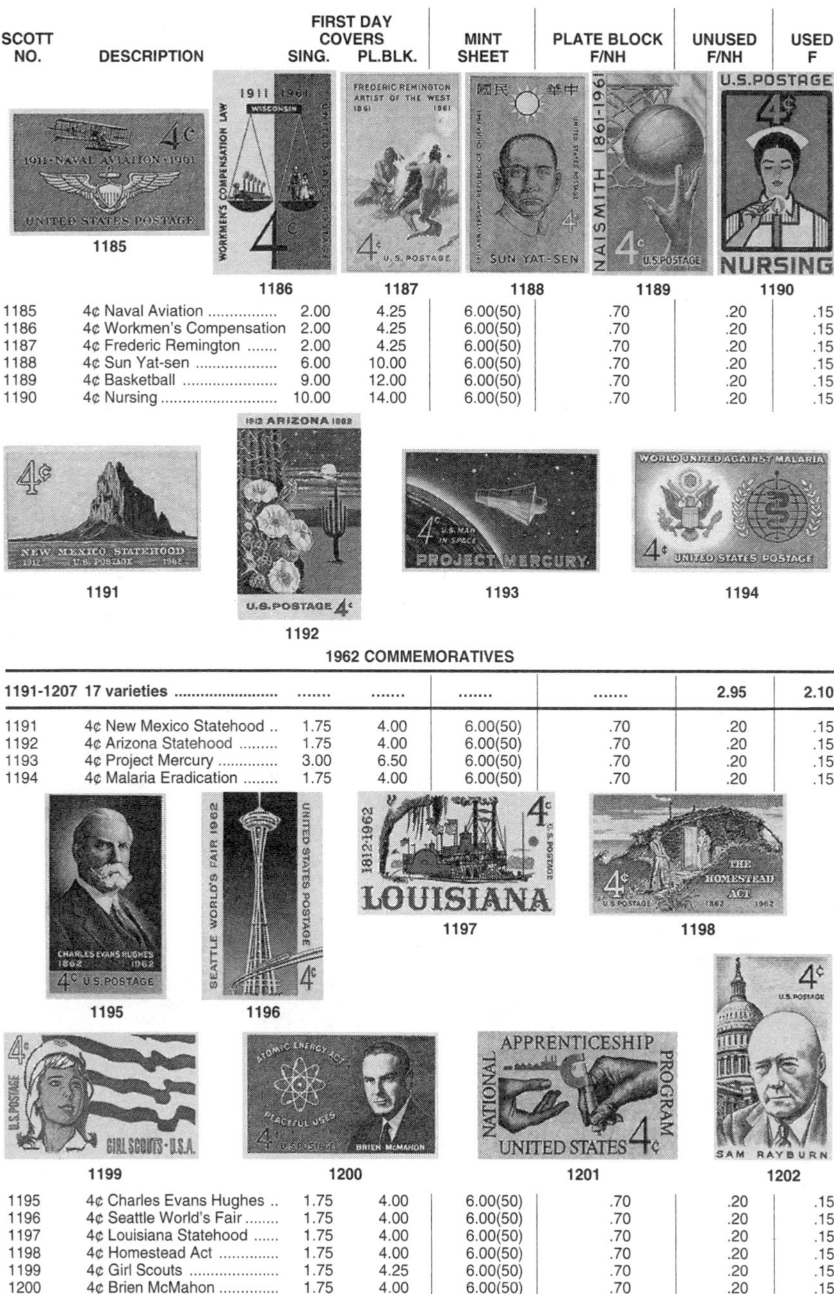

SCOTT NO.	DESCRIPTION	FIRST DAY COVERS SING.	FIRST DAY COVERS PL.BLK.	MINT SHEET	PLATE BLOCK F/NH	UNUSED F/NH	USED F
1185	4¢ Naval Aviation	2.00	4.25	6.00(50)	.70	.20	.15
1186	4¢ Workmen's Compensation	2.00	4.25	6.00(50)	.70	.20	.15
1187	4¢ Frederic Remington	2.00	4.25	6.00(50)	.70	.20	.15
1188	4¢ Sun Yat-sen	6.00	10.00	6.00(50)	.70	.20	.15
1189	4¢ Basketball	9.00	12.00	6.00(50)	.70	.20	.15
1190	4¢ Nursing	10.00	14.00	6.00(50)	.70	.20	.15

1962 COMMEMORATIVES

SCOTT NO.	DESCRIPTION	FIRST DAY COVERS SING.	FIRST DAY COVERS PL.BLK.	MINT SHEET	PLATE BLOCK F/NH	UNUSED F/NH	USED F
1191-1207	**17 varieties**	....	....	....	....	**2.95**	**2.10**
1191	4¢ New Mexico Statehood	1.75	4.00	6.00(50)	.70	.20	.15
1192	4¢ Arizona Statehood	1.75	4.00	6.00(50)	.70	.20	.15
1193	4¢ Project Mercury	3.00	6.50	6.00(50)	.70	.20	.15
1194	4¢ Malaria Eradication	1.75	4.00	6.00(50)	.70	.20	.15
1195	4¢ Charles Evans Hughes	1.75	4.00	6.00(50)	.70	.20	.15
1196	4¢ Seattle World's Fair	1.75	4.00	6.00(50)	.70	.20	.15
1197	4¢ Louisiana Statehood	1.75	4.00	6.00(50)	.70	.20	.15
1198	4¢ Homestead Act	1.75	4.00	6.00(50)	.70	.20	.15
1199	4¢ Girl Scouts	1.75	4.25	6.00(50)	.70	.20	.15
1200	4¢ Brien McMahon	1.75	4.00	6.00(50)	.70	.20	.15
1201	4¢ Apprenticeship	1.75	4.00	6.00(50)	.70	.20	.15
1202	4¢ Sam Rayburn	1.75	4.00	6.00(50)	.70	.20	.15

NOTE: To determine the VF price on stamps issued from 1941 to date, add 20% to the F/NH or F (used) price (minimum .03 per item). All VF unused stamps from 1941 date priced as NH.

U.S. Postage #1203-1233

1203 1205 1206 1207

SCOTT NO.	DESCRIPTION	FIRST DAY COVERS SING.	FIRST DAY COVERS PL.BLK.	MINT SHEET	PLATE BLOCK F/NH	UNUSED F/NH	USED F
1203	4¢ Dag Hammarskjold	1.75	4.00	6.00(50)	.70	.20	.15
1204	same, yellow inverted	5.00	10.25	6.00(50)	1.65	.20	.15
1205	4¢ Christmas 1962	1.75	4.00	11.00(50)	.70	.20	.15
1206	4¢ Higher Education	1.75	4.00	6.00(50)	.70	.20	.15
1207	4¢ Winslow Homer	1.75	4.00	6.00(50)	.70	.20	.15

1208

1209, 1225

1213, 1229

1962-66 REGULAR ISSUE

SCOTT NO.	DESCRIPTION	FIRST DAY COVERS SING.	FIRST DAY COVERS PL.BLK.	MINT SHEET	PLATE BLOCK F/NH	UNUSED F/NH	USED F
1208	5¢ Flag & White House (1963)	2.00	4.25	22.50(100)	1.10	.20	.15
1209	1¢ Andrew Jackson (1963) .	1.75	4.00	6.25(100)	.35	.20	.15
1213	5¢ Washington	1.75	4.00	22.50(100)	1.10	.20	.15
1213a	5¢ b. pane of 5—Slog. I	2.50	....	....	....	6.00	....
1213a	5¢ b. pane of 5—Slog. II (1963).......		....	....	....	16.00	....
1213a	5¢ b. pane of 5—Slog. III (1964).......		....	....	....	2.75	....
1213c	5¢ Tagged pane of 5 Slogan II (1963)	....	....	....	....	90.00	....
1213c	5¢ b. p. of 5—Slog. III (1963)	....	....	....	....	1.50	....

Slogan I—Your Mailman Deserves Your Help • Keep Harmful Objects Out of...
Slogan II—Add Zip to Your Mail • Use Zone Numbers for Zip Code.
Slogan III—Add Zip to Your Mail • Always Use Zip Code.

1962-66 COIL STAMPS Perf. 10 Vertically

SCOTT NO.	DESCRIPTION	FIRST DAY COVERS SING.	L.PR.	MINT SHEET	LINE PAIRS	UNUSED F/NH	USED F
1225	1¢ Andrew Jackson (1963) .	1.75	3.00	....	3.00	.20	.15
1229	5¢ George Washington	1.75	3.00	....	3.25	1.25	.15

1230

1231

1232

1233

1963 COMMEMORATIVES

SCOTT NO.	DESCRIPTION	FIRST DAY COVERS SING.	FIRST DAY COVERS PL.BLK.	MINT SHEET	PLATE BLOCK	UNUSED F/NH	USED F
1230-41	**12 varieties ....**	....	....	....	....	**2.00**	**1.50**
1230	5¢ Carolina Charter	1.75	4.00	6.50(50)	.70	.20	.15
1231	5¢ Food for Peace	1.75	4.00	6.50(50)	.70	.20	.15
1232	5¢ West Virginia Statehood	1.75	4.00	6.50(50)	.70	.20	.15
1233	5¢ Emancipation Proclamation	1.75	4.00	6.50(50)	.70	.20	.15

PLATE BLOCKS: are portions of a sheet of stamps adjacent to the number(s) indicating the printing plate number used to produce that sheet. Flat plate issues are usually collected in plate blocks of six (number opposite middle stamp) while rotary issues are normally corner blocks of four.

U.S. Postage #1234-1251

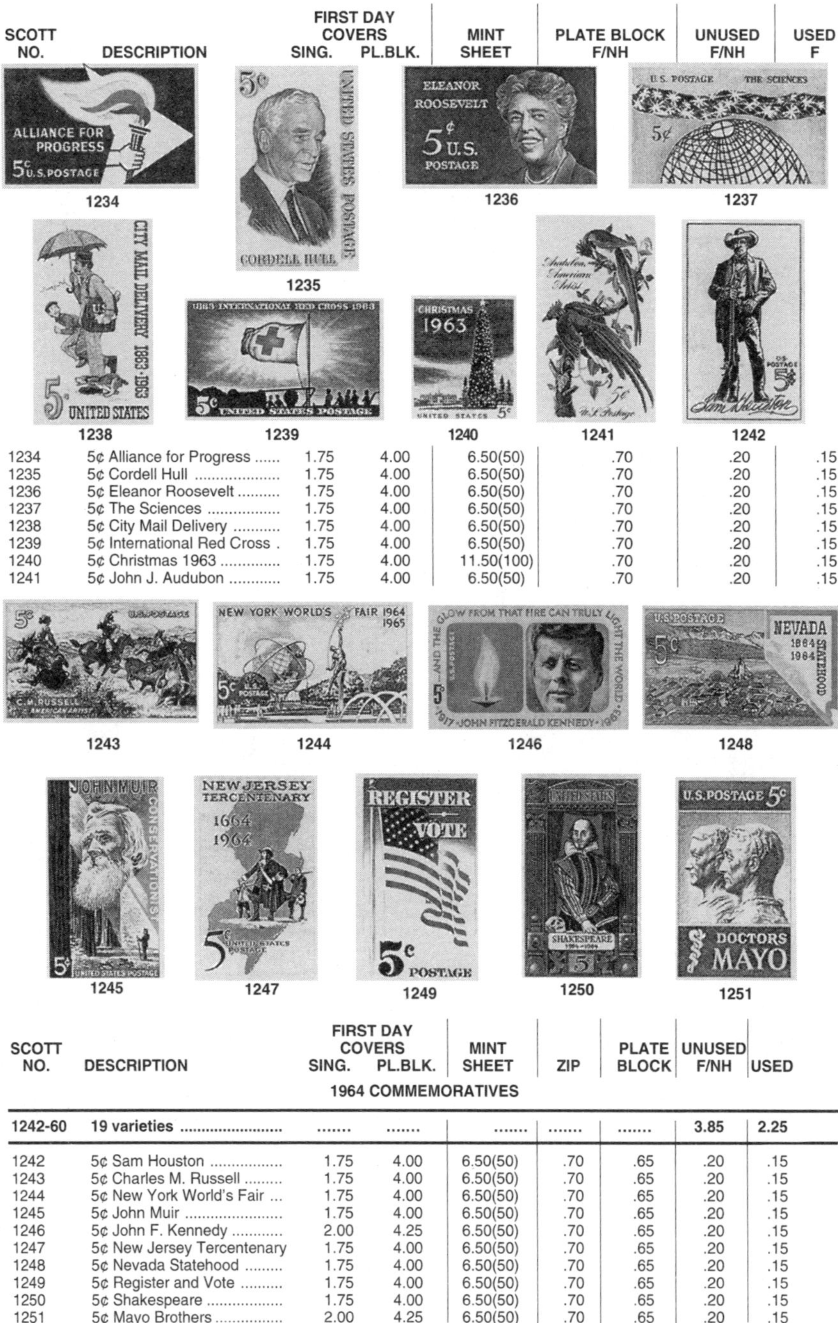

1234 1235 1236 1237 1238 1239 1240 1241 1242

1243 1244 1246 1248

1245 1247 1249 1250 1251

SCOTT NO.	DESCRIPTION	FIRST DAY COVERS SING.	FIRST DAY COVERS PL.BLK.	MINT SHEET	PLATE BLOCK F/NH	UNUSED F/NH	USED F
1234	5¢ Alliance for Progress	1.75	4.00	6.50(50)	.70	.20	.15
1235	5¢ Cordell Hull	1.75	4.00	6.50(50)	.70	.20	.15
1236	5¢ Eleanor Roosevelt	1.75	4.00	6.50(50)	.70	.20	.15
1237	5¢ The Sciences	1.75	4.00	6.50(50)	.70	.20	.15
1238	5¢ City Mail Delivery	1.75	4.00	6.50(50)	.70	.20	.15
1239	5¢ International Red Cross .	1.75	4.00	6.50(50)	.70	.20	.15
1240	5¢ Christmas 1963	1.75	4.00	11.50(100)	.70	.20	.15
1241	5¢ John J. Audubon	1.75	4.00	6.50(50)	.70	.20	.15

SCOTT NO.	DESCRIPTION	FIRST DAY COVERS SING.	FIRST DAY COVERS PL.BLK.	MINT SHEET	ZIP	PLATE BLOCK	UNUSED F/NH	USED
		1964 COMMEMORATIVES						
1242-60	**19 varieties ....**	**.......**	**.......**	**.......**	**.......**	**.......**	**3.85**	**2.25**
1242	5¢ Sam Houston	1.75	4.00	6.50(50)	.70	.65	.20	.15
1243	5¢ Charles M. Russell	1.75	4.00	6.50(50)	.70	.65	.20	.15
1244	5¢ New York World's Fair ...	1.75	4.00	6.50(50)	.70	.65	.20	.15
1245	5¢ John Muir	1.75	4.00	6.50(50)	.70	.65	.20	.15
1246	5¢ John F. Kennedy	2.00	4.25	6.50(50)	.70	.65	.20	.15
1247	5¢ New Jersey Tercentenary	1.75	4.00	6.50(50)	.70	.65	.20	.15
1248	5¢ Nevada Statehood	1.75	4.00	6.50(50)	.70	.65	.20	.15
1249	5¢ Register and Vote	1.75	4.00	6.50(50)	.70	.65	.20	.15
1250	5¢ Shakespeare	1.75	4.00	6.50(50)	.70	.65	.20	.15
1251	5¢ Mayo Brothers	2.00	4.25	6.50(50)	.70	.65	.20	.15

COMMEMORATIVES: Commemorative stamps are special issues released to honor or recognize persons, organizations, historical events or landmarks. They are usually issued in the current first class denomination to supplement regular issues.

U.S. Postage #1252-1266

1252 1253 1254 1255 1256 1257

SCOTT NO.	DESCRIPTION	FIRST DAY COVERS SING.	PL.BLK.	MINT SHEET	ZIP	PLATE BLOCK	UNUSED F/NH	USED
1252	5¢ American Music	1.75	4.00	6.50(50)	.65	.70	.20	.15
1253	5¢ Homemakers	1.75	4.00	6.50(50)	.65	.70	.20	.15
1254-57	5¢ Christmas, 4 varieties, attached	5.25	7.50	36.00(100)	1.70	1.75	1.50	1.25
1254	5¢ Holly	2.75	......	......	......	......	.35	.15
1255	5¢ Mistletoe	2.75	......	......	......	......	.35	.15
1256	5¢ Poinsettia	2.75	......	......	......	......	.35	.15
1257	5¢ Pine Cone	2.75	......	......	......	......	.35	.15

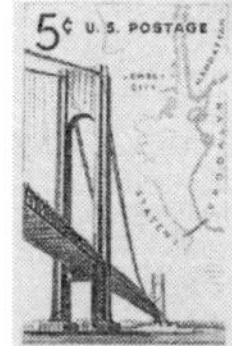

1258

1260

1262

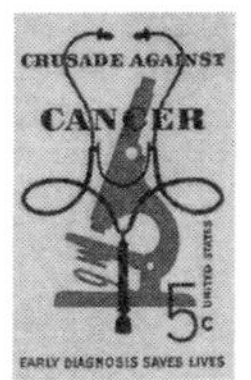

1263

1264

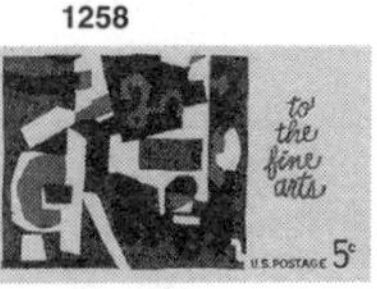

1259

1261

1265

1266

SCOTT NO.	DESCRIPTION	FIRST DAY COVERS SING.	PL.BLK.	MINT SHEET	ZIP	PLATE BLOCK	UNUSED F/NH	USED
1258	5¢ Verrazano-Narrows Bridge	1.75	4.00	6.50(50)	.65	.70	.20	.15
1259	5¢ Modern Art	1.75	4.00	6.50(50)	.65	.70	.20	.15
1260	5¢ Radio Amateurs	1.75	4.00	6.50(50)	.65	.70	.20	.15

1965 COMMEMORATIVES

SCOTT NO.	DESCRIPTION	FIRST DAY COVERS SING.	PL.BLK.	MINT SHEET	ZIP	PLATE BLOCK	UNUSED F/NH	USED
1261-76	**5¢-11¢, 16 varieties.**	......	......	......	......	......	**2.90**	**1.90**
1261	5¢ Battle of New Orleans	1.75	4.00	6.50(50)	.65	.70	.20	.15
1262	5¢ Physical Fitness	1.75	4.00	6.50(50)	.65	.70	.20	.15
1263	5¢ Crusade Against Cancer	1.75	4.00	6.50(50)	.65	.70	.20	.15
1264	5¢ Winston Churchill	1.75	4.00	6.50(50)	.65	.70	.20	.15
1265	5¢ Magna Carta	1.75	4.00	6.50(50)	.65	.70	.20	.15
1266	5¢ International Cooperation Year	1.75	4.00	6.50(50)	.65	.70	.20	.15

1267

1268

1269

1271

1273

1275

1270

1272

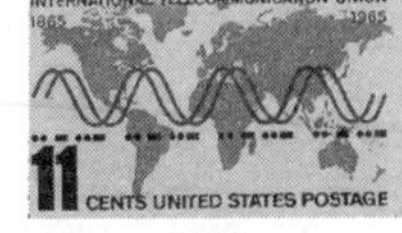

1274

1276

U.S. Postage #1267-1282

SCOTT NO.	DESCRIPTION	FIRST DAY COVERS SING.	PL.BLK.	MINT SHEET	ZIP	PLATE BLOCK	UNUSED F/NH	USED
1267	5¢ Salvation Army	1.75	4.00	6.50(50)	.65	.70	.20	.15
1268	5¢ Dante Alighieri	1.75	4.00	6.50(50)	.65	.70	.20	.15
1269	5¢ Herbert Hoover	1.75	4.00	6.50(50)	.65	.70	.20	.15
1270	5¢ Robert Fulton	1.75	4.00	6.50(50)	.65	.70	.20	.15
1271	5¢ Florida Settlement	1.75	4.00	6.50(50)	.65	.70	.20	.15
1272	5¢ Traffic Safety	1.75	4.00	6.50(50)	.65	.70	.20	.15
1273	5¢ John S. Copley	1.75	4.00	6.50(50)	.65	.70	.20	.15
1274	11¢ Telecommunication	1.75	4.00	26.50(50)	7.00	8.50	.45	.25
1275	5¢ Adlai Stevenson	1.75	4.00	6.50(50)	.....	.70	.20	.15
1276	5¢ Christmas 1965	1.75	4.00	11.50(50)	.65	.70	.20	.15

1278, 1299

1279

1280

1281, 1297

1282, 1303

1283, 1304

1283B, 1304C

1284, 1298

1285

1286

1286A

1287

1288, 1288B, 1288d
1305E, 1305Ei

1289

1290

1291

1292

1293

1294, 1305C

1295

1305

SCOTT NO.	DESCRIPTION	FIRST DAY COVERS SING.	PL.BLK.	MINT SHEET	MAIL EARLY	ZIP	PLATE BLOCK	UNUSED F/NH	USED
	1965-78 PROMINENT AMERICAN SERIES								
1278-95	**1¢-$5, 20 varieties, complete (No #1288B or d) ....**	**91.50**	**.....**	**.....**	**.....**		**103.00**	**21.50**	**5.25**
1278	1¢ Thomas Jefferson (1968)	1.75	4.00	5.50(100)	.60	.60	.60	.20	.15
1278a	1¢ booklet pane of 8	2.50	.....	.....	.....	.....	.....	1.00	.....
1278ae	1¢ test gum	90.00	.....	.....	.....	.....	.....	2.00	.....
1278b	1¢ booklet pane of 4 (1971)	18.00	.....	.....	.....	.....	.....	.70	.....
1279	1-1/4¢ Albert Gallatin (1967)	1.75	4.00	25.00(100)	.....	.....	15.25	.20	.15
1280	2¢ Frank L. Wright (1966)	1.75	4.00	6.00(100)	.60	.60	.60	.20	.15
1280a	2¢ booklet pane of 5 (1968)	2.50	.....	.....	.....	.....	.....	1.00	.....
1280c	2¢ booklet pane of 6 (1971)	18.00	.....	.....	.....	.....	.....	1.00	.....
1280ce	2¢ test gum	125.00	.....	.....	.....	.....	.....	1.00	.....
1281	3¢ Francis Parkman (1967)	1.75	4.00	8.00(100)	.90	.70	.70	.20	.15
1282	4¢ Abraham Lincoln	1.75	4.00	10.50(100)	.....	.....	.70	.20	.15

U.S. Postage #1283-1305C

SCOTT NO.	DESCRIPTION	FIRST DAY COVERS SING.	PL.BLK.	MINT SHEET	MAIL EARLY	ZIP	PLATE BLOCK	UNUSED F/NH	USED
1283	5¢ G. Washington (1966)...........	1.75	4.00	12.75(100)	.....	.....	.70	.20	.15
1283B	5¢ Washington, redrawn (1967)	1.75	4.00	12.25(100)	.....	.....	.70	.20	.15
1284	6¢ F.D. Roosevelt (1966)	1.75	4.00	16.50(100)	6.40	6.10	.80	.20	.15
1284b	6¢ booklet pane of 8 (1967)	3.00	.....	.....	.....	.....	.....	1.60	.....
1284c	6¢ booklet pane of 5 (1968)	150.00	.....	.....	.....	.....	.....	1.50	.....
1285	8¢ Albert Einstein (1966)...........	2.00	4.25	24.00(100)	1.50	1.00	1.00	.25	.15
1286	10¢ Andrew Jackson (1967)	2.00	4.25	28.00(100)	1.50	1.25	1.25	.30	.15
1286A	12¢ Henry Ford (1968)	2.00	4.25	33.25(100)	1.95	1.50	1.55	.35	.15
1287	13¢ John F. Kennedy (1967)	2.50	4.50	33.25(100)	.....	.....	1.55	.35	.15
1288	15¢ Oliver W. Holmes, die I (1968)	2.25	4.50	37.00(100)	2.50	1.90	2.00	.40	.15
1288d	15¢ Holmes, die II (1979)	.....	.....	90.00(100)	6.00	5.25	14.00	.95	.15
1288B	Same, from booklet pane (1978)	2.25	.....	.....	.....	.....	.....	.45	.15
1288Bc	15¢ booklet pane of 8	3.75	.....	.....	.....	.....	.....	3.75	.....
1289	20¢ G.C. Marshall (1967)...........	2.25	4.50	55.00(100)	3.10	2.50	2.75	.60	.15
1290	25¢ Frederick Douglass (1967) ..	2.50	5.00	62.50(100)	3.50	2.80	3.25	.75	.15
1291	30¢ John Dewey (1968)..............	2.50	5.00	67.50(100)	4.25	3.50	3.70	.80	.15
1292	40¢ Thomas Paine (1968)	2.50	5.00	97.50(100)	5.50	4.50	4.65	1.05	.15
1293	50¢ Lucy Stone (1968)	3.75	7.25	125.00(100)	6.50	6.00	6.25	1.50	.15
1294	$1 E. O'Neill (1967)....................	6.00	12.50	250.00(100)	15.00	10.50	11.25	2.75	.15
1295	$5 John Bassett Moore (1966) ..	50.00	115.00	.....	.....	.....	49.50	12.00	2.85

BOOKLET PANE SLOGANS

Slogan IV: Mail Early in the Day.
Slogan V: Use Zip Code.

#1278b—Slogans IV and V
#1280a, 1284c—Slogans IV or V

1966-81 COIL STAMPS

SCOTT NO.	DESCRIPTION	FIRST DAY COVERS SING.	LINE PAIR	MINT SHEET	MAIL EARLY	ZIP	LINE PAIR	UNUSED F/NH	USED
1297-1305C	**1¢-$1, 9 varieties, (No #1305Ei)**	.....	.....	.....	.....	.....	**14.00**	**4.60**	**1.90**
	Perf. 10 Horizontally								
1297	3¢ Francis Parkman (1975)........	1.75	2.75	.....	.....	.....	.70	.20	.15
1298	6¢ F.D. Roosevelt (1967)	1.75	2.75	.....	.....	.....	1.55	.20	.15
	Perf. 10 Vertically								
1299	1¢ T. Jefferson (1968)	1.75	2.75	.....	.....	.....	.45	.20	.15
1303	4¢ Abraham Lincoln	1.75	2.75	.....	.....	.....	.70	.20	.15
1304	5¢ George Washington	1.75	2.75	.....	.....	.....	.55	.20	.15
1304C	5¢ Washington, redrawn (1981)	1.75	2.75	.....	.....	.....	1.15	.20	.15
1305	6¢ F.D. Roosevelt (1968)	1.75	2.75	.....	.....	.....	.70	.20	.15
1305E	15¢ O.W. Holmes, die I (1978)....	2.00	3.25	.....	.....	.....	1.40	.45	.15
1305Ei	15¢ O.W. Holmes, die II (1979) ..	.....	.....	.....	.....	.....	1.80	.55	.30
1305C	$1 E. O'Neill (1973)	5.00	9.50	.....	.....	.....	5.75	2.50	1.00

ZIP BLOCKS: are generally corner Blocks of Four that contain a drawing of "Mr. Zip" and the legend "USE ZIP CODE" or a similar design. They were introduced in 1964 and are still in use today.

U.S. Postage #1306-1322

1306

1307

1308

1309

1310, 1311

1312

1313

1314

1315

1966 COMMEMORATIVES

SCOTT NO.	DESCRIPTION	FIRST DAY COVERS SING.	PL.BLK.	MINT SHEET	ZIP	PLATE BLOCK	UNUSED F/NH	USED
1306/22	(1306-10, 1312-22) 16 varieties	......	......	......	......	......	2.70	1.90
1306	5¢ Migratory Bird Treaty	2.00	4.25	6.50(50)	.65	.70	.20	.15
1307	5¢ A.S.P.C.A.	1.75	4.00	6.50(50)	.65	.70	.20	.15
1308	5¢ Indiana Statehood	1.75	4.00	6.50(50)	.65	.70	.20	.15
1309	5¢ American Circus	3.00	4.25	6.50(50)	.65	.70	.20	.15
1310	5¢ SIPEX, (single)	1.75	4.00	6.50(50)	.65	.70	.20	.15
1311	5¢ SIPEX Imperforate Souvenir Sheet	2.00	......	......	......	......	.20	.15
1312	5¢ Bill of Rights	1.75	4.00	8.00(50)	.80	.85	.20	.15
1313	5¢ Polish Millennium	1.75	4.00	6.50(50)	.65	.70	.20	.15
1314	5¢ National Park Service	1.75	4.00	6.50(50)	.65	.70	.20	.15
1315	5¢ Marine Corps Reserve	1.75	4.00	6.50(50)	.65	.70	.20	.15

1316

1317

1318

1319

1320

1321

1322

1323

SCOTT NO.	DESCRIPTION	FIRST DAY COVERS SING.	PL.BLK.	MINT SHEET	ZIP	PLATE BLOCK	UNUSED F/NH	USED
1316	5¢ Womens' Clubs	1.75	4.00	6.50(50)	.65	.70	.20	.15
1317	5¢ Johnny Appleseed	1.75	4.00	6.50(50)	.65	.70	.20	.15
1318	5¢ Beautification	1.75	4.00	6.50(50)	.65	.70	.20	.15
1319	5¢ Great River Road	1.75	4.00	6.50(50)	.65	.70	.20	.15
1320	5¢ Servicemen—Bonds	1.75	4.00	6.50(50)	.65	.70	.20	.15
1321	5¢ Christmas 1966	1.75	4.00	11.50(50)	.65	.70	.20	.15
1322	5¢ Mary Cassatt	1.75	4.00	8.00(50)	.80	.85	.20	.15

Note: All stamps from #1242 to date are priced for F/NH condition. For VF/NH price, add 20% to listed price.

MINT SHEETS: From 1935 to date, we list prices for standard size Mint Sheets in Fine, Never Hinged condition. The number of stamps in each sheet is noted in ( ).

U.S. Postage #1323-1334

SCOTT NO.	DESCRIPTION	FIRST DAY COVERS SING.	PL.BLK.	MINT SHEET	ZIP	PLATE BLOCK	UNUSED F/NH	USED
			1967 COMMEMORATIVES					
1323-37	**15 varieties, complete**	......	......	......	......	......	**4.00**	**1.90**
1323	5¢ National Grange	1.75	4.00	11.50(50)	1.10	1.10	.20	.15

1324

1325

1326

SCOTT NO.	DESCRIPTION	FIRST DAY COVERS SING.	PL.BLK.	MINT SHEET	ZIP	PLATE BLOCK	UNUSED F/NH	USED
1324	5¢ Canada Centennial	1.75	4.00	6.50(50)	.65	.70	.20	.15
1325	5¢ Erie Canal	1.75	4.00	6.50(50)	.65	.70	.20	.15
1326	5¢ Search for Peace	1.75	4.00	6.50(50)	.65	.70	.20	.15

1327

1328

1329

1330

SCOTT NO.	DESCRIPTION	FIRST DAY COVERS SING.	PL.BLK.	MINT SHEET	ZIP	PLATE BLOCK	UNUSED F/NH	USED
1327	5¢ Henry D. Thoreau	1.75	4.00	6.50(50)	.65	.70	.20	.15
1328	5¢ Nebraska Statehood	1.75	4.00	6.50(50)	.65	.70	.20	.15
1329	5¢ Voice of America	1.75	4.00	6.50(50)	.65	.70	.20	.15
1330	5¢ Davy Crockett	2.00	4.25	6.50(50)	.65	.70	.20	.15

1331

1332

SCOTT NO.	DESCRIPTION	FIRST DAY COVERS SING.	PL.BLK.	MINT SHEET	ZIP	PLATE BLOCK	UNUSED F/NH	USED
1331-32	Space, attached, 2 varieties ...	12.50	25.00	45.00(50)	4.50	4.75	2.25	1.50
1331	5¢ Astronaut	4.00	......	......	......	......	.65	.30
1332	5¢ Gemini 4 Capsule	4.00	......	......	......	......	.65	.30

1333

1334

SCOTT NO.	DESCRIPTION	FIRST DAY COVERS SING.	PL.BLK.	MINT SHEET	ZIP	PLATE BLOCK	UNUSED F/NH	USED
1333	5¢ Urban Planning	1.75	4.00	6.50(50)	.65	.70	.20	.15
1334	5¢ Finland Independence	1.75	4.00	6.50(50)	.65	.70	.20	.15

FOR YOUR CONVENIENCE IN ORDERING, COMPLETE SETS ARE LISTED BEFORE SINGLE STAMP LISTINGS!

U.S. Postage #1335-1340

SCOTT NO.	DESCRIPTION	FIRST DAY COVERS SING.	PL.BLK.	MINT SHEET	MAIL EARLY	ZIP	PLATE BLOCK	UNUSED F/NH	USED

1335

1336

1337

SCOTT NO.	DESCRIPTION	FIRST DAY COVERS SING.	PL.BLK.	MINT SHEET	MAIL EARLY	ZIP	PLATE BLOCK	UNUSED F/NH	USED
1335	5¢ Thomas Eakins	1.75	4.00	6.50(50)	......	......	.70	.20	.15
1336	5¢ Christmas 1967	1.75	4.00	6.50(50)	......	.65	.70	.20	.15
1337	5¢ Mississippi Statehood	1.75	4.00	6.50(50)	......	.65	.70	.20	.15

1338, 1338A-G

1339

1340

GIORI PRESS

1968 Design size: 18-1/2 x 22mm Perf. 11

SCOTT NO.	DESCRIPTION	FIRST DAY COVERS SING.	PL.BLK.	MINT SHEET	MAIL EARLY	ZIP	PLATE BLOCK	UNUSED F/NH	USED
1338	6¢ Flag & White House	1.75	4.00	14.50(100)	.90	.65	.70	.20	.15

HUCK PRESS Design Size: 18 x 21mm

1969 Coil Stamp Perf. 10 Vertically

SCOTT NO.	DESCRIPTION	FIRST DAY COVERS SING.	PL.BLK.	MINT SHEET	MAIL EARLY	ZIP	PLATE BLOCK	UNUSED F/NH	USED
1338A	6¢ Flag & White House	1.75	......	......	......	......	......	.20	.15

1970 Perf. 11 x 10-1/2

SCOTT NO.	DESCRIPTION	FIRST DAY COVERS SING.	PL.BLK.	MINT SHEET	MAIL EARLY	ZIP	PLATE BLOCK	UNUSED F/NH	USED
1338D	6¢ Flag & White House	2.00	4.25	14.50(100)	......	......	3.50(20)	.20	.15

1971 Perf. 11 x 10-1/2

SCOTT NO.	DESCRIPTION	FIRST DAY COVERS SING.	PL.BLK.	MINT SHEET	MAIL EARLY	ZIP	PLATE BLOCK	UNUSED F/NH	USED
1338F	8¢ Flag & White House	2.00	4.25	21.50(100)	......	......	4.75(20)	.25	.15

Coil Stamp Perf. 10 Vertically

SCOTT NO.	DESCRIPTION	FIRST DAY COVERS SING.	PL.BLK.	MINT SHEET	MAIL EARLY	ZIP	PLATE BLOCK	UNUSED F/NH	USED
1338G	8¢ Flag & White House	2.00	......	......	......	......	......	.30	.15

1968 COMMEMORATIVES

SCOTT NO.	DESCRIPTION	FIRST DAY COVERS SING.	PL.BLK.	MINT SHEET	MAIL EARLY	ZIP	PLATE BLOCK	UNUSED F/NH	USED
1339/64	**(1339-40, 1342-64) 25 varieties**	......	......	....	......	......	......	**6.95**	**4.50**
1339	6¢ Illinois Statehood	1.75	4.00	7.25(50)	......	.65	.70	.20	.15
1340	6¢ Hemisfair '68	1.75	4.00	7.25(50)	.90	.65	.70	.20	.15

1341

1342

1343

1344

U.S. Postage #1341-1359

SCOTT NO.	DESCRIPTION	FIRST DAY COVERS SING.	PL.BLK.	MINT SHEET	MAIL EARLY	ZIP	PLATE BLOCK	UNUSED F/NH	USED
1341	$1 Airlift to Servicemen	8.50	17.50	150.00(50)	21.00	13.50	13.50	3.25	1.95
1342	6¢ Support our Youth	1.75	4.00	7.25(50)	.90	.65	.70	.20	.15
1343	6¢ Law and Order	1.75	4.00	7.25(50)	.90	.65	.70	.20	.15
1344	6¢ Register and Vote	1.75	4.00	7.25(50)	.90	.65	.70	.20	.15

1345 1346 1347

1348 1349 1350 1351

1352 1353 1354

1968 HISTORIC AMERICAN FLAGS

SCOTT NO.	DESCRIPTION	FIRST DAY COVERS SING.	PL.BLK.	MINT SHEET	MAIL EARLY	ZIP	PLATE BLOCK	UNUSED F/NH	USED
1345-54	**10 varieties, complete, attached**	**11.50**	**......**	**19.75(50)**	**......**	**......**	**9.00**	**3.95**	**......**
1345-54	**Same, set of singles**	**57.50**	**......**	**.......**	**......**	**......**	**......**	**3.10**	**2.50**
1345-54	Inscription blocks	......	......	....	2.50	1.75	1.75	......	......
1345	6¢ Fort Moultrie Flag	6.00	......	....	......	......	......	.45	.40
1346	6¢ Fort McHenry Flag	6.00	......	....	......	......	......	.35	.35
1347	6¢ Washington's Cruisers	6.00	......	....	......	......	......	.30	.25
1348	6¢ Bennington Flag	6.00	......	....	......	......	......	.30	.25
1349	6¢ Rhode Island Flag	6.00	......	....	......	......	......	.30	.25
1350	6¢ First Stars & Stripes	6.00	......	....	......	......	......	.30	.25
1351	6¢ Bunker Hill Flag	6.00	......	....	......	......	......	.30	.25
1352	6¢ Grand Union Flag	6.00	......	....	......	......	......	.30	.25
1353	6¢ Philadelphia Light Horse	6.00	......	....	......	......	......	.30	.25
1354	6¢ First Navy Jack	6.00	......	....	......	......	......	.30	.25

NOTE: All 10 varieties of 1345-54 were printed on the same sheet; therefore, plate and regular blocks are not available for each variety separately. Plate blocks of 4 will contain two each of #1346, with number adjacent to #1345 only; Zip blocks will contain two each of #1353 and #1354, with inscription adjacent to #1354 only; Mail Early blocks will contain two each of #1347-49 with inscription adjacent to #1348 only. A plate strip of 20 stamps, with two of each variety will be required to have all stamps in plate block form and will contain all marginal inscription.

1355

1356

1357

1358

1359

1968 COMMEMORATIVES

SCOTT NO.	DESCRIPTION	FIRST DAY COVERS SING.	PL.BLK.	MINT SHEET	MAIL EARLY	ZIP	PLATE BLOCK	UNUSED F/NH	USED
1355	6¢ Walt Disney	30.00	40.00	24.50(50)	3.50	2.50	2.50	.55	.15
1356	6¢ Father Marquette	1.75	4.00	7.25(50)	1.00	.65	.70	.20	.15
1357	6¢ Daniel Boone	1.75	4.00	7.25(50)	1.00	.65	.70	.20	.15
1358	6¢ Arkansas River	1.75	4.00	7.25(50)	1.00	.65	.70	.20	.15
1359	6¢ Leif Erikson	1.75	4.00	7.25(50)	1.00	.65	.70	.20	.15

U.S. Postage #1360-1375

1360

1361

1363

1364

1362

SCOTT NO.	DESCRIPTION	FIRST DAY COVERS SING.	PL.BLK.	MINT SHEET	MAIL EARLY	ZIP	PLATE BLOCK	UNUSED F/NH	USED
1360	6¢ Cherokee Strip	1.75	4.00	7.25(50)	1.00	.70	.75	.20	.15
1361	6¢ Trumbull Art	1.75	4.00	7.25(50)	1.00	.70	.75	.20	.15
1362	6¢ Waterfowl Conservation	1.75	4.00	10.50(50)	1.60	1.20	1.25	.20	.15
1363	6¢ Christmas 1968	1.75	......	7.50(50)	......	......	1.75(10)	.20	.15
1364	6¢ Chief Joseph	1.75	4.00	10.50(50)	1.60	1.20	1.25	.20	.15

1365

1366

1367

1368

1969 COMMEMORATIVES

SCOTT NO.	DESCRIPTION	FIRST DAY COVERS SING.	PL.BLK.	MINT SHEET	MAIL EARLY	ZIP	PLATE BLOCK	UNUSED F/NH	USED
1365-86	**22 varieties, complete**	......	......	....	......	......	......	**8.00**	**2.95**
1365-68	Beautification, 4 varieties, attached	6.00	8.50	25.00(50)	3.50	2.50	2.50	2.20	2.20
1365	6¢ Azaleas & Tulips	3.00	......	....	......	......	......	.50	.15
1366	6¢ Daffodils	3.00	......	....	......	......	......	.50	.15
1367	6¢ Poppies	3.00	......	....	......	......	......	.50	.15
1368	6¢ Crabapple Trees	3.00	......	....	......	......	......	.50	.15

1369

1370

1371

1372

SCOTT NO.	DESCRIPTION	FIRST DAY COVERS SING.	PL.BLK.	MINT SHEET	MAIL EARLY	ZIP	PLATE BLOCK	UNUSED F/NH	USED
1369	6¢ American Legion	1.75	4.00	7.25(50)	1.00	.70	.70	.20	.15
1370	6¢ Grandma Moses	1.75	4.00	7.25(50)	1.00	.70	.70	.20	.15
1371	6¢ Apollo 8 Moon Orbit	2.50	5.00	11.75(50)	1.35	1.10	1.15	.25	.15
1372	6¢ W.C. Handy—Musician	2.25	4.25	8.00(50)	1.10	.80	.80	.20	.15

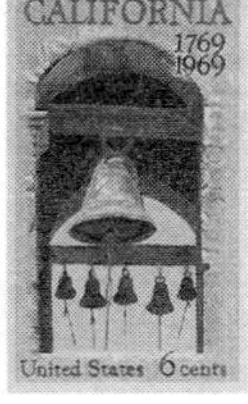

1373

1374

1375

SCOTT NO.	DESCRIPTION	FIRST DAY COVERS SING.	PL.BLK.	MINT SHEET	MAIL EARLY	ZIP	PLATE BLOCK	UNUSED F/NH	USED
1373	6¢ California Settlement	1.75	4.00	7.25(50)	1.00	.70	.70	.20	.15
1374	6¢ Major John W. Powell	1.75	4.00	7.25(50)	1.00	.70	.70	.20	.15
1375	6¢ Alabama Statehood	1.75	4.00	7.25(50)	1.00	.70	.70	.20	.15

AVERAGE QUALITY: From 1935 to date, deduct 20% from the Fine price to determine the price for an Average quality stamp.

U.S. Postage #1376-1386

SCOTT NO.	DESCRIPTION	FIRST DAY COVERS SING.	FIRST DAY COVERS PL.BLK.	MINT SHEET	MAIL EARLY	ZIP	PLATE BLOCK	UNUSED F/NH	USED

1376

1377

1378

1379

SCOTT NO.	DESCRIPTION	FDC SING.	FDC PL.BLK.	MINT SHEET	MAIL EARLY	ZIP	PLATE BLOCK	UNUSED F/NH	USED
1376-79	Botanical Congress, 4 Varieties, attached	7.00	9.50	32.50(50)	4.50	3.40	3.50	3.00	3.00
1376	6¢ Douglas Fir	3.00	....	....	....	....	....	.75	.20
1377	6¢ Lady's-slipper	3.00	....	....	....	....	....	.75	.20
1378	6¢ Ocotillo	3.00	....	....	....	....	....	.75	.20
1379	6¢ Franklinia	3.00	....	....	....	....	....	.75	.20

1380

1381

1382

SCOTT NO.	DESCRIPTION	FDC SING.	FDC PL.BLK.	MINT SHEET	MAIL EARLY	ZIP	PLATE BLOCK	UNUSED F/NH	USED
1380	6¢ Dartmouth College	1.75	4.00	7.25(50)	1.00	.70	.70	.20	.15
1381	6¢ Professional Baseball	16.00	25.00	38.50(50)	5.75	3.75	4.00	.90	.15
1382	6¢ College Football	7.00	13.50	13.75(50)	1.95	1.30	1.40	.40	.15

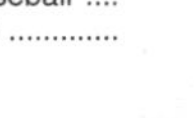

1383

1384

1385

1386

SCOTT NO.	DESCRIPTION	FDC SING.	FDC PL.BLK.	MINT SHEET	MAIL EARLY	ZIP	PLATE BLOCK	UNUSED F/NH	USED
1383	6¢ Eisenhower	1.75	4.00	4.75(32)	1.00	.70	.70	.20	.15
1384	6¢ Christmas 1969	1.75	....	7.25(50)	....	....	1.80(10)	.20	.15
1384a	6¢ precancelled	45.00	....	45.00(50)	....	....	17.50(10)	.70	....
1385	6¢ Rehabilitation	1.75	4.00	7.25(50)	1.00	.70	.70	.20	.15
1386	6¢ William M. Harnett	1.75	4.00	4.75(32)	1.00	.70	.70	.20	.15

1387

1388

1389

MINT SHEETS: From 1935 to date, we list prices for standard size Mint Sheets in Fine, Never Hinged condition. The number of stamps in each sheet is noted in ( ).

U.S. Postage #1387-1402

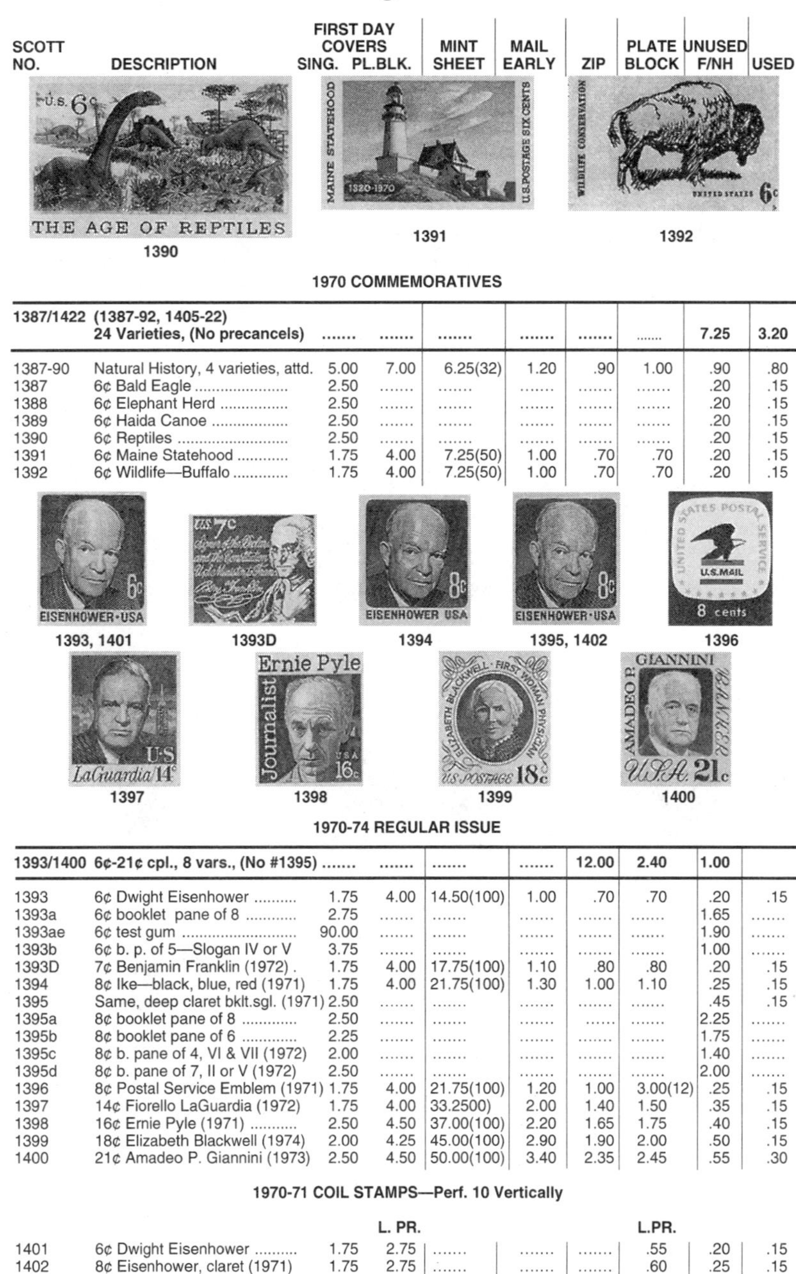

1390 1391 1392

1970 COMMEMORATIVES

SCOTT NO.	DESCRIPTION	FIRST DAY COVERS SING.	FIRST DAY COVERS PL.BLK.	MINT SHEET	MAIL EARLY	ZIP	PLATE BLOCK	UNUSED F/NH	USED
1387/1422	(1387-92, 1405-22) 24 Varieties, (No precancels)	....	....	....	....	....	....	7.25	3.20
1387-90	Natural History, 4 varieties, attd.	5.00	7.00	6.25(32)	1.20	.90	1.00	.90	.80
1387	6¢ Bald Eagle	2.50	....	....	....	....	....	.20	.15
1388	6¢ Elephant Herd	2.50	....	....	....	....	....	.20	.15
1389	6¢ Haida Canoe	2.50	....	....	....	....	....	.20	.15
1390	6¢ Reptiles	2.50	....	....	....	....	....	.20	.15
1391	6¢ Maine Statehood	1.75	4.00	7.25(50)	1.00	.70	.70	.20	.15
1392	6¢ Wildlife—Buffalo	1.75	4.00	7.25(50)	1.00	.70	.70	.20	.15

1393, 1401 1393D 1394 1395, 1402 1396

1397 1398 1399 1400

1970-74 REGULAR ISSUE

SCOTT NO.	DESCRIPTION	FIRST DAY COVERS SING.	FIRST DAY COVERS PL.BLK.	MINT SHEET	MAIL EARLY	ZIP	PLATE BLOCK	UNUSED F/NH	USED
1393/1400	6¢-21¢ cpl., 8 vars., (No #1395)	....	....	....	....	12.00	2.40	1.00	
1393	6¢ Dwight Eisenhower	1.75	4.00	14.50(100)	1.00	.70	.70	.20	.15
1393a	6¢ booklet pane of 8	2.75	....	....	....	....	....	1.65	....
1393ae	6¢ test gum	90.00	....	....	....	....	....	1.90	....
1393b	6¢ b. p. of 5—Slogan IV or V	3.75	....	....	....	....	....	1.00	....
1393D	7¢ Benjamin Franklin (1972) .	1.75	4.00	17.75(100)	1.10	.80	.80	.20	.15
1394	8¢ Ike—black, blue, red (1971)	1.75	4.00	21.75(100)	1.30	1.00	1.10	.25	.15
1395	Same, deep claret bklt.sgl. (1971)	2.50	....	....	....	....	....	.45	.15
1395a	8¢ booklet pane of 8	2.50	....	....	....	....	....	2.25	....
1395b	8¢ booklet pane of 6	2.25	....	....	....	....	....	1.75	....
1395c	8¢ b. pane of 4, VI & VII (1972)	2.00	....	....	....	....	....	1.40	....
1395d	8¢ b. pane of 7, II or V (1972)	2.50	....	....	....	....	....	2.00	....
1396	8¢ Postal Service Emblem (1971)	1.75	4.00	21.75(100)	1.20	1.00	3.00(12)	.25	.15
1397	14¢ Fiorello LaGuardia (1972)	1.75	4.00	33.2500)	2.00	1.40	1.50	.35	.15
1398	16¢ Ernie Pyle (1971)	2.50	4.50	37.00(100)	2.20	1.65	1.75	.40	.15
1399	18¢ Elizabeth Blackwell (1974)	2.00	4.25	45.00(100)	2.90	1.90	2.00	.50	.15
1400	21¢ Amadeo P. Giannini (1973)	2.50	4.50	50.00(100)	3.40	2.35	2.45	.55	.30

1970-71 COIL STAMPS—Perf. 10 Vertically

SCOTT NO.	DESCRIPTION	SING.	L. PR.	MINT SHEET	MAIL EARLY	ZIP	L.PR.	UNUSED F/NH	USED
1401	6¢ Dwight Eisenhower	1.75	2.75	....	....	....	.55	.20	.15
1402	8¢ Eisenhower, claret (1971)	1.75	2.75	....	....	....	.60	.25	.15

U.S. Postage #1405-1418a

1405

1406

1407

1408

1409

1970 COMMEMORATIVES

SCOTT NO.	DESCRIPTION	FIRST DAY COVERS SING.	FIRST DAY COVERS PL.BLK.	MINT SHEET	MAIL EARLY	ZIP	PLATE BLOCK	UNUSED F/NH	USED
1405	6¢ Edgar L. Master—Poet ..	1.75	4.00	14.00(50)	1.00	.70	.70	.20	.15
1406	6¢ Woman Suffrage	1.75	4.00	14.00(50)	1.00	.70	.70	.20	.15
1407	6¢ South Carolina Tercentenary	1.75	4.00	14.00(50)	1.00	.70	.70	.20	.15
1408	6¢ Stone Mountain Memorial	1.75	4.00	14.00(50)	1.00	.70	.70	.20	.15
1409	6¢ Fort Snelling	1.75	4.00	14.00(50)	1.00	.70	.70	.20	.15

1410

1411

1412

1413

SCOTT NO.	DESCRIPTION	FIRST DAY COVERS SING.	FIRST DAY COVERS PL.BLK.	MINT SHEET	MAIL EARLY	ZIP	PLATE BLOCK	UNUSED F/NH	USED
1410-13	Anti-Pollution, 4 Varieties, attd.	5.00	7.00	13.50(50)	2.50	1.75	3.35(10)	1.35	1.25
1410	6¢ Globe & Wheat	2.50	....	....	....	....	....	.25	.15
1411	6¢ Globe & City	2.50	....	....	....	....	....	.25	.15
1412	6¢ Globe & Bluegill	2.50	....	....	....	....	....	.25	.15
1413	6¢ Globe & Seagull	2.50	....	....	....	....	....	.25	.15

1414

1415

1416

1417

1418

SCOTT NO.	DESCRIPTION	FIRST DAY COVERS SING.	FIRST DAY COVERS PL.BLK.	MINT SHEET	MAIL EARLY	ZIP	PLATE BLOCK	UNUSED F/NH	USED
1414	6¢ Nativity	1.75	....	7.25(50)	1.15	.75	1.50(8)	.20	.15
1415-18	Christmas Toys, 4 Varieties, attached	5.50	....	30.00(50)	4.40	2.95	6.25(8)	2.75	2.25
1415	6¢ Locomotive	3.00	....	....	....	....	....	.50	.15
1416	6¢ Horse	3.00	....	....	....	....	....	.50	.15
1417	6¢ Tricycle	3.00	....	....	....	....	....	.50	.15
1418	6¢ Doll Carriage	3.00	....	....	....	....	....	.50	.15

Precancelled

SCOTT NO.	DESCRIPTION	FIRST DAY COVERS SING.	FIRST DAY COVERS PL.BLK.	MINT SHEET	MAIL EARLY	ZIP	PLATE BLOCK	UNUSED F/NH	USED
1414a	6¢ Nativity (precancelled) ...	12.00	....	8.50(50)	1.20	.85	2.75(8)	.20	.15
1415a-18a	Christmas Toys, precancelled 4 varieties attached	27.50	....	45.00(50)	7.50	5.50	9.50(8)	4.25	3.75
1415a	6¢ Locomotive	16.50	....	....	....	....	....	1.00	.20
1416a	6¢ Horse	16.50	....	....	....	....	....	1.00	.20
1417a	6¢ Tricycle	16.50	....	....	....	....	....	1.00	.20
1418a	6¢ Doll Carriage	16.50	....	....	....	....	....	1.00	.20

NOTE: Unused precancels are with original gum while used are without gum.

U.S. Postage #1419-1430

1419

1420

1421

HONORING U.S. SERVICEMEN PRISONERS OF WAR MISSING AND KILLED IN ACTION UNITED 6¢ STATES
1422

1423

1424

SCOTT NO.	DESCRIPTION	FIRST DAY COVERS SING.	PL.BLK.	MINT SHEET	MAIL EARLY	ZIP	PLATE BLOCK	UNUSED F/NH	USED
1419	6¢ U.N. 25th Anniversary	1.75	4.00	7.25(50)	1.00	.70	.70	.20	.15
1420	6¢ Pilgrim Landing......................	1.75	4.00	7.25(50)	1.00	.70	.70	.20	.15
1421-22	D.A.V. Servicemen, 2 Varieties, attached	2.00	3.75	9.75(50)	1.65	1.15	1.75	.45	.35
1421	6¢ Disabled Veterans..................	1.75	......	......	......	......	......	.20	.15
1422	6¢ Prisoners of War....................	1.75	......	......	......	......	......	.20	.15

1971 COMMEMORATIVES

SCOTT NO.	DESCRIPTION	FIRST DAY COVERS SING.	PL.BLK.	MINT SHEET	MAIL EARLY	ZIP	PLATE BLOCK	UNUSED F/NH	USED
1423-45	**6¢-8¢, 23 varieties, complete ..**	......	......	......	......	......	......	**5.50**	**3.25**
1423	6¢ Sheep	1.75	4.00	7.25(50)	1.00	.70	.70	.20	.15
1424	6¢ General D. MacArthur............	1.75	4.00	7.25(50)	1.00	.70	.70	.20	.15

1425

1426

1427

1428

1429

1430

SCOTT NO.	DESCRIPTION	FIRST DAY COVERS SING.	PL.BLK.	MINT SHEET	MAIL EARLY	ZIP	PLATE BLOCK	UNUSED F/NH	USED
1425	6¢ Blood Donors	1.75	4.00	7.25(50)	1.00	.70	.70	.20	.15
1426	8¢ Missouri Statehood................	1.75	4.00	10.25(50)	.95(4)	.95	2.75(12)	.25	.15
1427-30	Wildlife Conservation 4 vars., att'd.	3.75	5.50	7.75(32)	1.45	1.10	1.20	1.10	.95
1427	8¢ Trout	2.50	......	......	......	......	......	.25	.15
1428	8¢ Alligator.................................	2.50	......	......	......	......	......	.25	.15
1429	8¢ Polar Bear..............................	2.50	......	......	......	......	......	.25	.15
1430	8¢ Condor	2.50	......	......	......	......	......	.25	.15

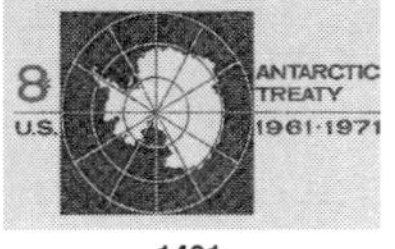

1431

1433

1434

1435

FIRST DAY COVERS: First Day Covers are envelopes cancelled on the "First Day of Issue" of the stamp used on the envelope. Usually they also contain a picture (cachet) on the left side designed to go with the theme of the stamp. From 1935 to 1949, prices listed are for cacheted, addressed covers. From 1950 to date, prices are for cacheted, unaddressed covers.

U.S. Postage #1431-1447

1432

1436

1437

1438

1439

SCOTT NO.	DESCRIPTION	FIRST DAY COVERS SING.	FIRST DAY COVERS PL.BLK.	MINT SHEET	MAIL EARLY	ZIP	PLATE BLOCK	UNUSED F/NH	USED
1431	8¢ Antarctic Treaty	1.75	4.00	10.25(50)	1.50	.95	1.00	.25	.15
1432	8¢ American Revolution	1.75	4.00	11.50(50)	1.60	1.10	1.20	.25	.15
1433	8¢ John Sloan—Artist	1.75	4.00	10.25(50)	1.50	.95	1.00	.25	.15
1434-35	Space Achievements, 2 varieties, attached	2.00	4.50	10.25(50)	1.50	1.00	1.10	.55	.40
1434	8¢ Moon, Earth, Sun & Landing Craft	1.75	......	......	......	......	......	.25	.15
1435	8¢ Lunar Rover	1.75	......	......	......	......	......	.25	.15
1436	8¢ Emilly Dickinson	1.75	4.00	10.25(50)	1.50	.95	1.00	.25	.15
1437	8¢ San Juan	1.75	4.00	10.25(50)	1.50	.95	1.00	.25	.15
1438	8¢ Drug Addiction	1.75	4.00	10.25(50)	1.50	.95	1.45(6)	.25	.15
1439	8¢ CARE	1.75	4.00	10.25(50)	1.50	.95	1.90(8)	.25	.15

1440

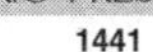

1441

1442

1444

1445

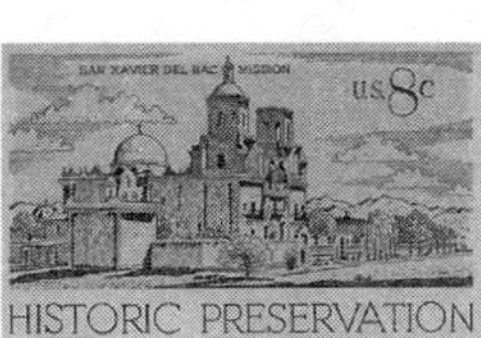

1443

1446

1447

SCOTT NO.	DESCRIPTION	FIRST DAY COVERS SING.	FIRST DAY COVERS PL.BLK.	MINT SHEET	MAIL EARLY	ZIP	PLATE BLOCK	UNUSED F/NH	USED
1440-43	Historic Preservation, 4 varieties attached	3.75	5.50	7.75(32)	1.45	1.10	1.20	1.10	.90
1440	8¢ Decatur House	2.50	......	......	......	......	......	.25	.15
1441	8¢ Whaling Ship	2.50	......	......	......	......	......	.25	.15
1442	8¢ Cable Car	2.50	......	......	......	......	......	.25	.15
1443	8¢ Mission	2.50	......	......	......	......	......	.25	.15
1444	8¢ Christmas Nativity	1.75	4.00	10.25(50)	1.05(4)	1.05	2.75(12)	.25	.15
1445	8¢ Christmas Partridge	1.75	4.00	10.25(50)	1.05(4)	1.05	2.75(12)	.25	.15

1972 COMMEMORATIVES

SCOTT NO.	DESCRIPTION	FIRST DAY COVERS SING.	FIRST DAY COVERS PL.BLK.	MINT SHEET	MAIL EARLY	ZIP	PLATE BLOCK	UNUSED F/NH	USED
1446-74	**29 varieties, complete**	......	......	......	......	......	......	**7.00**	**4.20**
1446	8¢ Sidney Lanier—Poet	1.75	4.00	10.25(50)	1.50	1.00	1.10	.25	.15
1447	8¢ Peace Corps	1.75	4.00	10.25(50)	1.50	1.00	1.65	.25	.15

SE-TENANTS: Beginning with the 1964 Christmas issue (#1254-57), the United States has issued numerous Se-Tenant stamps covering a wide variety of subjects. Se-Tenants are issues where two or more different stamp designs are produc on the same sheet in pair, strip or block form. Mint stamps are usually collected in attached blocks, etc.; used are genera saved as single stamps.

U.S. Postage #1448-1463a

1448-51

1452

1454

1453

1455

1972 NATIONAL PARKS CENTENNIAL

SCOTT NO.	DESCRIPTION	FIRST DAY COVERS SING.	FIRST DAY COVERS PL.BLK.	MINT SHEET	MAIL EARLY	ZIP	PLATE BLOCK	UNUSED F/NH	USED
1448-54	**2¢-15¢ complete, 7 varieties ....**	......	......	......	......	......	......	**1.50**	**.90**
1448-51	Cape Hatteras, 4 varieties, attached	1.75	2.50	11.00(100)	1.40(8)	.75	.85	.75	.45
1448	2¢ Ship's Hull	......	......	......	......	......	......	.15	.10
1449	2¢ Lighthouse	......	......	......	......	......	......	.15	.10
1450	2¢ Three Seagulls	......	......	......	......	......	......	.15	.10
1451	2¢ Two Seagulls	......	......	......	......	......	......	.15	.10
1452	6¢ Wolf Trap Farm Park	1.75	4.00	7.25(50)	1.00	.70	.70	.20	.15
1453	8¢ Yellowstone Park	1.75	4.00	7.50(32)	1.50	1.00	1.10	.25	.15
1454	15¢ Mt. McKinley	1.75	4.00	19.25(50)	2.45	1.65	1.75	.45	.25

1972 COMMEMORATIVES

SCOTT NO.	DESCRIPTION	FIRST DAY COVERS SING.	FIRST DAY COVERS PL.BLK.	MINT SHEET	MAIL EARLY	ZIP	PLATE BLOCK	UNUSED F/NH	USED
1455	8¢ Family Planning	1.75	4.00	10.25(50)	1.50	1.00	1.10	.25	.15

1456 1457 1458 1459

SCOTT NO.	DESCRIPTION	FIRST DAY COVERS SING.	FIRST DAY COVERS PL.BLK.	MINT SHEET	MAIL EARLY	ZIP	PLATE BLOCK	UNUSED F/NH	USED
1456-59	Colonial Craftsmen, 4 varieties, attached....................	3.75	4.75	12.00(50)	......	1.00	1.25	1.05	.90
1456-59	Bicent, Emblem block	......	......	1.50	......	......	......	......	
1456	8¢ Glassmaker	2.25	......	......	......	......	......	.25	.15
1457	8¢ Silversmith	2.25	......	......	......	......	......	.25	.15
1458	8¢ Wigmaker	2.25	......	......	......	......	......	.25	.15
1459	8¢ Hatter	2.25	......	......	......	......	......	.25	.15

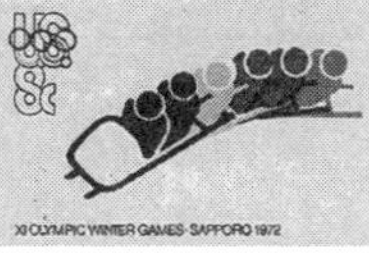

1460 1461 1462 1463

SCOTT NO.	DESCRIPTION	FIRST DAY COVERS SING.	FIRST DAY COVERS PL.BLK.	MINT SHEET	MAIL EARLY	ZIP	PLATE BLOCK	UNUSED F/NH	USED
1460	6¢ Olympics—Cycling	2.10	4.25	8.00(50)	1.05	.70	1.75(10)	.20	.15
1461	8¢ Olympics—Bob Sled Racing	2.10	4.25	10.25(50)	1.35	.90	2.75(10)	.25	.15
1462	15¢ Olympics—Foot Racing	2.10	4.25	19.25(50)	2.50	1.75	4.50(10)	.45	.35
1463	8¢ Parent-Teacher Association ..	1.75	4.00	10.25(50)	1.50	1.00	1.10	.25	.15
1463a	Same, Reversed Plate Number ..	1.75	4.00	10.75(50)	......	......	1.20	......	......

1464 1465 1466

U.S. Postage #1464-1475

1467

1468

SCOTT NO.	DESCRIPTION	FIRST DAY COVERS SING.	FIRST DAY COVERS PL.BLK.	MINT SHEET	MAIL EARLY	ZIP	PLATE BLOCK	UNUSED F/NH	USED
1464-67	Wildlife conservation, 4 varieties attached	2.75	3.50	9.00(32)	1.50	1.00	1.25	1.05	.90
1464	8¢ Fur Seal	1.75	....	....	....	....	....	.25	.15
1465	8¢ Cardinal	1.75	....	....	....	....	....	.25	.15
1466	8¢ Brown Pelican	1.75	....	....	....	....	....	.25	.15
1467	8¢ Bighorn Sheep	1.75	....	....	....	....	....	.25	.15
1468	8¢ Mail Order Business	1.75	4.00	10.25(50)	1.00(4)	1.00	3.00(12)	.25	.15

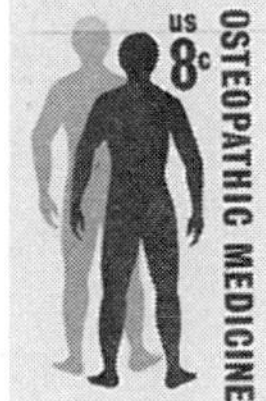

1469

1470

1471

1472

SCOTT NO.	DESCRIPTION	FIRST DAY COVERS SING.	FIRST DAY COVERS PL.BLK.	MINT SHEET	MAIL EARLY	ZIP	PLATE BLOCK	UNUSED F/NH	USED
1469	8¢ Osteopathic Medicine ...	2.00	4.25	10.25(50)	1.50	1.05	1.70(6)	.25	.15
1470	8¢ Tom Sawyer—Folklore .	1.75	4.00	10.25(50)	1.50	1.00	1.10(4)	.25	.15
1471	8¢ Christmas—Virgin Mother	1.75	4.00	10.25(50)	1.00	1.00	3.00(12)	.25	.15
1472	8¢ Christmas—Santa Claus	1.75	4.00	10.25(50)	1.00	1.00	3.00(12)	.25	.15

1473

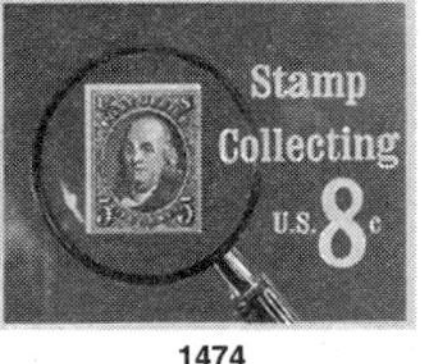

1474

1475

SCOTT NO.	DESCRIPTION	FIRST DAY COVERS SING.	FIRST DAY COVERS PL.BLK.	MINT SHEET	MAIL EARLY	ZIP	PLATE BLOCK	UNUSED F/NH	USED
1473	8¢ Pharmacy	2.25	4.50	10.25(50)	1.50	1.00	1.10(4)	.25	.15
1474	8¢ Stamp Collecting	2.00	4.25	9.50(40)	1.50	1.00	1.10(4)	.25	.15

1973 COMMEMORATIVES

SCOTT NO.	DESCRIPTION	FIRST DAY COVERS SING.	FIRST DAY COVERS PL.BLK.	MINT SHEET	MAIL EARLY	ZIP	PLATE BLOCK	UNUSED F/NH	USED
1475-1508	**34 varieties, complete .....**	....	....	....	....	....	....	**7.50**	**4.25**
1475	8¢ "Love"	2.25	5.00	10.25(50)	1.50	1.05	1.70(6)	.25	.15

1476 1477 1478 1479 1480 1481 1482 1483

U.S. Postage #1476-1488

SCOTT NO.	DESCRIPTION	FIRST DAY COVERS SING.	FIRST DAY COVERS PL.BLK.	MINT SHEET	MAIL EARLY	ZIP	PLATE BLOCK	UNUSED F/NH	USED
	COLONIAL COMMUNICATIONS								
1476	8¢ Pamphlet Printing	1.75	4.00	10.25(50)	1.50	1.00	1.10	.25	.15
1477	8¢ Posting Broadside	1.75	4.00	10.25(50)	1.50	1.00	1.10	.25	.15
1477	8¢ Bicent. Emblem block	....	....	....	1.50	....	....	....	....
1478	8¢ Colonial Post Rider	1.75	4.00	10.25(50)	1.50	1.00	1.10	.25	.15
1478	8¢ Bicent. Emblem block	....	....	....	1.50	....	....	....	....
1479	8¢ Drummer & Soldiers	1.75	4.00	10.25(50)	1.50	1.00	1.10	.25	.15
1479	8¢ Bicent. Emblem block	....	....	....	1.50	....	....	....	....
1480-83	Boston Tea Party, 4 varieties, attached	4.50	6.50	10.25(50)	1.60	1.10	1.20	1.05	.90
1480-83	8¢ Bicent. Emblem block	....	....	....	1.60	1.85	....	....	....
1480	8¢ Throwing Tea	2.25	....	....	....	....	....	.25	.15
1481	8¢ Ship	2.25	....	....	....	....	....	.25	.15
1482	8¢ Rowboats	2.25	....	....	....	....	....	.25	.15
1483	8¢ Rowboats & Dock	2.25	....	....	....	....	....	.25	.15

1484

1485

1488

1486

1487

SCOTT NO.	DESCRIPTION	FIRST DAY COVERS SING.	FIRST DAY COVERS PL.BLK.	MINT SHEET	MAIL EARLY	ZIP	PLATE BLOCK	UNUSED F/NH	USED
	AMERICAN ARTS								
1484	8¢ George Gershwin—Composer	1.75	4.00	9.00(40)	(combo)	1.00	2.75(12)	.25	.15
1485	8¢ Robinson Jeffers—Poet	1.75	4.00	9.00(40)	(combo)	1.00	2.75(12)	.25	.15
1486	8¢ Henry O. Tanner—Artist	1.75	4.00	9.00(40)	(combo)	1.00	2.75(12)	.25	.15
1487	8¢ Willa Cather—Novelist	1.75	4.00	9.00(40)	(combo)	1.00	2.75(12)	.25	.15
1488	8¢ Nicolaus Copernicus	1.75	4.00	10.25(40)	1.50	1.00	1.10	.25	.15

1489

1490

1491

1492

1493

1494

1495

1496

1497

1498

U.S. Postage #1489-1508

SCOTT NO.	DESCRIPTION	FIRST DAY COVERS SING.	FIRST DAY COVERS PL.BLK.	MINT SHEET	MAIL EARLY	ZIP	PLATE BLOCK	UNUSED F/NH	USED
	1973 POSTAL SERVICE EMPLOYEES								
1489-98	**10 varieties, attached, complete**	**6.50**	**......**	**18.00(50)**	**......**	**......**	**8.75(20)**	**2.50**	**2.50**
1489-98	**Set of singles, complete ....**	**22.00**	**......**	**......**	**......**	**......**	**......**	**2.35**	**1.40**
1489	8¢ Window Clerk	2.25	......	......	......	......	......	.25	.15
1490	8¢ Mail Pickup	2.25	......	......	......	......	......	.25	.15
1491	8¢ Conveyor Belt	2.25	......	......	......	......	......	.25	.15
1492	8¢ Sacking Parcels.......................	2.25	......	......	......	......	......	.25	.15
1493	8¢ Mail Cancelling	2.25	......	......	......	......	......	.25	.15
1494	8¢ Manual Sorting	2.25	......	......	......	......	......	.25	.15
1495	8¢ Machine Sorting	2.25	......	......	......	......	......	.25	.15
1496	8¢ Loading Truck	2.25	......	......	......	......	......	.25	.15
1497	8¢ Letter Carrier...........................	2.25	......	......	......	......	......	.25	.15
1498	8¢ Rural Delivery	2.25	......	......	......	......	......	.25	.15

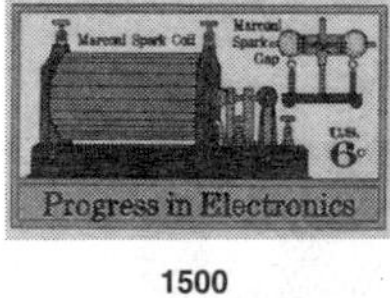

1500

1501

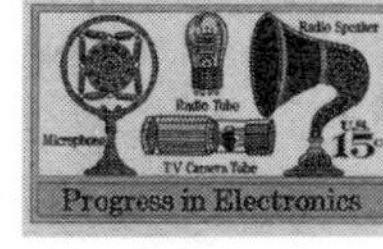

1502

1499

1504

1505

1506

1503

SCOTT NO.	DESCRIPTION	FIRST DAY COVERS SING.	FIRST DAY COVERS PL.BLK.	MINT SHEET	MAIL EARLY	ZIP	PLATE BLOCK	UNUSED F/NH	USED
	1973 COMMEMORATIVES								
1499	8¢ Harry S. Truman	1.75	4.00	7.50(32)	......	......	1.10	.25	.15
1500	6¢ Electronics	1.75	4.00	7.25(50)	1.00	.70	.70	.20	.15
1501	8¢ Electronics	1.75	4.00	10.25(50)	1.50	1.00	1.10	.25	.15
1502	15¢ Electronics	1.75	4.00	18.75(50)	2.60	1.75	1.85	.45	.30
1503	8¢ Lyndon B. Johnson	1.75	4.00	7.50(32)	......	......	3.00(12)	.25	.15
	1973-74 RURAL AMERICA								
1504	8¢ Angus Cattle	1.75	4.00	10.25(50)	1.50	1.00	1.10	.25	.15
1505	10¢ Chautauqua (1974)..............	1.75	4.00	13.00(50)	1.80	1.20	1.30	.30	.15
1506	10¢ Winter Wheat (1974)............	1.75	4.00	13.00(50)	1.80	1.20	1.30	.30	.15

1507

1508

1509, 1519

We hold these Truths...
UNITED STATES 10¢

1510, 1520

1511

1518

SCOTT NO.	DESCRIPTION	FIRST DAY COVERS SING.	FIRST DAY COVERS PL.BLK.	MINT SHEET	MAIL EARLY	ZIP	PLATE BLOCK	UNUSED F/NH	USED
	1973 CHRISTMAS								
1507	8¢ Madonna................................	1.75	3.25	18.00(50)	1.00(4)	1.00	3.00(12)	.25	.15
1508	8¢ Christmas Tree	1.75	3.25	18.00(50)	1.00(4)	1.00	3.00(12)	.25	.15

U.S. Postage #1509-1529

SCOTT NO.	DESCRIPTION	FIRST DAY COVERS SING.	FIRST DAY COVERS PL.BLK.	MINT SHEET	MAIL EARLY	ZIP	PLATE BLOCK	UNUSED F/NH	USED
	1973-74 REGULAR ISSUES								
1509	10¢ Crossed Flags	1.75	4.00	33.25(100)	....	....	7.25(20)	.35	.15
1510	10¢ Jefferson Memorial	1.75	4.00	28.00(100)	1.80	1.20	1.30	.30	.15
1510b	10¢ booklet pane of 5-Sl. VIII	1.95	....	....	....	....	....	1.60	....
1510c	10¢ booklet pane of 8	1.95	....	....	....	....	....	2.50	....
1510d	10¢ booklet pane of 6 (1974)	1.95	....	....	....	....	....	6.50	....
1511	10¢ Zip Code Theme (1974)	1.75	4.00	26.50(100)	1.80	1.20	2.30(8)	.30	.15

BOOKLET PANE SLOGANS

VI—Stamps in This Book.... **VII—This Book Contains 25...** **VIII—Paying Bills....**

COIL STAMPS Perf. 10 Vertically

SCOTT NO.	DESCRIPTION	FIRST DAY COVERS SING.	LINE PR	MINT SHEET	MAIL EARLY	ZIP	LINE PR	UNUSED F/NH	USED
1518	6.3¢ Liberty Bell	1.75	2.75	....	....	....	.65	.20	.15
1519	10¢ Crossed Flags	1.75	....	....	....	....	....	.35	.15
1520	10¢ Jefferson Memorial	1.75	2.75	....	....	....	.70	.30	.15

1525

1526

1527

1528

1529

1974 COMMEMORATIVES

SCOTT NO.	DESCRIPTION	FIRST DAY COVERS SING.	FIRST DAY COVERS PL.BLK.	MINT SHEET	MAIL EARLY	ZIP	PLATE BLOCK	UNUSED F/NH	USED
1525-52	**28 varieties, complete**	......	......	....	....	....	....	**8.15**	**4.00**
1525	10¢ Veterans of Foreign Wars	1.75	4.00	13.00(50)	1.80	1.20	1.30	.30	.15
1526	10¢ Robert Frost	1.75	4.00	13.00(50)	1.80	1.20	1.30	.30	.15
1527	10¢ Environment—Expo '74	1.75	4.00	13.00(40)	(combo)	1.20	3.75(12)	.30	.15
1528	10¢ Horse Racing	1.75	4.00	13.00(50)	1.20	1.20	3.75(12)	.30	.15
1529	10¢ Skylab Project	1.75	4.00	13.00(50)	1.80	1.20	1.30	.30	.15

1530

1531

1532

1533

MAIL EARLY BLOCKS: Contain the inscription "Mail Early in the Day", a post office slogan designed to encourage their patrons to post their mail early in the morning. Mail Early Blocks are usually blocks of 6 since they come from the center of the sheet margin and six presents a balanced appearance.

U.S. Postage #1530-1547

1534

1535

1536

1537

1974 UNIVERSAL POSTAL UNION

SCOTT NO.	DESCRIPTION	FIRST DAY COVERS SING.	FIRST DAY COVERS PL.BLK.	MINT SHEET	MAIL EARLY	ZIP	PLATE BLOCK	UNUSED F/NH	USED
1530-37	**8 varieties, attached**	**4.25**	....	**10.50(32)**	**(combo)**	**1.80(6)**	**4.75(16)**	**2.70(8)**	**2.70**
1530-37	**Set of singles, complete**	**13.50**	....	....	....	....	....	**2.30**	**1.55**
1530	10¢ Raphael	1.75	....	....	....	....	....	.30	.20
1531	10¢ Hokusai	1.75	....	....	....	....	....	.30	.20
1532	10¢ J.F. Peto	1.75	....	....	....	....	....	.30	.20
1533	10¢ J.E. Liotard	1.75	....	....	....	....	....	.30	.20
1534	10¢ G. Terborch	1.75	....	....	....	....	....	.30	.20
1535	10¢ J.B.S. Chardin	1.75	....	....	....	....	....	.30	.20
1536	10¢ T. Gainsborough	1.75	....	....	....	....	....	.30	.20
1537	10¢ F. de Goya	1.75	....	....	....	....	....	.30	.20

1538

1539

1540

1541

1974 COMMEMORATIVES

SCOTT NO.	DESCRIPTION	FIRST DAY COVERS SING.	FIRST DAY COVERS PL.BLK.	MINT SHEET	MAIL EARLY	ZIP	PLATE BLOCK	UNUSED F/NH	USED
1538-41	Mineral Heritage 4 varieties, attd	3.50	5.00	11.50(48)	1.60	1.10	1.20	1.10	1.10
1538	10¢ Petrified Wood	2.25	....	....	....	....	....	.25	.15
1539	10¢ Tourmaline	2.25	....	....	....	....	....	.25	.15
1540	10¢ Amethyst	2.25	....	....	....	....	....	.25	.15
1541	10¢ Rhodochrosite	2.25	....	....	....	....	....	.25	.15

1542

1543

1544

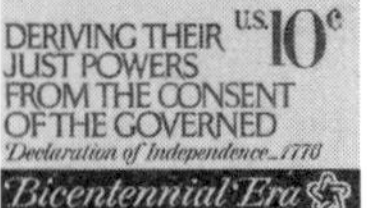

1545

1546

1547

SCOTT NO.	DESCRIPTION	FIRST DAY COVERS SING.	FIRST DAY COVERS PL.BLK.	MINT SHEET	MAIL EARLY	ZIP	PLATE BLOCK	UNUSED F/NH	USED
1542	10¢ Fort Harrod Bicentennial	1.75	4.00	13.00(50)	1.80	1.20	1.30	.30	.15
1543-46	Continental Congress, 4 varieties, attached	2.75	3.75	13.00(50)	1.60	1.20	1.30	1.20	1.00
1543-46	10¢ Bicentennial Emblem block..	....	....	....	1.70	....	....	....	....
1543	10¢ Carpenters' Hall	1.75	....	....	....	....	....	.25	.15
1544	10¢ Quote—First Congress	1.75	....	....	....	....	....	.25	.15
1545	10¢ Quote—Decl. of Independence	1.75	....	....	....	....	....	.25	.15
1546	10¢ Independence Hall	1.75	....	....	....	....	....	.25	.15
1547	10¢ Energy Conservation	1.75	4.00	13.00(50)	1.80	1.20	1.30	.30	.15

U.S. Postage #1548-1562

SCOTT NO.	DESCRIPTION	FIRST DAY COVERS SING.	FIRST DAY COVERS PL.BLK.	MINT SHEET	MAIL EARLY	ZIP	PLATE BLOCK	UNUSED F/NH	USED

1548

1549

1550

SCOTT NO.	DESCRIPTION	FIRST DAY COVERS SING.	FIRST DAY COVERS PL.BLK.	MINT SHEET	MAIL EARLY	ZIP	PLATE BLOCK	UNUSED F/NH	USED
1548	10¢ Sleepy Hollow	1.75	4.00	13.00(50)	1.80	1.20	1.30	.30	.15
1549	10¢ Retarded Children	1.75	4.00	13.00(50)	1.80	1.20	1.30	.30	.15

1551

1552

SCOTT NO.	DESCRIPTION	FIRST DAY COVERS SING.	FIRST DAY COVERS PL.BLK.	MINT SHEET	MAIL EARLY	ZIP	PLATE BLOCK	UNUSED F/NH	USED
1550	10¢ Christmas—Angel	1.75	4.00	13.00(50)	1.80	1.20	3.00	.30	.15
1551	10¢ Christmas—Currier & Ives ..	1.75	4.00	13.00(50)	1.20	1.20	3.00	.30	.15
1552	10¢ Christmas—Dove of Peace	1.75	4.00	13.00(50)	....	....	6.25	.30	.15
1552	Same	....	....	....	....	....	3.00(12)	....	....

1553

1554

1555

PIONEER ★ JUPITER

US 10c

1556

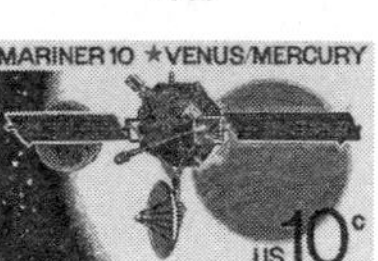

1557

1558

1975 COMMEMORATIVES

SCOTT NO.	DESCRIPTION	FIRST DAY COVERS SING.	FIRST DAY COVERS PL.BLK.	MINT SHEET	MAIL EARLY	ZIP	PLATE BLOCK	UNUSED F/NH	USED
1553-80	**8¢-10¢, 28 varieties, complete..**	....	....	....	....	....	....	**8.10**	**4.00**
1553	10¢ Benjamin West—Arts	1.75	4.00	13.00(50)	1.80	1.20	3.00(10)	.30	.15
1554	10¢ Paul Dunbar—Arts	1.75	4.00	13.00(50)	1.80	1.20	3.00(10)	.30	.15
1555	10¢ D.W. Griffith—Arts	1.75	4.00	13.00(50)	1.80	1.20	1.30	.30	.15
1556	10¢ Pioneer 10..........................	1.75	4.00	13.00(50)	1.90	1.50	1.40	.35	.15
1557	10¢ Mariner 10..........................	1.75	4.00	13.00(50)	1.90	1.30	1.40	.35	.15
1558	10¢ Collective Bargaining	1.75	4.00	13.00(50)	1.80	1.20	2.25(8)	.30	.15

1559

Salem Poor Gallant Soldier

1560

1561

1562

SCOTT NO.	DESCRIPTION	FIRST DAY COVERS SING.	FIRST DAY COVERS PL.BLK.	MINT SHEET	MAIL EARLY	ZIP	PLATE BLOCK	UNUSED F/NH	USED
1559	8¢ Sybil Ludington	1.75	4.00	10.25(50)	1.20	1.00	2.40(10)	.25	.15
1560	10¢ Salem Poor	1.75	4.00	13.00(50)	1.60	1.10	2.75(10)	.30	.15
1561	10¢ Haym Salomon	1.75	4.00	13.00(50)	1.60	1.10	2.75(10)	.30	.15
1562	18¢ Peter Francisco	1.75	4.00	22.25(50)	3.25	2.00	5.75(10)	.50	.20

U.S. Postage #1563-76

1563

1564

1565

1566

1567

1568

SCOTT NO.	DESCRIPTION	FIRST DAY COVERS SING.	FIRST DAY COVERS PL.BLK.	MINT SHEET	MAIL EARLY	ZIP	PLATE BLOCK	UNUSED F/NH	USED
1563	10¢ Lexington-Concord	1.75	4.00	9.50(40)	(combo)	1.10	3.00(12)	.30	.15
1564	10¢ Battle of Bunker Hill	1.75	4.00	9.50(40)	(combo)	1.10	3.00(12)	.30	.15
1565-68	Military Uniforms, 4 varieties attd.	2.75	3.75	14.00(50)	1.40(4)	1.40	3.75(12)	1.20	1.00
1565	10¢ Continental Army	1.75	....	....	....	....	....	.25	.15
1566	10¢ Continental Navy	1.75	....	....	....	....	....	.25	.15
1567	10¢ Continental Marines	1.75	....	....	....	....	....	.25	.15
1568	10¢ American Militia	1.75	....	....	....	....	....	.25	.15

1569

1570

SCOTT NO.	DESCRIPTION	SING.	PL.BLK.	MINT SHEET	MAIL EARLY	ZIP	PLATE BLOCK	UNUSED F/NH	USED
1569-70	Apollo-Soyuz Mission, 2 varieties, attached.....................	3.00	4.50	6.50(24)	(combo)	1.10	3.50(12)	.60	.55
1569	10¢ Docked	2.25	....	....	....	....	....	.25	.15
1570	10¢ Docking................................	2.25	....	....	....	....	....	.25	.15

1571

1572

1573

1574

1575

1576

SCOTT NO.	DESCRIPTION	SING.	PL.BLK.	MINT SHEET	MAIL EARLY	ZIP	PLATE BLOCK	UNUSED F/NH	USED
1571	10¢ International Women's Year	1.75	4.00	13.00(50)	1.10	1.10	1.75(6)	.30	1.5
1572-75	Postal Service Bicentennial 4 varieties, attached....................	2.75	3.75	13.00(50)	1.10(4)	1.10	3.75(12)	1.10	1.00
1572	10¢ Stagecoach & Trailer............	1.75	....	....	....	....	....	.25	.15
1573	10¢ Locomotives	1.75	....	....	....	....	....	.25	.15
1574	10¢ Airplanes..............................	1.75	....	....	....	....	....	.25	.15
1575	10¢ Satellite................................	1.75	....	....	....	....	....	.25	.15
1576	10¢ World Peace through Law....	1.75	4.00	13.00(50)	1.60	1.10	1.20	.30	.15

U.S. BICENTENNIAL: The U.S.P.S. issued stamps commemorating the 200th anniversary of the struggle for independence from 1775 through 1783. These include numbers: 1432, 1476-83, 1543-46, 1559-68, 1629-31, 1633-82, 1686-89, 1691-94, 1704, 1716-20, 1722, 1726, 1728-29, 1753, 1789, 1826, 1937-38, 1941, 2052 and C98.

U.S. Postage #1577-1585

SCOTT NO.	DESCRIPTION	FIRST DAY COVERS SING.	FIRST DAY COVERS PL.BLK.	MINT SHEET	MAIL EARLY	ZIP	PLATE BLOCK	UNUSED F/NH	USED

1577 1578

1579

1580

SCOTT NO.	DESCRIPTION	SING.	PL.BLK.	MINT SHEET	MAIL EARLY	ZIP	PLATE BLOCK	UNUSED F/NH	USED
1577-78	Banking & Commerce, 2 varieties, attached	2.50	3.75	11.00(40)	1.60	1.10	1.20	.55	.50
1577	10¢ Banking	1.75	....	....	....	....	....	.25	.15
1578	10¢ Commerce	1.75	....	....	....	....	....	.25	.15
1579	(10¢) Madonna	1.75	4.00	13.00(50)	1.10(4)	1.10	3.75(12)	.30	.15
1580	(10¢) Christmas Card	1.75	4.00	13.00(50)	1.10(4)	1.10	3.75(12)	.30	.15
1580b	(10¢) Christmas Card, pf.10-1/2x11	....	....	35.00(50)	3.00(4)	3.00	15.00(12)	.75	.30

1581, 1811 1582 1584 1585 1590, 1591, 1616

1592, 1617 1593 1594, 1816 1595, 1618 1596

1597, 1598, 1618C 1599, 1619 1603 1604 1605

1606 1608 1610 1611 1612

1975-81 AMERICANA ISSUE

SCOTT NO.	DESCRIPTION	SING.	PL.BLK.	MINT SHEET	MAIL EARLY	ZIP	PLATE BLOCK	UNUSED F/NH	USED
1581/1612	**1¢-$5, (no #1590, 1590a, 1595 or 1598) 19 varieties, complete**	**51.50**	....	....	....	....	**115.00**	**24.50**	**5.50**
1581	1¢ Inkwell & Quill (1977)	1.75	4.00	8.25(100)	1.00	.70	.70	.20	.15
1582	2¢ Speaker's Stand (1977)	1.75	4.00	8.25(100)	1.00	.70	.70	.20	.15
1584	3¢ Ballot Box (1977)	1.75	4.00	9.25(100)	1.00	.70	.70	.20	.15
1585	4¢ Books & Eyeglasses (1977)	1.75	4.00	10.50(100)	1.00	.60	.60	.20	.15

U.S. Postage #1590-1619

SCOTT NO.	DESCRIPTION	FIRST DAY COVERS SING.	PL.BLK.	MINT SHEET	MAIL EARLY	ZIP	PLATE BLOCK	UNUSED F/NH	USED
1590	9¢ Capitol, from bklt. p. (1977)	15.00	....	....	....	....	....	.40	.30
1590a	Same Perf 10 (1977)	15.00	....	....	....	....	....	31.50	15.00
1590, 1623	Attached Pair, from booklet pane	....	....	....	....	....	....	.75	....
1590a, 1623b	Attached Pair, Perf 10	....	....	....	....	....	....	32.50	....
1591	9¢ Capitol, grey paper	1.75	4.00	21.75(100)	1.60	1.10	1.10	.25	.15
1592	10¢ Justice (1977)	1.75	4.00	26.50(100)	1.80	1.20	1.30	.30	.15
1593	11¢ Printing Press	1.75	4.00	26.50(100)	1.80	1.20	1.30	.30	.15
1594	12¢ Torch (1981)	1.75	4.00	28.00(100)	2.60	2.00	2.10	.30	.15
1595	13¢ Liberty Bell from booklet p.	1.75	....	....	....	....	....	.35	.15
1595a	13¢ booklet pane of 6	2.25	....	....	....	....	....	2.25	....
1595b	13¢ booklet pane of 7—VIII	2.50	....	....	....	....	....	2.75	....
1595c	13¢ booklet pane of 8	2.50	....	....	....	....	....	2.75	....
1595d	13¢ booklet p. of 5—IX (1976)	1.75	....	....	....	....	....	2.25	....
	VIII—Paying Bills... IX—Collect Stamps...								
1596	13¢ Eagle & Shield..............	1.75	4.00	32.25(100)	1.25(4)	1.25	4.50(12)	.35	.15
1597	15¢ Fort McHenry Flag (1978)	1.75	4.00	38.00(100)	....	....	9.50(20)	.40	.15
1598	Same, from booklet pane (1978)	1.75	....	....	....	....	....	.60	.15
1598a	15¢ booklet pane of 8	3.00	....	....	....	....	....	5.00	....
1599	16¢ Statue of Liberty (1978)	1.75	4.00	51.75(100)	©4.10	2.40	2.50	.55	.15
1603	24¢ Old North Church	1.75	4.00	58.75(100)	6.50	2.75	2.75	.65	.15
1604	28¢ Fort Nisqually (1978)....	1.75	4.00	70.00(100)	©5.25	3.25	3.50	.75	.15
1605	29¢ Lighthouse (1978)	1.75	4.00	72.50(100)	©5.75	3.60	3.75	.80	.20
1606	30¢ School House (1979) ..	1.75	4.00	72.50(100)	©5.75	3.60	3.75	.80	.15
1608	50¢ "Betty" Lamp (1979)	2.50	5.25	112.50(100)	©5.75	5.75	6.00	1.40	.15
1610	$1 Rush Lamp (1979)	3.50	17.50	235.00(100)	©11.00	11.00	11.50	2.60	.15
1610c	same, candle flame inverted	....	....	....	....	....	....	17500.00	....
1611	$2 Kerosene Lamp (1978) ..	7.00	14.50	495.00(100)	©22.00	22.00	22.50	5.25	.70
1612	$5 Conductor's Lantern (1979)	15.00	31.50	1100.00(100)	©50.00	50.00	50.00	12.00	3.00

©—Copyright inscriptions replaced "Mail Early in the Day" inscriptions beginning in 1978; numbers 1599 and 1604-12 sheets all bear the Copyright inscription.

1613

1614

1615

1615C

1975-79 COIL STAMPS Perforated Vertically

							LINE PR.		
1613-19	**3.1¢-16¢, 9 varieties, complete**	....	....	....	....	....	**9.25**	**2.40**	**1.25**
1613	3.1¢ Guitar (1979)	1.75	2.75	....	....	....	.90	.20	.15
1614	7.7¢ Saxhorns (1976)	1.75	2.75	....	....	....	1.30	.30	.15
1615	7.9¢ Drum (1976)......................	1.75	2.75	....	....	....	.90	.30	.15
1615C	8.4¢ Piano (1978)	1.75	2.75	....	....	....	2.75	.30	.15
1616	9¢ Capitol (1976)	1.75	2.75	....	....	....	.90	.30	.15
1617	10¢ Justice (1977)	1.75	2.75	....	....	....	.90	.30	.15
1618	13¢ Liberty Bell	1.75	2.75	....	....	....	.90	.40	.15
1618C	15¢ Fort McHenry Flag (1978)....	1.75	....	....	....	....	....	.45	.15
1619	16¢ Statue of Liberty (1978)	1.75	2.75	....	....	....	1.40	.45	.30

COIL LINE PAIRS: are two connected coil stamps with a line the same color as the stamps printed between the two stamps. This line usually appears every twenty to thirty stamps on a roll depending on the issue.

U.S. Postage #1622-1682

SCOTT NO.	DESCRIPTION	FIRST DAY COVERS SING.	FIRST DAY COVERS PL.BLK.	MINT SHEET	MAIL EARLY	ZIP	PLATE BLOCK	UNUSED F/NH	USED

1622, 1625 1623, 1623b

1975-77 REGULAR ISSUES

SCOTT NO.	DESCRIPTION	FDC SING.	FDC PL.BLK.	MINT SHEET	MAIL EARLY	ZIP	PLATE BLOCK	UNUSED F/NH	USED
1622	13¢ Flag & Ind. Hall, 11x10-1/2 ..	1.75	4.00	35.00(100)	....	....	8.00(20)	.40	.15
1622c	Same, perf. 11 (1981)	....	....	160.00(100)	....	....	90.00(20)	1.00	....
1623	13¢ Flag & Capitol from booklet pane, perf. 11 x 10-1/2 (1977)	3.00	....	....	....	....	....	.35	.15
1623a	b. pane of 8, (1—1590, 7—1623)	45.00.......	....	....	....	....	2.50	....	
1623b	13¢ Flag & Capitol from booklet pane, perf. 10	1.75	....	....	....	....	....	.60	.55
1623c	b. pane of 8 (1—1590a, 7—1623b)	22.50	....	....	....	....	....	35.00	....

1975 COIL STAMP

SCOTT NO.	DESCRIPTION	FDC SING.	FDC PL.BLK.	MINT SHEET	MAIL EARLY	ZIP	PLATE BLOCK	UNUSED F/NH	USED
1625	13¢ Flag & Ind. Hall	1.75	....	....	....	....	....	.40	.15

1629 1630 1631

1632

1976 COMMEMORATIVES

SCOTT NO.	DESCRIPTION	FDC SING.	FDC PL.BLK.	MINT SHEET	MAIL EARLY	ZIP	PLATE BLOCK	UNUSED F/NH	USED
1629/1703	**(1629-32, 1683-85, 1690-1703) 21 varieties ....**	....	....	....	....	....	....	**8.75**	**2.75**
1629-31	Spirit of '76, 3 varieties, attached.	3.00	6.00	16.00(50)	(combo)	2.75(8)	4.50(12)	1.10	1.00
1629	13¢ Boy Drummer	2.00	....	....	....	....	....	.30	.15
1630	13¢ Older Drummer	2.00	....	....	....	....	....	.30	.15
1631	13¢ Fifer	2.00	....	....	....	....	....	.30	.15
1632	13¢ Interphil	1.75	4.00	18.75(50)	2.10	1.40	1.50	.40	.15

1976 BICENTENNIAL STATE FLAGS
Complete Set Printed in One Sheet of 50 Stamps

1633

1650

1633 *Delaware*
1634 *Pennsylvania*
1635 *New Jersey*
1636 *Georgia*
1637 *Connecticut*
1638 *Massachusetts*
1639 *Maryland*
1640 *South Carolina*
1641 *New Hampshire*
1642 *Virginia*
1643 *New York*
1644 *North Carolina*
1645 *Rhode Island*
1646 *Vermont*
1647 *Kentucky*
1648 *Tennessee*
1649 *Ohio*
1650 *Louisiana*
1651 *Indiana*
1652 *Mississippi*
1653 *Illinois*
1654 *Alabama*
1655 *Maine*
1656 *Missouri*
1657 *Arkansas*
1658 *Michigan*
1659 *Florida*
1660 *Texas*
1661 *Iowa*
1662 *Wisconsin*
1663 *California*
1664 *Minnesota*
1665 *Oregon*
1666 *Kansas*
1667 *West Virginia*
1668 *Nevada*
1669 *Nebraska*
1670 *Colorado*
1671 *North Dakota*
1672 *South Dakota*
1673 *Montana*
1674 *Washington*
1675 *Idaho*
1676 *Wyoming*
1677 *Utah*
1678 *Oklahoma*
1679 *New Mexico*
1680 *Arizona*
1681 *Alaska*
1682 *Hawaii*

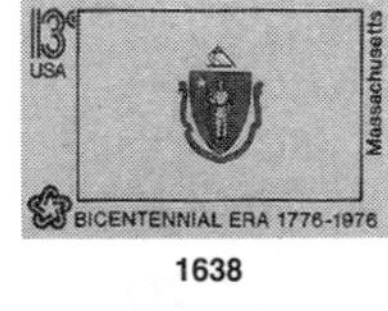

1638

1682

SCOTT NO.	DESCRIPTION	FDC SING.	FDC PL.BLK.	MINT SHEET	MAIL EARLY	ZIP	PLATE BLOCK	UNUSED F/NH	USED
1633-82	13¢ State Flags 50 varieties, attd	....	....	24.00(50)	....	....	5.00(12)	....	....
	Set of 50 Singles	95.00	....	....	....	....	....	....	15.75
	Singles of above..........................	2.00	....	....	....	....	....	.60	.35

U.S. Postage #1683-1694

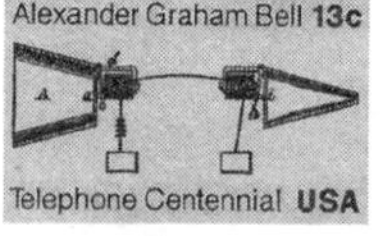

1683

1684

1685

SCOTT NO.	DESCRIPTION	FIRST DAY COVERS SING.	FIRST DAY COVERS PL.BLK.	MINT SHEET	MAIL EARLY	ZIP	PLATE BLOCK	UNUSED F/NH	USED
1683	13¢ Telephone	1.75	4.00	18.75(50)	2.10	1.40	1.50	.40	.15
1684	13¢ Aviation	1.75	4.00	18.75(50)	2.10	1.40	3.75	.40	.15
1685	13¢ Chemistry	1.75	4.00	18.75(50)	1.40	1.40	4.50	.40	.15

1686

1687

1976 BICENTENNIAL SOUVENIR SHEETS

SCOTT NO.	DESCRIPTION	FIRST DAY COVERS SING.	FIRST DAY COVERS PL.BLK.	MINT SHEET	MAIL EARLY	ZIP	PLATE BLOCK	UNUSED F/NH	USED
1686-89	4 varieties, complete	32.50	....	....	....	....	....	30.00	27.00
1686	13¢ Cornwallis Surrender	6.00	....	....	....	....	....	5.00	4.75
1686a-e	13¢ singles, each	3.50	....	....	....	....	....	1.20	1.10
1687	18¢ Independence	7.50	....	....	....	....	....	7.00	6.50
1687a-e	18¢ singles, each	3.75	....	....	....	....	....	1.60	1.50
1688	24¢ Washington Crossing Delaware	9.50	....	....	....	....	....	8.75	8.25
1688a-e	24¢ singles, each	4.25	....	....	....	....	....	1.90	1.80
1689	31¢ Washington at Valley Forge	11.50	....	....	....	....	....	11.00	10.50
1689a-e	31¢ singles, each	5.25	....	....	....	....	....	2.40	2.30

1690

1691 1692 1693 1694

SCOTT NO.	DESCRIPTION	FIRST DAY COVERS SING.	FIRST DAY COVERS PL.BLK.	MINT SHEET	MAIL EARLY	ZIP	PLATE BLOCK	UNUSED F/NH	USED
1690	13¢ Benjamin Franklin	1.75	4.00	18.75(50)	2.25	1.50	1.50	.40	.15
1691-94	Declaration of Independence 4 varieties, attached	5.00	10.00	24.00(50)	(combo)	1.60	9.50(16)	2.25	1.50
1691	13¢ Delegation members	1.75	....	....	....	....	....	.55	.15
1692	13¢ Adams, etc.	1.75	....	....	....	....	....	.55	.15
1693	13¢ Jefferson, Franklin, etc.	1.75	....	....	....	....	....	.55	.15
1694	13¢ Hancock, Thomson, etc.	1.75	....	....	....	....	....	.55	.15

MINT SHEETS: From 1935 to date, we list prices for our standard size Mint Sheets in Fine, Never Hinged condition. The number of stamps in each sheet is noted in ( ).

U.S. Postage #1695-1709

1695

1696

1697

1698

1699

1700

SCOTT NO.	DESCRIPTION	FIRST DAY COVERS SING.	FIRST DAY COVERS PL.BLK.	MINT SHEET	MAIL EARLY	ZIP	PLATE BLOCK	UNUSED F/NH	USED
1695-98	Olympic Games, 4 varieties, att'd.	2.50	3.50	21.50(50)	1.50	1.50	6.75(12)	2.10	1.50
1695	13¢ Diving	1.75	....	....	....	....	....	.50	.15
1696	13¢ Skiing	1.75	....	....	....	....	....	.50	.15
1697	13¢ Running	1.75	....	....	....	....	....	.50	.15
1698	13¢ Skating	1.75	....	....	....	....	....	.50	.15
1699	13¢ Clara Maass	1.75	4.00	14.25(40)	(combo)	1.40	4.50(12)	.40	.15
1700	13¢ Adolph S. Ochs	1.75	4.00	11.50(32)	2.10	1.40	1.50	.40	.15

1701

1702, 1703

1704

1705

SCOTT NO.	DESCRIPTION	SING.	PL.BLK.	MINT SHEET	MAIL EARLY	ZIP	PLATE BLOCK	UNUSED F/NH	USED
1701	13¢ Nativity	1.75	....	18.75(50)	1.40(4)	1.40	4.50(12)	.40	.15
1702	13¢ "Winter Pastime" (Andreati)	1.75	....	18.75(50)	2.10	1.40	3.75(10)	.40	.15
1703	13¢ "Winter Pastime" (Gravure Int.)	2.25	....	18.75(50)	....	....	7.50(20)	.40	.15

1702: Marginal Inscription 1/2 millimeters below design. Black lettering.
1703: Marginal Inscription 3/4 millimeters below design. Grey black lettering.

1977 COMMEMORATIVES

SCOTT NO.	DESCRIPTION	SING.	PL.BLK.	MINT SHEET	MAIL EARLY	ZIP	PLATE BLOCK	UNUSED F/NH	USED
1704-30	**27 varieties, complete**	....	....	....	....	....	....	**10.00**	**3.40**
1704	13¢ Princeton	1.75	4.00	14.00(40)	(combo)	1.40(16)	3.75(10)	.40	.15
1705	13¢ Sound Recording	1.75	4.00	18.75(50)	2.10	1.40	1.50	.40	.15

1706

1707

1708

1709

SCOTT NO.	DESCRIPTION	SING.	PL.BLK.	MINT SHEET	MAIL EARLY	ZIP	PLATE BLOCK	UNUSED F/NH	USED
1706-09	Pueblo Art, 4 varieties, attached	2.50	....	15.25(40)	(combo)	1.90	4.50	1.70	1.50
1706	13¢ Zia	1.75	....	....	....	....	....	.40	.15
1707	13¢ San Ildefonso	1.75	....	....	....	....	....	.40	.15
1708	13¢ Hopi	1.75	....	....	....	....	....	.40	.15
1709	13¢ Acoma	1.75	....	....	....	....	....	.40	.15

U.S. Postage #1710-1724

1710

1711

SCOTT NO.	DESCRIPTION	FIRST DAY COVERS SING.	FIRST DAY COVERS PL.BLK.	MINT SHEET	MAIL EARLY	ZIP	PLATE BLOCK	UNUSED F/NH	USED
1710	13¢ Transatlantic Flight	2.00	4.25	18.75(50)	1.40(4)	1.40	4.50(12)	.40	.15
1711	13¢ Colorado Statehood	1.75	4.00	18.75(50)	1.40(4)	1.40	4.50(12)	.40	.15

1712 1713

1716

1714 1715

SCOTT NO.	DESCRIPTION	FIRST DAY COVERS SING.	FIRST DAY COVERS PL.BLK.	MINT SHEET	MAIL EARLY	ZIP	PLATE BLOCK	UNUSED F/NH	USED
1712-15	Butterflies, 4 varieties, attached..	3.50	....	18.75(50)	1.70(4)	1.70	4.50(12)	1.70	1.50
1712	13¢ Swallowtail	1.75	....	....	....	....	....	.40	.15
1713	13¢ Checkerspot	1.75	....	....	....	....	....	.40	.15
1714	13¢ Dogface................................	1.75	....	....	....	....	....	.40	.15
1715	13¢ Orange-Tip	1.75	....	....	....	....	....	.40	.15
1716	13¢ Lafayette	1.75	4.00	14.25(50)	2.10	1.40	1.50	.40	.15

1717 1718 1719 1720

SCOTT NO.	DESCRIPTION	FIRST DAY COVERS SING.	FIRST DAY COVERS PL.BLK.	MINT SHEET	MAIL EARLY	ZIP	PLATE BLOCK	UNUSED F/NH	USED
1717-20	Skilled Hands, 4 varieties, attached	2.50	....	18.75(50)	1.70(4)	1.70	4.50(12)	1.70	1.50
1717	13¢ Seamstress	1.75	....	....	....	....	....	.40	.15
1718	13¢ Blacksmith............................	1.75	....	....	....	....	....	.40	.15
1719	13¢ Wheelwright	1.75	....	....	....	....	....	.40	.15
1720	13¢ Leatherworker	1.75	....	....	....	....	....	.40	.15

1721 1722 1723 1724

SCOTT NO.	DESCRIPTION	FIRST DAY COVERS SING.	FIRST DAY COVERS PL.BLK.	MINT SHEET	MAIL EARLY	ZIP	PLATE BLOCK	UNUSED F/NH	USED
1721	13¢ Peace Bridge........................	1.75	4.00	18.75(50)	2.10	1.40	1.50	.40	.15
1722	13¢ Herkimer at Oriskany	1.75	4.00	14.00(40)	(combo)	2.00(6)	3.75(10)	.40	.15
1723-24	Energy, 2 varieties, attached	2.50	....	14.00(40)	(combo)	1.40	4.50(12)	.75	.70
1723	13¢ Conservation........................	1.75	....	....	....	....	....	.35	.15
1724	13¢ Development	1.75	....	....	....	....	....	.35	.15

U.S. Postage #1725-1737a

1725

1726

1727

1728

SCOTT NO.	DESCRIPTION	FIRST DAY COVERS SING.	FIRST DAY COVERS PL.BLK.	MINT SHEET	MAIL EARLY	ZIP	PLATE BLOCK	UNUSED F/NH	USED
1725	13¢ Alta California	1.75	4.00	18.75(50)	2.10	1.40	1.50	.40	.15
1726	13¢ Articles of Confederation......	1.75	4.00	18.75(50)	2.10	1.40	1.50	.40	.15
1727	13¢ Talking Pictures	1.75	4.00	18.75(50)	2.10	1.40	1.50	.40	.15
1728	13¢ Surrender at Saratoga	1.75	....	14.50(40)	(combo)	2.25(6)	4.00(10)	.40	.15

1729

1730

1731

1732

1733

SCOTT NO.	DESCRIPTION	FIRST DAY COVERS SING.	FIRST DAY COVERS PL.BLK.	MINT SHEET	MAIL EARLY	ZIP	PLATE BLOCK	UNUSED F/NH	USED
1729	13¢ Washington, Christmas	2.50	....	37.00(100)	....	....	8.00(20)	.40	.15
1730	13¢ Rural Mailbox, Christmas	2.50	....	36.00(100)	2.10	1.40	3.75(10)	.40	.15

1978 COMMEMORATIVES

SCOTT NO.	DESCRIPTION	FIRST DAY COVERS SING.	FIRST DAY COVERS PL.BLK.	MINT SHEET	COPY-RIGHT	ZIP	PLATE BLOCK	UNUSED F/NH	USED
1731/69	**(1731-33, 1744-56, 1758-69) 28 varieties ....**	....	....	....	....	....	....	**11.40**	**3.50**
1731	13¢ Carl Sandburg......................	1.75	4.00	18.75(50)	1.40	1.40	1.50	.40	.15
1732-33	Captain Cook, 2 varieties, attached	2.00	....	18.75(50)	....	....	7.00(20)	1.00	.80
1732	13¢ Captain Cook (Alaska)	1.75	4.00	....	1.40	1.40	1.50	.35	.15
1733	13¢ "Resolution" (Hawaii)............	1.75	4.00	....	1.40	1.40	1.50	.35	.15

NOTE: The Plate Block set includes #1732 & 1733 Plate Blocks of four

1734

1735, 1736, 1743

1737

1738

1739

1740

1741

1742

1978-80 Definitives

SCOTT NO.	DESCRIPTION	FIRST DAY COVERS SING.	FIRST DAY COVERS PL.BLK.	MINT SHEET	COPY-RIGHT	ZIP	PLATE BLOCK	UNUSED F/NH	USED
1734	13¢ Indian Head Penny	1.75	4.00	52.50(150)	1.60	1.60	1.70	.40	.15
1735	(15¢) "A" Definitive (Gravure)......	1.75	4.00	35.00(100)	2.40(ME)	1.60	1.70	.40	.15
1736	same (Intaglio), from booklet pane	1.75	....	....	....	....	....	.40	.15
1736a	15¢ "A" booklet pane of 8............	3.50	....	....	....	....	....	3.00	....
1737	15¢ Roses	1.75	....	....	....	....	....	.40	.15
1737a	same, booklet pane of 8..............	4.00	....	....	....	....	....	3.50	....

U.S. Postage #1738-1752

SCOTT NO.	DESCRIPTION	FIRST DAY COVERS SING.	FIRST DAY COVERS PL.BLK.	MINT SHEET	MAIL EARLY	ZIP	PLATE BLOCK	UNUSED F/NH	USED
1738-42	Windmills, strip of 5, attached (1980)	3.75	....	....	....	....	....	2.25	....
1738	15¢ Virginia Windmill	1.75	....	....	....	....	....	.40	.15
1739	15¢ Rhode Island Windmill	1.75	....	....	....	....	....	.40	.15
1740	15¢ Massachusetts Windmill	1.75	....	....	....	....	....	.40	.15
1741	15¢ Illinois Windmill	1.75	....	....	....	....	....	.40	.15
1742	15¢ Texas Windmill......................	1.75	....	....	....	....	....	.40	.15
1742a	same, booklet pane of 10...........	4.50	....	....	....	....	....	4.50	....
	1978 COIL STAMP								
			LINE PR				LINE PR		
1743	(15¢) "A" Definitive	1.75	2.75	....	....	....	.95	.40	.15

1745

1746

1744

1747

1748

SCOTT NO.	DESCRIPTION	FIRST DAY COVERS SING.	FIRST DAY COVERS PL.BLK.	MINT SHEET	MAIL EARLY	ZIP	PLATE BLOCK	UNUSED F/NH	USED
1744	13¢ Harriet Tubman	1.75	4.00	25.75(50)	2.40	2.40	6.75(12)	.55	.15
1745-48	Quilts, 4 varieties, attached	3.50	....	19.50(48)	(combo)	1.70	5.50(12)	1.70	1.50
1745	13¢ Flowers	2.25	....	....	....	....	....	.40	.15
1746	13¢ Stars	2.25	....	....	....	....	....	.40	.15
1747	13¢ Stripes..................................	2.25	....	....	....	....	....	.40	.15
1748	13¢ Plaid	2.25	....	....	....	....	....	.40	.15

1749

1750

1751

1752

SCOTT NO.	DESCRIPTION	FIRST DAY COVERS SING.	FIRST DAY COVERS PL.BLK.	MINT SHEET	MAIL EARLY	ZIP	PLATE BLOCK	UNUSED F/NH	USED
1749-52	American Dance, 4 varieties, att'd.	3.50	....	19.50(48)	(combo)	1.70	5.50(12)	1.70	1.50
1749	13¢ Ballet	1.75	....	....	....	....	....	.40	.15
1750	13¢ Theater	1.75	....	....	....	....	....	.40	.15
1751	13¢ Folk	1.75	....	....	....	....	....	.40	.15
1752	13¢ Modern	1.75	....	....	....	....	....	.40	.15

1753

1754

1755

1756

U.S. Postage #1753-1763

SCOTT NO.	DESCRIPTION	FIRST DAY COVERS SING.	FIRST DAY COVERS PL.BLK.	MINT SHEET	MAIL EARLY	ZIP	PLATE BLOCK	UNUSED F/NH	USED
1753	13¢ French Alliance	1.75	4.00	14.25(40)	1.40	1.40	1.50	.40	.15
1754	13¢ Dr. Papanicolaou	1.75	4.00	18.75(50)	1.40	1.40	1.40	.40	.15
1755	13¢ Jimmie Rodgers	1.75	4.00	18.75(50)	1.40	1.40	4.50(12)	.40	.15
1756	15¢ George M. Cohan	1.75	4.00	21.25(50)	1.50	1.40	5.25(12)	.40	.15

1757

1758

1759

1978 CAPEX SOUVENIR SHEET

SCOTT NO.	DESCRIPTION	SING.	PL.BLK.	MINT SHEET	MAIL EARLY	ZIP	PLATE BLOCK	UNUSED F/NH	USED
1757	$1.04 CAPEX	4.25	....	14.75(6)	(combo)	3.25	3.50	3.00	2.25
1757a	13¢ Cardinal	1.75	....	....	....	....	....	.35	.25
1757b	13¢ Mallard	1.75	....	....	....	....	....	.35	.25
1757c	13¢ Canada Goose	1.75	....	....	....	....	....	.35	.25
1757d	13¢ Blue Jay	1.75	....	....	....	....	....	.35	.25
1757e	13¢ Moose	1.75	....	....	....	....	....	.35	.25
1757f	13¢ Chipmunk	1.75	....	....	....	....	....	.35	.25
1757g	13¢ Red Fox	1.75	....	....	....	....	....	.35	.25
1757h	13¢ Raccoon	1.75	....	....	....	....	....	.35	.25
1758	15¢ Photography	1.75	4.00	14.50(40)	(combo)	1.50	5.25(12)	.40	.15
1759	15¢ Viking Mission	1.75	4.00	21.00(50)	1.75	1.75	1.75	.45	.15

1760

1761

1762

1763

1768

1769

1764

1765

1766

1767

SCOTT NO.	DESCRIPTION	SING.	PL.BLK.	MINT SHEET	MAIL EARLY	ZIP	PLATE BLOCK	UNUSED F/NH	USED
1760-63	American Owls, 4 varieties, attached	3.50	4.75	20.00(50)	1.95	1.95	2.10	1.90	1.50
1760	15¢ Great Gray	1.75	....	....	....	....	....	.45	.15
1761	15¢ Saw-Whet	1.75	....	....	....	....	....	.45	.15
1762	15¢ Barred Owl	1.75	....	....	....	....	....	.45	.15
1763	15¢ Great Horned	1.75	....	....	....	....	....	.45	.15

U.S. Postage #1764-1786

SCOTT NO.	DESCRIPTION	FIRST DAY COVERS SING.	FIRST DAY COVERS PL.BLK.	MINT SHEET	MAIL EARLY	ZIP	PLATE BLOCK	UNUSED F/NH	USED
1764-67	Trees, 4 varieties, attached	3.50	....	16.00(40)	(combo)	1.75	5.50(12)	1.70	1.50
1764	15¢ Giant Sequoia	1.75	....	....	....	....	....	.40	.15
1765	15¢ Pine	1.75	....	....	....	....	....	.40	.15
1766	15¢ Oak	1.75	....	....	....	....	....	.40	.15
1767	15¢ Birch	1.75	....	....	....	....	....	.40	.15
1768	15¢ Madonna, Christmas	1.75	4.00	36.00(100)	1.50	1.50	5.25(12)	.40	.15
1769	15¢ Hobby Horse, Christmas	1.75	4.00	36.00(100)	1.50	1.50	5.25(12)	.40	.15

1770 1771 1772 1773 1774

1979 COMMEMORATIVES

SCOTT NO.	DESCRIPTION	FIRST DAY COVERS SING.	FIRST DAY COVERS PL.BLK.	MINT SHEET	MAIL EARLY	ZIP	PLATE BLOCK	UNUSED F/NH	USED
1770/1802 (1770-94, 1799-1802)	**29 varieties, complete ....**	....	....	....	....	....	....	**12.50**	**4.10**
1770	15¢ Robert F. Kennedy	1.75	4.00	17.00(48)	1.60	1.60	1.75	.40	.15
1771	15¢ Martin L. King, Jr.	1.75	4.00	18.25(50)	1.60	1.60	5.50(12)	.40	.15
1772	15¢ International Year of the Child	1.75	4.00	18.25(50)	1.60	1.60	1.75	.40	.15
1773	15¢ John Steinbeck	1.75	4.00	18.25(50)	1.60	1.60	1.75	.40	.15
1774	15¢ Albert Einstein	1.75	4.00	18.25(50)	1.60	1.60	1.75	.40	.15

1775 1776 1779 1780 1783 1784

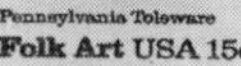

1781 1782

1777 1778 1785 1786

SCOTT NO.	DESCRIPTION	FIRST DAY COVERS SING.	FIRST DAY COVERS PL.BLK.	MINT SHEET	MAIL EARLY	ZIP	PLATE BLOCK	UNUSED F/NH	USED
1775-78	Pennsylvania Toleware, 4 varieties, attached	3.50	....	18.00(40)	(combo)	2.50(6)	5.00(10)	1.85	1.60
1775	15¢ Coffee Pot	1.75	....	....	....	....	....	.45	.15
1776	15¢ Tea Caddy	1.75	....	....	....	....	....	.45	.15
1777	15¢ Sugar Bowl	1.75	....	....	....	....	....	.45	.15
1778	15¢ Coffee Pot	1.75	....	....	....	....	....	.45	.15
1779-82	Architecture, 4 varieties, attached	3.50	4.75	22.50(48)	2.15	2.15	2.25	2.10	1.80
1779	15¢ Virginia Rotunda	1.75	....	....	....	....	....	.45	.15
1780	15¢ Baltimore Cathedral	1.75	....	....	....	....	....	.45	.15
1781	15¢ Boston State House	1.75	....	....	....	....	....	.45	.15
1782	15¢ Philadelphia Exchange	1.75	....	....	....	....	....	.45	.15
1783-86	Endangered Flora, 4 varieties, attd	3.50	....	19.50(50)	1.90	1.90	5.50(12)	1.85	1.70
1783	15¢ Trillium	1.75	....	....	....	....	....	.45	.15
1784	15¢ Broadbean	1.75	....	....	....	....	....	.45	.15
1785	15¢ Wallflower	1.75	....	....	....	....	....	.45	.15
1786	15¢ Primrose	1.75	....	....	....	....	....	.45	.15

U.S. Postage #1787-1802

1787

1788

1789, 1789a

1790

1791

1792

1793

1794

1795

1796

1797

1798

SCOTT NO.	DESCRIPTION	FIRST DAY COVERS SING.	FIRST DAY COVERS PL.BLK.	MINT SHEET	MAIL EARLY	ZIP	PLATE BLOCK	UNUSED F/NH	USED
1787	15¢ Guide Dog	1.75	....	18.25(50)	1.60	1.60	8.50(20)	.40	.15
1788	15¢ Special Olympics	1.75	....	18.25(50)	1.60	1.60	4.50(10)	.40	.15
1789	15¢ John Paul Jones, perf. 11x12	1.75	....	18.25(50)	1.60	1.60	4.50(10)	.40	.15
1789a	same, perf. 11	1.75	....	25.00(50)	2.00	2.00	6.50(10)	.50	.15

Note: #1789a may be included in year date sets and special offers and not 1789.

SCOTT NO.	DESCRIPTION	FIRST DAY COVERS SING.	FIRST DAY COVERS PL.BLK.	MINT SHEET	MAIL EARLY	ZIP	PLATE BLOCK	UNUSED F/NH	USED
1790	10¢ Summer Olympics, Javelin Thrower	1.75	4.00	14.50(50)	1.20	1.20	5.00(12)	.30	.15
1791-94	Summer Olympics, 4 varieties, att'd.	3.50	....	20.00(50)	1.75	1.75	6.50(12)	2.00	1.50
1791	15¢ Runners	1.75	....	....	....	....	....	.45	.15
1792	15¢ Swimmers	1.75	....	....	....	....	....	.45	.15
1793	15¢ Rowers	1.75	....	....	....	....	....	.45	.15
1794	15¢ Equestrian	1.75	....	....	....	....	....	.45	.15
			(1980)						
1795-98	Winter Olympics, 4 varieties, att'd.	3.50	....	20.00(50)	2.00	2.00	6.50(12)	2.00	1.50
1795	15¢ Skater	1.75	....	....	....	....	....	.45	.15
1796	15¢ Downhill Skier	1.75	....	....	....	....	....	.45	.15
1797	15¢ Ski Jumper	1.75	....	....	....	....	....	.45	.15
1798	15¢ Hockey	1.75	....	....	....	....	....	.45	.15
1795a-98a	same, perf. 11, attached	....	....	40.00(50)	5.50	5.50	15.00(12)	4.00	....
1795a	15¢ Skater	....	....	....	....	....	....	.90	....
1796a	15¢ Downhill Skier	....	....	....	....	....	....	.90	....
1797a	15¢ Ski Jumper	....	....	....	....	....	....	.90	....
1798a	15¢ Hockey	....	....	....	....	....	....	.90	....

1799

1800

1801

1802

1803

1804

1979 COMMEMORATIVES

SCOTT NO.	DESCRIPTION	FIRST DAY COVERS SING.	FIRST DAY COVERS PL.BLK.	MINT SHEET	MAIL EARLY	ZIP	PLATE BLOCK	UNUSED F/NH	USED
1799	15¢ Christmas—Madonna	1.75	....	36.25(100)	1.50	1.50	5.25(12)	.40	.15
1800	15¢ Christmas—Santa Claus	1.75	....	36.25(100)	1.50	1.50	5.25(12)	.40	.15
1801	15¢ Will Rogers	1.75	....	20.50(50)	1.80	1.80	5.25(12)	.40	.15
1802	15¢ Vietnam Veterans	2.50	5.25	20.50(50)	1.80	1.80	5.25(10)	.45	.15

U.S. Postage #1803-1820

SCOTT NO.	DESCRIPTION	FIRST DAY COVERS SING.	PL.BLK.	MINT SHEET	COPY-RIGHT	ZIP	PLATE BLOCK	UNUSED F/NH	USED
	1980 COMMEMORATIVES								
1795/1843	**(1795-98, 1803-10, 1821-43) 35 varieties, complete ....**	....	....	....	....	....	....	**14.50**	**4.50**
1803	15¢ W.C. Fields	1.75	4.00	20.00(50)	1.75	1.75	5.25(12)	.45	.15
1804	15¢ Benjamin Banneker	1.75	4.00	20.00(50)	1.75	1.75	5.25(12)	.45	.15

1805

1806, 1808, 1810

1807

1809

SCOTT NO.	DESCRIPTION	FIRST DAY COVERS SING.	PL.BLK.	MINT SHEET	COPY-RIGHT	ZIP	PLATE BLOCK	UNUSED F/NH	USED
1805-10	6 varieties, attached	4.50	....	27.50(60)	5.00(12)	5.00(12)	17.50(36)	2.50	2.35
1805-06	2 varieties, attached	2.50	....	....	....	....	....	....	....
1807-08	2 varieties, attached	2.50	....	....	....	....	....	....	....
1809-10	2 varieties, attached	2.50	....	....	....	....	....	....	....
1805	15¢ "Letters Preserve Memories"	1.75	....	....	....	....	....	.40	.15
1806	15¢ claret & multicolor	1.75	....	....	....	....	....	.40	.15
1807	15¢ "Letters Lift Spirits"	1.75	....	....	....	....	....	.40	.15
1808	15¢ green & multicolor	1.75	....	....	....	....	....	.40	.15
1809	15¢ "Letters Shape Opinions"	1.75	....	....	....	....	....	.40	.15
1810	15¢ red, white & blue	1.75	....	....	....	....	....	.40	.15

1813

1818, 1819, 1820

1980-81 Coil Stamps, Perf. 10 Vertically

SCOTT NO.	DESCRIPTION	SING.	L.PR.	MINT SHEET	COPY-RIGHT	ZIP	LINE PR.	UNUSED F/NH	USED
1811	1¢ Inkwell & Quill	1.75	2.75	....	....	....	.50	.20	.15
1813	3.5¢ Two Violins	1.75	2.75	....	....	....	1.40	.20	.15
1816	12¢ Torch (1981)	1.75	2.75	....	....	....	1.90	.35	.30
1818	(18¢) "B" definitive	2.50	3.50	47.50(100)	3.10(ME)	2.10	2.25	.55	.15
1819	(18¢) "B" definitive, from bklt pane	1.75	....	....	....	....	....	1.00	.15
1819a	(18¢) "B" booklet pane of 8	4.00	....	....	....	....	....	7.95	....

1981 Coil Stamp Perf. Vertically

SCOTT NO.	DESCRIPTION	SING.	LINE PR.	MINT SHEET	COPY-RIGHT	ZIP	LINE PR.	UNUSED F/NH	USED
1820	(18¢) "B" definitive	1.75	2.75	....	....	....	1.60	.55	.15

1821

1822

1823

1824

U.S. Postage #1821-1837

SCOTT NO.	DESCRIPTION	FIRST DAY COVERS SING.	FIRST DAY COVERS PL.BLK.	MINT SHEET	COPY-RIGHT	ZIP	PLATE BLOCK	UNUSED F/NH	USED
1821	15¢ Frances Perkins	1.75	4.00	18.25(50)	1.60	1.60	1.75	.40	.15
1822	15¢ Dolley Madison	1.75	4.00	55.00(150)	1.60	1.60	1.75	.40	.15
1823	15¢ Emily Bissell	1.75	4.00	18.25(50)	1.60	1.60	1.75	.40	.15
1824	15¢ Helen Keller & Anne Sullivan	1.75	4.00	18.25(50)	1.60	1.60	1.75	.40	.15

1825

1826

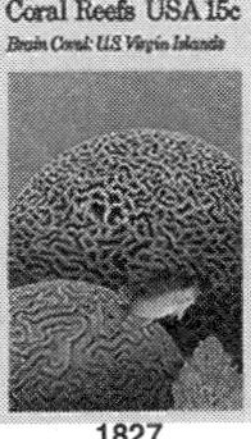

1827

1828

1829

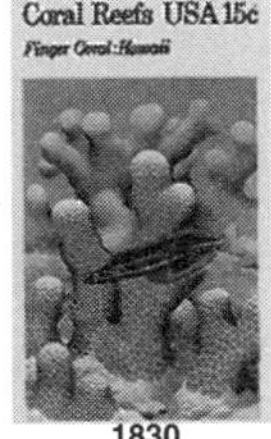

1830

SCOTT NO.	DESCRIPTION	FIRST DAY COVERS SING.	FIRST DAY COVERS PL.BLK.	MINT SHEET	COPY-RIGHT	ZIP	PLATE BLOCK	UNUSED F/NH	USED
1825	15¢ Veterans Administration	1.75	4.00	18.25(50)	1.60	1.60	1.75	.40	.15
1826	15¢ Gen. Bernardo deGalvez	1.75	4.00	18.25(50)	1.60	1.60	1.75	.40	.15
1827-30	Coral Reefs, 4 varieties, attached	3.50	....	19.00(50)	2.00	2.00	5.50(12)	1.75	1.75
1827	15¢ Brain Coral, Virgin Islands	1.75	....	....	....	....	....	.40	.15
1828	15¢ Elkhorn Coral, Florida	1.75	....	....	....	....	....	.40	.15
1829	15¢ Chalice Coral, Am. Samoa	1.75	....	....	....	....	....	.40	.15
1830	15¢ Finger Coral, Hawaii	1.75	....	....	....	....	....	.40	.15

1831

1832

1833

SCOTT NO.	DESCRIPTION	FIRST DAY COVERS SING.	FIRST DAY COVERS PL.BLK.	MINT SHEET	COPY-RIGHT	ZIP	PLATE BLOCK	UNUSED F/NH	USED
1831	15¢ Organized Labor	1.75	4.00	18.25(50)	1.60	1.60	5.25(12)	.40	.15
1832	15¢ Edith Wharton	1.75	4.00	18.25(50)	1.60	1.60	1.75	.40	.15
1833	15¢ Education	1.75	4.00	18.25(50)	1.60	1.60	2.60(6)	.40	.15

1834

1835

1836

1837

SCOTT NO.	DESCRIPTION	FIRST DAY COVERS SING.	FIRST DAY COVERS PL.BLK.	MINT SHEET	COPY-RIGHT	ZIP	PLATE BLOCK	UNUSED F/NH	USED
1834-37	American Folk Art, 4 varieties, attached	3.50	....	20.00(40)	(combo)	2.75	6.00(10)	2.00	1.85
1834	15¢ Bella Bella Tribe	1.75	....	....	....	....	....	.45	.15
1835	15¢ Chilkat Tlingit Tribe	1.75	....	....	....	....	....	.45	.15
1836	15¢ Tlingit Tribe	1.75	....	....	....	....	....	.45	.15
1837	15¢ Bella Coola Tribe	1.75	....	....	....	....	....	.45	.15

1838

1839

1840

1841

U.S. Postage #1838-1849

SCOTT NO.	DESCRIPTION	FIRST DAY COVERS SING.	PL.BLK.	MINT SHEET	COPY-RIGHT	ZIP	PLATE BLOCK	UNUSED F/NH	USED
1838-41	American Architecture, 4 varieties, attached	2.50	3.75	21.00(40)	2.25	2.25	2.25	2.10	2.00
1838	15¢ Smithsonian Inst.	1.75	....	....	....	....	....	.50	.15
1839	15¢ Trinity Church	1.75	....	....	....	....	....	.50	.15
1840	15¢ Penn Academy	1.75	....	....	....	....	....	.50	.15
1841	15¢ Lyndhurst	1.75	....	....	....	....	....	.50	.15

1842

1843

SCOTT NO.	DESCRIPTION	SING.	PL.BLK.	MINT SHEET	COPY-RIGHT	ZIP	PLATE BLOCK	UNUSED F/NH	USED
1842	15¢ Madonna	1.75	4.00	18.25(50)	1.60	1.60	5.25(12)	.40	.15
1843	15¢ Christmas Wreath & Toy ...	1.75	4.00	18.25(50)	....	....	8.50(20)	.40	.15

1844 1845 1846 1847 1848 1849 1850

1851 1852 1853 1854 1855 1856 1857

1858 1859 1860 1861 1862 1863

1864 1865 1866 1867 1868 1869

1980-85 GREAT AMERICANS

SCOTT NO.	DESCRIPTION	SING.	PL.BLK.	MINT SHEET	COPY-RIGHT	ZIP	PLATE BLOCK	UNUSED F/NH	USED
1844-69	**1¢-50¢, 26 varieties, complete**	....	....	....	....	....	....	**11.40**	**3.70**
1844	1¢ Dorothea Dix (1983)	1.75	4.00	8.25(100)	....	....	3.25(20)	.20	.15
1844a	same, Bullseye perf	....	....	....	....	....	2.25(20)	.20	....
1845	2¢ Igor Stravinsky (1982)	1.75	4.00	10.00(100)	.80	.80	.80	.20	.15
1846	3¢ Henry Clay (1983)	1.75	4.00	11.25(100)	.80	.80	.80	.20	.15
1847	4¢ Carl Schurz (1983)	1.75	4.00	12.00(100)	.80	.80	.80	.20	.15
1848	5¢ Pearl Buck (1983)................	1.75	4.00	13.25(100)	.80	.80	.80	.20	.15
1849	6¢ Walter Lippmann (1985)	1.75	4.00	11.75(100)	....	....	3.75(20)	.20	.15

U.S. Postage #1850-1879

SCOTT NO.	DESCRIPTION	FIRST DAY COVERS SING.	PL.BLK.	MINT SHEET	COPY-RIGHT	ZIP	PLATE BLOCK	UNUSED F/NH	USED
1850	7¢ Abraham Baldwin (1985)	1.75	4.00	15.00(100)	....	....	4.00(20)	.20	.15
1851	8¢ Henry Knox (1985)	1.75	4.00	23.50(100)	1.00	1.00	1.25	.25	.15
1852	9¢ Sylvanus Thayer (1985)	1.75	4.00	23.50(100)	....	....	5.25(20)	.25	.15
1853	10¢ Richard Russell (1984)	1.75	4.00	24.00(100)	....	....	6.5020)	.30	.15
1854	11¢ Partridge (1985)	1.75	4.00	24.00(100)	1.40	1.40	1.65	.30	.15
1855	13¢ Crazy Horse (1982)	1.75	4.00	36.00(100)	1.75	1.75	2.25	.40	.15
1856	14¢ Sinclair Lewis (1985)	1.75	4.00	36.00(100)	....	....	8.50(20)	.40	.15
1857	17¢ Rachel Carson (1981)	1.75	4.00	41.00(100)	2.00	2.00	2.25	.45	.15
1858	18¢ George Mason (1981)	1.75	4.00	48.50(100)	3.00	3.00	3.75	.55	.15
1859	19¢ Sequoyah	1.75	4.00	48.50(100)	2.50	2.50	3.00	.55	.15
1860	20¢ Ralph Bunche (1982)	1.75	4.00	54.00(100)	3.00	3.00	3.75	.60	.15
1861	20¢ Thomas Gallaudet (1983) .	1.75	4.00	54.00(100)	4.00	4.00	4.00	.60	.15
1862	20¢ Harry Truman (1984)	1.75	4.00	54.00(100)	....	....	13.50(20)	.65	.15
1862a	same, Bullseye perf	....	....	....	3.50	3.50	4.00	.65	....
1863	22¢ J. Audubon (1985)	1.75	4.00	50.00(100)	....	....	13.00(20)	.75	.15
1863a	same, Bullseye perf	....	....	....	5.00	5.00	5.50	.75	....
1864	30¢ Frank C. Laubach (1984) ..	1.75	4.00	65.00(100)	....	....	18.00(20)	.75	.15
1864a	same, Bullseye perf	....	....	....	4.50	4.50	5.00	.75	....
1865	35¢ Charles Drew (1981)	2.25	4.50	80.00(100)	4.00	4.00	4.25	.90	.15
1866	37¢ Robert Millikan (1982)	2.25	4.50	80.00(100)	4.00	4.00	4.25	.90	.15
1867	39¢ Grenville Clark (1985)	2.25	4.50	90.00(100)	5.00	5.00	20.00(20)	1.00	.15
1867a	same, Bullseye perf	....	....	....	5.00	5.00	5.25	1.00	....
1868	40¢ Lillian Gilbreth (1984)	2.25	4.50	90.00(100)	....	....	20.00(20)	1.00	.15
1868a	same, Bullseye perf	....	....	....	5.50	5.50	5.75	1.00	....
1869	50¢ Chester Nimitz (1985)	2.25	4.50	110.00(100)	6.25	6.25	6.75	1.25	.15
1869a	same, Bullseye perf	....	....	....	4.50	4.50	5.00	1.25	....

1874

1875

1981 COMMEMORATIVES

SCOTT NO.	DESCRIPTION	FIRST DAY COVERS SING.	PL.BLK.	MINT SHEET	COPY-RIGHT	ZIP	PLATE BLOCK	UNUSED F/NH	USED
1874/1945	**(1874-79, 1910-45) 42 varieties, complete ....**	**.......**	**.......**	**.......**	**.......**	**.......**	**.......**	**22.50**	**5.25**
1874	15¢ Everett Dirksen	1.75	4.00	18.25(50)	1.60	1.60	1.75	.40	.15
1875	15¢ Whitney Moore Young	1.75	4.00	18.25(50)	1.60	1.60	1.75	.40	.15

1876

1877

1878

1879

SCOTT NO.	DESCRIPTION	FIRST DAY COVERS SING.	PL.BLK.	MINT SHEET	COPY-RIGHT	ZIP	PLATE BLOCK	UNUSED F/NH	USED
1876-79	Flowers, 4 varieties, attached ..	2.50	3.75	30.00(48)	3.10	3.10	3.25	3.00	2.60
1876	18¢ Rose	1.75	....	....	....	....	....	.70	.15
1877	18¢ Camellia	1.75	....	....	....	....	....	.70	.15
1878	18¢ Dahlia	1.75	....	....	....	....	....	.70	.15
1879	18¢ Lily	1.75	....	....	....	....	....	.70	.15

1880, 1949

1881

1882

1883

1884

1885

1886

1887

1888

1889

U.S. Postage #1880-1896b

SCOTT NO.	DESCRIPTION	FIRST DAY COVERS SING.	FIRST DAY COVERS PL.BLK.	MINT SHEET	COPY-RIGHT	ZIP	PLATE BLOCK	UNUSED F/NH	USED
	1981 WILDLIFE DEFINITIVES								
1880-89	Wildlife, set of singles	17.00	....	....	....	....	....	9.25	1.50
1880	18¢ Bighorned Sheep	1.75	....	....	....	....	....	.95	.15
1881	18¢ Puma	1.75	....	....	....	....	....	.95	.15
1882	18¢ Harbor Seal	1.75	....	....	....	....	....	.95	.15
1883	18¢ Bison	1.75	....	....	....	....	....	.95	.15
1884	18¢ Brown Bear	1.75	....	....	....	....	....	.95	.15
1885	18¢ Polar Bear	1.75	....	....	....	....	....	.95	.15
1886	18¢ Elk	1.75	....	....	....	....	....	.95	.15
1887	18¢ Moose	1.75	....	....	....	....	....	.95	.15
1888	18¢ White-tailed Deer	1.75	....	....	....	....	....	.95	.15
1889	18¢ Pronghorned Antelope	1.75	....	....	....	....	....	.95	.15
1889a	Wildlife, booklet pane of 10	6.50	....	....	....	....	....	10.25	....
	1981 FLAG AND ANTHEM ISSUE								
1890	18¢ "Waves of Grain"	1.75	4.00	47.50(100)	....	....	14.50(20)	.50	.15
	1981 Coil Stamp Perf. 10 Vertically								
			PL # STRIP 3				**PL# STRIP 3**		
1891	18¢ "Shining Sea"	1.75	....	....	....	....	6.00	.50	.15
	1981								
1892	6¢ Stars, from booklet pane	1.75	....	....	....	....	....	.75	.15
1893	18¢ "Purple Mountains" from booklet pane	1.75	....	....	....	....	....	.50	.15
1892-93	6¢ & 18¢ as above, attached pair	....	....	....	....	....	....	1.25	....
1893a	2-1892, 6-1893 booklet pane of 8	5.25	....	....	....	....	....	4.25	....
			PL.BLK.				**PL. BLK.**		
1894	20¢ Flag & Supreme Court	1.75	4.00	49.50(100)	....	....	12.50(20)	.55	.15
			PL # STRIP 3				**PL # STRIP 3**		
1895	20¢ Flag & Supreme Court	1.75	50.00	....	....	....	4.50	.55	.15
1896	20¢ Flag & S.C., from bklt pane	1.75	....	....	....	....	....	.55	.15
1896a	20¢ booklet pane of 6	3.50	....	....	....	....	....	3.25	....
1896b	20¢ booklet pane of 10	5.50	....	....	....	....	....	5.25	....

1890 1891 1892 1893 1894, 1895, 1896

1897 1897A 1898 1898A

1899 1900 1901 1902 1903

COPYRIGHT BLOCKS: Starting in 1978, the U.S.P.S. replaced the Mail Early slogan with the standard copyright inscription seen in copyrighted publications, etc. This was a legal move to protect the design from copyright infringement. Copyright Blocks are collected as Blocks of Four.

U.S. Postage #1897-1911

1904 1905 1906 1907 1908

NOTE: #1898A—"Stagecoach 1890s" is 19-1/2 mm. long.

1981-84 Perf. 10 Vertically
TRANSPORTATION COILS

SCOTT NO.	DESCRIPTION	FIRST DAY COVERS SING.	FIRST DAY COVERS PL # STRIP 3	MINT SHEET	COPY-RIGHT	ZIP	PL# STRIP 3	UNUSED F/NH	USED
1897-1908	1¢-20¢, 14 varieties, complete	29.50	....	....	....	....	....	4.25	1.75
1897	1¢ Omnibus (1983)	2.25	17.50	....	....	....	.70	.20	.15
1897A	2¢ Locomotive (1982)	2.25	25.00	....	....	....	.75	.20	.15
1898	3¢ Handcar (1983)	2.25	25.00	....	....	....	1.05	.20	.15
1898A	4¢ Stagecoach (1982)	2.25	22.50	....	....	....	2.00	.20	.15
1899	5¢ Motorcycle (1983)	2.25	25.00	....	....	....	1.25	.20	.15
1900	5.2¢ Sleigh (1983)	2.25	37.50	....	....	....	8.00	.30	.15
1901	5.9¢ Bicycle (1982)	2.25	37.50	....	....	....	10.00	.30	.15
1902	7.4¢ Baby Buggy (1984)	2.25	25.00	....	....	....	9.50	.30	.15
1903	9.3¢ Mail Wagon	2.25	42.50	....	....	....	9.00	.30	.15
1904	10.9¢ Hansom Cab (1982)	2.25	40.00	....	....	....	17.00	.55	.15
1905	11¢ Caboose (1984)	2.25	40.00	....	....	....	4.00	.30	.15
1906	17¢ Electric Car	2.25	37.50	....	....	....	3.75	.40	.15
1907	18¢ Surrey	2.25	55.00	....	....	....	4.00	.55	.15
1908	20¢ Fire Pumper	2.25	55.00	....	....	....	3.75	.55	.15

NOTE: Plate # Strips of 3 have plate number under center stamp. Some issues also have lines between two of the stamps.

PRECANCELLED COILS

The following are for precancelled, unused, never hinged stamps. Stamps without gum sell for less.

SCOTT NO.		PL # STRIP 3	UN-USED	SCOTT NO.		PL # STRIP 3	UN-USED
1895e	20¢ Supreme Court	85.00	.75	1903a	9.3¢ Mail Wagon	4.50	.30
1898Ab	4¢ Stagecoach	8.50	.20	1904a	10.9¢ Hansom Cab	37.50	.40
1900a	5.2¢ Sleigh	13.00	.30	1905a	11¢ Caboose	4.00	.30
1901a	5.9¢ Bicycle	32.50	.30	1906a	17¢ Electric Car	5.00	.40
1902a	7.4¢ Baby Buggy	5.75	.30				

1909

1910

1911

SCOTT NO.	DESCRIPTION	FIRST DAY COVERS SING.	FIRST DAY COVERS PL.BLK.	MINT SHEET	COPY-RIGHT	ZIP	PLATE BLOCK	UN-USED	USED
	1983 EXPRESS MAIL BOOKLET SINGLE								
1909	$9.35 Eagle & Moon	95.00	....	....	....	....	....	27.50	22.50
1909a	$9.35 booklet pane of 3	300.00	....	....	....	....	....	80.00	....
	1981 COMMEMORATIVES (Continued)								
1910	18¢ American Red Cross	1.75	4.00	23.75(50)	2.10	2.10	2.25	.50	.15
1911	18¢ Savings & Loans Assoc.	1.75	4.00	23.75(50)	2.10	2.10	2.25	.50	.15

U.S. Postage #1912-1927

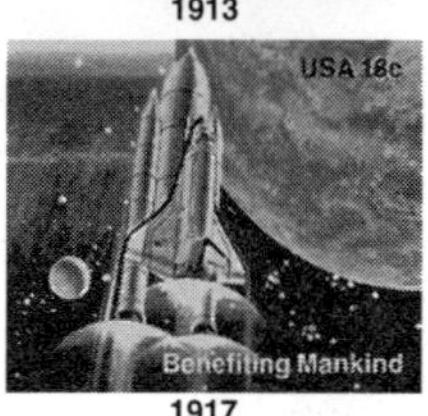

1912 1913 1914 1915 1916 1917 1918 1919

1981 COMMEMORATIVES (continued)

SCOTT NO.	DESCRIPTION	FIRST DAY COVERS SING.	PL.BLK.	MINT SHEET	COPY-RIGHT	ZIP	PLATE BLOCK	UNUSED F/NH	USED
1912-19	Space Achievement, 8 varieties, attached	6.00	9.00	32.00(48)	(combo)	5.25(8)	5.50(8)	5.25	4.75
1912-19	Same, set of singles	15.50	....	....	....	....	....	....	1.15
1912	18¢ Exploring the Moon	2.00	....	....	....	....	....	.60	.15
1913	18¢ Releasing Boosters	2.00	....	....	....	....	....	.60	.15
1914	18¢ Cooling Electric Systems	2.00	....	....	....	....	....	.60	.15
1915	18¢ Understanding the Sun	2.00	....	....	....	....	....	.60	.15
1916	18¢ Probing the Planets	2.00	....	....	....	....	....	.60	.15
1917	18¢ Shuttle and Rockets	2.00	....	....	....	....	....	.60	.15
1918	18¢ Landing	2.00	....	....	....	....	....	.60	.15
1919	18¢ Comprehending Universe	2.00	....	....	....	....	....	.60	.15

1920

1921

1922

1923

1924

SCOTT NO.	DESCRIPTION	FIRST DAY COVERS SING.	PL.BLK.	MINT SHEET	COPY-RIGHT	ZIP	PLATE BLOCK	UNUSED F/NH	USED
1920	18¢ Professional Management	1.75	4.00	23.50(50)	2.10	2.10	2.25	.50	.15
1921-24	Wildlife Habitats, 4 varieties, att'd.	2.75	3.75	27.50(50)	2.60	2.60	2.75	2.50	2.50
1921	18¢ Blue Heron	1.75	....	....	....	....	....	.60	.15
1922	18¢ Badger	1.75	....	....	....	....	....	.60	.15
1923	18¢ Grizzly Bear	1.75	....	....	....	....	....	.60	.15
1924	18¢ Ruffled Grouse	1.75	....	....	....	....	....	.60	.15

1925

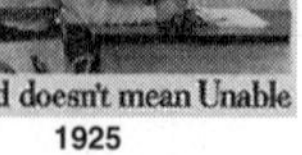

1926

1927

SCOTT NO.	DESCRIPTION	FIRST DAY COVERS SING.	PL.BLK.	MINT SHEET	COPY-RIGHT	ZIP	PLATE BLOCK	UNUSED F/NH	USED
1925	18¢ Disabled Persons	1.75	4.00	23.50(50)	2.10	2.10	2.25	.50	.15
1926	18¢ Edna St. Vincent Millay	1.75	4.00	23.50(50)	2.10	2.10	2.25	.50	.15
1927	18¢ Alcoholism	1.75	4.00	60.00(50)	....	....	47.50(20)	.65	.15

U.S. Postage #1928-1941

1928 1929 1930 1931

SCOTT NO.	DESCRIPTION	FIRST DAY COVERS SING.	PL.BLK.	MINT SHEET	COPY-RIGHT	ZIP	PLATE BLOCK	UNUSED F/NH	USED
1928-31	American Architecture, 4 varieties, attached	2.75	3.75	28.50(40)	2.90	2.90	3.00	2.75	2.50
1928	18¢ New York Univ. Library	1.75	....	....	....	....	....	.65	.15
1929	18¢ Biltmore House	1.75	....	....	....	....	....	.65	.15
1930	18¢ Palace of the Arts	1.75	....	....	....	....	....	.65	.15
1931	18¢ National Farmers Bank	1.75	....	....	....	....	....	.65	.15

1932 1933 1934

SCOTT NO.	DESCRIPTION	FIRST DAY COVERS SING.	PL.BLK.	MINT SHEET	COPY-RIGHT	ZIP	PLATE BLOCK	UNUSED F/NH	USED
1932	18¢ Babe Zaharias	9.00	12.00	23.50(50)	2.10	2.10	2.25	.50	.15
1933	18¢ Bobby Jones	12.50	15.00	65.00(50)	5.75	5.75	6.25	1.35	.20
1934	18¢ Coming Through the Rye ..	2.25	4.50	23.50(50)	2.10	2.10	2.25	.50	.15

1935 1936 1937 1938

SCOTT NO.	DESCRIPTION	FIRST DAY COVERS SING.	PL.BLK.	MINT SHEET	COPY-RIGHT	ZIP	PLATE BLOCK	UNUSED F/NH	USED
1935	18¢ James Hoban	1.75	4.00	23.50(50)	2.10	2.10	2.25	.50	.15
1936	20¢ James Hoban	1.75	4.00	26.00(50)	2.25	2.25	2.50	.55	.15
1937-38	18¢ Yorktown/Virginia Capes, 2 varieties, attached	2.00	4.00	26.00(50)	2.25	2.25	2.50	1.25	1.25
1937	18¢ Yorktown	1.75	....	....	....	....	....	.55	.15
1938	18¢ Virginia Capes	1.75	....	....	....	....	....	.55	.15

1939 1940 1941

SCOTT NO.	DESCRIPTION	FIRST DAY COVERS SING.	PL.BLK.	MINT SHEET	COPY-RIGHT	ZIP	PLATE BLOCK	UNUSED F/NH	USED
1939	(20¢) Madonna & Child	1.75	4.00	50.00(100)	2.25	2.25	2.50	.55	.15
1940	(20¢) Christmas Toy	1.75	4.00	26.00(50)	2.25	2.25	2.50	.55	.15
1941	20¢ John Hanson	1.75	4.00	26.00(50)	2.25	2.25	2.50	.55	.15

FIRST DAY COVERS: First Day Covers are envelopes cancelled on the "First Day of Issue" of the stamp used on the envelope. Usually they also contain a picture (cachet) on the left side designed to go with the theme of the stamp. From 1935 to 1949, prices listed are for cacheted, addressed covers. From 1950 to date, prices are for cacheted, unaddressed covers.

U.S. Postage #1942-1952

SCOTT NO.	DESCRIPTION	FIRST DAY COVERS SING.	FIRST DAY COVERS PL. BLK.	MINT SHEET	COPY-RIGHT	ZIP	PLATE BLOCK	UNUSED F/NH	USED

1942

1943

Opuntia basilaris
USA 20c
Beavertail Cactus

1944

1945

SCOTT NO.	DESCRIPTION	FDC SING.	FDC PL. BLK.	MINT SHEET	COPY-RIGHT	ZIP	PLATE BLOCK	UNUSED F/NH	USED
1942-45	Desert Plants, 4 varieties, attached	2.75	3.75	29.50(40)	2.90	2.90	3.00	2.80	2.00
1942	20¢ Barrel Cactus	1.75	....	....	....	....	....	.70	.15
1943	20¢ Agave	1.75	....	....	....	....	....	.70	.15
1944	20¢ Beavertail Cactus	1.75	....	....	....	....	....	.70	.15
1945	20¢ Saguaro	1.75	....	....	....	....	....	.70	.15

1981-1982 Regular Issues

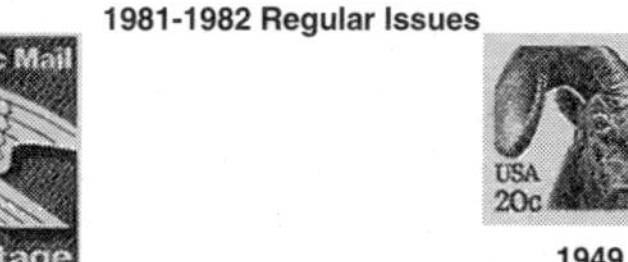

1946, 1947, 1948

1949

SCOTT NO.	DESCRIPTION	FDC SING.	FDC PL. BLK.	MINT SHEET	COPY-RIGHT	ZIP	PLATE BLOCK	UNUSED F/NH	USED
1946	(20¢) "C" Eagle, 11x10-1/2	1.75	4.00	49.50(100)	2.25	2.25	2.50	.55	.15
			LINE PR.				LINE PR.		
1947	(20¢) "C" Eagle, coil	1.75	2.75	....	....	....	2.25	.55	.15
1948	(20¢) "C" Eagle, from pane	1.75	....	....	....	....	....	.55	.15
1948a	same, booklet pane of 10	6.00	....	....	....	....	....	6.00	....
1949	20¢ Bighorned Sheep, blue, from booklet pane (1982)	1.75	....	....	....	....	....	.60	.15
1949a	same, booklet pane of 10	6.00	....	....	....	....	....	7.00	....
1949c	Type II, from booklet pane	....	....	....	....	....	....	0.60	0.20
1949d	same, booklet pane of 10	....	....	....	....	....	....	7.00	....

1950

1951

1982 COMMEMORATIVES

1952

SCOTT NO.	DESCRIPTION	FDC SING.	PLATE BLOCK	MINT SHEET	COPY-RIGHT	ZIP	PLATE BLOCK	UNUSED F/NH	USED
1950/2030	(1950-52, 2003-04, 2006-30) 30 varieties	....	....	....	....	....	....	19.95	4.40
1950	20¢ Franklin D. Roosevelt	1.75	4.00	30.50(48)	4.95	4.95	5.50	.60	.15
1951	20¢ LOVE, Perf. 11 x 10-1/2	1.85	4.25	51.75(50)	4.95	4.95	5.50	1.10	.30
1951a	Same, Perf. 11	....	....	30.50(50)	2.60	2.60	2.90	.65	.15

NOTE: Perforations will be mixed on Used #1951

SCOTT NO.	DESCRIPTION	FDC SING.	PLATE BLOCK	MINT SHEET	COPY-RIGHT	ZIP	PLATE BLOCK	UNUSED F/NH	USED
1952	20¢ George Washington	1.75	4.00	30.50(50)	2.45	2.45	2.70	.60	.15

BOOKLET PANE SINGLES: Traditionally, booklet panes have been collected only as intact panes since, other than the straight edged sides, they were identical to sheet stamps. However starting with the 1971 8¢ Eisenhower stamp, many issues differ from the comparative sheet stamp or may even be totally different issues (e.g. #1738-42 Windmills). These newer issues are now collected as booklet singles or panes—both methods being acceptable.

U.S. Postage #1953-2009

1953 1973 1966 2002

1982 STATE BIRDS AND FLOWERS

1953 Alabama
1954 Alaska
1955 Arizona
1956 Arkansas
1957 California
1958 Colorado
1959 Connecticut
1960 Delaware
1961 Florida
1962 Georgia
1963 Hawaii
1964 Idaho
1965 Illinois
1966 Indiana
1967 Iowa
1968 Kansas
1969 Kentucky
1970 Louisiana
1971 Maine
1972 Maryland
1973 Massachusetts
1974 Michigan
1975 Minnesota
1976 Mississippi
1977 Missouri
1978 Montana
1979 Nebraska
1980 Nevada
1981 New Hampshire
1982 New Jersey
1983 New Mexico
1984 New York
1985 North Carolina
1986 North Dakota
1987 Ohio
1988 Oklahoma
1989 Oregon
1990 Pennsylvania
1991 Rhode Island
1992 South Carolina
1993 South Dakota
1994 Tennessee
1995 Texas
1996 Utah
1997 Vermont
1998 Virginia
1999 Washington
2000 West Virginia
2001 Wisconsin
2002 Wyoming

Perf. 10-1/2 x 11

SCOTT NO.	DESCRIPTION	FIRST DAY COVERS SING.	FIRST DAY COVERS PL. BLK.	MINT SHEET	COPY-RIGHT	ZIP	PLATE BLOCK	UNUSED F/NH	USED
1953-2002	20¢, 50 varieties, attached	....	....	32.00(50)	....	....	....	37.50	....
	Set of singles	86.00	....	....	....	....	....	....	25.00
	Singles of above	2.00	....	....	....	....	....	.75	.65
1953a-2002a	Same, perf. 11	....	....	33.00(50)	....	....	....	33.00	....
	Singles of above	....	....	....	....	....	....	.75	....

NOTE: Used singles will not be sorted by perf. sizes.

2003 2004 2005

SCOTT NO.	DESCRIPTION	FIRST DAY COVERS SING.	FIRST DAY COVERS PL. BLK.	MINT SHEET	COPY-RIGHT	ZIP	PLATE BLOCK	UNUSED F/NH	USED
2003	20¢ USA/Netherlands	1.75	4.00	34.50(50)	....	....	17.00(20)	.60	.15
2004	20¢ Library of Congress	1.75	4.00	27.00(50)	2.35	2.35	2.60	.60	.15
			PL # STRIP 3				PL # STRIP 3		
2005	20¢ Consumer Education, coil	1.75	60.00	....	....	....	51.75	1.20	.15

2006 2007 2008 2009

SCOTT NO.	DESCRIPTION	FIRST DAY COVERS SING.	FIRST DAY COVERS PL. BLK.	MINT SHEET	COPY-RIGHT	ZIP	PLATE BLOCK	UNUSED F/NH	USED
2006-09	World's Fair, 4 varieties, attached	2.75	3.25	28.75(50)	3.45	3.45	3.95	2.80	2.00
2006	20¢ Solar Energy	1.75	....	....	....	....	....	.65	.15
2007	20¢ Synthetic Fuels	1.75	....	....	....	....	....	.65	.15
2008	20¢ Breeder Reactor	1.75	....	....	....	....	....	.65	.15
2009	20¢ Fossil Fuels	1.75	....	....	....	....	....	.65	.15

SE-TENANTS: Beginning with the 1964 Christmas issue (#1254-57), the United States has issued numerous Se-Tenant stamps covering a wide variety of subjects. Se-Tenants are issues where two or more different stamp designs are produced on the same sheet in pair, strip or block form. Mint stamps are usually collected in attached blocks, etc.—Used are generally saved as single stamps. Our Se-Tenant prices follow in this collecting pattern.

U.S. Postage #2010-2025

2010

2011

2012

2013

SCOTT NO.	DESCRIPTION	FIRST DAY COVERS SING.	PL. BLK.	MINT SHEET	COPY-RIGHT	ZIP	PLATE BLOCK	UNUSED F/NH	USED
2010	20¢ Horatio Alger	1.75	4.00	27.00(50)	2.25	2.25	2.50	.60	.15
2011	20¢ Aging Together	1.75	4.00	27.00(50)	2.25	2.25	2.50	.60	.15
2012	20¢ Barrymores	1.75	4.00	30.00(50)	2.50	2.50	2.75	.60	.15
2013	20¢ Dr. Mary Walker	1.75	4.00	27.00(50)	2.25	2.25	2.50	.60	.15

2014

2015

2016

2017

SCOTT NO.	DESCRIPTION	FIRST DAY COVERS SING.	PL. BLK.	MINT SHEET	COPY-RIGHT	ZIP	PLATE BLOCK	UNUSED F/NH	USED
2014	20¢ Peace Garden	1.75	4.00	27.00(50)	2.25	2.25	2.50	.60	.15
2015	20¢ America's Libraries	1.75	4.00	27.00(50)	2.25	2.25	2.50	.60	.15
2016	20¢ Jackie Robinson	7.00	13.50	90.00(50)	8.00	8.00	9.00	1.75	.15
2017	20¢ Touro Synagogue	1.75	4.00	34.50(50)	....	....	18.00(20)	.75	.15

2018

SCOTT NO.	DESCRIPTION	FIRST DAY COVERS SING.	PL. BLK.	MINT SHEET	COPY-RIGHT	ZIP	PLATE BLOCK	UNUSED F/NH	USED
2018	20¢ Wolf Trap Farm	1.75	4.00	27.00(50)	2.25	2.25	2.50	.60	.15

2019

2020

2021

2022

SCOTT NO.	DESCRIPTION	FIRST DAY COVERS SING.	PL. BLK.	MINT SHEET	COPY-RIGHT	ZIP	PLATE BLOCK	UNUSED F/NH	USED
2019-22	American Architecture. 4 varieties, attached	2.30	3.25	30.00(40)	2.95	2.95	3.25	2.90	2.00
2019	20¢ Fallingwater Mill Run ...	1.75	....	....	....	....	....	.65	.15
2020	20¢ Illinois Inst. Tech	1.75	....	....	....	....	....	.65	.15
2021	20¢ Gropius House	1.75	....	....	....	....	....	.65	.15
2022	20¢ Dulles Airport	1.75	....	....	....	....	....	.65	.15

2023

2024

2025

SCOTT NO.	DESCRIPTION	FIRST DAY COVERS SING.	PL. BLK.	MINT SHEET	COPY-RIGHT	ZIP	PLATE BLOCK	UNUSED F/NH	USED
2023	20¢ St. Francis of Assisi	1.75	4.00	30.00(50)	2.25	2.25	2.50	.60	.15
2024	20¢ Ponce de Leon	1.75	4.00	34.50(50)	....	....	18.00(20)	.75	.15
2025	13¢ Kitten & Puppy, Christmas	1.75	4.00	16.70(50)	1.80	1.80	2.00	.40	.15

U.S. Postage #2026-2035

SCOTT NO.	DESCRIPTION	FIRST DAY COVERS SING.	FIRST DAY COVERS PL. BLK.	MINT SHEET	COPY-RIGHT	ZIP	PLATE BLOCK	UNUSED F/NH	USED

2026

SCOTT NO.	DESCRIPTION	SING.	PL. BLK.	MINT SHEET	COPY-RIGHT	ZIP	PLATE BLOCK	UNUSED F/NH	USED
2026	20¢ Madonna & Child, Christmas	1.75	4.00	30.00(50)	....	....	16.50(20)	.60	.15

2027

2028

2029

2030

SCOTT NO.	DESCRIPTION	SING.	PL. BLK.	MINT SHEET	COPY-RIGHT	ZIP	PLATE BLOCK	UNUSED F/NH	USED
2027-30	Winter Scenes, Christmas 4 varieties, attached	2.75	3.25	43.00(50)	4.00	4.00	4.50	4.00	2.50
2027	20¢ Sledding	1.75	....	....	....	....	....	.85	.15
2028	20¢ Snowman	1.75	....	....	....	....	....	.85	.15
2029	20¢ Skating	1.75	....	....	....	....	....	.85	.15
2030	20¢ Decorating	1.75	....	....	....	....	....	.85	.15

1983 COMMEMORATIVES

SCOTT NO.	DESCRIPTION	SING.	PL. BLK.	MINT SHEET	COPY-RIGHT	ZIP	PLATE BLOCK	UNUSED F/NH	USED
2031-65	**13¢-20¢, 35 varieties, complete.......**		**.......**	**..... .**	**.....**	**.....**	**.......**	**24.25**	**5.00**

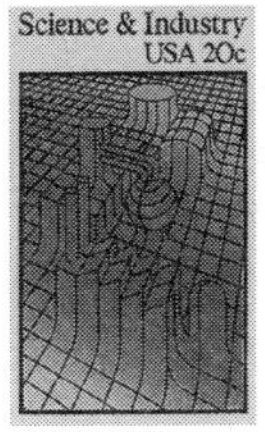

2031

SCOTT NO.	DESCRIPTION	SING.	PL. BLK.	MINT SHEET	COPY-RIGHT	ZIP	PLATE BLOCK	UNUSED F/NH	USED
2031	20¢ Science & Industry	1.75	4.00	27.00(50)	2.25	2.25	2.50	.60	.15

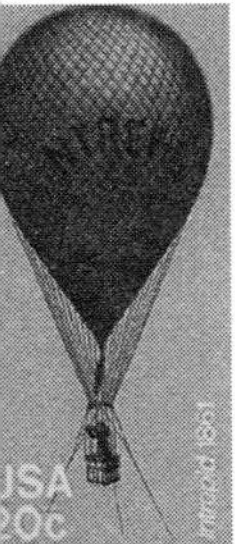

2032

2033

2034

2035

SCOTT NO.	DESCRIPTION	SING.	PL. BLK.	MINT SHEET	COPY-RIGHT	ZIP	PLATE BLOCK	UNUSED F/NH	USED
2032-35	20¢ Ballooning, 4 varieties, att'd.	2.75	3.25	26.00(40)	2.60	2.60	3.00	2.80	2.00
2032	20¢ Intrepid	1.75	....	....	....	....	....	.65	.15
2033	20¢ Red, white, & blue balloon	1.75	....	....	....	....	....	.65	.15
2034	20¢ Yellow, gold & gr. balloon	1.75	....	....	....	....	....	.65	.15
2035	20¢ Explorer II	1.75	....	....	....	....	....	.65	.15

PLATE BLOCKS: are portions of a sheet of stamps adjacent to the number(s) indicating the printing plate number used to produce that sheet. Flat plate issues are usually collected in plate blocks of six (number opposite middle stamp) while rotary issues are normally corner blocks of four.

U.S. Postage #2036-2051

2036

2037

2038

2039

SCOTT NO.	DESCRIPTION	FIRST DAY COVERS SING.	FIRST DAY COVERS PL. BLK.	MINT SHEET	COPY-RIGHT	ZIP	PLATE BLOCK	UNUSED F/NH	USED
2036	20¢ USA/Sweden	1.75	4.00	27.00(50)	2.25	2.25	2.50	.65	.15
2037	20¢ Civilian Conservation Corps	1.75	4.00	27.00(50)	2.25	2.25	2.50	.65	.15
2038	20¢ Joseph Priestley	1.75	4.00	27.00(50)	2.25	2.25	2.50	.65	.15
2039	20¢ Volunteerism	1.75	4.00	34.50(50)	....	....	18.00(20)	.65	.15

2040

2041

2042

2043

SCOTT NO.	DESCRIPTION	FIRST DAY COVERS SING.	FIRST DAY COVERS PL. BLK.	MINT SHEET	COPY-RIGHT	ZIP	PLATE BLOCK	UNUSED F/NH	USED
2040	20¢ German Immigrants	1.75	4.00	27.00(50)	2.25	2.25	2.50	.65	.15
2041	20¢ Brooklyn Bridge	1.75	4.00	30.00(50)	2.25	2.25	2.50	.65	.15
2042	20¢ Tennessee Valley Authority	1.75	4.00	34.50(50)	....	....	18.00(20)	.65	.15
2043	20¢ Physical Fitness	1.75	4.00	34.50(50)	....	....	18.00(20)	.65	.15

2044

2045

2046

2047

SCOTT NO.	DESCRIPTION	FIRST DAY COVERS SING.	FIRST DAY COVERS PL. BLK.	MINT SHEET	COPY-RIGHT	ZIP	PLATE BLOCK	UNUSED F/NH	USED
2044	20¢ Scott Joplin	1.75	4.00	30.00(50)	2.25	2.25	2.50	.70	.15
2045	20¢ Medal of Honor	1.75	4.00	27.00(40)	2.90	2.90	3.20	.70	.15
2046	20¢ Babe Ruth	8.00	16.00	97.50(50)	9.00	9.00	10.00	2.25	.15
2047	20¢ Nathaniel Hawthorne ...	1.75	4.00	27.00(50)	2.25	2.25	2.50	.65	.15

2048

2049

2050

2051

SCOTT NO.	DESCRIPTION	FIRST DAY COVERS SING.	FIRST DAY COVERS PL. BLK.	MINT SHEET	COPY-RIGHT	ZIP	PLATE BLOCK	UNUSED F/NH	USED
2048-51	13¢ Olympics, 4 varieties ...	2.75	3.25	22.00(50)	2.50	2.50	2.60	2.40	2.00
2048	13¢ Discus	1.75	....	....	......	....	....	.55	.15
2049	13¢ High Jump	1.75	....	....	......	....	....	.55	.15
2050	13¢ Archery	1.75	....	....	......	....	....	.55	.15
2051	13¢ Boxing	1.75	....	....	......	....	....	.55	.15

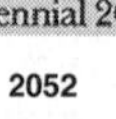
2052

2053

2054

U.S. Postage #2052-2070

SCOTT NO.	DESCRIPTION	FIRST DAY COVERS SING.	FIRST DAY COVERS PL. BLK.	MINT SHEET	COPY-RIGHT	ZIP	PLATE BLOCK	UNUSED F/NH	USED
2052	20¢ Treaty of Paris	1.75	4.00	24.00(40)	2.25	2.25	2.50	.60	.15
2053	20¢ Civil Service	1.75	4.00	34.50(50)	....	....	18.00(20)	.60	.15
2054	20¢ Metropolitan Opera	1.75	4.00	27.00(50)	2.25	2.25	2.50	.60	.15

2055 2056 2057 2058

SCOTT NO.	DESCRIPTION	FIRST DAY COVERS SING.	FIRST DAY COVERS PL. BLK.	MINT SHEET	COPY-RIGHT	ZIP	PLATE BLOCK	UNUSED F/NH	USED
2055-58	20¢ Inventors, 4 varieties, attd.	2.75	3.25	32.50(50)	3.75	3.75	4.00	3.50	2.00
2055	20¢ Charles Steinmetz	1.75	....	....	....	....	....	.80	.15
2056	20¢ Edwin Armstrong	1.75	....	....	....	....	....	.80	.15
2057	20¢ Nikola Tesla	1.75	....	....	....	....	....	.80	.15
2058	20¢ Philo T. Farnsworth	1.75	....	....	....	....	....	.80	.15

2059 2060 2061 2062

SCOTT NO.	DESCRIPTION	FIRST DAY COVERS SING.	FIRST DAY COVERS PL. BLK.	MINT SHEET	COPY-RIGHT	ZIP	PLATE BLOCK	UNUSED F/NH	USED
2059-62	20¢ Streetcars, 4 varieties, attd.	2.75	3.25	30.00(50)	3.25	3.25	3.50	3.00	2.00
2059	20¢ First Streetcar	1.75	....	....	....	....	....	.70	.15
2060	20¢ Electric Trolley	1.75	....	....	....	....	....	.70	.15
2061	20¢ "Bobtail"	1.75	....	....	....	....	....	.70	.15
2062	20¢ St. Charles Streetcar	1.75	....	....	....	....	....	.70	.15

2063 2064 2065 2066

SCOTT NO.	DESCRIPTION	FIRST DAY COVERS SING.	FIRST DAY COVERS PL. BLK.	MINT SHEET	COPY-RIGHT	ZIP	PLATE BLOCK	UNUSED F/NH	USED
2063	20¢ Madonna	1.75	4.00	27.00(50)	2.25	2.25	2.50	.60	.15
2064	20¢ Santa Claus	1.75	4.00	34.50(50)	....	....	18.00(20)	.60	.15
2065	20¢ Martin Luther	1.75	4.00	27.00(50)	2.25	2.25	2.50	.60	.15

1984 COMMEMORATIVES

SCOTT NO.	DESCRIPTION	FIRST DAY COVERS SING.	FIRST DAY COVERS PL. BLK.	MINT SHEET	COPY-RIGHT	ZIP	PLATE BLOCK	UNUSED F/NH	USED
2066-2109	**44 varieties, complete**	....	....	....	....	....	....	**32.00**	**6.25**
2066	20¢ Alaska Statehood	1.75	4.00	27.00(50)	3.75	3.75	3.95	.60	.15

2067 2068 2069 2070

SCOTT NO.	DESCRIPTION	FIRST DAY COVERS SING.	FIRST DAY COVERS PL. BLK.	MINT SHEET	COPY-RIGHT	ZIP	PLATE BLOCK	UNUSED F/NH	USED
2067-70	Winter Olympics, 4 varieties, attd.	2.75	3.25	35.00(50)	3.60	3.60	4.00	3.50	2.00
2067	20¢ Ice Dancing	1.75	....	....	....	....	....	.65	.15
2068	20¢ Downhill Skiing	1.75	....	....	....	....	....	.65	.15
2069	20¢ Cross Country Skiing	1.75	....	....	....	....	....	.65	.15
2070	20¢ Hockey	1.75	....	....	....	....	....	.65	.15

MINT SHEETS: From 1935 to date, we list prices for standard size Mint Sheets in Fine, Never Hinged condition. The Number of stamps in each sheet is noted in ( ).

U.S. Postage #2071-2085

2071 2072 2073 2074

SCOTT NO.	DESCRIPTION	FIRST DAY COVERS SING.	FIRST DAY COVERS PL. BLK.	MINT SHEET	COPY-RIGHT	ZIP	PLATE BLOCK	UNUSED F/NH	USED
2071	20¢ Federal Deposit Insur. Corp.	1.75	4.00	27.00(50)	2.25	2.25	2.50	.60	.15
2072	20¢ Love	1.95	4.00	34.50(50)	....	....	18.00(20)	.65	.15
2073	20¢ Carter G. Woodson	1.75	4.00	27.00(50)	2.25	2.25	2.50	.60	.15
2074	20¢ Conservation	1.75	4.00	27.00(50)	2.25	2.25	2.50	.60	.15

2075

2076

2077

2078

2079

SCOTT NO.	DESCRIPTION	FIRST DAY COVERS SING.	FIRST DAY COVERS PL. BLK.	MINT SHEET	COPY-RIGHT	ZIP	PLATE BLOCK	UNUSED F/NH	USED
2075	20¢ Credit Union	1.75	4.00	27.00(50)	2.25	2.25	2.50	.60	.15
2076-79	20¢ Orchids, 4 varieties, attached	2.75	3.25	34.00(48)	3.00	3.00	3.25	3.00	2.00
2076	20¢ Wildpink	1.75	....	....	....	....	....	.70	.15
2077	20¢ Lady's-slipper	1.75	....	....	....	....	....	.70	.15
2078	20¢ Spreading Pogonia	1.75	....	....	....	....	....	.70	.15
2079	20¢ Pacific Calypso	1.75	....	....	....	....	....	.70	.15

2080

2081

SCOTT NO.	DESCRIPTION	FIRST DAY COVERS SING.	FIRST DAY COVERS PL. BLK.	MINT SHEET	COPY-RIGHT	ZIP	PLATE BLOCK	UNUSED F/NH	USED
2080	20¢ Hawaii Statehood	1.75	4.00	30.00(50)	2.25	2.25	2.50	.60	.15
2081	20¢ National Archives	1.75	4.00	30.00(50)	2.25	2.25	2.50	.60	.15

2082

2083

2084

2085

SCOTT NO.	DESCRIPTION	FIRST DAY COVERS SING.	FIRST DAY COVERS PL. BLK.	MINT SHEET	COPY-RIGHT	ZIP	PLATE BLOCK	UNUSED F/NH	USED
2082-85	20¢ Olympics, 4 varieties, attd .	2.75	3.25	51.75(50)	5.10	5.10	5.25	5.00	3.00
2082	20¢ Men's Diving	1.75	....	....	....	....	....	1.15	.15
2083	20¢ Long Jump	1.75	....	....	....	....	....	1.15	.15
2084	20¢ Wrestling	1.75	....	....	....	....	....	1.15	.15
2085	20¢ Women's Kayak	1.75	....	....	....	....	....	1.15	.15

U.S. Postage #2086-2101

2086 2087 2088 2089

SCOTT NO.	DESCRIPTION	FIRST DAY COVERS SING.	FIRST DAY COVERS PL. BLK.	MINT SHEET	COPY-RIGHT	ZIP	PLATE BLOCK	UNUSED F/NH	USED
2086	20¢ Louisiana Exposition	1.75	4.00	21.85(40)	2.25	2.25	2.50	.60	.15
2087	20¢ Health Research	1.75	4.00	30.00(50)	2.25	2.25	2.50	.60	.15
2088	20¢ Douglas Fairbanks	1.75	4.00	34.50(50)	....	....	20.00	.60	.15
2089	20¢ Jim Thorpe	4.50	8.00	32.75(50)	2.70	2.70	3.00	.65	.15

2090 2091 2092 2093

SCOTT NO.	DESCRIPTION	FIRST DAY COVERS SING.	FIRST DAY COVERS PL. BLK.	MINT SHEET	COPY-RIGHT	ZIP	PLATE BLOCK	UNUSED F/NH	USED
2090	20¢ John McCormack	1.75	4.00	30.00(50)	2.25	2.25	2.50	.60	.15
2091	20¢ St. Lawrence Seaway	1.75	4.00	30.00(50)	2.70	2.70	3.00	.60	.15
2092	20¢ Preserving Wetlands	1.75	4.00	40.00(50)	2.25	2.25	2.50	.85	.15
2093	20¢ Roanoke Voyages	1.75	4.00	30.00(50)	2.25	2.25	2.50	.60	.15

2094 2095 2096 2097

SCOTT NO.	DESCRIPTION	FIRST DAY COVERS SING.	FIRST DAY COVERS PL. BLK.	MINT SHEET	COPY-RIGHT	ZIP	PLATE BLOCK	UNUSED F/NH	USED
2094	20¢ Herman Melville	1.75	4.00	27.00(50)	2.25	2.25	2.50	.60	.15
2095	20¢ Horace Moses	1.75	4.00	50.00(50)	2.70	2.70	25.00(20)	1.00	.15
2096	20¢ Smokey Bear	1.75	4.00	27.00(50)	2.70	2.70	3.00	.60	.15
2097	20¢ Roberto Clemente	12.00	20.00	100.00(50)	9.50	9.50	10.50	2.25	.15

2098 2099 2100 2101

SCOTT NO.	DESCRIPTION	FIRST DAY COVERS SING.	FIRST DAY COVERS PL. BLK.	MINT SHEET	COPY-RIGHT	ZIP	PLATE BLOCK	UNUSED F/NH	USED
2098-2101	20¢ American Dogs, attached ..	3.25	3.75	35.00(40)	3.50	3.50	4.00	3.25	2.50
2098	20¢ Beagle, Boston Terrier	1.75	....	....	....	....	....	.65	.15
2099	20¢ Chesapeake Bay Retriever, Cocker Spaniel	1.75	....	....	....	....	....	.65	.15
2100	20¢ Alaskan Malamute, Collie .	1.75	....	....	....	....	....	.65	.15
2101	20¢ Black & Tan Coonhound, American Foxhound	1.75	....	....	....	....	....	.65	.15

MINT SHEETS: From 1935 to date, we list prices for standard size Mint Sheets in Fine, Never Hinged condition. The number of stamps in each sheet is noted in ( ).

U.S. Postage #2102-2116a

2102

2103

2104

2105

2106

2107

2108

2109

SCOTT NO.	DESCRIPTION	FIRST DAY COVERS SING.	FIRST DAY COVERS PL.BLK.	MINT SHEET	COPY-RIGHT	ZIP	PLATE BLOCK	UNUSED F/NH	USED
2102	20¢ Crime Prevention	1.75	4.00	27.00(50)	2.25	2.25	2.50	.60	.15
2103	20¢ Hispanic Americans	1.75	4.00	21.85(40)	2.25	2.25	2.10	.60	.15
2104	20¢ Family Unity	1.75	4.00	34.50(50)	2.60	2.60	22.00(20)	.60	.15
2105	20¢ Eleanor Roosevelt	1.75	4.00	25.90(40)	2.25	2.25	2.50	.60	.15
2106	20¢ Nation of Readers	1.75	4.00	27.00(50)	2.25	2.25	2.50	.60	.15
2107	20¢ Madonna & Child	1.75	4.00	27.00(50)	2.25	2.25	2.50	.60	.15
2108	20¢ Santa Claus	1.35	4.00	27.00(50)	2.25	2.25	2.10	.20	.15
2109	20¢ Vietnam Veterans	1.75	4.00	24.00(40)	(combo)	5.50(6)	3.35	.60	.15

2110

2111, 2112, 2113

2114, 2115, 2115b

2116

1985 COMMEMORATIVES

SCOTT NO.	DESCRIPTION	FIRST DAY COVERS SING.	FIRST DAY COVERS PL.BLK.	MINT SHEET	COPY-RIGHT	ZIP	PLATE BLOCK	UNUSED F/NH	USED
2110/2166	**(2110, 2137-47, 2152-66) 27 vars........**		**.......**	**.......**	**.......**	**.......**	**.......**	**30.00**	**3.85**
2110	22¢ Jerome Kern	1.75	4.00	30.00(50)	2.70	2.70	3.00	.65	.15

1985 REGULAR ISSUES

SCOTT NO.	DESCRIPTION	FIRST DAY COVERS SING.	FIRST DAY COVERS PL.BLK.	MINT SHEET	COPY-RIGHT	ZIP	PLATE BLOCK	UNUSED F/NH	USED
2111	(22¢) "D" Eagle	1.75	4.00	92.00(100)	....	....	35.00(20)	.81	.15
			PL # STRIP 3				**PL # STRIP 3**		
2112	(22¢) "D" Eagle, coil	1.75	21.00	....	....	....	6.35	.70	.15
2113	(22¢) "D" Eagle from booklet pane	1.75	....	....	....	....	....	.95	.15
2113a	same, booklet pane of 10	5.75	....	....	....	....	....	9.50	....
			PL. BLK.				**PL. BLK.**		
2114	22¢ Flag over Capitol	1.75	4.00	46.00(100)	2.41	2.45	2.30	.20	.15
			PL # STRIP 3				**PL # STRIP 3**		
2115	22¢ Flag over Capitol, coil	1.75	27.50	....	....	....	3.25	.60	.15
2115b	22¢ Flag "T" coil (1985-87)	2.90	....	....	....	....	5.40	.60	.15
2116	22¢ Flag over Capitol from booklet pane	1.75	....	....	....	....	....	.90	.15
2116a	same, booklet pane of 5	2.90	....	....	....	....	....	4.50	....

U.S. Postage #2117-2136

2117 2118 2119 2120 2121

1985 SEASHELLS FROM BOOKLET PANE

SCOTT NO.	DESCRIPTION	FIRST DAY COVERS SING.	FIRST DAY COVERS PL.BLK.	MINT SHEET	COPY-RIGHT	ZIP	PLATE BLOCK	UNUSED F/NH	USED
2117-21	Shells, strip of 5, attached	3.00	....	....	....	....	....	3.10	....
2117	22¢ Frilled Dogwinkle	1.75	....	....	....	....	....	.60	.15
2118	22¢ Reticulated Helmet	1.75	....	....	....	....	....	.60	.15
2119	22¢ New England Neptune	1.75	....	....	....	....	....	.60	.15
2120	22¢ Calico Scallop	1.75	....	....	....	....	....	.60	.15
2121	22¢ Lightning Whelk	1.75	....	....	....	....	....	.60	.15
2121a	22¢ Seashells, booklet pane of 10	5.95	....	....	....	....	....	5.45	5.00

2122

1985 EXPRESS MAIL STAMP FROM BOOKLET PANE

SCOTT NO.	DESCRIPTION	FIRST DAY COVERS SING.	FIRST DAY COVERS PL.BLK.	MINT SHEET	COPY-RIGHT	ZIP	PLATE BLOCK	UNUSED F/NH	USED
2122	$10.75 Eagle & Moon	65.00	....	....	....	....		26.50	11.00
2122a	same, booklet pane of 3	160.00	....	....	....	....	....	75.00	....
2122b	Type II, from booklet pane	....	....	....	....	....	....	32.50	12.50
2122c	same, booklet pane of 3	....	....	....	....	....	....	95.00	....

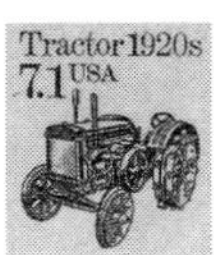

2123 2124 2125 2126 2127 2128 2129

2130 2131 2132 2133 2134 2135 2136

TRANSPORTATION COILS 1985-87 PERF. 10

SCOTT NO.	DESCRIPTION	FIRST DAY COVERS SING.	PL # STRIP 3	MINT SHEET	COPY-RIGHT	ZIP	PL # STRIP 3	UNUSED F/NH	USED
2123	3.4¢ School Bus	2.00	11.50	....	....	....	1.35	.20	.15
2124	4.9¢ Buckboard	2.00	14.00	....	....	....	1.25	.20	.15
2125	5.5¢ Star Route Truck (1986) ..	2.00	15.00	....	....	....	2.50	.20	.15
2126	6¢ Tricycle	2.00	14.00	....	....	....	2.00	.20	.15
2127	7.1¢ Tractor (1987)	2.00	15.00	....	....	....	3.15	.20	.15
2128	8.3¢ Ambulance	2.00	14.00	....	....	....	1.95	.20	.15
2129	8.5¢ Tow Truck (1987)	2.00	12.50	....	....	....	3.45	.25	.15
2130	10.1¢ Oil Wagon	2.00	12.50	....	....	....	2.75	.30	.15
2131	11¢ Stutz Bearcat	2.00	18.00	....	....	....	1.75	.30	.15
2132	12¢ Stanley Steamer	2.00	15.00	....	....	....	2.35	.35	.15
2133	12.5¢ Pushcart	2.00	15.00	....	....	....	3.00	.35	.15
2134	14¢ Iceboat	2.00	15.00	....	....	....	2.30	.40	.15
2135	17¢ Dog Sled (1986)	2.00	12.50	....	....	....	3.25	.55	.15
2136	25¢ Bread Wagon (1986)	2.00	15.00	....	....	....	4.00	.65	.15

U.S. Postage #2123a-2150a

PRECANCELLED COILS

The following prices are for precancelled, unused, never hinged stamps. Stamps without gum sell for less.

SCOTT NO.		PL # STRIP 3	UN-USED	SCOTT NO.		PL # STRIP 3	UN-USED
2123a	3.4¢ School Bus	7.50	.20	2129a	8.5¢ Tow Truck	4.00	.25
2124a	4.9¢ Buckboard	2.35	.20	2130a	10.1¢ Oil Wagon	3.25	.30
2125a	5.5¢ Star Route Truck	2.35	.20	2130av	10.1¢ Oil Wagon, red precancel (1988)	3.50	.30
2126a	6¢ Tricycle	2.30	.20	2132a	12¢ Stanley Steamer	3.15	.35
2127a	7.1¢ Tractor	4.00	.20	2132b	12¢ Stanley Steamer "B" Press	25.00	.85
2127av	7.1¢ Tractor, precancel (1989)	2.75	.20	2133a	12.5¢ Pushcart	4.00	.40
2128a	8.3¢ Ambulance	1.75	.25				

2137

2138

2139

2140

2141

2142

2143

2144

2145

2146

2147

1985 COMMEMORATIVES (continued)

SCOTT NO.	DESCRIPTION	FIRST DAY COVERS SING.	FIRST DAY COVERS PL.BLK.	MINT SHEET	COPY-RIGHT	ZIP	PLATE BLOCK	UNUSED F/NH	USED
2137	22¢ Mary Bethune	1.75	4.00	32.75(50)	2.70	2.70	3.00	.70	.15
2138-41	Duck Decoys, 4 varieties, attached	2.75	3.25	72.50(50)	8.00	8.00	9.00	7.50	4.00
2138	22¢ Broadbill	1.75	......	......	......	......	......	.85	.15
2139	22¢ Mallard	1.75	......	......	......	......	......	.85	.15
2140	22¢ Canvasback	1.75	......	......	......	......	......	.85	.15
2141	22¢ Redhead	1.75	......	......	......	......	......	.85	.15
2142	22¢ Winter Special Olympics	1.75	4.00	21.85(40)	2.70	2.70	3.00	.60	.15
2143	22¢ "LOVE"	1.95	4.00	30.00(50)	2.70	2.70	3.00	.65	.15
2144	22¢ Rural Electricity	1.75	......	51.75(50)	......	......	35.00(20)	.85	.15
2145	22¢ Ameripex '86	1.75	4.00	25.00(48)	2.50	2.50	2.80	.60	.15
2146	22¢ Abigail Adams	1.75	4.00	27.00(50)	2.50	2.50	2.80	.60	.15
2147	22¢ Frederic Bartholdi	1.75	4.00	27.00(50)	2.50	2.50	2.80	.60	.15

2149

2150

1985 REGULAR ISSUE COILS

SCOTT NO.	DESCRIPTION	FIRST DAY COVERS SING.	PLATE # STRIP 3	MINT SHEET	COPY-RIGHT	ZIP	PLATE # STRIP 3	UNUSED F/NH	USED
2149	18¢ G. Washington	1.75	50.00	......	......	......	4.00	.60	.15
2149a	18¢ G. Washington, precancel	......	......	......	......	......	4.25	.60	......
2150	21.1¢ Envelope	1.75	32.50	......	......	......	4.00	.55	1.00
2150a	21.1¢ Envelope, precancel	......	......	......	......	......	4.85	.55	......

U.S. Postage #2152-2167

2152

2153

2154

SCOTT NO.	DESCRIPTION	FIRST DAY COVERS SING.	FIRST DAY COVERS PL.BLK.	MINT SHEET	COPY-RIGHT	ZIP	PLATE BLOCK	UNUSED F/NH	USED
2152	22¢ Korean War Veterans ..	1.75	4.00	32.80(50)	2.70	2.70	3.00	.70	.15
2153	22¢ Social Security	1.75	4.00	27.00(50)	2.50	2.50	2.80	.60	.15
2154	22¢ World War I Veterans ...	1.75	4.00	32.80(50)	2.70	2.70	3.00	.70	.15

2155

2156

2157

2158

SCOTT NO.	DESCRIPTION	FIRST DAY COVERS SING.	FIRST DAY COVERS PL.BLK.	MINT SHEET	COPY-RIGHT	ZIP	PLATE BLOCK	UNUSED F/NH	USED
2155-58	American Horses, 4 varieties, attd	3.00	3.50	95.00(40)	10.25	10.25	11.00	10.00	4.00
2155	22¢ Quarter Horse	1.75	......	......	......	......	......	2.45	.15
2156	22¢ Morgan	1.75	......	......	......	......	......	2.45	.15
2157	22¢ Saddlebred	1.75	......	......	......	......	......	2.45	.15
2158	22¢ Appaloosa	1.75	......	......	......	......	......	2.45	.15

2159

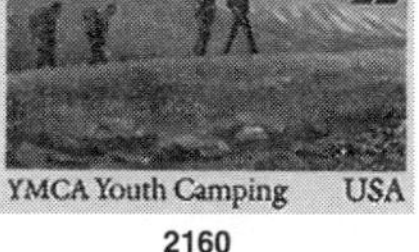

2160

2161

2162

2163

2164

SCOTT NO.	DESCRIPTION	FIRST DAY COVERS SING.	FIRST DAY COVERS PL.BLK.	MINT SHEET	COPY-RIGHT	ZIP	PLATE BLOCK	UNUSED F/NH	USED
2159	22¢ Public Education	1.75	4.00	27.00(50)	2.70	2.70	3.00	.60	.15
2160-63	Youth Year, 4 varieties, attached	3.00	3.50	50.00(50)	5.25	5.25	5.50	5.00	3.50
2160	22¢ YMCA	1.75	....	....	....	....	....	1.20	.15
2161	22¢ Boy Scouts	1.75	....	....	....	....	....	1.20	.15
2162	22¢ Big Brothers & Big Sisters .	1.75	....	....	....	....	....	1.20	.15
2163	22¢ Camp Fire	1.75	....	....	....	....	....	1.20	.15
2164	22¢ Help End Hunger	1.75	4.00	32.75(50)	2.55	2.55	2.80	.70	.15

2165

2166

2167

SCOTT NO.	DESCRIPTION	FIRST DAY COVERS SING.	FIRST DAY COVERS PL.BLK.	MINT SHEET	COPY-RIGHT	ZIP	PLATE BLOCK	UNUSED F/NH	USED
2165	22¢ Madonna & Child	1.75	4.00	27.00(50)	2.55	2.55	2.80	.60	.15
2166	22¢ Poinsettia	1.75	4.00	27.00(50)	2.55	2.55	2.80	.60	.15
2167	22¢ Arkansas Statehood	1.75	4.00	32.75(50)	2.55	2.55	2.80	.70	.15

U.S. Postage #2168-2197a

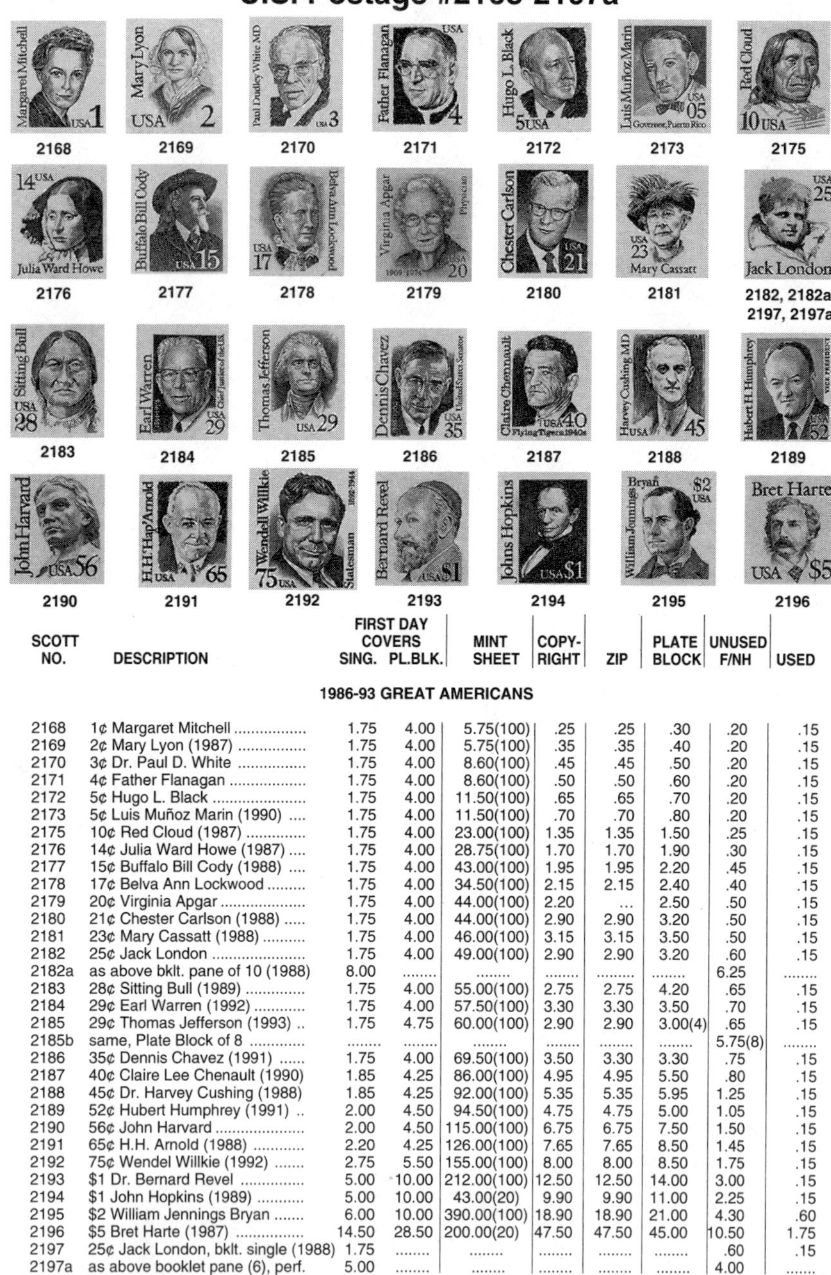

2168, 2169, 2170, 2171, 2172, 2173, 2175, 2176, 2177, 2178, 2179, 2180, 2181, 2182, 2182a, 2197, 2197a, 2183, 2184, 2185, 2186, 2187, 2188, 2189, 2190, 2191, 2192, 2193, 2194, 2195, 2196

SCOTT NO.	DESCRIPTION	FIRST DAY COVERS SING.	FIRST DAY COVERS PL.BLK.	MINT SHEET	COPY-RIGHT	ZIP	PLATE BLOCK	UNUSED F/NH	USED
	1986-93 GREAT AMERICANS								
2168	1¢ Margaret Mitchell	1.75	4.00	5.75(100)	.25	.25	.30	.20	.15
2169	2¢ Mary Lyon (1987)	1.75	4.00	5.75(100)	.35	.35	.40	.20	.15
2170	3¢ Dr. Paul D. White	1.75	4.00	8.60(100)	.45	.45	.50	.20	.15
2171	4¢ Father Flanagan	1.75	4.00	8.60(100)	.50	.50	.60	.20	.15
2172	5¢ Hugo L. Black	1.75	4.00	11.50(100)	.65	.65	.70	.20	.15
2173	5¢ Luis Muñoz Marin (1990)	1.75	4.00	11.50(100)	.70	.70	.80	.20	.15
2175	10¢ Red Cloud (1987)	1.75	4.00	23.00(100)	1.35	1.35	1.50	.25	.15
2176	14¢ Julia Ward Howe (1987)	1.75	4.00	28.75(100)	1.70	1.70	1.90	.30	.15
2177	15¢ Buffalo Bill Cody (1988)	1.75	4.00	43.00(100)	1.95	1.95	2.20	.45	.15
2178	17¢ Belva Ann Lockwood	1.75	4.00	34.50(100)	2.15	2.15	2.40	.40	.15
2179	20¢ Virginia Apgar	1.75	4.00	44.00(100)	2.20	...	2.50	.50	.15
2180	21¢ Chester Carlson (1988)	1.75	4.00	44.00(100)	2.90	2.90	3.20	.50	.15
2181	23¢ Mary Cassatt (1988)	1.75	4.00	46.00(100)	3.15	3.15	3.50	.50	.15
2182	25¢ Jack London	1.75	4.00	49.00(100)	2.90	2.90	3.20	.60	.15
2182a	as above bklt. pane of 10 (1988)	8.00	....	....	....	....	....	6.25	....
2183	28¢ Sitting Bull (1989)	1.75	4.00	55.00(100)	2.75	2.75	4.20	.65	.15
2184	29¢ Earl Warren (1992)	1.75	4.00	57.50(100)	3.30	3.30	3.50	.70	.15
2185	29¢ Thomas Jefferson (1993) ..	1.75	4.75	60.00(100)	2.90	2.90	3.00(4)	.65	.15
2185b	same, Plate Block of 8	....	....	....	....	....	....	5.75(8)	....
2186	35¢ Dennis Chavez (1991)	1.75	4.00	69.50(100)	3.50	3.30	3.30	.75	.15
2187	40¢ Claire Lee Chenault (1990)	1.85	4.25	86.00(100)	4.95	4.95	5.50	.80	.15
2188	45¢ Dr. Harvey Cushing (1988)	1.85	4.25	92.00(100)	5.35	5.35	5.95	1.25	.15
2189	52¢ Hubert Humphrey (1991) ..	2.00	4.50	94.50(100)	4.75	4.75	5.00	1.05	.15
2190	56¢ John Harvard	2.00	4.50	115.00(100)	6.75	6.75	7.50	1.50	.15
2191	65¢ H.H. Arnold (1988)	2.20	4.25	126.00(100)	7.65	7.65	8.50	1.45	.15
2192	75¢ Wendel Willkie (1992)	2.75	5.50	155.00(100)	8.00	8.00	8.50	1.75	.15
2193	$1 Dr. Bernard Revel	5.00	10.00	212.00(100)	12.50	12.50	14.00	3.00	.15
2194	$1 John Hopkins (1989)	5.00	10.00	43.00(20)	9.90	9.90	11.00	2.25	.15
2195	$2 William Jennings Bryan	6.00	10.00	390.00(100)	18.90	18.90	21.00	4.30	.60
2196	$5 Bret Harte (1987)	14.50	28.50	200.00(20)	47.50	47.50	45.00	10.50	1.75
2197	25¢ Jack London, bklt. single (1988)	1.75	....	....	....	....	....	.60	.15
2197a	as above booklet pane (6), perf.	5.00	....	....	....	....	....	4.00	....

FIRST DAY COVERS: First Day Covers are envelopes cancelled on the "First Day of Issue" of the stamp used on the envelope. Usually they also contain a picture (cachet) on the left side designed to go with the theme of the stamp. From 1935 to 1944, prices listed are for cacheted, addressed covers. From 1945 to date, prices are for cacheted, unaddressed covers.

U.S. Postage #2198-2211

SCOTT NO.	DESCRIPTION	FIRST DAY COVERS SING.	FIRST DAY COVERS PL.BLK.	MINT SHEET	COPY-RIGHT	ZIP	PLATE BLOCK	UNUSED F/NH	USE
	1986 COMMEMORATIVES								
2167/2245	(2167, 2202-04, 2210-11, 2220-24, 2235-45) 22 varieties.......		....	....	....	....	....	16.00	3.15

2198

2199

2200

2201

2202

2203

2204

SCOTT NO.	DESCRIPTION	FIRST DAY COVERS SING.	FIRST DAY COVERS PL.BLK.	MINT SHEET	COPY-RIGHT	ZIP	PLATE BLOCK	UNUSED F/NH	USE
2198	22¢ Cover & Handstamp	1.75	....	....	....	....	....	.70	.15
2199	22¢ Collector with Album	1.75	....	....	....	....	....	.70	.15
2200	22¢ No. 836 under magnifier ...	1.75	....	....	....	....	....	.70	.15
2201	22¢ President sheet	1.75	....	....	....	....	....	.70	.15
2201a	Stamp Collecting booklet pane, 4 varieties, attached	4.50	....	....	....	....	....	2.80	2.50
2202	22¢ Love	1.95	4.25	27.00(50)	2.55	2.55	2.80	.60	.15
2203	22¢ Sojourner Truth	1.75	4.00	30.50(50)	2.55	2.55	2.80	.65	.15
2204	22¢ Texas Republic	1.75	4.00	32.75(50)	2.55	2.55	2.80	.70	.15

2205

2206

2207

2208

2209

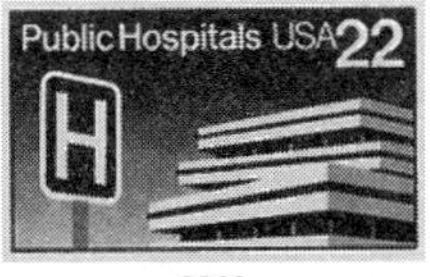
2210

2211

SCOTT NO.	DESCRIPTION	FIRST DAY COVERS SING.	FIRST DAY COVERS PL.BLK.	MINT SHEET	COPY-RIGHT	ZIP	PLATE BLOCK	UNUSED F/NH	USE
2205	22¢ Muskellunge	1.75	....	....	....	....	....	2.25	.15
2206	22¢ Altantic Cod	1.75	....	....	....	....	....	2.25	.15
2207	22¢ Largemouth Bass	1.75	....	....	....	....	....	2.25	.15
2208	22¢ Bluefin Tuna	1.75	....	....	....	....	....	2.25	.15
2209	22¢ Catfish	1.75	....	....	....	....	....	2.25	.15
2209a	22¢ Fish, bklt. pane 5 vars., att'd.	6.50	....	....	....	....	....	10.50	4.00
2210	22¢ Public Hospitals	1.75	4.00	27.00(50)	2.55	2.55	2.80	.60	.15
2211	22¢ Duke Ellington	1.75	4.00	30.50(50)	2.55	2.55	2.80	.65	.15

U.S. Postage #2216-2231

1986 PRESIDENTS MINIATURE SETS
Complete set printed on 4 miniature sheets of 9 stamps each.

2216a	*Washington*	**2218a**	*Hayes*
2216b	*Adams*	**2218b**	*Garfield*
2216c	*Jefferson*	**2218c**	*Arthur*
2216d	*Madison*	**2218d**	*Cleveland*
2216e	*Monroe*	**2218e**	*B. Harrison*
2216f	*J.Q. Adams*	**2218f**	*McKinley*
2216g	*Jackson*	**2218g**	*T. Roosevelt*
2216h	*Van Buren*	**2218h**	*Taft*
2216i	*W.H. Harrison*	**2218i**	*Wilson*
2217a	*Tyler*	**2219a**	*Harding*
2217b	*Polk*	**2219b**	*Coolidge*
2217c	*Taylor*	**2219c**	*Hoover*
2217d	*Fillmore*	**2219d**	*F.D. Roosevelt*
2217e	*Pierce*	**2219e**	*White House*
2217f	*Buchanan*	**2219f**	*Truman*
2217g	*Lincoln*	**2219g**	*Eisenhower*
2217h	*A. Johnson*	**2219h**	*Kennedy*
2217i	*Grant*	**2219i**	*L.B. Johnson*

SCOTT NO.	DESCRIPTION	FIRST DAY COVERS SING.	PL.BLK.	MINT SHEET	COPY-RIGHT	ZIP	PLATE BLOCK	UNUSED F/NH	USED
	1986 AMERIPEX '86 MINIATURE SHEETS								
2216-19	22¢ 36 vars., cpl. in 4 min. sheet	29.95	....	....	....	....	....	21.00	19.50
2216a-19i	set of 36 singles	70.00	....	....	....	....	....	....	11.50
2216	22¢ Wash.-Harrison, 9 varieties	10.00	....	....	....	....	....	5.00	5.00
2216a-i	22¢, any single	2.25	....	....	....	....	....	.50	.30
2217	22¢ Tyler-Grant, 9 varieties	10.00	....	....	....	....	....	5.00	5.00
2217a-i	22¢, any single	2.25	....	....	....	....	....	.50	.30
2218	22¢ Hayes-Wilson, 9 varieties .	10.00	....	....	....	....	....	5.00	5.00
2218a-i	22¢, any single	2.25	....	....	....	....	....	.50	.30
2219	22¢ Harding-Johnson, 9 varieties	10.00	....	....	....	....	....	5.00	5.00
2219a-i	22¢, any single	2.25	....	....	....	....	....	.50	.30

2220

2221

2224

2222

2223

SCOTT NO.	DESCRIPTION	FIRST DAY COVERS SING.	PL.BLK.	MINT SHEET	COPY-RIGHT	ZIP	PLATE BLOCK	UNUSED F/NH	USED
	1986 COMMEMORATIVES								
2220-23	Explorers, 4 varieties, attached	2.75	3.25	55.00(50)	6.00	6.00	7.50	5.50	3.00
2220	22¢ Elisha Kent Kane	1.75	....	....	....	....	....	1.00	.15
2221	22¢ Adolphus W. Greely	1.75	....	....	....	....	....	1.00	.15
2222	22¢ Vilhjalmur Stefansson	1.75	....	....	....	....	....	1.00	.15
2223	22¢ R.E. Peary, M. Henson	1.75	....	....	....	....	....	1.00	.15
2224	22¢ Statue of Liberty	1.75	4.00	27.00(50)	2.55	2.55	2.80	.60	.15

2225

2226, 2226a

2228

NOTE: #2225—"¢" sign eliminated. #1897 has "1¢". #2226—inscribed "2 USA". #1897A inscribed "USA 2¢". #2228—"Stagecoach 1890s" is 17 mm. long.

1986-91 TRANSPORTATION COILS—"B" Press
Perf. 10 Vertically

SCOTT NO.	DESCRIPTION	FIRST DAY COVERS SING.	PL# STRIP 3	MINT SHEET	COPY-RIGHT	ZIP	PL# STRIP 3	UNUSED F/NH	USED
2225	1¢ Omnibus		1.75	6.50	...	...	.85	.20	.15
2225a	1¢ Omnibus, untagged (1991)		...	...	...	...	1.25	.20	.15
2226	2¢ Locomotive (1987)		1.75	6.50	...	...	1.00	.20	.15
2226a	2¢ Locomotive, untagged (1994)		...	...	...	...	1.10	.20	.15
2228	4¢ Stagecoach		...	...	...	...	1.75	.20	.15
2228a	Same, overall tagging (1990)		...	...	...	...	20.00	.75	.15
2231	8.3¢ Ambulance Precancelled (1986) .		...	...	...	...	4.95	.30	.15

U.S. Postage #2235-2245

2235  2236  2237  2238  2239

1986 COMMEMORATIVES

SCOTT NO.	DESCRIPTION	FIRST DAY COVERS SING.	PL.BLK.	MINT SHEET	COPY-RIGHT	ZIP	PLATE BLOCK	UNUSED F/NH	USED
2235-38	Navajo Art, 4 varieties, att'd.	2.75	3.25	35.00(50)	3.60	3.60	3.75	3.50	3.00
2235	22¢ Navajo Art	1.75	....	....	....	....	....	.85	.15
2236	22¢ Navajo Art	1.75	....	....	....	....	....	.85	.15
2237	22¢ Navajo Art	1.75	....	....	....	....	....	.85	.15
2238	22¢ Navajo Art	1.75	....	....	....	....	....	.85	.15
2239	22¢ T.S. Eliot	1.75	4.00	27.00(50)	2.55	2.55	2.80	.60	.15

2240  2241  2242  2243  2244  2245

SCOTT NO.	DESCRIPTION	FIRST DAY COVERS SING.	PL.BLK.	MINT SHEET	COPY-RIGHT	ZIP	PLATE BLOCK	UNUSED F/NH	USED
2240-43	Woodcarved Figurines, 4 varieties, attached	2.75	3.25	35.00(50)	3.60	3.60	3.75	3.50	3.00
2240	22¢ Highlander Figure	1.75	....	....	....	....	....	.85	.15
2241	22¢ Ship Figurehead	1.75	....	....	....	....	....	.85	.15
2242	22¢ Nautical Figure	1.75	....	....	....	....	....	.85	.15
2243	22¢ Cigar Store Figure	1.75	....	....	....	....	....	.85	.15
2244	22¢ Madonna	1.75	4.00	51.75(100)	2.55	2.55	2.80	.60	.15
2245	22¢ Village Scene	1.75	4.00	51.75(100)	2.55	2.55	2.80	.60	.15

2246

2247

2248

2249

2250

2251

U.S. Postage #2246-2266

1987 COMMEMORATIVES

SCOTT NO.	DESCRIPTION	FIRST DAY COVERS SING.	FIRST DAY COVERS PL.BLK.	MINT SHEET	COPY-RIGHT	ZIP	PLATE BLOCK	UNUSED F/NH	USED
2246/2368	(2246-51, 2275, 2336-38, 2349-54, 2360-61, 2367-68) 20 varieties	....	....	....	....	....	....	15.00	2.50
2246	22¢ Michigan Statehood	1.75	4.00	30.00(50)	2.55	2.55	2.80	.60	.15
2247	22¢ Pan American Games	1.75	4.00	27.00(50)	2.55	2.55	2.80	.60	.15
2248	22¢ LOVE	1.95	4.25	51.75(100)	2.55	2.55	2.80	.60	.15
2249	22¢ Jean Baptiste Pointe du Sable	1.75	4.00	27.00(50)	2.55	2.55	2.80	.60	.15
2250	22¢ Enrico Caruso	1.75	4.00	30.00(50)	2.55	2.55	2.80	.60	.15
2251	22¢ Girl Scouts	1.75	4.00	27.00(50)	2.55	2.55	2.80	.60	.15

2252  2253  2254  2255  2256

2257  2258  2259  2260  2261

2262  2263  2264  2265  2266

1987-93 TRANSPORTATION COILS

SCOTT NO.	DESCRIPTION	FIRST DAY COVERS SING.	PLATE # STRIP	MINT SHEET	COPY-RIGHT	ZIP	PLATE # STRIP	UNUSED F/NH	USED
2252	3¢ Conestoga Wagon (1988) ...	1.75	9.00	....	....	....	1.25	.20	.15
2252a	same, untagged (1992)	....	9.00	....	....	....	1.75	.20	.20
2253	5¢ Milk Wagon	1.75	9.00	....	....	....	1.50	.20	.15
2254	5.3¢ Elevator, Precancel (1988)	1.75	9.00	....	....	....	1.90	.20	.15
2255	7.6¢ Carreta, Precancel (1988)	1.75	9.00	....	....	....	3.25	.20	.15
2256	8.4¢ Wheel Chair, Precancel (1988)	1.75	9.00	....	....	....	3.25	.25	.15
2257	10¢ Canal Boat	1.75	9.00	....	....	....	2.00	.30	.15
2257a	same, overall tagging (1993) ...	....	9.00	....	....	....	3.75	.30	.20
2258	13¢ Police Wagon, Precancel (1988)	1.75	9.00	....	....	....	3.45	.35	.15
2259	13.2¢ Railroad Coal Car, Precancel (1988)	1.75	9.00	....	....	....	3.50	.40	.15
2260	15¢ Tugboat (1988)	1.75	9.00	....	....	....	3.50	.40	.15
2260a	same, overall tagging (1990) ...	....	9.00	....	....	....	4.50	.40	.20
2261	16.7¢ Popcorn Wagon, Precancel (1988)	1.75	9.00	....	....	....	4.25	.40	.15
2262	17.5¢ Racing Car	1.75	9.00	....	....	....	4.75	.45	.15
2262a	17.5¢ Racing Car, Precancel (1988)	1.75	9.00	....	....	....	5.25	.45	.15
2263	20¢ Cable Car (1988)	1.75	9.00	....	....	....	4.50	.50	.15
2263b	same, overall tagging (1990) ...	....	9.00	....	....	....	6.50	.50	.20
2264	20.5¢ Fire Engine, Precancel (1988)	1.75	9.00	....	....	....	4.75	.60	.15
2265	21¢ Railroad Mail Car, Precancel (1988)	1.75	9.00	....	....	....	4.75	.60	.15
2266	24.1¢ Tandem Bicycle, Precancel (1988)	1.75	9.00	....	....	....	5.50	.60	.15

U.S. Postage #2267-2283

2267 2268 2269 2270

2271 2272 2273 2274

SCOTT NO.	DESCRIPTION	FIRST DAY COVERS SING.	PL.BLK.	MINT SHEET	COPY-RIGHT	ZIP	PLATE BLOCK	UNUSED F/NH	USED
	1987 SPECIAL OCCASIONS BOOKLET PANE								
2267	22¢ Congratulations!	1.75	....	....	....	....	....	2.25	.15
2268	22¢ Get Well!	1.75	....	....	....	....	....	2.25	.15
2269	22¢ Thank You!	1.75	....	....	....	....	....	2.25	.15
2270	22¢ Love You, Dad!	1.75	....	....	....	....	....	2.25	.15
2271	22¢ Best Wishes!	1.75	....	....	....	....	....	2.25	.15
2272	22¢ Happy Birthday!	1.75	....	....	....	....	....	2.25	.15
2273	22¢ Love You, Mother!	1.75	....	....	....	....	....	2.25	.15
2274	22¢ Keep in Touch!	1.75	....	....	....	....	....	2.25	.15
2274a	Special Occasions booklet pane of 10, attached	7.00	....	....	....	....	....	17.50	....

NOTE: #2274a contains 1 each of #2268-71, 2273-74 and 2 each of #2267 and 2272.

SCOTT NO.	DESCRIPTION	FIRST DAY COVERS SING.	PL.BLK.	MINT SHEET	COPY-RIGHT	ZIP	PLATE BLOCK	UNUSED F/NH	USED
	1987 COMMEMORATIVES (continued)								
2275	22¢ United Way	1.75	4.00	27.00(50)	2.55	2.55	2.80	.60	.15

2275

2276, 2276a

2277, 2279, 2282, 2282a

2278, 2285A, 2285Ac

2280 2281 2283, 2283a 2284 2285, 2285b

SCOTT NO.	DESCRIPTION	FIRST DAY COVERS SING.	PL.BLK.	MINT SHEET	COPY-RIGHT	ZIP	PLATE BLOCK	UNUSED F/NH	USED
	1987-88 REGULAR ISSUE								
2276	22¢ Flag & Fireworks	1.75	4.00	51.75(100)	2.55	2.55	2.80	.60	.15
2276a	booklet pane of 20	12.50	......	......	......	......	......	11.50	......
2277	(25¢) "E" Earth (1988)	1.75	4.00	60.00(100)	2.70	2.70	3.00	.60	.15
2278	25¢ Flag with Clouds (1988)	1.75	4.00	60.00(100)	2.70	2.70	3.00	.60	.15
			PL # STRIP 3				**PL # STRIP 3**		
2279	(25¢) "E" Earth coil (1988)	1.75	7.50	......	......	......	4.50	.60	.15
2280	25¢ Flag over Yosemite, coil (1988)	1.75	7.50	......	......	......	4.50	.60	.15
2280v	25¢ Flag over Yosemite, phosphor (1989)	1.75	......	......	......	......	4.75	.60	.15
2281	25¢ Honey Bee, coil (1988)	1.75	7.50	......	......	......	4.00	.60	.15
2282	(25¢) "E" Earth, booklet single (1988)	1.75	......	......	......	......	......	.60	.15
2282a	(25¢) "E" Earth, bklt. pane of 10	7.25	......	......	......	......	......	6.90	......
2283	25¢ Pheasant booklet single (1988)	1.75	......	......	......	......	......	.60	.15
2283a	25¢ Pheasant, bklt. pane of 10	7.25	......	......	......	......	......	6.35	......
2283b	25¢ Pheasant, (red omitted) booklet single	......	......	......	......	......	......	9.00	......
2283c	25¢ Pheasant, (red omitted) booklet pane of 10	......	......	......	......	......	......	92.50	......

U.S. Postage #2284-2335

SCOTT NO.	DESCRIPTION	FIRST DAY COVERS SING.	PL.BLK.	MINT SHEET	COPY-RIGHT	ZIP	PLATE BLOCK	UNUSED F/NH	USED
	1987-88 REGULAR ISSUE (Continued)						**PL # STRIP 3**		
2284	25¢ Grosbeak, booklet sgl.(1988)	1.75	......	......	......	......	......	.65	.15
2285	25¢ Owl booklet single	1.75	......	......	......	......	......	.65	.15
2285b	25¢ Owl/Grosbeak, booklet pane of 10	7.25	......	......	......	......	......	6.35	......
2285A	25¢ Flag with Clouds, booklet single	1.75	......	......	......	......	......	.65	.15
2285Ac	as above, booklet pane of 6 (1988)	4.00	......	......	......	......	......	4.00	......

1987 AMERICAN WILDLIFE

2286

2296

2286 *Barn Swallow*
2287 *Monarch Butterfly*
2288 *Bighorn Sheep*
2289 *Broad-tailed Hummingbird*
2290 *Cottontail*
2291 *Osprey*
2292 *Mountain Lion*
2293 *Luna Moth*
2294 *Mule Deer*
2295 *Gray Squirrel*
2296 *Armadillo*
2297 *Eastern Chipmunk*
2298 *Moose*
2299 *Black Bear*
2300 *Tiger Swallowtail*
2301 *Bobwhite*
2302 *Ringtail*
2303 *Red-winged Blackbird*
2304 *American Lobster*
2305 *Black-tailed Jack Rabbit*
2306 *Scarlet Tanager*
2307 *Woodchuck*
2308 *Roseate Spoonbill*
2309 *Bald Eagle*
2310 *Alaskan Brown Bear*
2311 *Iiwi*
2312 *Badger*
2313 *Pronghorn*
2314 *River Otter*
2315 *Ladybug*
2316 *Beaver*
2317 *White-tailed Deer*
2318 *Blue Jay*
2319 *Pika*
2320 *Bison*
2321 *Snowy Egret*
2322 *Gray Wolf*
2323 *Mountain Goat*
2324 *Deer Mouse*
2325 *Black-tailed Prairie Dog*
2326 *Box Turtle*
2327 *Wolverine*
2328 *American Elk*
2329 *California Sea Lion*
2330 *Mockingbird*
2331 *Raccoon*
2332 *Bobcat*
2333 *Black-footed Ferret*
2334 *Canada Goose*
2335 *Red Fox*

2325

2335

SCOTT NO.	DESCRIPTION	FIRST DAY COVERS SING.	PL.BLK.	MINT SHEET	COPY-RIGHT	ZIP	PLATE BLOCK	UNUSED F/NH	USED
2286-2335	22¢, 50 varieties, attached	70.00	....	60.00(50)	....	....	....	60.00	....
	set of singles	86.00	....	....	....	....	....	....	11.50
	singles of above, each	1.75	....	....	....	....	....	....	.30

2336

2337

2338

2339

2340

2341

2342

2343

2344

U.S. Postage #2336-2354

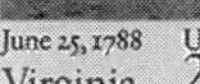

2345

2346

2347

2348

SCOTT NO.	DESCRIPTION	FIRST DAY COVERS SING.	PL.BLK.	MINT SHEET	COPY-RIGHT	ZIP	PLATE BLOCK	UNUSED F/NH	USED
	1987-90 COMMEMORATIVES								
2336	22¢ Delaware Statehood	1.75	4.00	30.00(50)	2.85	2.85	3.20	.65	.15
2337	22¢ Pennsylvania Statehood	1.75	4.00	40.00(50)	2.85	2.85	3.20	.85	.15
2338	22¢ New Jersey Statehood	1.75	4.00	32.75(50)	2.85	2.85	3.20	.70	.15
2339	22¢ Georgia Statehood (1988)	1.75	4.00	30.00(50)	2.85	2.85	3.20	.65	.15
2340	22¢ Connecticut Statehood (1988)	1.75	4.00	30.00(50)	2.85	2.85	3.20	.65	.15
2341	22¢ Massachusetts Statehood (1988)	1.75	4.00	30.00(50)	2.85	2.85	3.20	.65	.15
2342	22¢ Maryland Statehood (1988)	1.75	4.00	30.00(50)	2.85	2.85	3.20	.65	.15
2343	25¢ South Carolina Statehood (1988)	1.75	4.00	30.00(50)	2.85	2.85	3.20	.65	.15
2344	25¢ New Hampshire Statehood (1988)	1.75	4.00	30.00(50)	2.85	2.85	3.20	.65	.15
2345	25¢ Virginia Statehood (1988)	1.75	4.00	30.00(50)	2.85	2.85	3.20	.65	.15
2346	25¢ New York Statehood (1988)	1.75	4.00	30.00(50)	2.85	2.85	3.20	.65	.15
2347	25¢ North Carolina Statehood(1989) .	1.75	4.00	30.00(50)	2.85	2.85	3.20	.65	.15
2348	25¢ Rhode Island Statehood (1990) ..	1.75	4.00	30.00(50)	2.85	2.85	3.20	.65	.15

2349

2350

2351

2352

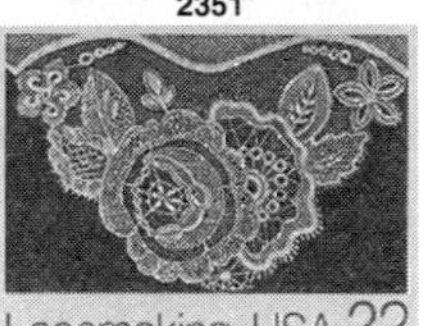

2353

2354

SCOTT NO.	DESCRIPTION	FIRST DAY COVERS SING.	PL.BLK.	MINT SHEET	COPY-RIGHT	ZIP	PLATE BLOCK	UNUSED F/NH	USED
2349	22¢ Morocco	1.75	4.00	27.00(50)	2.55	2.55	2.80	.60	.15
2350	22¢ William Faulkner	1.75	4.00	27.00(50)	2.55	2.55	2.80	.60	.15
2351-54	Lacemaking, 4 varieties, attached	2.75	3.25	35.00(40)	3.60	3.60	3.75	3.50	3.00
2351	22¢ Lace, Ruth Maxwell	1.75	....	....	....	....	....	.85	.15
2352	22¢ Lace, Mary McPeek	1.75	....	....	....	....	....	.85	.15
2353	22¢ Lace, Leslie K. Saari	1.75	....	....	....	....	....	.85	.15
2354	22¢ Lace, Trenna Ruffner	1.75	....	....	....	....	....	.85	.15

2355

2356

2357

2358

2359

U.S. Postage #2355-2368

2360

1987 COMMEMORATIVES (continued)

2361

SCOTT NO.	DESCRIPTION	FIRST DAY COVERS SING.	PL.BLK.	MINT SHEET	COPY-RIGHT	ZIP	PLATE BLOCK	UNUSED F/NH	USED
2355	22¢ "The Bicentennial"	1.75	....	....	....	....	....	.85	.15
2356	22¢ "We the people"	1.75	....	....	....	....	....	.85	.15
2357	22¢ "Establish justice"	1.75	....	....	....	....	....	.85	.15
2358	22¢ "And secure"	1.75	....	....	....	....	....	.85	.15
2359	22¢ "Do ordain"	1.75	....	....	....	....	....	.85	.15
2359a	Drafting of Constitution booklet pane, 5 varieties, attached	4.60	....	....	....	....	....	4.50	3.50
2360	22¢ Signing of U.S. Constitution	1.75	4.00	32.75(50)	2.90	2.90	3.20	.70	.15
2361	22¢ Certified Public Accountants	2.50	5.00	170.00(50)	14.25	14.25	15.00	3.50	.15

LOCOMOTIVES ISSUE

2362

2363

2364

2365

2366

2367

2368

SCOTT NO.	DESCRIPTION	FIRST DAY COVERS SING.	PL.BLK.	MINT SHEET	COPY-RIGHT	ZIP	PLATE BLOCK	UNUSED F/NH	USED
2362	22¢ "Stourbridge Lion, 1829"	1.75	....	....	....	....	....	.85	.15
2363	22¢ "Best Friend of Charleston, 1830"	1.75	....	....	....	....	....	.85	.15
2364	22¢ "John Bull, 1831"	1.75	....	....	....	....	....	.85	.15
2365	22¢ "Brother Jonathan, 1832"	1.75	....	....	....	....	....	.85	.15
2366	22¢ "Gowan + Marx, 1839"	1.75	....	....	....	....	....	.85	.15
2366a	Locomotives, booklet pane, 5 varieties, attached	4.60	....	....	....	....	....	4.50	4.00
2367	22¢ Madonna	1.75	4.00	46.00(100)	2.55	2.55	2.80	.60	.15
2368	22¢ Ornament	1.75	4.00	46.00(100)	2.55	2.55	2.80	.60	.15

2369

2370

2371

2372

2373

2374

2375

2376

U.S. Postage #2369-2385a

SCOTT NO.	DESCRIPTION	FIRST DAY COVERS SING.	FIRST DAY COVERS PL.BLK.	MINT SHEET	COPY-RIGHT	ZIP	PLATE BLOCK	UNUSED F/NH	USED
	1988 COMMEMORATIVES								
2339/2400	**(2339-46, 2369-80, 2386-93, 2399-2400) 30 varieties ....**	....	....	....	....	....	....	**22.50**	**4.25**
2369	22¢ Winter Olympics	1.75	4.00	40.00(50)	3.50	3.50	3.75	.85	.15
2370	22¢ Australia Bicentennial	1.75	4.00	21.85(50)	2.55	2.55	2.80	.60	.15
2371	22¢ James Weldon Johnson	1.75	4.00	27.00(50)	2.55	2.55	2.80	.60	.15
2372-75	Cats, 4 varieties, attached	2.75	3.25	32.50(40)	3.75	3.75	4.00	3.50	3.00
2372	22¢ Siamese, Exotic Shorthair .	1.75	....	....	....	....	....	.85	.15
2373	22¢ Abyssinian, Himalayan	1.75	....	....	....	....	....	.85	.15
2374	22¢ Maine Coon, Burmese	1.75	....	....	....	....	....	.85	.15
2375	22¢ American Shorthair, Persian	1.75	....	....	....	....	....	.85	.15
2376	22¢ Knute Rockne	3.00	6.00	31.00(50)	3.40	3.40	3.80	.75	.15

2377

2378

2379

2380

2381

2382

2383

2384

2385

SCOTT NO.	DESCRIPTION	FIRST DAY COVERS SING.	FIRST DAY COVERS PL.BLK.	MINT SHEET	COPY-RIGHT	ZIP	PLATE BLOCK	UNUSED F/NH	USED
2377	25¢ Francis Ouimet	3.00	6.00	45.00(50)	4.50	4.50	4.75	1.10	.15
2378	25¢ Love	1.75	4.00	60.00(100)	2.70	2.70	3.00	.65	.15
2379	45¢ Love	1.75	4.00	49.00(50)	4.95	4.95	5.50	1.05	.15
2380	25¢ Summer Olympics	1.75	4.00	40.00(50)	3.50	3.50	3.75	.85	.15
2381	25¢ Locomobile	1.75	....	....	....	....	....	2.00	.15
2382	25¢ Pierce-Arrow	1.75	....	....	....	....	....	2.00	.15
2383	25¢ Cord	1.75	....	....	....	....	....	2.00	.15
2384	25¢ Packard	1.75	....	....	....	....	....	2.00	.15
2385	25¢ Duesenberg	1.75	....	....	....	....	....	2.00	.15
2385a	Classic Automobiles booklet pane, 5 varieties, attached	4.60	....	....	....	....	....	10.50	4.00

2386

2387

2388

2389

2390

2391

2392

2393

2394

U.S. Postage #2386-2400

SCOTT NO.	DESCRIPTION	FIRST DAY COVERS SING.	PL.BLK.	MINT SHEET	COPY-RIGHT	ZIP	PLATE BLOCK	UNUSED F/NH	USED
1988 COMMEMORATIVES (continued)									
2386-89	Antarctic Explorers 4 vars., att'd.	2.75	3.25	50.00(50)	5.75	5.75	8.00	5.00	3.00
2386	25¢ Nathaniel Palmer	1.75	....	....	....	....	....	1.20	.15
2387	25¢ Lt. Charles Wilkes	1.75	....	....	....	....	....	1.20	.15
2388	25¢ Richard E. Byrd	1.75	....	....	....	....	....	1.20	.15
2389	25¢ Lincoln Ellsworth	1.75	....	....	....	....	....	1.20	.15
2390-93	Carousel Animals, 4 vars., att'd.	2.75	3.25	47.5050)	5.25	5.25	6.00	5.00	3.00
2390	25¢ Deer	1.75	....	....	....	....	....	1.20	.15
2391	25¢ Horse	1.75	....	....	....	....	....	1.20	.15
2392	25¢ Camel	1.75	....	....	....	....	....	1.20	.15
2393	25¢ Goat	1.75	....	....	....	....	....	1.20	.15
2394	$8.75 Express Mail	32.00	70.00	450.00(20)	....	....	110.00	25.00	9.00

2395

2396

2399

2397

2398

2400

SCOTT NO.	DESCRIPTION	SING.	PL.BLK.	MINT SHEET	COPY-RIGHT	ZIP	PLATE BLOCK	UNUSED F/NH	USED
2395-2398	Special Occasions bklt. singles.	7.00	....	....	....	....	....	3.00	.60
2396a	Booklet pane (6) with gutter 3—#2395 + 3—#2396	4.60	....	....	....	....	....	5.25	5.00
2398a	Booklet pane (6) with gutter 3—#2397 + 3—#2398	4.60	....	....	....	....	....	5.25	5.00
2399	25¢ Madonna and Child	1.75	4.00	30.00(50)	2.70	2.70	3.00	.65	.15
2400	25¢ One Horse Sleigh	1.75	4.00	30.00(50)	2.70	2.70	3.00	.65	.15

2401

2402

2403

2404

2405

2406

2407

2408

2409

U.S. Postage #2401-2417

SCOTT NO.	DESCRIPTION	FIRST DAY COVERS SING.	PL.BLK.	MINT SHEET	COPY-RIGHT	ZIP	PLATE BLOCK	UNUSED F/NH	USED
	1989 COMMEMORATIVES								
2347/2437	**(2347, 2401-4, 2410-14, 2416-18 2420-28, 2434-37) 26 varieties**	......	......	......	......	......	....	**20.50**	**3.70**
2401	25¢ Montana Statehood	1.75	4.00	30.00(50)	2.70	2.70	3.00	.65	.15
2402	25¢ A.P. Randolph	1.75	4.00	30.00(50)	2.70	2.30	3.00	.65	.15
2403	25¢ North Dakota Statehood ...	1.75	4.00	30.00(50)	2.70	2.30	3.00	.65	.15
2404	25¢ Washington Statehood	1.75	4.00	30.00(50)	2.70	2.70	3.00	.65	.15
2405	25¢ "Experiment ,1788-90"	1.75	......	......	......	......	......	.85	.15
2406	25¢ "Phoenix, 1809"	1.75	......	......	......	......	......	.85	.15
2407	25¢ "New Orleans, 1812"	1.75	......	......	......	......	.....	.85	.15
2408	25¢ "Washington, 1816"	1.75	......	......	......	......	......	.85	.15
2409	25¢ "Walk In The Water, 1818"	1.75	......	......	......	......	.....	.85	.15
2409a	Steamboat, booklet pane, 5 varieties, attached	6.00	......	......	......	......	......	4.50	.....
2409av	same, booklet pane, unfolded ..	....	....	....	....	....	....	15.00	3.50

2410

2411

2412

2413

2414

2415

2416

2417

SCOTT NO.	DESCRIPTION	FIRST DAY COVERS SING.	PL.BLK.	MINT SHEET	COPY-RIGHT	ZIP	PLATE BLOCK	UNUSED F/NH	USED
2410	25¢ World Stamp Expo '89	1.75	4.00	27.00(50)	2.30	2.70	3.00	.65	.15
2411	25¢ Arturo Toscanini	1.75	4.00	27.00(50)	2.70	2.70	3.00	.65	.15
2412	25¢ U.S. House of Representatives	1.75	4.00	27.00(50)	2.70	2.70	3.00	.65	.15
2413	25¢ U.S.Senate	1.75	4.00	27.00(50)	2.30	2.70	3.00	.65	.15
2414	25¢ Executive Branch	1.75	4.00	27.00(50)	2.70	2.70	3.00	.65	.15
2415	25¢ U.S. Supreme Court (1990)	1.75	4.00	27.00(50)	2.70	2.70	3.00	.65	.15
2416	25¢ South Dakota Statehood ...	1.75	4.00	27.00(50)	2.70	2.70	3.00	.65	.15
2417	25¢ Lou Gehrig	5.00	8.00	45.00(50)	3.90	3.90	4.75	.95	.20

2418

2419

2420

2421

2422

2423

2424

2425

2426

2427, 2427a

2428, 2429, 2429a

2431, 2431a, 2432

1989 COMMEMORATIVES (continued)

SCOTT NO.	DESCRIPTION	FIRST DAY COVERS SING.	PL.BLK.	MINT SHEET	COPY-RIGHT	ZIP	PLATE BLOCK	UNUSED F/NH	USED
2418	25¢ Ernest Hemingway	1.75	4.00	30.00(50)	2.70	2.70	3.00	.65	.15
2419	$2.40 Moon Landing	7.50	15.75	105.00(20)	......	......	25.00	5.50	4.00
2420	25¢ Letter Carriers	1.75	4.00	22.00(50)	2.70	2.70	3.00	.65	.15
2421	25¢ Bill of Rights	1.75	4.00	50.00(50)	4.00	4.00	4.50	1.00	.15
2422-25	Prehistoric Animals, 4 attached	2.75	3.25	52.50(40)	5.75	5.75	6.25	5.50	3.00
2422	25¢ Tyrannosaurus Rex	1.75	......	......	......	......	......	1.35	.15
2423	25¢ Pteranodon	1.75	......	......	......	......	......	1.35	.15
2424	25¢ Stegosaurus	1.75	......	......	......	......	......	1.35	.15
2425	25¢ Brontosaurus	1.35	......	......	......	......	......	1.35	.15
2426	25¢ Kachina Doll	1.75	4.00	30.00(50)	2.70	2.70	3.00	.65	.15
2427	25¢ Madonna & Child	1.75	4.00	30.00(50)	2.70	2.70	3.00	.65	.15
2427a	same, booklet pane of 10	7.25	......	......	......	......	......	7.00	......
2427av	same, booklet pane, unfolded ..	....	......	......	......	......	......	12.75	......
2428	25¢ Sleigh full of Presents	1.75	4.00	30.00(50)	2.70	2.70	3.00	.65	.15
2429	25¢ Sleigh full of Presents booklet single	1.75	......	......	......	......	......	.75	.20
2429a	same, booklet pane of 10	7.25	......	......	......	......	......	8.00	......
2429av	same, booklet pane, unfolded ..	......	......	......	......	......	......	12.75	......
2431	25¢ Eagle & Shield, self-adhesive	1.95		......	......	......	......	.75	.20
2431a	same, booklet pane of 18	13.50	......	......	......	......	......	13.00	......
2431	same, coil	......	......	......	......	......	3.00(3)	.75	....

2433

2434

2435

2436

2437

SCOTT NO.	DESCRIPTION	FIRST DAY COVERS SING.	PL.BLK.	MINT SHEET	COPY-RIGHT	ZIP	PLATE BLOCK	UNUSED F/NH	USED
2433	$3.60 World Stamp Expo, Imperforate Souvenir Sheet	12.00	.....	......	......	......	......	20.00	11.00
2434-37	Classic Mail Delivery, 4 attached	2.75	3.25	45.00(40)	4.60	4.60	5.00	4.50	3.00
2434	25¢ Stagecoach	1.75	......	......	......	......	......	1.10	.15
2435	25¢ Paddlewheel Steamer	1.75	......	......	......	......	......	1.10	.15
2436	25¢ Biplane	1.75	......	......	......	......	......	1.10	.15
2437	25¢ Automobile	1.75	......	......	......	......	......	1.10	.15
2438	$1.00 Classic Mail Del. Imp. S.S.	4.50	......	......	......	......	......	6.50	4.00

SCOTT NO.	DESCRIPTION	FIRST DAY COVERS SING.	PL.BLK.	MINT SHEET	COPY-RIGHT	ZIP	PLATE BLOCK	UNUSED F/NH	USED

2439

2440, 2441, 2441a

2442

1990 COMMEMORATIVES

SCOTT NO.	DESCRIPTION	FIRST DAY COVERS SING.	PL.BLK.	MINT SHEET	COPY-RIGHT	ZIP	PLATE BLOCK	UNUSED F/NH	USED
2348/2515	(2348, 2415, 2439-40, 2442, 2444-49, 2496-2500, 2506-15) 26 varieties.......		....	....	....	....		23.50	3.50
2439	25¢ Idaho Statehood	1.75	4.00	28.75(50)	2.70	2.70	3.00	.65	.15
2440	25¢ LOVE	1.75	4.00	28.75(50)	2.70	2.70	3.00	.65	.15
2441	25¢ LOVE, booklet single	1.75	....	....	....	....	....	.75	.15
2441a	25¢ LOVE, booklet pane of 10 .	8.65	....	....	....	....	....	7.25	....
2441av	same, booklet pane, unfolded ..	....	....	....	....	....	....	39.50	....
2442	25¢ Ida B.Wells	1.75	4.00	28.75(50)	2.70	2.70	3.00	.65	.15

2443

2445

2446

2449

2444

2447

2448

SCOTT NO.	DESCRIPTION	FIRST DAY COVERS SING.	PL.BLK.	MINT SHEET	COPY-RIGHT	ZIP	PLATE BLOCK	UNUSED F/NH	USED
2443	15¢ Umbrella, booklet single	1.75	......	......	......	......	......	.35	.15
2443a	15¢ Umbrella, booklet pane of 10	5.75	......	......	......	......	......	3.40	3.40
2443av	same, booklet pane, unfolded ..	......	......	......	......	......	......	9.00	......
2444	25¢ Wyoming Statehood	8.00	10.00	28.75(50)	2.70	2.70	3.00	.65	.15
2445-48	Classic Films, 4 varieties, att'd.	4.00	6.00	77.50(40)	8.25	8.25	9.00	8.00	4.50
2445	25¢ Wizard of Oz	4.00	......	......	......	......	......	1.95	.15
2446	25¢ Gone with the Wind	4.00	......	......	......	......	......	1.95	.15
2447	25¢ Beau Geste	4.00	....	......	......	......	......	1.95	.15
2448	25¢ Stagecoach	4.00	......	......	......	......	......	1.95	.15
2449	25¢ Marianne Craig Moore	1.75	4.00	28.75(50)	2.70	2.70	3.00	.65	.15

2451

2452, 2452B, 2452D

2453, 2454

2457, 2458

2463

2464

2466

2468

1990-95 TRANSPORTATION COILS

SCOTT NO.	DESCRIPTION	FIRST DAY COVERS SING.	PLATE # STRIP 3	MINT SHEET	COPY-RIGHT	ZIP	PLATE # STRIP 3	UNUSED F/NH	USED
2451	4¢ Steam Carriage (1991)	1.75	6.50	......	......	......	1.50	.20	.15
2451b	4¢ Steam Carriage, untagged ..	......	......	......	......	......	1.50	.20	.15
2452	5¢ Circus Wagon	1.75	6.50	......	......	......	1.75	.20	.15
2452a	5¢ Circus Wagon, untagged	......	......	......	......	......	1.85	.20	.15
2452B	5¢ Circus Wagon, Gravure (1992)	1.75	6.50	......	......	......	1.85	.20	.15
2452D	5¢ Circus Wagon, coil (Reissue, 1995 added)	1.95	10.00	......	......	......	1.85	.20	.15

U.S. Postage #2453-2484av

SCOTT NO.	DESCRIPTION	FIRST DAY COVERS SING.	FIRST DAY COVERS PL.BLK.	MINT SHEET	COPY-RIGHT	ZIP	PLATE BLOCK	UNUSED F/NH	USED
	1990-95 TRANSPORTATION COILS (Continued)								
2453	5¢ Canoe, Precancel, brown (1991) ..	1.75	6.50	....	....	....	1.85	.20	.15
2454	5¢ Canoe, Precancel, red (1991)	1.75	6.50	....	....	....	1.85	.20	.15
2457	10¢ Tractor Trailer (1991)	1.75	6.50	....	....	....	1.85	.25	.15
2458	10¢ Tractor Trailer, Gravure (1994) ...	1.75	6.50	....	....	....	1.85	.25	.15
2463	20¢ Cog Railway Car, coil	1.95	10.00	....	....	....	4.75	.50	.15
2464	23¢ Lunch Wagon (1991)	1.75	6.50	....	....	....	4.50	.60	.15
2466	32¢ Ferryboat, coil	1.95	10.00	....	....	....	5.75	.70	.15
2468	$1 Seaplane Coil	3.00	10.00	....	....	....	9.25	2.10	.60

2470 2471 2472 2473 2474 2475

SCOTT NO.	DESCRIPTION	FIRST DAY COVERS SING.	FIRST DAY COVERS PL.BLK.	MINT SHEET	COPY-RIGHT	ZIP	PLATE BLOCK	UNUSED F/NH	USED
2470	25¢ Admiralty Head Lighthouse	2.25	....	....	....	....	....	.90	.15
2471	25¢ Cape Hatteras Lighthouse	2.25	....	....	....	....	....	.90	.15
2472	25¢ West Quoddy Head Lighthouse ..	2.25	....	....	....	....	....	.90	.15
2473	25¢ American Shoals Lighthouse	2.25	....	....	....	....	....	.90	.15
2474	25¢ Sandy Hook Lighthouse	2.25	....	....	....	....	....	.90	.15
2474a	25¢ Lighthouse, booklet pane, 5 vars.	4.60	....	....	....	....	....	4.75	3.75
2474av	same, booklet pane, unfolded ...	....	....	....	....	....	....	8.50	....
2475	25¢ ATM Plastic Stamp, single.	1.75	....	....	....	....	....	.80	.15
2475a	same, pane of 12	20.00	....	....	....	....	....	9.00	....

2476 2477 2478 2479 2480 2481

2482 2483 2484, 2485 2486 2487, 2493, 2495

2488, 2494, 2495A 2489 2490 2491

SCOTT NO.	DESCRIPTION	FIRST DAY COVERS SING.	FIRST DAY COVERS PL.BLK.	MINT SHEET	COPY-RIGHT	ZIP	PLATE BLOCK	UNUSED F/NH	USED
	1990-95 REGULAR ISSUE								
2476	1¢ Kestrel	1.75	4.00	6.00(100)	.75	.75	.75	.20	.15
2477	1¢ Kestrel (redesign 1¢)	1.75	4.00	6.00(100)	....	....	.75	.20	.15
2478	3¢ Bluebird (1993)	1.75	4.00	8.00(100)	.75	.75	.75	.20	.15
2479	19¢ Fawn (1993)	1.75	4.00	62.50(100)	3.65	3.65	4.00	.45	.15
2480	30¢ Cardinal (1993)	1.75	4.00	62.50(100)	3.25	3.25	3.50	.65	.15
2481	45¢ Pumpkinseed Sunfish (1992)	2.00	4.50	95.00(100)	4.10	4.10	4.50	1.00	.15
2482	$2 Bobcat	6.00	14.00	82.50(20)	....	....	19.50	4.30	.40
2483	20¢ Blue Jay, booklet single (1991) ..	1.95	....	....	....	....	....	.50	.20
2483a	same, booklet pane of 10	6.00	....	....	....	....	....	5.25	....
2483av	same, booklet pane, unfolded	....	....	....	....	....	....	6.00	....
2484	29¢ Wood Duck, bklt. sgl.(BEP) (1991)	1.75	....	....	....	....	....	.75	.15
2484a	same, booklet pane of 10 (BEP)	6.50	....	....	....	....	....	7.35	....
2484av	same, booklet pane, unfolded	....	....	....	....	....	....	9.75	....

U.S. Postage #2485-2500

SCOTT NO.	DESCRIPTION	FIRST DAY COVERS SING.	PL.BLK.	MINT SHEET	COPY-RIGHT	ZIP	PLATE BLOCK	UNUSED F/NH	USED
2485	29¢ Wood Duck, bklt. sgl. (KCS) (1991) ..	1.75	....	....	....	....	....	1.00	.20
2485a	same, booklet pane of 10 (KCS)	6.50	....	....	....	....	....	9.75	....
2485av	same, booklet pane, unfolded	....	....	....	....	....	....	12.50	....
2486	29¢ African Violet, booklet single	1.75	....	....	....	....	....	.65	.20
2486a	same, booklet pane of 10	6.50	....	....	....	....	....	6.35	....
2486av	same, booklet pane, unfolded	....	....	....	....	....	....	7.00	....
2487	32¢ Peach, booklet single	1.95	....	....	....	....	....	.70	.20
2488	32¢ Pear, booklet single	1.95	....	....	....	....	....	.70	.20
2488a	32¢ Peach and Pear, booklet pane of 10	7.25	....	....	....	....	....	7.00	....
2488av	same, booklet pane, unfolded	....	....	....	....	....	....	9.75	....
2489	29¢ Red Squirrel, self-adhesive (1993) ...	1.75	....	....	....	....	....	.75	.20
2489a	same, booklet pane of 18	13.50	....	....	....	....	....	13.00	....
2489v	same, coil	....	....	....	....	....	3.00(3)	.75	....
2490	29¢ Rose, self-adhesive (1993)	1.75	....	....	....	....	....	.75	.20
2490a	same, booklet pane of 18	13.50	....	....	....	....	....	13.00	....
2491	29¢ Pine Cone, self-adhesive	1.75	....	....	....	....	....	.75	.20
2491a	same, booklet pane of 18	13.50	....	....	....	....	....	13.00	....
2492	32¢ Pink Rose, self-adhesive	1.95	....	....	....	....	....	.70	.20
2492a	same, booklet pane of 20	14.50	....	....	....	....	....	13.50	....
2492b	same, booklet pane of 15	11.50	....	....	....	....	....	11 .00	....
2493	32¢ Peach, self-adhesive	1.95	....	....	....	....	....	.70	.20
2494	32¢ Pear, self-adhesive	1.95	....	....	....	....	....	.70	.20
2494a	32¢ Peach and Pear, self-adhesive, booklet pane of 20	14.50	....	....	....	....	....	13.50	....
2495	32¢ Peach, self-adhesive coil (1993)	1.95	....	....	....	....	7.00(3)	.70	.20
2495A	32¢ Pear, self-adhesive coil	1.95	....	....	....	....	....	.70	.20

2496

2497

2498

2499

2500

SCOTT NO.	DESCRIPTION	SING.	PL.BLK.	MINT SHEET	COPY-RIGHT	ZIP	PLATE BLOCK	UNUSED F/NH	USED
2496-2500	Olympians, strip of 5, attached	4.00	12.50	38.00(35)	16.50(15)	11.00(10)	12.50(10)	5.50	3.00
2496	25¢ Jesse Owens	2.40	......	......	......	......	......	1.05	.20
2497	25¢ Ray Ewry	2.40	......	......	......	......	......	1.05	.20
2498	25¢ Hazel Wightman	2.40	......	......	......	......	......	1.05	.20
2499	25¢ Eddie Eagan	2.40	......	......	......	......	......	1.05	.20
2500	25¢ Helene Madison	2.40	......	......	......	......	......	1.05	.20

2501

2502

2503

2504

2505

U.S. Postage #2501-2517

SCOTT NO.	DESCRIPTION	FIRST DAY COVERS SING.	FIRST DAY COVERS PL.BLK.	MINT SHEET	COPY-RIGHT	ZIP	PLATE BLOCK	UNUSED F/NH	USED
2501-2505	Indian Headdresses, 5 vars., attd	3.95	......	......	......	......	......	4.00	2.75
2501	25¢ Assiniboin	2.40	......	......	......	......	......	.75	.20
2502	25¢ Cheyenne	2.40	......	......	......	......	......	.75	.20
2503	25¢ Comanche	2.40	......	......	......	......	......	.75	.20
2504	25¢ Flathead	2.40	......	......	......	......	......	.75	.20
2505	25¢ Shoshone	2.40	......	......	......	......	......	.75	.20
2505a	25¢ booklet pane of 10	7.85	......	......	......	......	......	7.75	......
2505av	same, booklet pane, unfolded ..	......	......	......	......	......	......	22.50	......

2506

2507

SCOTT NO.	DESCRIPTION	FIRST DAY COVERS SING.	FIRST DAY COVERS PL.BLK.	MINT SHEET	COPY-RIGHT	ZIP	PLATE BLOCK	UNUSED F/NH	USED
2506-07	Micronesia + Marshall Islands 2 varieties, attached	2.50	4.00	35.00(50)	3.60	3.60	4.00	1.75	1.00
2506	25¢ Micronesia	1.75	......	......	......	......	......	.85	.20
2507	25¢ Marshall Islands	1.75	......	......	......	......	......	.85	.20

2508

2509

2510

2511

2512

2513

2514

2515, 2516

1990 REGULAR ISSUES

SCOTT NO.	DESCRIPTION	FIRST DAY COVERS SING.	FIRST DAY COVERS PL.BLK.	MINT SHEET	COPY-RIGHT	ZIP	PLATE BLOCK	UNUSED F/NH	USED
2508-11	Sea Creature, 4 varieties, att'd. ..	3.00	3.50	35.00(40)	3.60	3.60	4.00	3.50	2.50
2508	25¢ Killer Whales	2.00	......	......	......	......	......	.85	.15
2509	25¢ Northern Sea Lions	2.00	......	......	......	......	......	.85	.15
2510	25¢ Sea Otter	2.00	......	......	......	......	......	.85	.15
2511	25¢ Common Dolphin	2.00	......	......	......	......	......	.85	.15
2512	25¢ Americas Issue (Grand Canyon)	1.75	4.00	28.75(50)	2.70	2.70	3.00	.65	.15
2513	25¢ Dwight D. Eisenhower	1.75	4.00	24.75(40)	2.70	2.70	3.00	.65	.15
2514	25¢ Madonna & Child—Antonello	1.75	4.00	28.75(50)	Combo	2.70	3.00	.65	.15
2514a	same, booklet pane of 10	6.50	......	......	......	......	......	6.50	......
2514av	same, booklet pane, unfolded ..	....	......	......	......	......	......	10.00	......
2515	25¢ Christmas Tree	1.75	4.00	28.75(50)	2.70	2.70	3.00	.65	.15
2516	25¢ Christmas Tree booklet single	1.75	......	......	......	......	......	.65	.15
2516a	same, booklet pane of 10	6.00	......	......	......	......	......	6.50	......
2516av	same, booklet pane, unfolded ..	......	......	......	......	......	......	10.00	......

2517, 2518, 2519, 2520

1991 REGULAR ISSUES

SCOTT NO.	DESCRIPTION	FIRST DAY COVERS SING.	FIRST DAY COVERS PL.BLK.	MINT SHEET	COPY-RIGHT	ZIP	PLATE BLOCK	UNUSED F/NH	USED
2517	(29¢) "F" Flower	1.75	4.25	62.50(100)	2.90	2.90	3.25	.70	.15

U.S. Postage #2518-2531Ab

SCOTT NO.	DESCRIPTION	FIRST DAY COVERS SING.	FIRST DAY COVERS PL.BLK.	MINT SHEET	COPY-RIGHT	ZIP	PLATE BLOCK	UNUSED F/NH	USED
	1991 REGULAR ISSUES (Continued)								
			PLATE # STRIP 3				**PLATE# STRIP 3**		
2518	(29¢) "F" Flower coil	1.75	10.00	......	......	......	5.50	.70	.15
2519	(29¢) "F" Flower, booklet single (BEP)	1.75	......	......	......	......	......	.70	.15
2519a	same, booklet pane of 10 (BEP)	6.50	......	......	......	......	......	7.50	......
2520	(29¢) "F" Flower, booklet single (KCS)	1.75	......	......	......	......	......	2.25	.15
2520a	same, booklet pane of 10 (KCS)	6.50	......	......	......	......	......	20.00	......

2521 2522 2523, 2523A

SCOTT NO.	DESCRIPTION	FIRST DAY COVERS SING.	FIRST DAY COVERS PL.BLK.	MINT SHEET	COPY-RIGHT	ZIP	PLATE BLOCK	UNUSED F/NH	USED
			PL. BLK.				**PL. BLK.**		
2521	(4¢) "F" Make-up Rate	1.75	4.25	8.50(100)	.75	.75	.75	.20	.15
2522	(29¢) "F" ATM Plastic Stamp, single	1.75	......	......	......	......	......	.80	.25
2522a	same, pane of 12	9.00	......	......	......	......	......	9.25	......
			PLATE # STRIP 3				**PLATE# STRIP 3**		
2523	29¢ Flag over Mt. Rushmore, coil	1.75	10.00	......	......	......	6.00	.70	.15
2523A	29¢ Flag over Mt. Rushmore, photogravure coil	1.75	10.00	......	......	......	6.25	.70	.15

2524-27 2528 2529-29C 2530 2531 2531A

SCOTT NO.	DESCRIPTION	FIRST DAY COVERS SING.	FIRST DAY COVERS PL.BLK.	MINT SHEET	COPY-RIGHT	ZIP	PLATE BLOCK	UNUSED F/NH	USED
2524	29¢ Flower	1.75	4.25	65.00(100)	2.90	2.90	3.50	.70	.15
2524a	29¢ Flower, perf. 13	......	......	......	......	......	3.50	.70	.20
			PLATE # STRIP 3				**PLATE # STRIP 3**		
2525	29¢ Flower, coil rouletted	1.75	10.00	......	......	......	5.50	.70	.15
2526	29¢ Flower, coil, perf (1992)	1.75	10.00	......	......	......	5.50	.70	.15
2527	29¢ Flower, booklet single	1.75	......	......	......	......	......	.70	.15
2527a	same, booklet pane of 10	6.50	......	......	......	......	......	7.00	......
2527av	same booklet pane, unfolded ...	......	......	......	......	......	......	9.00	....
2528	29¢ Flag with Olympic Rings, booklet single	1.75	......	......	......	......	......	.70	.15
2528a	same, booklet pane of 10	6.50	......	......	......	......	......	7.00	......
2528av	same, booklet pane, unfolded ..	......	......	......	......	......	......	9.00	......
2529	19¢ Fishing Boat Type I	1.75	10.00	......	......	......	4.50	.45	.15
2529a	same, Type II (1993)	......	......	......	......	......	4.50	.45	.20
2529C	19¢ Fishing Boat (reengraved)	1.75	10.00	......	......	......	5.00	.45	.20
2530	19¢ Hot-Air Balloon booklet single	1.75	......	......	......	......	......	.45	.15
2530a	same, booklet pane of 10	5.50	......	......	......	......	......	4.25	.15
2530av	same, booklet pane, unfolded ..	......	......	......	......	......	......	5.50	......
2531	29¢ Flags on Parade	1.75	4.25	65.00(100)	2.90	2.90	3.25	.70	.15
2531A	29¢ Liberty Torch ATM Stamp .	1.75	......	......	......	......	......	.70	.25
2531Ab	same, pane of 18	12.50	......	......	......	......	......	12.00	......

2532

2533

2534

2535

U.S. Postage #2532-2544A

SCOTT NO.	DESCRIPTION	FIRST DAY COVERS SING.	FIRST DAY COVERS PL.BLK.	MINT SHEET	COPY-RIGHT	ZIP	PLATE BLOCK	UNUSED F/NH	USED
	1991 COMMEMORATIVES								
2532/2579	**(2532-35, 2537-38, 2550-51, 2553-61, 2567, 2578-79) 29 varieties ....**	......	......	......	......	......	......	**21.00**	**4.00**
2532	50¢ Switzerland	2.25	5.00	41.25(40)	5.10	5.10	5.25	1.10	.25
2533	29¢ Vermont Statehood	1.75	4.25	32.50(50)	2.90	2.90	3.25	.70	.20
2534	29¢ Savings Bonds	1.75	4.25	32.50(50)	2.90	2.90	3.25	.70	.20
2535	29¢ Love	1.75	4.25	32.50(50)	Combo	2.75	3.00	.70	.20

2537

2538

2539

2540

SCOTT NO.	DESCRIPTION	FIRST DAY COVERS SING.	FIRST DAY COVERS PL.BLK.	MINT SHEET	COPY-RIGHT	ZIP	PLATE BLOCK	UNUSED F/NH	USED
2536	29¢ Love, booklet single	1.75	......	......	......	......	......	.70	.20
2536a	same, booklet pane of 10	6.50	......	......	......	......	......	6.50	......
2536av	same, booklet pane, unfolded ..	......	......	......	......	......	......	8.50	......
2537	52¢ Love	2.25	5.00	52.25(50)	5.10	5.10	5.25	1.10	.35
2538	29¢ William Saroyan	1.75	4.25	32.50(50)	2.90	2.90	3.00	.20	.20
2539	$1 USPS/Olympic Rings	3.00	6.50	45.00(20)	10.00	10.00	12.00	2.50	.35
2540	$2.90 Eagle and Olympic Rings	7.50	16.50	130.00(20)	......	......	30.00	7.00	2.50

2541

2542

2543

2544

2544A

2545

2546

2547

2548

2549

2550

2551, 2552

SCOTT NO.	DESCRIPTION	FIRST DAY COVERS SING.	FIRST DAY COVERS PL.BLK.	MINT SHEET	COPY-RIGHT	ZIP	PLATE BLOCK	UNUSED F/NH	USED
2541	$9.95 Express Mail	27.00	50.00	350.00(20)	......	......	85.00	20.75	7.00
2542	$14 Express Mail	35.00	67.50	525.00(20)	......	......	125.00	28.50	25.00
2543	$2.90 Space Vehicle, priority mail	8.00	17.50	225.00(40)	24.50	24.50	25.00	6.00	2.25
2544	$3 Challenger Shuttle, priority mail (1995)	8.00	17.50	115.00(20)	......	......	27.00	6.25	3.00
2544A	$10.75 Endeavour Shuttle, express mail (1995)	27.50	57.50	425.00(20)	......	......	87.50	22.50	8.00

SCOTT NO.	DESCRIPTION	FIRST DAY COVERS SING.	PL.BLK.	MINT SHEET	COPY-RIGHT	ZIP	PLATE BLOCK	UNUSED F/NH	USED
	1991 COMMEMORATIVES (Continued)								
2545	29¢ "Royal Wulff"	1.75	......	......	......	......	......	.95	.20
2546	29¢ "Jock Scott"	1.75	......	......	......	......	......	.95	.20
2547	29¢ "Apte Tarpon"	1.75	......	......	......	......	......	.95	.20
2548	29¢ "Lefty's Deceiver"	1.75	......	......	......	......	......	.95	.20
2549	29¢ "Muddler Minnow"	1.75	......	......	......	......	......	.95	.20
2549a	29¢ Fishing Flies, booklet pane, 5 varieties, attached	4.50	......	......	......	......	......	5.00	3.50
2549av	same, booklet pane, unfolded	......	......	......	......	......	......	6.50	......
2550	29¢ Cole Porter	1.75	4.25	35.00(50)	3.10	3.10	3.50	.75	.20
2551	29¢ Desert Storm	1.75	4.25	32.50(50)	2.90	2.90	3.25	.70	.20
2552	29¢ Desert Storm, booklet single	1.75	......	......	......	......	......	.70	.20
2552a	same, booklet pane of 5	4.75	......	......	......	......	......	3.75	.20
2552av	same, booklet pane, unfolded	......	......	......	......	......	......	9.00	......

2553 2554 2555

2556 2557

SCOTT NO.	DESCRIPTION	FIRST DAY COVERS SING.	PL.BLK.	MINT SHEET	COPY-RIGHT	ZIP	PLATE BLOCK	UNUSED F/NH	USED
2553-57	Summer Olympics, 5 vars., att'd.	4.50	......	32.50(40)	......	......	9.50(10)	4.50	2.50
2553	29¢ Pole Vault	1.75	......	......	......	......	......	.85	.20
2554	29¢ Discus	1.75	......	......	......	......	......	.85	.20
2555	29¢ Sprinters	1.75	......	......	......	......	......	.85	.20
2556	29¢ Javelin	1.75	......	......	......	......	......	.85	.20
2557	29¢ Hurdles	1.75	......	......	......	......	......	.85	.20

2558

SCOTT NO.	DESCRIPTION	FIRST DAY COVERS SING.	PL.BLK.	MINT SHEET	COPY-RIGHT	ZIP	PLATE BLOCK	UNUSED F/NH	USED
2558	29¢ Numismatics	1.75	4.25	39.50(50)	3.50	3.50	4.00	.85	.20
2559	$2.90 World War II, 1941 souvenir sheet of 10	7.50	......	14.00(20)	......	......	......	7.00	7.00
2559a	29¢ Burma Road	1.75	......	......	......	......	......	.70	.40
2559b	29¢ Peacetime Draft	1.75	......	......	......	......	......	.70	.40
2559c	29¢ Lend-Lease Act	1.75	......	......	......	......	......	.70	.40
2559d	29¢ Atlantic Charter	1.75	......	......	......	......	......	.70	.40
2559e	29¢ "Arsenal of Democracy"	1.75	......	......	......	......	......	.70	.40
2559f	29¢ Destroyer "Reuben James"	1.75	......	......	......	......	......	.70	.40
2559g	29¢ Civil Defense	1.75	......	......	......	......	......	.70	.40
2559h	29¢ Liberty Ship	1.75	......	......	......	......	......	.70	.40
2559i	29¢ Pearl Harbor	1.75	......	......	......	......	......	.70	.40
2559j	29¢ Declaration of War on Japan	1.75	......	......	......	......	......	.70	.40

U.S. Postage #2560-2567

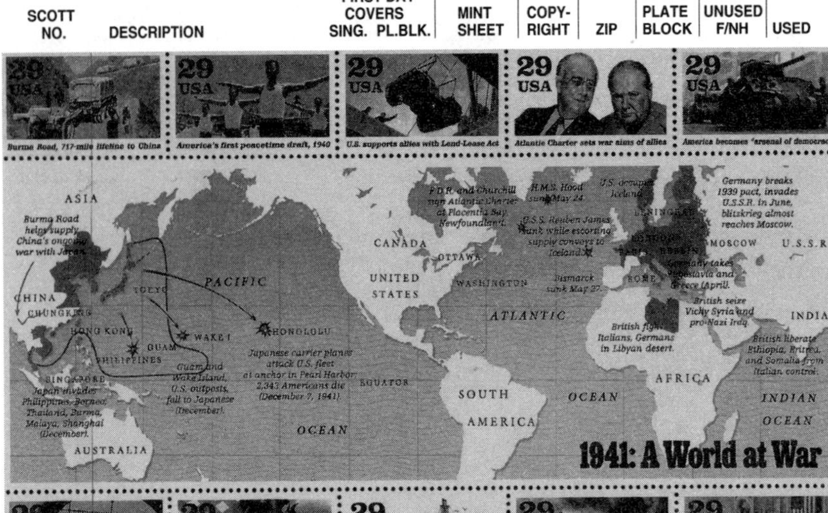

2559

2560

2561

2562

2563

2564

2565

2566

Jan E. Matzeliger
29
Black Heritage USA

2567

SCOTT NO.	DESCRIPTION	FIRST DAY COVERS SING.	FIRST DAY COVERS PL.BLK.	MINT SHEET	COPY-RIGHT	ZIP	PLATE BLOCK	UNUSED F/NH	USED
2560	29¢ Basketball	2.00	4.50	42.50(50)	3.75	3.75	4.25	.90	.40
2561	29¢ District of Columbia	1.75	4.25	32.50(50)	2.90	2.90	3.25	.70	.20
2562	29¢ Laurel and Hardy	1.75	......	......	......	......	......	.70	.20
2563	29¢ Bergen and McCarthy	1.75	......	......	......	......	......	.70	.20
2564	29¢ Jack Benny	1.75	......	......	......	......	......	.70	.20
2565	29¢ Fanny Brice	1.75	......	......	......	......	......	.70	.20
2566	29¢ Abbott and Costello	1.75	......	......	......	......	......	.70	.20
2566a	29¢ Comedians, bklt. pane of 10	6.00	......	......	......	......	......	7.00	6.00
2566av	same, booklet pane, unfolded	......	......	......	......	......	......	8.00	......
2567	29¢ Jan Matzeliger	1.75	4.25	32.50(50)	2.90	2.90	3.25	.70	.20

U.S. Postage #2568-2585av

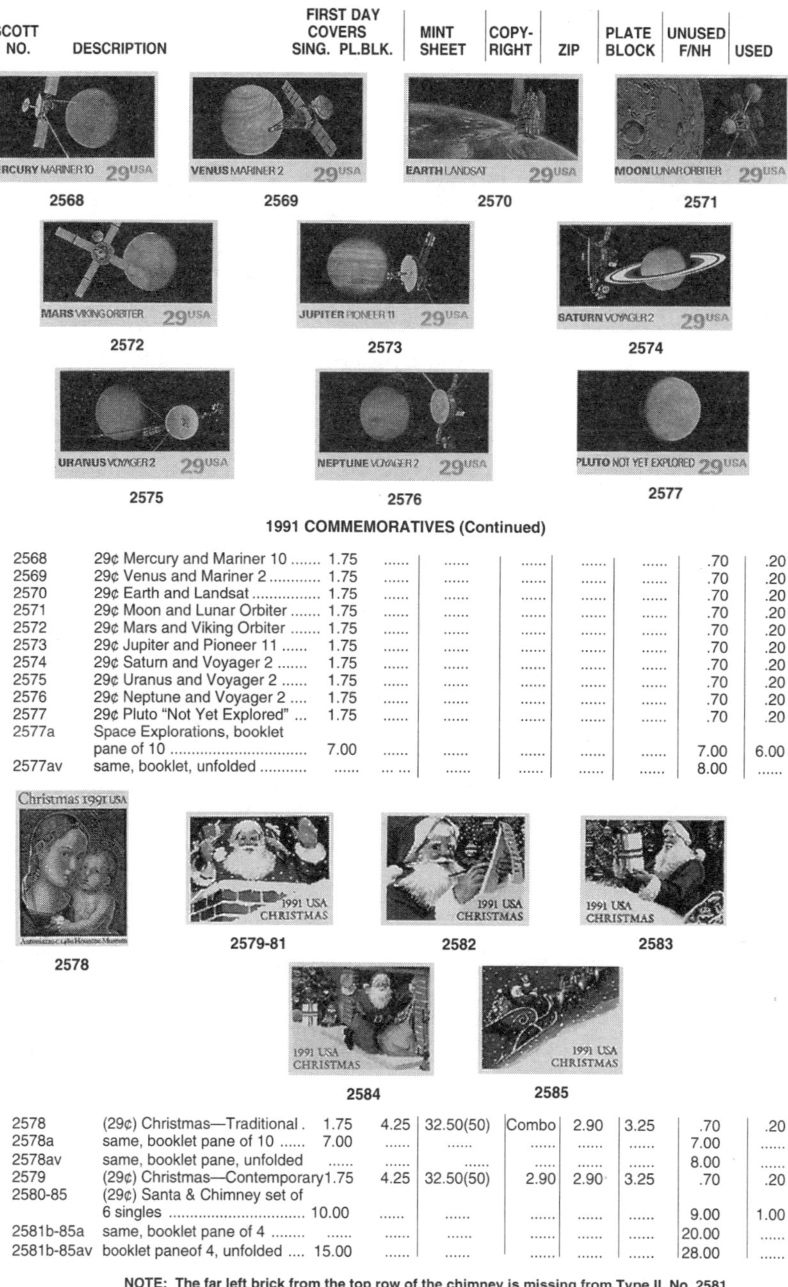

SCOTT NO.	DESCRIPTION	FIRST DAY COVERS SING.	FIRST DAY COVERS PL.BLK.	MINT SHEET	COPY-RIGHT	ZIP	PLATE BLOCK	UNUSED F/NH	USED
	1991 COMMEMORATIVES (Continued)								
2568	29¢ Mercury and Mariner 10	1.75	......	......	......	......	......	.70	.20
2569	29¢ Venus and Mariner 2	1.75	......	......	......	......	......	.70	.20
2570	29¢ Earth and Landsat	1.75	......	......	......	......	......	.70	.20
2571	29¢ Moon and Lunar Orbiter	1.75	......	......	......	......	......	.70	.20
2572	29¢ Mars and Viking Orbiter	1.75	......	......	......	......	......	.70	.20
2573	29¢ Jupiter and Pioneer 11	1.75	......	......	......	......	......	.70	.20
2574	29¢ Saturn and Voyager 2	1.75	......	......	......	......	......	.70	.20
2575	29¢ Uranus and Voyager 2	1.75	......	......	......	......	......	.70	.20
2576	29¢ Neptune and Voyager 2	1.75	......	......	......	......	......	.70	.20
2577	29¢ Pluto "Not Yet Explored" ...	1.75	......	......	......	......	......	.70	.20
2577a	Space Explorations, booklet pane of 10	7.00	......	......	......	......	......	7.00	6.00
2577av	same, booklet, unfolded	......	... ...	......	......	......	......	8.00	......

SCOTT NO.	DESCRIPTION	FIRST DAY COVERS SING.	FIRST DAY COVERS PL.BLK.	MINT SHEET	COPY-RIGHT	ZIP	PLATE BLOCK	UNUSED F/NH	USED
2578	(29¢) Christmas—Traditional .	1.75	4.25	32.50(50)	Combo	2.90	3.25	.70	.20
2578a	same, booklet pane of 10	7.00	......	......	......	......	......	7.00	......
2578av	same, booklet pane, unfolded	......	......	......	......	......	......	8.00	......
2579	(29¢) Christmas—Contemporary	1.75	4.25	32.50(50)	2.90	2.90	3.25	.70	.20
2580-85	(29¢) Santa & Chimney set of 6 singles	10.00	......	......	......	......	......	9.00	1.00
2581b-85a	same, booklet pane of 4	......	......	......	......	......	......	20.00	......
2581b-85av	booklet paneof 4, unfolded	15.00	......	......	......	......	......	28.00	......

NOTE: The far left brick from the top row of the chimney is missing from Type II, No. 2581

U.S. Postage #2587-2599v

2587

2590

2593, 2594

2592

1992-95 Regular Issues

SCOTT NO.	DESCRIPTION	FIRST DAY COVERS SING.	FIRST DAY COVERS PL.BLK.	MINT SHEET	COPY-RIGHT	ZIP	PLATE BLOCK	UNUSED F/NH	USED
2587	32¢ James K. Polk (1995)	1.95	4.75	65.00(100)	....	....	3.25	.70	.20
2590	$1 "Surrender at Saratoga" (1994)	3.00	6.50	37.50(20)	....	....	10.25	2.10	1.50
2592	$5 "Washington & Jackson" (1994)	14.50	28.50	195.00(20)	....	....	47.50	10.50	3.50
2593	29¢ Pledge of Allegiance (black) booklet single	1.75	....	....	....	....	....	.70	.15
2593a	same, booklet pane of 10	7.00	....	....	....	....	....	7.00	....
2593av	same, booklet pane, unfolded	....	....	....	....	....	....	7.25	....
2594	29¢ Pledge of Allegiance (red) booklet single (1993)	1.75	....	....	....	....	....	.70	.15
2594a	same, booklet pane of 10	7.00	....	....	....	....	....	7.00	....
2594av	same, booklet pane, unfolded	....	....	....	....	....	....	7.25	....

2595-97

2598

2599

1992-94 Self-Adhesive Stamps

SCOTT NO.	DESCRIPTION	FIRST DAY COVERS SING.	FIRST DAY COVERS PL.BLK.	MINT SHEET	COPY-RIGHT	ZIP	PLATE BLOCK	UNUSED F/NH	USED
2595	29¢ Eagle & Shield (brown) booklet single	1.75	....	....	....	....	....	.85	.15
2595a	same, booklet pane of 17	7.00	....	....	....	....	....	12.50	....
2595v	same, coil	2.50	....	....	....	....	3.25(3)	.85	.15
2596	29¢ Eagle & Shield (green) booklet single	1.75	....	....	....	....	....	.85	.15
2596a	same, booklet pane of 17	7.00	....	....	....	....	....	12.50	....
2596v	same, coil	2.50	....	....	....	....	3.25(3)	.85	.15
2597	29¢ Eagle & Shield (red) booklet single	1.75	....	....	....	....	....	.85	.15
2597a	same, booklet pane of 17	7.00	....	....	....	....	....	12.50	....
2597v	same, coil	2.50	....	....	....	....	3.25(3)	.85	.15
2598	29¢ Eagle (1994)	1.75	....	....	....	....	....	.70	.15
2598a	same, booklet pane of 18	13.50	....	....	....	....	....	11.50	....
2598v	29¢ Eagle, coil	2.50	....	....	....	....	7.00(3)	.80	....
2599	29¢ Statue of Liberty (1994)	1.75	....	....	....	....	....	.70	.20
2599a	same, booklet pane of 18	13.50	....	....	....	....	....	11.50	....
2599v	29¢ Statue of Liberty, coil	2.50	....	....	....	....	7.00(3)	.80	....

2602

2603, 2604

2605

2606-08

2609

U.S. Postage #2602-2619

SCOTT NO.	DESCRIPTION	FIRST DAY COVERS SING.	FIRST DAY COVERS PL.BLK.	MINT SHEET	COPY-RIGHT	ZIP	PLATE BLOCK	UNUSED F/NH	USED
	1991-93 Regular Issue								
							PLATE # STRIP 3		
2602	(10¢) Eagle, Bulk-Rate coil	1.75	10.00	....	....	....	3.75	.25	.15
2603	(10¢) Eagle, Bulk-Rate coil (BEP) (orange-yellow) (1993)	1.75	10.00	....	....	....	4.25	.25	.15
2604	(10¢) Eagle, Bulk-Rate coil (Stamp Venturers) (gold) (1993)	1.75	10.00	....	....	....	3.00	.25	.15
2605	23¢ Flag, Presort First-Class	1.75	10.00	....	....	....	5.00	.55	.15
2606	23¢ USA, Presort First-Class (ABN) (1992)	1.75	10.00	....	....	....	5.75	.55	.15
2607	23¢ USA, Presort First-Class (BEP) (1992)	1.75	10.00	....	....	....	5.75	.55	.15
2608	23¢ USA, Presort First-Class (Stamp Venturers) (1993)	1.75	10.00	....	....	....	5.75	.55	.15
2609	29¢ Flag over White House, coil (1992)	1.75	10.00	....	....	....	6.00	.70	.15

2611 2612 2613

2614 2615

1992 COMMEMORATIVES

SCOTT NO.	DESCRIPTION	FIRST DAY COVERS SING.	FIRST DAY COVERS PL.BLK.	MINT SHEET	COPY-RIGHT	ZIP	PLATE BLOCK	UNUSED F/NH	USED
2611/2720	**(2611-23, 2630-41, 2692-2704, 2710-14, 2720) 48 varieties**		....	....	....	....	....	**35.00**	**6.75**
2611-15	Winter Olympics, 5 varieties, attached	4.50		31.50(35)			9.00(10)	4.50	2.75
2611	29¢ Hockey	1.75	....	....	....	....	....	.85	.15
2612	29¢ Figure Skating	1.75	....	....	....	....	....	.85	.15
2613	29¢ Speed Skating	1.75	....	....	....	....	....	.85	.15
2614	29¢ Skiing	1.75	....	....	....	....	....	.85	.15
2615	29¢ Bobsledding	1.75	....	....	....	....	....	.85	.15

2616 2617 2618 2619

SCOTT NO.	DESCRIPTION	FIRST DAY COVERS SING.	FIRST DAY COVERS PL.BLK.	MINT SHEET	COPY-RIGHT	ZIP	PLATE BLOCK	UNUSED F/NH	USED
2616	29¢ World Columbian Expo	1.75	4.25	32.50(50)	2.90	2.90	3.25	.70	.15
2617	29¢ W.E.B. Du Bois	1.75	4.25	32.50(50)	2.90	2.90	3.25	.70	.15
2618	29¢ Love	1.75	4.25	32.50(50)	2.90	2.90	3.25	.70	.15
2619	29¢ Olympic Baseball	2.50	5.50	57.50(50)	5.10	5.10	5.50	1.25	.15

U.S. Postage #2620-2636

2620

2621

2622

2623

SCOTT NO.	DESCRIPTION	FIRST DAY COVERS SING.	FIRST DAY COVERS PL.BLK.	MINT SHEET	COPY-RIGHT	ZIP	PLATE BLOCK	UNUSED F/NH	USED
2620-23	First Voyage of Columbus	3.00	4.25	35.00(40)	3.60	3.60	4.00	3.50	2.50
2620	29¢ Seeking Isabella's Support ..	1.75	....	....	....	....	....	.85	.15
2621	29¢ Crossing the Atlantic............	1.75	....	....	....	....	....	.85	.15
2622	29¢ Approaching Land................	1.75	....	....	....	....	....	.85	.15
2623	29¢ Coming Ashore.....................	1.75	....	....	....	....	....	.85	.15

2625 2626 2627

SCOTT NO.	DESCRIPTION	FIRST DAY COVERS SING.	FIRST DAY COVERS PL.BLK.	MINT SHEET	COPY-RIGHT	ZIP	PLATE BLOCK	UNUSED F/NH	USED
2624-29	1¢-$5 Columbian Souvenir Sheets (6)	55.00	....	....	....	....	....	38.50	33.50
2624a-29a	same, set of 16 singles	105.00	....	....	....	....	....	39.50	28.50

2630

2631 2632

2633 2634

2635

2636

SCOTT NO.	DESCRIPTION	FIRST DAY COVERS SING.	FIRST DAY COVERS PL.BLK.	MINT SHEET	COPY-RIGHT	ZIP	PLATE BLOCK	UNUSED F/NH	USED
2630	29¢ NY Stock Exchange	1.75	4.25	25.75(40)	2.90	2.90	3.25	.70	.15
2631-34	Space, US/Russian Joint Issue ..	3.00	4.75	35.00(50)	3.60	3.60	4.00	3.50	2.50
2631	29¢ Cosmonaut & Space Shuttle	1.75	....	....	....	....	....	.85	.15
2632	29¢ Astronaut & Mir Space Station	1.75	....	....	....	....	....	.85	.15
2633	29¢ Apollo Lunar Module & Sputnik	1.75	....	....	....	....	....	.85	.15
2634	29¢ Soyoz, Mercury & Gemini Space Craft	1.75	....	....	....	....	....	.85	.15
2635	29¢ Alaska Highway	1.75	4.75	32.50(50)	2.90	2.90	3.25	.70	.15
2636	29¢ Kentucky Statehood	1.75	4.75	32.50(50)	2.90	2.90	3.25	.70	.15

U.S. Postage #2637-2646av

2637 2638 2639

2640 2641

SCOTT NO.	DESCRIPTION	FIRST DAY COVERS SING.	FIRST DAY COVERS PL.BLK.	MINT SHEET	COPY-RIGHT	ZIP	PLATE BLOCK	UNUSED F/NH	USED
2637-41	Summer Olympics, 5 varieties, attd	4.50	....	31.50(35)	....	....	9.25(10)	4.50	2.75
2637	29¢ Soccer	1.75	....	....	....	....	....	.85	.15
2638	29¢ Women's Gymnastics	1.75	....	....	....	....	....	.85	.15
2639	29¢ Volleyball	1.75	....	....	....	....	....	.85	.15
2640	29¢ Boxing	1.75	....	....	....	....	....	.85	.15
2641	29¢ Swimming	1.75	....	....	....	....	....	.85	.15

2642 2643 2644 2645 2646

SCOTT NO.	DESCRIPTION	FIRST DAY COVERS SING.	FIRST DAY COVERS PL.BLK.	MINT SHEET	COPY-RIGHT	ZIP	PLATE BLOCK	UNUSED F/NH	USED
2642	29¢ Ruby-throated Hummingbird	1.75	....	....	....	....	....	.85	.15
2643	29¢ Broad-billed Hummingbird	1.75	....	....	....	....	....	.85	.15
2644	29¢ Costa's Hummingbird	1.75	....	....	....	....	....	.85	.15
2645	29¢ Rufous Hummingbird	1.75	....	....	....	....	....	.85	.15
2646	29¢ Calliope Hummingbird	1.75	....	....	....	....	....	.85	.15
2646a	29¢ Hummingbirds, booklet pane, 5 varieties, attached	4.50	....	....	....	....	....	4.50	....
2646av	same, booklet pane, unfolded	....	....	....	....	....	....	5.50	....

U.S. Postage #2647-2696

1992 Wildflowers

2647

2647	Indian Paintbrush	2672	Fringed Gentian	2672	
2648	Fragrant Water Lily	2673	Yellow Lady's Slipper		
2649	Meadow Beauty	2674	Passionflower		
2650	Jack-in-the-Pulpit	2675	Bunchberry		
2651	California Poppy	2676	Pasqueflower		
2652	Large-Flowered Trillium	2677	Round-lobed Hepatica		
2653	Tickseed	2678	Wild Columbine		
2654	Shooting Star	2679	Fireweed		
2655	Stream Violet	2680	Indian Pond Lily		
2656	Bluets	2681	Turk's Cap Lily		
2657	Herb Robert	2682	Dutchman's Breeches		
2658	Marsh Marigold	2683	Trumpet Honeysuckle		
2659	Sweet White Violet	2684	Jacob's Ladder		
2660	Claret Cup Cactus	2685	Plains Prickly Pear		
2661	White Mountain Avens	2686	Moss Campion		
2662	Sessile Bellwort	2687	Bearberry		
2663	Blue Flag	2688	Mexican Hat		
2664	Harlequin Lupine	2689	Harebell		
2665	Twinflower	2690	Desert Five Spot		
2666	Common Sunflower	2691	Smooth Solomon's Seal		
2667	Sego Lily	2692	Red Maids		
2668	Virginia Bluebells	2693	Yellow Skunk Cabbage		
2669	Ohi'a Lehua	2694	Rue Anemone		
2670	Rosebud Orchid	2695	Standing Cypress		
2671	Showy Evening Primrose	2696	Wild Flax		

2649

2648

2650

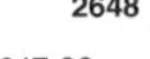

SCOTT NO.	DESCRIPTION	FIRST DAY COVERS SING.	FIRST DAY COVERS PL.BLK.	MINT SHEET	COPY-RIGHT	ZIP	PLATE BLOCK	UNUSED F/NH	USED
2647-96	29¢ Wildflowers, 50 varieties, attached	70.00	....	37.50(50)	....	....	37.50(50)	....	....
	set of singles	86.00	....	....	....	....	....	....	19.50
	singles of above, each	1.75	....	....	....	....	....	1.00	.40

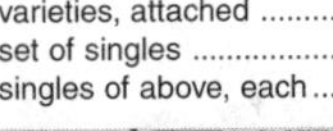

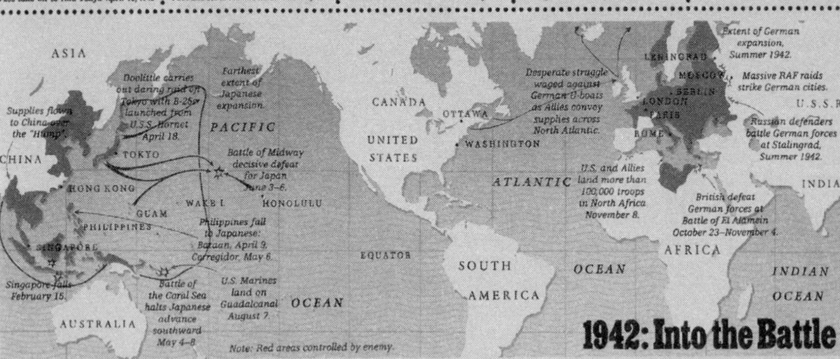

2697

U.S. Postage #2697-2704

SCOTT NO.	DESCRIPTION	FIRST DAY COVERS SING.	PL.BLK.	MINT SHEET	COPY-RIGHT	ZIP	PLATE BLOCK	UNUSED F/NH	USED
2697	$2.90 World War II (1942) Souvenir Sheet of 10	7.50	....	....	....	....	....	7.00	....
2697a	29¢ Tokyo Raid	1.75	....	....	....	....	....	.70	.40
2697b	29¢ Commodity Rationing	1.75	....	....	....	....	....	.70	.40
2697c	29¢ Battle at Coral Sea	1.75	....	....	....	....	....	.70	.40
2697d	29¢ Fall of Corregidor	1.75	....	....	....	....	....	.70	.40
2697e	29¢ Japan Invades Aleutians	1.75	....	....	....	....	....	.70	.40
2697f	29¢ Allies Break Codes	1.75	....	....	....	....	....	.70	.40
2697g	29¢ USS Yorktown Lost	1.75	....	....	....	....	....	.70	.40
2697h	29¢ Women Join War Effort	1.75	....	....	....	....	....	.70	.40
2697i	29¢ Marines on Guadalcanal	1.75	....	....	....	....	....	.70	.40
2697j	29¢ Allies Land in North Africa	1.75	....	....	....	....	....	.70	.40

2698

2699

2700 2701

2702 2703

2704

SCOTT NO.	DESCRIPTION	FIRST DAY COVERS SING.	PL.BLK.	MINT SHEET	COPY-RIGHT	ZIP	PLATE BLOCK	UNUSED F/NH	USED
2698	29¢ Dorothy Parker	1.75	4.75	32.50(50)	2.90	2.90	3.25	.70	.15
2699	29¢ Dr. Theodore von Karman	1.75	4.75	32.50(50)	2.90	2.90	3.25	.70	.15
2700-03	Minerals, 4 varieties, attached	3.00	4.75	35.00(40)	3.60	3.60	4.00	3.50	2.50
2700	29¢ Azurite	1.75	....	....	....	....	....	.85	.15
2701	29¢ Copper	1.75	....	....	....	....	....	.85	.15
2702	29¢ Variscite	1.75	....	....	....	....	....	.85	.15
2703	29¢ Wulfenite	1.75	....	....	....	....	....	.85	.15
2704	29¢ Juan Rodriguez Cabrillo	1.75	4.75	32.50(50)	2.90	2.90	3.25	.70	.15

2705

2706

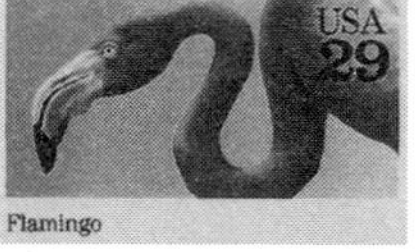

2707

2708

2709

U.S. Postage #2705-2720

SCOTT NO.	DESCRIPTION	FIRST DAY COVERS SING.	FIRST DAY COVERS PL.BLK.	MINT SHEET	COPY-RIGHT	ZIP	PLATE BLOCK	UNUSED F/NH	USED
2705	29¢ Giraffe	1.75	....	....	....	....	....	.75	.15
2706	29¢ Giant Panda	1.75	....	....	....	....	....	.75	.15
2707	29¢ Flamingo	1.75	....	....	....	....	....	.75	.15
2708	29¢ King Penguins	1.75	....	....	....	....	....	.75	.15
2709	29¢ White Bengal Tiger	1.75	....	....	....	....	....	.75	.15
2709a	29¢ Wild Animals, booklet pane of 5	4.50	....	....	....	....	....	4.00	3.50
2709av	same, booklet pane, unfolded	....	....	....	....	....	....	5.00	....

2711, 2715

2712, 2716, 2719

2710

2713, 2717

2714, 2718

2720

SCOTT NO.	DESCRIPTION	FIRST DAY COVERS SING.	FIRST DAY COVERS PL.BLK.	MINT SHEET	COPY-RIGHT	ZIP	PLATE BLOCK	UNUSED F/NH	USED
2710	29¢ Christmas—Traditional	1.75	4.75	32.50(50)	2.90	2.90	3.25	.70	.15
2710a	same, booklet pane of 10	7.00	....	....	....	....	....	7.00	....
2710av	same, booklet pane, unfolded	....	....	....	....	....	....	7.50	....
2711-14	Christmas Toys, 4 varieties, attached	3.00	4.75	35.00(50)	3.60	3.60	4.00	3.50	2.00
2711	29¢ Hobby Horse	1.75	....	....	....	....	....	.85	.15
2712	29¢ Locomotive	1.75	....	....	....	....	....	.85	.15
2713	29¢ Fire Engine	1.75	....	....	....	....	....	.85	.15
2714	29¢ Steamboat	1.75	....	....	....	....	....	.85	.15
2715	29¢ Hobby Horse (gravure) booklet single	1.75	....	....	....	....	....	.85	.15
2716	29¢ Locomotive (gravure) booklet single	1.75	....	....	....	....	....	.85	.15
2717	29¢ Fire Engine (gravure) booklet single	1.75	....	....	....	....	....	.85	.15
2718	29¢ Steamboat (gravure) booklet single	1.75	....	....	....	....	....	.85	.15
2718a	29¢ Christmas Toys (gravure) booklet pane of 4	3.00	....	....	....	....	....	3.50	3.25
2718av	same, booklet pane, unfolded	....	....	....	....	....	....	4.00	....
2719	29¢ Locomotive ATM, self-adhesive	1.75	....	....	....	....	....	.70	.15
2719a	same, booklet, pane of 18	13.50	....	....	....	....	....	13.00	....
2720	29¢ Happy New Year	1.75	4.75	13.00(20)	2.90	2.90	3.25	.70	.15

2721

2722

2723

2724, 2731

2725, 2732

2726, 2733

U.S. Postage #2721-2737bv

2727, 2734

2728, 2735

2729, 2736

2730, 2737

1993 COMMEMORATIVES

SCOTT NO.	DESCRIPTION	FIRST DAY COVERS SING.	FIRST DAY COVERS PL.BLK.	MINT SHEET	COPY-RIGHT	ZIP	PLATE BLOCK	UNUSED F/NH	USED
2721-2806	**(2721-30, 2746-59, 2765-66, 2771-74, 2779-89, 2791-94, 2804-06) 57 varieties**	....	....	....	....	....	....	40.25	12.50
2721	29¢ Elvis Presley	2.00	5.00	26.50(40)	2.90	2.90	3.25	.70	.20
2722	29¢ "Oklahoma!"	1.75	4.75	26.50(40)	2.90	2.90	3.25	.70	.20
2723	29¢ Hank Williams	1.75	4.75	26.50(40)	2.90	2.90	3.25	.70	.20
2723a	29¢ Hank Williams, perf. 11.2x11.4	....	....	950.00(40)	....	....	150.00	25.00	4.00
2724-30	Rock & Roll/Rhythm & Blues 7 varieties, attached	8.00	....	21.50(35)	....	....	6.50(8)	5.00	2.50
2724-30	same, Top Plate Block of 10	....	....	....	....	....	8.00(10)	....	....
2724	29¢ Elvis Presley	2.00	....	....	....	....	.....	.70	.20
2725	29¢ Bill Haley	2.00	....	....	....	....	.....	.70	.20
2726	29¢ Clyde McPhatter	2.00	....	....	....	....	.....	.70	.20
2727	29¢ Ritchie Valens	2.00	....	....	....	....	.....	.70	.20
2728	29¢ Otis Redding	2.00	....	....	....	....	.....	.70	.20
2729	29¢ Buddy Holly	2.00	....	....	....	....	.....	.70	.20
2730	29¢ Dinah Washington	2.00	....	....	....	....	.....	.70	.20
2731	29¢ Elvis Presley, booklet single	2.00	....	....	....	....	.....	.70	.20
2732	29¢ Bill Haley, booklet single	2.00	....	....	....	....	.....	.70	.20
2733	29¢ Clyde McPhatter, booklet single	2.00	....	....	....	....	.....	.70	.20
2734	29¢ Ritchie Valens, booklet single	2.00	....	....	....	....	.....	.70	.20
2735	29¢ Otis Redding, booklet single	2.00	....	....	....	....	.....	.70	.20
2736	29¢ Buddy Holly, booklet single	2.00	....	....	....	....	.....	.70	.20
2737	29¢ Dinah Washington, booklet single	2.00	....	....	....	....	.....	.70	.20
2737a	same, booklet pane of 8	8.00	....	....	....	....	.....	3.50	....
2737av	same, booklet pane, unfolded	....	....	....	....	....	.....	4.00	....
2737b	same, booklet pane of 4	5.00	....	....	....	....	.....	6.00	....
2737bv	same, booklet pane, unfolded	....	....	....	....	....	....	7.00	....

U.S. Postage #2741-2754

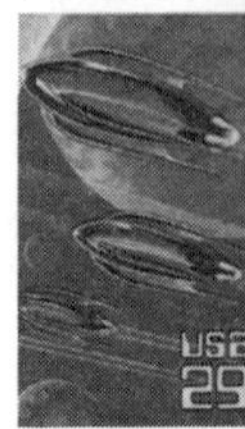

2741 2742 2743 2744 2745

SCOTT NO.	DESCRIPTION	FIRST DAY COVERS SING.	FIRST DAY COVERS PL.BLK.	MINT SHEET	COPY-RIGHT	ZIP	PLATE BLOCK	UNUSED F/NH	USE
2741	29¢ Saturn & 3 Rockets	1.75	....	....	....	....	.....	.75	.2
2742	29¢ 2 Flying Saucers	1.75	....	....	....	....	.....	.75	.2
2743	29¢ 2 Rocketeers	1.75	....	....	....	....	.....	.75	.2
2744	29¢ Winged Spaceship	1.75	....	....	....	....	.....	.75	.2
2745	29¢ 3 Space Ships	1.75	....	....	....	....	.....	.75	.2
2745a	29¢ Space Fantasy, booklet pane 5	4.50	....	....	....	....	.....	4.00	.2
2745av	same, booklet pane, unfolded	....	....	....	....	.....	.....	5.00	.....

2746

2747

2748

2749

SCOTT NO.	DESCRIPTION	FIRST DAY COVERS SING.	FIRST DAY COVERS PL.BLK.	MINT SHEET	COPY-RIGHT	ZIP	PLATE BLOCK	UNUSED F/NH	USE
2746	29¢ Percy Lavon Julian	1.75	4.75	32.50(50)	2.90	2.90	3.25	.70	.2
2747	29¢ Oregon Trail	1.75	4.75	32.50(50)	2.90	2.90	3.25	.70	.2
2748	29¢ World University Games	1.75	4.75	32.50(50)	2.90	2.90	3.25	.70	.2
2749	29¢ Grace Kelly	1.75	4.75	32.50(50)	2.90	2.90	3.25	.70	.2

2750-53

2754

SCOTT NO.	DESCRIPTION	FIRST DAY COVERS SING.	FIRST DAY COVERS PL.BLK.	MINT SHEET	COPY-RIGHT	ZIP	PLATE BLOCK	UNUSED F/NH	USED
2750-53	Circus, 4 varieties, attached	3.00	4.75	28.00(40)	3.10	3.10	6.00(6)	3.00	2.00
2750	29¢ Clown	1.75	....	....	....	....	.....	.70	.20
2751	29¢ Ringmaster	1.75	....	....	....	....	.....	.70	.20
2752	29¢ Trapeze Artist	1.75	....	....	....	....	.....	.70	.20
2753	29¢ Elephant	1.75	....	....	....	....	.....	.70	.20
2754	29¢ Cherokee Strip	1.75	4.75	32.50(50)	2.90	2.90	3.25	.70	.20

U.S. Postage #2755-2764av

SCOTT NO.	DESCRIPTION	FIRST DAY COVERS SING.	FIRST DAY COVERS PL.BLK.	MINT SHEET	COPY-RIGHT	ZIP	PLATE BLOCK	UNUSED F/NH	USED

2755

2756 2757

2758 2759

SCOTT NO.	DESCRIPTION	FIRST DAY COVERS SING.	FIRST DAY COVERS PL.BLK.	MINT SHEET	COPY-RIGHT	ZIP	PLATE BLOCK	UNUSED F/NH	USED
2755	29¢ Dean Acheson	1.75	4.75	32.50(50)	2.90	2.90	3.25	.70	.20
2756-59	Sporting Horses, 4 varieties, attached	3.00	4.75	32.50(40)	3.60	3.60	4.00	3.50	2.00
2756	29¢ Steeplechase	1.75	....	....	....	....	.....	.85	.20
2757	29¢ Thoroughbred	1.75	....	....	....	....	.....	.85	.20
2758	29¢ Harness	1.75	....	....	....	....	.....	.85	.20
2759	29¢ Polo....................................	1.75	....	....	....	....	.....	.85	.20

2760 2761 2762 2763 2764

SCOTT NO.	DESCRIPTION	FIRST DAY COVERS SING.	FIRST DAY COVERS PL.BLK.	MINT SHEET	COPY-RIGHT	ZIP	PLATE BLOCK	UNUSED F/NH	USED
2760	29¢ Hyacinth	1.75	....	....	....	....	.....	.85	.20
2761	29¢ Daffodil	1.75	....	....	....	....	.....	.85	.20
2762	29¢ Tulip....................................	1.75	....	....	....	....	.....	.85	.20
2763	29¢ Iris......................................	1.75	....	....	....	....	.....	.85	.20
2764	29¢ Lilac	1.75	....	....	....	....	.....	.85	.20
2764a	29¢ Garden Flowers, booklet pane of 5..	4.50	....	....	....	....	.....	4.00	.....
2764av	same, booklet pane, unfolded	....	....	....	....	....	.....	5.00	.....

U.S. Postage #2765-2765j

SCOTT NO.	DESCRIPTION	FIRST DAY COVERS SING.	PL.BLK.	MINT SHEET	COPY-RIGHT	ZIP	PLATE BLOCK	UNUSED F/NH	USED

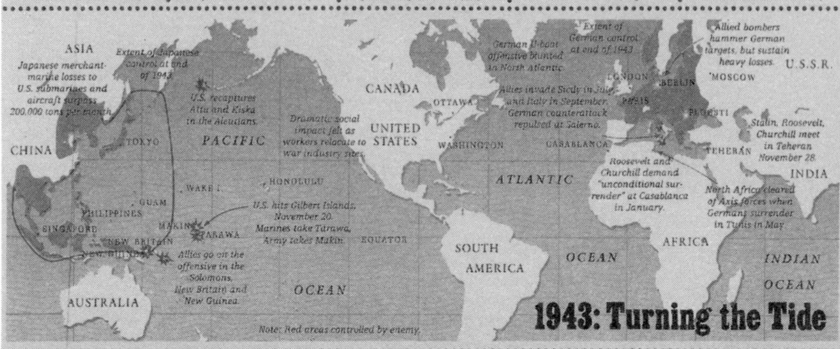

2765

SCOTT NO.	DESCRIPTION	FIRST DAY COVERS SING.	PL.BLK.	MINT SHEET	COPY-RIGHT	ZIP	PLATE BLOCK	UNUSED F/NH	USED
2765	$2.90 World War II, 1943 Souvenir Sheet of 10	7.50	....	....	....	....	.....	7.00	.....
2765a	29¢ Allies battle U-boats	1.75	....	....	....	....	.....	.70	.40
2765b	29¢ Medics treat wounded	1.75	....	....	....	....	.....	.70	.40
2765c	29¢ Allies attack Sicily	1.75	....	....	....	....	.....	.70	.40
2765d	29¢ B-24s hit Ploesti refineries	1.75	....	....	....	....	.....	.70	.40
2765e	29¢ V-Mail	1.75	....	....	....	....	.....	.70	.40
2765f	29¢ Italy invaded by Allies	1.75	....	....	....	....	.....	.70	.40
2765g	29¢ Bonds and Stamps help	1.75	....	....	....	....	.....	.70	.40
2765h	29¢ "Willie and Joe"	1.75	....	....	....	....	.....	.70	.40
2765i	29¢ Gold Stars	1.75	....	....	....	....	.....	.70	.40
2765j	29¢ Marines assault Tarawa	1.75	....	....	....	....	.....	.70	.40

2766

2767

2768

2769

2770

U.S. Postage #2766-2784

SCOTT NO.	DESCRIPTION	FIRST DAY COVERS SING.	PL.BLK.	MINT SHEET	COPY-RIGHT	ZIP	PLATE BLOCK	UNUSED F/NH	USED
2766	29¢ Joe Louis	1.75	4.75	35.00(50)	3.10	3.10	3.50	.75	.20
2767	29¢ "Show Boat"	1.75	....	....	....	....	......	.75	.20
2768	29¢ "Porgy & Bess"	1.75	....	....	....	....	......	.75	.20
2769	29¢ "Oklahoma!"	1.75	....	....	....	....	......	.75	.20
2770	29¢ "My Fair Lady".....................	1.75	....	....	....	....	......	.75	.20
2770a	Broadway Musicals, booklet pane of 4	3.75	....	....	....	....	......	3.00	......
2770av	same, booklet pane, unfolded ..	......	......	....	....	....	......	3.75	......

2771 2772 2773 2774

SCOTT NO.	DESCRIPTION	FIRST DAY COVERS SING.	PL.BLK.	MINT SHEET	COPY-RIGHT	ZIP	PLATE BLOCK	UNUSED F/NH	USED
2771-74	Country Music, 4 varieties, attached	3.00	4.75	13.00(20)	....	....	3.50	3.00	2.50
2771	29¢ Hank Williams	1.75	....	....	....	....	....	.70	.20
2772	29¢ Patsy Cline	1.75	....	....	....	....	....	.70	.20
2773	29¢ The Carter Family	1.75	....	....	....	....	....	.70	.20
2774	29¢ Bob Wills	1.75	....	....	....	....	....	.70	.20
2775	29¢ Hank Williams, booklet single ..	1.75	....	....	....	....	....	.70	.20
2776	29¢ The Carter Family, bklt. single..	1.75	....	....	....	....	....	.70	.20
2777	29¢ Patsy Cline, booklet single	1.75	....	....	....	....	....	.70	.20
2778	29¢ Bob Wills, booklet single	1.75	....	....	....	....	....	.70	.20
2778a	Country Music, booklet pane of 4 ..	5.00	....	....	....	....	....	3.00	2.50
2778av	same, booklet pane, unfolded	......	....	....	....	....	....	3.75	....

2779 2780 2781 2782

2783 2784

SCOTT NO.	DESCRIPTION	FIRST DAY COVERS SING.	PL.BLK.	MINT SHEET	COPY-RIGHT	ZIP	PLATE BLOCK	UNUSED F/NH	USED
2779-82	National Postal Museum, 4 varieties, attached	3.00	4.75	15.00(20)	....	....	3.50	3.25	2.50
2779	29¢ Ben Franklin	1.75	....	....	....	....	....	.80	.20
2780	29¢ Soldier & Drum	1.75	....	....	....	....	....	.80	.20
2781	29¢ Lindbergh	1.75	....	....	....	....	....	.80	.20
2782	29¢ Stamps & Bar Code	1.75	....	....	....	....	....	.80	.20
2783-84	Amer. Sign Language/Deaf Comm., 2 varieties, attached	2.50	4.75	13.00(20)	....	....	3.50	1.50	1.00
2783	29¢ Mother/Child	1.75	....	....	....	....	....	.70	.20
2784	29¢ Hand Sign	1.75	....	....	....	....	....	.70	.20

U.S. Postage #2785-2803a

2785 2786 2787 2788

SCOTT NO.	DESCRIPTION	FIRST DAY COVERS SING.	FIRST DAY COVERS PL.BLK.	MINT SHEET	COPY-RIGHT	ZIP	PLATE BLOCK	UNUSED F/NH	USED
2785-88	29¢ Youth Classics, 4 varieties, att'd.	3.00	4.75	32.50(40)	....	....	4.25	3.50	2.50
2785	29¢ Rebecca of Sunnybrook Farm	1.75	....	....	....	....	......	.85	.20
2786	29¢ Little House on the Prairie	1.75	....	....	....	....	......	.85	.20
2787	29¢ Adventures of Huckleberry Finn	1.75	....	....	....	....	......	.85	.20
2788	29¢ Little Women	1.75	....	....	....	....	......	.85	.20

2789, 2790

2791, 2798, 2801

2792, 2797, 2802

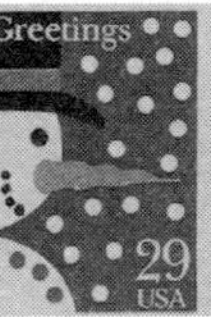

2793, 2796, 2799, 2803

2794, 2795, 2800

SCOTT NO.	DESCRIPTION	FIRST DAY COVERS SING.	FIRST DAY COVERS PL.BLK.	MINT SHEET	COPY-RIGHT	ZIP	PLATE BLOCK	UNUSED F/NH	USED
2789	29¢ Christmas—Traditional........	1.75	4.75	32.50(50)	combo	2.90	3.25	.70	.20
2790	29¢ Christmas—Traditional, booklet single	1.75	......	....	....	....	....	.70	.20
2790a	same, booklet pane of 4	3.00	......	....	....	....	....	2.75	....
2790av	same, booklet pane, unfolded....	......	......	....	....	....	....	3.50	....
2791-94	Christmas—Contemporary, 4 varieties, attached......................	3.00	4.75	29.75(50)	combo	3.10	3.50	3.00	2.50
2791	29¢ Jack-in-the-Box	1.75	......	....	....	....	....	.70	.20
2792	29¢ Red-Nosed Reindeer..........	1.75	......	....	....	....	....	.70	.20
2793	29¢ Snowman............................	1.75	......	....	....	....	....	.70	.20
2794	29¢ Toy Soldier Blowing Horn....	1.75	......	....	....	....	....	.70	.20
2795	29¢ Toy Soldier Blowing Horn, booklet single	1.75	......	....	....	....	....	.70	.20
2796	29¢ Snowman, booklet single....	1.75	......	....	....	....	....	.70	.20
2797	29¢ Red-Nosed Reindeer, booklet single	1.75	......	....	....	....	....	.70	.20
2798	29¢ Jack-in-the-Box, booklet single	1.75	......	....	....	....	....	.70	.20
2798a	same, booklet pane of 10	7.00	......	....	....	....	....	7.00	....
2798av	same, booklet pane, unfolded....	....	......	....	....	....	....	7.50	....
2799-2802v	29¢ Christmas—Contemporary, coil	......	......	....	....	....	....	2.80(4)	....
2799	29¢ Snowman, self-adhesive (3 buttons).................................	1.75	......	....	....	....	....	.70	.20
2800	29¢ Toy Soldier Blowing Horn, self-adhesive..............................	1.75	......	....	....	....	....	.70	.20
2801	29¢ Jack-in-the-Box, self-adhesive	1.75	......	....	....	....	....	.70	.20
2802	29¢ Red-Nosed Reindeer, self-adhesive....................................	1.75	......	....	....	....	....	.70	.20
2802a	same, booklet pane of 12	9.00	......	....	....	....	....	8.25	....
2803	29¢ Snowman, self-adhesive (2 buttons)	1.75	......	....	....	....	....	.70	.20
2803a	same, booklet pane of 18	13.50	......	....	....	....	....	12.50	....

U.S. Postage #2804-2815

2804

2805

2806

SCOTT NO.	DESCRIPTION	FIRST DAY COVERS SING.	FIRST DAY COVERS PL.BLK.	MINT SHEET	COPY-RIGHT	ZIP	PLATE BLOCK	UNUSED F/NH	USED
2804	29¢ Commonwealth of North Mariana Islands	1.75	4.75	13.00(20)	....	....	3.25	.70	.20
2805	29¢ Columbus Landing in Puerto Rico	1.75	4.75	32.50(50)	4.00	2.90	3.25	.70	.20
2806	29¢ AIDS Awareness	1.75	4.75	32.50(50)	combo	2.90	3.25	.70	.20
2806a	29¢ AIDS Awareness, booklet single	1.75	....	....	....	....	....	.70	.20
2806b	same, booklet pane of 5................	4.00	....	....	....	....	....	3.50	....
2806bv	same, booklet pane, unfolded	....	....	....	....	....	....	4.50	....

2807

2808

2809

2810

2811

2812

1994 COMMEMORATIVES

SCOTT NO.	DESCRIPTION	FIRST DAY COVERS SING.	FIRST DAY COVERS PL.BLK.	MINT SHEET	COPY-RIGHT	ZIP	PLATE BLOCK	UNUSED F/NH	USED
2807-76	**(2807-12, 2814C-28, 2834-36, 2838-39, 2841a, 2848-68, 2871-72, 2876) 60 varieties ....**		**.......**	**.......**	**.......**	**.......**	**.......**	**43.00**	**13.25**
2807-11	Winter Olympics, 5 varieties, att'd.	3.75	....	14.00(20)	....	....	8.00(10)	3.75	3.00
2807	29¢ Alpine Skiing	1.75	....	....	....	....	....	.70	.20
2808	29¢ Luge..	1.75	....	....	....	....	....	.70	.20
2809	29¢ Ice Dancing	1.75	....	....	....	....	....	.70	.20
2810	29¢ Cross Country Skiing	1.75	....	....	....	....	....	.70	.20
2811	29¢ Ice Hockey..................................	1.75	....	....	....	....	....	.70	.20
2812	29¢ Edward R. Murrow......................	1.75	4.75	32.50(50)	4.50(6)	....	3.25	.70	.20

2813

2814

2815

2816

2817

SCOTT NO.	DESCRIPTION	FIRST DAY COVERS SING.	FIRST DAY COVERS PL.BLK.	MINT SHEET	COPY-RIGHT	ZIP	PLATE BLOCK	UNUSED F/NH	USED
2813	29¢ Love (sunrise), self-adhesive......	1.75	....	....	....	....	....	.70	.20
2813a	same, booklet pane of 18................	13.50	....	....	....	....	....	12.50	....
2813v	29¢ Love (sunrise), self-adhesive coil	2.50	....	....	....	....	2.40(3)	.80	....
2814	29¢ Love (dove), booklet single	1.75	....	....	....	....	....	.70	.20
2814a	same, booklet pane of 10..................	7.00	....	....	....	....	....	7.00	....
2814av	same, booklet pane, unfolded		....	....	....	....	....	7.50	....
2814C	29¢ Love (dove)	1.75	4.75	32.50(50)	....	....	3.25	.70	.20
2815	52¢ Love (dove)	2.00	4.50	48.50(50)	....	....	5.00(4)	1.05	.20
....	same, plate block of 10		....	....	....	....	11.50(10)	....	....

U.S. Postage #2816-2833av

SCOTT NO.	DESCRIPTION	FIRST DAY COVERS SING.	PL.BLK.	MINT SHEET	COPY-RIGHT	ZIP	PLATE BLOCK	UNUSED F/NH	USED
2816	29¢ Allison Davis	1.75	4.75	13.00(20)	....	....	3.25	.70	.20
2817	29¢ Chinese New Year of the Dog	1.75	4.75	13.00(20)	....	....	3.25	.70	.20

2818 2819 2820 2821 2822

2823 2824 2825 2826 2827 2828

SCOTT NO.	DESCRIPTION	FIRST DAY COVERS SING.	PL.BLK.	MINT SHEET	COPY-RIGHT	ZIP	PLATE BLOCK	UNUSED F/NH	USED
2818	29¢ Buffalo Soldiers	1.75	4.75	13.00(20)	....	....	3.25	.70	.20
2819	29¢ Rudolph Valentino	1.75	....	....	....	....	....	.70	.20
2820	29¢ Clara Bow	1.75	....	....	....	....	....	.70	.20
2821	29¢ Charlie Chaplin	1.75	....	....	....	....	....	.70	.20
2822	29¢ Lon Chaney	1.75	....	....	....	....	....	.70	.20
2823	29¢ John Gilbert	1.75	....	....	....	....	....	.70	.20
2824	29¢ Zasu Pitts	1.75	....	....	....	....	....	.70	.20
2825	29¢ Harold Lloyd	1.75	....	....	....	....	....	.70	.20
2826	29¢ Keystone Cops	1.75	....	....	....	....	....	.70	.20
2827	29¢ Theda Bara	1.75	....	....	....	....	....	.70	.20
2828	29¢ Buster Keaton	1.75	....	....	....	....	....	.70	.20
2828a	29¢ Silent Screen Stars, 10 varieties, attached	7.00	....	27.50(40)	....	....	10.00(10)	7.50	5.00

2829 2830 2831 2832 2833

SCOTT NO.	DESCRIPTION	FIRST DAY COVERS SING.	PL.BLK.	MINT SHEET	COPY-RIGHT	ZIP	PLATE BLOCK	UNUSED F/NH	USED
2829	29¢ Lily	1.75	....	....	....	....	....	.75	.20
2830	29¢ Zinnia	1.75	....	....	....	....	....	.75	.20
2831	29¢ Gladiola	1.75	....	....	....	....	....	.75	.20
2832	29¢ Marigold	1.75	....	....	....	....	....	.75	.20
2833	29¢ Rose	1.75	....	....	....	....	....	.75	.20
2833a	29¢ Summer Garden flowers, booklet pane of 5	4.50	......	......	......	......	......	4.00	3.50
2833av	same, booklet pane, unfolded	....	......	......	......	......	......	5.00	......

U.S. Postage #2834-2837

2834

2835

2836

2837

SCOTT NO.	DESCRIPTION	FIRST DAY COVERS SING.	PL.BLK.	MINT SHEET	COPY-RIGHT	ZIP	PLATE BLOCK	UNUSED F/NH	USED
2834	29¢ World Cup Soccer	1.75	4.75	13.00(20)	....	....	3.25	.70	.20
2835	40¢ World Cup Soccer	1.75	4.75	16.00(20)	....	....	4.00	.85	.20
2836	50¢ World Cup Soccer	2.00	4.50	21.00(20)	....	....	5.00	1.10	.25
2837	29¢-50¢ World Cup Soccer Souvenir Sheet	3.50	....	....	....	....	....	3.00	2.50

U.S. Postage #2838-2840d

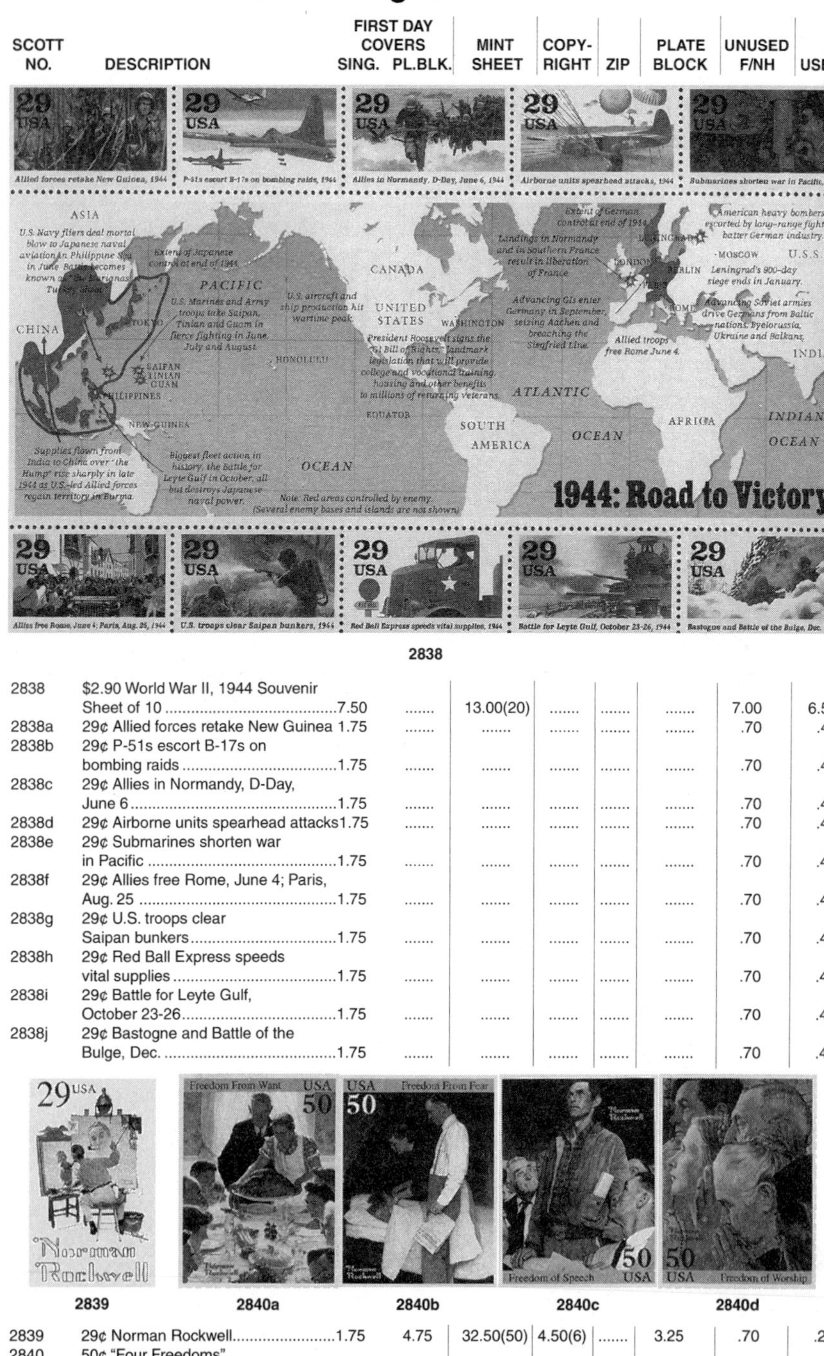

2838

SCOTT NO.	DESCRIPTION	FIRST DAY COVERS SING.	PL.BLK.	MINT SHEET	COPY-RIGHT	ZIP	PLATE BLOCK	UNUSED F/NH	USED
2838	$2.90 World War II, 1944 Souvenir Sheet of 10	7.50	....	13.00(20)	....	....	....	7.00	6.50
2838a	29¢ Allied forces retake New Guinea	1.75	....	....	....	....	....	.70	.40
2838b	29¢ P-51s escort B-17s on bombing raids	1.75	....	....	....	....	....	.70	.40
2838c	29¢ Allies in Normandy, D-Day, June 6	1.75	....	....	....	....	....	.70	.40
2838d	29¢ Airborne units spearhead attacks	1.75	....	....	....	....	....	.70	.40
2838e	29¢ Submarines shorten war in Pacific	1.75	....	....	....	....	....	.70	.40
2838f	29¢ Allies free Rome, June 4; Paris, Aug. 25	1.75	....	....	....	....	....	.70	.40
2838g	29¢ U.S. troops clear Saipan bunkers	1.75	....	....	....	....	....	.70	.40
2838h	29¢ Red Ball Express speeds vital supplies	1.75	....	....	....	....	....	.70	.40
2838i	29¢ Battle for Leyte Gulf, October 23-26	1.75	....	....	....	....	....	.70	.40
2838j	29¢ Bastogne and Battle of the Bulge, Dec.	1.75	....	....	....	....	....	.70	.40

2839 2840a 2840b 2840c 2840d

SCOTT NO.	DESCRIPTION	FIRST DAY COVERS SING.	PL.BLK.	MINT SHEET	COPY-RIGHT	ZIP	PLATE BLOCK	UNUSED F/NH	USED
2839	29¢ Norman Rockwell	1.75	4.75	32.50(50)	4.50(6)	....	3.25	.70	.20
2840	50¢ "Four Freedoms" Souvenir Sheet	5.00	....	....	....	....	....	4.50	3.50
2840a-d	same, set of 4 singles	9.00	....	....	....	....	....	4.25	2.75

U.S. Postage #2841-2853

2843

2844

2845

2841

2846

2847

2842

2848

SCOTT NO.	DESCRIPTION	FIRST DAY COVERS SING.	PL.BLK.	MINT SHEET	COPY-RIGHT	ZIP	PLATE BLOCK	UNUSED F/NH	USED
2841	29¢ Moon Landing 25th Anniv. Sheet of 12	....	....	....	....	....	....	8.00	....
2841a	29¢ Moon Landing 25th Anniv. single stamp	1.75	....	....	....	....	....	.70	.85
2842	$9.95 Moon Landing Express Mail Stamp	20.00	50.00	350.00(20)	....	....	85.00	20.75	12.50
2843	29¢ Hudson's General	1.75	....	....	....	....	....	.70	.20
2844	29¢ McQueen's Jupiter	1.75	....	....	....	....	....	.70	.20
2845	29¢ Eddy's No. 242	1.75	....	....	....	....	....	.70	.20
2846	29¢ Ely's No. 10	1.75	....	....	....	....	....	.70	.20
2847	29¢ Buchanan's No. 999	1.75	....	....	....	....	....	.70	.20
2847a	29¢ Locomotives, booklet pane of 5	4.50	....	....	....	....	....	3.75	3.50
2847av	same, booklet pane, unfolded	....	....	....	....	....	....	5.00	....
2848	29¢ George Meany	1.75	4.75	32.50(50)	4.50(6)	....	3.25	.70	.20

2849

2850

2851

2852

2853

SCOTT NO.	DESCRIPTION	FIRST DAY COVERS SING.	PL.BLK.	MINT SHEET	COPY-RIGHT	ZIP	PLATE BLOCK	UNUSED F/NH	USED
2849-53	29¢ Popular Singers, 5 vars., att'd.	4.50	....	13.00(20)	....	....	4.75(6)	3.50	3.00
2849	29¢ Al Jolson	1.75	....	....	....	....	....	.70	.20
2850	29¢ Bing Crosby	1.75	....	....	....	....	....	.70	.20
2851	29¢ Ethel Waters	1.75	....	....	....	....	....	.70	.20
2852	29¢ Nat "King" Cole	1.75	....	....	....	....	....	.70	.20
2853	29¢ Ethel Merman	1.75	....	....	....	....	....	.70	.20
....	same, Plate Block of 12	....	....	....	....	....	9.00(12)	....	....

U.S. Postage #2854-2866

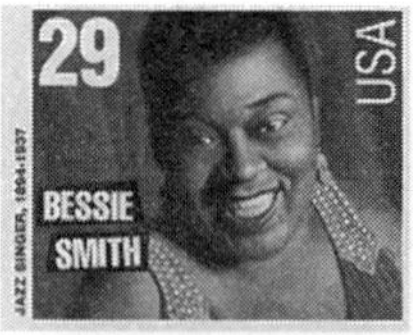

2854 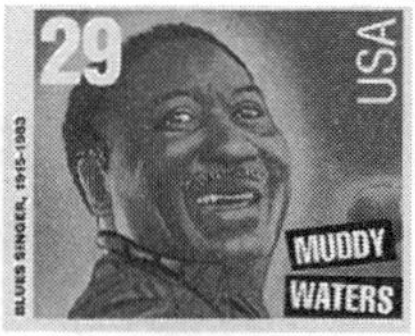 2855 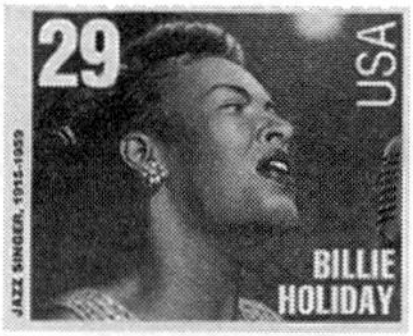 2856 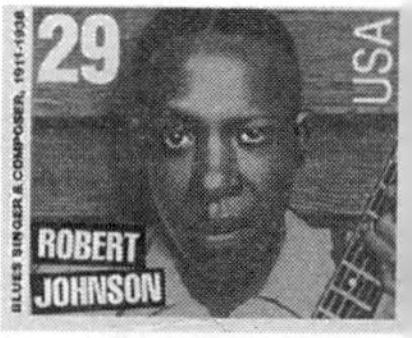 2857

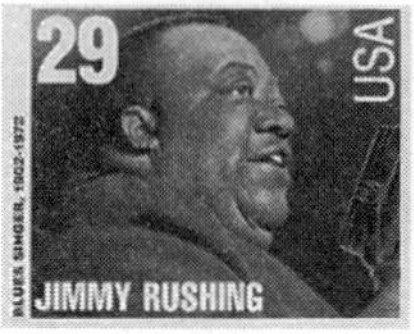

2858 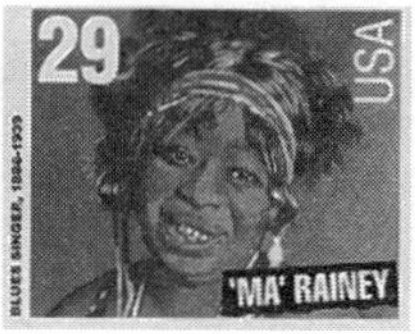 2859 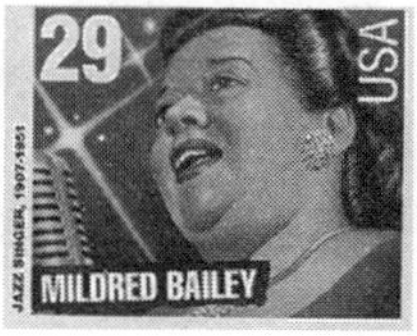 2860 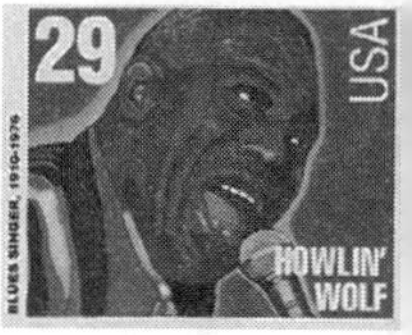 2861

SCOTT NO.	DESCRIPTION	FIRST DAY COVERS SING.	PL.BLK.	MINT SHEET	COPY-RIGHT	ZIP	PLATE BLOCK	UNUSED F/NH	USED
2854-61	29¢ Blues & Jazz Singers, 8 varieties, attached	6.00	....	22.50(35)	....	....	8.00(10)	7.25	4.50
....	same, Horizontal Plate Block of 10 w/Top Label		....	....	....	....	8.50(10)	....	....
2854	29¢ Bessie Smith	1.75	....	....	....	....	....	.70	.20
2855	29¢ Muddy Waters	1.75	....	....	....	....	....	.70	.20
2856	29$ Billie Holiday	1.75	....	....	....	....	....	.70	.20
2857	29¢ Robert Johnson	1.75	....	....	....	....	....	.70	.20
2858	29¢ Jimmy Rushing	1.75	....	....	....	....	....	.70	.20
2859	29¢ "Ma" Rainey	1.75	....	....	....	....	....	.70	.20
2860	29¢ Mildred Bailey	1.75	....	....	....	....	....	.70	.20
2861	29¢ Howlin' Wolf	1.75	....	....	....	....	....	.70	.20

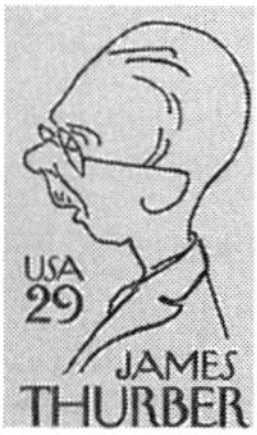

2862

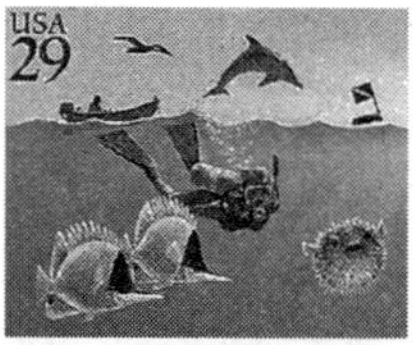

2863 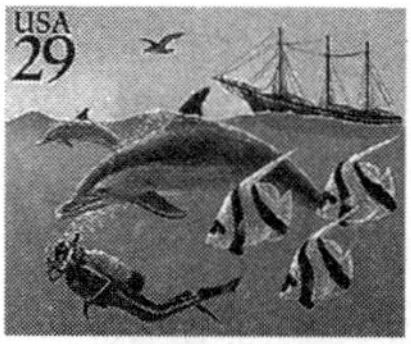 2864

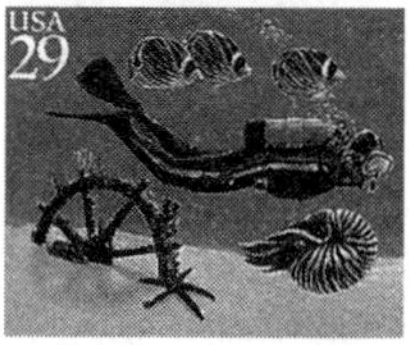

2865 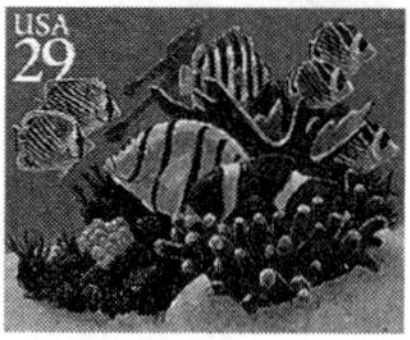 2866

SCOTT NO.	DESCRIPTION	FIRST DAY COVERS SING.	PL.BLK.	MINT SHEET	COPY-RIGHT	ZIP	PLATE BLOCK	UNUSED F/NH	USED
2862	29¢ James Thurber	1.75	4.75	32.50(50)	4.50(6)	....	3.25	.70	.20
2863-66	29¢ Wonders of the Sea, 4 varieties, attached	3.00	4.75	16.00(24)	....	....	3.50	3.00	2.50
2863	29¢ Diver & Motorboat	1.75	....	....	....	....	....	.70	.20
2864	29¢ Diver & Ship	1.75	....	....	....	....	....	.70	.20
2865	29¢ Diver & Ship's Wheel	1.75	....	....	....	....	....	.70	.20
2866	29¢ Diver & Coral	1.75	....	....	....	....	....	.70	.20

U.S. Postage #2867-2870

SCOTT NO.	DESCRIPTION	FIRST DAY COVERS SING.	FIRST DAY COVERS PL.BLK.	MINT SHEET	COPY-RIGHT	ZIP	PLATE BLOCK	UNUSED F/NH	USED

2867

2868

SCOTT NO.	DESCRIPTION	FIRST DAY COVERS SING.	FIRST DAY COVERS PL.BLK.	MINT SHEET	COPY-RIGHT	ZIP	PLATE BLOCK	UNUSED F/NH	USED
2867-68	29¢ Cranes	2.50	4.75	12.00(20)	....	....	3.50	1.40	1.00
2867	29¢ Black-Necked Crane	1.75	....	....	....	....	....	.70	.20
2868	29¢ Whooping Crane	1.75	....	....	....	....	....	.70	.20

Legends of the West

2869g

2869a	*Home on the Range*	**2869k**	*Nellie Cashman*
2869b	*Buffalo Bill Cody*	**2869l**	*Charles Goodnight*
2869c	*Jim Bridger*	**2869m**	*Geronimo*
2869d	*Annie Oakley*	**2869n**	*Kit Carson*
2869e	*Native American Culture*	**2869o**	*Wild Bill Hickok*
2869f	*Chief Joseph*	**2869p**	*Western Wildlife*
2869g	*Bill Pickett*	**2869q**	*Jim Beckwourth*
2869h	*Bat Masterson*	**2869r**	*Bill Tilghman*
2869i	*John Fremont*	**2869s**	*Sacagawea*
2869j	*Wyatt Earp*	**2869t**	*Overland Mail*

2870g

SCOTT NO.	DESCRIPTION	FIRST DAY COVERS SING.	FIRST DAY COVERS PL.BLK.	MINT SHEET	COPY-RIGHT	ZIP	PLATE BLOCK	UNUSED F/NH	USED
2869	29¢ Legends of the West, 20 varieties, attached		....	13.00(20)	....	....	....	13.00	10.00
....	set of singles	31.50	....	....	....	....	....	....	8.50
....	singles of above, each	1.75	....	....	....	....	....	.85	.45
2869v	same as above, uncut sheet of 120 (6 panes)		....	80.00(120)	....	....	....	80.00	....
....	block of 40 with vertical or horizontal, gutter between (2 panes)		....	27.50(40)	....	....	....	27.50	....
....	block of 24 with vertical gutter		....	20.75(24)	....	....	....	20.75	....
....	block of 25 with horizontal gutter		....	21.50(25)	....	....	....	21.50	....
....	cross gutter block of 20		....	....	....	....	....	31.00	....
....	cross gutter block of 4		....	....	....	....	....	17.00	....
....	vertical pair with horizontal gutter		....	....	....	....	....	2.25	....
....	horizontal, pair with vert. gutter		....	....	....	....	....	2.25	....
2870	29¢ Legends of the West (Recalled), 20 varieties, attached		....	295.00(20)	....	....	....	295.00	....

2871

2872

2873

2874

2875

U.S. Postage #2871-2892

SCOTT NO.	DESCRIPTION	FIRST DAY COVERS SING.	FIRST DAY COVERS PL.BLK.	MINT SHEET	COPY-RIGHT	ZIP	PLATE BLOCK	UNUSED F/NH	USED
2871	29¢ Christmas—Traditional	1.75	4.75	32.50(50)	4.50(6)	....	3.25	.70	.20
2871a	29¢ Christmas—Traditional, booklet single	1.75	....	....	....	....	....	.70	.20
2871b	same, booklet pane of 10	7.00	....	....	....	....	....	7.00	....
2871bv	same, booklet pane, unfolded		....	....	....	....	....	7.50	....
2872	29¢ Christmas Stocking	1.75	4.75	32.50(50)	4.50(6)	....	3.25	.70	.20
2872v	29¢ Christmas Stocking, bklt. single	1.75	....	....	....	....	....	.70	.20
2872a	same, booklet pane of 20		....	....	....	....	....	13.00	....
2872av	same, booklet pane, unfolded		....	....	....	....	....	15.00	....
2873	29¢ Santa Claus, self-adhesive	1.75	....	....	....	....	....	.70	.20
2873a	same, booklet pane of 12	9.00	....	....	....	....	....	8.25	....
2874	29¢ Cardinal in Snow, self-adhesive	1.75	....	....	....	....	....	.70	.20
2874a	same, booklet pane of 18	13.50	....	....	....	....	....	12.00	....
2875	$2 B.E.P. souvenir sheet of 4 (Madison)	16.50	....	....	....	....	....	17.00	12.00
2875a	single from above ($2 Madison)	6.00	....	....	....	....	....	4.25	2.50

2876

2877, 2878

2879, 2880

2881-2885, 2889-2892

2886, 2887

2888

SCOTT NO.	DESCRIPTION	FIRST DAY COVERS SING.	FIRST DAY COVERS PL.BLK.	MINT SHEET	COPY-RIGHT	ZIP	PLATE BLOCK	UNUSED F/NH	USED
2876	29¢ Year of the Boar	1.75	4.75	13.00(20)	....	....	3.25	.70	.20
2877	(3¢) "G" Make-up Rate (ABN, bright blue)	1.75	4.75	8.50(100)	.80	.80	.85	.20	.15
2878	(3¢) "G" Make-up Rate (SVS, dark blue)	1.75	4.75	8.50(100)	.80	.80	.85	.20	.15
2879	(20¢) "G" Old Glory Postcard Rate (BEP, black "G")	1.75	4.75	44.00(100)	2.20	2.20	2.50	.50	.15
2880	(20¢) "G" Old Glory Postcard Rate (SVS, red "G")	1.75	4.75	44.00(100)	2.20	2.20	2.50	.50	.15
2881	(32¢) "G" Old Glory (BEP, black "G")	1.75	4.75	65.00(100)	3.00	3.00	3.25	.70	.20
2882	(32¢) "G" Old Glory (SVS, red "G")	1.75	4.75	65.00(100)	3.00	3.00	3.25	.70	.20
2883	(32¢) "G" Old Glory, booklet single (BEP, black "G")	1..75	....	....	....	....	....	.70	.20
2883a	same, booklet pane of 10	7.25	....	....	....	....	....	7.00	....
2883av	same, booklet pane, unfolded		....	....	....	....	....	8.00	....
2884	(32¢) "G" Old Glory, booklet single (ABN, blue "G")	1.75	....	....	....	....	....	.70	.20
2884a	same, booklet pane of 10	7.25	....	....	....	....	....	7.00	....
2884av	same, booklet pane, unfolded		....	....	....	....	....	8.00	....
2885	(32¢) "G" Old Glory, booklet single (KCS, red "G")	1.75	....	....	....	....	....	.70	.20
2885a	same, booklet pane of 10	7.25	....	....	....	....	....	7.00	....
2885av	same, booklet pane, unfolded		....	....	....	....	....	8.00	....
2886	(32¢) "G" Old Glory, self-adhesive	1.75	....	....	....	....	....	.70	.20
2886a	same, booklet pane of 18	13.50	....	....	....	....	....	12.50	....
2887	(32¢) "G" Old Glory, self-adhesive (blue shading)	1.75	....	....	....	....	....	.70	.20
2887a	same, booklet pane of 18	13.50	....	....	....	....	....	12.50	....
			PLATE # STRIP 3				PLATE # STRIP 3		
2888	(25¢) "G" Old Glory First-Class Presort, coil	1.75	10.00	....	....	....	5.75	.65	.20
2889	(32¢) "G" Old Glory, coil (BEP, black "G")	1.75	10.00	....	....	....	6.00	.70	.20
2890	(32¢) "G" Old Glory, coil (ABN, blue "G")	1.75	10.00	....	....	....	5.00	.70	.20
2891	(32¢) "G" Old Glory, coil (SVS, red "G")	1.75	10.00	....	....	....	5.00	.70	.20
2892	(32¢) "G" Old Glory, coil (SVS, red "G"), rouletted	1.75	10.00	....	....	....	6.00	.70	.20

U.S. Postage #2893-2915D

2893 | 2897, 2913-16 | 2902 | 2903, 2904

2905, 2906 | 2907 | 2908-10 | 2911, 2912

1995-97 Regular Issues

SCOTT NO.	DESCRIPTION	FIRST DAY COVERS SING.	FIRST DAY COVERS PL.BLK.	MINT SHEET	COPY-RIGHT	ZIP	PLATE BLOCK	UNUSED F/NH	USED
2893	(5¢) "G" Old Glory, Nonprofit, coil	1.95	10.00	....	....	....	1.75	.20	.20
2897	32¢ Flag over Porch	1.95	4.75	65.00(100)	....	....	3.25	.70	.20

1995-97 Regular Issue Coils

SCOTT NO.	DESCRIPTION	FIRST DAY COVERS SING.	PLATE # STRIP 3	MINT SHEET	COPY-RIGHT	ZIP	PLATE # STRIP 3	UNUSED F/NH	USED
2902	(5¢) Butte, Nonprofit, coil	1.95	10.00	....	....	....	1.75	.20	.20
2902B	(5¢) Butte, self-adhesive coil	1.95	......	......	......	......	2.50	.20	.20
2903	(5¢) Mountain (BEP, violet 1996)	1.95	10.00	....	....	....	1.75	.20	.20
2904	(5¢) Mountain (SVS, blue 1996)	1.95	10.00	....	....	....	1.75	.20	.20
2904A	(5¢) Mountain, self-adhesive coil	1.95	......	......	......	......	2.50	.20	.20
2904B	(5¢) Mountain, self-adhesive coil (1997)	1.95	......	......	......	......	2.50	.20	.20
2905	(10¢) Automobile, Bulk Rate, coil	1.95	10.00	....	....	....	2.50	.25	.20
2906	(10¢) Automobile, self-adhesive coil	1.95	......	......	......	......	2.50	.25	.20
2907	(10¢) Eagle, bulk-rate, coil (1996)	1.95	......	......	......	......	3.00	.25	.20
2908	(15¢) Auto Tail Fin, Presorted First-Class Card, coil (BEP)	1.95	10.00	....	....	....	3.50	.40	.25
2909	(15¢) Auto Tail Fin, Presorted First-Class Card, coil (SVS)	1.95	10.00	....	....	....	3.50	.40	.25
2910	(15¢) Automobile Tail Fin, self-adhesive coil	1.95	......	......	......	......	3.50	.40	.20
2911	(25¢) Juke Box, Presorted First-Class, coil (BEP)	1.95	10.00	....	....	....	5.00	.70	.35
2912	(25¢) Juke Box, Presorted First-Class, coil (SVS)	1.95	10.00	....	....	....	5.00	.70	.35
2912A	(25¢) Juke Box, self-adhesive coil	1.95	......	......	......	......	5.00	.60	.25
2912B	(25¢) Juke Box, self-adhesive coil (1997)	1.95	......	......	......	......	5.00	.60	.25
2913	32¢ Flag over Porch, coil (BEP, red date)	1.95	10.00	....	....	....	5.75	.70	.25
2914	32¢ Flag over Porch, coil (SVS, blue date)	1.95	10.00	....	....	....	5.75	.80	.25
2915	32¢ Flag over Porch, self-adhesive coil (Die Cut 8.7)	1.95	....	....	....	....	8.00	.80	.25
2915A	32¢ Flag over Porch, self-adhesive coil (1996, Die Cut 9.8)	1.95	....	....	....	....	8.00	1.00	.25
2915B	32¢ Flag over Porch, self-adhesive coil (1996, Die Cut 11.5)	1.95	....	....	....	....	8.00	.90	.25
2915C	32¢ Flag over Porch, self-adhesive coil (1996, Die Cut 10.9)	1.95	....	....	....	....	25.00	2.50	.75
2915D	32¢ Flag over Porch, self-adhesive coil (1997)	1.95	......	......	......	......	8.00	.85	.20

U.S. Postage #2916-2954

2919 2920, 2921 2933 2934 2938 2940 2943

1995-97 Booklet Panes

SCOTT NO.	DESCRIPTION	FIRST DAY COVERS SING.	FIRST DAY COVERS PL.BLK.	MINT SHEET	COPY-RIGHT	ZIP	PLATE BLOCK	UNUSED F/NH	USED
2916	32¢ Flag over Porch, booklet single	1.95	....	....	....	....	....	.70	.20
2916a	same, booklet pane of 10	7.25	....	....	....	....	....	7.00	....
2916av	same, booklet pane, unfolded		....	....	....	....	....	8.00	....
2919	32¢ Flag over Field, self-adhesive	1.95	....	....	....	....	....	.70	.25
2919a	same, booklet pane of 18	13.50	....	....	....	....	....	12.50	....
2920	32¢ Flag over Porch, self-adhesive (large "1995")	1.95	....	....	....	....	....	.70	.25
2920a	same, booklet pane of 20	14.50	....	....	....	....	....	13.50	....
2920b	32¢ Flag over Porch, self-adhesive (small "1995")	1.95	....	....	....	....	....	2.25	.80
2920c	same, booklet pane of 20	14.50	....	....	....	....	....	40.00	....
2920d	32¢ Flag over Porch ("1996" date), self-adhesive	1.95	....	....	....	....	....	.70	.25
2920e	same, booklet pane of 10	6.95	....	....	....	....	....	7.00	....
2921	32¢ Flag over Porch, self-adhesive (1996, Die Cut 9.8)	1.95	....	....	....	....	....	.70	.25
2921a	same, booklet pane of 10	7.00	....	....	....	....	....	7.00	....
2921av	same, booklet pane, unfolded		....	....	....	....	....	8.00	....
2921b	same, booklet pane of 5	5.50	....	....	....	....	....	3.75	....
2933	32¢ Milton S. Hershey	1.95	4.75	65.00(100)	....	....	3.25	.70	.20
2934	32¢ Cal Farley	1.95	4.75	65.00(100)	....	....	3.25	.70	.20
2938	46¢ Ruth Benedict	2.25	5.00	95.00(100)	....	....	5.00	1.00	.25
2940	55¢ Alice Hamilton	2.25	5.00	115.00(100)	....	....	5.75	1.20	.20
2943	78¢ Alice Paul	2.95	5.50	155.00(100)	....	....	8.25	1.65	.25

2948 2949 2950

SCOTT NO.	DESCRIPTION	FIRST DAY COVERS SING.	FIRST DAY COVERS PL.BLK.	MINT SHEET	COPY-RIGHT	ZIP	PLATE BLOCK	UNUSED F/NH	USED
2948	(32¢) Love (Cherub)	1.95	4.75	31.50(50)	4.00(6)	....	3.25	.70	.20
2949	(32¢) Love (Cherub), self-adhesive	1.95	....	....	....	....	....	.70	.20
2949a	same, booklet pane of 20	14.50	....	....	....	....	....	13.50	....
2950	32¢ Florida Statehood	1.95	4.75	13.75(20)	....	....	3.25	.70	.20

2951 2952 2953 2954

SCOTT NO.	DESCRIPTION	FIRST DAY COVERS SING.	FIRST DAY COVERS PL.BLK.	MINT SHEET	COPY-RIGHT	ZIP	PLATE BLOCK	UNUSED F/NH	USED
2951-54	32¢ Kids Care About Environment, 4 varieties, attached	4.00	4.75	11.75(16)	....	....	3.25	3.00	2.50
2951	32¢ Earth in a Bathtub	1.95	....	....	....	....	....	.70	.20
2952	32¢ Solar Energy	1.95	....	....	....	....	....	.70	.20
2953	32¢ Tree Planting	1.95	....	....	....	....	....	.70	.20
2954	32¢ Beach Clean-Up	1.95	....	....	....	....	....	.70	.20

U.S. Postage #2955-2968

2955 2956 2957, 2959 2958 2960

SCOTT NO.	DESCRIPTION	FIRST DAY COVERS SING.	PL.BLK.	MINT SHEET	COPY-RIGHT	ZIP	PLATE BLOCK	UNUSED F/NH	USED
2955	32¢ Richard M. Nixon	1.95	4.75	31.50(50)	....	....	3.25	.70	.20
2956	32¢ Bessie Coleman	1.95	4.75	31.50(50)	....	....	3.25	.70	.20
2957	32¢ Love (Cherub)	1.95	4.75	31.50(50)	....	....	3.25	.70	.20
2958	55¢ Love (Cherub)	2.50	5.00	60.00(50)	....	....	....	1.20	.35
2959	32¢ Love (Cherub), booklet single	1.95	....	....	....	....	....	.70	.20
2959a	same, booklet pane of 10	7.25	....	....	....	....	....	7.00	....
2959av	same, booklet pane, unfolded		....	....	....	....	....	8.00	....
2960	55¢ Love (Cherub), self-adhesive	2.50	....	....	....	....	....	1.20	.35
2960a	same, booklet pane of 20	23.50	....	....	....	....	....	23.00	....

2961 2962 2963 2964 2965 2966 2967

SCOTT NO.	DESCRIPTION	FIRST DAY COVERS SING.	PL.BLK.	MINT SHEET	COPY-RIGHT	ZIP	PLATE BLOCK	UNUSED F/NH	USED
2961-65	32¢ Recreational Sports, 5 varieties, attached	5.50	....	13.75(20)	....	....	8.50(10)	3.75	2.75
2961	32¢ Volleyball	1.95	....	....	....	....	....	.70	.20
2962	32¢ Softball	1.95	....	....	....	....	....	.70	.20
2963	32¢ Bowling	1.95	....	....	....	....	....	.70	.20
2964	32¢ Tennis	1.95	....	....	....	....	....	.70	.20
2965	32¢ Golf	1.95	....	....	....	....	....	.70	.20
2966	32¢ POW & MIA	1.95	4.75	13.75(20)	....	....	3.25	.70	.20
2967	32¢ Marilyn Monroe	1.95	4.75	13.75(20)	....	....	3.25	.70	.20

2968

SCOTT NO.	DESCRIPTION	FIRST DAY COVERS SING.	PL.BLK.	MINT SHEET	COPY-RIGHT	ZIP	PLATE BLOCK	UNUSED F/NH	USED
2968	32¢ Texas Statehood	1.95	4.75	13.75(20)	....	....	3.25	.70	.20

U.S. Postage #2969-2974

2969 2970 2971 2972 2973 2974

SCOTT NO.	DESCRIPTION	FIRST DAY COVERS SING.	FIRST DAY COVERS PL.BLK.	MINT SHEET	COPY-RIGHT	ZIP	PLATE BLOCK	UNUSED F/NH	USED
2969	32¢ Split Rock Lighthouse	1.95	....	....	....	....	....	.70	.20
2970	32¢ St. Joseph Lighthouse	1.95	....	....	....	....	....	.70	.20
2971	32¢ Spectacle Reef Lighthouse	1.95	....	....	....	....	....	.70	.20
2972	32¢ Marblehead Lighthouse	1.95	....	....	....	....	....	.70	.20
2973	32¢ Thirty Mile Point Lighthouse	1.95	....	....	....	....	....	.70	.20
2973a	32¢ Great Lakes Lighthouses, booklet pane of 5	5.50	....	....	....	....	....	4.00	3.50
2973av	same, booklet pane, unfolded		....	....	....	....	....	4.75	....
2974	32¢ United Nations	1.75	4.75	13.75(20)	....	....	3.25	.70	.20

U.S. Postage #2975a-2975t

SCOTT NO.	DESCRIPTION	FIRST DAY COVERS SING.	PL.BLK.	MINT SHEET	COPY-RIGHT	ZIP	PLATE BLOCK	UNUSED F/NH	USED

2975

Civil War

2975a	*Monitor–Virginia*	**2975h**	*Frederick Douglass*	**2975o**	*Mary Chestnut*
2975b	*Robert E. Lee*	**2975i**	*Raphael Semmes*	**2975p**	*Chancellorsville*
2975c	*Clara Barton*	**2975j**	*Abraham Lincoln*	**2975q**	*William T. Sherman*
2975d	*Ulysses S. Grant*	**2975k**	*Harriet Tubman*	**2975r**	*Phoebe Pember*
2975e	*Shiloh*	**2975l**	*Stand Watie*	**2975s**	*"Stonewall" Jackson*
2975f	*Jefferson Davis*	**2975m**	*Joseph E. Johnston*	**2975t**	*Gettysburg*
2975g	*David Farragut*	**2975n**	*Winfield Hancock*		

U.S. Postage #2975-2981c

SCOTT NO.	DESCRIPTION	FIRST DAY COVERS SING.	PL.BLK.	MINT SHEET	COPY-RIGHT	ZIP	PLATE BLOCK	UNUSED F/NH	USED
2975	32¢ Civil War, 20 varieties, attached		....	13.75(20)	....	....	....	13.75	10.00
....	set of singles	35.00	....	....	....	....	....	....	9.25
....	single of above, each	1.95	....	....	....	....	....	.90	.55
2975v	same as above, uncut sheet of 120 (6 panes)		....	82.50(120)	....	....	....	82.50	....
....	block of 40 with vertical or horizontal gutter between (2 panes)		....	29.00(40)	....	....	....	29.00	....
....	block of 24 with vertical gutter		....	21.50(24)	....	....	....	21.50	....
....	block of 25 with horizontal gutter		....	22.50(25)	....	....	....	22.50	....
....	cross gutter block of 20		....	....	....	....	....	32.00	....
....	cross gutter block of 4		....	....	....	....	....	17.25	....
....	vertical pair with horizontal gutter	....	....	....	....	....	....	2.25	....
....	horizontal pair with vertical gutter	....	....	....	....	....	....	2.25	....

2976 2977 2978 2979 2980

SCOTT NO.	DESCRIPTION	FIRST DAY COVERS SING.	PL.BLK.	MINT SHEET	COPY-RIGHT	ZIP	PLATE BLOCK	UNUSED F/NH	USED
2976-79	32¢ Carousel Horses, 4vars., att'd.	4.00	4.75	13.75(20)	....	....	3.25	3.00	2.50
2976	32¢ Palamino	1.95	....	....	....	....	....	.70	.20
2977	32¢ Pinto Pony	1.95	....	....	....	....	....	.70	.20
2978	32¢ Armored Jumper	1.95	....	....	....	....	....	.70	.20
2979	32¢ Brown Jumper	1.95	....	....	....	....	....	.70	.20
2980	32¢ Women's Suffrage	1.95	4.75	27.00(40)	....	....	3.25	.70	.20

2981

SCOTT NO.	DESCRIPTION	FIRST DAY COVERS SING.	PL.BLK.	MINT SHEET	COPY-RIGHT	ZIP	PLATE BLOCK	UNUSED F/NH	USED
2981	$3.20 World War II (1945) Souvenir Sheet of 10	8.25	....	13.75(20)	....	....	....	7.00	7.00
2981a	32¢ Marines raise flag on Iwo Jima	1.95	....	....	....	....	....	.70	.50
2981b	32¢ Fierce fighting frees Manila	1.95	....	....	....	....	....	.70	.50
2981c	32¢ Okinawa, the last big battle	1.95	....	....	....	....	....	.70	.50

U.S. Postage #2981d-2992

SCOTT NO.	DESCRIPTION	FIRST DAY COVERS SING.	FIRST DAY COVERS PL.BLK.	MINT SHEET	COPY-RIGHT	ZIP	PLATE BLOCK	UNUSED F/NH	USED
2981d	32¢ U.S. & Soviets link up at Elbe River	1.95	....	....	....	....	....	.70	.50
2981e	32¢ Allies liberate Holocaust survivors	1.95	....	....	....	....	....	.70	.50
2981f	32¢ Germany surrenders at Reims	1.95	....	....	....	....	....	.70	.50
2981g	32¢ By 1945, World War II has uprooted millions	1.95	....	....	....	....	....	.70	.50
2981h	32¢ Truman announces Japan's surrender	1.95	....	....	....	....	....	.70	.50
2981i	32¢ News of victory hits home	1.95	....	....	....	....	....	.70	.50
2981j	32¢ Hometowns honor their returning veterans	1.95	....	....	....	....	....	.70	.50

2982, 2984

2983

2985

2986

2987

2988

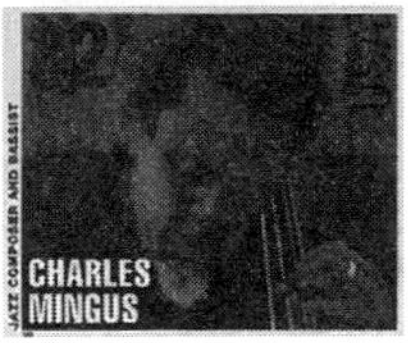

2989

2990

2991

2992

SCOTT NO.	DESCRIPTION	FIRST DAY COVERS SING.	FIRST DAY COVERS PL.BLK.	MINT SHEET	COPY-RIGHT	ZIP	PLATE BLOCK	UNUSED F/NH	USED
2982	32¢ Louis Armstrong	1.95	4.75	13.75(20)	....	....	3.25	.70	.20
2983-92	32¢ Jazz Musicians	8.25	....	13.75(20)	....	....	8.50(10)	7.50	6.50
2983	32¢ Coleman Hawkins	1.95	....	....	....	....	....	.70	.35
2984	32¢ Louis Armstrong	1.95	....	....	....	....	....	.70	.35
2985	32¢ James P. Johnson	1.95	....	....	....	....	....	.70	.35
2986	32¢ "Jelly Roll" Morton	1.95	....	....	....	....	....	.70	.35
2987	32¢ Charlie Parker	1.95	....	....	....	....	....	.70	.35
2988	32¢ Eubie Blake	1.95	....	....	....	....	....	.70	.35
2989	32¢ Charles Mingus	1.95	....	....	....	....	....	.70	.35
2990	32¢ Thelonius Monk	1.95	....	....	....	....	....	.70	.35
2991	32¢ John Coltrane	1.95	....	....	....	....	....	.70	.35
2992	32¢ Erroll Garner	1.95	....	....	....	....	....	.70	.35

U.S. Postage #2993-2999

2993 2994 2995 2996 2997

2998

SCOTT NO.	DESCRIPTION	FIRST DAY COVERS SING.	FIRST DAY COVERS PL.BLK.	MINT SHEET	COPY-RIGHT	ZIP	PLATE BLOCK	UNUSED F/NH	USED
2993	32¢ Aster	1.95	....	....	....	....	....	.70	.20
2994	32¢ Chrysanthemum	1.95	....	....	....	....	....	.70	.20
2995	32¢ Dahlia	1.95	....	....	....	....	....	.70	.20
2996	32¢ Hydrangea	1.95	....	....	....	....	....	.70	.20
2997	32¢ Rudbeckia	1.95	....	....	....	....	....	.70	.20
2997a	Fall Garden Flowers, booklet pane of 5	5.50	....	....	....	....	....	4.00	3.50
2997av	same, booklet pane, unfolded		....	....	....	....	....	4.75	....
2998	60¢ Eddie Rickenbacker	2.25	5.00	65.00(50)	....	....	6.75	1.35	.40

2999

SCOTT NO.	DESCRIPTION	FIRST DAY COVERS SING.	FIRST DAY COVERS PL.BLK.	MINT SHEET	COPY-RIGHT	ZIP	PLATE BLOCK	UNUSED F/NH	USED
2999	32¢ Republic of Palau	1.95	4.75	31.50(50)	....	....	3.25	.70	.20

SCOTT NO.	DESCRIPTION	FIRST DAY COVERS SING. PL.BLK.	MINT SHEET	COPY-RIGHT	ZIP	PLATE BLOCK	UNUSED F/NH	USED

COMIC STRIP CLASSICS

3000

Comic Strips

3000a	*The Yellow Kid*	**3000h**	*Gasoline Alley*	**3000o**	*Nancy*
3000b	*Katzenjammer Kids*	**3000i**	*Barney Google*	**3000p**	*Flash Gordon*
3000c	*Little Nemo*	**3000j**	*Little Orphan Annie*	**3000q**	*Li'l Abner*
3000d	*Bringing Up Father*	**3000k**	*Popeye*	**3000r**	*Terry and the Pirates*
3000e	*Krazy Kat*	**3000l**	*Blondie*	**3000s**	*Prince Valiant*
3000f	*Rube Goldberg*	**3000m**	*Dick Tracy*	**3000t**	*Brenda Starr*
3000g	*Toonerville Folks*	**3000n**	*Alley Oop*		

U.S. Postage #3000-3011a

SCOTT NO.	DESCRIPTION	FIRST DAY COVERS SING.	FIRST DAY COVERS PL.BLK.	MINT SHEET	COPY-RIGHT	ZIP	PLATE BLOCK	UNUSED F/NH	USED
3000	32¢ Comic Strips, 20 varieties, attached		....	13.75(20)	....	....	....	13.75	10.00
....	set of singles	35.00	....	....	....	....	....	....	9.25
....	single of above, each	1.95	....	....	....	....	....	.90	.55
3000v	same as above, uncut sheet of 120 (6 panes)		....	82.50(120)	....	....	....	82.50	....
....	block of 40 with vertical or horizontal gutter between (2 panes)		....	29.00(40)	....	....	....	29.00	....
....	block of 24 with vertical gutter		....	21.50(24)	....	....	....	21.50	....
....	block of 25 with horizontal gutter		....	22.50(25)	....	....	....	22.50	....
....	cross gutter block of 20		....	....	....	....	....	32.00	....
....	cross gutter block of 4		....	....	....	....	....	17.25	....
....	vertical pair with horizontal gutter		....	....	....	....	....	2.25	....
....	horizontal pair with vertical gutter		....	....	....	....	....	2.25	....

3001

3002

SCOTT NO.	DESCRIPTION	FIRST DAY COVERS SING.	FIRST DAY COVERS PL.BLK.	MINT SHEET	COPY-RIGHT	ZIP	PLATE BLOCK	UNUSED F/NH	USED
3001	32¢ Naval Academy	1.95	4.75	13.75(20)	....	....	3.25	.70	.20
3002	32¢ Tennessee Williams	1.95	4.75	13.75(20)	....	....	3.25	.70	.20

3003

3004, 3010, 3016

3005, 3009, 3015

3006, 3011, 3017

3007, 3008, 3014

3012, 3018

SCOTT NO.	DESCRIPTION	FIRST DAY COVERS SING.	FIRST DAY COVERS PL.BLK.	MINT SHEET	COPY-RIGHT	ZIP	PLATE BLOCK	UNUSED F/NH	USED
3003	32¢ Madonna & Child	1.95	4.75	31.50(50)	....	....	3.25	.70	.20
3003a	32¢ Madonna & Child, booklet single	1.95	....	....	....	....	....	.70	.20
3003b	Same, booklet pane of 10	7.25	....	....	....	....	....	7.00	....
3003bv	same, booklet pane, unfolded		....	....	....	....	....	8.00	....
3004-07	32¢ Santa & Children with Toys, 4 varieties, attached	4.00	4.75	31.50(50)	....	....	3.25	3.00	2.50
3004	32¢ Santa at Chimney	1.95	....	....	....	....	....	.70	.20
....	same, booklet single	1.95	....	....	....	....	....	.70	.20
3005	32¢ Girl holding Jumping Jack	1.95	....	....	....	....	....	.70	.20
....	same, booklet single	1.95	....	....	....	....	....	.70	.20
3006	32¢ Boy holding Toy Horse	1.95	....	....	....	....	....	.70	.20
....	same, booklet single	1.95	....	....	....	....	....	.70	.20
3007	32¢ Santa working on Sled	1.95	....	....	....	....	....	.70	.20
....	same, booklet single	1.95	....	....	....	....	....	.70	.20
3007b	32¢ Santa & Children with Toys, booklet pane of 10 (3 each of 3004-05)	7.25	....	....	....	....	....	7.00	....
....	same, booklet pane, unfolded		....	....	....	....	....	8.00	....
3007c	32¢ Santa & Children with Toys, booklet pane of 10 (3 each of 3006-07)	7.25	....	....	....	....	....	7.00	....
....	same, booklet pane, unfolded		....	....	....	....	....	8.00	....
3008	32¢ Santa working on Sled, self-adhesive	1.95	....	....	....	....	....	.70	.20
3009	32¢ Girl holding Jumping Jack, self-adhesive	1.95	....	....	....	....	....	.70	.20
3010	32¢ Santa at Chimney, self-adhesive	1.95	....	....	....	....	....	.70	.20
3011	32¢ Boy holding Toy Horse, self-adhesive	1.95	....	....	....	....	....	.70	.20
3011a	32¢ Santa & Children with Toys, self-adhesive, pane of 20	14.50	....	....	....	....	....	13.50	....

U.S. Postage #3012-3023

SCOTT NO.	DESCRIPTION	FIRST DAY COVERS SING.	FIRST DAY COVERS PL.BLK.	MINT SHEET	COPY-RIGHT	ZIP	PLATE BLOCK	UNUSED F/NH	USED
3012	32¢ Midnight Angel, self-adhesive	1.95	....	....	....	....	....	.70	.20
3012a	same, booklet pane of 20	14.50	....	....	....	....	....	13.50	....

3013

SCOTT NO.	DESCRIPTION	FIRST DAY COVERS SING.	FIRST DAY COVERS PL.BLK.	MINT SHEET	COPY-RIGHT	ZIP	PLATE BLOCK	UNUSED F/NH	USED
3013	32¢ Children Sledding, self-adhesive	1.95	....	....	....	....	....	.70	.20
3013a	same, booklet pane of 18	13.00	....	....	....	....	....	12.25	....
3014-17	32¢ Santa & Children With Toys, self-adhesive, coil strip of 4		....	....	....	....	....	2.95	....
3014	32¢ Santa working on Sled, self-adhesive coil	1.95	....	....	....	....	....	.70	.20
3015	32¢ Girl holding Jumping Jack, self-adhesive coil	1.95	....	....	....	....	....	.70	.20
3016	32¢ Santa at Chimney, self-adhesive coil	1.95	....	....	....	....	....	.70	.20
3017	32¢ Boy holding Toy Horse, self-adhesive coil	1.95	....	....	....	....	....	.70	.20
3018	32¢ Midnight Angel, self-adhesive coil	1.95	....	....	....	....	....	.70	.20

3019

3020

3021

3022

3023

SCOTT NO.	DESCRIPTION	FIRST DAY COVERS SING.	FIRST DAY COVERS PL.BLK.	MINT SHEET	COPY-RIGHT	ZIP	PLATE BLOCK	UNUSED F/NH	USED
3019-23	32¢ Antique Automobiles, 5 varieties, attached	5.50	....	13.75(20)	....	....	8.50(10)	3.75	2.75
3019	32¢ 1893 Duryea	1.95	....	....	....	....	....	.70	.20
3020	32¢ 1894 Haynes	1.95	....	....	....	....	....	.70	.20
3021	32¢ 1898 Columbia	1.95	....	....	....	....	....	.70	.20
3022	32¢ 1899 Winton	1.95	....	....	....	....	....	.70	.20
3023	32¢ 1901 White	1.95	....	....	....	....	....	.70	.20

3024

3025 3026 3027 3028 3029

U.S. Postage #3024-3058

SCOTT NO.	DESCRIPTION	FIRST DAY COVERS SING.	PL.BLK.	MINT SHEET	COPY-RIGHT	ZIP	PLATE BLOCK	UNUSED F/NH	USE
	1996								
3024	32¢ Utah Statehood	1.95	4.75	31.50(50)	....	....	3.25	.70	.2
3025	32¢ Crocus	1.95	....	....	....	....	....	.70	.2
3026	32¢ Winter Aconite	1.95	....	....	....	....	....	.70	.2
3027	32¢ Pansy	1.95	....	....	....	....	....	.70	.2
3028	32¢ Snowdrop	1.95	....	....	....	....	....	.70	.2
3029	32¢ Anemone	1.95	....	....	....	....	....	.70	.2
3029a	32¢ Winter Garden Flowers, booklet pane of 5	5.50	....	....	....	....	....	4.00	3.0
3029av	same, booklet pane, unfolded		....	....	....	....	....	4.75	....

3030

3032

3033

3044

3048

3049

3058

SCOTT NO.	DESCRIPTION	FIRST DAY COVERS SING.	PL.BLK.	MINT SHEET	COPY-RIGHT	ZIP	PLATE BLOCK	UNUSED F/NH	USE
3030	32¢ Love (Cherub), self-adhesive	1.95	....	....	....	....	....	.70	.2
3030a	same, booklet pane of 20	14.50	....	....	....	....	....	13.50	.....
3030b	same, booklet pane of 15	11.50	....	....	....	....	....	11.00	.....
3032	2¢ Red-headed Woodpecker	1.95	4.75	5.75(100)	....	....	.75	.20	.2
3033	3¢ Eastern Bluebird (redesign 3¢)	1.95	4.75	8.50(100)	....	....	.75	.20	.2
3044	1¢ Kestrel, coil	1.95	10.00	....	....	....	1.00	.20	.2
3048	20¢ Blue Jay, self-adhesive	1.95	......	......	......	......	......	.50	.2
3048a	same, booklet pane of 10	5.50	......	......	......	......	......	5.00	....
3049	32¢ Yellow Rose, self-adhesive	1.95	......	......	......	......	......	.70	.2
3049a	same, booklet pane of 20	14.50	......	......	......	......	......	13.50	....
3053	20¢ Blue Jay, self-adhesive coil	1.95	....	....	....	....	4.75	.50	.2
3058	32¢ Ernest Just	1.95	4.75	13.75(20)	....	....	3.25	.70	.2

3059

3060

3061

3062

3063

3064

3065

U.S. Postage #3059-3067

SCOTT NO.	DESCRIPTION	FIRST DAY COVERS SING.	FIRST DAY COVERS PL.BLK.	MINT SHEET	COPY-RIGHT	ZIP	PLATE BLOCK	UNUSED F/NH	USED
3059	32¢ Smithsonian Institution	1.95	4.75	13.75(20)	....	....	3.25	.70	.20
3060	32¢ Year of the Rat	1.95	4.75	13.75(20)	....	....	3.25	.70	.20
3061-64	32¢ Pioneers of Communication, 4 varieties, attached	4.00	4.75	11.75(16)	....	....	3.25	3.00	2.50
3061	32¢ Eadweard Muybridge	1.95	....	....	....	....	....	.70	.20
3062	32¢ Ottmar Mergenthaler	1.95	....	....	....	....	....	.70	.20
3063	32¢ Frederic E. Ives	1.95	....	....	....	....	....	.70	.20
3064	32¢ William Dickson	1.95	....	....	....	....	....	.70	.20
3065	32¢ Fulbright Scholarships	1.95	4.75	31.50(50)	....	....	3.25	.70	.20

3066

3067

SCOTT NO.	DESCRIPTION	FIRST DAY COVERS SING.	FIRST DAY COVERS PL.BLK.	MINT SHEET	COPY-RIGHT	ZIP	PLATE BLOCK	UNUSED F/NH	USED
3066	50¢ Jacqueline Cochran	2.25	5.00	52.00(50)	....	....	5.25	1.10	.25
3067	32¢ Marathon	1.95	4.75	13.75(20)	....	....	3.25	.70	.20

SCOTT NO.	DESCRIPTION	FIRST DAY COVERS SING.	PL.BLK.	MINT SHEET	COPY-RIGHT	ZIP	PLATE BLOCK	UNUSED F/NH	USED

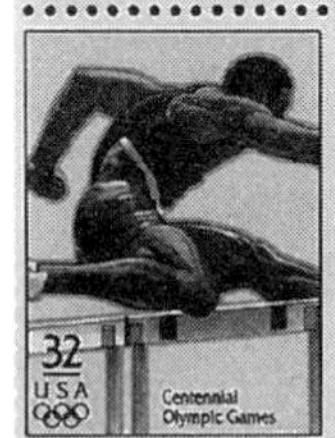

3068

1996 SUMMER OLYMPICS GAMES

3068a	*Decathlon*	**3068h**	*Women's sailboarding*	**3068o**	*Women's softball*
3068b	*Men's canoeing*	**3068i**	*Men's shot put*	**3068p**	*Men's hurdles*
3068c	*Women's running*	**3068j**	*Women's soccer*	**3068q**	*Men's swimming*
3068d	*Women's diving*	**3068k**	*Beach volleyball*	**3068r**	*Men's gymnastics*
3068e	*Men's cycling*	**3068l**	*Men's rowing*	**3068s**	*Equestrian*
3068f	*Freestyle wrestling*	**3068m**	*Men's sprints*	**3068t**	*Men's basketball*
3068g	*Women's gymnastics*	**3068n**	*Women's swimming*		

U.S. Postage #3068-3080a

SCOTT NO.	DESCRIPTION	FIRST DAY COVERS SING.	FIRST DAY COVERS PL.BLK.	MINT SHEET	COPY-RIGHT	ZIP	PLATE BLOCK	UNUSED F/NH	USED
3068	32¢ Centennial Olympic Games, 20 varieties, attached		....	13.75(20)	....	....	....	13.75	10.00
....	set of singles	35.00	....	....	....	....	....	....	9.25
....	single of above, each	1.95	....	....	....	....	....	.90	.55
....	32¢ Cal Farley	1.95	4.75	65.00(100)	....	....	3.25	.70	.20
....	(10¢) Eagle, bulk-rate, coil (1996)	1.95	10.00	....	....	....	3.00	.25	.20

3069

3070, 3071

SCOTT NO.	DESCRIPTION	FIRST DAY COVERS SING.	FIRST DAY COVERS PL.BLK.	MINT SHEET	COPY-RIGHT	ZIP	PLATE BLOCK	UNUSED F/NH	USED
3069	32¢ Georgia O'Keefe	1.95	....	10.25(15)	....	....	....	.70	.20
3070	32¢ Tennessee Statehood	1.95	4.75	31.50(50)	....	....	3.25	.70	.20
3071	32¢ Tennessee Statehood, self-adhesive	1.95	....	....	....	....	....	.70	.20
3071a	same, booklet pane of 20	14.50	....	....	....	....	....	13.50	....

3072

3073

3074

3075

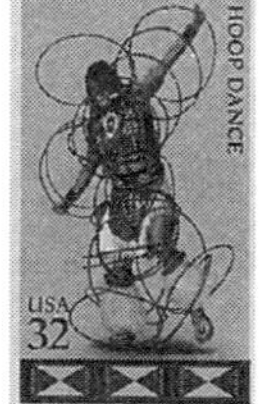

3076

SCOTT NO.	DESCRIPTION	FIRST DAY COVERS SING.	FIRST DAY COVERS PL.BLK.	MINT SHEET	COPY-RIGHT	ZIP	PLATE BLOCK	UNUSED F/NH	USED
3072-76	32¢ American Indian Dances, 5 varieties, attached	5.50	....	13.75(20)	....	....	8.50(10)	3.75	2.75
3072	32¢ Fancy Dance	1.95	......	......	......	......	......	.70	.20
3073	32¢ Butterfly Dance	1.95	......	......	......	......	......	.70	.20
3074	32¢ Traditional Dance	1.95	......	......	......	......	......	.70	.20
3075	32¢ Raven Dance	1.95	......	......	......	......	......	.70	.20
3076	32¢ Hoop Dance	1.95	......	......	......	......	......	.70	.20

3077

3078

3079

3080

SCOTT NO.	DESCRIPTION	FIRST DAY COVERS SING.	FIRST DAY COVERS PL.BLK.	MINT SHEET	COPY-RIGHT	ZIP	PLATE BLOCK	UNUSED F/NH	USED
3077-80	32¢ Prehistoric Animals, 4 varieties, attached	4.00	4.75	13.75(20)	....	....	3.25	3.00	2.50
3077	32¢ Eohippus	1.95	......	......	......	......	......	.70	.20
3078	32¢ Woolly Mammoth	1.95	......	......	......	......	......	.70	.20
3079	32¢ Mastodon	1.95	......	......	......	......	......	.70	.20
3080	32¢ Saber-tooth Cat	1.95	......	......	......	......	......	.70	.20

U.S. Postage #3081-3095

3081 3082 3083 3084 3085 3086

SCOTT NO.	DESCRIPTION	FIRST DAY COVERS SING.	PL.BLK.	MINT SHEET	COPY-RIGHT	ZIP	PLATE BLOCK	UNUSED F/NH	USED
3081	32¢ Breast Cancer Awareness	1.95	4.75	13.75(20)	....	....	3.25	.70	.20
3082	32¢ James Dean	1.95	4.75	13.75(20)	....	....	3.25	.70	.20
3083-86	32¢ Folk Heroes, 4 varieties, attached	4.00	4.75	13.75(20)	....	....	3.25	3.00	2.50
3083	32¢ Mighty Casey	1.95	......	......	......	......	......	.70	.20
3084	32¢ Paul Bunyan	1.95	......	....	......	......	......	.70	.20
3085	32¢ John Henry	1.95	......	....	......	......	......	.70	.20
3086	32¢ Pecos Bill	1.95	......	....	......	......	......	.70	.20

3087 3088, 3089 3090

SCOTT NO.	DESCRIPTION	FIRST DAY COVERS SING.	PL.BLK.	MINT SHEET	COPY-RIGHT	ZIP	PLATE BLOCK	UNUSED F/NH	USED
3087	32¢ Olympic Discus Thrower	1.95	4.75	13.75(20)	....	....	3.25	.70	.20
3088	32¢ Iowa Statehood	1.95	4.75	31.50(50)	....	....	3.25	.70	.20
3089	32¢ Iowa Statehood, self-adhesive	1.95	....	....	....	....	....	.70	.20
3089a	same, booklet pane of 20	14.50	....	....	....	....	....	13.50	....
3090	32¢ Rural Free Delivery	1.95	4.75	31.50(50)	....	....	3.25	.70	.20

3091 3092 3093

3094 3095

SCOTT NO.	DESCRIPTION	FIRST DAY COVERS SING.	PL.BLK.	MINT SHEET	COPY-RIGHT	ZIP	PLATE BLOCK	UNUSED F/NH	USED
3091-95	32¢ Riverboats, 5 varieties attached	5.50	....	13.75(20)	....	....	8.50(10)	3.75	2.75
3091	32¢ Robt. E. Lee	1.95	....	....	....	....	....	.70	.20
3092	32¢ Sylvan Dell	1.95	....	....	....	....	....	.70	.20
3093	32¢ Far West	1.95	....	....	....	....	....	.70	.20
3094	32¢ Rebecca Everingham	1.95	....	....	....	....	....	.70	.20
3095	32¢ Bailey Gatzert	1.95	....	....	....	....	....	.70	.20

U.S. Postage #3096-3104

3096 3097 3098 3099

SCOTT NO.	DESCRIPTION	FIRST DAY COVERS SING.	FIRST DAY COVERS PL.BLK.	MINT SHEET	COPY-RIGHT	ZIP	PLATE BLOCK	UNUSED F/NH	USED
3096-99	32¢ Big Band Leaders, 4 varieties, attached	4.00	4.75	13.75(20)	......	......	3.25	3.00	2.50
3096	32¢ Count Basie	1.95	......	......	......	......	......	.70	.20
3097	32¢ Tommy & Jimmy Dorsey	1.95	......	......	......	......	......	.70	.20
3098	32¢ Glenn Miller	1.95	......	......	......	......	......	.70	.20
3099	32¢ Benny Goodman	1.95	......	......	......	......	......	.70	.20

3100 3101 3102 3103

SCOTT NO.	DESCRIPTION	FIRST DAY COVERS SING.	FIRST DAY COVERS PL.BLK.	MINT SHEET	COPY-RIGHT	ZIP	PLATE BLOCK	UNUSED F/NH	USED
3100-03	32¢ Songwriters, 4 varieties, attached	4.00	4.75	13.75(20)	......	......	3.25	3.00	2.50
3100	32¢ Harold Arlen	1.95	......	......	......	......	......	.70	.20
3101	32¢ Johnny Mercer	1.95	......	......	......	......	......	.70	.20
3102	32¢ Dorothy Fields	1.95	......	......	......	......	......	.70	.20
3103	32¢ Hoagy Carmichael	1.95	......	......	......	......	......	.70	.20

3104

SCOTT NO.	DESCRIPTION	FIRST DAY COVERS SING.	FIRST DAY COVERS PL.BLK.	MINT SHEET	COPY-RIGHT	ZIP	PLATE BLOCK	UNUSED F/NH	USED
3104	23¢ F. Scott Fitzgerald	1.95	4.75	31.50(50)	......	......	3.25	.70	.20

3105

ENDANGERED SPECIES

3105a	*32¢ Black-footed ferret*	**3105i**	*32¢ California condor*
3105b	*32¢ Thick-billed parrot*	**3105j**	*32¢ Gila trout*
3105c	*32¢ Hawaiian monk seal*	**3105k**	*32¢ San Francisco garter snake*
3105d	*32¢ American crocodile*	**3105l**	*32¢ Woodland caribou*
3105e	*32¢ Ocelot*	**3105m**	*32¢ Florida panther*
3105f	*32¢ Schaus swallowtail butterfly*	**3105n**	*32¢ Piping plover*
3105g	*32¢ Wyoming toad*	**3105o**	*32¢ Florida manatee*
3105h	*32¢ Brown pelican*		

SCOTT NO.	DESCRIPTION	FIRST DAY COVERS SING.	PL.BLK.	MINT SHEET	COPY-RIGHT	ZIP	PLATE BLOCK	UNUSED F/NH	USED
3105	32¢ Endangered Species, 15 varieties, attached	......	......	10.25(15)	......	......	......	10.25	8.50
......	set of singles.	27.50	......	......	......	......	......	......	6.50
......	singles of above, each	1.95	......	......	......	......	......	.90	.45

U.S. Postage #3106-3118

3106

3107, 3112

3108, 3113

3109, 3114

3110, 3115

3111, 3116

SCOTT NO.	DESCRIPTION	FIRST DAY COVERS SING.	FIRST DAY COVERS PL.BLK.	MINT SHEET	COPY-RIGHT	ZIP	PLATE BLOCK	UNUSED F/NH	USED
106	32¢ Computer Technology	1.95	4.75	26.00(40)	......	......	3.25	.70	.20
107	32¢ Madonna & Child	1.95	4.75	31.50(50)	......	......	3.25	.70	.20
108-11	32¢ Christmas Family Scenes, 4 varieties, attached	4.00	4.75	31.50(50)	......	......	3.25	3.00	2.50
108	32¢ Family at Fireplace	1.95	......	......	......	......	......	.70	.20
109	32¢ Decorating Tree	1.95	......	......	......	......	......	.70	.20
110	32¢ Dreaming of Santa Claus	1.95	......	......	......	......	......	.70	.20
111	32¢ Holiday Shopping	1.95	......	......	......	......	......	.70	.20
112	32¢ Madonna & Child, self-adhesive	1.95	......	......	......	......	......	.70	.20
112a	same, booklet pane of 20	14.50	......	......	......	......	......	13.50	......
113	32¢ Family at Fireplace, self-adhesive	1.95	......	......	......	......	......	.70	.20
114	32¢ Decorating Tree, self-adhesive	1.95	......	......	......	......	......	.70	.20
115	32¢ Dreaming of Santa Claus, self-adhesive	1.95	......	......	......	......	......	.70	.20
116	32¢ Holiday Shopping, self-adhesive	1.95	......	......	......	......	......	.70	.20
116a	32¢ Christmas Family Scenes, self-adhesive, booklet pane of 20	14.50	......	......	......	......	......	13.50	......

3117

3118

SCOTT NO.	DESCRIPTION	FIRST DAY COVERS SING.	FIRST DAY COVERS PL.BLK.	MINT SHEET	COPY-RIGHT	ZIP	PLATE BLOCK	UNUSED F/NH	USED
117	32¢ Skaters, self-adhesive	1.95	......	......	......	......	......	.70	.20
117a	same, booklet pane of 18	13.00	......	......	......	......	......	.70	.20
118	32¢ Hanukkah, self-adhesive	1.95	......	13.75(20)	......	......	3.25	.70	.20

U.S. Postage #3119-3119b

SCOTT NO.	DESCRIPTION	FIRST DAY COVERS SING.	PL.BLK.	MINT SHEET	COPY-RIGHT	ZIP	PLATE BLOCK	UNUSED F/NH	USED

3119

SCOTT NO.	DESCRIPTION	FIRST DAY COVERS SING.	PL.BLK.	MINT SHEET	COPY-RIGHT	ZIP	PLATE BLOCK	UNUSED F/NH	USED
3119	50¢ Cycling, sheet of 2	3.00	......	......	......	......	......	2.25	2.00
3119a-b	same, set of 2 single	4.25	......	......	......	......	......	2.10	.60

3120

3121

3122

3123

3124

3125

3126

3127

3130

3131

3132

U.S. Postage #3120-3135

3134

3135

1997

SCOTT NO.	DESCRIPTION	FIRST DAY COVERS SING.	FIRST DAY COVERS PL.BLK.	MINT SHEET	COPY-RIGHT	ZIP	PLATE BLOCK	UNUSED F/NH	USED
3120	32¢ Year of the Ox	1.95	......	13.75(20)	......	......	3.25	.70	.20
3121	32¢ Benjamin O. Davis, Sr.	1.95	4.75	13.75(20)	......	......	3.25	.70	.20
3122	32¢ Statue of Liberty, self-adhesive (1997)	1.95	......	......	......	......	......	.70	.20
3122a	same, booklet pane of 20	14.50	......	......	......	......	......	13.50	......
3122b	same, booklet pane of 4	3.00	......	......	......	......	......	2.75	......
3122c	same, booklet pane of 5	3.75	......	......	......	......	......	3.40	......
3122d	same, booklet pane of 6	4.50	......	......	......	......	......	4.15	......
3123	32¢ Swans, self-adhesive	1.95	......	......	......	......	......	.70	.20
3123a	same, booklet pane of 20	14.50	......	......	......	......	......	13.50	......
3124	55¢ Swans, self-adhesive	2.50	......	......	......	......	......	1.20	.35
3124a	same, booklet pane of 20	19.75	......	......	......	......	......	23.50	......
3125	32¢ Helping Children Learn	1.95	4.75	13.75(20)	......	......	3.25	.70	.20
3126	32¢ Citron, Moth, Larvae, Pupa, Beetle, self-adhesive (Die Cut 10.9x10.2)	1.95	......	......	......	......	......	.70	.20
3127	32¢ Flowering Pineapple, Cockroaches, self-adhesive, (Die Cut 10.9x10.2)	1.95	......	......	......	......	......	.70	.20
3127a	same, booklet pane of 20 (10 #3126, 10 #3127)	14.50	......	......	......	......	......	13.50	......
3128	32¢ Citron, Moth, Larvae, Pupa, Beetle, self-adhesive (Die Cut 11.2x10.8)	1.95	......	......	......	......	......	.70	.20
3128a	same, stamp sideways	1.95	......	......	......	......	......	.70	.20
3128b	same, booklet pane of 5 (2 #3128 & 3129, 1 #3128a)	5.50	......	......	......	......	......	4.00	......
3129	32¢ Flowering Pineapple, Cockroaches, self-adhesive (Die Cut 11.2x10.8)	1.95	......	......	......	......	......	.70	.20
3129a	same, stamp sideways	1.95	......	......	......	......	......	.70	.20
3129b	same, booklet pane of 5 (2 #3128 & #3129, 1 #3129a)	5.50	......	......	......	......	......	4.00	......
3130-31	32¢ Stagecoach & Ship, (Pacific '97) 2 varieties, attached	3.00	4.75	11.00(16)	......	......	3.25	1.50	1.00
3130	32¢ Ship	1.95	......	......	......	......	......	.70	.20
3131	32¢ Stagecoach	1.95	......	......	......	......	......	.70	.20
3132	(25¢) Juke Box, self-adhesive linerless coil	1.95	......	......	......	......	5.00	.60	.20
3133	32¢ Flag Over Porch, self-adhesive linerless coil	1.95	......	......	......	......	8.00	.70	.20
3134	32¢ Thornton Wilder	1.95	4.75	13.75(20)	......	......	3.25	.70	.20
3135	32¢ Raoul Wallenberg	1.95	4.75	13.75(20)	......	......	3.25	.70	.20

U.S. Postage #3136a-3136o

Dinosaurs

3136a *Ceratosaurus*
3136b *Camptosaurus*
3136c *Camarasaurus*
3136d *Brachiosaurus*
3136e *Goniopholis*
3136f *Stegosaurus*
3136g *Allosaurus*
3136h *Opisthias*
3136i *Edmontonia*
3136j *Einiosaurus*
3136k *Daspletosaurus*
3136l *Palaeosaniwa*
3136m *Corythosaurus*
3136n *Ornithominus*
3136o *Parasaurolophus*

SCOTT NO.	DESCRIPTION	FIRST DAY COVERS SING.	FIRST DAY COVERS PL.BLK.	MINT SHEET	COPY-RIGHT	ZIP	PLATE BLOCK	UNUSED F/NH	USED
3136	32¢ Dinosaurs, 15 varieties, attached	11.50	......	......	......	......	......	10.75	9.00
......	set of singles	26.50	......	......	......	......	......	....	8.50
......	singles of above, each	1.95	......	......	......	......	......	.90	.45

3137, 3138

3139

3140

3141

U.S. Postage #3137-New Issues

SCOTT NO.	DESCRIPTION	FIRST DAY COVERS SING.	FIRST DAY COVERS PL.BLK.	MINT SHEET	COPY-RIGHT	ZIP	PLATE BLOCK	UNUSED F/NH	USED
3137	32¢ Bugs Bunny, self-adhesive, pane of 10	9.50	......	......	......	......	......	7.25	......
3137a	same, single from pane	1.95	......	......	......	......	......	.70	.20
3137b	same, pane of 9 (#3137a)		......	......	......	......	......	6.50	......
3137c	same, pane of 1 (#3137a)	....	......	......	......	......	......	1.50	......
3138	32¢ Bugs Bunny, self-adhesive, Die Cut, pane of 10	10.00	......	......	......	......	......	8.25	......
3138a	same, single from pane	1.95	......	......	......	......	......	.80	.20
3138b	same, pane of 9 (#3138a)	....	......	......	......	......	......	7.50	......
3138c	same, pane of 1 (#3138a)	....	......	......	......	......	......	2.00	....
3139	50¢ Benjamin Franklin, souvenir sheet of 12 (Pacific '97)	14.00	......	......	......	......	......	13.50	......
3139a	same, single from sheet	2.25	......	......	......	......	......	1.25	.35
3140	60¢ George Washington, souvenir sheet of 12 (Pacific '97)	16.00	......	......	......	......	......	15.50	......
3140a	same, single from sheet	2.25	5.00	......	......	......	......	1.40	.40
3141	32¢ Marshall Plan	1.95	4.75	13.75(20)	......	......	3.25	.70	.20
......	32¢ Classic American Aircraft, 20 varieties, attached	14.50	......	......	......	......	......	13.75	10.00
......	32¢ Legendary Football Coaches, 4 varieties, attached	4.00	4.75	13.75(20)	......	......	3.25	3.00	2.50
......	32¢ Classic American Dolls, 15 varieties, attached	....	......	10.25(15)	......	......	......	10.25	8.50
......	32¢ Humphrey Bogart	1.95	......	13.75(20)	......	......	3.25	.70	.20
......	32¢ Yellow Rose, self-adhesive coil	1.95	......	......	......	......	8.00	.70	.20
......	32¢ Vince Lombardi	1.95	......	13.75(20)	......	......	3.25	.70	.20
......	32¢ Paul "Bear" Bryant	1.95	......	13.75(20)	......	......	3.25	.70	.20
......	32¢ Glenn "Pop" Warner	1.95	......	13.75(20)	......	......	3.25	.70	.20
......	32¢ George Halas	1.95	......	13.75(20)	......	......	3.25	.70	.20
......	32¢ "The Stars & Stripes Forever"1.954.75		31.50(50)	......	......	3.25	.70	.20	
......	32¢ Opera Singers, 4 varieties, attached	4.00	4.75	13.75(20)	......	......	3.25	3.00	2.50
......	32¢ Composers & Conductors, 8 varieties, attached	7.00	......	13.75(20)	......	......	......	5.75	4.50

U.S. Air Post #C1-C12

SCOTT NO.	DESCRIPTION	UNUSED O.G VF	UNUSED O.G F	UNUSED O.G AVG	USED VF	USED F	USED AVG

AIR MAIL STAMPS

C1-C3
Curtiss Jenny Biplane

C4
Airplane Propeller

C5
Badge of Air Service

C6
Airplane

C7-C9
Map of U.S. and Airplanes

1918 (C1-12 NH + 30%)

SCOTT NO.	DESCRIPTION	UNUSED O.G VF	UNUSED O.G F	UNUSED O.G AVG	USED VF	USED F	USED AVG
C1-3	**6¢-24¢, 3 varieties, complete**	**360.00**	**270.00**	**187.50**	**152.00**	**113.50**	**74.00**
C1	6¢ orange	100.00	75.00	52.50	48.50	36.00	24.75
C2	16¢ green	140.00	105.00	72.50	52.00	38.50	25.75
C3	24¢ carmine rose & blue	140.00	105.00	72.50	60.00	45.00	27.50
C3a	same, center inverted	....	140000.00	....	....	....	....

SCOTT NO.		CENTER LINE BLOCKS F/NH	CENTER LINE BLOCKS F/OG	CENTER LINE BLOCKS A/OG	ARROW BLOCKS F/NH	ARROW BLOCKS F/OG	ARROW BLOCKS A/OG
C1	6¢ orange	350.00	280.00	225.00	300.00	240.00	190.00
C2	16¢ green	500.00	400.00	325.00	450.00	360.00	285.00
C3	24¢ carmine rose & blue	500.00	400.00	325.00	435.00	350.00	275.00

1923

SCOTT NO.	DESCRIPTION	UNUSED O.G VF	UNUSED O.G F	UNUSED O.G AVG	USED VF	USED F	USED AVG
C4-6	**8¢-24¢, 3 varieties, complete**	**320.00**	**237.00**	**160.00**	**110.00**	**81.25**	**55.00**
C4	8¢ dark green	40.00	29.50	20.50	20.50	15.00	10.00
C5	16¢ dark blue	142.00	105.00	71.50	54.00	40.00	28.00
C6	24¢ carmine	155.00	115.00	77.50	41.25	30.50	20.50

1926-27

SCOTT NO.	DESCRIPTION	UNUSED O.G VF	UNUSED O.G F	UNUSED O.G AVG	USED VF	USED F	USED AVG
C7-9	**10¢-20¢, 3 varieties, complete**	**19.95**	**15.25**	**7.60**	**5.35**	**4.15**	**2.80**
C7	10¢ dark blue	4.00	3.05	2.20	.55	.40	.25
C8	15¢ olive brown	4.75	3.60	2.75	2.85	2.20	1.50
C9	20¢ yellow green (1927)	12.25	9.35	6.05	2.25	1.75	1.20

C10
Lindbergh's Airplane "Spirit of St. Louis"

C11
Beacon and Rocky Mountains

C12, C16, C17, C19
Winged Globe

1927 LINDBERGH TRIBUTE ISSUE

SCOTT NO.	DESCRIPTION	UNUSED O.G VF	UNUSED O.G F	UNUSED O.G AVG	USED VF	USED F	USED AVG
C10	10¢ dark blue	10.75	8.25	5.50	2.85	2.20	1.40
C10a	same, booklet pane of 3	125.00	95.00	67.50	....	....	....

1928 BEACON

SCOTT NO.	DESCRIPTION	UNUSED O.G VF	UNUSED O.G F	UNUSED O.G AVG	USED VF	USED F	USED AVG
C11	5¢ carmine & blue	5.00	3.85	2.75	.55	.40	.25

1930 Flat Plate Printing, Perf. 11

SCOTT NO.	DESCRIPTION	UNUSED O.G VF	UNUSED O.G F	UNUSED O.G AVG	USED VF	USED F	USED AVG
C12	5¢ violet	12.35	9.50	6.05	.55	.40	.25

U.S. Air Post #C13-C24

SCOTT NO.	DESCRIPTION	UNUSED O.G VF	UNUSED O.G F	UNUSED O.G AVG	USED VF	USED F	USED AVG

C13

C14
Graf Zeppeliin

C15

1930 GRAF ZEPPELIN ISSUE (NH + 20%)

SCOTT NO.	DESCRIPTION	UNUSED O.G VF	UNUSED O.G F	UNUSED O.G AVG	USED VF	USED F	USED AVG
C13-15	**65¢-$2.60, 3 varieties, cpl.**	**2495.00**	**2080.00**	**1550.00**	**1625.00**	**1350.00**	**1125.00**
C13	65¢ green	355.00	285.00	235.00	275.00	230.00	192.50
C14	$1.30 brown	895.00	745.00	575.00	630.00	525.00	440.00
C15	$2.60 blue	1375.00	1150.00	825.00	800.00	665.00	550.00
	1931-32 Rotary Press Printing. Perf. 10-1/2 x 11, Designs as #C12						
C16	5¢ violet	7.15	5.50	3.60	.60	.45	.30
C17	8¢ olive bistre	2.95	2.25	1.65	.40	.30	.20

C18
Graf Zeppelin

SCOTT NO.	DESCRIPTION	UNUSED O.G VF	UNUSED O.G F	UNUSED O.G AVG	USED VF	USED F	USED AVG
	1933 CENTURY OF PROGRESS ISSUE						
C18	50¢ green	117.50	97.50	77.50	97.50	80.00	55.00
	1934 DESIGN OF 1930						
C19	6¢ dull orange	3.30	2.75	1.95	.25	.20	.15

C20-22
China Clipper

C23
Eagle

C24
Winged Globe

SCOTT NO.	DESCRIPTION	UNUSED O.G VF	UNUSED O.G F	UNUSED O.G AVG	USED VF	USED F	USED AVG
	1935 TRANS-PACIFIC ISSUE						
C20	25¢ blue	1.50	1.25	.95	1.15	.95	.75
	1937. Type of 1935 Issue, Date Omitted						
C21	20¢ green	9.95	8.25	6.60	2.00	1.65	1.25
C22	50¢ carmine	13.25	11.00	8.75	5.40	4.50	3.50
	1938						
C23	6¢ dark blue & carmine	.55	.45	.35	.25	.20	.15
	1939 TRANS-ATLANTIC ISSUE						
C24	30¢ dull blue	12.60	10.50	8.40	1.70	1.40	1.10

C25-C31

C32

Air Post Plate Blocks #C1-C24

SCOTT NO.	DESCRIPTION	UNUSED NH VF	F	AVG	UNUSED O.G. VF	F	AVG
C1 (6)	6¢ orange	1550.00	1150.00	925.00	1115.00	825.00	550.00
C2 (6)	16¢ green	2665.00	1975.00	1575.00	2000.00	1485.00	1100.00
C3 (12)	24¢ carmine rose & blue	3100.00	2300.00	1825.00	2450.00	1815.00	1250.00
C4 (6)	8¢ dark green	610.00	450.00	360.00	445.00	330.00	260.00
C5 (6)	16¢ dark blue	3845.00	2850.00	2250.00	2975.00	2200.00	1650.00
C6 (6)	24¢ carmine	4790.00	3550.00	2825.00	3700.00	2750.00	2100.00
C7 (6)	10¢ dark blue	71.50	55.00	44.00	54.00	41.50	27.50
C8 (6)	15¢ olive brown	85.00	66.00	52.75	65.00	50.00	33.00
C9 (6)	20¢ yellow green	200.00	155.00	125.00	145.00	110.00	85.00
C10 (6)	10¢ dark blue	265.00	205.00	165.00	195.00	150.00	110.00
C11 (6)	5¢ carmine & blue	82.00	63.25	50.00	60.00	46.50	31.50
C12 (6)	5¢ violet	285.00	220.00	175.00	215.00	165.00	120.00
C13 (6)	65¢ green	3600.00	3000.00	2400.00	2975.00	2475.00	1950.00
C14 (6)	$1.30 brown	8250.00	6875.00	5500.00	1250.00	6050.00	4675.00
C15 (6)	$2.60 blue	13800.00	11500.00	9200.00	10890.00	9075.00	7250.00
C16 (4)	5¢ violet	175.00	135.00	105.00	125.00	95.00	65.00
C17 (4)	8¢ olive bistre	58.50	45.00	36.00	40.00	30.00	24.00
C18 (6)	5¢ green	1075.00	900.00	720.00	955.00	795.00	635.00
C19 (4)	6¢ dull orange	39.50	33.00	26.00	30.00	25.00	20.00
C20 (6)	25¢ blue	33.00	27.50	22.00	26.50	22.00	17.50
C21 (6)	20¢ green	185.00	155.00	122.50	150.00	125.00	100.00
C22 (6)	50¢ carmine	180.00	150.00	115.00	145.00	120.00	90.00
C23 (4)	6¢ dark blue & carmine .	11.50	9.50	7.50	8.50	7.15	5.50
C24 (6)	30¢ dull blue	250.00	210.00	160.00	200.00	165.00	130.00

U.S. Air Post #C25-C41

SCOTT NO.	DESCRIPTION	FIRST DAY COVERS SING	FIRST DAY COVERS PL. BLK.	MINT SHEET	PLATE BLOCK F/NH	PLATE BLOCK F	UNUSED F/NH	UNUSED F	USED F
	1941-44 TRANSPORT ISSUE								
C25-31	**6¢-50¢, 7 varieties, complete**	....	....	....	**137.00**	**120.00**	**23.95**	**20.00**	**5.60**
C25	6¢ Transport Plane	4.50	8.75	8.35(50)	1.05	.80	.20	.15	.15
C25a	same, booklet pane of 3	20.00	....	....	....	....	4.25	3.40	....
C26	8¢ Transport Plane	4.50	11.25	11.50(50)	2.20	1.95	.25	.20	.15
C27	10¢ Transport Plane	6.00	12.50	82.50(50)	10.50	9.25	1.65	1.30	.20
C28	15¢ Transport Plane	6.00	13.75	150.00(50)	13.95	12.50	3.50	3.10	.40
C29	20¢ Transport Plane	8.00	16.00	125.00(50)	12.65	11.25	2.60	2.25	.35
C30	30¢ Transport Plane	13.00	27.00	140.00(50)	14.00	12.50	3.00	2.60	.40
C31	50¢ Transport Plane	28.50	68.75	625.00(50)	90.00	80.00	14.00	12.50	4.25
	1946								
C32	5¢ DC-4 Skymaster	1.75	4.25	6.65(50)	.75	.70	.20	.15	.15

C33, C37, C39, C41 — C34 — C35 — C36

SCOTT NO.	DESCRIPTION	FIRST DAY COVERS SING	FIRST DAY COVERS PL. BLK.	MINT SHEET	PLATE BLOCK F/NH	PLATE BLOCK F	UNUSED F/NH	UNUSED F	USED F
	1947								
C33-36	**5¢-25¢, 4 varieties, complete**	....	....	....	....	....	**1.85**	**1.50**	**.55**
C33	5¢ DC-4 Skymaster	1.75	4.25	13.35(100)	.75	.70	.20	.15	.15
C34	10¢ Pan American Bldg.	1.75	4.25	11.75(50)	1.50	1.35	.30	.25	.15
C35	15¢ New York Skyline	1.75	4.25	19.50(50)	1.85	1.65	.40	.35	.15
C36	25¢ Plane over Bridge	2.00	5.00	50.00(50)	4.75	4.00	1.05	.95	.15
	1948 **Rotary Press Coil Perf. 10 Horiz.**								
		LINE PR.			**LINE PAIR**				
C37	5¢ DC-4 Skymaster................	1.75	4.25	....	9.50	8.50	.95	.85	.85

C38 — C40

SCOTT NO.	DESCRIPTION	FIRST DAY COVERS SING	FIRST DAY COVERS PL. BLK.	MINT SHEET	PLATE BLOCK F/NH	PLATE BLOCK F	UNUSED F/NH	UNUSED F	USED F
		PL. BLK.			**PLATE BLOCK**				
C38	5¢ New York Jubilee	1.75	4.25	16.50(100)	5.75	5.00	.20	.15	.15
	1949								
C39	6¢ DC-4 Skymaster (as #C33)	1.75	4.25	13.50(100)	.75	.70	.20	.15	.15
C39a	same, booklet pane of 6	6.50	....	....	....	....	11.50	10.00	....
C40	6¢ Alexandria, Virginia	1.75	4.25	7.25(50)	.75	.70	.20	.15	.15
	Rotary Press Coil Perf. 10 Horiz.								
		LINE PR.			**LINE PAIR**				
C41	DC-4 Skymaster (as #C37)	1.75	4.25	....	14.00	12.50	3.50	3.00	.15

NOTE: Unused Air Mail coil pairs can be supplied at two times the singles price.

C42

C43

C44

U.S. Air Post #C42-C56

SCOTT NO.	DESCRIPTION	FIRST DAY COVERS SING	FIRST DAY COVERS PL. BLK.	MINT SHEET	PLATE BLOCK F/NH	PLATE BLOCK F	UNUSED F/NH	UNUSED F	USED F
			1949 U.P.U. ISSUES						
C42-44	**10¢-25¢, 3 varieties, complete**	....	....	....	....	....	**1.10**	**.95**	**1.05**
C42	10¢ Post Office	1.75	4.25	13.50(50)	1.70	1.50	.30	.25	.30
C43	15¢ Globe & Doves	2.00	5.00	17.00(50)	1.50	1.30	.35	.30	.35
C44	25¢ Plane & Globe	2.50	6.25	31.50(50)	7.25	6.50	.55	.50	.50

C45

C46

C47

SCOTT NO.	DESCRIPTION	FDC SING	FDC PL. BLK.	MINT SHEET	PLATE BLOCK F/NH	PLATE BLOCK F	UNUSED F/NH	UNUSED F	USED F
			1949-58						
C45-51	**7 varieties, complete**	....	....	....	....	....	**8.75**	**7.75**	**2.30**
			1949						
C45	6¢ Wright Bros.	1.75	4.25	9.00(50)	.80	.70	.20	.15	.15
			1952						
C46	80¢ Hawaii	15.00	35.00	350.00(50)	35.00	30.00	8.00	7.25	1.50
			1953						
C47	6¢ Powered Flight	1.75	4.25	7.25(50)	.75	.70	.20	.15	.15

C48, C50

C49

C51, C52, C60, C61

SCOTT NO.	DESCRIPTION	FDC SING	FDC PL. BLK.	MINT SHEET	PLATE BLOCK F/NH	PLATE BLOCK F	UNUSED F/NH	UNUSED F	USED F
			1954						
C48	4¢ Eagle	1.75	4.25	12.25(100)	1.95	1.75	.20	.15	.15
			1957						
C49	6¢ Air Force	1.75	4.25	7.25(50)	.75	.70	.20	.15	.15
			1958						
C50	5¢ Eagle	1.75	4.25	13.25(100)	1.85	1.70	.20	.15	.15
C51	7¢ Silhouette of Jet, blue	1.75	4.25	16.50(100)	.75	.70	.20	.15	.15
C51a	same, booklet pane of 6	8.00	....	....	....	....	12.00	11.00	....
			Rotary Press Coil Perf. 10 Horiz.						
			LINE PR.		**LINE PAIR**				
C52	7¢ Silhouette of Jet, blue	1.75	3.25	....	17.50	16.00	2.50	2.35	.15

C53

C54

C55

C56

SCOTT NO.	DESCRIPTION	FDC SING	FDC PL. BLK.	MINT SHEET	PLATE BLOCK F/NH	PLATE BLOCK F	UNUSED F/NH	UNUSED F	USED F
			1959 COMMEMORATIVES						
			PL. BLK.		**PLATE BLOCK**				
C53-56	**4 varieties, complete**	....	....	....	....	....	**.85**	**.65**	**.70**
C53	7¢ Alaska Statehood	1.75	4.25	7.25(50)	.75	.70	.20	.15	.15
C54	7¢ Balloon Jupiter	1.75	4.25	7.25(50)	.75	.70	.20	.15	.15
C55	7¢ Hawaii Statehood	1.75	4.25	7.25(50)	.75	.70	.20	.15	.15
C56	10¢ Pan-Am Games	1.75	4.25	11.75(50)	1.70	1.55	.30	.25	.30

U.S. Air Post #C57-C69

C57, C62 | C58 | C59 | C63

SCOTT NO.	DESCRIPTION	FIRST DAY COVERS SING	PL. BLK.	MINT SHEET	PLATE BLOCK F/NH	F	UNUSED F/NH	F	USED F
	1959-1966 REGULAR ISSUES								
C57/63	**(C57-60, C62-63) 6 varieties**	....	....	....	**16.40**	**13.00**	**3.65**	**2.80**	**1.65**
	1959-66								
C57	10¢ Liberty Bell (1960)	1.75	4.25	85.00(50)	8.00	6.50	1.75	1.35	1.00
C58	15¢ Statue of Liberty	1.75	4.25	22.50(50)	1.95	1.50	.45	.35	.15
C59	25¢ Abraham Lincoln (1960)	1.75	4.25	28.00(50)	2.75	2.10	.60	.45	.15
	1960. Design of 1958								
C60	7¢ Jet Plane, carmine	1.75	4.25	17.00(100)	.75	.60	.20	.15	.15
C60a	same, booklet pane of 6	9.00	....	....	....	....	15.00	12.50	....
	Rotary Press Coil—Perf. 10 Horiz.		**LINE PR.**		**LINE PAIR**				
C61	7¢ Jet Plane, carmine	1.75	3.25	....	45.00	37.50	5.00	4.00	.35
	1961-67		**PL. BLK.**		**PLATE BLOCK**				
C62	13¢ Liberty Bell	1.75	4.25	21.50(50)	2.10	1.75	.45	.35	.15
C63	15¢ Statue re-drawn	1.75	4.25	17.25(50)	1.70	1.35	.40	.30	.15

C64, C65

C66

C67

C68

C69

SCOTT NO.	DESCRIPTION	FIRST DAY COVERS SING	PL. BLK.	MINT SHEET	PLATE BLOCK F/NH	F	UNUSED F/NH	F	USED F
	1962-64								
C64/69	**(C64, C66-69) 5 varieties**	....	....	....	**10.35**	**8.50**	**1.85**	**1.45**	**1.25**
	1962								
C64	8¢ Plane & Capitol	1.75	4.25	21.00(100)	1.00	.80	.25	.20	.15
C64b	same, booklet pane of 5, Sl. 1 .	1.95	....	....	....	....	5.25	4.25	....
C64b	booklet pane of 5, Slogan II (1963).......		....	....	....	....	58.00	47.50	....
C64b	booklet pane of 5, Slogan III (1964).......		....	....	....	....	11.75	9.50	....
C64c	booklet pane of 5, tagged, Slogan III (1964)	....	....	....	....	....	1.70	1.35	....

SLOGAN I—Your Mailman Deserves Your Help... **SLOGAN II—Use Zone Numbers...**
SLOGAN III—Always Use Zip Code...

SCOTT NO.	DESCRIPTION	FIRST DAY COVERS SING	PL. BLK.	MINT SHEET	PLATE BLOCK F/NH	F	UNUSED F/NH	F	USED F
	Rotary Press Coil—Perf. 10 Horiz.		**LINE PR.**		**LINE PR.**				
C65	8¢ Plane & Capitol................	1.75	3.25	....	5.75	4.75	.45	.35	.15
	1963		**PL. BLK.**		**PLATE BLOCK**				
C66	15¢ Montgomery Blair............	1.75	4.25	33.50(50)	4.00	3.25	.75	.60	.60
C67	6¢ Bald Eagle........................	1.75	4.25	16.50(100)	2.25	1.90	.20	.15	.15
C68	8¢ Amelia Earhart...............	1.75	4.25	10.50(50)	1.40	1.10	.25	.20	.20
	1964								
C69	8¢ Dr. Robert H. Goddard.........	2.00	5.00	23.75(50)	2.25	1.90	.50	.40	.20
C69	Zip Block..............................	....	....	....	2.25	1.90	....	....	....

ZIP BLOCKS: are generally corner Blocks of Four that contain a drawing of "Mr. Zip" and the legend "USE ZIP CODE" or a similar design. They were introduced in 1964 and are still in use today.

U.S. Air Post #C70-C83

SCOTT NO.	DESCRIPTION	FIRST DAY COVERS SING.	FIRST DAY COVERS PL.BLK.	MINT SHEET	MAIL EARLY	ZIP	PLATE BLOCK	UNUSED F/NH	USED

C70

C71

C72, C73

C74

C75, C81

1967-69

SCOTT NO.	DESCRIPTION	FDC SING.	FDC PL.BLK.	MINT SHEET	MAIL EARLY	ZIP	PLATE BLOCK	UNUSED F/NH	USED
C70/76	**(C70-72, C74-76) 6 varieties**	....	....	....	....	....	....	**2.60**	**1.00**

1967-68

SCOTT NO.	DESCRIPTION	FDC SING.	FDC PL.BLK.	MINT SHEET	MAIL EARLY	ZIP	PLATE BLOCK	UNUSED F/NH	USED
C70	8¢ Alaska Purchase	1.75	4.25	13.50(50)	....	1.80	1.95	.30	.20
C71	20¢ "Columbia Jays"	1.75	4.25	48.00(50)	....	4.50	4.50	1.00	.15
C72	10¢ 50-Stars (1968)	1.75	4.25	24.00(100)	6.00	5.00	1.15	.25	.15
C72b	same, booklet pane of 8	3.00	....	....	....	....	....	2.50	....
C72c	same, b. pane of 5, Sl. IV or V .	140.00	....	....	....	....	....	4.00	....

SLOGAN IV—Mail Early in the Day... **SLOGAN V—Use Zip Code...**

1968 Rotary Press Coil—Perf. 10 Vert.

SCOTT NO.	DESCRIPTION	FDC SING.	LINE PR.	MINT SHEET	MAIL EARLY	ZIP	LINE PR.	UNUSED F/NH	USED
C73	10¢ 50-Stars........................	1.75	3.25	....	....	....	2.25	.35	.15

SCOTT NO.	DESCRIPTION	FDC SING.	PL. BLK.	MINT SHEET	MAIL EARLY	ZIP	PL. BLK.	UNUSED F/NH	USED
C74	10¢ Air Mail Anniversary.........	1.75	4.25	15.00(50)	2.90	2.35	3.10	.30	.15
C75	20¢ "USA" & Plane...............	1.75	4.25	28.00(50)	3.35	2.35	2.50	.55	.20

1969

SCOTT NO.	DESCRIPTION	FDC SING.	FDC PL.BLK.	MINT SHEET	MAIL EARLY	ZIP	PLATE BLOCK	UNUSED F/NH	USED
C76	10¢ Man on the Moon..............	6.00	14.50	10.50(32)	1.80	1.20	1.70	.35	.20

C76

C77

C78, C82

C79, C83

C80

1971-73

SCOTT NO.	DESCRIPTION	FDC SING.	FDC PL.BLK.	MINT SHEET	MAIL EARLY	ZIP	PLATE BLOCK	UNUSED F/NH	USED
C77-81	**9¢-21¢, 5 varieties, complete**	....	....	....	....	....	....	**1.80**	**.80**
C77	9¢ Delta Winged Plane	1.75	4.25	19.00(100)	1.35	.95	1.05	.25	.25
C78	11¢ Silhouette of Plane	1.75	4.25	25.00(100)	1.75	1.15	1.25	.30	.15
C78b	same, precanceled	....	....	....	....	....	....	....	.50
C78a	11¢ booklet pane of 4	2.25	....	....	....	....	....	1.20	....
C79	13¢ Letter (1973)	1.75	4.25	32.50(100)	1.75	1.15	1.55	.35	.15
C79b	same, precanceled	....	....	....	....	....	....	....	.60
C79a	13¢ booklet pane of 5	2.25	....	....	....	....	....	1.50	....
C80	17¢ Liberty Head	1.75	4.25	22.50(50)	2.75	2.00	2.25	.50	.15
C81	21¢ "USA" & Plane	1.75	4.25	21.00(50)	2.60	1.75	1.95	.50	.15

Rotary Press Coils Perf. 10 Vertically

SCOTT NO.	DESCRIPTION	FDC SING.	LINE PR.	MINT SHEET	MAIL EARLY	ZIP	LINE PR.	UNUSED F/NH	USED
C82	11¢ Silhouette of Jet	1.75	3.25	....	....	....	.90	.30	.15
C83	13¢ Letter	1.75	3.25	....	....	....	1.15	.35	.15

U.S. Air Post #C84-C96

C85

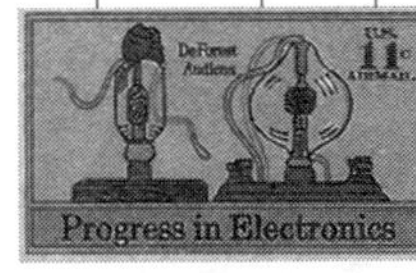

C86

C87

C84

C88

C89

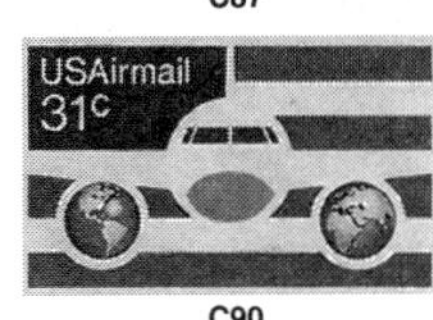

C90

SCOTT NO.	DESCRIPTION	FIRST DAY COVERS SING.	PL.BLK.	MINT SHEET	MAIL EARLY	ZIP	PLATE BLOCK	UNUSED F/NH	USED
		1972-76							
C84-90	**11¢-31¢, 7 varieties, complete**		....	....	....	....	....	**3.10**	**1.20**
		1972							
C84	11¢ City of Refuge	1.75	4.25	11.75(50)	1.65	1.10	1.10	.30	.15
C85	11¢ Olympics	1.75	4.25	12.75(50)	1.85	1.25	3.10(10)	.30	.15
		1973							
C86	11¢ Electronics	1.75	4.25	11.75(50)	1.65	1.10	1.10	.30	.15
		1974							
C87	18¢ Statue of Liberty	1.75	4.25	22.50(50)	3.35	2.25	2.25	.50	.40
C88	26¢ Mt. Rushmore	1.75	4.25	27.50(50)	3.50	2.50	2.75	.60	.15
		1976							
C89	25¢ Plane & Globes	1.75	4.25	27.50(50)	3.50	2.50	2.75	.60	.15
C90	31¢ Plane, Flag & Globes	1.75	4.25	31.50(50)	4.50	3.00	3.00	.65	.15

C91

C92

C93

C94

C95

C96

SCOTT NO.	DESCRIPTION	FIRST DAY COVERS SING.	PL.BLK.	MINT SHEET	COPY-RIGHT	ZIP	PLATE BLOCK	UNUSED F/NH	USED
		1978-80							
C91-100	**21¢-40¢, 10 varieties, complete**		....	....	....	....	....	**10.00**	**2.15**
C91-92	Wright Bros., 2 varieties, att'd. .	2.40	5.00	85.00(100)	3.25	3.25	4.00	1.85	1.10
C91	31¢ Wright Bros. & Plane	1.75	....	....	....	....	....	.90	.20
C92	31¢ Wright Bros. & Shed	1.75	....	....	....	....	....	.90	.20
		1979							
C93-94	Octave Chanute, 2 varieties, att'd.	2.40	5.00	85.00(100)	4.50	4.50	4.50	1.85	1.20
C93	21¢ Chanute & Plane	1.75	....	....	....	....	....	.90	.30
C94	21¢ Chanute & 2 Planes	1.75	....	....	....	....	....	.90	.30
C95-96	Wiley Post, 2 varieties, attached	2.40	5.00	165.00(100)	12.00	12.00	13.50	3.50	1.75
C95	25¢ Post & Plane	1.75	....	....	....	....	....	1.70	.20
C96	25¢ Plane & Post	1.75	....	....	....	....	....	1.70	.20

U.S. Air Post #C97-C112

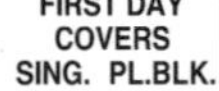

SCOTT NO.	DESCRIPTION	FIRST DAY COVERS SING.	PL.BLK.	MINT SHEET	MAIL EARLY	ZIP	PLATE BLOCK	UNUSED F/NH	USED

C97

C98

C99

C100

SCOTT NO.	DESCRIPTION	FIRST DAY COVERS SING.	PL.BLK.	MINT SHEET	MAIL EARLY	ZIP	PLATE BLOCK	UNUSED F/NH	USED
C97	31¢ High Jumper	1.75	4.25	36.00(50)	3.75	3.75	12.00(12)	.80	.30
	1980								
C98	40¢ Philip Mazzei	1.75	4.25	45.00(50)	4.15	4.15	11.25(12)	1.00	.15
C99	28¢ Blanche S. Scott	1.75	4.25	32.50(50)	3.00	3.00	8.25(12)	.70	.20
C100	35¢ Glenn Curtiss	1.75	4.25	42.00(50)	3.60	3.60	10.50(12)	.90	.20

C101

C102

C103

C104

1983-85

SCOTT NO.	DESCRIPTION	FIRST DAY COVERS SING.	PL.BLK.	MINT SHEET	MAIL EARLY	ZIP	PLATE BLOCK	UNUSED F/NH	USED
C101-16	**28¢-44¢, 16 varieties, complete**		....	....	....	....	....	**20.50**	**4.35**
	1983								
C101-04	28¢ Summer Olympics, 4 varieties, attached.	3.50	4.50	50.00(50)	3.85	3.85	5.50	5.00	2.50
C101	28¢ Women's Gymnastics	1.75	....	....	....	....	....	1.20	.25
C102	28¢ Hurdles	1.75	....	....	....	....	....	1.20	.25
C103	28¢ Womens Basketball	1.75	....	....	....	....	....	1.20	.25
C104	28¢ Soccer	1.75	....	....	....	....	....	1.20	.25

C105

C106

C107

C108

SCOTT NO.	DESCRIPTION	FIRST DAY COVERS SING.	PL.BLK.	MINT SHEET	MAIL EARLY	ZIP	PLATE BLOCK	UNUSED F/NH	USED
C105-08	40¢ Summer Olympics, 4 varieties, attached	4.50	5.75	60.00(50)	5.00	5.00	6.75	6.00	2.50
C105	40¢ Shot Put	1.85	....	....	....	....	....	1.45	.30
C106	40¢ Men's Gymnastics	1.85	....	....	....	....	....	1.45	.30
C107	40¢ Womens Swimming	1.85	....	....	....	....	....	1.45	.30
C108	40¢ Weight-Lifting	1.85	....	....	....	....	....	1.45	.30

C109

C110

C111

C112

SCOTT NO.	DESCRIPTION	FIRST DAY COVERS SING.	PL.BLK.	MINT SHEET	MAIL EARLY	ZIP	PLATE BLOCK	UNUSED F/NH	USED
C109-12	35¢ Summer Olympics, 4 varieties, attached	4.00	5.00	52.50(50)	6.25	6.25	8.00	6.00	2.50
C109	35¢ Fencing	1.75	....	....	....	....	....	1.45	.35
C110	35¢ Cycling	1.75	....	....	....	....	....	1.45	.35
C111	35¢ Volleyball	1.75	....	....	....	....	....	1.45	.35
C112	35¢ Pole Vault	1.75	....	....	....	....	....	1.25	.35

U.S. Air Post #C113-C126

C113

C114

C115

C116

SCOTT NO.	DESCRIPTION	FIRST DAY COVERS SING.	FIRST DAY COVERS PL.BLK.	MINT SHEET	MAIL EARLY	ZIP	PLATE BLOCK	UNUSED F/NH	USED
	1985								
C113	33¢ Alfred Verville	1.75	4.25	39.50(50)	3.60	3.60	4.00	.85	.20
C114	39¢ Lawrence and Elmer Sperry	1.75	4.25	45.00(50)	4.25	4.25	4.50	1.00	.25
C115	44¢ Transpacific	1.75	4.25	50.00(50)	4.50	4.50	5.00	1.10	.25
C116	44¢ Junipero Serra	1.75	4.25	65.00(50)	6.50	6.50	9.00	1.40	.25

C117

C118

C119

SCOTT NO.	DESCRIPTION	FIRST DAY COVERS SING.	FIRST DAY COVERS PL.BLK.	MINT SHEET	MAIL EARLY	ZIP	PLATE BLOCK	UNUSED F/NH	USED
	1988								
C117	44¢ New Sweden	1.75	4.25	55.00(50)	6.00	6.00	8.00	1.20	.25
C118	45¢ Samuel Langley	1.75	4.25	55.00(50)	4.90	4.90	5.25	1.20	.25
C119	36¢ Igor Sikorsky	1.75	4.25	42.00(50)	3.85	3.85	4.00	.90	.25

C120

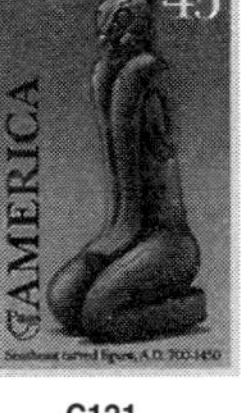

C121

C122

C123

C124

C125

SCOTT NO.	DESCRIPTION	FIRST DAY COVERS SING.	FIRST DAY COVERS PL.BLK.	MINT SHEET	MAIL EARLY	ZIP	PLATE BLOCK	UNUSED F/NH	USED
	1989								
C120-25	**6 varieties, complete ....**	**......**	**......**	**......**	**......**	**......**	**......**	**8.40**	**1.45**
C120	45¢ French Revolution	1.75	4.25	34.50(30)	4.90	4.90	5.25	1.20	.25
C121	45¢ Americas Issue (Key Marco Cat)	1.75	4.25	55.00(50)	4.90	4.90	5.25	1.20	.25
C122-25	Futuristic Mail Delivery	5.00	6.00	65.00(40)	6.60	6.60	7.00	6.50	4.00
C122	45¢ Spacecraft	1.75	.....	.....	.....	.....	.....	1.60	.25
C123	45¢ Air Suspended Hover	1.75	.....	.....	.....	.....	.....	1.60	.25
C124	45¢ Moon Rover	1.75	.....	.....	.....	.....	.....	1.60	.25
C125	45¢ Space Shuttle	1.75	.....	.....	.....	.....	.....	1.60	.25
C126	$1.80 Futuristic Mail Imp. S.S. ...	6.50	.....	.....	.....	.....	.....	6.50	.....

C127

C128

C129

C130

C131

SCOTT NO.	DESCRIPTION	FIRST DAY COVERS SING.	FIRST DAY COVERS PL.BLK.	MINT SHEET	MAIL EARLY	ZIP	PLATE BLOCK	UNUSED F/NH	USED
	1990								
C127	45¢ Americas Issue (Island Beach)	1.75	4.25	55.000(50)	4.90	4.90	5.50	1.20	.25
	1991-93								
C128	50¢ Harriet Quimby	1.75	4.25	65.00(50)	5.75	5.75	6.25	1.40	.25
C128b	50¢ Harriet Quimby, reissue, bullseye perf. (1993)	...	...	65.00(50)	5.75	8.50(6)	6.25	1.40	.25
C129	40¢ William Piper	1.75	4.25	45.00(50)	4.25	4.25	5.00	1.00	.25
C130	50¢ Antarctic Treaty	1.75	4.25	65.00(50)	5.75	5.75	6.25	1.40	.25
C131	50¢ America (Bering Strait) (1991)	1.75	4.25	65.00(50)	5.75	5.75	6.25	1.40	.25
C132	40¢ William Piper, reissue, bullseye perf. (1993)	...	...	55.00(50)	4.90	4.90	5.25	1.20	.25

Special Delivery #CE1-2; E1-4

AIR MAIL SPECIAL DELIVERY STAMPS

771, CE1, CE2

SCOTT NO.	DESCRIPTION	PLATE BLOCK F/NH	PLATE BLOCK F	PLATE BLOCK AVG	UNUSED F/NH	UNUSED F	UNUSED AVG	USED F	USED AVG
CE1	16¢ dark blue (1934)	(6)20.50	18.00	14.50	.80	.70	.55	.70	.55
CE2	16¢ red & blue (1936)	8.00	6.00	4.50	.45	.40	.30	.25	.20
CE2	same, center line block	2.75	2.15	1.75	....	....	....	....	....
CE2	same, arrow block of 4	2.50	1.95	1.50	....	....	....	....	....

SPECIAL DELIVERY STAMPS

E1

E2, E3

E4, E5

SCOTT NO.	DESCRIPTION	UNUSED NH. F	UNUSED NH. AVG	UNUSED OG F	UNUSED OG AVG	USED F	USED AVG
	1885 Inscribed "Secures Immediate Delivery at Special Delivery Office" Perf. 12						
E1	10¢ blue	335.00	265.00	235.00	140.00	31.00	18.00
	1888 Inscribed "Secures Immediate Delivery at any Post Office"						
E2	10¢ blue	325.00	255.00	230.00	135.00	8.50	5.00
	1893						
E3	10¢ orange	225.00	175.00	140.00	90.00	15.00	9.00
	1894 Same type as preceding issue, but with line under "Ten Cents" Unwatermarked						
E4	10¢ blue	825.00	625.00	610.00	385.00	18.25	10.00

Special Delivery #E5-E19

SCOTT NO.	DESCRIPTION	UNUSED NH F	UNUSED NH AVG	UNUSED O.G. F	UNUSED O.G. AVG	USED F	USED AVG
	1895 Double Line Watermark						
E5	10¢ blue	165.00	130.00	115.00	70.00	2.80	1.55

E6, E8-11

E7

SCOTT NO.	DESCRIPTION	UNUSED NH F	UNUSED NH AVG	UNUSED O.G. F	UNUSED O.G. AVG	USED F	USED AVG
	1902						
E6	10¢ ultramarine	100.00	75.00	67.50	46.50	2.75	1.65
	1908						
E7	10¢ green	78.50	62.50	52.50	35.00	29.50	19.50
	1911 Single Line Watermark						
E8	10¢ ultramarine	105.00	82.50	68.50	50.00	4.15	3.00
	1914 Perf. 10						
E9	10¢ ultramarine	205.00	160.00	135.00	90.00	5.50	4.00
	1916 Unwatermarked Perf. 10						
E10	10¢ pale ultra	360.00	280.00	250.00	160.00	19.00	13.00
	1917 Perf. 11						
E11	10¢ ultramarine	20.00	15.50	14.00	8.50	.45	.30
E11	same, plate block of 6	225.00	175.00	165.00	120.00	....	....

E12, E13, E15-E18

E14, E19

1922-25 Flat Plate Printing Perf. 11

E12	10¢ gray violet	(6) 385.00	275.00	185.00	28.00	21.00	13.50	.20	.15
E13	15¢ deep orange (1925)	(6) 275.00	195.00	135.00	28.00	21.00	13.00	1.15	.70
E14	20¢ black (1925)	(6) 45.00	31.50	23.00	3.35	2.75	1.70	1.40	1.00

SCOTT NO.	DESCRIPTION	FIRST DAY COVERS SING	FIRST DAY COVERS PL. BLK.	MINT SHEET	PLATE BLOCK F/NH	PLATE BLOCK F	UNUSED F/NH	UNUSED F	USED F
	1927-51 Rotary Press Printing Perf. 11 x 10-1/2								
E15-19	**10¢-20¢, 5 varieties**	....	....	....	**85.00**	**75.50**	**12.65**	**10.95**	**6.15**
E15	10¢ gray violet	....	....	42.50(50)	6.75	5.00	.85	.60	.15
E16	15¢ orange (1931)	....	....	45.00(50)	4.75	3.35	.90	.70	.15
E17	13¢ blue (1944)	9.00	20.00	35.00(50)	4.00	2.75	.70	.50	.15
E18	17¢ orange yellow (1944)	12.00	28.00	165.00(50)	28.00	21.00	4.00	2.75	2.25
E19	20¢ black (1951)	5.00	12.50	97.50(50)	8.00	6.00	1.95	1.35	.15

E20, E21

E22, E23

U.S. Special Delivery #E20-E23, Registration & Certified

SCOTT NO.	DESCRIPTION	FIRST DAY COVERS SING	PL. BLK.	MINT SHEET	PLATE BLOCK F/NH	F	UNUSED F/NH	F	USED F
				1954-57					
E20	20¢ deep blue	2.50	6.25	26.00(50)	2.80	2.25	.55	.45	.15
E21	30¢ lake (1957)	2.50	6.25	31.50(50)	3.10	2.50	.70	.50	.15

SCOTT NO.	DESCRIPTION	FIRST DAY COVERS SING.	PL.BLK.	MINT SHEET	MAIL EARLY	ZIP	PLATE BLOCK	UNUSED F/NH	USED
				1969-71					
E22	45¢ carmine & violet blue	2.50	6.25	63.50(50)	10.50	7.25	7.25	1.40	.35
E23	60¢ violet blue & carmine (1971)	2.75	6.75	55.00(50)	7.75	5.25	5.25	1.20	.15

REGISTRATION STAMP

F1

SCOTT NO.	DESCRIPTION	UNUSED NH F	AVG	UNUSED OG F	AVG	USED F	AVG
			1911 Registration				
F1	10¢ ultramarine	85.00	65.00	57.50	35.00	5.00	3.50

U.S. Certified

CERTIFIED MAIL STAMP

FA1

SCOTT NO.	DESCRIPTION	FIRST DAY COVERS SING	PL. BLK.	MINT SHEET	PLATE BLOCK F/NH	F	UNUSED F/NH	F	USED F
				1955 Certified Mail					
FA1	15¢ red	2.50	6.25	19.50(50)	4.25	3.25	.35	.25	.25

PLATE BLOCKS: are portions of a sheet of stamps adjacent to the number(s) indicating the printing plate number used to produce that sheet. Flat plate issues are usually collected in plate blocks of six (number opposite middle stamp) while rotary issues are normally corner blocks of four.

U.S. Postage Due #J1-J50

J1-J28

J29-J68

SCOTT NO.	DESCRIPTION	UNUSED NH F	UNUSED NH AVG	UNUSED OG F	UNUSED OG AVG	USED F	USED AVG
	1879 Unwatermarked Perf. 12						
J1	1¢ brown	45.00	30.00	30.00	20.00	6.00	3.50
J2	2¢ brown	275.00	165.00	185.00	110.00	5.00	2.75
J3	3¢ brown	33.00	21.00	22.00	14.00	3.10	1.75
J4	5¢ brown	410.00	250.00	275.00	170.00	40.00	20.00
J5	10¢ brown	500.00	295.00	335.00	195.00	13.00	9.00
J6	30¢ brown	250.00	150.00	165.00	100.00	30.00	18.00
J7	50¢ brown	315.00	185.00	210.00	125.00	36.50	21.50
	1884-89						
J15	1¢ red brown	46.50	27.00	31.00	18.00	3.10	1.90
J16	2¢ red brown	58.00	33.00	38.75	22.00	3.10	1.90
J17	3¢ red brown	675.00	395.00	450.00	275.00	95.00	55.00
J18	5¢ red brown	335.00	195.00	225.00	130.00	13.00	8.00
J19	10¢ red brown	330.00	225.00	220.00	150.00	10.50	7.00
J20	30¢ red brown	160.00	95.00	110.00	65.00	28.00	20.00
J21	50¢ red brown	1375.00	825.00	925.00	550.00	115.00	75.00
	1891						
J22	1¢ bright claret	18.00	11.00	12.00	7.50	.60	.35
J23	2¢ bright claret	21.00	12.00	14.00	8.00	.55	.35
J24	3¢ bright claret	45.75	24.75	30.50	16.50	4.00	2.75
J25	5¢ bright claret	54.00	30.00	36.00	21.00	4.00	2.75
J26	10¢ bright claret	95.00	60.00	65.00	40.00	10.00	6.50
J27	30¢ bright claret	345.00	185.00	230.00	125.00	95.00	47.50
J28	50¢ bright claret	390.00	220.00	260.00	145.00	95.00	47.50
	1894 Unwatermarked Perf. 12 (†)						
J29	1¢ pale vermillion	925.00	600.00	625.00	400.00	160.00	95.00
J30	2¢ dark vermillion	410.00	275.00	275.00	190.00	60.00	40.00
J31	1¢ deep claret	30.00	21.00	20.00	14.00	4.10	2.75
J32	2¢ deep claret	27.00	18.00	18.00	12.00	2.30	1.75
J33	3¢ deep claret	115.00	70.00	71.50	45.00	18.75	12.00
J34	5¢ deep claret	150.00	90.00	100.00	60.00	25.00	17.00
J35	10¢ deep claret	150.00	90.00	100.00	60.00	16.50	11.00
J36	30¢ deep claret	305.00	225.00	215.00	150.00	55.00	35.00
J36b	30¢ pale rose	285.00	195.00	195.00	130.00	50.00	35.00
J37	50¢ deep claret	745.00	495.00	495.00	325.00	130.00	100.00
	1895 Double Line Watermark Perf. 12 (†)						
J38	1¢ deep claret	9.00	5.50	4.95	3.50	.40	.30
J39	2¢ deep claret	9.00	5.50	4.95	3.50	.25	.20
J40	3¢ deep claret	50.00	35.00	30.00	20.00	1.25	.90
J41	5¢ deep claret	55.00	35.00	33.50	20.00	1.25	.90
J42	10¢ deep claret	55.00	37.50	36.50	22.50	2.60	1.80
J43	30¢ deep claret	445.00	350.00	295.00	200.00	27.50	19.00
J44	50¢ deep claret	275.00	190.00	175.00	120.00	22.50	15.00
	1910-12 Single Line Watermark Perf. 12						
J45	1¢ deep claret	27.50	19.50	17.50	12.50	2.30	1.60
J46	2¢ deep claret	27.50	19.50	17.50	12.00	.25	.20
J47	3¢ deep claret	500.00	325.00	330.00	210.00	18.25	12.00
J48	5¢ deep claret	82.50	52.50	52.50	35.00	4.00	2.50
J49	10¢ deep claret	105.00	67.50	65.00	45.00	8.50	6.00
J50	50¢ deep claret (1912)	850.00	510.00	550.00	325.00	75.00	47.50

U.S. Postage Due #J52-J87

SCOTT NO.	DESCRIPTION	UNUSED NH F	UNUSED NH AVG	UNUSED OG F	UNUSED OG AVG	USED F	USED AVG
	1914 Single Line Watermark Perf. 10						
J52	1¢ carmine lake	57.50	37.50	36.50	25.00	7.50	5.25
J53	2¢ carmine lake	41.50	29.00	27.50	19.50	.25	.20
J54	3¢ carmine lake	600.00	375.00	400.00	250.00	20.00	14.00
J55	5¢ carmine lake	33.50	20.00	21.00	13.00	1.85	1.20
J56	10¢ carmine lake	55.00	35.00	36.00	22.00	1.05	.75
J57	30¢ carmine lake	200.00	120.00	135.00	80.00	14.50	9.00
J58	50¢ carmine lake	....	....	5500.00	3750.00	400.00	250.00
	1916 Unwatermarked Perf. 10						
J59	1¢ rose	1500.00	1050.00	1050.00	700.00	195.00	125.00
J60	2¢ rose	120.00	80.00	80.00	55.00	11.00	7.00

SCOTT NO.	DESCRIPTION	PLATE BLOCK F/NH	PLATE BLOCK F/OG	PLATE BLOCK AVG/OG	UNUSED F/NH	UNUSED F/OG	UNUSED AVG/OG	USED F	USED AVG
	1917 Unwatermarked Perf. 11								
J61	1¢ carmine rose	(6) 50.00	40.00	27.50	2.50	1.55	1.10	.20	.15
J62	2¢ carmine rose	(6) 40.00	32.00	25.00	2.35	1.40	.95	.20	.15
J63	3¢ carmine rose	(6) 120.00	95.00	70.00	11.00	7.50	4.75	.20	.15
J64	5¢ carmine	(6) 120.00	95.00	70.00	11.00	7.50	4.75	.20	.15
J65	10¢ carmine rose	(6) 160.00	125.00	100.00	16.50	11.00	5.50	.20	.15
J66	30¢ carmine rose	....	....	....	85.00	50.00	35.00	.55	.35
J67	50¢ carmine rose	....	....	....	100.00	65.00	45.00	.20	.15
	1925								
J68	1/2¢ dull red	(6) 12.50	10.00	7.50	.80	.60	.40	.20	.15

J69-J76, J79-J86

J77, J78, J87

J88-J104

SCOTT NO.	DESCRIPTION	PLATE BLOCK F/NH	PLATE BLOCK F/OG	PLATE BLOCK AVG/OG	UNUSED F/NH	UNUSED F/OG	UNUSED AVG/OG	USED F	USED AVG
	1930 Perf. 11								
J69	1/2¢ carmine	(6) 40.00	32.00	25.00	3.60	2.50	1.70	.85	.50
J70	1¢ carmine	(6) 32.50	26.00	21.00	3.10	2.15	1.50	.20	.15
J71	2¢ carmine	(6) 45.00	36.00	28.50	4.50	3.35	2.40	.20	.15
J72	3¢ carmine	(6) 300.00	240.00	190.00	31.50	22.00	15.00	1.25	.75
J73	5¢ carmine	(6) 250.00	200.00	160.00	25.00	17.50	12.00	1.80	1.25
J74	10¢ carmine	(6) 475.00	380.00	300.00	58.00	38.00	25.00	.70	.45
J75	30¢ carmine	....	....	....	140.00	95.00	70.00	1.25	.85
J76	50¢ carmine	....	....	....	165.00	115.00	80.00	.40	.30
J77	$1 scarlet	(6) 325.00	260.00	210.00	35.00	22.00	17.00	.20	.15
J78	$5 scarlet	(6) 425.00	340.00	275.00	46.50	30.50	22.50	.20	.15
	1931 Rotary Press Printing Perf. 11 x 10-1/2								
J79-86	**1/2¢-50¢, 8 varieties, complete**		....	....	**20.25**	**16.25**	**11.50**	**1.50**	**1.15**
J79	1/2¢ dull carmine	25.00	20.00	14.00	1.15	.95	.65	.20	.15
J80	1¢ dull carmine	2.25	1.80	1.25	.25	.20	.15	.20	.15
J81	2¢ dull carmine	2.25	1.80	1.25	.25	.20	.15	.20	.15
J82	3¢ dull carmine	3.10	2.50	1.75	.30	.25	.20	.20	.15
J83	5¢ dull carmine	4.25	3.40	2.40	.40	.35	.25	.20	.15
J84	10¢ dull carmine	8.50	6.75	4.75	1.25	1.00	.70	.20	.15
J85	30¢ dull carmine	47.50	38.00	26.50	8.50	6.75	4.75	.20	.15
J86	50¢ dull carmine	60.00	48.00	33.50	9.50	7.50	5.25	.20	.15
	1956 Rotary Press Printing Perf. 10-1/2 x 11								
J87	$1.00 scarlet	260.00	210.00	....	38.50	30.00	....	.20	....

NEVER HINGED: From 1893 to 1965, Unused OG or Unused prices are for stamps with original gum that have been hinged. If you desire Never Hinged stamps, order from the NH listings.

U.S. Postage Due #J88-J104, Offices in China

SCOTT NO.	DESCRIPTION	MINT SHEET	PLATE BLOCK F/NH	PLATE BLOCK F	UNUSED F/NH	UNUSED F	USED F
		1959					
J88-101	**1/2¢-$5, 14 varieties, complete**	....	....	....	**16.50**	**14.50**	**3.25**
J88	1/2¢ carmine rose & black	400.00(100)	210.00	175.00	1.70	1.50	1.40
J89	1¢ carmine rose & black	3.25(100)	.40	.35	.20	.15	.15
J90	2¢ carmine rose & black	4.25(100)	.45	.40	.20	.15	.15
J91	3¢ carmine rose & black	6.25(100)	.50	.45	.20	.15	.15
J92	4¢ carmine rose & black	8.00(100)	.85	.75	.20	.15	.15
J93	5¢ carmine rose & black	9.50(100)	.80	.70	.20	.15	.15
J94	6¢ carmine rose & black	11.50(100)	1.10	1.00	.20	.15	.15
J95	7¢ carmine rose & black	13.50(100)	1.20	1.10	.20	.15	.15
J96	8¢ carmine rose & black	16.00(100)	1.60	1.45	.20	.15	.15
J97	10¢ carmine rose & black	18.50(100)	1.70	1.55	.20	.15	.15
J98	30¢ carmine rose & black	57.50(100)	4.75	4.25	.60	.55	.15
J99	50¢ carmine rose & black	90.00(100)	5.75	5.25	1.00	.90	.15
J100	$1 carmine rose & black	175.00(100)	10.00	9.00	2.15	1.95	.15
J101	$5 carmine rose & black	800.00(100)	47.50	42.50	10.00	9.00	.20
		1978-1985					
J102	11¢ carmine rose & black	22.00(100)	4.00	....	.35	....	.20
J103	13¢ carmine rose & black	25.00(100)	2.60	....	.35	....	.25
J104	17¢ carmine rose & black (1985)	75.00(100)	33.50	....	.45	....	.35

OFFICES IN CHINA

SHANGHAI
2¢
CHINA
1919

K1-16: U.S. Postage 498-518 surcharged

SHANGHAI
2 Cts.
CHINA
1922

K17-18: U.S. Postage 498-528B with local surcharge

SCOTT NO.	DESCRIPTION	UNUSED NH F	UNUSED NH AVG	UNUSED OG F	UNUSED OG AVG	USED F	USED AVG
		1919					
K1	2¢ on 1¢ green	27.50	16.50	17.50	10.00	22.00	13.50
K2	4¢ on 2¢ rose	27.50	16.50	17.50	10.00	22.00	13.50
K3	6¢ on 3¢ violet	52.50	31.50	36.00	22.00	50.00	30.00
K4	8¢ on 4¢ brown	65.00	40.00	41.50	25.00	50.00	30.00
K5	10¢ on 5¢ blue	70.00	40.00	47.50	28.00	55.00	33.00
K6	12¢ on 6¢ red orange	87.50	50.00	58.00	36.00	70.00	42.50
K7	14¢ on 7¢ black	90.00	55.00	60.00	37.00	85.00	52.50
K8	16¢ on 8¢ olive bister	70.00	40.00	47.50	27.50	55.00	33.00
K8a	16¢ on 8¢ olive green	70.00	40.00	45.00	26.00	50.00	30.00
K9	18¢ on 9¢ salmon red	70.00	40.00	47.50	27.50	61.50	35.00
K10	20¢ on 10¢ orange yellow	67.50	41.00	45.00	25.00	55.00	33.00
K11	24¢ on 12¢ brown carmine	75.00	45.00	50.00	30.00	62.50	37.50
K11a	24¢ on 12¢ claret brown	105.00	60.00	72.50	45.00	80.00	47.50
K12	30¢ on 15¢ gray	90.00	55.00	60.00	36.00	77.00	46.00
K13	40¢ on 20¢ deep ultramarine ...	135.00	80.00	90.00	57.50	120.00	70.00
K14	60¢ on 30¢ orange red	120.00	70.00	85.00	52.50	110.00	67.50
K15	$1 on 50¢ light violet	575.00	440.00	400.00	335.00	460.00	310.00
K16	$2 on $1 violet brown	450.00	300.00	325.00	235.00	400.00	280.00
		1922 LOCAL ISSUES					
K17	2¢ on 1¢ green	115.00	80.00	80.00	47.50	75.00	45.00
K18	4¢ on 2¢ carmine	100.00	70.00	71.50	45.00	67.50	50.00

U.S. Official #O1-O34

OFFICIAL STAMPS

O1-O9, O94, O95

O10-O14

O15-O24, O96-O103

O25-O34, O106, O107

Except for the Post Office Department, portraits for the various denominations are the same as on the regular issues of 1870-73

1873 Printed by the Continental Bank Note Co.
Thin hard paper
(OG + 30%)

SCOTT NO.	DESCRIPTION	UNUSED F	UNUSED AVG	USED F	USED AVG
	DEPARTMENT OF AGRICULTURE				
O1	1¢ yellow	82.50	52.00	66.00	40.50
O2	2¢ yellow	64.00	40.50	22.00	16.50
O3	3¢ yellow	60.50	38.00	5.00	3.50
O4	6¢ yellow	71.50	46.00	19.00	12.50
O5	10¢ yellow	137.50	86.50	82.50	55.00
O6	12¢ yellow	194.00	115.00	91.00	57.50
O7	15¢ yellow	143.00	92.00	88.00	57.50
O8	24¢ yellow	165.00	103.50	77.00	48.50
O9	30¢ yellow	212.50	121.00	115.50	75.00
	EXECUTIVE DEPARTMENT				
O10	1¢ carmine	330.00	213.00	198.00	126.50
O11	2¢ carmine	214.50	138.00	99.00	63.50
O12	3¢ carmine	269.50	172.50	93.50	57.50
O13	6¢ carmine	396.00	241.50	286.00	178.50
O14	10¢ carmine	363.00	241.50	231.00	144.00
	DEPARTMENT OF THE INTERIOR				
O15	1¢ vermillion	21.50	13.00	5.00	3.50
O16	2¢ vermillion	20.00	11.50	3.00	2.50
O17	3¢ vermillion	27.50	17.50	3.50	2.50
O18	6¢ vermillion	21.50	13.00	3.50	2.50
O19	10¢ vermillion	21.50	13.00	7.50	5.00
O20	12¢ vermillion	32.50	19.00	5.50	3.50
O21	15¢ vermillion	49.50	30.00	12.00	7.70
O22	24¢ vermillion	39.50	22.50	8.50	5.50
O23	30¢ vermillion	49.50	30.00	10.50	6.50
O24	90¢ vermillion	110.00	69.00	20.50	13.00
	DEPARTMENT OF JUSTICE				
O25	1¢ purple	60.50	38.00	41.00	27.50
O26	2¢ purple	93.50	60.00	38.50	25.50
O27	3¢ purple	93.50	60.00	10.50	6.50
O28	6¢ purple	88.00	57.50	14.50	9.50
O29	10¢ purple	103.00	57.50	35.50	23.00
O30	12¢ purple	77.00	49.00	19.00	12.50
O31	15¢ purple	165.00	103.50	66.00	43.50
O32	24¢ purple	434.50	276.00	154.00	98.00
O33	30¢ purple	396.00	241.50	99.00	63.50
O34	90¢ purple	577.50	345.00	220.00	144.00

OFFICIAL STAMPS: From 1873 to 1879, Congress authorized the use of Official Stamps to prepay postage on government mail. Separate issues were produced for each department so that mailing costs could be assigned to that department's budget. Penalty envelopes replaced Official Stamps on May 1, 1879.

U.S. Official #O35-O71

O35-O45

O47-O56, O108

O57-O67

O68-O71
Seward

NAVY DEPARTMENT
(OG + 30%)

SCOTT NO.	DESCRIPTION	UNUSED F	UNUSED AVG	USED F	USED AVG
O35	1¢ ultramarine	42.50	29.00	14.50	9.50
O36	2¢ ultramarine	36.50	24.50	12.50	8.50
O37	3¢ ultramarine	36.50	23.00	5.50	3.50
O38	6¢ ultramarine	36.50	23.00	8.50	5.00
O39	7¢ ultramarine	220.00	155.50	79.00	52.00
O40	10¢ ultramarine	48.50	32.00	15.50	9.50
O41	12¢ ultramarine	60.50	40.50	13.00	8.50
O42	15¢ ultramarine	97.00	57.50	33.50	22.50
O43	24¢ ultramarine	97.00	57.50	38.50	25.50
O44	30¢ ultramarine	85.00	52.00	19.00	11.50
O45	90¢ ultramarine	434.50	287.50	97.00	63.50

POST OFFICE DEPARTMENT

SCOTT NO.	DESCRIPTION	UNUSED F	UNUSED AVG	USED F	USED AVG
O47	1¢ black	8.50	5.50	4.50	3.50
O48	2¢ black	10.50	7.00	3.50	2.50
O49	3¢ black	3.00	2.00	1.50	1.00
O50	6¢ black	8.50	5.00	2.50	1.50
O51	10¢ black	42.50	26.50	22.50	14.00
O52	12¢ black	24.50	15.00	7.00	4.50
O53	15¢ black	27.50	16.50	11.00	6.50
O54	24¢ black	36.50	23.00	13.00	8.50
O55	30¢ black	36.50	23.00	12.50	8.50
O56	90¢ black	54.50	34.50	16.00	10.50

DEPARTMENT OF STATE

SCOTT NO.	DESCRIPTION	UNUSED F	UNUSED AVG	USED F	USED AVG
O57	1¢ dark green	60.50	40.50	17.00	9.50
O58	2¢ dark green	121.00	80.50	33.50	20.00
O59	3¢ bright green	49.50	31.50	11.50	7.00
O60	6¢ bright green	46.50	29.00	12.50	7.50
O61	7¢ dark green	88.00	52.00	24.00	14.00
O62	10¢ dark green	79.00	44.50	19.50	11.50
O63	12¢ dark green	104.50	63.50	43.00	26.50
O64	15¢ dark green	110.00	75.00	31.00	20.00
O65	24¢ dark green	225.50	144.00	85.00	52.00
O66	30¢ dark green	225.50	144.00	66.00	40.50
O67	90¢ dark green	451.00	299.00	143.00	92.00
O68	$2 green & black	598.50	348.00	374.00	241.50
O69	$5 green & black	4537.50	2875.00	2178.00	1552.50
O70	$10 green & black	3025.00	1736.50	1485.00	1035.00
O71	$20 green & black	2359.50	1391.50	1149.50	664.50

O72-O82, O109-O113

O83-O93, O114-O120

ORIGINAL GUM: Prior to 1893, the Unused price is for stamps either without gum or with partial gum. If you require original gum, add the OG percentage. Never Hinged quality is scarce on these issues—please write for specific quotations if NH is required.

U.S. Official #O72-O120

SCOTT NO.	DESCRIPTION	UNUSED F	UNUSED AVG	USED F	USED AVG
	TREASURY DEPARTMENT (OG + 30%)				
O72	1¢ brown	21.50	12.50	2.50	1.50
O73	2¢ brown	24.50	15.00	2.50	1.50
O74	3¢ brown	15.50	9.50	2.00	1.00
O75	6¢ brown	22.50	13.00	2.00	1.50
O76	7¢ brown	54.50	34.50	15.00	9.00
O77	10¢ brown	60.50	37.00	6.50	4.00
O78	12¢ brown	60.50	37.00	4.50	3.00
O79	15¢ brown	48.50	28.50	6.50	4.00
O80	24¢ brown	242.00	161.00	51.50	31.50
O81	30¢ brown	82.00	52.00	7.00	4.00
O82	90¢ brown	88.00	52.00	7.00	4.00
	WAR DEPARTMENT				
O83	1¢ rose	82.50	57.50	5.50	3.50
O84	2¢ rose	71.50	46.00	8.00	4.50
O85	3¢ rose	68.50	40.50	2.50	1.50
O86	6¢ rose	272.50	161.00	5.00	3.00
O87	7¢ rose	71.50	46.00	39.50	25.50
O88	10¢ rose	24.50	15.00	6.00	4.00
O89	12¢ rose	73.00	46.00	5.50	3.50
O90	15¢ rose	21.50	12.50	4.00	2.50
O91	24¢ rose	21.50	12.50	4.50	2.50
O92	30¢ rose	24.50	15.00	4.00	2.50
O93	90¢ rose	51.50	34.50	15.50	9.00
	1879 Printed by American Bank Note Co. Soft Porous Paper DEPARTMENT OF AGRICULTURE				
O94	1¢ yellow	1485.00	949.00	....	....
O95	3¢ yellow	212.00	126.50	39.50	25.50
	DEPARTMENT OF INTERIOR				
O96	1¢ vermillion	151.50	92.00	88.00	57.50
O97	2¢ vermillion	3.00	2.00	1.50	1.00
O98	3¢ vermillion	2.50	1.50	1.00	1.00
O99	6¢ vermillion	3.50	2.00	2.50	1.50
O100	10¢ vermillion	36.50	23.00	27.50	21.00
O101	12¢ vermillion	79.00	44.50	38.50	26.50
O102	15¢ vermillion	181.50	109.50	85.00	52.00
O103	24¢ vermillion	1815.00	1207.50	....	....
	DEPARTMENT OF JUSTICE				
O106	3¢ bluish purple	57.50	32.00	25.50	16.50
O107	6¢ bluish purple	121.00	70.00	82.50	55.50
	POST OFFICE DEPARTMENT				
O108	3¢ black	10.50	6.00	2.50	1.50
	TREASURY DEPARTMENT				
O109	3¢ brown	30.50	17.50	5.00	3.00
O110	6¢ brown	57.50	34.50	20.00	12.50
O111	10¢ brown	73.00	46.00	20.50	13.00
O112	30¢ brown	797.50	517.50	157.50	92.00
O113	90¢ brown	817.00	489.00	157.50	92.00
	WAR DEPARTMENT				
O114	1¢ rose red	2.50	1.50	1.50	1.50
O115	2¢ rose red	4.00	2.50	1.50	1.50
O116	3¢ rose red	3.50	2.00	1.00	1.00
O117	6¢ rose red	4.00	2.50	1.00	1.00
O118	10¢ rose red	24.50	15.00	16.50	11.50
O119	12¢ rose red	18.50	11.50	4.50	3.00
O120	30¢ rose red	54.50	32.50	33.00	23.00

U.S. Official #O121-O148

O121-O126

O127-O136

O138-O143

SCOTT NO.	DESCRIPTION	UNUSED O.G. F	UNUSED O.G. AVG	UNUSED F	UNUSED AVG	USED F	USED AVG
	1910-11 Double Line Watermark						
O121	2¢ black	14.85	10.00	10.00	5.50	2.00	1.00
O122	50¢ dark green	154.00	105.00	115.00	60.50	36.50	23.00
O123	$1 ultramarine	148.50	100.00	109.00	57.50	11.00	6.50
	Single Line Watermark						
O124	1¢ dark violet	7.15	4.25	4.50	3.00	1.50	1.00
O125	2¢ black	44.00	28.00	33.50	21.00	5.00	3.00
O126	10¢ carmine	13.75	8.50	9.50	5.50	1.50	1.00

SCOTT NO.	DESCRIPTION	FIRST DAY COVERS SING	FIRST DAY COVERS PL. BLK.	MINT SHEET	PLATE BLOCK	UN-USED	USED
	1983-1989						
O127	1¢ Great Seal	1.75	4.25	8.25(100)	.45	.20	.20
O128	4¢ Great Seal	1.75	4.25	8.25(100)	.55	.20	.25
O129	13¢ Great Seal	1.75	4.25	24.25(100)	1.50	.30	.85
O129A	14¢ Great Seal (1985)	1.75	....	30.25(100)	....	.35	.60
O130	17¢ Great Seal	1.75	4.25	33.00(100)	1.95	.40	.45
O132	$1.00 Great Seal	5.75	14.25	195.00(100)	9.35	2.05	1.75
O133	$5.00 Great Seal	16.50	41.25	875.00(100)	41.25	9.90	6.00
			PL. # ST. 3		**PLATE # STRIP 3**		
O135	20¢ Great Seal, coil	1.75	80.00	....	19.50	1.05	1.25
O136	22¢ Seal, coil (1985)	1.75	....	....	....	.95	1.00
	1985 Non-Denominated Issues						
			PL. BLK.		**PL. BLK.**		
O138	(14¢) Great Seal, postcard D	1.75	30.00	325.00(100)	37.50	3.25	2.00
O138A	15¢ Great Seal, coil (1988)	1.75	....	....	....	.40	.75
O138B	20¢ Great Seal, coil (1988)	1.75	....	....	....	.50	.90
			PL. # ST. 3		**PLATE # STRIP 3**		
O139	(22¢) Great Seal,"D" coil (1985)	1.75	80.00	....	60.00	3.00	2.00
O140	(25¢) Great Seal "E", coil (1988)	1.75	....	....	....	1.10	1.75
O141	25¢ Great Seal, coil (1988)	1.75	....	....	....	.60	.40
O143	1¢ Great Seal (1989)	1.75	....	8.25(100)	....	.20	.25

O144 O145 O146 O146A O147 O148

SCOTT NO.	DESCRIPTION	FIRST DAY COVERS SING	FIRST DAY COVERS PL. BLK.	MINT SHEET	PLATE BLOCK	UN-USED	USED
	1991-94						
O144	(29¢) Great Seal "F", coil	1.75	....	....	....	1.75	.60
O145	29¢ Great Seal, coil	1.75	....	....	....	.95	.50
O146	4¢ Great Seal	1.75	....	9.00(100)	....	.20	.35
O146A	10¢ Great Seal	1.75	....	27.50(100)	....	.30	.50
O147	19¢ Great Seal	1.75	....	41.25(100)	....	.45	.50
O148	23¢ Great Seal	1.75	....	49.50(100)	....	.55	.50

U.S. Official #O151-O156

O151

O152

O153 O154 O155 O156

SCOTT NO.	DESCRIPTION	FIRST DAY COVERS SING	FIRST DAY COVERS PL. BLK.	MINT SHEET	PLATE BLOCK	UN-USED	USED
	1993						
O151	$1 Great Seal	1.75	....	195.00(100)	....	2.10	2.00
	1994						
O152	(32¢) Great Seal "G", coil	2.75	....	....	....	.70	....
	1995						
O153	32¢ Official Mail	1.95	....	....	....	.70	....
O154	1¢ Official Mail	1.95	....	8.25(100)	....	.20	....
O155	20¢ Official Mail	1.95	....	42.00(100)	....	.45	....
O156	23¢ Official Mail	1.95	....	49.50(100)	....	.55	....

Parcel Post; Parcel Post Due; Special Handling

SCOTT NO.	DESCRIPTION	UNUSED NH F	UNUSED NH AVG	UNUSED OG F	UNUSED OG AVG	USED F	USED AVG

PARCEL POST STAMPS

Q1-Q12 Various Designs

PARCEL POST DUE STAMPS

JQ1-JQ5

SPECIAL HANDLING STAMPS

QE1-QE4

1912-13 Parcel Post—All Printed in Carmine Rose

SCOTT NO.	DESCRIPTION	UNUSED NH F	UNUSED NH AVG	UNUSED OG F	UNUSED OG AVG	USED F	USED AVG
Q1	1¢ P.O. Clerk	5.00	3.40	3.00	2.00	1.20	.80
Q2	2¢ City Carrier	6.00	4.25	3.50	2.35	1.00	.65
Q3	3¢ Railway Clerk	10.50	7.25	6.00	4.25	5.00	3.40
Q4	4¢ Rural Carrier	28.50	20.00	17.50	12.00	2.50	1.75
Q5	5¢ Mail Train	28.00	19.50	17.50	12.00	2.00	1.40
Q6	10¢ Steamship	52.50	36.00	28.50	19.50	2.25	1.50
Q7	15¢ Auto Service	62.50	43.50	40.00	27.50	9.50	6.50
Q8	20¢ Airplane	135.00	95.00	90.00	62.50	17.50	11.50
Q9	25¢ Manufacturing	70.00	47.50	42.00	28.50	6.00	4.00
Q10	50¢ Dairying	260.00	175.00	175.00	137.00	35.00	24.50
Q11	75¢ Harvesting	85.00	60.00	55.00	37.50	25.00	17.50
Q12	$1 Fruit Growing	415.00	280.00	280.00	190.00	20.00	13.50

1912 Parcel Post Due

SCOTT NO.	DESCRIPTION	UNUSED NH F	UNUSED NH AVG	UNUSED OG F	UNUSED OG AVG	USED F	USED AVG
JQ1	1¢ dark green	12.00	8.50	7.25	5.00	3.50	2.40
JQ2	2¢ dark green	95.00	65.00	60.00	42.50	15.00	10.50
JQ3	5¢ dark green	14.50	9.75	9.00	6.50	3.50	2.50
JQ4	10¢ dark green	190.00	125.00	135.00	95.00	35.00	24.50
JQ5	25¢ dark green	110.00	75.00	77.50	42.50	4.00	2.75

1925-29 Special Handling

SCOTT NO.	DESCRIPTION	UNUSED NH F	UNUSED NH AVG	UNUSED OG F	UNUSED OG AVG	USED F	USED AVG
QE1	10¢ yellow green	1.75	1.25	1.25	.85	1.00	.70
QE2	15¢ yellow green	2.00	1.35	1.40	.95	1.00	.70
QE3	20¢ yellow green	3.00	2.10	1.75	1.20	1.95	1.35
QE4	25¢ yellow green	22.50	15.50	16.50	11.50	8.00	5.00
QE4a	25¢ deep green	31.50	22.00	21.50	14.75	5.00	3.40

PLATE BLOCKS

SCOTT NO.	UNUSED N.H. F	UNUSED N.H. AVG	UNUSED O.G. F	UNUSED O.G. AVG
O121	(6)250.00	180.00	200.00	130.00
O124	(6)135.00	95.00	105.00	75.00
O126	(6)295.00	200.00	225.00	150.00
Q1	(6)85.00	60.00	65.00	45.00
Q2	(6)100.00	67.50	70.00	47.50
Q3	(6)175.00	115.00	135.00	95.00
Q4	(6)850.00	575.00	650.00	435.00
Q5	(6)850.00	575.00	635.00	420.00
JQ1	(6)600.00	375.00	450.00	275.00
JQ3	(6)700.00	450.00	475.00	295.00
QE1	(6)30.00	18.50	24.00	16.50
QE2	(6)40.00	24.50	32.00	22.50
QE3	(6)45.00	28.50	35.00	25.00
QE4	(6)275.00	190.00	220.00	150.00
QE4a	(6)360.00	245.00	285.00	195.00

POSTAL NOTE STAMPS

PN1-P18

All values printed in black

SCOTT NO.	DESCRIPTION	UNUSED F/NH	UNUSED F/OG	USED F
PN1-18	1¢-90¢, 18 varieties, complete	35.00	24.50	2.50

U.S. Postal Stationery #U1-U73

ENVELOPES

U1-U18
Washington

U19-W25, U28, U29
Franklin

U26-U33
Washington

1853-55

SCOTT NO.	DESCRIPTION	UNUSED ENTIRE	UNUSED CUT SQ.	USED CUT SQ.
U1	3¢ red on white, die 1	1320.00	225.00	18.50
U2	3¢ red on buff, die 1	840.00	96.00	9.00
U3	3¢ red on white, die 2	3300.00	900.00	45.00
U4	3¢ red on buff, die 2	1680.00	270.00	18.00
U5	3¢ red on white, die 3	......	......	510.00
U6	3¢ red on buff, die 3	1080.00	180.00	36.50
U7	3¢ red on white, die 4	6000.00	720.00	120.00
U8	3¢ red on buff, die 4	5400.00	1750.00	120.00
U9	3¢ red on white, die 5	72.00	21.50	2.15
U10	3c red on buff, die 5	60.00	16.50	2.25
U11	6¢ red on white	270.00	180.00	80.00
U12	6¢ red on buff	240.00	120.00	72.00
U13	6¢ green on white	360.00	240.00	120.00
U14	6¢ green on buff	390.00	240.00	108.00
U15	10¢ green on white, die 1	330.00	180.00	78.00
U16	10¢ green on buff, die 1	228.00	78.00	60.00
U17	10¢ green on white, die 2	420.00	240.00	132.00
U18	10¢ green on buff, die 2	198.00	120.00	75.00

1860-61

SCOTT NO.	DESCRIPTION	UNUSED ENTIRE	UNUSED CUT SQ.	USED CUT SQ.
U19	1¢ blue on buff, die 1	66.00	33.00	16.50
W20	1¢ blue on buff, die 1	120.00	72.00	60.00
W21	1¢ blue on manila, die 1	96.00	51.00	51.00
W22	1¢ blue on orange, die 1	2850.00	1650.00	......
U23	1¢ blue on orange, die 2	600.00	540.00	540.00
U24	1¢ blue on buff, die 3	420.00	270.00	120.00
U26	3¢ red on white	42.00	30.00	15.00
U27	3¢ red on buff	33.00	21.50	13.20
U28	3¢ & 1¢ red & blue on white	660.00	480.00	330.00
U29	3¢ & 1¢ red & blue on buff	600.00	360.00	300.00
U30	6¢ red on white	3600.00	3000.00	1800.00
U31	6¢ red on buff	4200.00	2100.00	1200.00
U32	10¢ green on white	....	1200.00	360.00
U33	10¢ green on buff	3000.00	1075.00	325.00

U34-U39

U40-U45

Washington

1861

SCOTT NO.	DESCRIPTION	UNUSED ENTIRE	UNUSED CUT SQ.	USED CUT SQ.
U34	3¢ pink on white	48.00	21.00	6.00
U35	3¢ pink on buff	48.00	18.00	6.00
U36	3¢ pink on blue (letter sheet)	240.00	82.50	60.00
U37	3¢ pink on orange	4250.00	2650.00	......
U38	6¢ pink on white	180.00	120.00	110.00
U39	6¢ pink on buff	130.00	78.00	78.00
U40	10¢ yellow green on white	72.00	36.00	33.00
U41	10¢ yellow green on buff	72.00	36.00	27.00
U42	12¢ brown & red on buff	540.00	240.00	198.00
U43	20¢ blue & red on buff ...	600.00	225.00	198.00
U44	24¢ green & red on buff	780.00	240.00	198.00
U45	40¢ red & black on buff .	960.00	360.00	360.00

U46-U49

U50-W57

Jackson

1863-64

SCOTT NO.	DESCRIPTION	UNUSED ENTIRE	UNUSED CUT SQ.	USED CUT SQ.
U46	2¢ black on buff, die 1	65.00	36.00	18.00
W47	2¢ black on dark manila, die 1	78.00	48.50	42.00
U48	2¢ black on buff, die 2	4200.00	2100.00	......
U49	2¢ black on orange, die 2 ..	2700.00	1300.00	......
U50	2¢ black on buff, die 3	30.00	10.50	9.60
W51	2¢ black on buff, die 3	315.00	200.00	204.00
U52	2¢ black on orange, die 3	29.50	13.20	8.40
W53	2¢ black on dark manila, die 3	132.00	36.00	24.00
U54	2¢ black on buff, die 4	27.00	13.25	10.80
W55	2¢ black on buff, die 4	150.00	90.00	60.00
U56	2¢ black on orange, die 4	19.25	12.00	8.40
W57	2¢ black on light manila, die 4	29.50	13.80	12.00

U58-U65

U66-U73

Washington

1864-65

SCOTT NO.	DESCRIPTION	UNUSED ENTIRE	UNUSED CUT SQ.	USED CUT SQ.
U58	3¢ pink on white	10.80	7.20	1.80
U59	3¢ pink on buff	11.50	5.40	1.20
U60	3¢ brown on white	96.00	48.00	27.00
U61	3¢ brown on buff	96.00	48.00	27.00
U62	6¢ pink on white	100.00	60.00	33.00
U63	6¢ pink on buff	100.00	39.00	27.00
U64	6¢ purple on white	84.00	48.00	27.00
U65	6¢ purple on buff	69.00	42.50	24.00
U66	9¢ lemon on buff	690.00	420.00	300.00
U67	9¢ orange on buff	240.00	108.00	102.00
U68	12¢ brown on buff	690.00	420.00	270.00
U69	12¢ red brown on buff	165.00	108.00	70.00
U70	18¢ red on buff	270.00	108.00	108.00
U71	24c blue on buff	270.00	108.00	102.00
U72	30¢ green on buff	225.00	72.00	72.00
U73	40¢ rose on buff	330.00	84.00	300.00

U74-W77, U108-U121
Franklin

U78-W81, U122-W158
Jackson

U82-U84, U159-U169
Washington

U.S. Postal Stationery #U74-U179

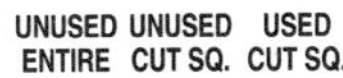

U172-U180
Taylor

U85-U87, U181-U184
Lincoln

U88, U185, U186
Stanton

U89-U92, U187-U194
Jefferson

U93-U95, U195-U197
Clay

U96-U98, U198-U200
Webster

U99-U101, U201-U203
Scott

U102-U104, U204-U210, U336-U341
Hamilton

U105-U107, U211-U217, U342-U347
Perry

1870-71 REAY ISSUE

SCOTT NO.	DESCRIPTION	UNUSED ENTIRE	UNUSED CUT SQ.	USED CUT SQ.
U74	1¢ blue on white	66.00	36.00	30.00
U74a	1¢ ultramarine on white	100.00	72.00	36.00
U75	1¢ blue on amber	66.00	36.00	30.00
U75a	1¢ ultramarine on amber	75.00	60.00	36.00
U76	1¢ blue on orange	30.00	15.50	12.00
W77	1¢ blue on manila	84.00	48.00	36.00
U78	2¢ brown on white	66.00	42.00	15.50
U79	2¢ brown on amber	36.00	18.00	9.00
U80	2¢ brown on orange	15.00	9.60	6.00
W81	2¢ brown on manila	54.00	27.00	21.00
U82	3¢ green on white	13.20	7.20	.90
U83	3¢ green on amber	13.20	5.50	2.00
U84	3¢ green on cream	18.00	9.00	3.60
U85	6¢ dark red on white	33.00	18.50	15.00
U86	6¢ dark red on amber	48.00	25.00	17.00
U87	6¢ dark red on cream	54.00	30.00	17.00
U88	7¢ vermillon on amber	66.00	48.00	240.00
U89	10¢ olive black on white	540.00	420.00	420.00
U90	10¢ olive black on amber	540.00	420.00	420.00
U91	10¢ brown on white	90.00	60.00	90.00
U92	10¢ brown on amber	108.00	84.00	60.00
U93	12¢ plum on white	285.00	135.00	84.00
U94	12¢ plum on amber	270.00	130.00	120.00
U95	12¢ plum on cream	450.00	270.00	270.00
U96	15¢ red orange on white	198.00	72.00	90.00
U97	15¢ red orange on amber	480.00	198.00	240.00
U98	15¢ red orange on cream	420.00	300.00	300.00
U99	24¢ purple on white	210.00	150.00	108.00
U100	24¢ purple on amber	465.00	210.00	360.00
U101	24¢ purple on cream	468.00	210.00	360.00
U102	30¢ black on white	375.00	90.00	120.00
U103	30¢ black on amber	690.00	210.00	300.00
U104	30¢ black on cream	540.00	270.00	480.00
U105	90¢ carmine on white	240.00	165.00	270.00
U106	90¢ carmine on amber	975.00	360.00	480.00
U107	90¢ carmine on cream	1100.00	420.00	600.00

1874-86 PLIMPTON ISSUE

SCOTT NO.	DESCRIPTION	UNUSED ENTIRE	UNUSED CUT SQ.	USED CUT SQ.
U108	1¢ dark blue on white, die 1	132.00	108.00	48.00
U109	1¢ dark blue on amber, die 1	170.00	120.00	78.00
U110	1¢ dark blue on cream, die 1	......	900.00	......
U111	1¢ dark blue on orange, die 1	33.00	20.00	18.00
U111a	1¢ light blue on orange, die 1	25.00	24.00	12.00
W112	1¢ dark blue on manila, die 1	78.00	48.00	36.00
U113	1¢ light blue on white, die 2	2.40	1.50	.90
U113a	1¢ dark blue on white, die 2	19.50	8.40	6.00
U114	1¢ light blue on amber, die 2	6.00	4.50	4.80
U115	1¢ blue on cream, die 2	7.20	4.50	4.80
U116	1¢ light blue on orange, die 2	.75	.60	.50
U116a	1¢ dark blue on orange, die 2	8.40	2.00	1.25
U117	1¢ light blue on blue, die 2	8.40	6.00	4.80
U118	1¢ light blue on fawn, die 2	7.20	6.00	4.80
U119	1¢ light blue on manila, die 2	7.20	6.00	3.60
W120	1¢ light blue on manila, die 2	2.40	1.50	1.20
W120a	1¢ dark blue on manila, die 2	9.50	4.80	3.00
U121	1¢ blue on amber manila, die 2	16.00	12.00	10.80
U122	2¢ brown on white, die 1	120.00	100.00	48.00
U123	2¢ brown on amber, die 1	90.00	60.00	48.00
U124	2¢ brown on cream, die 1	......	900.00	......
W126	2¢ brown on manila, die 1	120.00	108.00	48.00
W127	2¢ vermillon on manila, die 1	2100.00	1500.00	360.00
U128	2¢ brown on white, die 2	96.00	48.00	30.00
U129	2¢ brown on amber, die 2	96.00	78.00	42.00
W131	2¢ brown on manila, die 2	24.00	16.50	16.50
U132	2¢ brown on white, die 3	96.00	72.00	30.00
U133	2¢ brown on amber, die 3	260.00	240.00	72.00
U134	2¢ brown on white, die 4	960.00	840.00	150.00
U135	2¢ brown on amber, die 4	720.00	525.00	150.00
U136	2¢ brown on orange, die 4	720.00	36.00	36.00
W137	2¢ brown on manila, die 4	78.00	66.00	36.00
U139	2¢ brown on white, die 5	60.00	48.00	42.00
U140	2¢ brown on amber, die 5	108.00	84.00	72.00
W141	2¢ brown on manila, die 5	48.00	42.00	30.00
U142	2¢ vermillon on white, die 5	7.20	6.00	2.50
U143	2¢ vermillon on amber, die 5	7.20	6.00	2.50
U144	2¢ vermillon on cream, die 5	15.60	12.00	6.00
U146	2¢ vermillon on blue, die 5	240.00	150.00	38.50
U147	2¢ vermillon on fawn, die 5	13.00	7.20	4.80
W148	2¢ vermillon on manila, die 5	7.00	3.75	3.60
U149	2¢ vermillon on white, die 6	72.00	48.00	30.00
U150	2¢ vermillon on amber, die 6	36.00	24.00	16.50
U151	2¢ vermillon on blue, die 6	12.00	9.60	8.40
U152	2¢ vermillon on fawn, die 6	13.80	10.50	4.20
U153	2¢ vermillon on white, die 7	84.00	54.00	24.00
U154	2¢ vermillon on amber, die 7	450.00	360.00	96.00
W155	2¢ vermillon on manila, die 7	48.00	20.00	9.90
U156	2¢ vermillon on white, die 8	825.00	725.00	150.00
W158	2¢ vermillon on manila,die 8	168.00	90.00	72.00
U159	3¢ green on white, die 1	38.50	24.00	6.00
U160	3¢ green on amber, die 1	48.00	28.80	10.80
U161	3¢ green on cream, die 1	54.00	42.00	12.00
U163	3¢ green on white, die 2	2.40	1.20	.40
U164	3¢ green on amber, die 2	2.75	1.50	.60
U165	3¢ green on cream, die 2	10.80	6.60	6.00
U166	3¢ green on blue,die 2	12.00	7.25	4.80
U167	3¢ green on fawn, die 2	8.40	4.80	3.00
U168	3¢ green on white, die 3	2200.00	600.00	48.00
U169	3¢ green on amber, die 3	360.00	240.00	120.00
U172	5¢ blue on white, die 1	11.75	9.00	8.25
U173	5¢ blue on amber, die 1	12.60	8.60	9.00
U174	5¢ blue on cream, die 1	150.00	108.00	54.00
U175	5¢ blue on blue, die 1	21.60	16.50	16.50
U176	5¢ blue on fawn, die 1	225.00	132.00	72.00
U177	5¢ blue on white, die 2	11.40	6.50	6.50
U178	5¢ blue on amber, die 2	13.00	7.20	7.00
U179	5¢ blue on blue, die 2	18.00	13.00	8.40

U.S. Postal Stationery #U180-U276

SCOTT NO.	DESCRIPTION	UNUSED ENTIRE	UNUSED CUT SQ.	USED CUT SQ.
U180	5¢ blue on fawn, die 2	135.00	96.00	60.00
U181	6¢ red on white	10.80	6.00	6.00
U182	6¢ red on amber	18.00	6.00	6.00
U183	6¢ red on cream	24.00	19.80	12.00
U184	6¢ red on fawn	30.00	21.00	12.00
U185	7¢ vermilion on white	......	650.00	......
U186	7¢ vermilion on amber	150.00	105.00	78.00
U187	10¢ brown on white,die 1	60.00	36.00	21.00
U188	10¢ brown on amber, die 1	108.00	72.00	30.00
U189	10¢ chocolate on white, die 2	9.60	6.00	3.50
U190	10¢ chocolate on amber, die 2	9.60	7.20	6.50
U191	10¢ brown on buff, die 2 .	11.10	9.30	7.20
U192	10¢ brown on blue, die 2 .	12.00	10.80	7.20
U193	10¢ brown on manila, die 2	14.40	11.40	9.00
U194	10¢ brown/amber manila, die 2	16.00	13.50	7.20
U195	12¢ plum on white	228.00	190.00	108.00
U196	12¢ plum on amber	330.00	178.00	178.00
U197	12¢ plum on cream	1020.00	240.00	210.00
U198	15¢ orange on white	150.00	42.00	36.00
U199	15¢ orange on amber	240.00	150.00	120.00
U200	15¢ orange on cream	1200.00	480.00	480.00
U201	24¢ purple on white	300.00	190.00	150.00
U202	24¢ purple on amber	300.00	190.00	150.00
U203	24¢ purple on cream	990.00	210.00	150.00
U204	30¢ black on white	90.00	72.00	36.00
U205	30¢ black on amber	150.00	78.00	72.00
U206	30¢ black on cream	1050.00	590.00	540.00
U207	30¢ black on oriental buff	168.00	120.00	102.00
U208	30¢ black on blue	150.00	120.00	102.00
U209	30¢ black on manila	150.00	108.00	102.00
U210	30¢ black on amber manila	168.00	150.00	102.00
U211	90¢ carmine on white	168.00	140.00	102.00
U212	90¢ carmine on amber	318.00	210.00	275.00
U213	90¢ carmine on cream	2700.00	1700.00	......
U214	90¢ carmine on oriental buff	325.00	240.00	328.00
U215	90¢ carmine on blue	325.00	210.00	300.00
U216	90¢ carmine on manila	275.00	150.00	300.00
U217	90¢ carmine on amber manila	275.00	150.00	240.00

U218-U221, U582
Pony Express Rider and Train

U222-U226
Garfield

Die 1. Single thick line under "POSTAGE"
Die 2. Two thin lines under "POSTAGE"

1876 CENTENNIAL ISSUE

SCOTT NO.	DESCRIPTION	UNUSED ENTIRE	UNUSED CUT SQ.	USED CUT SQ.
U218	3¢ red on white, die 1	84.00	72.00	30.00
U219	3¢ green on white, die 1	72.00	54.00	19.00
U221	3¢ green on white, die 2	96.00	72.00	21.00

1882-86

SCOTT NO.	DESCRIPTION	UNUSED ENTIRE	UNUSED CUT SQ.	USED CUT SQ.
U222	5¢ brown on white	7.20	3.90	2.40
U223	5¢ brown on amber	8.40	4.50	2.75
U224	5¢ brown on oriental buff ...	150.00	120.00	90.00
U225	5¢ brown on blue	105.00	60.00	45.00
U226	5¢ brown on fawn	360.00	270.00	......

NOTE: For details on die or silmilar appearing varieties of envelopes, please refer to the Scott Specialized Catalogue.

U227-U230

U231-U429, U260-W292
Washington

U250-U259
Jackson

1883 OCTOBER

SCOTT NO.	DESCRIPTION	UNUSED ENTIRE	UNUSED CUT SQ.	USED CUT SQ.
U227	2¢ red on white	7.20	3.90	1.80
U228	2¢ red on amber	8.40	4.80	2.10
U229	2¢ red on blue	9.30	6.90	4.80
U230	2¢ red on fawn	9.60	5.00	3.00

1883 NOVEMBER
Four Wavy Lines in Oval

SCOTT NO.	DESCRIPTION	UNUSED ENTIRE	UNUSED CUT SQ.	USED CUT SQ.
U231	2¢ red on white	7.20	3.00	1.50
U232	2¢ red on amber	7.20	3.00	1.50
U233	2¢ red on blue	12.00	7.25	4.80
U234	2¢ red on fawn	7.20	12.00	5.40
W235	2¢ red on manila	21.00	21.00	4.20

1884 JUNE

SCOTT NO.	DESCRIPTION	UNUSED ENTIRE	UNUSED CUT SQ.	USED CUT SQ.
U236	2¢ red on white	9.60	6.00	3.60
U237	2¢ red on amber	15.50	10.20	8.40
U238	2¢ red on blue	23.00	15.00	8.40
U239	2¢ red on fawn	14.40	10.80	7.80
U240	2¢ red on white(3-1/2links)	81.00	48.00	36.00
U241	2¢ red on amber(3-1/2links)	1200.00	750.00	360.00
U243	2¢ red on white .. (2 links)	108.00	72.00	48.00
U244	2¢ red on amber .. (2links)	198.00	150.00	84.00
U245	2¢ red on blue ..... (2links)	540.00	330.00	135.00
U246	2¢ red on fawn .... (2links)	420.00	330.00	135.00
U247	2¢ red on white (round O)	1620.00	1080.00	300.00
U249	2¢ red on fawn (round O)	990.00	600.00	360.00

1883-86

SCOTT NO.	DESCRIPTION	UNUSED ENTIRE	UNUSED CUT SQ.	USED CUT SQ.
U250	4¢ green on white, die 1 ..	5.60	3.00	3.00
U251	4¢ green on amber,die 1 .	6.00	4.20	3.00
U252	4¢ green on buff, die 1	10.80	7.20	7.20
U253	4¢ green on blue, die 1 ...	10.80	7.20	6.00
U254	4¢ green on manila, die 1	12.00	8.50	6.00
U255	4¢ green/amber manila,die 1	30.00	21.00	10.80
U256	4¢ green on white, die 2 ..	12.00	4.80	3.60
U257	4¢ green on amber, die 2	15.75	9.50	6.00
U258	4¢ green on manila, die 2	13.75	9.00	6.00
U259	4¢ green/amber manila,die 2	13.25	9.00	6.00

1884 MAY

SCOTT NO.	DESCRIPTION	UNUSED ENTIRE	UNUSED CUT SQ.	USED CUT SQ.
U260	2¢ brown on white	16.80	13.25	4.95
U261	2¢ brown on amber	14.50	12.00	6.00
U262	2¢ brown on blue	16.80	12.75	9.75
U263	2¢ brown on fawn	14.50	10.80	9.00
W264	2¢ brown on manila	20.50	12.75	9.75

1884 JUNE

SCOTT NO.	DESCRIPTION	UNUSED ENTIRE	UNUSED CUT SQ.	USED CUT SQ.
U265	2¢ brown on white	19.75	13.25	4.95
U266	2¢ brown on amber	77.00	60.00	45.00
U267	2¢ brown on blue	14.50	10.75	6.00
U268	2¢ brown on fawn	15.75	10.75	9.75
W269	2¢ brown on manila	33.00	21.00	14.50
U270	2¢ brown on white (2links)	120.00	90.00	48.00
U271	2¢ brown on amber .... (2links)	360.00	240.00	120.00
U273	2¢ brown on white .... (round O)	168.00	150.00	78.00
U274	2¢ brown on amber (round O)	192.00	168.00	78.00
U276	2¢ brown on fawn . (round O)	1175.00	810.00	540.00

U.S. Postal Stationery #U277-U351

SCOTT NO.	DESCRIPTION	UNUSED ENTIRE	UNUSED CUT SQ.	USED CUT SQ.
	1884-86			
	Two Wavy Lines in Oval			
U277	2¢ brown on white, die 1 .	.85	.50	.25
U277a	2¢ brown lake on white, die 1	24.00	21.00	14.50
U278	2¢ brown on amber, die 1	1.50	.75	.50
U279	2¢ brown on buff, die 1 ...	4.50	3.00	1.80
U280	2¢ brown on blue, die 1 ...	3.25	2.50	1.50
U281	2¢ brown on fawn, die 1 ..	3.90	3.00	1.80
U282	2¢ brown on manila, die 1	13.80	10.25	3.60
W283	2¢ brown on manila, die 1	7.95	5.50	5.40
U284	2¢ brown/amber manila, die 1	10.25	6.00	6.00
U285	2¢ red on white, die 1	960.00	720.00	......
U286	2¢ red on blue, die 1	390.00	300.00	......
W287	2¢ red on manila, die 1 ...	170.00	120.00	......
U288	2¢ brown on white, die 2 .	540.00	210.00	42.00
U289	2¢ brown on amber, die 2	18.00	13.25	12.00
U290	2¢ brown on blue, die 2 ...	1020.00	900.00	180.00
U291	2¢ brown on fawn, die 2 ..	33.50	24.00	19.25
W292	2¢ brown on manila, die 2	33.50	25.25	19.25

U293
Grant

SCOTT NO.	DESCRIPTION	UNUSED ENTIRE	UNUSED CUT SQ.	USED CUT SQ.
	1886			
U293	2¢ green on white	27.00	22.50	10.25
	Entire letter sheet	54.00	52.50	19.50

U294-U304, U352-W357
Franklin

U305-U323, U358-U370
Washington

U324-U329
Jackson

U330-U335, U377-U378
Grant

SCOTT NO.	DESCRIPTION	UNUSED ENTIRE	UNUSED CUT SQ.	USED CUT SQ.
	1887-94			
U294	1¢ blue on white	.90	.60	.25
U295	1¢ dark blue on white	11.40	7.80	3.00
U296	1¢ blue on amber	4.80	3.00	1.50
U297	1¢ dark blue on amber	60.00	48.00	27.00
U300	1¢ blue on manila	1.15	.75	.30
W301	1¢ blue on manila	.90	.50	.30
U302	1¢ dark blue on manila	33.00	24.00	10.75
W303	1¢ dark blue on manila	27.00	14.50	12.00
U304	1¢ blue on amber manila	8.40	4.80	3.25
U305	2¢ green on white, die 1 ..	21.00	19.75	8.50
U306	2¢ green on amber, die 1	30.00	24.00	14.50
U307	2¢ green on buff, die 1	108.00	78.00	36.00
U308	2¢ green on blue, die 1 ...	......	3600.00	900.00
U309	2¢ green on manila, die 1 ..	7200.00	2400.00	600.00
U311	2¢ green on white, die 2 ..	.60	.30	.15
U312	2¢ green on amber, die 2 .	.65	.45	.15
U313	2¢ green on buff, die 2	1.00	.60	.25
U314	2¢ green on blue, die 2 ...	1.05	.60	.25
U315	2¢ green on manila, die 2	2.25	1.75	.60
W316	2¢ green on manila, die 2	5.00	1.80	1.25
U317	2¢ green/amber manila, die 2	4.80	2.00	1.80
U318	2¢ green on white, die 3 ..	168.00	120.00	15.00
U319	2¢ green on amber, die 3	192.00	168.00	24.00
U320	2¢ green on buff, die 3	228.00	180.00	48.00
U321	2¢ green on blue, die 3 ...	240.00	198.00	71.50
U322	2¢ green on manila, die 3	225.00	180.00	90.00
U323	2¢ green/amber manila, die 3	480.00	420.00	108.00
U324	4¢ carmine on white	3.60	1.75	1.30
U325	4¢ carmine on amber	4.80	2.40	2.10
U326	4¢ carmine on oriental buff	9.60	6.00	3.00
U327	4¢ carmine on blue	6.75	4.75	4.25
U328	4¢ carmine on manila	9.00	6.85	6.00
U329	4¢ carmine on amber/manila	8.40	4.80	3.00
U330	5¢ blue on white, die 1	6.00	3.60	3.00
U331	5¢ blue on amber, die 1 ..	7.25	3.60	2.25
U332	5¢ blue on oriental buff, die 1	9.90	3.90	3.60
U333	5¢ blue on blue, die 1	10.80	6.00	4.80
U334	5¢ blue on white, die 2	15.00	10.75	5.40
U335	5¢ blue on amber, die 2 ..	16.75	10.75	6.00
U336	30¢ red brown on white ...	54.00	42.00	48.00
U337	30¢ red brown on amber .	60.00	54.00	72.00
U338	30¢ red brown/oriental buff	54.00	42.00	54.00
U339	30¢ red brown on blue	48.00	42.00	48.00
U340	30¢ red brown on manila	54.00	48.00	48.00
U341	30¢ red brown/amber manila	60.00	54.00	36.00
U342	90¢ purple on white	84.00	66.00	84.00
U343	90¢ purple on amber	108.00	84.00	84.00
U344	90¢ purple on oriental buff	108.00	84.00	90.00
U345	90¢ purple on blue	120.00	84.00	96.00
U346	90¢ purple on manila	120.00	84.00	96.00
U347	90¢ purple on amber manila	135.00	90.00	96.00

U348-U351
Columbus and Liberty, with Shield and Eagle

SCOTT NO.	DESCRIPTION	UNUSED ENTIRE	UNUSED CUT SQ.	USED CUT SQ.
	1893 COLUMBIAN ISSUE			
U348	1¢ deep blue on white	3.00	2.50	1.25
U349	2¢ violet on white	2.75	2.50	.60
U350	5¢ chocolate on white	15.00	9.60	9.00
U351	10¢ slate brown on white	65.00	48.00	36.00

U.S. Postal Stationery #U352-U423

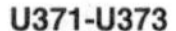

U371-U373 U374-W376
Lincoln

1899

SCOTT NO.	DESCRIPTION	UNUSED ENTIRE	UNUSED CUT SQ.	USED CUT SQ.
U352	1¢ green on white	1.25	.60	.25
U353	1¢ green on amber	7.75	4.80	1.80
U354	1¢ green on oriental buff	14.00	10.80	3.00
U355	1¢ green on blue	11.40	9.60	8.40
U356	1¢ green on manila	6.00	2.10	1.10
W357	1¢ green on manila	8.40	2.10	1.10
U358	2¢ carmine on white, die 1	8.00	2.60	1.10
U359	2¢ carmine on amber, die 1	24.00	18.00	12.00
U360	2¢ carmine on buff, die 1	25.00	16.00	9.60
U361	2¢ carmine on blue, die 1	72.00	60.00	30.00
U362	2¢ carmine on white,die 2	.60	.30	.25
U363	2¢ carmine on amber. die 2	2.75	1.10	.20
U364	2¢ carmine on buff, die 2	2.75	1.10	.20
U365	2¢ carmine on blue, die 2	3.60	1.30	.60
W366	2¢ carmine on manila, die 2	11.40	5.40	3.00
U367	2¢ carmine on white, die 3	9.00	4.80	2.10
U368	2¢ carmine on amber, die 3	14.40	9.00	6.25
U369	2¢ carmine on buff, die 3	31.50	24.00	15.00
U370	2¢ carmine on blue, die 3	24.00	12.00	8.40
U371	4¢ brown on white, die 1	27.00	14.50	13.25
U372	4¢ brown on amber, die 1	33.00	18.00	13.25
U373	4¢ brown on white, die 2	5250.00	4800.00	450.00
U374	4¢ brown on white, die 3	19.25	9.60	7.25
U375	4¢ brown on amber, die 3	51.00	43.00	15.00
W376	4¢ brown on manila, die 3	21.75	16.80	9.00
U377	5¢ blue on white, die 3	15.00	10.25	10.25
U378	5¢ blue on amber, die 3	20.50	15.00	11.50

U379-W384
Franklin

U385-W389, U395-W399
Washington

U390-W392
Grant

U393, U394
Lincoln

1903

SCOTT NO.	DESCRIPTION	UNUSED ENTIRE	UNUSED CUT SQ.	USED CUT SQ.
U379	1¢ green on white	.90	.60	.15
U380	1¢ green on amber	18.00	12.00	4.80
U381	1¢ green on oriental buff	16.80	12.00	2.30
U382	1¢ green on blue	13.80	13.80	2.40
U383	1¢ green on manila	3.70	3.70	1.20
W384	1¢ green on manila	1.70	1.20	.50
U385	2¢ carmine on white	.60	.45	.20
U386	2¢ carmine on amber	3.60	1.80	1.20
U387	2¢ carmine on oriental buff	2.40	1.80	.35
U388	2¢ carmine on blue	3.60	1.50	.60
W389	2¢ carmine on manila	19.25	16.75	8.50
U390	4¢ chocolate on white	24.00	21.00	12.00
U391	4¢ chocolate on amber	24.00	19.25	12.00
W392	4¢ chocolate on manila	24.00	19.25	10.80
U393	5¢ blue on white	24.00	19.25	10.80
U394	5¢ blue on amber	24.00	19.25	12.00

1904 RECUT DIE

SCOTT NO.	DESCRIPTION	UNUSED ENTIRE	UNUSED CUT SQ.	USED CUT SQ.
U395	2¢ carmine on white	1.15	.50	.25
U396	2¢ carmine on amber	10.80	7.80	.60
U397	2¢ carmine on oriental buff	7.80	6.00	1.50
U398	2¢ carmine on blue	4.80	3.60	3.00
W399	2¢ carmine on manila	21.00	12.60	7.80

U400-W405, U416, U417
Franklin

U406-W415, U418, U419
Washington

1907-16

SCOTT NO.	DESCRIPTION	UNUSED ENTIRE	UNUSED CUT SQ.	USED CUT SQ.
U400	1¢ green on white	.45	.30	.15
U401	1¢ green on amber	1.20	.80	.50
U402	1¢ green on oriental buff	4.80	3.60	1.20
U403	1¢ green on blue	6.00	4.80	1.80
U404	1¢ green on manila	4.50	3.30	2.10
W405	1¢ green on manila	.60	.50	.30
U406	2¢ brown red on white	1.70	.85	.20
U407	2¢ brown red on amber	7.50	6.00	3.00
U408	2¢ brown red on oriental buff	10.80	7.50	1.80
U409	2¢ brown red on blue	6.00	4.20	2.10
W410	2¢ brown red on manila	60.00	48.00	36.00
U411	2¢ carmine on white	.60	.25	.20
U412	2¢ carmine on amber	.95	.25	.15
U413	2¢ carmine on oriental buff	.60	.50	.25
U414	2¢ carmine on blue	1.25	.50	.15
W415	2¢ carmine on manila	7.80	4.80	2.40
U416	4¢ black on white	9.00	3.60	1.20
U417	4¢ black on amber	10.80	6.00	3.00
U418	5¢ blue on white	12.00	7.20	2.85
U419	5¢ blue on amber	18.00	14.50	13.25

U420-U428, U440-U442
Franklin

U429-U439, U443-U445, U481-U485, U529-U531
Washington

1916-32

SCOTT NO.	DESCRIPTION	UNUSED ENTIRE	UNUSED CUT SQ.	USED CUT SQ.
U420	1¢ green on white	.25	.10	.10
U421	1¢ green on amber	.55	.45	.35
U422	1¢ green on oriental buff	2.30	1.80	1.20
U423	1¢ green on blue	.70	.50	.10

U.S. Postal Stationery #U424-U482

SCOTT NO.	DESCRIPTION	UNUSED ENTIRE	UNUSED CUT SQ.	USED CUT SQ.
U424	1¢ green on manila	9.00	7.20	4.80
W425	1¢ green on manila	.20	.15	.10
U426	1¢ green on brown (glazed)	42.00	30.00	19.25
W427	1¢ green on brown (glazed)	90.00	78.00	......
U428	1¢ green on brown (unglazed)	12.00	9.00	9.00
U429	2¢ carmine on white	.25	.10	.10
U430	2¢ carmine on amber	.35	.15	.10
U431	2¢ carmine on oriental buff	3.60	2.10	.55
U432	2¢ carmine on blue	.50	.15	.10
W433	2¢ carmine on manila	.30	.25	.20
W434	2¢ carmine on brown (glazed)	120.00	96.00	72.00
W435	2¢ carmine/brown (unglazed)	120.00	96.00	72.00
U436	3¢ dark violet on white	.75	.60	.20
U436f	3¢ purple on white (1932)	.45	.15	.10
U436h	3¢ carmine on white (error)	39.00	33.00	33.00
U437	3¢ dark violet on amber ..	6.00	2.70	1.20
U437a	3¢ purple on amber (1932)	.65	.20	.10
U437g	3¢ carmine on amber (error)	480.00	420.00	300.00
U437h	3¢ black on amber (error)	240.00	198.00	......
U438	3¢ dark violet on buff	30.00	24.00	1.80
U439	3¢ dark violet on blue	10.80	7.20	1.70
U439a	3¢ purple on blue (1932) .	.80	.25	.10
U439g	3¢ carmine on blue (error)	480.00	390.00	390.00
U440	4¢ black on white	2.40	1.20	.60
U441	4¢ black on amber	4.80	3.00	.90
U442	4¢ black on blue	5.40	3.00	1.95
U443	5¢ blue on white	6.00	3.20	1.10
U444	5¢ blue on amber	5.50	3.60	1.70
U445	5¢ blue on blue	8.40	4.20	1.20

1920-21 SURCHARGED

Type 1

SCOTT NO.	DESCRIPTION	UNUSED ENTIRE	UNUSED CUT SQ.	USED CUT SQ.
U446	2¢ on 3¢ dark violet on white .... (U436)	15.00	12.00	11.75

Type 2 **Type 3**

Surcharge on Envelopes of 1916-21 Type 2

SCOTT NO.	DESCRIPTION	UNUSED ENTIRE	UNUSED CUT SQ.	USED CUT SQ.
U447	2¢ on 3¢ dark violet on white, rose .... (U436)	9.00	8.40	6.60
U448	2¢ on 3¢ dark violet on white .... (U436)	3.00	2.40	2.10
U449	2¢ on 3¢ dark violet on amber .... (U437)	7.20	6.00	6.00
U450	2¢ on 3¢ dark violet on oriental buff .... (U438)	21.40	14.80	14.80
U451	2¢ on 3¢ dark violet on blue .... (U439)	13.80	12.00	12.00

Surcharge on Envelopes of 1874-1921
Type 3 bars 2mm apart

SCOTT NO.	DESCRIPTION	UNUSED ENTIRE	UNUSED CUT SQ.	USED CUT SQ.
U454	2¢ on 2¢ carmine on white .... (U429)	132.00	110.00	......
U455	2¢ on 2¢ carmine on amber .... (U430)	1200.00	1140.00	......
U456	2¢ on 2¢ carmine on oriental buff .. (U431)	270.00	210.00	......
U457	2¢ on 2¢ carmine on blue .... (U432)	300.00	240.00	......
U458	2¢ on 3¢ dark violet on white .... (U436)	.75	.55	.40
U459	2¢ on 3¢ dark violet on amber .... (U437)	4.50	3.00	1.20
U460	2¢ on 3¢ dark violet on oriental buff .. (U438)	3.95	3.15	1.20
U461	2¢ on 3¢ dark violet on blue .... (U439)	6.60	4.80	1.20
U462	2¢ on 4¢ chocolate on white .... (U390)	480.00	420.00	210.00
U463	2¢ on 4¢ chocolate on amber .... (U391)	450.00	390.00	120.00
U464	2¢ on 5¢ blue on white (U443)	1200.00	1050.00	......

Type 4 like Type 3, but bars 1-1/2 mm apart

SCOTT NO.	DESCRIPTION	UNUSED ENTIRE	UNUSED CUT SQ.	USED CUT SQ.
U465	2¢ on 1¢ green on white .... (U420)	1200.00	1050.00	......
U466A	2¢ on 2¢ carmine on white .... (U429)	330.00	270.00	......
U467	2¢ on 3¢ green on white .... (U163)	360.00	300.00	......
U468	2¢ on 3¢ dark violet on white .... (U436)	.95	.75	.45
U469	2¢ on 3¢ dark violet on amber .... (U437)	4.80	3.60	2.50
U470	2¢ on 3¢ dark violet on oriental buff .. (U438)	7.20	5.10	3.00
U471	2¢ on 3¢ dark violet on blue .... (U439)	9.60	4.80	1.50
U472	2¢ on 4¢ chocolate on white .... (U390)	27.00	11.25	9.60
U473	2¢ on 4¢ chocolate on amber .... (U391)	21.00	15.60	10.80
U474	2¢ on 1¢ on 3¢ dark violet on white .... (U436)	300.00	270.00	......
U475	2¢ on 1¢ on 3¢ dark violet on amber .... (U437)	300.00	270.00	......

Type 5 **Type 6** **Type 7**

Surcharge on Envelope of 1916-21 Type 5

SCOTT NO.	DESCRIPTION	UNUSED ENTIRE	UNUSED CUT SQ.	USED CUT SQ.
U476	2¢ on 3¢ dark violet on amber .... (U437)	150.00	120.00	......

Surcharge on Envelope of 1916-21 Type 6

SCOTT NO.	DESCRIPTION	UNUSED ENTIRE	UNUSED CUT SQ.	USED CUT SQ.
U477	2¢ on 3¢ dark violet on white .... (U436)	150.00	120.00	......
U478	2¢ on 3¢ dark violet on amber .... (U437)	240.00	210.00	......

Surcharge on Envelope of 1916-21 Type 7

SCOTT NO.	DESCRIPTION	UNUSED ENTIRE	UNUSED CUT SQ.	USED CUT SQ.
U479	2¢ on 3¢ dark violet on white (black) .... (U436)	420.00	360.00	......

1925

SCOTT NO.	DESCRIPTION	UNUSED ENTIRE	UNUSED CUT SQ.	USED CUT SQ.
U481	1-1/2¢ brown on white	.60	.15	.10
U481b	1-1/2¢ purple on white (error)	120.00	105.00	......
U482	1-1/2¢ brown on amber ...	1.75	1.10	.25

U.S. Postal Stationery #U483-U522a

SCOTT NO.	DESCRIPTION	UNUSED ENTIRE	UNUSED CUT SQ.	USED CUT SQ.
U483	1-1/2¢ brown on blue	2.10	1.80	.90
U484	1-1/2¢ brown on manila ..	13.25	7.25	3.75
W485	1-1/2¢ brown on manila ..	1.25	.90	.25

Type 8 Type 9

Surcharge on Envelopes of 1887 Type 8

SCOTT NO.	DESCRIPTION	UNUSED ENTIRE	UNUSED CUT SQ.	USED CUT SQ.
U486	1-1/2¢ on 2¢ green on white .... (U311)	720.00	720.00	......
U487	1-1/2¢ on 2¢ green on amber .... (U312)	960.00	840.00	......

Surcharge on Envelopes of 1899 Type 8

SCOTT NO.	DESCRIPTION	UNUSED ENTIRE	UNUSED CUT SQ.	USED CUT SQ.
U488	1-1/2¢ on 1¢ green on white .... (U352)	780.00	660.00	......
U489	1-1/2¢ on 1¢ green on amber .... (U353)	132.00	96.00	90.00

Surcharge on Envelopes of 1907-10 Type 8

SCOTT NO.	DESCRIPTION	UNUSED ENTIRE	UNUSED CUT SQ.	USED CUT SQ.
U490	1-1/2¢ on 1¢ green on white .... (U400)	6.00	4.20	4.20
U491	1-1/2¢ on 1¢ green on amber .... (U401)	13.25	9.00	3.00
U492	1-1/2¢ on 1¢ green on oriental buff (U402a)	240.00	235.00	105.00
U493	1-1/2¢ on 1¢ green on blue .... (U403c)	120.00	102.00	78.00
U494	1-1/2¢ on 1¢ green on manila .... (U404)	300.00	250.00	110.00

Surcharge on Envelopes of 1916-21 Type 8

SCOTT NO.	DESCRIPTION	UNUSED ENTIRE	UNUSED CUT SQ.	USED CUT SQ.
U495	1-1/2¢ on 1¢ green on white .... (U420)	.60	.30	.20
U496	1-1/2¢ on 1¢ green on amber .... (U421)	22.80	16.75	16.75
U497	1-1/2¢ on 1¢ green on oriental buff .. (U422)	5.40	3.25	2.50
U498	1-1/2¢ on 1¢ green on blue .... (U423)	2.25	1.25	.90
U499	1-1/2¢ on 1¢ green on manila .... (U424)	19.20	12.00	8.40
U500	1-1/2¢ on 1¢ green on brown (unglazed) .... (U428)	72.00	66.00	42.00
U501	1-1/2¢ on 1¢ green on brown (glazed) (U426)	72.00	66.00	36.00
U502	1-1/2¢ on 2¢ carmine on white .... (U429)	360.00	300.00	......
U503	1-1/2¢ on 2¢ carmine on oriental buff (U431) ..	360.00	230.00	......
U504	1-1/2¢ on 2¢ carmine on blue .... (U432)	360.00	300.00	......

Surcharge on Envelopes of 1925 Type 8

SCOTT NO.	DESCRIPTION	UNUSED ENTIRE	UNUSED CUT SQ.	USED CUT SQ.
U505	1-1/2¢ on 1-1/2¢ brown on white .... (U481)	600.00	480.00	.....
U506	1-1/2¢ on 1-1/2¢ brown on blue .... (U483)	480.00	420.00	.....

Surcharge on Envelopes of 1899 Type 9

SCOTT NO.	DESCRIPTION	UNUSED ENTIRE	UNUSED CUT SQ.	USED CUT SQ.
U508	1-1/2¢ on 1¢ green on amber .... (U353)	72.00	60.00	.....

Surcharge on Envelopes of 1903 Type 9

SCOTT NO.	DESCRIPTION	UNUSED ENTIRE	UNUSED CUT SQ.	USED CUT SQ.
U508A	1-1/2¢ on 1¢ green on white .... (U379)	1800.00	1500.00	.....
U509	1-1/2¢ on 1¢ green on amber .... (U380)	27.00	12.00	12.00
U509B	1-1/2¢ on 1¢ green on oriental buff .. (U381)	78.00	60.00	55.00

Surcharge on Envelopes of 1907-10 Type 9

SCOTT NO.	DESCRIPTION	UNUSED ENTIRE	UNUSED CUT SQ.	USED CUT SQ.
U510	1-1/2¢ on 1¢ green on white .... (U400)	3.90	2.50	1.50
U511	1-1/2¢ on 1¢ green on amber .... (U401)	240.00	210.00	110.00
U512	1-1/2¢ on 1¢ green on oriental buff .. (U402)	10.75	6.60	4.75
U513	1-1/2¢ on 1¢ green on blue .... (U403)	8.25	5.50	3.00
U514	1-1/2¢ on 1¢ green on manila .... (U404)	36.00	21.00	12.00
U515	1-1/2¢ on 1¢ green on white .... (U420)	.65	.35	.25
U516	1-1/2¢ on 1¢ green on amber .... (U421)	60.00	48.00	36.00
U517	1-1/2¢ on 1¢ green on oriental buff .. (U422)	6.00	4.80	1.50
U518	1-1/2¢ on 1¢ green on blue .... (U423)	6.00	4.80	1.50
U519	1-1/2¢ on 1¢ green on manila .... (U424)	24.00	15.00	13.25
U520	1-1/2¢ on 2¢ carmine on white .... (U429)	240.00	210.00	.....
U521	1-1/2¢ on 1¢ green on white, magenta surcharged .... (U420)	5.40	4.80	4.20

U522 U523-U528

U522: Die 1, "E" of "POSTAGE" has center bar shorter than top bar.

U522a: Die 2, "E" of "POSTAGE" has center and top bars same length.

U525: Die 1 "S" of "POSTAGE" even with "T".

U525a: Die 2 "S" of "POSTAGE" higher than "T".

1926 SESQUICENTENNIAL EXPOSITION

SCOTT NO.	DESCRIPTION	UNUSED ENTIRE	UNUSED CUT SQ.	USED CUT SQ.
U522	2¢ carmine on white, die 1	3.00	1.80	.60
U522a	2¢ carmine on white, die 2	14.50	10.25	7.25

U.S. Postal Stationery #U523-U555

SCOTT NO.	DESCRIPTION	UNUSED ENTIRE	UNUSED CUT SQ.	USED CUT SQ.
	1932 WASHINGTON BICENTENNIAL			
U523	1¢ olive green on white ...	3.00	2.10	1.25
U524	1-1/2¢ chocolate on white	4.50	4.20	1.80
U525	2¢ carmine on white, die 1	.75	.50	.10
U525a	2¢ carmine on white, die 2	135.00	110.00	18.00
U526	3¢ violet on white	5.50	4.25	.45
U527	4¢ black on white	35.00	30.00	18.00
U528	5¢ dark blue on white	7.00	6.00	3.90
	1932 Designs of 1916-32			
U529	6¢ orange on white	10.00	5.75	3.30
U530	6¢ orange on amber	17.50	13.20	9.60
U531	6¢ orange on blue	16.80	13.25	9.75

U532, U536 *Franklin* U533, U534 U535 *Washington*

SCOTT NO.	DESCRIPTION	FIRST DAY COVER	UNUSED ENTIRE	USED CUT SQ.
	1950			
U532	1¢ green	2.00	7.00	2.10
U533	2¢ carmine	2.00	1.25	.15
U534	3¢ dark violet	2.00	.50	.15
	1952			
U535	1-1/2¢ brown	....	5.75	4.00

U537, U538, U552, U556 U539, U540, U545, U553

Surcharge on Envelopes of 1916-32, 1950, 1965, 1971

SCOTT NO.	DESCRIPTION	FIRST DAY COVER	UNUSED ENTIRE	USED CUT SQ.
	1958			
U536	4¢ red violet	1.75	1.00	.15
U537	2¢&2¢(4¢) carmine ... (U429)	......	4.00	2.00
U538	2¢&2¢(4¢) carmine ... (U533)	......	1.00	.20
U539	3¢&1¢(4¢) purple, die1 (U436a)	......	18.50	13.80
U539a	3¢&1¢(4¢) purple, die 7(U436e)	......	16.50	12.00
U539b	3¢&1¢(4¢) purple,die 9 (U436f)	......	36.00	21.00
U540	3¢&1¢(4¢) dark violet (U534)	......	.70	.15

U541 *Franklin* U542 *Washington* U544 *Lincoln*

U543 U546

SCOTT NO.	DESCRIPTION	FIRST DAY COVER	UNUSED ENTIRE	USED CUT SQ.
	1960			
U541	1-1/4¢ turquoise	1.75	.85	.60
U542	2-1/2¢ dull blue	1.75	1.00	.60
U543	4¢ Pony Express	2.00	.70	.35
	1962			
U544	5¢ dark blue	1.75	.95	.25
	Surcharge on Envelope of 1958			
U545	4¢+1¢ red violet ...... (U536)	......	1.80	.60
	1964			
U546	5¢ N.Y. World's Fair	1.75	.75	.45

U547, U548, U548A, U556 U549

U550 U551

SCOTT NO.	DESCRIPTION	FIRST DAY COVER	UNUSED ENTIRE	USED CUT SQ.
	1965-69			
U547	1-1/4¢ brown	1.75	.95	.15
U548	1-4/10¢ brown (1968)	1.75	1.00	.15
U548A	1-6/10¢ orange (1969)	1.75	.90	.15
U549	4¢ bright blue	1.75	.95	.15
U550	5¢ bright purple	1.75	.90	.15
U551	6¢ light green (1968)	1.75	.85	.15
	1968			
	1958 Type Surcharges on Envelopes of 1965			
U552	4¢ & 2¢ (6¢) blue .... (U549)	9.00	4.75	2.25
U553	5¢ & 1¢ (6¢) purple . (U550)	9.00	4.00	2.50

U554 U555

SCOTT NO.	DESCRIPTION	FIRST DAY COVER	UNUSED ENTIRE	USED CUT SQ.
	1970			
U554	6¢ Moby Dick	1.75	.60	.20
	1971			
U555	6¢ Conference on Youth	1.75	.90	.20

U.S. Postal Stationery #U556-U575

U557

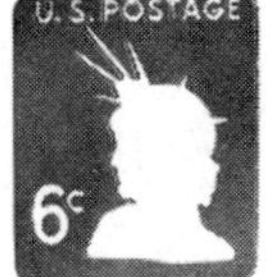

U561, U562 (on U551, U555)

SCOTT NO.	DESCRIPTION	FIRST DAY COVER	UNUSED ENTIRE	USED CUT SQ
U556	1-7/10¢ deep lilac	1.75	.40	.15
U557	8¢ ultramarine	1.75	.50	.15

U561 & U562 Surcharge

U563

SCOTT NO.	DESCRIPTION	FIRST DAY COVER	UNUSED ENTIRE	USED CUT SQ
U561	6¢ & (2¢) (8¢) green (on U551)	4.00	1.25	.40
U562	6¢ & (2¢) (8¢) blue .. (on U555)	4.00	3.00	1.10
U563	8¢ Bowling	1.75	.70	.15

U564

U565

SCOTT NO.	DESCRIPTION	FIRST DAY COVER	UNUSED ENTIRE	USED CUT SQ
U564	8¢ Conference on Aging	1.75	.70	.15

1972

SCOTT NO.	DESCRIPTION	FIRST DAY COVER	UNUSED ENTIRE	USED CUT SQ
U565	8¢ Transpo '72	1.75	.80	.15

U567

U568

1973

SCOTT NO.	DESCRIPTION	FIRST DAY COVER	UNUSED ENTIRE	USED CUT SQ
U566	8¢ & 2¢ ultramarine .. (on U557)	3.00	.55	.15
U567	10¢ emerald	1.75	.45	.15

U569

1974

SCOTT NO.	DESCRIPTION	FIRST DAY COVER	UNUSED ENTIRE	USED CUT SQ
U568	1-8/10¢ blue green	1.75	.35	.15
U569	10¢ Tennis Centenary	2.50	.60	.15

CUT SQUARES: From 1947 to date, Unused Envelope Cut Squares can be supplied at the Unused Entire Price.

U571

U572

U573

U574

U575

1975-76 BICENTENNIAL ERA

SCOTT NO.	DESCRIPTION	FIRST DAY COVER	UNUSED ENTIRE	USED CUT SQ
U571	10¢ Seafaring	1.75	.55	.20
U572	13¢ Homemaker (1976)	1.75	.55	.20
U573	13¢ Farmer (1976)	1.75	.55	.20
U574	13¢ Doctor (1976)	1.75	.55	.20
U575	13¢ Craftsman (1976) ...	1.75	.55	.20

U.S. Postal Stationery #U576-U594

U576

U577

U578

U579

U580

U581

1975

SCOTT NO.	DESCRIPTION	FIRST DAY COVER	UNUSED ENTIRE	USED CUT SQ
U576	13¢ orange brown	1.75	.50	.15

1976-78

SCOTT NO.	DESCRIPTION	FIRST DAY COVER	UNUSED ENTIRE	USED CUT SQ
U577	2¢ red	1.75	.35	.15
U578	2.1¢ green (1977)	1.75	.35	.15
U579	2.7¢ green (1978)	1.75	.40	.15
U580	(15¢) "A" orange (1978)	1.75	.60	.20
U581	15¢ red & white (1978)	1.75	.60	.20

1976

SCOTT NO.	DESCRIPTION	FIRST DAY COVER	UNUSED ENTIRE	USED CUT SQ
U582	13¢ Bicentennial (design of U218)	1.75	.55	.20

U581

1977

SCOTT NO.	DESCRIPTION	FIRST DAY COVER	UNUSED ENTIRE	USED CUT SQ
U583	13¢ Golf	8.00	.80	.20

U584

U585

SCOTT NO.	DESCRIPTION	FIRST DAY COVER	UNUSED ENTIRE	USED CUT SQ
U584	13¢ Energy Conservation ..	1.75	.50	.20
U585	13¢ Energy Development ..	1.75	.50	.20

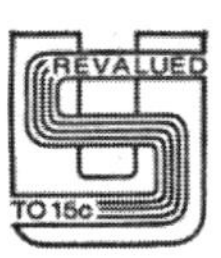

U586, U588

U586

1978

SCOTT NO.	DESCRIPTION	FIRST DAY COVER	UNUSED ENTIRE	USED CUT SQ
U586	15¢ on 16¢ blue & white	1.75	.55	.20

U587

SCOTT NO.	DESCRIPTION	FIRST DAY COVER	UNUSED ENTIRE	USED CUT SQ
U587	15¢ Auto Racing	2.00	.75	.20
U588	15¢ on 13¢ white, orange brown .... (U576)	1.75	.55	.20

U589

U590

1979

SCOTT NO.	DESCRIPTION	FIRST DAY COVER	UNUSED ENTIRE	USED CUT SQ
U589	3.1¢ ultramarine & white	1.75	.30	.15

1980

SCOTT NO.	DESCRIPTION	FIRST DAY COVER	UNUSED ENTIRE	USED CUT SQ
U590	3.5¢ purple	1.75	.30	.15

U591

U592

USA18c

U593

U594

1981-82

SCOTT NO.	DESCRIPTION	FIRST DAY COVER	UNUSED ENTIRE	USED CUT SQ
U591	5.9¢ brown (1982)	1.85	.30	.15
U592	(18¢) "B" violet & white	1.75	.60	.25
U593	18¢ white & dark blue	1.75	.60	.25
U594	(20¢) "C" brown & white	1.75	60	.15

U.S. Postal Stationery #U595-U614

U595

U596

U597

U598

U599

SCOTT NO.	DESCRIPTION	FIRST DAY COVER	UNUSED ENTIRE	USED CUT SQ
	1979			
U595	15¢ Veterinarians	1.75	.60	.20
U596	15¢ Moscow Olympics ..	1.75	.90	.20
	1980			
U597	15¢ Bicycle	1.75	.55	.20
U598	15¢ America's Cup	1.75	.55	.20
U599	15¢ Honeybee	1.75	.55	.20

Remember the Blinded Veteran

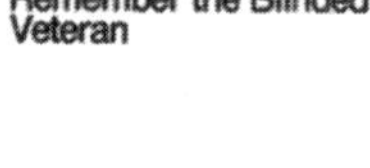

U600

U601

U602

The Purple Heart 1782 1982 USA 20c

U603

U604

Remember Our Paralyzed Veterans USA 20c

U605

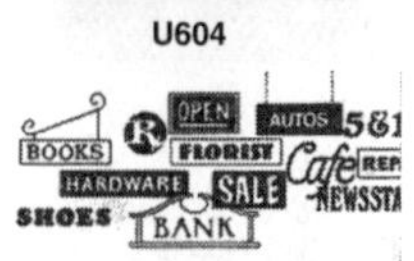

U606

SCOTT NO.	DESCRIPTION	FIRST DAY COVER	UNUSED ENTIRE	USED CUT SQ
	1981			
U600	18¢ Blinded Veterans	1.75	.60	.20
U601	20¢ deep magenta & white	1.75	.60	.15
	1982			
U602	20¢ black, blue & magenta	1.75	.60	.15
U603	20¢ Purple Heart	1.75	.60	.15
	1983			
U604	5.2¢ orange & white	1.75	.30	.15
U605	20¢ Paralyzed Veterans	1.75	.60	.15
	1984			
U606	20¢ Small Business	2.00	.60	.15

U607 U608 U609

SCOTT NO.	DESCRIPTION	FIRST DAY COVER	UNUSED ENTIRE	USED CUT SQ
	1985			
U607	(22¢) "D"	1.75	.60	.15
U608	22¢ Bison	1.75	.60	.15
U609	6¢ Old Ironsides	1.75	.30	.15

U610 U611

U612

SCOTT NO.	DESCRIPTION	FIRST DAY COVER	UNUSED ENTIRE	USED CUT SQ
	1986			
U610	8.5¢ Mayflower	1.75	.30	.15
	1988			
U611	25¢ Stars	1.75	.55	.15
U612	8.4¢ Constellation	1.75	.30	.15

U613 U614

SCOTT NO.	DESCRIPTION	FIRST DAY COVER	UNUSED ENTIRE	USED CUT SQ
U613	25¢ Snowflake	1.75	.55	.30
	1989			
U614	25¢ Stamped Return Envelope	1.75	.55	.30

U.S. Postal Stationery #U615-U627

U615 U616

SCOTT NO.	DESCRIPTION	FIRST DAY COVER	UNUSED ENTIRE	USED CUT SQ
U615	25¢ "USA" and Stars	1.75	.60	.30
U616	25¢ LOVE	1.75	.60	.30

U617, U639

SCOTT NO.	DESCRIPTION	FIRST DAY COVER	UNUSED ENTIRE	USED CUT SQ
U617	25¢ Shuttle Docking Hologram	1.75	.60	.30

U618

1990

SCOTT NO.	DESCRIPTION	FIRST DAY COVER	UNUSED ENTIRE	USED CUT SQ
U618	25¢ Football Hologram	2.75	.65	.30

1991

U619

SCOTT NO.	DESCRIPTION	FIRST DAY COVER	UNUSED ENTIRE	USED CUT SQ
U619	29¢ Star	1.75	.70	.30

U620

SCOTT NO.	DESCRIPTION	FIRST DAY COVER	UNUSED ENTIRE	USED CUT SQ
U620	11.1¢ Birds on Wire	1.75	.25	.20

U621

SCOTT NO.	DESCRIPTION	FIRST DAY COVER	UNUSED ENTIRE	USED CUT SQ
U621	29¢ Love	1.75	.70	.30

U622

U623

SCOTT NO.	DESCRIPTION	FIRST DAY COVER	UNUSED ENTIRE	USED CUT SQ
U622	29¢ Magazine Industry	1.75	.70	.30
U623	29¢ Star	1.75	.70	.30

U624

SCOTT NO.	DESCRIPTION	FIRST DAY COVER	UNUSED ENTIRE	USED CUT SQ
U624	29¢ Country Geese	1.75	.70	.30

U625

1992

SCOTT NO.	DESCRIPTION	FIRST DAY COVER	UNUSED ENTIRE	USED CUT SQ
U625	29¢ Space Station	1.75	.70	.30

Western Americana

U626

SCOTT NO.	DESCRIPTION	FIRST DAY COVER	UNUSED ENTIRE	USED CUT SQ
U626	29¢ Saddle & Blanket	1.75	.70	.30

Protect the Environment

U627

SCOTT NO.	DESCRIPTION	FIRST DAY COVER	UNUSED ENTIRE	USED CUT SQ
U627	29¢ Protect the Environment	1.75	.70	.30

U.S. Postal Stationery #U628-U639

SCOTT NO.	DESCRIPTION	FIRST DAY COVER	UNUSED ENTIRE	USED CUT SQ

U628

U628	19.8¢ Star	1.75	.60	.30

U629

U629	29¢ Americans With Disabilities	1.75	.70	.30

1993

U630

U630	29¢ Kitten	1.75	.70	.30

1994

U631

U631	29¢ Football	1.75	.70	.30

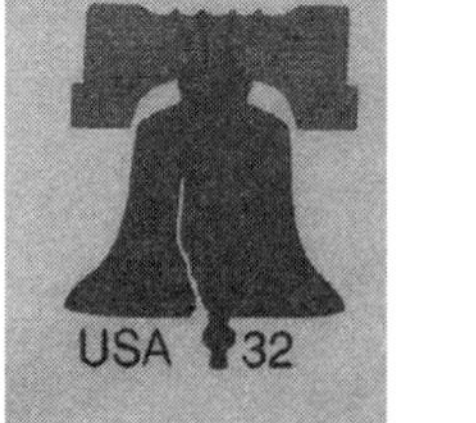

U632, U638

1995

U632	32¢ Liberty Bell	1.95	.75	.35

SCOTT NO.	DESCRIPTION	FIRST DAY COVER	UNUSED ENTIRE	USED CUT SQ

U633

U633	(32¢) "G" Old Glory (Design size 49x38mm)	1.95	.75	.35
U634	(32¢) "G" Old Glory (Design size 53x44mm)	1.95	.75	.35

U635

U635	(5¢) Sheep, Nonprofit	1.95	.30	.35

U636

U636	(10¢) Graphic Eagle, Bulk Rate	1.95	.40	.35

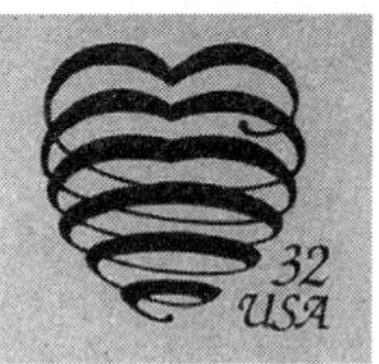

U637

U637	32¢ Spiral Heart	1.95	.75	.35
U638	32¢ Liberty Bell, security ...	1.95	.75	.35
U639	32¢ Space Station	1.95	.75	.35

U.S. Postal Stationery #U640-U641

SCOTT NO.	DESCRIPTION	FIRST DAY COVER	UNUSED ENTIRE	USED CUT SQ

U640

1996

SCOTT NO.	DESCRIPTION	FIRST DAY COVER	UNUSED ENTIRE	USED CUT SQ
U640	32¢ Save our Environment	1.95	.75	.35

U641

SCOTT NO.	DESCRIPTION	FIRST DAY COVER	UNUSED ENTIRE	USED CUT SQ
U641	32¢ Paralympic Games	1.95	.75	.35

U.S. Postal Stationery Air Mail #UC1-UC26

SCOTT NO.	DESCRIPTION	UNUSED ENTIRE	UNUSED CUT SQ.	USED CUT SQ.

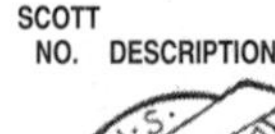

UC1 UC2-UC7

Airplane in Circle

Die 1. Vertical rudder not semi-circular, but slopes to the left. Tail projects into "G".
Die 2. Vertical rudder is semi-circular. Tail only touches "G" Die 2a. "6" is 6-1/2mm. wide.
Die 2b. "6" is 6mm. wide.
Die 2c. "6" is 5-1/2mm. wide.
Die 3. Vertical rudder leans forward. "S" closer to "O" than to "T" of "POSTAGE" and "E" has short center bar.

1929-44

UC1	5¢ blue, die 1	4.50	3.25	2.00
UC2	5¢ blue, die 2	18.00	13.00	6.00
UC3	6¢ orange, die 2a	1.60	1.30	.30
UC3n	6¢, die 2a, no border	2.00	1.30	.30
UC4	6¢, die 2b, with border	55.00	3.00	1.50
UC4n	6¢, die 2b, no border	4.80	3.00	1.50
UC5	6¢, die 2c, no border	1.25	1.00	.40
UC6	6¢ orange on white, die 3 ..	2.00	1.25	.45
UC6n	6¢, die 3, no border	3.00	1.50	.50
UC7	8¢ olive green	18.00	14.50	4.00

Envelopes of 1916-32 surcharged

1945

UC8	6¢ on 2¢ carmine on white .... (U429)	1.75	1.40	.75
UC9	6¢ on 2¢ carmine on white .... (U525)	120.00	90.00	45.00

REVALUED
5¢
P.O. DEPT.

UC14, UC15, UC18, UC26
DC-4 Skymaster

UC14: Die 1. Small projection below rudder is rounded.
UC15: Die 2. Small projection below rudder is sharp pointed.

1946

UC10	5¢ on 6¢, die 2a	. (UC3n)	4.00	3.00	1.75
UC11	5¢ on 6¢, die 2b	. (UC4n)	11.00	10.75	5.50
UC12	5¢ on 6¢, die 2c	(UC5)	1.50	.90	.60
UC13	5¢ on 6¢, die 3	(UC6n)	1.15	.95	.75

SCOTT NO.	DESCRIPTION	FIRST DAY COVER	UNUSED ENTIRE	USED CUT SQ
UC14	5¢ carmine, die 1	2.50	1.10	.25
UC15	5¢ carmine, die 2	......	1.10	.30

UC16
DC-4 Skymaster

UC17
Washington and Franklin, Mail-carrying Vehicles

1947

UC16	10¢ red on blue, Entire "Air Letter" on face, 2-line inscription on back ...	6.00	8.00	6.50
UC16a	Entire, "Air Letter" on face, 4-line inscription on back ...	......	13.50	......
UC16c	Entire "Air Letter" and "Aerogramme" on face, 4-line inscription on back ...	......	60.00	......
UC16d	Entire "Air Letter" and "Aerogramme" on face, 3-line inscription on back ...	......	8.25	......

1947 CIPEX COMMEMORATIVE

UC17	5¢ carmine	3.00	.60	.35

1950 Design of 1946

UC18	6¢ carmine	1.75	.60	.15

REVALUED
6¢
P. O. DEPT.
ENVELOPE of 1946 Surcharged

REVALUED
6¢
P. O. DEPT.
ENVELOPE of 1946-47 Surcharged

1951 (Shaded Numeral)

UC19	6¢ on 5¢, die 1 ... (UC14)		1.35	.60
UC20	6¢ on 5¢, die 2 ... (UC15)		1.25	.60

1952 (Solid Numeral)

UC21	6¢ on 5¢, die 1 .... (UC14)	......	37.50	16.00
UC22	6¢ on 5¢, die 2 .... (UC15)	......	5.75	2.75
UC23	6¢ on 5¢ .... (UC17)	......	1200.00	......

Surcharge on Envelopes of 1934 to 1956

UC25 **UC27-UC31**

1956 FIPEX COMMEMORATIVE

UC25	6¢ red	1.75	1.10	.60

1958 Design of 1946

UC26	7¢ blue	1.75	1.10	.60

1958

SCOTT NO.	DESCRIPTION	FIRST DAY COVER	UNUSED ENTIRE	USED CUT SQ
UC27	6¢ & 1¢ (7¢) orange, die 2a .... (UC3n)	......	240.00	......
UC28	6¢ & 1¢ (7¢), die 2b .... (UC4n)	......	80.00	82.50
UC29	6¢ & 1¢ (7¢) orange, die 2c .... (UC5)	......	48.50	52.50
UC30	6¢ & 1¢ (7¢) carmine . ... (UC18)	......	1.35	.60
UC31	6¢ & 1¢ (7¢) red .... (UC25)	......	1.40	.60

UC32

UC33, UC34

1958-59

SCOTT NO.	DESCRIPTION	FIRST DAY COVER	UNUSED ENTIRE	USED CUT SQ
UC32	10¢ blue & red Entire letter sheet, 2-line inscription on back (1959)	......	7.00	5.25
UC32a	Entire letter sheet, 3 line inscription on back	2.25	12.00	5.25

1958

SCOTT NO.	DESCRIPTION	FIRST DAY COVER	UNUSED ENTIRE	USED CUT SQ
UC33	7¢ blue	1.75	.80	.15

1960

SCOTT NO.	DESCRIPTION	FIRST DAY COVER	UNUSED ENTIRE	USED CUT SQ
UC34	7¢ carmine	1.75	.75	.15

UC35

UC36

1961

SCOTT NO.	DESCRIPTION	FIRST DAY COVER	UNUSED ENTIRE	USED CUT SQ
UC35	11¢ red & blue	3.25	2.50	1.75

1962

SCOTT NO.	DESCRIPTION	FIRST DAY COVER	UNUSED ENTIRE	USED CUT SQ
UC36	8¢ red	1.75	.85	.15

UC37

UC38, UC39

1965

SCOTT NO.	DESCRIPTION	FIRST DAY COVER	UNUSED ENTIRE	USED CUT SQ
UC37	8¢ red	1.75	.60	.15
UC38	11¢ J.F. Kennedy	1.75	4.00	1.10

1967

SCOTT NO.	DESCRIPTION	FIRST DAY COVER	UNUSED ENTIRE	USED CUT SQ
UC39	13¢ J.F. Kennedy	1.75	3.50	.85

UC40

UC41 (on UC37)

1968

SCOTT NO.	DESCRIPTION	FIRST DAY COVER	UNUSED ENTIRE	USED CUT SQ
UC40	10¢ red	1.75	.85	.15
UC41	8¢ & 2¢ (10¢) red	12.00	.95	.20

UC42

SCOTT NO.	DESCRIPTION	FIRST DAY COVER	UNUSED ENTIRE	USED CUT SQ
UC42	13¢ Human Rights Year	1.75	8.00	2.25

AIR MAIL

UC43

1971

SCOTT NO.	DESCRIPTION	FIRST DAY COVER	UNUSED ENTIRE	USED CUT SQ
UC43	11¢ red & blue	1.75	.70	.15

UC44

SCOTT NO.	DESCRIPTION	FIRST DAY COVER	UNUSED ENTIRE	USED CUT SQ
UC44	15¢ gray, red, blue	1.75	1.60	1.00
UC44a	Aerogramme added ...	1.75	1.60	1.00

UC45 (on UC40)

1971 Revalued

SCOTT NO.	DESCRIPTION	FIRST DAY COVER	UNUSED ENTIRE	USED CUT SQ
UC45	10 & (1¢) (11¢) red	6.00	2.00	.25

UC47

1973

SCOTT NO.	DESCRIPTION	FIRST DAY COVER	UNUSED ENTIRE	USED CUT SQ
UC46	15¢ Ballooning	1.75	.85	.50
UC47	13¢ rose red	1.75	1.50	.15

U.S. Postal Stationery Air Mail #UC48-UC58

SCOTT NO.	DESCRIPTION	FIRST DAY COVER	UNUSED ENTIRE	USED CUT SQ

UC48

UC49

1974

SCOTT NO.	DESCRIPTION	FIRST DAY COVER	UNUSED ENTIRE	USED CUT SQ
UC48	18¢ red & blue	1.75	.85	.35
UC49	18¢ NATO 25th Anniv.	1.75	.85	.30

UC50

1976

SCOTT NO.	DESCRIPTION	FIRST DAY COVER	UNUSED ENTIRE	USED CUT SQ
UC50	22¢ red, white & blue	1.75	.85	.30

UC51

1978

SCOTT NO.	DESCRIPTION	FIRST DAY COVER	UNUSED ENTIRE	USED CUT SQ
UC51	22¢ blue	1.75	.85	.30

UC52

UC53, UC54

1979

SCOTT NO.	DESCRIPTION	FIRST DAY COVER	UNUSED ENTIRE	USED CUT SQ
UC52	22¢ Moscow Olympics	1.75	1.70	.30

1980-81

SCOTT NO.	DESCRIPTION	FIRST DAY COVER	UNUSED ENTIRE	USED CUT SQ
UC53	30¢ red, blue & brown	1.75	.85	.35
UC54	30¢ yellow, magenta, blue & black (1981)	1.75	.85	.35

UC55

1982

SCOTT NO.	DESCRIPTION	FIRST DAY COVER	UNUSED ENTIRE	USED CUT SQ
UC55	30¢ Made in U.S.A.	1.75	.85	.35

UC56

UC57

1983

SCOTT NO.	DESCRIPTION	FIRST DAY COVER	UNUSED ENTIRE	USED CUT SQ
UC56	30¢ Communications	1.75	.85	.35
UC57	30¢ Olympics	1.75	.85	.35

UC58

1985

SCOTT NO.	DESCRIPTION	FIRST DAY COVER	UNUSED ENTIRE	USED CUT SQ
UC58	36¢ Landsat Satellite	1.75	.85	.45

CUT SQUARES: From 1947 to date, Unused Envelope Cut Squares can be supplied at the Unused Entire Price.

U.S. Postal Stationery Air Mail #UC59-UC64

UC59

UC60

SCOTT NO.	DESCRIPTION	FIRST DAY COVER	UNUSED ENTIRE	USED CUT SQ
UC59	36¢ Travel	1.75	.85	.45
UC60	36¢ Mark Twain, Halley's Comet	1.75	.85	.45

UC61

UC62

1986

SCOTT NO.	DESCRIPTION	FIRST DAY COVER	UNUSED ENTIRE	USED CUT SQ
UC61	39¢ Letters	1.75	.90	.45

1989

SCOTT NO.	DESCRIPTION	FIRST DAY COVER	UNUSED ENTIRE	USED CUT SQ
UC62	39¢ Blair & Lincoln	1.75	.90	.45

UC63

1991

SCOTT NO.	DESCRIPTION	FIRST DAY COVER	UNUSED ENTIRE	USED CUT SQ
UC63	45¢ Eagle	1.75	1.00	.45

UC64

1995

SCOTT NO.	DESCRIPTION	FIRST DAY COVER	UNUSED ENTIRE	USED CUT SQ
UC64	50¢ Thaddeus Lowe	1.95	1.10	.50

U.S. Official Postal Stationery #UO1-UO74

OFFICIAL ENVELOPES

NOTE: For details on similar appearing varieties please refer to the Scott Specialized Catalogue

UO1-UO13

UO14-UO17

POST OFFICE DEPARTMENT

1873 SMALL NUMERALS

SCOTT NO.	DESCRIPTION	UNUSED ENTIRE	UNUSED CUT SQ.	USED CUT SQ.
UO1	2¢ black on lemon	15.50	12.00	7.20
UO2	3¢ black on lemon	10.80	6.00	4.80
UO4	6¢ black on lemon	16.80	14.00	9.25

1874-79 LARGE NUMERALS

SCOTT NO.	DESCRIPTION	UNUSED ENTIRE	UNUSED CUT SQ.	USED CUT SQ.
UO5	2¢ black on lemon	7.50	4.20	3.60
UO6	2¢ black on white	47.50	45.00	39.50
UO7	3¢ black on lemon	7.95	3.00	.80
UO8	3¢ black on white	980.00	860.00	860.00
UO9	3¢ black on amber	60.00	48.50	39.50
UO12	6¢ black on lemon	7.20	4.25	2.50
UO13	6¢ black on white	795.00	625.00	......

1877 POSTAL SERVICE

SCOTT NO.	DESCRIPTION	UNUSED ENTIRE	UNUSED CUT SQ.	USED CUT SQ.
UO14	black on white	6.00	4.20	3.60
UO15	black on amber	95.00	30.00	21.00
UO16	blue on amber	96.00	36.00	23.00
UO17	blue on blue	9.00	6.00	6.00

UO18-UO69
Washington

UO70-UO72

Portraits for the various denominations are the same as on the regular issue of 1870-73

WAR DEPARTMENT

1873 REAY ISSUE

SCOTT NO.	DESCRIPTION	UNUSED ENTIRE	UNUSED CUT SQ.	USED CUT SQ.
UO18	1¢ dark red on white	840.00	650.00	300.00
UO19	2¢ dark red on white	840.00	720.00	360.00
UO20	3¢ dark red on white	78.00	60.00	48.00
UO22	3¢ dark red on cream	600.00	480.00	210.00
UO23	6¢ dark red on white	260.00	210.00	78.00
UO24	6¢ dark red on cream	3000.00	1800.00	420.00
UO25	10¢ dark red on white	5400.00	3000.00	330.00
UO26	12¢ dark red on white	155.00	120.00	48.00
UO27	15¢ dark red on white	155.00	120.00	54.00
UO28	24¢ dark red on white	198.00	150.00	42.00
UO29	30¢ dark red on white	480.00	420.00	120.00
UO30	1¢ vermillion on white	300.00	180.00	......
WO31	1¢ vermillion on manila	15.00	10.00	3.75
UO32	2¢ vermillion on white	5400.00	270.00	......
WO33	2¢ vermillion on manila	300.00	210.00	......
UO34	3¢ vermillion on white	168.00	90.00	45.00
UO35	3¢ vermillion on amber	288.00	102.00	......
UO36	3¢ vermillion on cream	36.00	15.00	4.80
UO37	6¢ vermillion on white	120.00	96.00	......
UO38	6¢ vermillion on cream	7800.00	420.00	......
UO39	10¢ vermillion on white	420.00	240.00	......
UO40	12¢ vermillion on white	220.00	150.00	......
UO41	15¢ vermillion on white	2700.00	240.00	......
UO42	24¢ vermillion on white	450.00	420.00	......
UO43	30¢ vermillion on white	675.00	480.00	......

1875 PLIMPTON ISSUE

SCOTT NO.	DESCRIPTION	UNUSED ENTIRE	UNUSED CUT SQ.	USED CUT SQ.
UO44	1¢ red on white	132.00	120.00	102.00
UO45	1¢ red on amber	......	840.00	......
WO46	1¢ red on manila	6.80	3.00	1.10
UO47	2¢ red on white	120.00	102.00	......
UO48	2¢ red on amber	36.00	30.00	9.00
UO49	2¢ red on orange	48.00	42.00	15.00
WO50	2¢ red on manila	110.00	80.00	60.00
UO51	3¢ red on white	12.75	10.75	7.25
UO52	3¢ red on amber	15.00	12.00	7.25
UO53	3¢ red on cream	7.80	6.00	3.00
UO54	3¢ red on blue	4.25	3.00	2.45
UO55	3¢ red on fawn	6.60	4.80	.90
UO56	6¢ red on white	85.00	36.00	27.00
UO57	6¢ red on amber	90.00	80.00	30.00
UO58	6¢ red on cream	240.00	210.00	84.00
UO59	10¢ red on white	165.00	150.00	102.00
UO60	10¢ red on amber	1500.00	1320.00	......
UO61	12¢ red on white	110.00	42.00	42.00
UO62	12¢ red on amber	840.00	780.00	......
UO63	12¢ red on cream	840.00	660.00	......
UO64	15¢ red on white	210.00	180.00	132.50
UO65	15¢ red on amber	870.00	692.00	......
UO66	15¢ red on cream	775.00	725.00	......
UO67	30¢ red on white	200.00	185.00	132.50
UO68	30¢ red on amber	1275.00	1150.00	......
UO69	30¢ red on cream	1200.00	1100.00	......

1911 POSTAL SAVINGS

SCOTT NO.	DESCRIPTION	UNUSED ENTIRE	UNUSED CUT SQ.	USED CUT SQ.
UO70	1¢ green on white	90.00	72.00	12.00
UO71	1¢ green on oriental buff	240.00	198.00	60.00
UO72	2¢ carmine on white	12.00	9.00	2.40

UO73

UO74

1983

SCOTT NO.	DESCRIPTION	FIRST DAY COVER	UNUSED ENTIRE	USED CUT SQ
UO73	20¢ blue and white	2.50	1.40	......

1985

SCOTT NO.	DESCRIPTION	FIRST DAY COVER	UNUSED ENTIRE	USED CUT SQ
UO74	22¢ blue and white	2.00	.90	......

UO75

U.S. Official Postal Stationery #UO75-UO87

SCOTT NO.	DESCRIPTION	FIRST DAY COVER	UNUSED ENTIRE	USED CUT SQ
	1987 Design Similar to UO74			
UO75	22¢ Savings Bond	3.25	.90	......

1988

UO76

SCOTT NO.	DESCRIPTION	FIRST DAY COVER	UNUSED ENTIRE	USED CUT SQ
UO76	(25¢) "E" black and blue Savings Bonds	2.00	.90	......

UO77

SCOTT NO.	DESCRIPTION	FIRST DAY COVER	UNUSED ENTIRE	USED CUT SQ
UO77	25¢ black and blue	2.00	.80	......

UO78

SCOTT NO.	DESCRIPTION	FIRST DAY COVER	UNUSED ENTIRE	USED CUT SQ
UO78	25¢ black and blue Savings Bonds	2.00	.80	......
	1990			
UO79	45¢ black & blue seal	2.25	1.40	......
UO80	65¢ black & blue seal	3.00	1.95	......

UO81

SCOTT NO.	DESCRIPTION	FIRST DAY COVER	UNUSED ENTIRE	USED CUT SQ
UO81	45¢ Self-sealing Envelope	2.25	1.40	......
UO82	65¢ Self-sealing Envelope	3.00	1.95	......

UO83

1991

SCOTT NO.	DESCRIPTION	FIRST DAY COVER	UNUSED ENTIRE	USED CUT SQ
UO83	(29¢) "F" black and blue Savings Bond	2.00	1.25	......

UO84

SCOTT NO.	DESCRIPTION	FIRST DAY COVER	UNUSED ENTIRE	USED CUT SQ
UO84	29¢ black and blue	2.00	.80	......

UO85

SCOTT NO.	DESCRIPTION	FIRST DAY COVER	UNUSED ENTIRE	USED CUT SQ
UO85	29¢ black and blue Savings Bond	2.00	.80	......

UO86, UO87

1992

SCOTT NO.	DESCRIPTION	FIRST DAY COVER	UNUSED ENTIRE	USED CUT SQ
UO86	52¢ Consular Service	2.50	3.00	......
UO87	75¢ Consular Service	3.00	5.00	......

UO88

1995

SCOTT NO.	DESCRIPTION	FIRST DAY COVER	UNUSED ENTIRE	USED CUT SQ
UO88	32¢ red and blue	2.00	.90	......

U.S. Postal Stationery #UX1-UX26

POSTAL CARDS

Prices Are For Entire Cards

MINT: As Issued, no printing or writing added.
UNUSED: Uncancelled, with printing or writing added.

UX1, UX3, UX65

UX4, UX5, UX7
Liberty

UX6, UX13, UX16

1873

SCOTT NO.	DESCRIPTION	MINT	UNUSED	USED
UX1	1¢ brown, large watermark	350.00	45.00	24.00
UX3	1¢ brown, small watermark	70.00	14.00	2.25

1875 Inscribed "Write the Address", etc.

SCOTT NO.	DESCRIPTION	MINT	UNUSED	USED
UX4	1¢ black, watermarked	2100.00	575.00	280.00
UX5	1¢ black, unwatermarked ...	55.00	5.00	.50

1879

SCOTT NO.	DESCRIPTION	MINT	UNUSED	USED
UX6	2¢ blue on buff	23.00	7.50	18.50

1881 Inscribed "Nothing but the Address", etc.

SCOTT NO.	DESCRIPTION	MINT	UNUSED	USED
UX7	1¢ black on buff	50.00	4.25	.50

UX8 UX9
Jefferson

1885

SCOTT NO.	DESCRIPTION	MINT	UNUSED	USED
UX8	1¢ brown on buff	42.00	7.00	1.50

1886

SCOTT NO.	DESCRIPTION	MINT	UNUSED	USED
UX9	1¢ black on buff	12.00	1.25	.65

UX10, UX11
Grant

UX12

UX14
Jefferson

1891

SCOTT NO.	DESCRIPTION	MINT	UNUSED	USED
UX10	1¢ black on buff	30.00	4.50	1.55
UX11	1¢ blue on grayish white	11.00	2.00	2.00

1894 Small Wreath and Name below

SCOTT NO.	DESCRIPTION	MINT	UNUSED	USED
UX12	1¢ black on buff	32.50	1.40	.50

UX15
John Adams

UX18
McKinley

UX19, UX20

1897 Large Wreath and Name below

SCOTT NO.	DESCRIPTION	MINT	UNUSED	USED
UX13	2¢ blue on cream	135.00	70.00	82.50
UX14	1¢ black on buff	22.00	2.50	.30

1898

SCOTT NO.	DESCRIPTION	MINT	UNUSED	USED
UX15	1¢ black on buff	35.00	10.00	16.00
UX16	2¢ black on buff	11.00	6.25	11.00

1902 Profile Background

SCOTT NO.	DESCRIPTION	MINT	UNUSED	USED
UX18	1¢ black on buff	10.00	1.75	.40

1907

SCOTT NO.	DESCRIPTION	MINT	UNUSED	USED
UX19	1¢ black on buff	30.00	2.00	.60

1908 Correspondence Space at Left

SCOTT NO.	DESCRIPTION	MINT	UNUSED	USED
UX20	1¢ black on buff	45.00	7.00	4.50

UX21

UX22, UX24

UX23, UX26

UX25

UX27

1910 Background Shaded

SCOTT NO.	DESCRIPTION	MINT	UNUSED	USED
UX21	1¢ blue on bluish	100.00	18.00	7.00

White Portrait Background

SCOTT NO.	DESCRIPTION	MINT	UNUSED	USED
UX22	1¢ blue on bluish	13.50	1.65	.30

1911

SCOTT NO.	DESCRIPTION	MINT	UNUSED	USED
UX23	1¢ red on cream	7.00	3.25	6.00
UX24	1¢ red on cream	8.00	1.50	.35
UX25	2¢ red on cream	1.50	.75	9.00

1913

SCOTT NO.	DESCRIPTION	MINT	UNUSED	USED
UX26	1¢ green on cream	8.00	2.50	6.50

U.S. Postal Stationery #UX27-UX55

SCOTT NO.	DESCRIPTION	MINT	UNUSED	USED
	1914			
UX27	1¢ green on buff	.35	.20	.15

UX28, UX43   UX29, UX30   UX32, UX33

SCOTT NO.	DESCRIPTION	MINT	UNUSED	USED
	1917-18			
UX28	1¢ green on cream	1.70	.40	.40
UX29	2¢ red on buff, die 1	42.00	5.00	1.80
UX30	2¢ red on cream,die 2 (1918)	20.00	4.00	1.80

NOTE: On UX29 end of queue slopes sharply down to right while on UX30 it extends nearly horizontally.

1920 UX29 & UX30 Revalued

SCOTT NO.	DESCRIPTION	MINT	UNUSED	USED
UX32	1¢ on 2¢ red, die 1	45.00	13.00	11.00
UX33	1¢ on 2¢ red, die 2	7.00	1.85	1.75

UX37   UX38   UX39-42

SCOTT NO.	DESCRIPTION	MINT	UNUSED	USED
	1926			
UX37	3¢ red on buff	3.50	2.00	10.00

SCOTT NO.	DESCRIPTION	FIRST DAY COVER	MINT	USED
	1951			
UX38	2¢ carmine rose	1.75	.40	.35

1952 UX27 & UX28 Surcharged by cancelling machine, light green

SCOTT NO.	DESCRIPTION	FIRST DAY COVER	MINT	USED
UX39	2¢ on 1¢ green	......	.60	.35
UX40	2¢ on 1¢ green	......	.70	.35

UX27 & UX28 Surcharge Typographed, dark green

SCOTT NO.	DESCRIPTION	FIRST DAY COVER	MINT	USED
UX41	2¢ on 1¢ green	......	4.00	1.85
UX42	2¢ on 1¢ green	......	5.25	2.25

1952 Design of 1917

SCOTT NO.	DESCRIPTION	FIRST DAY COVER	MINT	USED
UX43	2¢ carmine	1.75	.30	1.00

UX44   UX45, UY16   UX46, UY17

1956 FIPEX COMMEMORATIVE

SCOTT NO.	DESCRIPTION	FIRST DAY COVER	MINT	USED
UX44	2¢ deep carmine & dark violet	1.75	.35	1.00

1956 INTERNATIONAL CARD

SCOTT NO.	DESCRIPTION	FIRST DAY COVER	MINT	USED
UX45	4¢ deep red & ultramarine .	1.75	1.75	.30

SCOTT NO.	DESCRIPTION	FIRST DAY COVER	MINT	USED
	1958			
UX46	3¢ purple	1.75	.50	.25

As above, but with printed precancel lines

SCOTT NO.	DESCRIPTION	FIRST DAY COVER	MINT	USED
UX46c	3¢ purple	......	4.00	2.50

ONE CENT ADDITIONAL PAID

UX47   UX48, UY18

1958 UX38 Surcharged

SCOTT NO.	DESCRIPTION	FIRST DAY COVER	MINT	USED
UX47	2¢ & 1¢ carmine rose	......	165.00	300.00

Mint *UX47 has advertising

1962-66

SCOTT NO.	DESCRIPTION	FIRST DAY COVER	MINT	USED
UX48	4¢ red violet	1.75	.30	.25
UX48a	4¢ luminescent (1966)	3.00	.60	.25

UX50

UX49, UX54, UX59, UY19, UY20

SCOTT NO.	DESCRIPTION	FIRST DAY COVER	MINT	USED
	1963			
UX49	7¢ Tourism	1.75	2.00	25.00
	1964			
UX50	4¢ Customs Service	1.75	.50	1.00

UX51   UX52

SCOTT NO.	DESCRIPTION	FIRST DAY COVER	MINT	USED
UX51	4¢ Social Security	1.75	.50	1.00
	1965			
UX52	4¢ Coast Guard	1.75	.45	1.00

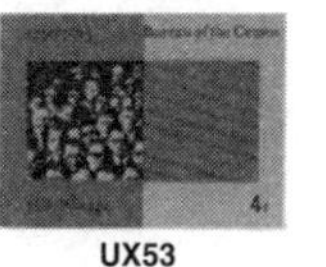

UX53

UX55, UY21

SCOTT NO.	DESCRIPTION	FIRST DAY COVER	MINT	USED
UX53	4¢ Census Bureau	1.75	.45	1.00
	1967 Design of UX49			
UX54	8¢ Tourism	1.75	2.00	25.00
	1968			
UX55	5¢ emerald	1.75	.30	.40

U.S. Postal Stationery #UX56-UX67

UX56

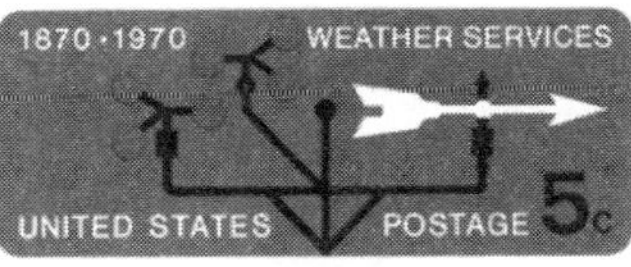

UX57

UX58, UY22

SCOTT NO.	DESCRIPTION	FIRST DAY COVER	MINT	USED
UX56	5¢ Women Marines	1.75	.40	1.00
	1970			
UX57	5¢ Weather Bureau	1.75	.35	1.00
	1971			
UX58	6¢ Paul Revere	1.75	.30	1.00
	Design of UX49			
UX59	10¢ Tourism	1.75	2.00	25.00

UX60

SCOTT NO.	DESCRIPTION	FIRST DAY COVER	MINT	USED
UX60	6¢ New York Hospital	1.75	.35	1.00

UX61

UX62

UX63

1972

SCOTT NO.	DESCRIPTION	FIRST DAY COVER	MINT	USED
UX61	6¢ U.S.F. Constellation	1.75	.45	2.50
UX62	6¢ Monument Valley	1.75	.45	2.50
UX63	6¢ Gloucester, Mass.	1.75	.45	2.50

NOTE: A Postal Card is a card with the postage preapplied (printed) on the card. A Post Card requires that you add postage stamps.

UX64, UY23

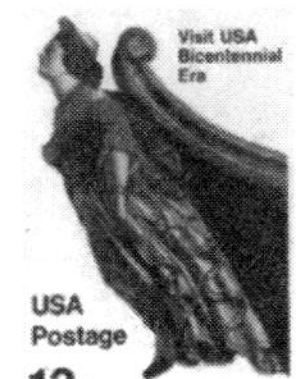

UX67

UX66, UY24

SCOTT NO.	DESCRIPTION	FIRST DAY COVER	MINT	USED
UX64	6¢ John Hanson	1.75	.35	1.00
	1973 Design of 1873			
UX65	6¢ Liberty, magenta	1.75	.35	1.00
UX66	8¢ Samuel Adams	1.75	.35	1.00
	1974			
UX67	12¢ Visit USA	1.75	.45	20.00

UX68, UY25

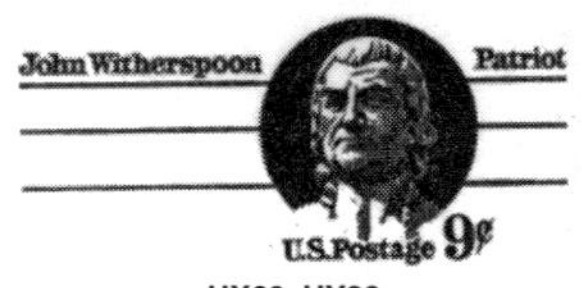

UX69, UY26

U.S. Postal Stationery #UX68-UX81

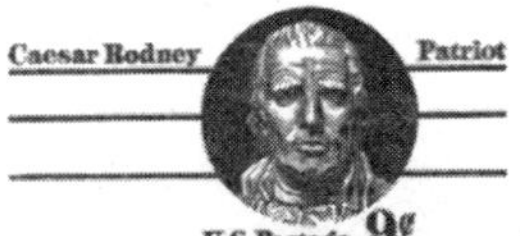

UX70, UY27

1975-76

SCOTT NO.	DESCRIPTION	FIRST DAY COVER	MINT	USED
UX68	7¢ Charles Thomson	1.75	.35	4.00
UX69	9¢ J. Witherspoon	1.75	.35	1.00
UX70	9¢ Caesar Rodney	1.75	.35	1.00

UX71

UX72, UY28

1977

SCOTT NO.	DESCRIPTION	FIRST DAY COVER	MINT	USED
UX71	9¢ Federal Court House	1.75	.50	1.00
UX72	9¢ Nathan Hale	1.75	.55	1.00

UX73

UX74, UX75, UY29, UY30

US Coast Guard Eagle USA 14c

UX76

1978

SCOTT NO.	DESCRIPTION	FIRST DAY COVER	MINT	USED
UX73	10¢ Music Hall	1.75	.35	1.00
UX74	(10¢) John Hancock	1.75	.35	1.00
UX75	10¢ John Hancock	1.75	.35	1.00
UX76	14¢ "Eagle"	1.75	.40	1.00

Molly Pitcher, Monmouth, 1778

UX77

SCOTT NO.	DESCRIPTION	FIRST DAY COVER	MINT	USED
UX77	10¢ multicolored	1.75	.50	.15

George Rogers Clark, Vincennes, 1779

UX78

Casimir Pulaski, Savannah, 1779

UX79

UX80

Historic Preservation

UX81

1979

SCOTT NO.	DESCRIPTION	FIRST DAY COVER	MINT	USED
UX78	10¢ Fort Sackville	1.75	.35	1.00
UX79	10¢ Casimir Pulaski	1.75	.35	1.00
UX80	10¢ Moscow Olympics ..	1.75	.60	1.00
UX81	10¢ Iolani Palace	1.75	.35	1.00

UX82

UX83

U.S. Postal Stationery #UX82-UX94

Landing of Rochambeau, 1780

UX84

Battle of Kings Mountain, 1780

UX85

Drake's Golden Hinde 1580

UX86

Battle of Cowpens, 1781

UX87

1980

SCOTT NO.	DESCRIPTION	FIRST DAY COVER	MINT	USED
UX82	14¢ Winter Olympics	1.75	.60	7.50
UX83	10¢ Salt Lake Temple ...	1.75	.35	1.00
UX84	10¢ Count Rochambeau	1.75	.35	1.00
UX85	10¢ Kings Mountain	1.75	.35	1.00
UX86	19¢ Sir Francis Drake ...	1.75	.50	7.50

1981

SCOTT NO.	DESCRIPTION	FIRST DAY COVER	MINT	USED
UX87	10¢ Cowpens	1.75	.35	2.00

UX88, UY31

UX89, UY32

Nathanael Greene, Eutaw Springs, 1781

UX90

Lewis and Clark Expedition, 1806

UX91

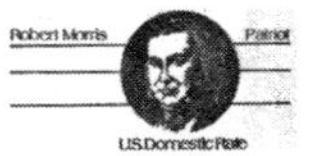

UX92, UY33

UX93, UY34

"Swamp Fox" Francis Marion, 1782

UX94

SCOTT NO.	DESCRIPTION	FIRST DAY COVER	MINT	USED
UX88	"B" (12¢) violet & white ..	1.75	.35	.50
UX89	12¢ Isaiah Thomas	1.75	.35	.50
UX90	12¢ Eutaw Springs	1.75	.35	1.00
UX91	12¢ Lewis & Clark	1.75	.35	2.00
UX92	(13¢) Robert Morris	1.75	.35	.50
UX93	13¢ Robert Morris	1.75	.35	.50

1982

SCOTT NO.	DESCRIPTION	FIRST DAY COVER	MINT	USED
UX94	13¢ Francis Marion	1.75	.35	.65

La Salle claims Louisiana, 1682

UX95

U.S. Postal Stationery #UX95-UX106

UX96

Historic Preservation

UX97

SCOTT NO.	DESCRIPTION	FIRST DAY COVER	MINT	USED
UX95	13¢ La Salle	1.75	.35	.75
UX96	13¢ Academy of Music	1.75	.35	.75
UX97	13¢ St. Louis Post Office ...	1.75	.35	.75

Landing of Oglethorpe, Georgia, 1733

UX98

1983

SCOTT NO.	DESCRIPTION	FIRST DAY COVER	MINT	USED
UX98	13¢ Gen. Oglethorpe	1.75	.35	.75

Old Post Office, Washington, D.C.

UX99

UX100

SCOTT NO.	DESCRIPTION	FIRST DAY COVER	MINT	USED
UX99	13¢ Washington Post Office	1.75	.35	.75
UX100	13¢ Olympics	1.75	.35	.75

Ark and Dove, Maryland, 1634

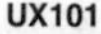

UX101

UX102

Frederic Baraga, Michigan, 1835

UX103

1984

SCOTT NO.	DESCRIPTION	FIRST DAY COVER	MINT	USED
UX101	13¢ "Ark" & "Dove"	1.75	.35	.75
UX102	13¢ Olympics	1.75	.35	.75
UX103	13¢ Frederic Baraga	1.75	.35	.75

UX104

SCOTT NO.	DESCRIPTION	FIRST DAY COVER	MINT	USED
UX104	13¢ Historic Preservation ...	1.75	.35	.75

Charles Carroll Patriot

U.S. Domestic Rate

UX105, UX106, UY35, UY36

1985

SCOTT NO.	DESCRIPTION	FIRST DAY COVER	MINT	USED
UX105	(14¢) Charles Carroll	1.75	.35	.60
UX106	14¢ Charles Carroll	1.75	.35	.25

U.S. Postal Stationery #UX107-UX116

SCOTT NO.	DESCRIPTION	FIRST DAY COVER	MINT	USED

UX107

UX107	25¢ Flying Cloud	1.75	.65	4.00

UX108

UX108	14¢ George Wythe	1.75	.35	.50

UX109

1986

UX109	14¢ Connecticut	1.75	.35	.65

UX110

UX110	14¢ Stamp Collecting	1.75	.35	.65

UX111

UX111	14¢ Francis Vigo	1.75	.35	.65

SCOTT NO.	DESCRIPTION	FIRST DAY COVER	MINT	USED

UX112

UX112	14¢ Rhode Island	1.75	.35	.65

UX113

UX113	14¢ Wisconsin	1.75	.35	.65

UX114

UX114	14¢ National Guard	1.75	.35	.65

UX115

1987

UX115	14¢ Steel Plow	1.75	.35	.50

UX116

UX116	14¢ Constitution	1.75	.35	.50

U.S. Postal Stationery #UX117-UX127

UX117

SCOTT NO.	DESCRIPTION	FIRST DAY COVER	MINT	USED
UX117	14¢ Flag	1.75	.35	.50

UX118

SCOTT NO.	DESCRIPTION	FIRST DAY COVER	MINT	USED
UX118	14¢ Take Pride in America	1.75	.35	.50

UX119

SCOTT NO.	DESCRIPTION	FIRST DAY COVER	MINT	USED
UX119	14¢ Timberline Lodge	1.75	.35	.50

UX120

1988

SCOTT NO.	DESCRIPTION	FIRST DAY COVER	MINT	USED
UX120	15¢ America the Beautiful	1.75	.35	.20

UX121

SCOTT NO.	DESCRIPTION	FIRST DAY COVER	MINT	USED
UX121	15¢ Blair House	1.75	.35	.20

UX122

SCOTT NO.	DESCRIPTION	FIRST DAY COVER	MINT	USED
UX122	28¢ Yorkshire	1.75	.65	1.00

UX123

SCOTT NO.	DESCRIPTION	FIRST DAY COVER	MINT	USED
UX123	15¢ Iowa Territory	1.75	.35	.20

UX124

SCOTT NO.	DESCRIPTION	FIRST DAY COVER	MINT	USED
UX124	15¢ Northwest Territory	1.75	.35	.20

UX125

SCOTT NO.	DESCRIPTION	FIRST DAY COVER	MINT	USED
UX125	15¢ Hearst Castle	1.75	.35	.20

UX126

SCOTT NO.	DESCRIPTION	FIRST DAY COVER	MINT	USED
UX126	15¢ Federalist Papers	1.75	.35	.20

UX127

1989

SCOTT NO.	DESCRIPTION	FIRST DAY COVER	MINT	USED
UX127	15¢ The Desert	1.75	.35	.20

U.S. Postal Stationery #UX128-UX142

UX128

SCOTT NO.	DESCRIPTION	FIRST DAY COVER	MINT	USED
UX128	15¢ Healy Hall	1.75	.35	.20

UX129

SCOTT NO.	DESCRIPTION	FIRST DAY COVER	MINT	USED
UX129	15¢ The Wet Lands	1.75	.35	.20

UX130

SCOTT NO.	DESCRIPTION	FIRST DAY COVER	MINT	USED
UX130	15¢ Oklahoma Territory	1.75	.35	.20

UX131

SCOTT NO.	DESCRIPTION	FIRST DAY COVER	MINT	USED
UX131	21¢ The Mountains	1.75	.50	1.00

UX132

SCOTT NO.	DESCRIPTION	FIRST DAY COVER	MINT	USED
UX132	15¢ The Seashore	1.75	.35	.20

UX133

SCOTT NO.	DESCRIPTION	FIRST DAY COVER	MINT	USED
UX133	15¢ The Woodlands	1.75	.35	.20

UX134

SCOTT NO.	DESCRIPTION	FIRST DAY COVER	MINT	USED
UX134	15¢ Hull House	1.75	.35	.20

UX135

SCOTT NO.	DESCRIPTION	FIRST DAY COVER	MINT	USED
UX135	15¢ Philadelphia Cityscape	1.75	.35	.20

UX136

SCOTT NO.	DESCRIPTION	FIRST DAY COVER	MINT	USED
UX136	15¢ Baltimore Cityscape	1.75	.35	.20

UX137

SCOTT NO.	DESCRIPTION	FIRST DAY COVER	MINT	USED
UX137	15¢ New York Cityscape	1.75	.35	.20

UX138

SCOTT NO.	DESCRIPTION	FIRST DAY COVER	MINT	USED
UX138	15¢ Washington Cityscape	1.75	.35	.20
UX139-42	15¢ Cityscape sheet of 4 postcards	8.00	10.00	......

U.S. Postal Stationery #UX143-UX156

SCOTT NO.	DESCRIPTION	FIRST DAY COVER	MINT	USED
	UX143			
UX143	15¢ White House	1.75	1.10	1.50
	UX144			
UX144	15¢ Jefferson Memorial	1.75	1.10	1.50
	UX145			
	1990			
UX145	15¢ Papermaking	1.75	.35	.20
	UX146			
UX146	15¢ Literacy	1.75	.35	.20
	UX147			
UX147	15¢ Bingham	1.75	1.10	1.50
	UX148			
UX148	15¢ Isaac Royall House	1.75	.35	.20
	UX150			

SCOTT NO.	DESCRIPTION	FIRST DAY COVER	MINT	USED
UX150	15¢ Stanford University	1.75	.35	.20
	UX151			
UX151	15¢ DAR Memorial Hall	1.75	1.10	1.50
	UX152			
UX152	15¢ Chicago Orchestra Hall	1.75	.35	.20
	UX153			
	1991			
UX153	19¢ Flag	1.75	.45	.20
	UX154			
UX154	19¢ Carnegie Hall	1.75	.45	.20
	UX155			
UX155	19¢ Old Red Admin. Bldg. .	1.75	.45	.20
	UX156			
UX156	19¢ Bill of Rights	1.75	.45	.20

U.S. Postal Stationery #UX157-UX168

SCOTT NO.	DESCRIPTION	FIRST DAY COVER	MINT	USED
UX157	19¢ Univ.of Notre Dame, Admin. Bldg.	1.75	.45	.20
UX158	30¢ Niagara Falls	1.75	.65	.50
UX159	19¢ Old Mill U of VT	1.75	.45	.25
	1992			
UX160	19¢ Wadsworth Atheneum	1.75	.45	.25
UX161	19¢ Cobb Hall U of Chicago	1.75	.45	.25
UX162	19¢ Waller Hall	1.75	.45	.25

UX157

UX158

UX159

UX160

UX161

UX162

SCOTT NO.	DESCRIPTION	FIRST DAY COVER	MINT	USED
UX163	19¢ America's Cup	1.75	1.10	.75
UX164	19¢ Columbia River Gorge	1.75	.45	.25
UX165	19¢ Great Hall, Ellis Island	1.75	.45	.25
	1993			
UX166	19¢ National Cathedral	1.75	.45	.25
UX167	19¢ Wren Building	1.75	.45	.25
UX168	19¢ Holocaust Memorial	2.00	.45	.75

UX163

UX164

UX165

UX166

UX167

UX168

UX169

U.S. Postal Stationery #UX169-UX198

SCOTT NO.	DESCRIPTION	FIRST DAY COVER	MINT	USED
UX169	19¢ Fort Recovery	1.75	.45	.25

UX170

SCOTT NO.	DESCRIPTION	FIRST DAY COVER	MINT	USED
UX170	19¢ Playmakers Theatre	1.75	.45	.35

UX171

SCOTT NO.	DESCRIPTION	FIRST DAY COVER	MINT	USED
UX171	19¢ O'Kane Hall	1.75	.45	.35

UX172

SCOTT NO.	DESCRIPTION	FIRST DAY COVER	MINT	USED
UX172	19¢ Beecher Hall	1.75	.45	.35

UX173

SCOTT NO.	DESCRIPTION	FIRST DAY COVER	MINT	USED
UX173	19¢ Massachusetts Hall	1.75	.45	.35

UX174

1994

SCOTT NO.	DESCRIPTION	FIRST DAY COVER	MINT	USED
UX174	19¢ Abraham Lincoln Home	1.75	.45	.35

UX175

SCOTT NO.	DESCRIPTION	FIRST DAY COVER	MINT	USED
UX175	19¢ Myers Hall	1.75	.45	.35

UX176

SCOTT NO.	DESCRIPTION	FIRST DAY COVER	MINT	USED
UX176	19¢ Canyon de Chelly	1.75	.45	.35

UX177

SCOTT NO.	DESCRIPTION	FIRST DAY COVER	MINT	USED
UX177	19¢ St. Louis Union Station	1.75	.45	.35

Legends of the West

UX178

UX178	*Home on the Range*
UX179	*Buffalo Bill*
UX180	*Jim Bridger*
UX181	*Annie Oakley*
UX182	*Native American Culture*
UX183	*Chief Joseph*
UX184	*Bill Pickett*
UX185	*Bat Masterson*
UX186	*John Fremont*
UX187	*Wyatt Earp*
UX188	*Nellie Cashman*
UX189	*Charles Goodnight*
UX190	*Geronimo*
UX191	*Kit Carson*
UX192	*Wild Bill Hickok*
UX193	*Western Wildlife*
UX194	*Jim Beckwourth*
UX195	*Bill Tilghman*
UX196	*Sacagawea*
UX197	*Overland Mail*

SCOTT NO.	DESCRIPTION	FIRST DAY COVER	MINT	USED
UX178-97	19¢ Legends of the West, set of 20	35.00	17.50	25.00

UX198

1995

SCOTT NO.	DESCRIPTION	FIRST DAY COVER	MINT	USED
UX198	20¢ Red Barn	1.75	.45	.35

U.S. Postal Stationery #UX199-UX261

SCOTT NO.	DESCRIPTION	FIRST DAY COVER	MINT	USED

UX199

UX199	(20¢) "G" Old Glory	1.75	.45	.35

Civil War

UX200

UX200	*Monitor-Virginia*
UX201	*Lee*
UX202	*Barton*
UX203	*Grant*
UX204	*Shiloh*
UX205	*Davis*
UX206	*Farragut*
UX207	*Douglass*
UX208	*Semmes*
UX209	*Lincoln*
UX210	*Tubman*
UX211	*Watie*
UX212	*Johnston*
UX213	*Hancock*
UX214	*Chestnut*
UX215	*Chancellorsville*
UX216	*Sherman*
UX217	*Pember*
UX218	*Jackson*
UX219	*Gettysburg*

UX200-19	20¢ Civil War, set of 20	35.00	17.50	25.00

UX220

UX220	20¢ American Clipper Ships	1.75	.45	.35

UX221

SCOTT NO.	DESCRIPTION	FIRST DAY COVER	MINT	USED

American Comic Strips

UX221	*Yellow Kid*	**UX231**	*Popeye*
UX222	*Katzenjammer Kids*	**UX232**	*Blondie*
UX223	*Little Nemo*	**UX233**	*Dick Tracy*
UX224	*Bring Up Father*	**UX234**	*Alley Oop*
UX225	*Krazy Kat*	**UX235**	*Nancy*
UX226	*Rube Goldberg*	**UX236**	*Flash Gordon*
UX227	*Toonerville Folks*	**UX237**	*Li'l Abner*
UX228	*Gasoline Alley*	**UX238**	*Terry/Pirates*
UX229	*Barney Google*	**UX239**	*Prince Valiant*
UX230	*Little Orphan Annie*	**UX240**	*Brenda Starr*

UX221-40	20¢ American Comic Strips, set of 20	35.00	17.50	25.00

UX241

1996

UX241	20¢ Winter Farm Scene	1.75	.45	.35

Centennial Olympic Games

UX242

UX242	*Men's cycling*
UX243	*Women's diving*
UX244	*Women's running*
UX245	*Men's canoeing*
UX246	*Decathlon*
UX247	*Women's soccer*
UX248	*Men's shot put*
UX249	*Women's sailboarding*
UX250	*Women's gymnastics*
UX251	*Freestyle wrestling*
UX252	*Women's softball*
UX253	*Women's swimming*
UX254	*Men's sprints*
UX255	*Men's rowing*
UX256	*Beach volleyball*
UX257	*Men's basketball*
UX258	*Equestrian*
UX259	*Men's gymnastics*
UX260	*Men's swimming*
UX261	*Men's hurdles*

UX242-61	20¢ Centennial Olympic Games, set of 20	35.00	17.50	25.00

U.S. Postal Stationery #UX262-New Issue

SCOTT NO.	DESCRIPTION	FIRST DAY COVER	MINT	USED

UX262

UX262	20¢ McDowell Hall	1.75	.45	.35

UX263

UX263	20¢ Alexander Hall	1.75	.45	.35

UX264

Engandered Species

UX264 *Florida panther*
UX265 *Black-footed ferret*
UX266 *American crocodile*
UX267 *Piping plover*
UX268 *Gila trout*
UX269 *Florida manatee*
UX270 *Schaus swallowtail butterfly*
UX271 *Woodland caribou*
UX272 *Thick-billed parrot*
UX273 *San Francisco garter snake*
UX274 *Ocelot*
UX275 *Wyoming toad*
UX276 *California condor*
UX277 *Hawaiian monk seal*
UX278 *Brown pelican*

UX264-78	20¢ Endangered Species, set of 15	26.50	13.50	18.75

SCOTT NO.	DESCRIPTION	FIRST DAY COVER	MINT	USED

UX279

1997

UX279	20¢ Swans, set of 12 .	20.00(8)	14.50	20.00
UX280	20¢ Shepard Hall	1.75	.45	.35
UX281	20¢ Bugs Bunny	1.75	.45	.35
UX282	20¢ Golden Gate Bridge	1.75	.45	.35
UX283	50¢ Golden Gate Bridge at Sunset	1.95	1.10	.50
......	20¢ Fort McHenry	1.75	.45	.35

U.S. Postal Stationery #UXC1-UXC15

AIR POST POSTAL CARDS

UXC1 UXC2, UXC3

1949

SCOTT NO.	DESCRIPTION	FIRST DAY COVER	MINT	USED
UXC1	4¢ orange	2.50	.45	.65

1958 No border on card

SCOTT NO.	DESCRIPTION	FIRST DAY COVER	MINT	USED
UXC2	5¢ red	2.50	2.00	.65

1960
Type of 1958 re-engraved: with border on card

UXC4

UXC5, UXC8, UXC11

SCOTT NO.	DESCRIPTION	FIRST DAY COVER	MINT	USED
UXC3	5¢ red	2.50	6.25	1.75

1963

SCOTT NO.	DESCRIPTION	FIRST DAY COVER	MINT	USED
UXC4	6¢ red	2.50	.45	.65

1966

SCOTT NO.	DESCRIPTION	FIRST DAY COVER	MINT	USED
UXC5	11¢ SIPEX	1.75	.60	10.00

UXC6

UXC7

1967

SCOTT NO.	DESCRIPTION	FIRST DAY COVER	MINT	USED
UXC6	6¢ Virgin Islands	1.75	.40	5.00
UXC7	6¢ Boy Scout Jamboree	2.50	.40	5.00
UXC8	13¢ AAM Convention	1.75	1.40	7.00

UXC9, UXC10

1968-71 Precancels

SCOTT NO.	DESCRIPTION	FIRST DAY COVER	MINT	USED
UXC9	8¢ blue & red	1.75	.60	1.50
UXC9at	8¢ luminescent (1969)	20.00	2.25	2.75
UXC10	9¢ red & blue (1971)	1.75	.55	1.00

1971 Inscribed U.S. Air Mail

SCOTT NO.	DESCRIPTION	FIRST DAY COVER	MINT	USED
UXC11	15¢ Travel Service	1.75	1.50	10.00

UXC12

UXC13

1972
Issued with various designs on reverse

SCOTT NO.	DESCRIPTION	FIRST DAY COVER	MINT	USED
UXC12	9¢ Grand Canyon	1.75	.50	7.00
UXC13	15¢ Niagara Falls	1.75	.60	12.50

UXC14

UXC15

1974

SCOTT NO.	DESCRIPTION	FIRST DAY COVER	MINT	USED
UXC14	11¢ red & ultramarine	1.75	.70	1.75
UXC15	18¢ Visit USA	1.75	.85	6.00

UXC16

1975

SCOTT NO.	DESCRIPTION	FIRST DAY COVER	MINT	USED
UXC16	21¢ Visit USA	1.75	.80	6.50

U.S. Postal Stationery #UXC16-UXC25

SCOTT NO.	DESCRIPTION	FIRST DAY COVER	MINT	USED

UXC17

1978

UXC17 21¢ Curtiss Jenny .... 1.75 .80 5.00

UXC18

1979

UXC18 21¢ Moscow Olympics ..... 1.75 .90 8.00

UXC19

1981

UXC19 28¢ Pacific Flight .... 1.75 .90 3.00

UXC20

1982

UXC20 28¢ Gliders .... 1.75 .80 2.00

SCOTT NO.	DESCRIPTION	FIRST DAY COVER	MINT	USED

UXC21

1983

UXC21 28¢ Olympics .... 1.75 .80 2.00

UXC22

1985

UXC22 33¢ China Clipper .... 1.75 .85 2.00

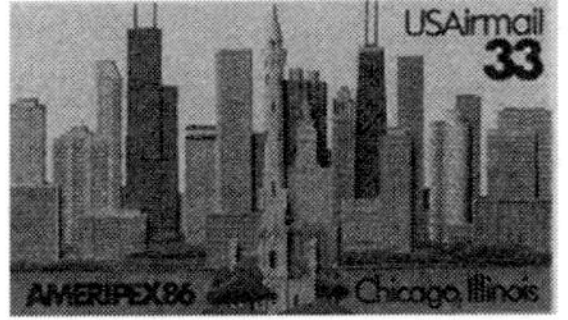

UXC23

1986

UXC23 33¢ Ameripex '86 .... 1.75 .85 2.00

UXC24

1988

UXC24 36¢ DC-3 .... 1.75 .85 1.00

UXC25

1991

UXC25 40¢ Yankee Clipper .... 1.75 .90 1.00

U.S. Postal Stationery #UXC26

SCOTT NO.	DESCRIPTION	FIRST DAY COVER	MINT	USED

UXC26

1995

SCOTT NO.	DESCRIPTION	FIRST DAY COVER	MINT	USED
UXC26	50¢ Soaring Eagle	1.75	1.10	1.25

SCOTT NO.	DESCRIPTION	FIRST DAY COVER	MINT	USED

U.S. Postal Stationery #UY1-UY20

PAID REPLY CARDS: Consist of two halves—one for your message and one for the other party to use to reply.

UY1m, UY3m — UY2m, UY11m — UY4m

UY1r, UY3r — UY2r, UY11r — UY4r

SCOTT NO.	DESCRIPTION	MINT	UNUSED	USED
	1892 Card Framed			
UY1	1¢ & 1¢ unsevered	40.00	15.00	9.00
UY1m	1¢ black (Message)	6.50	3.25	1.50
UY1r	1¢ black (Reply)	6.50	3.25	1.50
	1893			
UY2	2¢ & 2¢ unsevered	20.00	12.00	22.00
UY2m	2¢ blue (Message)	6.00	2.00	6.50
UY2r	2¢ blue (Reply)	6.00	2.00	6.50
	1898 Designs of 1892 Card Unframed			
UY3	1¢ & 1¢ unsevered	75.00	12.50	15.00
UY3m	1¢ black (Message)	15.50	5.00	3.00
UY3r	1¢ black (Reply)	15.50	5.00	3.00
	1904			
UY4	1¢ & 1¢ unsevered	50.00	10.00	3.25
UY4m	1¢ black (Message)	10.00	4.00	1.20
UY4r	1¢ black (Reply)	10.00	4.00	1.20

UY5m, UY6m, UY7m, UY13m — UY8m — UY12m

UY5r, UY6r, UY7r, UY13r — UY8r — UY12r

SCOTT NO.	DESCRIPTION	MINT	UNUSED	USED
	1910			
UY5	1¢ & 1¢ unsevered	160.00	35.00	22.00
UY5m	1¢ blue (Message)	12.00	6.00	3.60
UY5r	1¢ blue (Reply)	12.00	6.00	3.60
	1911 Double Line Around Instructions			
UY6	1¢ & 1¢ unsevered	160.00	50.00	25.00
UY6m	1¢ green (Message)	25.00	12.00	6.00
UY6r	1¢ green (Reply)	25.00	12.00	6.00
	1915 Single Frame Line Around Instruction			
UY7	1¢ & 1¢ unsevered	1.50	.50	.60
UY7m	1¢ green (Message)	.35	.20	.25
UY7r	1¢ green (Reply)	.35	.20	.25
	1918			
UY8	2¢ & 2¢ unsevered	85.00	30.00	45.00
UY8m	2¢ red (Message)	24.00	9.00	9.00
UY8r	2¢ red (Reply)	24.00	9.00	9.00
	1920 UY8 Surcharged			
UY9	1¢/2¢ & 1¢/2¢ unsevered	22.50	9.00	10.00
UY9m	1¢ on 2¢ red (Message)	6.00	2.50	3.00
UY9r	1¢ on 2¢ red (Reply)	6.00	2.50	3.00
	1924 Designs of 1893			
UY11	2¢ & 2¢ unsevered	3.00	1.50	32.50
UY11m	2¢ red (Message)	.75	.50	12.00
UY11r	2¢ red (Reply)	.75	.50	12.00
	1926			
UY12	3¢ & 3¢ unsevered	16.50	5.00	30.00
UY12m	3¢ red (Message)	3.25	1.35	7.00
UY12r	3¢ red (Reply)	3.25	1.35	7.00

SCOTT NO.	DESCRIPTION	FIRST DAY COVERS	MINT	USED
	1951 Design of 1910 Single Line Frame			
UY13	2¢ & 2¢ unsevered	2.10	1.00	2.25
UY13m	2¢ carmine (Message)	....	.45	1.00
UY13r	2¢ carmine (Reply)	....	.45	1.00
	1952 UY7 Surcharged by cancelling machine, light green			
UY14	2¢/1¢ & 2¢/1¢ unsevered	....	2.00	2.25
UY14m	2¢ on 1¢ green (Message)	....	.50	1.00
UY14r	2¢ on 1¢ green (Reply)	....	.50	1.00
	1952 UY7 Surcharge Typographed, dark green			
UY15	2¢/1¢ & 2¢/1¢ unsevered	....	140.00	50.00
UY15m	2¢ on 1¢ green (Message)	....	20.00	12.00
UY15r	2¢ on 1¢ green (Reply)	....	20.00	12.00
	1956 Design of UX45			
UY16	4¢ & 4¢ unsevered	1.75	2.00	40.00
UY16m	4¢ carmine (Message)	....	.50	27.50
UY16r	4¢ carmine (Reply)	....	.50	27.50
	1958 Design of UX46			
UY17	3¢ & 3¢ purple, unsevered	1.75	5.00	2.50
	1962 Design of UX48			
UY18	4¢ & 4¢ red violet, unsevered	1.75	5.00	2.25
	1963 Design of UX49			
UY19	7¢ & 7¢ unsevered	1.75	3.00	30.00
UY19m	7¢ blue & red (Message)	....	1.00	25.00
UY19r	7¢ blue & red (Reply)	....	1.00	25.00
	1967 Design of UX54			
UY20	8¢ & 8¢ unsevered	1.75	3.00	32.50
UY20m	8¢ blue & red (Message)	....	1.00	25.00
UY20r	8¢ blue & red (Reply)	....	1.00	25.00

U.S. Postal Stationery #UY21-UY41; UZ1-UZ6

SCOTT NO.	DESCRIPTION	FIRST DAY COVERS	MINT	USED
	1968 Design of UX55			
UY21	5¢ & 5¢ emerald	1.75	1.75	2.00
	1971 Design of UX58			
UY22	6¢ & 6¢ brown	1.75	1.75	2.00
	1972 Design of UX64			
UY23	6¢ & 6¢ blue	1.75	1.25	2.00
	1973 Design of UX66			
UY24	8¢ & 8¢ orange	1.75	1.25	2.00
	1975			
UY25	7¢ & 7¢ design of UX68	1.75	1.25	4.00
UY26	9¢ & 9¢ design of UX69	1.75	1.25	2.00
	1976			
UY27	9¢ & 9¢ design of UX70	1.75	1.25	2.00
	1977			
UY28	9¢ & 9¢ design of UX72	1.75	1.25	2.00
	1978			
UY29	(10¢ & 10¢) design of UX74	3.00	11.00	10.00
UY30	10¢ & 10¢ design of UX75	1.75	1.25	.40
	1981			
UY31	(12¢ & 12¢) "B" Eagle, design of UX88	1.75	1.25	2.00
UY32	12¢ & 12¢ light blue, design of UX89	1.75	1.25	2.00
UY33	(13¢ & 13¢) buff, design of UX92	1.75	1.85	2.00
UY34	13¢ & 13¢ buff, design of UX93	1.75	1.25	.25
	1985			
UY35	(14¢ & 14¢) Carroll, design of UX105	1.75	2.00	2.00
UY36	14¢ & 14¢ Carroll, design of UX106	1.75	1.25	2.00
UY37	14¢ & 14¢ Wythe, design of UX108	1.75	1.25	2.00
	1987			
UY38	14¢ & 14¢ Flag, design of UX117	1.75	1.25	2.00
	1988			
UY39	15¢ & 15¢ America the Beautiful, design of UX120	1.75	1.25	1.00
	1991			
UY40	19¢ & 19¢ Flag	1.75	1.35	1.00
	1995			
UY41	20¢ & 20¢ Red Barn	1.75	1.35	1.00

OFFICIAL POSTAL CARDS

Official Mall USA

USA 13c

UZ1 UZ2

SCOTT NO.	DESCRIPTION	FIRST DAY COVERS	MINT	USED
	1913			
UZ1	1¢ black (Printed Address)	......	325.00	185.00
	1983			
UZ2	13¢ Great Seal	1.75	.45	30.00
	1985			
UZ3	14¢ Great Seal	1.75	.50	25.00

Official Mail 15 USA

UZ4

SCOTT NO.	DESCRIPTION	FIRST DAY COVERS	MINT	USED
	1988			
UZ4	15¢ Great Seal	1.75	.45	2.50

Official Mail USA 19

UZ5

SCOTT NO.	DESCRIPTION	FIRST DAY COVERS	MINT	USED
	1991			
UZ5	19¢ Great Seal	1.75	.50	2.50

Official Mail USA 20

UZ6

SCOTT NO.	DESCRIPTION	FIRST DAY COVERS	MINT	USED
	1995			
UZ6	20¢ Great Seal	1.75	.50	2.50

U.S. Revenues #R1-R42

1862-71 FIRST ISSUE

When ordering from this issue be sure to indicate whether the "a", "b" or "c" variety is wanted. Example: R27c. Prices are for used singles.

R1-R4

R5-R15

R16-R42

R43-R53

R54-R65

R66-R76

SCOTT NO.	DESCRIPTION	IMPERFORATE (a) F	IMPERFORATE (a) AVG	PART. PERF. (b) F	PART. PERF. (b) AVG	PERFORATED (c) F	PERFORATED (c) AVG
R1	1¢ Express	52.25	27.50	35.75	19.25	1.00	.55
R2	1¢ Playing Cards	742.50	412.50	385.00	230.00	93.50	49.50
R3	1¢ Proprietary	495.00	275.00	99.00	55.00	.40	.25
R4	1¢ Telegraph	275.00	155.00	....	....	7.45	4.15
R5	2¢ Bank Check, blue	.85	.50	1.00	.60	.20	.15
R6	2¢ Bank Check, orange	....	....	71.50	41.25	.20	.15
R7	2¢ Certificate, blue	10.45	5.50	....	....	27.50	12.10
R8	2¢ Certificate, orange	....	....	....	....	24.75	12.10
R9	2¢ Express, blue	10.45	5.50	14.85	8.00	.30	.15
R10	2¢ Express, orange	....	....	....	....	6.00	3.30
R11	2¢ Playing Cards, blue	....	....	110.00	60.50	2.50	1.40
R12	2¢ Playing Cards, orange	....	....	....	....	24.75	13.75
R13	2¢ Proprietary, blue	....	....	93.50	52.25	.35	.20
R14	2¢ Proprietary, orange	....	....	....	....	33.00	17.60
R15	2¢ U.S. Internal Revenue	....	....	....	....	.20	.15
R16	3¢ Foreign Exchange	....	....	143.00	82.50	2.30	1.10
R17	3¢ Playing Cards	....	....	....	....	99.00	52.25
R18	3¢ Proprietary	....	....	181.50	110.00	1.65	.80
R19	3¢ Telegraph	41.25	22.00	13.75	7.70	2.60	1.40
R20	4¢ Inland Exchange	....	....	....	....	1.65	.95
R21	4¢ Playing Cards	....	....	....	....	357.50	181.50
R22	4¢ Proprietary	....	....	181.50	104.50	2.75	1.40
R23	5¢ Agreement	....	....	....	....	.30	.15
R24	5¢ Certificate	2.50	1.40	8.80	4.95	.20	.15
R25	5¢ Express	3.70	2.20	4.70	2.90	.35	.20
R26	5¢ Foreign Exchange	....	....	....	....	.35	.20
R27	5¢ Inland Exchange	3.60	2.15	3.60	2.15	.25	.15
R28	5¢ Playing Cards	....	....	....	....	12.10	6.60
R29	5¢ Proprietary	....	....	....	....	18.70	8.80
R30	6¢ Inland Exchange	....	....	....	....	1.05	.55
R32	10¢ Bill of Lading	46.75	24.75	143.00	77.00	.85	.40
R33	10¢ Certificate	82.50	44.00	110.00	60.50	.35	.20
R34	10¢ Contract, blue	....	....	99.00	55.00	.35	.20
R35	10¢ Foreign Exchange	....	....	....	....	4.70	2.75
R36	10¢ Inland Exchange	120.00	66.00	3.05	1.85	.25	.15
R37	10¢ Power of Attorney	302.50	165.00	18.15	11.00	.40	.25
R38	10¢ Proprietary	....	....	....	....	13.20	6.60
R39	15¢ Foreign Exchange	....	....	....	....	12.10	6.60
R40	15¢ Inland Exchange	24.75	13.75	11.00	6.05	1.00	.55
R41	20¢ Foreign Exchange	42.50	23.65	....	....	29.25	15.40
R42	20¢ Inland Exchange	12.65	7.15	16.50	9.35	.40	.25

U.S. Revenues #R43-R87

SCOTT NO.	DESCRIPTION	IMPERFORATE (a) F	AVG	PART. PERF. (b) F	AVG	PERFORATED (c) F	AVG
R43	25¢ Bond	96.25	52.25	5.80	3.50	1.65	.95
R44	25¢ Certificate	6.35	3.30	5.50	3.05	.20	.15
R45	25¢ Entry of Goods	16.50	9.35	33.00	18.15	.55	.30
R46	25¢ Insurance	8.80	4.95	9.90	5.50	.30	.15
R47	25¢ Life Insurance	31.50	17.60	99.00	55.00	4.70	2.50
R48	25¢ Power of Attorney	5.50	3.30	16.50	9.35	.30	.15
R49	25¢ Protest	22.00	12.10	137.50	74.25	5.50	3.05
R50	25¢ Warehouse Receipt	35.75	19.80	137.50	77.00	21.45	11.55
R51	30¢ Foreign Exchange	52.25	23.60	440.00	247.50	33.00	18.25
R52	30¢ Inland Exchange	38.50	22.00	41.25	22.00	2.15	1.20
R53	40¢ Inland Exchange	425.00	247.50	4.15	2.50	2.50	1.40
R54	50¢ Conveyance, blue	9.90	5.50	1.20	.75	.20	.15
R55	50¢ Entry of Goods	....	....	11.00	6.00	.30	.15
R56	50¢ Foreign Exchange	36.85	20.35	31.35	17.50	4.15	2.20
R57	50¢ Lease	21.45	12.10	55.00	30.25	5.25	2.75
R58	50¢ Life Insurance	27.50	15.40	52.25	28.50	.85	.50
R59	50¢ Mortgage	9.35	4.95	1.65	1.00	.40	.25
R60	50¢ Original Process	2.50	1.40	....	....	.35	.20
R61	50¢ Passage Ticket	66.00	35.75	104.50	55.00	.55	.30
R62	50¢ Probate of Will	31.35	17.60	44.00	24.25	16.50	9.35
R63	50¢ Surety Bond, blue	110.00	60.50	2.60	1.45	.30	.15
R64	60¢ Inland Exchange	77.00	42.35	44.00	24.50	4.95	2.75
R65	70¢ Foreign Exchange	291.50	165.00	82.50	46.75	4.95	2.75
R66	$1 Conveyance	10.45	5.80	247.50	137.50	2.50	1.20
R67	$1 Entry of Goods	24.75	13.75	....	....	1.55	.90
R68	$1 Foreign Exchange	49.50	26.95	....	....	.75	.45
R69	$1 Inland Exchange	10.45	5.80	220.00	120.00	.55	.30
R70	$1 Lease	32.45	17.60	....	....	1.40	.85
R71	$1 Life Insurance	137.50	79.75	....	....	4.70	2.50
R72	$1 Manifest	49.50	27.50	....	....	20.90	12.10
R73	$1 Mortgage	15.95	9.35	....	....	126.50	66.00
R74	$1 Passage Ticket	154.00	88.00	....	....	137.50	68.75
R75	$1 Power of Attorney	57.75	31.35	....	....	1.75	1.00
R76	$1 Probate of Will	55.00	30.25	....	....	33.00	18.25

R77-R80

R81-R87

R88-R96

R97-R101

Washington

SCOTT NO.	DESCRIPTION	IMPERFORATE (a) F	AVG	PART. PERF. (b) F	AVG	PERFORATED (c) F	AVG
R77	$1.30 Foreign Exchange	....	....	....	....	44.00	24.75
R78	$1.50 Inland Exchange	21.00	11.55	....	....	2.90	1.60
R79	$1.60 Foreign Exchange	550.00	302.50	....	....	88.00	46.75
R80	$1.90 Foreign Exchange	1650.00	990.00	....	....	60.50	30.25
R81	$2 Conveyance	88.00	49.50	850.00	500.00	1.90	1.05
R82	$2 Mortgage	77.00	42.35	....	....	2.50	1.40
R83	$2 Probate of Will	....	....	....	....	41.25	22.00
R84	$2.50 Inland Exchange	962.50	535.00	....	....	3.05	1.65
R85	$3 Charter Party	90.75	52.25	....	....	3.60	2.00
R86	$2 Manifest	88.00	49.50	....	....	20.90	11.55
R87	$3.50 Inland Exchange	1000.00	650.00	....	....	44.00	24.75

U.S. Revenues #R88-R121

R102

SCOTT NO.	DESCRIPTION	IMPERFORATE (a) F	AVG	PART. PERF. (b) F	AVG	PERFORATED (c) F	AVG
R88	$5 Charter Party	214.50	120.00	....	....	4.70	2.75
R89	$5 Conveyance	30.25	16.50	....	....	4.70	2.75
R90	$5 Manifest	82.50	45.50	....	....	82.50	45.65
R91	$5 Mortgage	79.75	44.00	....	....	16.50	9.10
R92	$5 Probate of Will	375.00	209.00	....	....	16.50	9.10
R93	$10 Charter Party	412.50	220.00	....	....	20.90	11.55
R94	$10 Conveyance	77.00	43.50	....	....	55.00	30.25
R95	$10 Mortgage	302.50	165.00	....	....	20.90	11.55
R96	$10 Probate of Will	935.00	522.50	....	....	20.90	11.55
R97	$15 Mortgage, blue	852.50	478.50	....	....	90.75	49.50
R98	$20 Conveyance	55.00	30.25	....	....	31.35	18.25
R99	$20 Probate of Will	852.50	478.50	....	....	795.00	440.00
R100	$25 Mortgage	700.00	396.00	....	....	82.50	46.75
R101	$50 U.S. Internal Revenue	154.00	88.00	....	....	77.00	44.00
R102	$200 U.S. Int. Revenue	990.00	550.00	....	....	522.50	302.50

1871 SECOND ISSUE

NOTE: The individual denominations vary in design from the illustrations shown which are more typical of their relative size.

R103, R104, R134, R135, R151

R105-R111, R136-R139

R112-R114

R115-R117, R142-R143

R118-R122, R144

R123-R126, R145-R147

R127, R128, R148, R149

R129-R131, R150

SCOTT NO.	DESCRIPTION	USED F	AVG
R103	1¢ blue and black	24.75	13.75
R104	2¢ blue and black	1.05	.60
R105	3¢ blue and black	12.10	6.60
R106	4¢ blue and black	41.25	22.00
R107	5¢ blue and black	1.05	.60
R108	6¢ blue and black	66.00	35.75
R109	10¢ blue and black	.90	.50
R110	15¢ blue and black	19.80	11.00
R111	20¢ blue and black	4.40	2.50
R112	25¢ blue and black	.65	.35
R113	30¢ blue and black	49.50	27.50
R114	40¢ blue and black	27.50	15.25
R115	50¢ blue and black	.65	.40
R116	60¢ blue and black	57.75	31.50
R117	70¢ blue and black	23.50	12.95
R118	$1 blue and black	3.05	1.65
R119	$1.30 blue and black	220.00	121.00
R120	$1.50 blue and black	11.00	6.05
R121	$1.60 blue and black	275.00	154.00

U.S. Revenues #R122-R174

SCOTT NO.	DESCRIPTION	USED F	USED AVG
R122	$1.90 blue and black	120.00	66.00
R123	$2.00 blue and black	10.45	5.80
R124	$2.50 blue and black	19.25	10.75
R125	$3.00 blue and black	30.25	17.05
R126	$3.50 blue and black	110.00	55.00
R127	$5 blue and black	16.50	9.35
R128	$10 blue and black	82.50	49.50
R129	$20 blue and black	265.00	143.00
R130	$25 blue and black	265.00	143.00
R131	$50 blue and black	302.50	165.00

1871-72 THIRD ISSUE

SCOTT NO.	DESCRIPTION	USED F	USED AVG
R134	1¢ claret and black	22.00	12.10
R135	2¢ orange and black	.15	.15
R135b	2¢ orange and black (center inverted)	325.00	225.00
R136	4¢ brown and black	27.50	14.85
R137	5¢ orange and black	.30	.15
R138	6¢ orange and black	27.50	15.50
R139	15¢ brown and black	9.90	5.50
R140	30¢ orange and black	10.45	6.00
R141	40¢ brown and black	22.00	12.65
R142	60¢ orange and black	46.75	26.25
R143	70¢ green and black	30.25	16.50
R144	$1 green and black	1.35	.75
R145	$2 vermillion and black	19.80	10.45
R146	$2.50 claret and black	29.15	15.95
R147	$3 green and black	31.35	17.60
R148	$5 vermillion and black	17.60	9.65
R149	$10 green and black	66.00	38.50
R150	$20 orange and black	368.50	203.50

1874 on greenish paper

SCOTT NO.	DESCRIPTION	USED F	USED AVG
R151	2¢ orange and black	.20	.15
R151a	2¢ orange and black (center inverted)	395.00	295.00

R152
Liberty

I. R.

R153

I. R.

R154, R155

R161-R172

R173-R178, R182, R183

SCOTT NO.	DESCRIPTION	UNUSED F	UNUSED AVG	USED F	USED AVG
	1875-78				
R152a	2¢ blue on blue silk paper	....	....	.20	.15
R152b	2¢ watermarked ("USIR") paper	....	....	.20	.15
R152c	2¢ watermarked, rouletted	....	....	27.50	13.75
	1898 Postage Stamps 279 & 267 Surcharged				
R153	1¢ green, small I.R.	1.05	.55	.60	.35
R154	1¢ green, large I.R.	.25	.20	.20	.15
R155	2¢ carmine, large I.R.	.25	.20	.60	.35

DOCUMENTARY STAMPS

Newspaper Stamp PR121 Surcharged

INT. REV.
$5.
DOCUMENTARY.

SCOTT NO.	DESCRIPTION	UNUSED F	UNUSED AVG	USED F	USED AVG
R159	$5 dark blue, red surcharge reading down ..	176.00	99.00	126.50	68.75
R160	$5 dark blue, red surcharge reading up	82.50	44.00	55.00	30.25
	1898 Battleships Inscribed "Documentary"				
R161	1/2¢ orange	2.00	3.85	6.05	3.85
R162	1/2¢ dark gray	.25	.20	.20	.15
R163	1¢ pale blue	.25	.20	.20	.15
R164	2¢ carmine	.25	.20	.20	.15
R165	3¢ dark blue	.90	.50	.20	.15
R166	4¢ pale rose	.40	.25	.20	.15
R167	5¢ lilac	.25	.20	.20	.15
R168	10¢ dark brown	.40	.25	.20	.15
R169	25¢ purple brown	.40	.25	.20	.15
R170	40¢ blue lilac .... (cut cancel .25)	52.25	30.25	1.20	.75
R171	50¢ slate violet	4.15	2.20	.20	.15
R172	80¢ bistre .... (cut cancel .15)	22.00	13.75	.40	.25
R173	$1 dark green	3.85	2.20	.20	.15
R174	$3 dark brown .... (cut cancel .20)	9.35	4.95	.45	.30

U.S. Revenues #R175-R205

SCOTT NO.	DESCRIPTION	UNUSED F	UNUSED AVG	USED F	USED AVG
R175	$5 orange red (cut cancel .25)	11.00	7.15	1.10	.65
R176	$10 black (cut cancel .70)	33.00	20.35	2.75	1.65
R177	$30 red (cut cancel 25.00)	115.50	66.00	74.25	44.00
R178	$50 gray brown (cut cancel 1.50)	55.00	31.35	3.60	1.95

R179, R225, R246, R248 *Washington*

R180, R226, R249 *Hamilton*

R181, R224, R227, R247, R250 *Madison*

R195-R216

R217-R223

1899 Various Portraits Inscribed "Series of 1898"

SCOTT NO.	DESCRIPTION	UNUSED F	UNUSED AVG	USED F	USED AVG
R179	$100 yellow brown & black (cut cancel 11.50)	57.75	35.75	27.50	15.40
R180	$500 carmine lake & black (cut cancel 180.00)	544.50	357.50	440.00	275.00
R181	$1000 green & black (cut cancel 95.00)	440.00	265.00	330.00	265.00

1900

SCOTT NO.	DESCRIPTION	UNUSED F	UNUSED AVG	USED F	USED AVG
R182	$1 carmine (cut cancel .15)	6.33	3.60	.55	.35
R183	$3 lake (cut cancel 7.00)	66.00	38.50	41.25	24.75

R184-R189

Designs of R173-78 surcharged

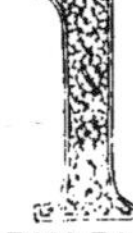

R190-R194

R228-239, R251-256, R260-263

R240-245, R257-259

Surcharged

SCOTT NO.	DESCRIPTION	UNUSED F	UNUSED AVG	USED F	USED AVG
R184	$1 gray (cut cancel .15)	3.60	1.95	.20	.15
R185	$2 gray (cut cancel .15)	3.05	1.65	.20	.15
R186	$3 gray (cut cancel 1.00)	31.35	16.50	10.45	6.00
R187	$5 gray (cut cancel .35)	18.15	10.45	4.40	2.75
R188	$10 gray (cut cancel 3.00)	38.50	23.10	9.65	6.00
R189	$50 gray (cut cancel 70.00)	550.00	302.50	330.00	181.50

1902

SCOTT NO.	DESCRIPTION	UNUSED F	UNUSED AVG	USED F	USED AVG
R190	$1 green (cut cancel .30)	7.15	3.85	2.20	1.40
R191	$2 green (cut cancel .25)	6.60	3.85	1.00	.60
R191a	$2 surcharged as R185	85.00	60.00	85.00	60.00
R192	$5 green (cut cancel 1.50)	44.00	24.75	14.85	8.25
R192a	$5 surcharge omitted	70.00	47.50	....	....
R193	$10 green (cut cancel 22.50)	214.50	120.00	143.00	77.00
R194	$50 green (cut cancel 200.00)	962.50	545.00	687.50	385.00

1914 Inscribed "Series of 1914" Single Line Watermark "USPS"

SCOTT NO.	DESCRIPTION	UNUSED F	UNUSED AVG	USED F	USED AVG
R195	1/2¢ rose	4.70	2.75	2.30	1.40
R196	1¢ rose	1.10	.60	.20	.15
R197	2¢ rose	1.10	.60	.15	.15
R198	3¢ rose	27.50	14.85	18.70	10.45
R199	4¢ rose	6.05	3.30	.95	.55
R200	5¢ rose	2.30	1.30	.20	.15
R201	10¢ rose	2.15	1.20	.15	.15
R202	25¢ rose	13.75	7.45	.50	.30
R203	40¢ rose	7.15	4.15	.55	.35
R204	50¢ rose	3.60	1.95	.15	.15
R205	80¢ rose	38.50	20.35	6.00	3.70

U.S. Revenues #R206-R263

SCOTT NO.	DESCRIPTION	UNUSED F	UNUSED AVG	USED F	USED AVG
	1914 Double Line Watermark "USIR"				
R206	1/2¢ rose	1.10	.55	.55	.35
R207	1¢ rose	.25	.20	.20	.15
R208	2¢ rose	.25	.20	.20	.15
R209	3¢ rose	1.10	.55	.25	.20
R210	4¢ rose	1.95	1.05	.35	.20
R211	5¢ rose	1.10	.55	.20	.15
R212	10¢ rose	.40	.25	.20	.15
R213	25¢ rose	3.05	1.75	.80	.50
R214	40¢ rose (cut cancel .60)	35.75	19.25	7.15	3.85
R215	50¢ rose	7.15	3.85	.20	.15
R216	80¢ rose (cut cancel 1.00)	41.25	21.50	8.00	4.80
R217	$1 green (cut cancel .15)	13.20	8.25	.20	.15
R218	$2 carmine (cut cancel .15)	24.75	13.75	.20	.15
R219	$3 purple (cut cancel .25)	35.75	19.25	1.10	.55
R220	$5 blue (cut cancel .65)	31.35	16.50	1.95	1.10
R221	$10 orange (cut cancel 1.00)	71.50	38.50	4.40	2.65
R222	$30 vermillion (cut cancel 2.25)	121.00	71.50	9.65	5.80
R223	$50 violet (cut cancel 200.00)	865.00	480.00	632.50	345.00
	1914-15 Various Portraits Inscribed "Series of 1914" or "Series of 1915"				
R224	$60 brown (cut cancel 45.00)	....	....	110.00	66.00
R225	$100 green (cut cancel 15.00)	....	....	41.25	22.00
R226	$500 blue (cut cancel 200.00)	....	....	495.00	275.00
R227	$1000 orange (cut cancel 200.00)	....	....	495.00	275.00
	1917 Perf. 11				
R228	1¢ carmine rose	.25	.20	.20	.15
R229	2¢ carmine rose	.25	.20	.20	.15
R230	3¢ carmine rose	.30	.20	.25	.15
R231	4¢ carmine rose	.25	.20	.20	.15
R232	5¢ carmine rose	.25	.20	.20	.15
R233	8¢ carmine rose	1.35	.85	.20	.15
R234	10¢ carmine rose	.25	.20	.20	.15
R235	20¢ carmine rose	.35	.20	.20	.15
R236	25¢ carmine rose	.60	.40	.20	.15
R237	40¢ carmine rose	.85	.50	.20	.15
R238	50¢ carmine rose	1.05	.60	.20	.15
R239	80¢ carmine rose	2.75	1.65	.20	.15
	Same design as issue of 1914-15 Without dates.				
R240	$1 yellow green	3.85	2.04	.20	.15
R241	$2 rose	8.00	4.70	.20	.15
R242	$3 violet (cut cancel .15)	22.00	13.75	.50	.30
R243	$4 yellow brown (cut cancel .20)	13.20	7.70	1.10	.65
R244	$5 dark blue .... (cut cancel .10) (perf. in. 15)	8.80	4.95	.25	.15
R245	$10 orange (cut cancel .20)	17.60	9.65	.65	.40
	Types of 1899 Various Portraits Perf. 12				
R246	$30 deep orange, Grant (cut cancel .70)	27.50	16.50	2.20	1.35
R247	$60 brown, Lincoln (cut cancel 95)	35.75	21.45	7.15	4.40
R248	$100 green, Washington (cut cancel .45)	22.00	12.65	.85	.50
R249	$500 blue, Hamilton (cut cancel 10.00)	....	....	33.00	19.25
R249a	$500 Numerals in orange	....	....	60.00	42.50
R250	$1000 orange, Madison (Perf. In. 3.00) (cut cancel 3.50)	90.75	52.25	11.00	6.60
	1928-29 Perf. 10				
R251	1¢ carmine rose	1.85	1.10	1.00	.60
R252	2¢ carmine rose	.55	.35	.20	.15
R253	4¢ carmine rose	5.25	2.75	3.30	2.05
R254	5¢ carmine rose	1.10	.50	.35	.20
R255	10¢ carmine rose	1.65	1.00	.95	.60
R256	20¢ carmine rose	5.25	3.05	4.15	2.50
R257	$1 green (cut cancel 2.00)	57.75	33.00	27.50	16.50
R258	$2 rose	14.85	8.25	1.65	1.00
R259	$10 orange (cut cancel 7.00)	79.75	46.75	24.75	16.50
	1929-30 Perf. 11 x 10				
R260	2¢ carmine rose	2.50	1.40	1.95	1.20
R261	5¢ carmine rose	1.95	1.20	1.10	.75
R262	10¢ carmine rose	7.15	3.85	6.05	3.85
R263	20¢ carmine rose	13.75	8.25	8.25	4.95

U.S. Revenues #R733-R734; RB1-RB23

SCOTT NO.	DESCRIPTION	PLATE BLOCK F/NH	UNUSED F/NH	USED F

R733, R734

1962 CENTENNIAL INTERNAL REVENUE. Inscribed "Established 1862"

SCOTT NO.	DESCRIPTION	PLATE BLOCK F/NH	UNUSED F/NH	USED F
R733	10¢ violet blue & green	13.50	1.25	.50
	1964 Without Inscription Date			
R734	10¢ violet blue & green	25.00	3.50	.50

RB1-2

RB3-7

RB11-12

RB13-19

PROPRIETARY STAMPS

1871-74 Perforated 12

SCOTT NO.	DESCRIPTION	VIOLET PAPER (a) F	VIOLET PAPER (a) AVG	GREEN PAPER (b) F	GREEN PAPER (b) AVG
RB1	1¢ green & black	3.60	2.15	5.50	3.30
RB2	2¢ green & black	4.15	2.50	12.10	7.15
RB3	3¢ green & black	11.00	6.60	35.75	19.25
RB4	4¢ green & black	6.90	3.85	11.00	6.60
RB5	5¢ green & black	104.50	57.75	110.00	60.50
RB6	6¢ green & black	26.95	15.25	82.50	45.75
RB7	10¢ green & black	143.00	82.50	33.00	18.15
RB8	50¢ green & black (large)	632.50	357.50	900.00	495.00

1875-81 NATIONAL BANK NOTE

SCOTT NO.	DESCRIPTION	SILK PAPER(a) F	SILK PAPER(a) AVG	WMKD., PERF. (b) F	WMKD., PERF. (b) AVG	ROULETTE(c) F	ROULETTE(c) AVG
RB11	1¢ green	1.40	.85	.35	.20	38.50	20.35
RB12	2¢ brown	1.95	1.10	1.20	.65	49.50	27.50
RB13	3¢ orange	8.25	4.40	2.15	1.40	55.00	30.25
RB14	4¢ red brown	4.40	2.50	3.85	2.15	....	....
RB15	4¢ red	....	....	3.85	2.15	55.00	30.25
RB16	5¢ black	96.25	55.00	71.50	35.75	....	101.75
RB17	6¢ violet blue	18.70	11.00	12.65	7.15	148.50	82.50
RB18	6¢ violet	....	....	19.25	11.00	181.50	101.75
RB19	10¢ blue	....	....	187.00	104.50	....	....

RB20-31

RB32-64

RB65-73

1898 Battleship Inscribed "Proprietary"

SCOTT NO.	DESCRIPTION	UNUSED F	UNUSED AVG	USED F	USED AVG
RB20	1/8¢ yellow green	.25	.20	.20	.15
RB21	1/4¢ brown	.25	.20	.20	.15
RB22	3/8¢ deep orange	.25	.20	.20	.15
RB23	5/8¢ deep ultramarine	.25	.20	.20	.15

U.S. Revenues #RB24-RB73; RC1-RC5

SCOTT NO.	DESCRIPTION	UNUSED F	UNUSED AVG	USED F	USED AVG
RB24	1¢ dark green	.40	.25	.25	.15
RB25	1-1/4¢ violet	.25	.20	.20	.15
RB26	1-7/8¢ dull blue	2.05	1.10	.85	.50
RB27	2¢ violet brown	.40	.25	.25	.15
RB28	2-1/2¢ lake	.85	.45	.20	.15
RB29	3-3/4¢ olive gray	8.25	4.95	2.95	1.75
RB30	4¢ purple	2.75	1.65	.95	.55
RB31	5¢ brown orange	2.75	1.65	.85	.50
	1914 Watermarked "USPS"				
RB32	1/8¢ black	.25	.20	.20	.15
RB33	1/4¢ black	1.10	.65	.95	.55
RB34	3/8¢ black	.25	.20	.20	.15
RB35	5/8¢ black	2.30	1.35	1.65	1.00
RB36	1-1/4¢ black	1.50	.95	.75	.45
RB37	1-7/8¢ black	23.65	13.75	14.85	8.80
RB38	2-1/2¢ black	3.30	1.95	2.15	1.65
RB39	3-1/8¢ black	66.00	38.50	46.75	27.50
RB40	3-3/4¢ black	23.65	13.75	17.10	10.45
RB41	4¢ black	41.25	24.75	25.85	15.10
RB43	5¢ black	85.25	49.50	57.75	33.00
	1914 Watermarked "USIR"				
RB44	1/8¢ black	.25	.20	.20	.15
RB45	1/4¢ black	.25	.20	.20	.15
RB46	3/8¢ black	.60	.35	.35	.20
RB47	1/2¢ black	2.50	1.50	1.95	1.20
RB48	5/8¢ black	.25	.20	.20	.15
RB49	1¢ black	3.30	1.85	2.50	1.40
RB50	1-1/4¢ black	.35	.20	.25	.15
RB51	1-1/2¢ black	3.05	1.75	2.20	1.20
RB52	1-7/8¢ black	.85	.50	.55	.35
RB53	2¢ black	4.70	3.05	3.60	2.15
RB54	2-1/2¢ black	1.20	.75	1.00	.60
RB55	3¢ black	3.30	1.85	2.50	1.50
RB56	3-1/8¢ black	3.85	2.30	2.75	1.65
RB57	3-3/4¢ black	8.55	4.95	6.90	4.15
RB58	4¢ black	.30	.20	.25	.15
RB59	4-3/8¢ black	9.90	5.80	6.90	4.15
RB60	5¢ black	2.50	1.35	2.15	1.20
RB61	6¢ black	44.00	26.40	35.75	21.45
RB62	8¢ black	12.10	7.15	9.90	6.05
RB63	10¢ black	8.55	4.95	6.60	3.85
RB64	20¢ black	16.50	9.90	13.75	8.25
	1919 Offset Printing				
RB65	1¢ dark blue	.25	.20	.15	.15
RB66	2¢ dark blue	.25	.20	.15	.15
RB67	3¢ dark blue	.95	.55	.55	.35
RB68	4¢ dark blue	.95	.55	.50	.30
RB69	5¢ dark blue	1.10	.65	.55	.35
RB70	8¢ dark blue	9.90	6.05	8.00	4.70
RB71	10¢ dark blue	2.75	1.85	1.95	1.20
RB72	20¢ dark blue	4.40	3.05	2.75	1.65
RB73	40¢ dark blue	21.75	12.95	9.35	5.50

FUTURE DELIVERY STAMPS

FUTURE
DELIVERY
Type 1

Documentary Stamps of 1917 Overprinted

FUTURE
DELIVERY
Type II

1918-34 Perforated 11, Type 1 Overprint Lines 8mm. Apart

SCOTT NO.	DESCRIPTION	UNUSED F	UNUSED AVG	USED F	USED AVG
RC1	2¢ carmine rose	1.40	.85	.20	.15
RC2	3¢ carmine rose (cut cancel 12.50)	27.50	16.50	19.80	12.10
RC3	4¢ carmine rose	1.75	1.00	.20	.15
RC3A	5¢ carmine rose	35.75	23.65	2.75	1.65
RC4	10¢ carmine rose	4.40	2.75	.20	.15
RC5	20¢ carmine rose	4.40	2.75	.20	.15

U.S. Revenues #RC6-RC26; RD1-RD32

SCOTT NO.	DESCRIPTION	UNUSED F	UNUSED AVG	USED F	USED AVG
RC6	25¢ carmine rose .... (cut cancel .10)	10.45	6.25	.50	.35
RC7	40¢ carmine rose .... (cut cancel .10)	10.45	4.50	.50	.35
RC8	50¢ carmine rose	3.60	1.60	.20	.15
RC9	80¢ carmine rose .... (cut cancel .85)	16.50	10.75	6.00	3.85
RC10	$1 green .... (cut cancel .10)	......	......	.20	.15
RC11	$2 rose .... (cut cancel .10)	......	......	.20	.15
RC12	$3 violet .... (cut cancel .15)	......	......	1.25	.80
RC13	$5 dark blue .... (cut cancel .10)	......	......	.30	.20
RC14	$10 orange .... (cut cancel .20)	......	......	.60	.40
RC15	$20 olive bistre .... (cut cancel .55)	......	......	3.65	2.35
	Perforated 12				
RC16	$30 vermillon .... (cut cancel 1.25)	......	......	3.35	2.15
RC17	$50 olive green .... (cut cancel 1.50)	......	......	1.10	.70
RC18	$60 brown .... (cut cancel .90)	......	......	1.75	1.10
RC19	$100 yellow green .... (cut cancel 6.00)	......	......	24.50	16.00
RC20	$500 blue .... (cut cancel 4.25)	60.00	38.75	9.50	6.25
RC21	$1000 orange .... (cut cancel 1.75)	......	......	4.25	2.75
RC22	1¢ carmine rose (lines 2mm apart)	.45	.30	.20	.15
RC23	80¢ carmine rose (lines 2mm apart)(cut cancel .25)	......	......	1.50	.95
	1925-34 Perforated 11 Type II Overprint				
RC25	$1 green .... (cut cancel .10)	6.00	3.85	.60	.40
RC26	$10 orange .... (cut cancel 5.75)	......	......	12.00	7.75

STOCK TRANSFER STAMPS

STOCK TRANSFER

Type I

Documentary Stamps of 1917 Overprinted

STOCK TRANSFER

Type II

SCOTT NO.	DESCRIPTION	UNUSED F	UNUSED AVG	USED F	USED AVG
	1918-22 Perforated 11 Type I Overprint				
RD1	1¢ carmine rose	.30	.20	.20	.15
RD2	2¢ carmine rose	.20	.15	.20	.15
RD3	4¢ carmine rose	.20	.15	.20	.15
RD4	5¢ carmine rose	.20	.15	.20	.15
RD5	10¢ carmine rose	.20	.15	.20	.15
RD6	20¢ carmine rose	.25	.20	.20	.15
RD7	25¢ carmine rose .... (cut cancel .10)	.70	.45	.20	.15
RD8	40¢ carmine rose	.60	.40	.20	.15
RD9	50¢ carmine rose	.30	.20	.20	.15
RD10	80¢ carmine rose .... (cut cancel .10)	.75	.50	.25	.20
RD11	$1 green (red ovverprint) .... (cut cancel .55)	30.00	19.50	7.50	4.75
RD12	$1 green (black overprint)	1.50	.95	.20	.15
RD13	$2 rose	1.50	.95	.20	.15
RD14	$3 violet .... (cut cancel .25)	5.25	3.50	.90	.60
RD15	$4 yellow brown .... (cut cancel .10)	3.75	2.50	.20	.15
RD16	$5 dark blue .... (cut cancel .10)	2.50	1.60	.20	.15
RD17	$10 orange .... (cut cancel .10)	3.75	2.50	.20	.15
RD18	$20 olive bistre .... (cut cancel 3.50)	35.00	22.50	17.50	11.50
	Perforated 12				
RD19	$30 vermillion .... (cut cancel 1.20)	13.50	8.75	4.25	2.75
RD20	$50 olive green .... (cut cancel 12.00)	70.00	45.00	35.00	35.00
RD21	$60 brown .... (cut cancel 6.00)	55.00	35.00	16.50	10.75
RD22	$100 green .... (cut cancel 1.75)	14.75	9.50	4.75	3.00
RD23	$500 blue .... (cut cancel 47.50)	......	......	110.00	70.00
RD24	$1000 orange .... (cut cancel 27.50)	......	......	77.50	50.00
	1928 Perforated 10 Type I Overprint				
RD25	2¢ carmine rose	.30	.20	.20	.15
RD26	4¢ carmine rose	.30	.20	.20	.15
RD27	10¢ carmine rose	.35	.25	.20	.15
RD28	20¢ carmine rose	.55	.35	.20	.15
RD29	50¢ carmine rose	1.00	.65	.20	.15
RD30	$1 green	1.65	1.10	.20	.15
RD31	$2 carmine rose	1.65	1.10	.20	.15
RD32	$10 orange .... (cut cancel .10)	7.50	4.75	.20	.15

U.S. Revenues #RD33-RD41; RG1-RG27; RJ1-RJ11

SCOTT NO.	DESCRIPTION	UNUSED F	UNUSED AVG	USED F	USED AVG
RD33	2¢ carmine rose	2.65	1.75	.50	.35
RD34	10¢ carmine rose	.40	.25	.20	.15
RD35	20¢ carmine rose	.45	.30	.20	.15
RD36	50¢ carmine rose	1.00	.65	.20	.15
RD37	$1 green (cut cancel .30)	12.00	7.85	5.50	3.50
RD38	$2 rose (cut cancel .30)	8.75	5.75	5.50	3.50

1920-28 Perforated 10 Type II overprint

SCOTT NO.	DESCRIPTION	UNUSED F	UNUSED AVG	USED F	USED AVG
RD39	2¢ carmine rose	2.75	1.75	.30	.20
RD40	10¢ carmine rose	.75	.50	.20	.15
RD41	20$ carmine rose	1.00	.65	.20	.15

SILVER TAX STAMPS

Documentary Stamps of 1917 Overprinted 1934-36

SCOTT NO.	DESCRIPTION	UNUSED F	UNUSED AVG	USED F	USED AVG
RG1	1¢ carmine rose	.75	.50	.35	.25
RG2	2¢ carmine rose	1.10	.70	.40	.30
RG3	3¢ carmine rose	1.20	.80	.50	.35
RG4	4¢ carmine rose	1.20	.80	.60	.40
RG5	5¢ carmine rose	1.50	1.00	.90	.60
RG6	8¢ carmine rose	2.00	1.30	1.25	.80
RG7	10¢ carmine rose	2.00	1.30	1.25	.80
RG8	20¢ carmine rose	4.50	2.95	3.00	1.95
RG9	25¢ carmine rose	4.50	2.95	3.50	2.25
RG10	40¢ carmine rose	6.00	3.85	5.25	3.35
RG11	50¢ carmine rose	7.00	4.50	5.75	3.75
RG12	80¢ carmine rose	11.00	7.00	7.00	4.50
RG13	$1 green	11.00	7.00	8.25	5.50
RG14	$2 rose	14.50	9.50	12.00	8.00
RG15	$3 violet	30.00	19.50	25.00	16.00
RG16	$4 yellow brown	20.00	13.00	15.00	10.00
RG17	$5 dark blue	26.50	17.50	14.50	9.50
RG18	$10 orange	45.00	28.75	14.50	9.50
RG19	$30 vermillion (cut cancel 20.00)	......	......	35.00	22.50
RG20	$60 brown (cut cancel 30.00)	......	......	60.00	38.75
RG21	$100 green	105.00	70.00	35.00	22.50
RG22	$500 blue (cut cancel 110.00)	300.00	200.00	235.00	160.00
RG23	$1000 orange (cut cancel 70.00)	......	......	120.00	77.50
RG26	$100 green, 11mm spacing	130.00	85.00	60.00	38.75
RG27	$1000 orange, 11mm spacing	......	......	575.00	375.00

TOBACCO SALE TAX STAMPS

Documentary Stamps of 1917 Overprinted

1934

SCOTT NO.	DESCRIPTION	UNUSED F	UNUSED AVG	USED F	USED AVG
RJ1	1¢ carmine rose	.40	.25	.20	.15
RJ2	2¢ carmine rose	.45	.30	.25	.20
RJ3	5¢ carmine rose	1.40	.90	.45	.30
RJ4	10¢ carmine rose	1.75	1.15	.45	.30
RJ5	25¢ carmine rose	4.75	3.00	1.85	1.20
RJ6	50¢ carmine rose	4.75	3.00	1.85	1.20
RJ7	$1 green	8.00	3.00	1.85	1.20
RJ8	$2 rose	15.00	9.50	2.15	1.40
RJ9	$5 dark blue	17.50	11.00	4.75	3.00
RJ10	$10 orange	30.00	19.00	12.00	7.75
RJ11	$20 olive bistre	70.00	45.00	15.00	9.75

U.S. Revenues #RW1-RW5
HUNTING PERMIT STAMPS

RW1 RW2 RW3

RW4 RW5 RW6

RW7 RW8 RW9

RW10 RW11 RW12

RW13 RW14 RW15

SCOTT NO.	DESCRIPTION	UNUSED VF	UNUSED F	UNUSED AVG	USED VF	USED F	USED AVG
	1934-1938 Inscribed: DEPARTMENT OF AGRICULTURE (NH + 50%)						
RW1	1934 $1 Mallards	540.00	365.00	245.00	140.00	110.00	85.00
RW2	1935 $1 Canvasbacks	500.00	335.00	230.00	200.00	135.00	95.00
RW3	1936 $1 Canada Geese	250.00	165.00	120.00	110.00	72.50	50.00
RW4	1937 $1 Scaup Ducks	200.00	135.00	95.00	65.00	45.00	29.50
RW5	1938 $1 Pintail Drake	215.00	145.00	105.00	75.00	50.00	32.50

U.S. Revenues #RW6-RW25

RW16

RW17

RW18

RW19

RW20

RW21

RW22

RW23

RW24

RW25

SCOTT NO.	DESCRIPTION	UNUSED VF	UNUSED F	UNUSED AVG	USED VF	USED F	USED AVG
	Note: NH premiums RW6-9 (50%) RW10-16 (40%) RW17-25 (25%)						
	1939-1958 Inscribed: DEPARTMENT OF INTERIOR						
RW6	1939 $1 Green-Winged Teal	150.00	100.00	67.50	40.00	27.50	17.00
RW7	1940 $1 Black Mallards	150.00	100.00	67.50	40.00	27.50	17.00
RW8	1941 $1 Ruddy Ducks	150.00	100.00	67.50	40.00	27.50	17.00
RW9	1942 $1 Baldpates	150.00	100.00	67.50	40.00	27.50	17.00
RW10	1943 $1 Wood Ducks	60.00	40.00	28.00	33.50	22.00	15.50
RW11	1944 $1 White Fronted Geese ...	60.00	40.00	28.00	33.50	22.00	15.50
RW12	1945 $1 Shoveller Ducks	40.00	27.50	19.50	27.00	18.00	14.00
RW13	1946 $1 Redhead Ducks	40.00	27.50	19.50	21.00	15.00	10.50
RW14	1947 $1 Snow Geese	40.00	27.50	19.50	21.00	15.00	10.50
RW15	1948 $1 Buffleheads	43.00	31.00	20.50	21.00	15.00	10.50
RW16	1949 $2 Goldeneye Ducks	46.50	33.50	24.00	15.50	11.00	7.50
RW17	1950 $2 Trumpeter Swans	55.00	38.50	26.00	15.50	11.00	7.50
RW18	1951 $2 Gadwall Ducks	55.00	38.50	26.00	11.50	8.25	5.75
RW19	1952 $2 Harlequin Ducks	55.00	38.50	26.00	11.50	8.25	5.75
RW20	1953 $2 Blue-Winged Teal	55.00	38.50	26.00	11.50	8.25	5.75
RW21	1954 $2 Ringed-Necked Ducks .	55.00	38.50	26.00	11.50	8.25	5.75
RW22	1955 $2 Blue Geese	55.00	38.50	26.00	11.50	8.25	5.75
RW23	1956 $2 American Merganser ...	55.00	38.50	26.00	11.50	8.25	5.75
RW24	1957 $2 American Eider	55.00	38.50	26.00	11.50	8.25	5.75
RW25	1958 $2 Canada Geese	55.00	38.50	26.00	11.50	8.25	5.75

Notes on Hunting Permit Stamps

1. Unused stamps without gum (uncancelled) are priced at one-half gummed price.
2. The date printed on the stamp is one year later than the date of issue listed above.
3. #RW1-RW25 and RW31 are plate blocks of 6.

U.S. Revenues #RW26-RW38

RW26

RW27

RW28

RW29

RW30

RW31

RW32

RW33

RW34

RW35

RW36

RW37

RW38

SCOTT NO.	DESCRIPTION	UNUSED VF	UNUSED F	USED VF	USED F
	1959-1971 (NH + 40%)				
RW26	1959 $3 Dog & Mallard	65.00	47.50	11.50	8.25
RW27	1960 $3 Redhead Ducks	65.00	47.50	11.50	8.25
RW28	1961 $3 Mallard Hen & Ducklings	70.00	50.00	11.50	8.25
RW29	1962 $3 Pintail Drakes	80.00	57.50	14.25	10.00
RW30	1963 $3 Brant Ducks Landing	80.00	57.50	14.25	10.00
RW31	1964 $3 Hawaiian Nene Goose	80.00	57.50	14.25	10.00
RW32	1965 $3 Canvasback Drakes	80.00	57.50	14.25	10.00
RW33	1966 $3 Whistling Swans	80.00	57.50	14.25	10.00
RW34	1967 $3 Old Squaw Ducks	80.00	57.50	14.25	10.00
RW35	1968 $3 Hooded Mergansers	50.00	36.00	14.25	10.00
RW36	1969 $3 White-Winged Scoters	50.00	36.00	9.50	6.75
RW37	1970 $3 Ross's Geese	47.00	33.50	9.50	6.75
RW38	1971 $3 Three Cinnamon Teal	33.00	23.75	9.50	6.75

U.S. Revenues #RW39-RW45

RW39

RW40

RW41

RW42

RW43

RW44

RW45

RW46

SCOTT NO.	DESCRIPTION	UNUSED/NH VF	F	USED VF	F
			1972-1978		
RW39	1972 $5 Emperor Geese	32.00	25.00	9.00	7.50
RW40	1973 $5 Steller's Eider	29.00	22.00	9.00	7.50
RW41	1974 $5 Wood Ducks	22.00	17.00	9.00	7.50
RW42	1975 $5 Canvasbacks	18.75	14.50	9.00	7.50
RW43	1976 $5 Canada Geese	18.75	14.50	9.00	7.50
RW44	1977 $5 Pair of Ross's Geese	18.75	14.50	9.00	7.50
RW45	1978 $5 Hooded Merganser Drake	18.75	14.50	9.00	7.50

PLATE BLOCKS RW1-RW25

SCOTT NO.	UNUSED NH F	UNUSED NH AVG	UNUSED OG F	UNUSED OG AVG	SCOTT NO.	UNUSED NH F	UNUSED NH AVG	UNUSED OG F	UNUSED OG AVG
	PLATE BLOCKS OF 6					PLATE BLOCKS OF 6			
RW1(6)	7000.00	5650.00	5750.00	4200.00	RW14(6)	275.00	220.00	195.00	155.00
RW2(6)	8250.00	6600.00	6750.00	5250.00	RW15(6)	305.00	245.00	205.00	165.00
RW3(6)	3000.00	2400.00	2750.00	2200.00	RW16(6)	325.00	260.00	215.00	170.00
RW4(6)	2100.00	1650.00	1800.00	1400.00	RW17(6)	385.00	305.00	260.00	205.00
RW5(6)	2150.00	1725.00	1850.00	1450.00	RW18(6)	385.00	305.00	260.00	205.00
RW6(6)	1500.00	1200.00	1200.00	950.00	RW19(6)	385.00	305.00	260.00	205.00
RW7(6)	1325.00	1050.00	1100.00	875.00	RW20(6)	385.00	305.00	260.00	205.00
RW8(6)	1200.00	950.00	1000.00	800.00	RW21(6)	385.00	305.00	260.00	205.00
RW9(6)	1200.00	950.00	1000.00	800.00	RW22(6)	385.00	305.00	260.00	205.00
RW10(6)	435.00	350.00	325.00	250.00	RW23(6)	385.00	305.00	260.00	205.00
RW11(6)	415.00	325.00	305.00	240.00	RW24(6)	385.00	305.00	260.00	205.00
RW12(6)	275.00	220.00	195.00	155.00	RW25(6)	385.00	305.00	260.00	205.00
RW13(6)	275.00	220.00	195.00	155.00					

Notes on Hunting Permit Stamps

1. Unused stamps without gum (uncancelled) are priced at one-half gummed price.
2. The date printed on the stamp is one year later than the date of issue listed above.
3. #RW1-RW25 and RW31 are plate blocks of 6.

U.S. Revenues #RW46-RW58

RW47

RW48

RW49

RW50

RW51

RW52

RW53

RW54

RW55

RW56

RW57

RW58

SCOTT NO.	DESCRIPTION	UNUSED/NH VF	UNUSED/NH F	USED VF	USED F
	1979-1986				
RW46	1979 $7.50 Green-Winged Teal	22.00	17.00	9.00	7.50
RW47	1980 $7.50 Mallards.	22.00	17.00	9.00	7.50
RW48	1981 $7.50 Ruddy Ducks	22.00	17.00	9.00	7.50
RW49	1982 $7.50 Canvasbacks.	22.00	17.00	9.00	7.50
RW50	1983 $7.50 Pintails	22.00	17.00	9.00	7.50
RW51	1984 $7.50 Widgeon.	22.00	17.00	9.00	7.50
RW52	1985 $7.50 Cinnamon Teal	22.00	17.00	9.00	7.50
RW53	1986 $7.50 Fulvous Whistling	22.00	17.00	9.00	7.50
	1987-1991				
RW54	1987 $10.00 Redhead Ducks	26.00	21.00	13.00	10.00
RW55	1988 $10.00 Snow Goose	26.00	21.00	13.00	10.00
RW56	1989 $12.50 Lesser Scaup	30.00	24.00	13.00	10.00
RW57	1990 $12.50 Black Bellied Whistling Duck	30.00	24.00	13.00	10.00
RW58	1991 $15.00 King Eiders	35.00	30.00	17.75	13.75

U.S. Revenues #RW59-New Issue

RW59

RW60

RW61

RW62

RW63

SCOTT NO.	DESCRIPTION	UNUSED/NH VF	UNUSED/NH F	USED VF	USED F
	1992-1997				
RW59	1992 $15.00 Spectacled Eider	35.00	30.00	17.75	13.75
RW60	1993 $15.00 Canvasbacks	35.00	30.00	17.75	13.75
RW61	1994 $15.00 Red-breasted Merganser	35.00	30.00	17.75	13.75
RW62	1995 $15.00 Mallards	35.00	30.00	17.75	13.75
RW63	1996 $15.00 Surf Scoters	35.00	30.00	17.75	13.75
......	1997 $15.00 Canada Goose	35.00	30.00	17.75	13.75

U.S. Revenues Plate Blocks #RW26-New Issue

SCOTT NO.		UNUSED NH F	UNUSED OG F
RW26	1959 $3.00 Dog & Mallard	330.00	250.00
RW27	1960 $3.00 Redhead Ducks	330.00	250.00
RW28	1961 $3.00 Mallard Hen &Ducklings	360.00	250.00
RW29	1962 $3.00 Pintail Drakes	415.00	275.00
RW30	1963 $3.00 Brant Ducks Landing	415.00	285.00
RW31(6)	1964 $3.00 Hawaiian Nene Goose	1975.00	1550.00
RW32	1965 $3.00 Canvasback Drakes	385.00	275.00
RW33	1966 $3.00 Whistling Swans	385.00	275.00
RW34	1967 $3.00 Old Squaw Ducks	385.00	275.00
RW35	1968 $3.00 Hooded Mergansers	230.00	175.00
RW36	1969 $3.00 White-Winged Scoters	230.00	175.00
RW37	1970 $3.00 Ross's Geese	230.00	175.00
RW38	1971 $3.00 Three Cinnamon Teal	155.00	110.00
RW39	1972 $5.00 Emperor Geese	110.00	......
RW40	1973 $5.00 Steller's Eider	105.00	......
RW41	1974 $5.00 Wood Ducks	82.50	......
RW42	1975 $5.00 Canvasbacks	60.00	......
RW43	1976 $5.00 Canada Geese	60.00	......
RW44	1977 $5.00 Pair of Ross's Geese	60.00	......
RW45	1978 $5.00 Hooded Merganser Drake	60.00	......
RW46	1979 $7.50 Green-Winged Teal	72.50	......
RW47	1980 $7.50 Mallards	72.50	......
RW48	1981 $7.50 Ruddy Ducks	72.50	......
RW49	1982 $7.50 Canvasbacks	72.50	......
RW50	1983 $7.50 Pintails	72.50	......
RW51	1984 $7.50 Widgeon	72.50	......
RW52	1985 $7.50 Cinnamon Teal	72.50	......
RW53	1986 $7.50 Fulvous Whistling	72.50	......
RW54	1987 $10.00 Redhead Ducks	82.50	......
RW55	1988 $10.00 Snow Goose	82.50	......
RW56	1989 $12.50 Lesser Scaup	100.00	......
RW57	1990 $12.50 Black Bellied Whistling Duck	100.00	......
RW58	1991 $15.00 King Eiders	150.00	......
RW59	1992 $15.00 Spectacled Eider	150.00	......
RW60	1993 $15.00 Canvasbacks	150.00	......
RW61	1994 $15.00 Red-breasted Merganser	150.00	......
RW62	1995 $15.00 Mallards	150.00	......
RW63	1996 $15.00 Surf Scoters	150.00	......
......	1997 $15.00 Canada Goose	150.00	......

Note: #RW1-RW25 and RW31 are plate blocks of six. All others are plate blocks of four.

State Duck Stamps #AL1-CA24

STATE HUNTING PERMIT

AL7

ALABAMA

NO.	DESCRIPTION	F-VF NH
AL1	'79 $5 Wood Ducks	9.00
AL2	'80 $5 Mallards	8.00
AL3	'81 $5 Canada Geese	8.00
AL4	'82 $5 Green-Winged Teal	8.00
AL5	'83 $5 Widgeons	11.00
AL6	'84 $5 Buffleheads	11.00
AL7	'85 $5 Wood Ducks	14.00
AL8	'86 $5 Canada Geese	14.00
AL9	'87 $5 Pintails	15.00
AL10	'88 $5 Canvasbacks	11.00
AL11	'89 $5 Hooded Mergansers	9.50
AL12	'90 $5 Wood Ducks	8.50
AL13	'91 $5 Redheads	8.50
AL14	'92 $5 Cinnamon Teal	8.00
AL15	'93 $5 Green-Winged Teal	8.00
AL16	'94 $5 Canvasbacks	8.00
AL17	'95 $5 Canada Geese	8.00
AL18	'96 $5 Wood Ducks	8.00
Alabama Set 1979-96 (18)		**155.00**

AK1

ALASKA

NO.	DESCRIPTION	F-VF NH
AK1	'85 $5 Emperor Geese	14.00
AK2	'86 $5 Steller's Eiders	11.00
AK3	'87 $5 Spectacled Eiders	10.00
AK4	'88 $5 Trumpeter Swans	10.00
AK5	'89 $5 Barrow's Goldeneyes	8.50
AK6	'90 $5 Old Squaws	8.50
AK7	'91 $5 Snow Geese	8.00
AK8	'92 $5 Canvasbacks	8.00
AK9	'93 $5 Tule White Front Geese	7.50
AK10	'94 $5 Harlequin Ducks	7.50
AK11	'95 $5 Pacific Brant	7.50
AK12	'96 $5 Aleutian Canada Geese	7.50
Alaska Set 1985-96 (12)		**97.00**

AZ1

ARIZONA

NO.	DESCRIPTION	F-VF NH
AZ1	'87 $5.50 Pintails	12.00
AZ2	'88 $5.50 Green-Winged Teal	10.00
AZ3	'89 $5.50 Cinnamon Teal	9.00
AZ4	'90 $5.50 Canada Geese	9.00
AZ5	'91 $5.50 Blue-Winged Teal	8.00
AZ6	'92 $5.50 Buffleheads	8.00
AZ7	'93 $5.50 Mexican Ducks	7.50
AZ8	'94 $5.50 Mallards	7.50
AZ9	'95 $5.50 Widgeon	7.50
AZ10	'96 $5.50 Canvasback	7.50
Arizona Set 1987-96 (10)		**77.00**

AR5

ARKANSAS

NO.	DESCRIPTION	F-VF NH
AR1	'81 $5.50 Mallards	47.50
AR2	'82 $5.50 Wood Ducks	42.50
AR3	'83 $5.50 Green-Winged Teal	52.50
AR4	'84 $5.50 Pintails	20.00
AR5	'85 $5.50 Mallards	12.00
AR6	'86 $5.50 Black Swamp Mallards	11.00
AR7	'87 $7 Wood Ducks	11.00
AR8	'88 $7 Pintails	9.50
AR9	'89 $7 Mallards	9.50
AR10	'90 $7 Black Ducks & Mallards	9.50
AR11	'91 $7 Sulphur River Widgeons	9.50
AR12	'92 $7 Shirey Bay Shovelers	9.50
AR13	'93 $7 Grand Prairie Mallards	9.00
AR14	'94 $7 Canada Goose	9.00
AR15	'95 $7 White River Mallards	9.00
AR16	'96 $7 Black Lab	9.00
Arkansas Set 1981-96 (16)		**250.00**

CA16

CALIFORNIA

NO.	DESCRIPTION	F-VF NH
CA1	'71 $1 Pintails	750.00
CA2	'72 $1 Canvasbacks	3,250.00
CA3	'73 $1 Mallards	15.00
CA4	'74 $1 White-Fronted Geese	4.50
CA5	'75 $1 Green-Winged Teal	35.00
CA6	'76 $1 Widgeons	15.00
CA7	'77 $1 Cinnamon Teal	50.00
CA8	'78 $5 Cinnamon Teal	9.00
CA9	'78 $5 Hooded Mergansers	150.00
CA6	'76 $1 Widgeons	15.00
CA7	'77 $1 Cinnamon Teal	50.00
CA8	'78 $5 Cinnamon Teal	9.00
CA9	'78 $5 Hooded Mergansers	150.00
CA10	'79 $5 Wood Ducks	7.50
CA11	'80 $5 Pintails	7.00
CA12	'81 $5 Canvasbacks	7.50
CA13	'82 $5 Widgeons	7.50
CA14	'83 $5 Green-Winged Teal	7.50
CA15	'84 $7.50 Mallard Decoy	10.00
CA16	'85 $7.50 Ring-Necked Ducks	10.00
CA17	'86 $7.50 Canada Goose	10.00
CA18	'87 $7.50 Redheads	10.00
CA19	'88 $7.50 Mallards	10.00
CA20	'89 $7.50 Cinnamon Teal	10.00
CA21	'90 $7.50 Canada Goose	10.00
CA22	'91 $7.50 Gadwalls	10.00
CA23	'92 $7.90 White-Fronted Goose	10.00
CA24	'93 $10.50 Pintails	13.00

State Duck Stamps #CA25-ID11

NO.	DESCRIPTION	F-VF NH
CA25	'94 $10.50 Wood Duck	13.00
CA26	'95 $10.50 Snow Geese	13.00
CA27	'96 $10.50 Mallard	13.00
California Set 1973-96 (25)		**410.00**

CO1

COLORADO

NO.	DESCRIPTION	F-VF NH
CO1	'90 $5 Canada Geese	12.50
CO2	'91 $5 Mallards	10.00
CO3	'92 $5 Pintails	8.50
CO4	'93 $5 Green-Winged Teal	7.50
CO5	'94 $5 Wood Ducks	7.50
CO6	'95 $5 Buffleheads	7.50
CO7	'96 $5 Cinnamon Teal	7.50
Colorado Set 1990-96 (7)		**55.00**

CONNECTICUT

NO.	DESCRIPTION	F-VF NH
CT1	'93 $5 Black Ducks	8.00
CT2	'94 $5 Canvasbacks	8.00
CT3	'95 $5 Mallards	8.00
CT4	'96 $5 Old Squaw	8.00
Connecticut Set 1993-96 (4)		**28.75**

DE1

DELAWARE

NO.	DESCRIPTION	F-VF NH
DE1	'80 $5 Black Ducks	95.00
DE2	'81 $5 Snow Geese	85.00
DE3	'82 $5 Canada Geese	80.00
DE4	'83 $5 Canvasbacks	55.00
DE5	'84 $5 Mallards	25.00
DE6	'85 $5 Pintail	14.00
DE7	'86 $5 Widgeons	12.00
DE8	'87 $5 Redheads	10.00
DE9	'88 $5 Wood Ducks	8.50
DE10	'89 $5 Buffleheads	8.00
DE11	'90 $5 Green-Winged Teal	8.00
DE12	'91 $5 Hooded Merganser	8.00
DE13	'92 $5 Blue-Winged Teal	7.50
DE14	'93 $5 Goldeneye	7.50
DE15	'94 $5 Blue Goose	7.50
DE16	'95 ($5) Scaup	8.00
DE17	'96 $6 Gadwall	8.00
Delaware Set 1980-96 (17)		**400.00**

FLORIDA

NO.	DESCRIPTION	F-VF NH
FL1	'79 $3.25 Green-Winged Teal	175.00
FL2	'80 $3.25 Pintails	25.00
FL3	'81 $3.25 Widgeon	25.00
FL4	'82 $3.25 Ring-Necked Ducks	35.00
FL5	'83 $3.25 Buffleheads	60.00
FL6	'84 $3.25 Hooded Merganser	20.00
FL7	'85 $3.25 Wood Ducks	18.00
FL8	'86 $3 Canvasbacks	10.00
FL9	'87 $3.50 Mallards	7.50
FL10	'88 $3.50 Redheads	7.50
FL11	'89 $3.50 Blue-Winged Teal	6.50
FL12	'90 $3.50 Wood Ducks	6.00
FL13	'91 $3.50 Northern Pintails	6.00
FL14	'92 $3.50 Ruddy Duck	6.00

FL1

NO.	DESCRIPTION	F-VF NH
FL15	'93 $3.50 American Widgeon	6.00
FL16	'94 $3.50 Mottled Duck	6.00
FL17	'95 $3.50 Fulvous Whistling Duck	6.00
FL18	'96 $3.50 Goldeneyes	6.00
Florida Set 1979-96 (18)		**388.00**

GA1

GEORGIA

NO.	DESCRIPTION	F-VF NH
GA1	'85 $5.50 Wood Ducks	13.00
GA2	'86 $5.50 Mallards	10.00
GA3	'87 $5.50 Canada Geese	7.50
GA4	'88 $5.50 Ring-Necked Ducks	7.50
GA5	'89 $5.50 Duckling & Golden Retriever Puppy	9.00
GA6	'90 $5.50 Wood Ducks	8.00
GA7	'91 $5.50 Green-Winged Teal	7.50
GA8	'92 $5.50 Buffleheads	7.50
GA9	'93 $5.50 Mallards	7.50
GA10	'94 $5.50 Ring-Necked Ducks	7.50
GA11	'95 $5.50 Widgeons, Labrador Retriever	7.50
GA12	'96 $5.50 Black Ducks	7.50
Georgia Set 1985-96 (12)		**90.00**

HAWAII

NO.	DESCRIPTION	F-VF NH
HI1	'96 $5 Nene Geese	7.50

ID1

IDAHO

NO.	DESCRIPTION	F-VF NH
ID1	'87 $5.50 Cinnamon Teal	20.00
ID2	'88 $5.50 Green-Winged Teal	10.00
ID3	'89 $6 Blue-Winged Teal	10.00
ID4	'90 $6 Trumpeter Swans	10.00
ID6	'91 $6 Widgeons	8.50
ID7	'92 $6 Canada Geese	8.00
ID8	'93 $6 Common Goldeneye	8.00
ID9	'94 $6 Harlequin Ducks	8.00
ID10	'95 $6 Wood Ducks	8.00
ID11	'96 $6 Mallard	8.00
Idaho Set 1987-96 (10)		**88.50**

State Duck Stamps #IL1-KS10

NO.	DESCRIPTION	F-VF NH

IL11

ILLINOIS

NO.	DESCRIPTION	F-VF NH
IL1	'75 $5 Mallard	700.00
IL2	'76 $5 Wood Ducks	300.00
IL3	'77 $5 Canada Goose	200.00
IL4	'78 $5 Canvasbacks	110.00
IL5	'79 $5 Pintail	110.00
IL6	'80 $5 Green-Winged Teal	110.00
IL7	'81 $5 Widgeons	110.00
IL8	'82 $5 Black Ducks	60.00
IL9	'83 $5 Lesser Scaup	57.50
IL10	'84 $5 Blue-Winged Teal	52.50
IL11	'85 $5 Redheads	21.00
IL12	'86 $5 Gadwalls	12.00
IL13	'87 $5 Buffleheads	10.00
IL14	'88 $5 Common Goldeneyes	9.00
IL15	'89 $5 Ring-Necked Ducks	8.00
IL16	'90 $10 Lesser Snow Geese	15.00
IL17	'91 $10 Labrador Retriever & Canada Goose	14.00
IL18	'92 $10 Retriever & Mallards	14.00
IL19	'93 $10 Pintail Decoys & Puppy	14.00
IL20	'94 $10 Canvasbacks & Retrievers	14.00
IL21	'95 $10 Retriever, Green-Winged Teal, Decoys	14.00
IL22	'96 $10 Wood Ducks	14.00
Ilinois Set 1975-96 (22)		**1,770.00**

IN10

INDIANA

NO.	DESCRIPTION	F-VF NH
IN1	'76 $5 Green-Winged Teal	7.50
IN2	'77 $5 Pintail	7.50
IN3	'78 $5 Canada Geese	7.50
IN4	'79 $5 Canvasbacks	7.50
IN5	'80 $5 Mallard Ducklings	7.50
IN6	'81 $5 Hooded Mergansers	7.50
IN7	'82 $5 Blue-Winged Teal	7.50
IN8	'83 $5 Snow Geese	7.50
IN9	'84 $5 Redheads	7.50
IN10	'85 $5 Pintail	7.50
IN11	'86 $5 Wood Duck	7.50
IN12	'87 $5 Canvasbacks	7.50
IN13	'88 $6.75 Redheads	9.00
IN14	'89 $6.75 Canada Goose	9.00
IN15	'90 $6.75 Blue-Winged Teal	9.00
IN16	'91 $6.75 Mallards	9.00
IN17	'92 $6.75 Green-Winged Teal	9.00
IN18	'93 $6.75 Wood Ducks	9.00
IN19	'94 $6.75 Pintail	9.00
IN20	'95 $6.75 Goldeneyes	9.00
IN21	'96 $6.75 Black Ducks	9.00
Indiana Set 1976-96 (21)		**153.50**

NO.	DESCRIPTION	F-VF NH

IA14

IOWA

NO.	DESCRIPTION	F-VF NH
IA1	'72 $1 Mallards	175.00
IA2	'73 $1 Pintails	42.50
IA3	'74 $1 Gadwalls	75.00
IA4	'75 $1 Canada Geese	100.00
IA5	'76 $1 Canvasbacks	19.00
IA6	'77 $1 Lesser Scaup	19.00
IA7	'78 $1 Wood Ducks	55.00
IA8	'79 $5 Buffleheads	400.00
IA9	'80 $5 Redheads	40.00
IA10	'81 $5 Green-Winged Teal	35.00
IA11	'82 $5 Snow Geese	15.00
IA12	'83 $5 Widgeons	15.00
IA13	'84 $5 Wood Ducks	32.50
IA14	'85 $5 Mallard & Mallard Decoy	16.00
IA15	'86 $5 Blue-Winged Teal	15.00
IA16	'87 $5 Canada Goose	12.00
IA17	'88 $5 Pintails	10.00
IA18	'89 $5 Blue-Winged Teal	10.00
IA19	'90 $5 Canvasbacks	8.50
IA20	'91 $5 Mallards	8.00
IA21	'92 $5 Labrador Retriever & Ducks	8.00
IA22	'93 $5 Mallards	7.50
IA23	'94 $5 Green-Winged Teal	7.50
IA24	'95 $5 Canada Geese	7.50
IA25	'96 $5 Canvasbacks	7.50
Iowa Set 1972-96 (25)		**1,025.00**

KS1

KANSAS

NO.	DESCRIPTION	F-VF NH
KS1	'87 $3 Green-Winged Teal	8.00
KS2	'88 $3 Canada Geese	6.00
KS3	'89 $3 Mallards	5.50
KS4	'90 $3 Wood Ducks	5.50
KS5	'91 $3 Pintail	5.25
KS6	'92 $3 Canvasbacks	5.50
KS7	'93 $3 Mallards	5.25
KS8	'94 $3 Blue-Winged Teal	5.25
KS9	'95 $3 Barrow's Goldeneye	5.25
KS10	'96 $3 Widgeon	5.25
Kansas Set 1987-96 (10)		**51.00**

KY1

State Duck Stamps #KY1-MI7

NO.	DESCRIPTION	F-VF NH
	KENTUCKY	
KY1	'85 $5.25 Mallards	12.00
KY2	'86 $5.25 Wood Ducks	8.50
KY3	'87 $5.25 Black Ducks	8.50
KY4	'88 $5.25 Canada Geese	8.50
KY5	'89 $5.25 Retriever & Canvasbacks	8.50
KY6	'90 $5.25 Widgeons	8.50
KY7	'91 $5.25 Pintails	8.50
KY8	'92 $5.25 Green-Winged Teal	8.00
KY9	'93 $5.25 Canvasback & Decoy	8.50
KY10	'94 $5.25 Canada Goose	7.50
KY11	'95 $7.50 Retriever, Decoy, Ringnecks	9.50
KY12	'96 $7.50 Blue-Winged Teal	9.50
Kentucky Set 1985-96 (12)		**95.00**

LA1

NO.	DESCRIPTION	F-VF NH
	LOUISIANA	
LA1	'89 $5 Blue-Winged Teal	10.00
LA2	'89 $7.50 Blue-Winged Teal	12.50
LA3	'90 $5 Green-Winged Teal	8.50
LA4	'90 $7.50 Green-Winged Teal	12.00
LA5	'91 $5 Wood Ducks	8.50
LA6	'91 $7.50 Wood Ducks	10.00
LA7	'92 $5 Pintails	8.00
LA8	'92 $7.50 Pintails	10.00
LA9	'93 $5 American Widgeon	7.50
LA10	'93 $7.50 American Widgeon	10.00
LA11	'94 $5 Mottled Duck	7.50
LA12	'94 $7.50 Mottled Duck	10.00
LA13	'95 $5 Speckle Bellied Goose	7.50
LA14	'95 $7.50 Speckle Bellied Goose	10.00
LA15	'96 $5 Gadwall	7.50
Louisiana Set 1989-96 (15)		**118.00**

ME2

NO.	DESCRIPTION	F-VF NH
	MAINE	
ME1	'84 $2.50 Black Ducks	25.00
ME2	'85 $2.50 Common Eiders	45.00
ME3	'86 $2.50 Wood Ducks	10.00
ME4	'87 $2.50 Buffleheads	8.00
ME5	'88 $2.50 Green-Winged Teal	8.00
ME6	'89 $2.50 Common Goldeneyes	5.50
ME7	'90 $2.50 Canada Geese	5.50
ME8	'91 $2.50 Ring-Necked Duck	5.00
ME9	'92 $2.50 Old Squaw	5.00
ME10	'93 $2.50 Hooded Merganser	5.00
ME11	'94 $2.50 Mallards	5.00
ME12	'95 $2.50 White-Winged Scoters	5.00
ME13	'96 $2.50 Blue-Winged Teal	5.00
Maine Set 1984-96 (13)		**123.00**

MD1

NO.	DESCRIPTION	F-VF NH
	MARYLAND	
MD1	'74 $1.10 Mallards	14.00
MD2	'75 $1.10 Canada Geese	7.50
MD3	'76 $1.10 Canvasbacks	9.00
MD4	'77 $1.10 Greater Scaup	9.00
MD5	'78 $1.10 Redheads	9.00
MD6	'79 $1.10 Wood Ducks	7.00
MD7	'80 $1.10 Pintail Decoy	7.00
MD8	'81 $3 Widgeon	5.50
MD9	'82 $3 Canvasback	7.00
MD10	'83 $3 Wood Duck	9.00
MD11	'84 $6 Black Ducks	8.00
MD12	'85 $6 Canada Geese	8.00
MD13	'86 $6 Hooded Mergansers	8.00
MD14	'87 $6 Redheads	8.00
MD15	'88 $6 Ruddy Ducks	8.00
MD16	'89 $6 Blue-Winged Teal	8.00
MD17	'90 $6 Lesser Scaup	8.00
MD18	'91 $6 Shovelers	8.00
MD19	'92 $6 Bufflehead	8.00
MD20	'93 $6 Canvasbacks	8.00
MD21	'94 $6 Redheads	8.00
MD22	'95 $6 Mallards	8.00
MD23	'96 $6 Canada Geese	8.00
Maryland Set 1974-96 (23)		**169.00**

MA12

NO.	DESCRIPTION	F-VF NH
	MASSACHSETTS	
MA1	'74 $1.25 Wood Duck Decoy	14.00
MA2	'75 $1.25 Pintail Decoy	10.00
MA3	'76 $1.25 Canada Goose Decoy	10.00
MA4	'77 $1.25 Goldeneye Decoy	10.00
MA5	'78 $1.25 Black Duck Decoy	10.00
MA6	'79 $1.25 Ruddy Turnstone Duck Decoy	10.00
MA7	'80 $1.25 Old Squaw Decoy	10.00
MA8	'81 $1.25 Red-Breasted Merganser Decoy	8.00
MA9	'82 $1.25 Greater Yellowlegs Decoy	8.00
MA10	'83 $1.25 Redhead Decoy	7.50
MA11	'84 $1.25 White-Winged Scoter Decoy	7.50
MA12	'85 $1.25 Ruddy Duck Decoy	7.50
MA13	'86 $1.25 Preening Bluebill Decoy	7.50
MA14	'87 $1.25 American Widgeon Decoy	7.50
MA15	'88 $1.25 Mallard Decoy	7.50
MA16	'89 $1.25 Brant Decoy	5.00
MA17	'90 $1.25 Whistler Hen Decoy	5.00
MA18	'91 $5 Canvasback Decoy	8.00
MA19	'92 $5 Black-Bellied Plover Decoy	8.00
MA20	'93 $5 Red-Breasted Merganser Decoy	8.00
MA21	'94 $5 White-Winged Scoter Decoy	8.00
MA22	'95 $5 Female Hooded Merganser Decoy	8.00
MA23	'96 $5 Eider Decoy	8.00
Massachusetts Set 1974-96 (23)		**173.50**
	MICHIGAN	
MI1	'76 $2.10 Wood Duck	5.00
MI2	'77 $2.10 Canvasbacks	325.00
MI3	'78 $2.10 Mallards	22.50
MI4	'79 $2.10 Canada Geese	42.50
MI5	'80 $3.75 Lesser Scaup	20.00
MI6	'81 $3.75 Buffleheads	20.00
MI7	'82 $3.75 Redheads	25.00

State Duck Stamps #MI8-MT44

1985 U 006476 $3.75
MICHIGAN WATERFOWL
Issued Mo. ____ Day ____

MI10

NO.	DESCRIPTION	F-VF NH
MI8	'83 $3.75 Wood Ducks	25.00
MI9	'84 $3.75 Pintails	25.00
MI10	'85 $3.75 Ring-Necked Ducks	20.00
MI11	'86 $3.75 Common Goldeneyes	14.00
MI12	'87 $3.85 Green-Winged Teal	10.00
MI13	'88 $3.85 Canada Geese	10.00
MI14	'89 $3.85 Widgeons	7.50
MI15	'90 $3.85 Wood Ducks	7.50
MI16	'91 $3.85 Blue-Winged Teal	7.00
MI17	'92 $3.85 Red-Breasted Merganser	6.50
MI18	'93 $3.85 Hooded Merganser	6.00
MI19	'94 $3.85 Black Duck	6.00
MI20	'95 $4.35 Blue Winged Teal	7.50
MI21	'96 $4.35 Canada Geese	8.00
Michigan Set 1976-96 (21)		**555.00**

MN1

MINNESOTA

NO.	DESCRIPTION	F-VF NH
MN1	'77 $3 Mallards	15.00
MN2	'78 $3 Lesser Scaup	9.00
MN3	'79 $3 Pintails	9.00
MN4	'80 $3 Canvasbacks	9.00
MN5	'81 $3 Canada Geese	9.00
MN6	'82 $3 Redheads	9.00
MN7	'83 $3 Blue Geese & Snow Goose	9.00
MN8	'84 $3 Wood Ducks	9.00
MN9	'85 $3 White-Fronted Geese	9.00
MN10	'86 $5 Lesser Scaup	9.00
MN11	'87 $5 Common Goldeneyes	10.00
MN12	'88 $5 Buffleheads	10.00
MN13	'89 $5 Widgeons	10.00
MN14	'90 $5 Hooded Mergansers	15.00
MN15	'91 $5 Ross's Geese	7.50
MN16	'92 $5 Barrow's Goldeneyes	7.50
MN17	'93 $5 Blue-Winged Teal	7.50
MN18	'94 $5 Ringneck Duck	7.50
MN19	'95 $5 Gadwall	7.50
MN20	'96 $5 Greater Scaup	7.50
Minnesota Set 1977-96 (20)		**167.00**

MISSISSIPPI

NO.	DESCRIPTION	F-VF NH
MS1	'76 $2 Wood Duck	15.00
MS2	'77 $2 Mallards	8.00
MS3	'78 $2 Green-Winged Teal	8.00
MS4	'79 $2 Canvasbacks	8.00
MS5	'80 $2 Pintails	8.00
MS6	'81 $2 Redheads	8.00
MS7	'82 $2 Canada Geese	8.00
MS8	'83 $2 Lesser Scaup	8.00
MS9	'84 $2 Black Ducks	8.00
MS10	'85 $2 Mallards	8.00
MS11	'86 $2 Widgeons	8.00
MS12	'87 $2 Ring-Necked Ducks	8.00
MS13	'88 $2 Snow Geese	8.00

MS10

NO.	DESCRIPTION	F-VF NH
MS14	'89 $2 Wood Ducks	7.00
MS15	'90 $2 Snow Geese	12.00
MS16	'91 $2 Labrador Retriever & Canvasbacks	5.00
MS17	'92 $2 Green-Winged Teal	4.50
MS18	'93 $2 Mallards	7.00
MS19	'94 $2 Canvasbacks	7.00
MS20	'95 $5 Blue-Winged Teal	7.00
MS21	'96 $5 Hooded Merganser	7.00
Mississippi Set 1976-96 (21)		**150.00**

MO7

MISSOURI

NO.	DESCRIPTION	F-VF NH
MO1	'79 $3.40 Canada Geese	625.00
MO2	'80 $3.40 Wood Ducks	140.00
MO3	'81 $3 Lesser Scaup	72.50
MO4	'82 $3 Buffleheads	47.50
MO5	'83 $3 Blue-Winged Teal	42.50
MO6	'84 $3 Mallards	37.50
MO7	'85 $3 American Widgeons	25.00
MO8	'86 $3 Hooded Mergansers	12.50
MO9	'87 $3 Pintails	10.00
MO10	'88 $3 Canvasback	8.50
MO11	'89 $3 Ring-Necked Ducks	8.00
MO12	'90 $5 Redheads	7.50
MO13	'91 $5 Snow Geese	7.50
MO14	'92 $5 Gadwalls	7.50
MO15	'93 $5 Green-Winged Teal	7.50
MO16	'94 $5 White-Fronted Goose	7.50
MO17	'95 $5 Goldeneyes	7.50
MO18	'96 $5 Black Duck	7.50
Missouri Set 1979-96 (18)		**970.00**

MT34

MONTANA

NO.	DESCRIPTION	F-VF NH
MT34	'86 $5 Canada Geese	17.50
MT35	'87 $5 Redheads	12.50
MT36	'88 $5 Mallards	10.00
MT37	'89 $5 Black Labrador Retriever & Pintail	10.00
MT38	'90 $5 Blue-Winged & CinnamonTeal	9.00
MT39	'91 $5 Snow Geese	8.50
MT40	'92 $5 Wood Ducks	8.00
MT41	'93 $5 Harlequin Ducks	7.50
MT42	'94 $5 Widgeons	7.50
MT43	'95 $5 Tundra Swans	7.50
MT44	'96 $5 Canvasbacks	7.50
Montana Set 1986-96 (11)		**94.75**

State Duck Stamps #NE1-NY3

NE1

NEBRASKA

NO.	DESCRIPTION	F-VF NH
NE1	'91 $6 Canada Geese	9.00
NE2	'92 $6 Pintails	8.50
NE3	'93 $6 Canvasbacks	8.50
NE4	'94 $6 Mallards	8.50
NE5	'95 $6 Wood Ducks	8.50
Nebraska Set 1991-95 (5)		**38.75**

NV7

NEVADA

NO.	DESCRIPTION	F-VF NH
NV1	'79 $2 Canvasbacks & Decoy	55.00
NV2	'80 $2 Cinnamon Teal	10.00
NV3	'81 $2 Whistling Swans	10.00
NV4	'82 $2 Shovelers	10.00
NV5	'83 $2 Gadwalls	10.00
NV6	'84 $2 Pintails	10.00
NV7	'85 $2 Canada Geese	10.00
NV8	'86 $2 Redheads	11.00
NV9	'87 $2 Buffleheads	10.00
NV10	'88 $2 Canvasbacks	10.00
NV11	'89 $2 Ross's Geese	7.00
NV12	'90 $5 Green-Winged Teal	8.00
NV13	'91 $5 White-Faced Ibis	7.50
NV14	'92 $5 American Widgeon	8.00
NV15	'93 $5 Common Goldeneye	7.50
NV16	'94 $5 Mallards	7.50
NV17	'95 $5 Wood Duck	7.50
NV18	'96 $5 Ring Necked Duck	7.50
Nevada Set 1979-96 (18)		**185.50**

NH2

NEW HAMPSHIRE

NO.	DESCRIPTION	F-VF NH
NH1	'83 $4 Wood Ducks	150.00
NH2	'84 $4 Mallards	110.00
NH3	'85 $4 Blue-Winged Teal	110.00
NH4	'86 $4 Hooded Mergansers	25.00
NH5	'87 $4 Canada Geese	17.50
NH6	'88 $4 Buffleheads	10.00
NH7	'89 $4 Black Ducks	8.50
NH8	'90 $4 Green-Winged Teal	7.50
NH9	'91 $4 Golden Retriever & Mallards	7.50
NH10	'92 $4 Ring-Necked Ducks	6.50
NH11	'93 $4 Hooded Mergansers	6.00
NH12	'94 $4 Common Goldeneyes	6.00
NH13	'95 $4 Northern Pintails	6.00
NH14	'96 $4 Surf Scoters	6.00
New Hampshire Set 1983-96 (14)		**428.50**

NJ1

NEW JERSEY

NO.	DESCRIPTION	F-VF NH
NJ1	'84 $2.50 Canvasbacks	50.00
NJ2	'84 $5 Canvasbacks	60.00
NJ3	'85 $2.50 Mallards	18.00
NJ4	'85 $5 Mallards	20.00
NJ5	'86 $2.50 Pintails	10.00
NJ6	'86 $5 Pintails	14.00
NJ7	'87 $2.50 Canada Geese	10.00
NJ8	'87 $5 Canada Geese	12.00
NJ9	'88 $2.50 Green-Winged Teal	9.00
NJ10	'88 $5 Green-Winged Teal	10.00
NJ11	'89 $2.50 Snow Geese	5.00
NJ12	'89 $5 Snow Geese	10.00
NJ13	'90 $2.50 Wood Ducks	4.50
NJ14	'90 $5 Wood Ducks	9.00
NJ17	'91 $2.50 Atlantic Brant	4.50
NJ18	'91 $5 Atlantic Brant	9.00
NJ19	'92 $2.50 Bluebills	5.00
NJ20	'92 $5 Bluebills	8.50
NJ21	'93 $2.50 Buffleheads	5.00
NJ22	'93 $5 Buffleheads	7.50
NJ23	'94 $2.50 Black Ducks	5.00
NJ24	'94 $5 Black Ducks	7.50
NJ25	'95 $2.50 Widgeon, Lighthouse	5.00
NJ26	'95 $5 Widgeon, Lighthouse	7.50
NJ27	'96 $2.50 Goldeneyes	5.00
New Jersey Set 1984-96 (25)		**275.00**

NM1

NEW MEXICO

NO.	DESCRIPTION	F-VF NH
NM1	'91 $7.50 Pintails	11.00
NM2	'92 $7.50 American Widgeon	10.00
NM3	'93 $7.50 Mallard	10.00
NM4	'94 $7.50 Green-Winged Teal	10.00
New Mexico Set 1991-94 (4)		**36.75**

NY1

NEW YORK

NO.	DESCRIPTION	F-VF NH
NY1	'85 $5.50 Canada Geese	14.00
NY2	'86 $5.50 Mallards	12.00
NY3	'87 $5.50 Wood Ducks	10.00

State Duck Stamps #NY4-OR14

NO.	DESCRIPTION	F-VF NH
NY4	'88 $5.50 Pintails	9.00
NY5	'89 $5.50 Greater Scaup	8.00
NY6	'90 $5.50 Canvasbacks	8.00
NY7	'91 $5.50 Redheads	8.00
NY8	'92 $5.50 Wood Ducks	7.50
NY9	'93 $5.50 Blue-Winged Teal	7.50
NY10	'94 $5.50 Canada Geese	7.50
NY11	'95 $5.50 Common Goldeneye	7.50
NY12	'96 $5.50 Common Loon	7.50
New York Set 1985-96 (12)		**95.75**

NC1

NORTH CAROLINA

NO.	DESCRIPTION	F-VF NH
NC1	'83 $5.50 Mallards	85.00
NC2	'84 $5.50 Wood Ducks	55.00
NC3	'85 $5.50 Canvasbacks	35.00
NC4	'86 $5.50 Canada Geese	15.00
NC5	'87 $5.50 Pintails	12.00
NC6	'88 $5 Green-Winged Teal	10.00
NC7	'89 $5 Snow Geese	10.00
NC8	'90 $5 Redheads	9.00
NC9	'91 $5 Blue-Winged Teal	8.00
NC10	'92 $5 American Widgeon	8.00
NC11	'93 $5 Tundra Swans	7.50
NC12	'94 $5 Buffleheads	7.50
NC13	'95 $5 Brant, Lighthouse	7.50
NC14	'96 $5 Pintails	7.50
North Carolina Set 1983-96 (14)		**249.50**

ND32

NORTH DAKOTA

NO.	DESCRIPTION	F-VF NH
ND32	'82 $9 Canada Geese	150.00
ND35	'83 $9 Mallards	80.00
ND38	'84 $9 Canvasbacks	32.50
ND41	'85 $9 Bluebills	25.00
ND44	'86 $9 Pintails	20.00
ND47	'87 $9 Snow Geese	16.00
ND50	'88 $9 White-Winged Scoters	15.00
ND53	'89 $6 Redheads	10.00
ND56	'90 $6 Labrador Retriever & Mallard	10.00
ND59	'91 $6 Green-Winged Teal	9.00
ND62	'92 $6 Blue-Winged Teal	8.00
ND65	'93 $6 Wood Ducks	8.00
ND67	'94 $6 Canada Geese	8.00
ND69	'95 $6 Widgeon	8.00
ND70	'96 $6 Mallards	8.00
North Dakota Set 1982-96 (15)		**366.75**

OHIO

NO.	DESCRIPTION	F-VF NH
OH1	'82 $5.75 Wood Ducks	85.00
OH2	'83 $5.75 Mallards	85.00
OH3	'84 $5.75 Green-Winged Teal	75.00
OH4	'85 $5.75 Redheads	50.00
OH5	'86 $5.75 Canvasback	20.00
OH6	'87 $6 Blue-Winged Teal	15.00
OH7	'88 $6 Common Goldeneyes	12.00
OH8	'89 $6 Canada Geese	10.00

OH4

NO.	DESCRIPTION	F-VF NH
OH9	'90 $9 Black Ducks	13.00
OH10	'91 $9 Lesser Scaup	12.00
OH11	'92 $9 Wood Duck	12.00
OH12	'93 $9 Buffleheads	11.00
OH13	'94 $11 Mallards	13.00
OH14	'95 $11 Pintails	13.50
OH15	'96 $11 Hooded Mergansers	13.50
Ohio Set 1982-96 (15)		**396.00**

OK4

OKLAHOMA

NO.	DESCRIPTION	F-VF NH
OK1	'80 $4 Pintails	45.00
OK2	'81 $4 Canada Goose	27.50
OK3	'82 $4 Green-Winged Teal	12.00
OK4	'83 $4 Wood Ducks	10.00
OK5	'84 $4 Ring-Necked Ducks	7.50
OK6	'85 $4 Mallards	7.50
OK7	'86 $4 Snow Geese	7.50
OK8	'87 $4 Canvasbacks	7.50
OK9	'88 $4 Widgeons	7.50
OK10	'89 $4 Redheads	7.00
OK11	'90 $4 Hooded Merganser	7.00
OK12	'91 $4 Gadwalls	7.00
OK13	'92 $4 Lesser Scaup	6.50
OK14	'93 $4 White-Fronted Geese	6.00
OK15	'94 $4 Blue-Winged Teal	6.00
OK16	'95 $4 Ruddy Ducks	6.00
OK17	'96 $4 Buffleheads	6.00
Oklahoma Set 1980-96 (17)		**165.00**

OR1

OREGON

NO.	DESCRIPTION	F-VF NH
OR1	'84 $5 Canada Geese	35.00
OR2	'85 $5 Lesser Snow Goose	45.00
OR3	'86 $5 Pacific Brant	17.50
OR4	'87 $5 White-Fronted Geese	12.00
OR5	'88 $5 Great Basin Canada Geese	10.00
OR7	'89 $5 Black Labrador Retriever & Pintails	10.00
OR8	'90 $5 Mallards & Golden Retriever	9.00
OR9	'91 $5 Buffleheads & Chesapeake Bay Retriever	8.50
OR10	'92 $5 Green-Winged Teal	8.50
OR11	'93 $5 Mallards	8.00
OR12	'94 $5 Pintails	8.00
OR14	'95 $5 Wood Ducks	8.00

NO.	DESCRIPTION	F-VF NH
OR16	'96 $5 Mallard/Widgeon/Pintail	8.00
Oregon Set 1984-96 (13)		**168.75**

PA1

PENNSYLVANIA

NO.	DESCRIPTION	F-VF NH
PA1	'83 $5.50 Wood Ducks	25.00
PA2	'84 $5.50 Canada Geese	22.50
PA3	'85 $5.50 Mallards	12.00
PA4	'86 $5.50 Blue-Winged Teal	10.00
PA5	'87 $5.50 Pintails	10.00
PA6	'88 $5.50 Wood Ducks	10.00
PA7	'89 $5.50 Hooded Mergansers	8.00
PA8	'90 $5.50 Canvasbacks	8.00
PA9	'91 $5.50 Widgeons	8.00
PA10	'92 $5.50 Canada Geese	8.00
PA11	'93 $5.50 Northern Shovelers	7.50
PA12	'94 $5.50 Pintails	7.50
PA13	'95 $5.50 Buffleheads	7.50
PA14	'96 $5.50 Black Ducks	7.50
Pennsylvania Set 1983-96 (14)		**136.25**

RI1

RHODE ISLAND

NO.	DESCRIPTION	F-VF NH
RI1	'89 $7.50 Canvasbacks	12.50
RI2	'90 $7.50 Canada Geese	12.00
RI3	'91 $7.50 Wood Ducks & Labrador Retriever	11.00
RI4	'92 $7.50 Blue-Winged Teal	10.00
RI5	'93 $7.50 Pintails	9.50
RI6	'94 $7.50 Wood Ducks	9.50
RI7	'95 $7.50 Hooded Mergansers	9.50
RI8	'96 $7.50 Harlequin	9.50
Rhode Island Set 1989-96 (8)		**75.00**

SC5

SOUTH CAROLINA

NO.	DESCRIPTION	F-VF NH
SC1	'81 $5.50 Wood Ducks	75.00
SC2	'82 $5.50 Mallards	110.00
SC3	'83 $5.50 Pintails	110.00
SC4	'84 $5.50 Canada Geese	70.00
SC5	'85 $5.50 Green-Winged Teal	65.00
SC6	'86 $5.50 Canvasbacks	30.00
SC7	'87 $5.50 Black Ducks	20.00
SC8	'88 $5.50 Widgeon & Spaniel	25.00
SC9	'89 $5.50 Blue-Winged Teal	15.00
SC10	'90 $5.50 Wood Ducks	10.00
SC11	'91 $5.50 Labrador Retriever, Pintails & Decoy	9.00
SC12	'92 $5.50 Buffleheads	9.50
SC13	'93 $5.50 Lesser Scaup	8.00
SC14	'94 $5.50 Canvasbacks	8.00
SC15	'95 $5.50 Shovelers, Lighthouse	8.00
SC16	'96 $5.50 Redheads, Lighthouse	8.00
South Carolina Set 1981-96 (16)		**522.50**

SD6

SOUTH DAKOTA

NO.	DESCRIPTION	F-VF NH
SD3	'76 $1 Mallards	30.00
SD4	'77 $1 Pintails	16.00
SD5	'78 $1 Canvasbacks	12.00
SD6	'86 $2 Canada Geese	12.00
SD7	'87 $2 Blue Geese	8.00
SD8	'88 $2 White-Fronted Geese	6.00
SD9	'89 $2 Mallards	5.00
SD10	'90 $2 Blue-Winged Teal	4.00
SD11	'91 $2 Pintails	4.00
SD12	'92 $2 Canvasbacks	4.00
SD13	'93 $2 Lesser Scaup	4.00
SD14	'94 $2 Redheads	4.00
SD15	'95 $2 Wood Ducks	4.00
SD16	'96 $2 Canada Goose	4.00
South Dakota Set 1976-96 (14)		**105.00**

TN9

TENNESSEE

NO.	DESCRIPTION	F-VF NH
TN1	'79 $2.30 Mallards	175.00
TN2	'79 $5 Mallards, Non-Resident	1,200.00
TN3	'80 $2.30 Canvasbacks	65.00
TN4	'80 $5 Canvasbacks, Non-Resident	525.00
TN5	'81 $2.30 Wood Ducks	50.00
TN6	'82 $6.50 Canada Geese	65.00
TN7	'83 $6.50 Pintails	60.00
TN8	'84 $6.50 Black Ducks	70.00
TN9	'85 $6.50 Blue-Winged Teal	25.00
TN10	'86 $6.50 Mallard	15.00
TN11	'87 $6.50 Canada Geese	15.00
TN12	'88 $6.50 Canvasbacks	12.00
TN13	'89 $6.50 Green-Winged Teal	9.00
TN14	'90 $13 Redheads	17.00
TN15	'91 $13 Mergansers	17.00
TN16	'92 $14 Wood Ducks	17.00
TN17	'93 $14 Pintails & Decoy	17.00
TN18	'94 $16 Mallard	19.00
TN19	'95 $16 Ring-Necked Duck	19.00
TN20	'96 $17 Black Ducks	21.00
Tennessee Set 1979-96 (20)		**2,170.00**
Tennessee Set 1979-96 (18) w/o Non-Resident		**640.00**

TEXAS

NO.	DESCRIPTION	F-VF NH
TX1	'81 $5 Mallards	55.00
TX2	'82 $5 Pintails	40.00
TX3	'83 $5 Widgeons	190.00

State Duck Stamps #TX4-WV14

TX5

NO.	DESCRIPTION	F-VF NH
TX4	'84 $5 Wood Ducks	35.00
TX5	'85 $5 Snow Geese	15.00
TX6	'86 $5 Green-Winged Teal	12.00
TX7	'87 $5 White-Fronted Geese	9.00
TX8	'88 $5 Pintails	9.00
TX9	'89 $5 Mallards	9.00
TX10	'90 $5 American Widgeons	9.00
TX11	'91 $7 Wood Duck	10.00
TX12	'92 $7 Canada Geese	10.00
TX13	'93 $7 Blue-Winged Teal	9.50
TX14	'94 $7 Shovelers	9.50
TX15	'95 $7 Buffleheads	9.50
TX16	'96 $3 Gadwalls	12.00
Texas Set 1981-96 (16)		**399.00**

UT1

UTAH

NO.	DESCRIPTION	F-VF NH
UT1	'86 $3.30 Whistling Swans	10.00
UT2	'87 $3.30 Pintails	8.50
UT3	'88 $3.30 Mallards	7.00
UT4	'89 $3.30 Canada Geese	7.00
UT5	'90 $3.30 Canvasbacks	6.00
UT6	'91 $3.30 Tundra Swans	6.00
UT7	'92 $3.30 Pintails	6.00
UT8	'93 $3.30 Canvasbacks	6.00
UT9	'94 $3.30 Chesapeake Retriever & Ducks	6.00
UT10	'95 $3.30 Green-Winged Teal	6.00
UT11	'96 $7.50 White-Fronted Goose	10.00
Utah Set 1986-96 (11)		**70.50**

VT1

VERMONT

NO.	DESCRIPTION	F-VF NH
VT1	'86 $5 Wood Ducks	14.00
VT2	'87 $5 Common Goldeneyes	10.00
VT3	'88 $5 Black Ducks	10.00
VT4	'89 $5 Canada Geese	9.00
VT5	'90 $5 Green-Winged Teal	9.00
VT6	'91 $5 Hooded Mergansers	8.00
VT7	'92 $5 Snow Geese	8.00
VT8	'93 $5 Mallards	7.00
VT9	'94 $5 Ring-Necked Duck	7.00
VT10	'95 $5 Bufflehead	7.00
VT11	'96 $5 Bluebills	7.00
Vermont Set 1986-96 (11)		**86.50**

VA1

VIRGINIA

NO.	DESCRIPTION	F-VF NH
VA1	'88 $5 Mallards	15.00
VA2	'89 $5 Canada Geese	12.00
VA3	'90 $5 Wood Ducks	9.00
VA4	'91 $5 Canvasbacks	8.50
VA5	'92 $5 Buffleheads	8.00
VA6	'93 $5 Black Ducks	7.50
VA7	'94 $5 Lesser Scaup	7.50
VA8	'95 $5 Snow Geese	7.50
VA9	'96 $5 Hooded Mergansers	7.50
Virginia Set 1988-96 (9)		**74.25**

WA1

WASHINGTON

NO.	DESCRIPTION	F-VF NH
WA1	'86 $5 Mallards	12.50
WA2	'87 $5 Canvasbacks	12.50
WA3	'88 $5 Harlequin	10.00
WA4	'89 $5 American Widgeons	9.00
WA5	'90 $5 Pintails & Sour Duck	9.00
WA6	'91 $5 Wood Duck	9.00
WA8	'92 $6 Labrador Puppy & Canada Geese	9.00
WA9	'93 $6 Snow Geese	8.00
WA10	'94 $6 Black Brant	8.00
WA11	'95 $6 Mallards	8.00
WA12	'96 $6 Redheads	8.00
Washington Set 1986-96 (11)		**92.50**

WV1

WEST VIRGINIA

NO.	DESCRIPTION	F-VF NH
WV1	'87 $5 Canada Geese	15.00
WV2	'87 $5 Canada Geese, Non-Resident	15.00
WV3	'88 $5 Wood Ducks	12.00
WV4	'88 $5 Wood Ducks, Non-Resident	12.00
WV5	'89 $5 Decoys	10.00
WV6	'89 $5 Decoys, Non-Resident	10.00
WV7	'90 $5 Labrador Retriever & Decoy	9.00
WV8	'90 $5 Labrador Retriever & Decoy, Non-Resident	9.00
WV9	'91 $5 Mallards	8.50
WV10	'91 $5 Mallards, Non-Resident	8.50
WV11	'92 $5 Canada Geese	8.50
WV12	'92 $5 Canada Geese, Non-Resident	8.50
WV13	'93 $5 Pintails	8.50
WV14	'93 $5 Pintails, Non-Resident	8.50

NO.	DESCRIPTION	F-VF NH
WV15	'94 $5 Green-Winged Teal	8.50
WV16	'94 $5 Green-Winged Teal, Non-Resident	8.50
WV17	'95 $5 Mallards	8.50
WV18	'95 $5 Mallards, Non-Resident	8.50
WV19	'96 $5 American Widgeons	8.50
West Virginia Set 1987-96 (19)		**165.00**

WI3

WISCONSIN

NO.	DESCRIPTION	F-VF NH
WI1	'78 $3.25 Wood Ducks	125.00
WI2	'79 $3.25 Buffleheads	45.00
WI3	'80 $3.25 Widgeons	15.00
WI4	'81 $3.25 Lesser Scaup	11.00
WI5	'82 $3.25 Pintails	8.00
WI6	'83 $3.25 Blue-Winged Teal	8.00
WI7	'84 $3.25 Hooded Merganser	8.00
WI8	'85 $3.25 Lesser Scaup	9.00
WI9	'86 $3.25 Canvasbacks	9.00
WI10	'87 $3.25 Canada Geese	6.00
WI11	'88 $3.25 Hooded Merganser	6.00
WI12	'89 $3.25 Common Goldeneye	6.00
WI13	'90 $3.25 Redheads	6.00
WI14	'91 $5.25 Green-Winged Teal	7.50
WI15	'92 $5.25 Tundra Swans	7.50
WI16	'93 $5.25 Wood Ducks	7.50
WI17	'94 $5.25 Pintails	7.50
WI18	'95 $5.25 Mallards	7.50
WI19	'96 $5.25 Green-Winged Teal	7.50
Wisconsin Set 1978-96 (19)		**276.00**

WYOMING

NO.	DESCRIPTION	F-VF NH
WY1	'84 $5 Meadowlark	25.00
WY2	'85 $5 Canada Geese	25.00
WY3	'86 $5 Antelope	25.00
WY4	'87 $5 Grouse	25.00
WY5	'88 $5 Fish	25.00
WY6	'89 $5 Deer	25.00
WY7	'90 $5 Bear	25.00
WY8	'91 $5 Rams	25.00
WY9	'92 $5 Bald Eagle	25.00
WY10	'93 $5 Elk	9.50
WY11	'94 $5 Bobcat	9.50
WY12	'95 $5 Moose	9.50
WY13	'96 $5 Turkey	9.50
Wyoming Set 1984-96 (13)		**236.50**

NO.	DESCRIPTION	F-VF NH

Canal Zone #4-8; 70-99

CANAL ZONE

1904
U.S. Stamp 300, 319, 304, 306-07 overprinted

CANAL ZONE

PANAMA

SCOTT NO.	DESCRIPTION	UNUSED NH F	UNUSED NH AVG	UNUSED OG F	UNUSED OG AVG	USED F	USED AVG
4	1¢ blue green	38.00	22.50	25.00	15.00	25.00	15.00
5	2¢ carmine	38.50	23.00	22.00	11.00	20.00	12.00
6	5¢ blue	125.00	75.00	80.00	55.00	65.00	40.00
7	8¢ violet black	205.00	125.00	125.00	70.00	95.00	60.00
8	10¢ pale red brown	225.00	135.00	140.00	80.00	100.00	60.00

1924-25
U.S. Stamps 551-54, 557, 562, 564-66, 569-71 overprinted

CANAL
ZONE

Type 1 Flat Tops on Letters "A". Perf. 11

SCOTT NO.	DESCRIPTION	UNUSED NH F	UNUSED NH AVG	UNUSED OG F	UNUSED OG AVG	USED F	USED AVG
70	1/2¢ olive brown	1.20	.75	.70	.45	.75	.45
71	1¢ deep green	2.25	1.35	1.50	.95	.50	.30
71e	same, booklet pane of 6	170.00	105.00	130.00	80.00	......	......
72	1-1/2¢ yellow brown	3.00	1.75	2.10	1.10	1.25	.80
73	2¢ carmine	12.00	7.25	8.00	5.50	1.75	1.00
73a	same, booklet pane of 6	210.00	125.00	150.00	90.00	......	......
74	5¢ dark blue	30.00	17.50	21.00	12.50	9.00	5.50
75	10¢ orange	62.00	37.00	40.00	25.00	19.00	11.50
76	12¢ brown violet	55.00	33.00	35.00	22.00	27.00	19.50
77	14¢ dark blue	33.50	19.50	22.00	12.00	17.00	10.00
78	15¢ gray	72.00	43.00	50.00	30.00	33.00	22.00
79	30¢ olive brown	45.00	27.00	33.00	20.00	28.00	16.50
80	50¢ lilac	95.00	57.00	65.00	35.00	42.00	25.00
81	$1 violet brown	335.00	200.00	225.00	135.00	125.00	80.00

1925-28
U.S. Stamps 554-55, 557, 564-66, 623, 567, 569-71, overprinted

CANAL
ZONE

Type II Pointed Tops on Letters "A"

SCOTT NO.	DESCRIPTION	UNUSED NH F	UNUSED NH AVG	UNUSED OG F	UNUSED OG AVG	USED F	USED AVG
84	2¢ carmine	45.00	27.00	30.00	20.00	10.00	6.00
84d	same, booklet pane of 6	300.00	175.00	220.00	140.00	......	......
85	3¢ violet	6.25	3.75	4.50	2.75	2.75	1.75
86	5¢ dark blue	6.00	3.50	4.00	2.50	2.75	1.75
87	10¢ orange	50.00	30.00	35.00	22.00	10.00	6.00
88	12¢ brown violet	36.50	22.00	25.00	16.50	14.00	9.00
89	14¢ dark blue	32.00	19.25	22.00	14.50	18.00	11.00
90	15¢ gray	10.00	6.00	7.00	4.50	3.35	2.00
91	17¢ black	6.00	3.50	4.25	2.50	3.00	1.95
92	20¢ carmine rose	10.00	6.00	7.00	4.50	4.50	2.65
93	30¢ olive brown	8.50	5.50	6.00	3.75	4.00	2.50
94	50¢ lilac	335.00	200.00	230.00	165.00	140.00	82.50
95	$1 violet brown	150.00	90.00	105.00	72.50	50.00	31.50

1926 Type II overprint on U.S. Stamp 627

SCOTT NO.	DESCRIPTION	UNUSED NH F	UNUSED NH AVG	UNUSED OG F	UNUSED OG AVG	USED F	USED AVG
96	2¢ carmine rose	6.75	4.00	4.50	2.60	3.75	2.30

1927 Type II overprint on U.S.Stamps 583-84, 591
Rotary Press Printing, Perf. 10

SCOTT NO.	DESCRIPTION	UNUSED NH F	UNUSED NH AVG	UNUSED OG F	UNUSED OG AVG	USED F	USED AVG
97	2¢ carmine	67.50	40.00	45.00	22.00	10.50	6.00
98	3¢ violet	12.50	7.50	9.00	5.25	5.00	3.00
99	10¢ orange	21.50	12.95	15.00	9.25	6.75	4.00

VERY FINE QUALITY: To determine the Very Fine price, add the difference between the Fine and Average prices to the Fine quailty price. For example: if the Fine price is $10.00 and the Average price is $6.00, the Very Fine price would be $14.00. From 1935 to date, add 20% to the Fine price to arrive at the Very Fine price.

Canal Zone #100-117a

SCOTT NO.	DESCRIPTION	PLATE BLOCK F/NH	PLATE BLOCK F	PLATE BLOCK AVG	UNUSED F/NH	UNUSED F	UNUSED AVG	USED F	USED AVG
	1927-31 **Type II overprint on U.S.Stamps 632, 634-35, 637, 642, Rotary Press printing, Perf. 11 x 10-1/2**								
100	1¢ green	25.00	20.00	16.00	2.65	1.95	1.15	1.30	.80
101	2¢ carmine	30.00	24.50	19.00	2.75	2.00	1.20	.90	.55
101a	same, booklet pane of 6	......	......	......	275.00	210.00	135.00	......	......
102	3¢ violet (1931)	110.00	85.00	68.00	6.50	4.50	2.25	3.50	2.25
103	5¢ dark blue	185.00	155.00	125.00	30.00	22.00	11.00	11.00	7.25
104	10¢ orange (1930)	225.00	180.00	145.00	25.00	17.00	11.00	12.00	8.00

105,160 106 107 108, 161 109

110 111 112 113 114

1928-40 Builders Issue

SCOTT NO.	DESCRIPTION	PLATE BLOCK F/NH	PLATE BLOCK F	PLATE BLOCK AVG	UNUSED F/NH	UNUSED F	UNUSED AVG	USED F	USED AVG
105-14	**1¢ to 50¢ complete,10 varieties.....**		**.....**	**.....**	**10.40**	**8.05**	**4.95**	**5.70**	**3.45**
105	1¢ Gorgas	1.15(6)	.80	.50	.30	.25	.20	.20	.15
106	2¢ Goethals	3.00(6)	2.25	1.30	.30	.25	.20	.20	.15
106a	same, booklet pane of 6	......	......	......	18.00	13.00	8.50	......	......
107	5¢ Gaillard Cut (1929)	17.00(6)	10.00	6.50	1.70	1.35	.85	.80	.45
108	10¢ Hodges (1932)	8.00(6)	6.00	3.50	.40	.30	.20	.25	.15
109	12¢ Gaillard (1929)	14.50(6)	11.00	6.50	1.35	1.05	.60	.85	.50
110	14¢ Sibert (1937)	11.50(6)	12.50	7.50	1.40	1.10	.70	1.10	.70
111	15¢ Smith (1932)	10.00(6)	6.50	4.00	.65	.50	.30	.50	.30
112	20¢ Rousseau (1932)	11.00(6)	7.50	4.50	.95	.75	.45	.30	.20
113	30¢ Williamson (1940)	13.50(6)	10.00	6.00	1.30	1.00	.60	.95	.55
114	50¢ Blackburn (1929)	22.00(6)	16.00	9.50	2.60	1.95	1.10	.85	.50
	1933 **Type II overprint on U.S. Stamps 720 & 695 Rotary Press Printing, Perf. 11 x 10-1/2**								
115	3¢ Washington	37.50	27.00	16.00	4.00	2.75	1.95	.35	.25
116	14¢ Indian	72.50	50.00	36.00	8.00	6.00	4.00	3.35	2.00

117, 153

SCOTT NO.	DESCRIPTION	PLATE BLOCK F/NH	PLATE BLOCK F	PLATE BLOCK AVG	UNUSED F/NH	UNUSED F	UNUSED AVG	USED F	USED AVG
	1934								
117	3¢ Goethals	2.00(6)	1.50	1.00	.30	.25	.20	.20	.15
117a	same, booklet pane of 6	......	......	......	70.00	52.00	35.00	......	......

PLATE BLOCKS: are portions of a sheet of stamps adjacent to the number(s) indicating the printing plate number used to produce that sheet. Flat plate issues are usually collected in plate blocks of six (number opposite the middle stamp) while rotary issues are normally corner blocks of four.

Canal Zone #118-145

SCOTT NO.	DESCRIPTION	PLATE BLOCK F/NH	PLATE BLOCK F/OG	UNUSED F/NH	UNUSED F/OG	USED F
	1939 U.S. Stamps 803, 805 overprinted					
118	1/2¢ red orange	2.75	2.25	.30	.25	.15
119	1-1/2 bistre brown	2.75	2.25	.30	.25	.15

122 *Gaillard Cut—Before* **123** *After*
124 *Bas Obispo—Before* **125** *After*
126 *Gatun Locks—Before* **127** *After*
128 *Canal Channel—Before* **129** *After*
130 *Gamboa—Before* **131** *After*
132 *Pedro Miguel Locks—Before* **133** *After*
134 *Gatun Spillway—Before* **135** *After*

120
Balboa—Before

121
Balboa—After

1939 25th ANNIVERSARY ISSUE

SCOTT NO.	DESCRIPTION	PLATE BLOCK F/NH	PLATE BLOCK F/OG	UNUSED F/NH	UNUSED F/OG	USED F
120-35	**1¢-50¢ complete, 16 varieties**	......	......	**117.50**	**85.25**	**60.00**
120	1¢ yellow green	11.00(6)	9.00	.50	.40	.40
121	2¢ rose carmine	12.00(6)	10.00	.60	.50	.50
122	3¢ purple	11.00(6)	9.00	.50	.40	.25
123	5¢ dark blue	20.00(6)	16.00	1.20	.90	.85
124	6¢ red orange	38.50(6)	33.00	2.75	1.95	1.95
125	7¢ black	38.50(6)	33.00	2.75	1.95	1.95
126	8¢ green	50.00(6)	41.00	4.00	2.75	3.00
127	10¢ ultramarine	50.00(6)	41.00	4.00	2.75	2.25
128	11¢ blue green	120.00(6)	100.00	9.00	6.75	7.00
129	12¢ brown carmine	100.00(6)	75.00	7.25	5.25	6.00
130	14¢ dark violet	110.00(6)	87.50	8.00	5.50	6.00
131	15¢ olive green	130.00(6)	110.00	12.00	8.00	4.75
132	18¢ rose pink	125.00(6)	105.00	11.00	7.25	8.00
133	20¢ brown	165.00(6)	130.00	14.00	10.50	4.00
134	25¢ orange	275.00(6)	220.00	20.00	15.00	11.50
135	50¢ violet brown	305.00(6)	240.00	26.50	19.50	4.75

136 **137** **138** **139** **140**

1945-49

SCOTT NO.	DESCRIPTION	PLATE BLOCK F/NH	PLATE BLOCK F/OG	UNUSED F/NH	UNUSED F/OG	USED F
136-40	**1/2¢-25¢ complete, 5 varieties**	......	......	**2.70**	**2.15**	**1.55**
136	1/2¢ Major General Davis (1948)	3.00(6)	2.50	.40	.30	.25
137	1-1/2¢ Gov. Magoon (1948)	3.00(6)	2.50	.40	.30	.25
138	2¢ T.Roosevelt (1948)	.70(6)	.50	.25	.20	.15
139	5¢ Stevens	4.00(6)	2.75	.45	.40	.15
140	25¢ J.F. Wallace (1948)	13.50(6)	9.50	1.35	1.10	.85

141 **142** **143** **144** **145**

1948 CANAL ZONE BIOLOGICAL AREA

SCOTT NO.	DESCRIPTION	PLATE BLOCK F/NH	PLATE BLOCK F/OG	UNUSED F/NH	UNUSED F/OG	USED F
141	10¢ Map & Coati-mundi	14.00(6)	10.00	1.60	1.30	1.10

1949 CALIFORNIA GOLD RUSH

SCOTT NO.	DESCRIPTION	PLATE BLOCK F/NH	PLATE BLOCK F/OG	UNUSED F/NH	UNUSED F/OG	USED F
142-45	**3¢-18¢ complete, 4 varieties**	......	......	**6.55**	**4.85**	**4.50**
142	3¢ "Forty Niners"	7.00(6)	5.00	.80	.65	.45
143	6¢ Journey—Las Cruces	8.25(6)	6.00	.85	.65	.60
144	12¢ Las Cruces—Panama Trail	19.50(6)	13.75	2.20	1.60	1.35
145	18¢ Departure—San Francisco	25.00(6)	21.00	3.05	2.20	2.35

Canal Zone #146-162

146

147

148

149

150

151

152, 154

SCOTT NO.	DESCRIPTION	PLATE BLOCK F/NH	PLATE BLOCK F/OG	UNUSED F/NH	UNUSED F/OG	USED F
	1951-58					
146	10¢ West Indian Labor	33.50(6)	25.00	3.60	2.75	2.75
147	3¢ Panama Railroad (1955)	9.00(6)	6.50	.90	.80	.65
148	3¢ Gorgas Hospital (1957)	5.00	3.50	.60	.50	.45
149	4¢ S.S. Ancon (1958)	3.50	2.60	.55	.45	.40
150	4¢ T. Roosevelt (1958)	4.00	3.00	.60	.50	.45
	1960-62					
151	4¢ Boy Scout Badge	5.00	3.75	.60	.50	.45
152	4¢ Administration Building	1.10	.80	.30	.25	.20
	LINE PAIR					
153	3¢ G.W. Goethals, coil	1.00	.85	.25	.20	.15
154	4¢ Administration Building, coil	1.25	1.05	.25	.20	.20
155	5¢ J.F. Stevens, coil (1962)	1.50	1.20	.35	.30	.25

156

157

158

159

SCOTT NO.	DESCRIPTION	PLATE BLOCK F/NH	PLATE BLOCK F/OG	UNUSED F/NH	UNUSED F/OG	USED F
	PLATE BLOCK					
156	4¢ Girl Scout Badge (1962)	3.00	2.20	.45	.40	.35
157	4¢ Thatcher Ferry Bridge (1962)	3.50	2.75	.40	.35	.30
157a	same, silver omitted (bridge)	......	......	8500.00	......	......
	1968-78					
158	6¢ Goethals Memorial	2.50	......	.40	......	.20
159	8¢ Fort San Lorenzo (1971)	3.00	......	.50	......	.25
	LINE PAIR					
160	1¢ W.C.Gorgas, coil (1975)	1.00	......	.20	......	.15
161	10¢ H.F.Hodges, coil (1975)	5.00	......	.80	......	.45
162	25¢ J.F.Wallace, coil (1975)	24.00	......	3.25	......	2.20

Canal Zone #163-165

163

165

SCOTT NO.	DESCRIPTION	PLATE BLOCK F/NH	PLATE BLOCK F/OG	UNUSED F/NH	UNUSED F/OG	USED F
	PLATE BLOCK					
163	13¢ Cascadas Dredge (1976)	2.50	......	.50	......	.40
163a	same, booklet pane 4	......	......	2.75	......	......
164	5¢ J.F.Stevens (#139) Rotary Press (1977)	5.00	......	1.00	......	.40
165	15¢ Locomotive (1978)	2.20	......	.50	......	.45

AVERAGE QUALITY: From 1935 to date, deduct 20% from the Fine price to determine the price for an Average quality stamp.

Canal Zone #C1-C20

AIR MAIL

25 CENTS 25

AIR MAIL STAMPS
105 & 106 Surcharged

1929-31

SCOTT NO.	DESCRIPTION	PLATE BLOCK F/NH	PLATE BLOCK F	PLATE BLOCK AVG	UNUSED F/NH	UNUSED F	UNUSED AVG	USED F	USED AVG
C1	15¢ on 1¢ green,Type I	150.00(6)	120.00	85.00	13.50	8.00	5.00	6.25	4.00
C2	15¢ on 1¢ y. green, Type II (1931)	......	......	......	135.00	100.00	55.00	90.00	55.00
C3	25¢ on 2¢ carmine	140.00	115.00	82.50	6.00	4.00	2.40	2.30	1.35

AIR MAIL

10c

1929

SCOTT NO.	DESCRIPTION	PLATE BLOCK F/NH	PLATE BLOCK F	PLATE BLOCK AVG	UNUSED F/NH	UNUSED F	UNUSED AVG	USED F	USED AVG
C4	10¢ on 50¢ lilac	150.00(6)	120.00	85.00	13.50	9.50	5.50	9.00	5.25
C5	20¢ on 2¢ carmine	125.00(6)	100.00	70.00	9.50	6.00	3.95	2.00	1.20

C6-14

C15

C16

C17

C18

C19

C20

1931-49

SCOTT NO.	DESCRIPTION	PLATE BLOCK F/NH	PLATE BLOCK F	PLATE BLOCK AVG	UNUSED F/NH	UNUSED F	UNUSED AVG	USED F	USED AVG
C6-14	**4¢-$1 complete, 9 varieties ...**	......	......	......	**28.25**	**21.25**	**14.00**	**7.60**	**4.80**
C6	4¢ Gaillard Cut, red violet (1949)	7.00(6)	5.00	3.35	1.10	.85	.55	.85	.55
C7	5¢ same, yellow green	5.50(6)	4.50	2.75	.75	.55	.40	.40	.25
C8	6¢ same, yellow brown (1946) .	7.75(6)	5.50	3.35	1.10	.85	.55	.40	.25
C9	10¢ same, orange	12.50(6)	9.50	6.00	1.30	1.00	.65	.40	.25
C10	15¢ same, blue	13.50(6)	10.50	7.00	1.60	1.20	.80	.30	.20
C11	20¢ same, red violet	21.00(6)	16.00	11.00	2.85	2.20	1.40	.30	.20
C12	30¢ same, rose lake (1941)	40.00(6)	30.00	20.00	4.50	3.25	2.15	1.30	.80
C13	40¢ same, yellow	40.00(6)	30.00	20.00	4.50	3.50	2.30	1.30	.80
C14	$1 same, black	105.00(6)	82.50	55.00	12.00	9.00	6.00	2.75	1.75

1939 25th ANNIVERSARY ISSUE

SCOTT NO.	DESCRIPTION	PLATE BLOCK F/NH	PLATE BLOCK F/OG	UNUSED F/NH	UNUSED F/OG	USED F
C15-20	**5¢-$1 complete, 6 varieties ....**	......	......	**74.00**	**54.25**	**48.00**
C15	5¢ Plane over Sosa Hill	35.00(6)	27.00	4.25	3.00	3.00
C16	10¢ Map of Central America	40.00(6)	30.00	4.25	3.00	2.95
C17	15¢ Scene near Fort Amador	44.00(6)	35.00	4.40	3.25	1.30
C18	25¢ Clipper at Cristobal Harbor	170.00(6)	130.00	16.00	12.00	9.00
C19	39¢ Clipper over Gaillard Cut	125.00(6)	95.00	12.50	9.50	8.00
C20	$1 Clipper Alighting	410.00(6)	300.00	36.50	26.50	26.50

Canal Zone #C21-C47

C21-31, C34

C32

C33

C35

SCOTT NO.	DESCRIPTION	PLATE BLOCK F/NH	PLATE BLOCK F/OG	UNUSED F/NH	UNUSED F/OG	USED F
	1951					
C21-26	**4¢-80¢ complete, 6 varieties**	......	......	**29.25**	**23.25**	**13.00**
C21	4¢ Globe & Wing, red violet	8.00(6)	6.00	1.00	.75	.50
C22	6¢ same, light brown	6.00(6)	4.50	1.00	.75	.40
C23	10¢ same, light red orange	10.50(6)	8.50	1.25	1.00	.50
C24	21¢ same, light blue	90.00(6)	70.00	10.00	8.00	5.00
C25	31¢ same, cerise	95.00(6)	70.00	10.00	8.00	5.00
C26	80¢ same, light gray black	50.00(6)	38.00	7.50	6.00	2.25
	1958					
C27-31	**5¢-35¢ complete, 5 varieties**	.....	.....	**28.50**	**22.90**	**9.65**
C27	5¢ Globe & Wing, yellow green	8.00	5.50	1.40	1.10	.85
C28	7¢ same, olive	6.00	4.50	1.20	1.00	.65
C29	15¢ same , brown violet	33.50	26.50	5.50	4.50	2.40
C30	25¢ same, orange yellow	90.00	72.50	12.00	9.50	3.25
C31	35¢ same, dark blue	57.50	45.00	10.00	8.00	4.00

1961-63

SCOTT NO.	DESCRIPTION	PLATE BLOCK F/NH	PLATE BLOCK F/OG	UNUSED F/NH	UNUSED F/OG	USED F
C32	15¢ Emblem Caribbean School	16.00	13.00	1.95	1.55	1.20
C33	7¢ Anti-Malaria (1962)	4.50	3.35	.80	.60	.55
C34	8¢ Globe & Wing, carmine (1963)	6.00	5.00	.85	.65	.40
C35	15¢ Alliance for Progress (1963)	15.00	11.50	1.90	1.50	1.10

C36

C37

C38

C39

C40

C41

C42-C53

SCOTT NO.	DESCRIPTION	PLATE BLOCK F/NH	PLATE BLOCK F/OG	UNUSED F/NH	UNUSED F/OG	USED F
	1964. 50th ANNIVERSARY ISSUE					
C36-C41	**6¢-80¢ complete, 6 varieties**	......	......	**15.50**	**11.00**	**10.00**
C36	6¢ Cristobal	3.35	2.75	.60	.45	.55
C37	8¢ Gatun Locks	4.00	3.25	.75	.55	.50
C38	15¢ Madden Dam	9.50	7.75	1.60	1.25	.85
C39	20¢ Gaillard Cut	12.50	10.00	2.50	1.75	1.20
C40	30¢ Miraflores Locks	20.00	16.00	4.00	2.75	3.00
C41	80¢ Balboa	35.00	28.00	7.00	4.95	4.50
	1965					
C42-C47	**6¢-80¢ complete, 6 varieties**	......	......	**6.95**	......	**3.60**
C42	6¢ Gov. Seal, green & black	2.60	......	.45	......	.40
C43	8¢ same, rose red & black	3.00	......	.50	......	.20
C44	15¢ same, blue & black	3.35	......	.50	......	.40
C45	20¢ same, lilac & black	3.50	......	.90	......	.55
C46	30¢ same, reddish brown & black	6.00	......	1.20	......	.60
C47	80¢ same, bistre & black	19.50	......	3.75	......	1.65

Canal Zone #C48-C53; CO1-CO14; J1-J24

SCOTT NO.	DESCRIPTION	PLATE BLOCK F/NH	PLATE BLOCK F/OG	UNUSED F/NH	UNUSED F/OG	USED F
	1968-76					
C48-C53	**10¢-35¢ complete, 6 varieties**	**......**	**......**	**6.40**	**......**	**2.70**
C48	10¢ Gov. Seal, dull orange & black	2.20	......	.45	......	.25
C48a	same, booklet pane of 4	......	......	4.50	......	......
C49	11¢ Seal, olive & black (1971)	2.75	......	.55	......	.30
C49a	same, booklet pane of 4	......	......	3.50	......	......
C50	13¢ Seal, emerald & black (1974)	6.00	......	1.20	......	.45
C50a	same, booklet pane of 4	......	......	6.00	......	......
C51	22¢ Seal, violet & black (1976)	6.50	......	1.30	......	.55
C52	25¢ Seal, pale yellow green & black	6.50	......	1.30	......	.55
C53	35¢ Seal, salmon & black (1976)	10.50	......	1.60	......	.75

AIR MAIL OFFICIAL STAMPS

C7-14 Overprinted

1941-42 Overprint 19 to 20-1/2 mm. long

OFFICIAL
PANAMA CANAL

SCOTT NO.	DESCRIPTION	PLATE BLOCK F/NH	PLATE BLOCK F/OG	UNUSED F/NH	UNUSED F/OG	USED F
CO1-7	**5¢-$1 complete, 7 varieties**	**......**	**......**	**136.50**	**97.75**	**49.00**
CO1	5¢ Gaillard Cut, yellow green (C7)	......	......	6.50	5.00	2.50
CO2	10¢ same, orange (C9)	......	......	12.00	9.50	3.15
CO3	15¢ same, blue (C10)	......	......	15.50	12.00	4.50
CO4	20¢ same, red violet (C11)	......	......	19.00	15.00	7.00
CO5	30¢ same, rose lake (1942) (C12)	......	......	23.00	17.50	7.00
CO6	40¢ same, yellow (C13)	......	......	27.50	20.00	11.00
CO7	$1 same, black (C14)	......	......	40.00	25.00	16.50
	1947 Overprint 19 to 20-1/2mm. Long					
CO14	6¢ yellow brown (C8)	......	......	15.00	11.00	6.25

POSTAGE DUE STAMPS

1914
U.S. Postage Due Stamps
J45-46, 49 overprinted

CANAL ZONE

SCOTT NO.	DESCRIPTION	UNUSED NH F	UNUSED NH AVG	UNUSED F	UNUSED AVG	USED F	USED AVG
J1	1¢ rose carmine	100.00	70.00	70.00	40.00	17.00	10.00
J2	2¢ rose carmine	275.00	190.00	185.00	105.00	55.00	35.00
J3	10¢ rose carmine	900.00	625.00	650.00	350.00	55.00	35.00
	1924 Type I overprint on U.S. Postage Due Stamps J61-62, 65						
J12	1¢ carmine rose	175.00	120.00	120.00	70.00	30.00	20.00
J13	2¢ deep claret	110.00	75.00	65.00	45.00	15.00	9.00
J14	10¢ deep claret	385.00	270.00	260.00	160.00	45.00	30.00
	1925 Canal Zone Stamps 71, 73, 75 overprinted (POSTAGE DUE)						
J15	1¢ deep green	140.00	95.00	100.00	55.00	19.00	11.50
J16	2¢ carmine	35.00	24.50	25.00	15.00	7.50	4.50
J17	10¢ orange	70.00	49.50	45.00	27.50	11.50	6.50
	1925 Type II overprint on U.S. Postage Due Stamps J61-62, 65						
J18	1¢ carmine rose	14.00	9.25	9.50	5.50	3.00	1.75
J19	2¢ carmine rose	22.00	15.00	15.00	10.00	5.00	3.00
J20	10¢ carmine rose	175.00	120.00	120.00	75.00	20.00	12.00
	1929-39 107 surcharged (POSTAGE DUE -1-)						
J21	1¢ on 5¢ blue	5.50	3.85	4.00	2.75	2.20	1.40
J22	2¢ on 5¢ blue	10.00	7.00	6.50	4.50	3.50	2.00
J23	5¢ on 5¢ blue	10.00	7.00	6.50	4.50	4.00	2.35
J24	10¢ on 5¢ blue	10.00	7.00	6.50	4.50	4.00	2.35

Canal Zone #J25-J29; O1-O9; U16-UXC5

J25-29

SCOTT NO.	DESCRIPTION	UNUSED NH F	UNUSED NH AVG	UNUSED F	UNUSED AVG	USED F	USED AVG
	1932-41						
J25-29	**1¢-15¢ complete, 5 varieties .**	**5.25**	**3.75**	**4.15**	**2.75**	**3.60**	**2.50**
J25	1¢ claret	.25	.20	.20	.15	.20	.15
J26	2¢ claret	.25	.20	.20	.15	.20	.15
J27	5¢ claret	.60	.45	.50	.35	.35	.25
J28	10¢ claret	2.50	1.75	1.95	1.25	1.75	1.20
J29	15¢ claret (1941)	1.95	1.35	1.50	1.00	1.30	.90

OFFICIAL STAMPS

OFFICIAL
PANAMA
CANAL

1941
105, 107, 108, 111, 112, 114, 117, 139 overprinted

OFFICIAL
PANAMA CANAL

"PANAMA" 10mm. Long

SCOTT NO.	DESCRIPTION	UNUSED F/NH	UNUSED F	USED F
O1/9	**1¢-50¢ (O1-2, O4-7, O9) 7 varieties**	**120.00**	**86.50**	**23.00**
O1	1¢ yellow green (105)	2.25	1.60	.60
O2	3¢ deep violet (117)	4.50	3.35	1.10
O3	5¢ blue (107)	......	......	40.00
O4	10¢ orange (108)	7.50	5.00	2.75
O5	15¢ gray black (111)	17.00	13.00	3.35
O6	20¢ olive brown (112)	20.00	15.00	4.00
O7	50¢ lilac (114)	65.00	45.00	8.00
	1947			
O9	5¢ deep blue (139)	11.00	8.00	4.50

CANAL ZONE MINT POSTAL STATIONERY ENTIRES

SCOTT NO.	DESCRIPTION	MINT ENTIRE
	ENVELOPES	
U16	1934, 3¢ purple	1.30
U17	1958, 4¢ blue	1.50
U18	1969, 4¢ +1¢ blue	1.50
U19	1969, 4¢ + 2¢ blue	3.00
U20	1971, 8¢ Gaillard Cut	.90
U21	1974, 8¢ + 2¢ Gaillard Cut	1.25
U22	1976,13¢ Gaillard Cut	.90
U23	1978, 13¢ + 2¢ Gaillard Cut	.90
	AIR MAIL ENVELOPES	
UC3	1949, 6¢ DC-4 Skymaster	4.50
UC4	1958, 7¢ DC-4 Skymaster	5.00
UC5	1963, 3¢ + 5¢ purple	7.00
UC6	1964, 8¢ Tail Assembly	2.75
UC7	1965, 4¢ + 4¢ blue	5.00
UC8	1966, 8¢ Tail Assembly	5.50
UC9	1968, 8¢ + 2¢ Tail Assembly	3.25
UC10	1968, 4¢ + 4¢ + 2¢ Tail Assembly	2.50
UC11	1969, 10¢ Tail Assembly	4.50
UC12	1971, 4¢ + 5¢ + 2¢ blue	4.50
UC13	1971, 10¢ + 1¢ Tail Assembly	4.50
UC14	1971, 11¢ Tail Assembly	1.25
UC15	1974, 11¢ + 2¢ Tail Assembly	1.75
UC16	1975, 8¢ +2¢ +3¢ emerald	1.50

SCOTT NO.	DESCRIPTION	MINT ENTIRE
	POSTAL CARDS	
UX10	1935,1¢ ov.print on U.S.#UX27	1.75
UX11	1952, 2¢ ov.print on U.S.#UX38	2.50
UX12	1958, 3¢ Ship in Lock	1.75
UX13	1963, 3¢ + 1¢ Ship in Lock	4.50
UX14	1964, 4¢ Ship in Canal	4.00
UX15	1965, 4¢ Ship in Lock	1.25
UX16	1968, 4¢ + 1¢ Ship in Lock	1.25
UX17	1969, 5¢ Ship in Lock	1.25
UX18	1971, 5¢ + 1¢ Ship in Lock	.95
UX19	1974, 8¢ Ship in Lock	.75
UX20	1976, 8¢ + 1¢ Ship in Lock	.60
UX21	1978, 8¢ + 2¢ Ship in Lock	.65
	AIR MAIL POSTAL CARDS	
UXC1	1958, 5¢ Plane, Flag & Map	4.00
UXC2	1963, 5¢ + 1¢ Plane, Flag & Map	10.50
UXC3	1965, 4¢ + 2¢ Ship in Lock	4.50
UXC4	1968, 4¢ + 4¢ Ship in Lock	3.25
UXC5	1971, 5¢ + 4¢ Ship in Lock	.90

Confederate States #1-14

CONFEDERATE STATES

1, 4
Jefferson Davis

2, 5
Thomas Jefferson

3
Andrew Jackson

6, 7
Jefferson Davis
6: Fine Print
7: Coarse Print

SCOTT NO.	DESCRIPTION	UNUSED OG F	UNUSED OG AVG	UNUSED F	UNUSED AVG	USED F	USED AVG
	1861						
1	5¢ green	210.00	130.00	150.00	95.00	105.00	60.00
2	10¢ blue	275.00	155.00	195.00	110.00	150.00	95.00
	1862						
3	2¢ green	595.00	365.00	425.00	260.00	450.00	350.00
4	5¢ blue	145.00	85.00	105.00	60.00	80.00	50.00
5	10¢ rose	1025.00	625.00	725.00	450.00	475.00	275.00
6	5¢ light blue, London Print .	11.25	7.75	8.00	5.50	16.50	11.00
7	5¢ blue, Local Print	15.50	9.00	11.00	6.50	9.00	6.00

8
Andrew Jackson

9

10, 11
(Die A)
Jefferson Davis

12 (Die B)

13
George Washington

14
John C. Calhoun

SCOTT NO.	DESCRIPTION	UNUSED OG F	UNUSED OG AVG	UNUSED F	UNUSED AVG	USED F	USED AVG
	1863						
8	2¢ brown red	61.50	35.00	44.00	25.00	250.00	160.00
9	10¢ blue (TEN)	975.00	595.00	700.00	425.00	450.00	275.00
10	10¢ blue (with frame line) . .	......	......	2500.00	1650.00	1200.00	700.00
11	10¢ blue (no frame)	12.50	8.50	9.00	6.00	14.00	8.00
12	10¢ blue, filled corner	12.50	8.50	9.00	6.00	14.00	8.00
13	20¢ green	49.00	30.50	35.00	22.00	350.00	250.00
	1862						
14	1¢ orange	97.50	63.00	70.00	45.00	......	......

Cuba #221-231, E1-E2, J1-J4; Guam #1-12; E1

SCOTT NO.	DESCRIPTION	UNUSED NH F	UNUSED NH AVG	UNUSED OG F	UNUSED OG AVG	USED F	USED AVG

CUBA

U.S. Administration

CUBA

1899

U.S. Stamps of
267, 279, 279B
268, 281, 282C surcharged

1 c.
de PESO.

SCOTT NO.	DESCRIPTION	UNUSED NH F	UNUSED NH AVG	UNUSED OG F	UNUSED OG AVG	USED F	USED AVG
221	1¢ on 1¢ yellow green	5.50	3.85	3.65	2.50	.65	.40
222	2¢ on 2¢ carmine	5.50	3.85	3.65	2.50	.55	.35
223	2-1/2¢ on 2¢ carmine	5.00	3.50	2.75	1.95	.65	.40
224	3¢ on 3¢ purple	11.00	7.75	6.50	4.25	1.60	.95
225	5¢ on 5¢ blue	11.00	7.75	6.50	4.25	1.60	.95
226	10¢ on 10¢ brown	26.00	18.25	19.00	12.00	8.00	5.00

227 228 229 230 231

Republic under U.S Military Rule Watermarked US-C

SCOTT NO.	DESCRIPTION	UNUSED NH F	UNUSED NH AVG	UNUSED OG F	UNUSED OG AVG	USED F	USED AVG
227	1¢ Columbus	3.65	2.50	2.40	1.60	.25	.15
228	2¢ Coconut Palms	3.65	2.50	2.40	1.60	.25	.15
229	3¢ Allegory "Cuba"	3.65	2.50	2.40	1.60	.35	.20
230	5¢ Ocean Liner	5.50	3.85	3.65	2.75	.40	.25
231	10¢ Cane Field	13.00	9.00	9.00	5.75	.85	.50

SPECIAL DELIVERY

1899; Surcharge of 1899 on U.S. E5

SCOTT NO.	DESCRIPTION	UNUSED NH F	UNUSED NH AVG	UNUSED OG F	UNUSED OG AVG	USED F	USED AVG
E1	10¢ on 10¢ blue	135.00	95.00	95.00	60.00	85.00	50.00

Republic under U.S. Military Rule
Watermarked US-C Inscribed "Immediate"

E2
Special Delivery Messenger

SCOTT NO.	DESCRIPTION	UNUSED NH F	UNUSED NH AVG	UNUSED OG F	UNUSED OG AVG	USED F	USED AVG
E2	10¢ orange	60.00	42.00	35.00	24.00	12.50	7.50

POSTAGE DUE STAMP

1899 Surcharge of 1899 on U.S. J38-39, J41-42

SCOTT NO.	DESCRIPTION	UNUSED NH F	UNUSED NH AVG	UNUSED OG F	UNUSED OG AVG	USED F	USED AVG
J1	1¢ on 1¢ deep claret	35.00	24.50	24.00	16.00	4.00	2.50
J2	2¢ on 2¢ deep claret	35.00	24.50	24.00	16.00	4.00	2.50
J3	5¢ on 5¢ deep claret	35.00	24.50	24.00	16.00	3.50	2.60
J4	10¢ on 10¢ deep claret	35.00	24.50	24.00	16.00	1.75	1.10

GUAM

1899

U.S. Stamps of 279, 267, 268, 272, 280-82c,
284, 275, 276 overprinted

GUAM

SCOTT NO.	DESCRIPTION	UNUSED NH F	UNUSED NH AVG	UNUSED OG F	UNUSED OG AVG	USED F	USED AVG
1	1¢ deep green	30.00	21.00	20.00	13.00	30.00	17.00
2	2¢ red	26.50	18.50	19.00	11.00	29.00	17.00
3	3¢ purple	165.00	115.00	110.00	65.00	140.00	90.00
4	4¢ lilac brown	165.00	115.00	110.00	65.00	140.00	90.00
5	5¢ blue	40.00	28.00	25.00	17.00	40.00	22.00
6	6¢ lake	165.00	115.00	110.00	65.00	130.00	85.00
7	8¢ violet brown	165.00	115.00	110.00	65.00	135.00	90.00
8	10¢ brown (Type I)	60.00	36.00	40.00	24.00	60.00	37.50
10	15¢ olive green	175.00	120.00	125.00	70.00	165.00	100.00
11	50¢ orange	305.00	210.00	210.00	125.00	275.00	165.00
12	$1 black (Type I)	500.00	350.00	350.00	210.00	450.00	260.00

SPECIAL DELIVERY

U.S. Stamp E5 Overprint

GUAM

SCOTT NO.	DESCRIPTION	UNUSED NH F	UNUSED NH AVG	UNUSED OG F	UNUSED OG AVG	USED F	USED AVG
E1	10¢ blue	205.00	140.00	130.00	80.00	170.00	110.00

Hawaii #23-47

23, 24

25, 26

SCOTT NO.	DESCRIPTION	UNUSED OG F	UNUSED OG AVG	UNUSED F	UNUSED AVG	USED F	USED AVG
	1864 Laid Paper						
23	1¢ black	195.00	115.00	150.00	90.00	......	......
24	2¢ black	195.00	115.00	150.00	90.00	......	......
	1865 Wove Paper						
25	1¢ dark blue	200.00	125.00	150.00	95.00	......	......
26	2¢ dark blue	175.00	110.00	135.00	85.00	......	......

27-29, 50, 51
King Kamehameha IV

30
Princess Kamamalu

31
King Kamehameha IV

32, 39, 52C

33
King Kamehameha V

34
Mataia Kekuanaoa

SCOTT NO.	DESCRIPTION	UNUSED OG F	UNUSED OG AVG	UNUSED F	UNUSED AVG	USED F	USED AVG
	1861-63						
27	2¢ pale rose, horizontal laid ppr.	180.00	120.00	150.00	100.00	100.00	60.00
28	2¢ pale rose, vertical laid paper	180.00	120.00	150.00	100.00	100.00	60.00
	1869 Engraved						
29	2¢ red, thin wove paper	55.00	33.50	45.00	28.00	......	......
	1864-71 Wove Paper						
30	1¢ purple	8.50	5.50	7.00	4.50	5.50	3.35
31	2¢ rose vermillion	12.00	7.25	10.00	6.00	6.00	3.75
32	5¢ blue	78.00	48.00	65.00	40.00	16.00	11.00
33	6¢ yellow green	19.25	12.00	16.00	10.00	5.50	3.35
34	18¢ dull rose	105.00	55.00	85.00	45.00	13.00	9.00

35, 38, 43
King David Kalakaua

36, 46
Prince William Pitt Leleichoku

37, 42
Princess Likelike

40, 44, 45
King David Kalakaua

SCOTT NO.	DESCRIPTION	UNUSED OG F	UNUSED OG AVG	UNUSED F	UNUSED AVG	USED F	USED AVG
	1875						
35	2¢ brown	6.60	4.00	5.50	3.35	2.20	1.40
36	12¢ black	45.00	30.00	37.50	25.00	19.50	12.50

41
Queen Kapiolani

47
Statue of King Kamehameha I

48
King William Lunalilo

49
Queen Emma Kaleleonalani

52
Queen Liliuokalani

SCOTT NO.	DESCRIPTION	UNUSED OG F	UNUSED OG AVG	UNUSED F	UNUSED AVG	USED F	USED AVG
	1882						
37	1¢ blue	4.50	3.00	3.75	2.50	6.00	4.00
38	2¢ lilac rose	90.00	60.00	75.00	50.00	28.00	18.00
39	5¢ ultramarine	13.75	9.00	11.50	7.50	2.10	1.40
40	10¢ black	26.50	18.00	22.00	15.00	15.00	9.50
41	15¢ red brown	45.00	28.75	37.50	24.00	22.00	13.50
	1883-86						
42	1¢ green	2.50	1.65	2.10	1.40	1.40	.80
43	2¢ rose	4.00	2.50	3.35	2.10	.85	.50
44	10¢ red brown	21.00	12.50	17.50	10.50	6.50	4.25
45	10¢ vermillion	26.50	15.00	22.00	12.50	11.50	7.75
46	12¢ red lilac	66.00	42.00	55.00	35.00	30.00	19.50
47	25¢ dark violet	95.00	60.00	80.00	50.00	41.50	26.50

Hawaii #48-82; O1-O6

SCOTT NO.	DESCRIPTION	UNUSED OG F	UNUSED OG AVG	UNUSED F	UNUSED AVG	USED F	USED AVG
48	50¢ red	155.00	105.00	130.00	85.00	70.00	45.00
49	$1 rose red	235.00	145.00	195.00	120.00	85.00	50.00
	1890-91						
52	2¢ dull violet	7.25	3.00	6.00	2.50	1.20	.80
52C	5¢ deep indigo	135.00	70.00	100.00	60.00	72.50	45.00
	1893 Provisional Government Red Overprint						
53	1¢ purple	4.75	2.85	4.00	2.40	3.40	2.10
54	1¢ blue	4.75	2.85	4.00	2.40	6.00	3.40
55	1¢ green	1.80	1.05	1.50	.85	2.75	1.65
56	2¢ brown	6.00	3.35	5.00	2.75	10.50	7.00
57	2¢ dull violet	1.80	1.10	1.50	.90	1.30	.85
58	5¢ deep indigo	10.75	6.25	9.00	5.25	16.00	10.50
59	5¢ ultramarine	5.50	3.35	4.50	2.75	3.25	1.95
60	6¢ green	11.50	6.50	9.50	5.50	17.00	11.00
61	10¢ black	7.75	4.50	6.50	3.75	8.00	5.00
62	12¢ black	8.75	5.30	7.25	4.50	12.00	7.50
63	12¢ red lilac	145.00	85.00	120.00	72.50	155.00	95.00
64	25¢ dark violet	24.00	14.50	20.00	12.00	25.00	17.00
	Black Overprint						
65	2¢ rose vermillon	55.00	36.00	45.00	30.00	45.00	30.00
66	2¢ rose	1.45	.95	1.20	.80	2.50	1.50
67	10¢ vermillion	12.00	7.75	10.00	6.50	20.00	12.00
68	10¢ red brown	7.25	4.50	6.00	3.75	10.00	6.00
69	12¢ red lilac	250.00	155.00	210.00	130.00	285.00	175.00
70	15¢ red brown	19.25	12.50	16.00	10.50	28.75	17.50
71	18¢ dull rose	25.00	14.50	21.00	12.00	33.75	20.00
72	50¢ red	62.50	36.00	52.50	30.00	85.00	51.50
73	$1 rose red	120.00	72.50	100.00	60.00	140.00	85.00

74, 80
Coat of Arms

75, 81
View of Honolulu

76
Statue of King Kamehameha I

77
Star and Palm

78
S.S."Arawa"

79
Pres. S.B. Dole

82
Statue of King Kamehameha I

O1-6
Lorrin A. Thurston

SCOTT NO.	DESCRIPTION	UNUSED OG F	UNUSED OG AVG	UNUSED F	UNUSED AVG	USED F	USED AVG
	1894						
74	1¢ yellow	3.00	2.10	2.00	1.20	1.40	.85
75	2¢ brown	3.10	2.20	2.15	1.25	.80	.45
76	5¢ rose lake	6.00	4.20	4.00	2.40	1.90	1.20
77	10¢ yellow green	7.25	5.00	5.00	3.00	5.00	3.00
78	12¢ blue	16.00	11.00	10.00	6.00	12.00	7.25
79	25¢ deep blue	16.00	11.00	10.00	6.00	12.00	7.25
	1899						
80	1¢ dark green	2.50	1.75	1.60	1.00	1.30	.85
81	2¢ rose	2.50	1.75	1.60	1.00	1.30	.85
82	5¢ blue	7.25	5.00	5.00	3.00	3.35	2.00
	1896 OFFICIAL STAMPS						
O1	2¢ green	45.00	31.50	30.00	18.00	18.00	11.75
O2	5¢ black brown	45.00	31.50	30.00	18.00	18.00	11.75
O3	6¢ deep ultramarine	60.00	42.00	40.00	22.00	18.00	11.75
O4	10¢ bright rose	45.00	31.50	30.00	18.00	18.00	11.75
O5	12¢ orange	95.00	65.00	60.00	35.00	18.00	11.75
O6	25¢ gray violet	120.00	85.00	82.50	50.00	18.00	11.75

Marshall Islands #31-62

MARSHALL ISLANDS

The Marshall Islands are a part of the U.S. administered Trust Territories of the Pacific formed in 1947. They were granted postal autonomy in 1984 on their way to independence.

31

35

50

54

58

59

63

70

65

SCOTT NO.	DESCRIPTION	UNUSED F/NH
	1984 COMMEMORATIVES	
31-34	20¢ Postal Independence, attached...	2.75
	1984-85 MAPS & NAVIGATION	
35-49A	**1¢-$1, 16 varieties**	**11.00**
35	1¢ Mili Atoll	
36	3¢ Likiep Atoll	
37	5¢ Ebon Atoll	
38	10¢ Jaluit Atoll	
39	13¢ Alinginae Atoll	
40	14¢ Wotho Atoll (1985)	
41	20¢ Kwajalein Atoll	
42	22¢ Enewetok (1985)	
43	28¢ Ailinglaplap Atoll	
44	30¢ Majuro Atoll	
45	33¢ Namu Atoll (1985)	
46	37¢ Rongelap Atoll	
47	39¢ Utirik & Taka (1985)	
48	44¢ Ujelang Atoll (1985)	
49	50¢ Maloelap & Aur (1985)	
49A	$1.00 Arno Atoll	
	1984-85 BOOKLET PANES	
39a	13¢ Ailingingae (10)	10.00
40a	14¢ Wotho Atoll (10)	10.00
41a	20¢ Kwajalein (10)	10.00
41b	13¢ (5) & 20¢ (5)	13.00
42a	22¢ Eniwetok (10)	10.00
42b	14¢ (5) & 22¢ (5)	13.00
	1984 COMMEMORATIVES	
50-53	40¢ U.P.U.—Hamburg, attached	3.50
54-57	20¢ Dolphins, attached	2.25
58	20¢ Christmas, strip of 4	2.10
59-62	20¢ Constitution, attached	2.25

74

78

82

Marshall Islands #63-131

86

91

SCOTT NO.	DESCRIPTION	UNUSED F/NH
	1985 COMMEMORATIVES	
63-64	22¢ Audubon Birds, attached	1.40
65-69	22¢ Seashells, attached	2.75
70-73	22¢ Decade for Women, attached ...	2.25
74-77	22¢ Reef Fish, attached	2.25
78-81	22¢ Youth Year, attached	2.25
82-85	14¢-44¢ Christmas, 4 varieties	2.75
86-90	22¢ Halley's Comet, strip of 5	6.00
91-94	22¢ Medicinal Plants, attached	2.25
	1986-87 MAPS & NAVIGATION	
107	$2 Wotje & Erikub	4.75
108	$5 Bikini Atoll	11.00
109	$10 Stick Chart (1987)	19.50

110

114

115

124

128

SCOTT NO.	DESCRIPTION	UNUSED F/NH
	1986 COMMEMORATIVES	
110-13	14¢ Marine Invertebrates, attached .	2.10
114	$1 AMERIPEX '86 Souvenir Sheet ..	3.40
115-18	22¢ Operation Crossroads, Atomic Tests, attached	2.50
119-23	22¢ Seashells, designs as #65-69, attached	2.50
124-27	22¢ Game Fish, attached.	2.25
128-31	22¢ Christmas, Peace, attached	2.25

132

136

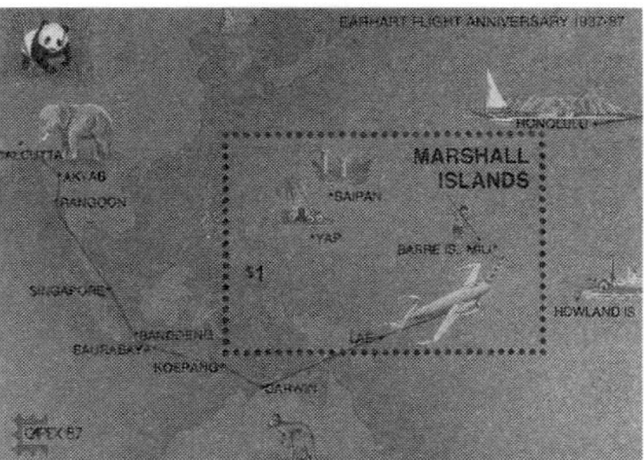

142

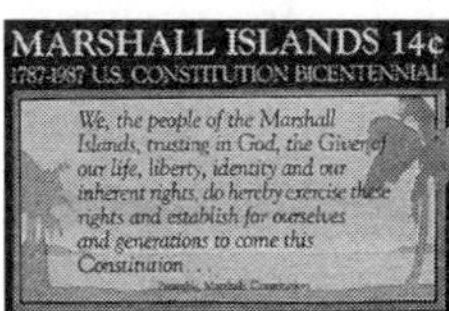

143

157

Marshall Islands #132-208

160

1987 COMMEMORATIVES

SCOTT NO.	DESCRIPTION	UNUSED F/NH
132-35	22¢ Whaling Ships, attached	2.50
136-41	33¢, 39¢, 44¢ Historic Aircraft, 3 attached pairs	5.50
142	$1 CAPEX '87 Souvenir Sheet	3.00
143-51	14¢-44¢ U.S. Constitution, 3 attached strips of 3	5.25
152-56	22¢ Seashells, attached	2.50
157-59	44¢ Copra Industry, attached	2.75
160-63	14¢-44¢ Christmas	2.75

164

168

1988

SCOTT NO.	DESCRIPTION	UNUSED F/NH
164-67	44¢ Marine Birds	4.25

1988-89 Definitives

SCOTT NO.	DESCRIPTION	UNUSED F/NH
168-83	1¢-$5 Fish, 16 singles complete set	22.50
184	$10 Blue Jack (1989)	19.25

Booklet Panes 1987-89

SCOTT NO.	DESCRIPTION	UNUSED F/NH
170a	14¢ Hawkfish pane (10)	4.50
171a	15¢ Balloonfish pane (10)	6.25
173a	22¢ Lyretail wrasse pane (10)	5.50
173b	5 (14¢) & 5 (22¢) pane (10)	4.75
174a	25¢ Parrotfish pane (10)	7.00
174b	5 (15¢) & 5 (25¢) pane (10)	6.00

188

189

190a

191

195

202

208a

1988 COMMEMORATIVES (continued)

SCOTT NO.	DESCRIPTION	UNUSED F/NH
188-89	15¢-25¢ Olympics 2 attached strip of 5	5.00
190	25¢ Stevenson, sheetlet of 9	7.00
191-94	25¢ Ships & Flags, attached	2.75
195-99	25¢ Christmas, strip of 5	3.00
200-04	25¢ J.F.K. Tribute, strip of 5	3.50
205-08	25¢ Space Shuttle, strip of 4	2.75

209

Marshall Islands #209-254

SCOTT NO.	DESCRIPTION	UNUSED F/NH

213

221

222

226

230a

232

1989 COMMEMORATIVES

SCOTT NO.	DESCRIPTION	UNUSED F/NH
209-12	45¢ Links to Japan, attached	4.25
213-15	45¢ Alaska Anniv., strip of 3	3.00
216-20	25¢ Seashells, strip of 5	3.25
221	$1 Japanese Art Souvenir Sheet	2.40
222-25	45¢ Migrant Birds, attached	4.00
226-29	45¢ Postal Service, attached	4.00
230	$1.50 PHILEX-FRANCE Souv. Sheet	12.00
231	$1.00 Postal Service Centenary Souvenir Sheet	12.00
232-38	25¢-$1 20th Anniversary First Moon Landing	16.00
238a	booklet pane of 232-38	16.50

239

1989 WWII Anniversary Issues

SCOTT NO.	DESCRIPTION	UNUSED F/NH
239	25¢ Invasion of Poland	.60
240	45¢ Sinking of HMS Royal Oak	1.00
241	45¢ Invasion of Finland	1.00
242-45	45¢ Battle of River Plate, 4 attached	4.00

248

1990 WWII Anniversary Issues

SCOTT NO.	DESCRIPTION	UNUSED F/NH
246-47	25¢ Invasion of Denmark and Norway	1.10
248	25¢ Katyn Forest Massacre	.60
249-50	25¢ Bombing of Rotterdam/ 25¢ Invasion of Belgium	1.20
251	45¢ Winston Churchill	1.00
252-53	45¢ Evacuation at Dunkirk, 2 attached	2.00
254	45¢ Occupation of Paris	1.00

Marshall Islands #255-390

SCOTT NO.	DESCRIPTION	UNUSED F/NH
255	25¢ Battle of Mers-el-Kebir	.60
256	25¢ Battles for Burma Road	.60
257-60	45¢ U.S. Destroyers, 4 attached	4.00
261-64	45¢ Battle for Britain, 4 attached	4.00
265	45¢ Tripartite Pact 1940	1.00
266	25¢ Roosevelt Reelected	.60
267-70	25¢ Battle of Taranto, 4 attached	2.25

1991 WWII Anniversary Issues

SCOTT NO.	DESCRIPTION	UNUSED F/NH
271-74	30¢ Roosevelt's Four Freedoms of Speech, 4 attached	2.50
275	30¢ Battle of Beda Fomm	.70
276-77	29¢ Invasion of Greece and Yugoslavia, 2 attached	1.20
278-81	50¢ Sinking of the Bismarck, 4 attached	4.40
282	30¢ Germany Invades Russia	.70
283-84	29¢ Atlantic Charter, 2 attached	1.20
285	29¢ Siege of Moscow	.70
286-87	30¢ Sinking of the USS Reuben James, 2 attached	1.20
288-91	50¢ Japanese Attack Pearl Harbor, 4 attached	4.40
288-91b	same, 2nd printing (1 title corrected)	4.40
292	29¢ Japanese Capture Guam	.70
293	29¢ Fall of Singapore	.70
294-95	50¢ Flying Tigers, 2 attached	2.25
296	29¢ Fall of Wake Island	.70

1992 WWII Anniversary Issues

SCOTT NO.	DESCRIPTION	UNUSED F/NH
297	29¢ Arcadia Conference	.70
298	50¢ Fall of Manila	1.10
299	29¢ Japanese take Rabaul	.70
300	29¢ Battle of Java Sea	.70
301	50¢ Fall of Rangoon	1.10
302	29¢ Japanese on New Guinea	.70
303	29¢ MacArthur evacuated from Corregidor	.70
304	29¢ Raid on Saint-Nazaire	.70
305	29¢ Bataan/Death March	.70
306	50¢ Doolittle Raid on Tokyo	1.10
307	29¢ Fall of Corregidor	.70
308-11	50¢ Battle of the Coral Sea, 4 attached	4.40
308-11b	same, 2nd printing (4 titles corrected)	4.40
312-15	50¢ Battle of Midway, 4 attached	4.40
316	29¢ Village of Lidice destroyed	.70
317	29¢ Fall of Sevastopol	.70
318-19	29¢ Convoy PQ 17 Destroyed, 2 attached	1.20
320	29¢ Marines on Guadalcanal	.70
321	29¢ Battle of Savo Island	.70
322	29¢ Dieppe Raid	.70
323	50¢ Battle of Stalingrad	1.10
324	29¢ Battle of Eastern Solomons	.70
325	50¢ Battle of Cape Esperance	1.10
326	29¢ Battle of El Alamein	.70
327-28	29¢ Battle of Barents Sea, 2 attached	1.10

1993 WWII Anniversary Issues

SCOTT NO.	DESCRIPTION	UNUSED F/NH
329	29¢ Casablanca Conference	.70
330	29¢ Liberation of Kharkov	.70
331-34	50¢ Battle of Bismarck Sea, 4 attached	4.40
335	50¢ Interception of Admiral Yamamoto	1.10
336-37	29¢ Battle of Kursk, 2 attached	1.20

341

345a

1989

SCOTT NO.	DESCRIPTION	UNUSED F/NH
341-44	25¢ Christmas 1989, 4 attached	4.50
345	45¢ Milestones in space (25)	40.00

346

356

1990

SCOTT NO.	DESCRIPTION	UNUSED F/NH
346-65A	1¢/$2 Birds (21)	20.50
361a	Essen '90 Germany, miniature sheet of 4 (347, 350, 353, 361)	2.75

366

SCOTT NO.	DESCRIPTION	UNUSED F/NH
366-69	25¢ Children's Games, 4 attached	3.50

370

SCOTT NO.	DESCRIPTION	UNUSED F/NH
370-76	25¢, $1 Penny Black, singles	11.00
376a	booklet pane of 370-76	12.00
377-80	25¢ Endangered Wildlife, 4 attached	5.00
381	25¢ Joint Issue (US & Micronesia)	1.00
382	45¢ German Reunification	1.40
383-86	25¢ Christmas 1990, 4 attached	3.50
387-90	25¢ Breadfruit, 4 attached	3.50

Marshall Islands #391-410

SCOTT NO.	DESCRIPTION	UNUSED F/NH

377

381

382

383

387

391

1991

SCOTT NO.	DESCRIPTION	UNUSED F/NH
391-94	50¢ 10th Anniv. of Space Shuttle, 4 attached	5.00
395-98	52¢ Flowers, 4 attached	5.00
398a	52¢ Phila Nippon, sheet of 4	5.00

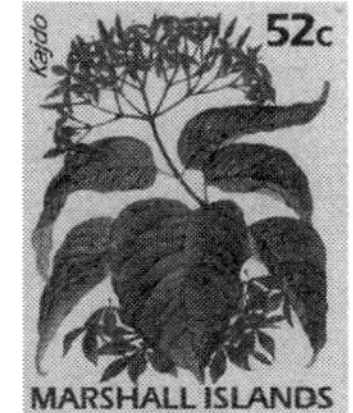

395

399

400

407

411

412

413

SCOTT NO.	DESCRIPTION	UNUSED F/NH
399	29¢ Operation Desert Storm	.85
400-06	29¢, $1 Birds, set of 7 singles	12.00
406a	same, booklet pane of 7	12.50
407-10	12¢-50¢ Air Marshall Islands Aircraft, set of 4	4.25

Marshall Islands #411-563

SCOTT NO.	DESCRIPTION	UNUSED F/NH
411	29¢ Admission to the United Nations	.85
412	30¢ Christmas 1991, Dove	.85
413	29¢ Peace Corps	.85

414

418

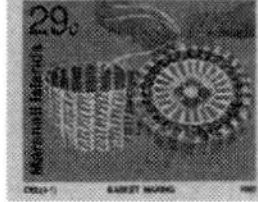

425

429

1992

SCOTT NO.	DESCRIPTION	UNUSED F/NH
414-17	29¢ Ships, strip of 4	3.50
418-24	50¢, $1 Columbus, set of 7 singles	12.00
424a	same, booklet pane of 7	12.50
425-28	29¢ Handicrafts, 4 attached	3.50
429	29¢ Christmas, 1992	.85
430-33	9-45¢ Birds, set of 4	3.00

434

1993

SCOTT NO.	DESCRIPTION	UNUSED F/NH
434-40	50¢, $1 Reef Life, set of 7 singles	10.00
440a	same, booklet pane of 7	10.50

442

466A

1993-95

SCOTT NO.	DESCRIPTION	UNUSED F/NH
441-66B	10¢-$10 Ships & Sailing Vessels, 26 varieties.	70.00
466C	"Hong Kong '94" miniature sheet of 4 (#464d-64g)	4.00

1993 WWII Anniversary Issues (continued)

SCOTT NO.	DESCRIPTION	UNUSED F/NH
467-70	52¢ Invasion of Sicily, 4 attached	4.60
471	50¢ Bombing of Schweinfurt ..	1.10
472	29¢ Liberation of Smolensk ...	.70
473	29¢ Landings at Bougainville .	.70
474	50¢ Invasion of Tarawa	1.10
475	52¢ Teheran Conference, 1943	1.10
476-77	29¢ Battle of North Cape, 2 attached	1.20

1994 WWII Anniversary Issues

SCOTT NO.	DESCRIPTION	UNUSED F/NH
478	29¢ Gen. Dwight D. Eisenhower	.70
479	50¢ Invasion of Anzio	1.10
480	52¢ Siege of Leningrad lifted	1.10
481	29¢ US Liberates Marshall Islands ..	.70
482	29¢ Japanese Defeated at Truk	.70
483	52¢ US Bombs Germany	1.10
484	50¢ Lt. Gen. Mark Clark, Rome Falls to the Allies	1.10
485-88	75¢ D-Day—Allied Landings at Normandy, 4 attached	6.25
485-88b	same, 2nd printing (3 titles corrected)	6.25
489	50¢ V-1 Bombardment of England Begins	1.10
490	29¢ US Marines Land on Saipan	.70
491	50¢ 1st Battle of Philippine Sea	1.10
492	29¢ US Liberates Guam	.70
493	50¢ Warsaw Uprising	1.10
494	50¢ Liberation of Paris	1.10
495	29¢ US Marines land on Peliliu	1.10
496	52¢ MacArthur returns to the Philippines	1.10
497	52¢ Battle of Leyte Gulf	1.10
498-99	50¢ Battleship Tirpitz Sunk, 2 attached	2.25
500-03	50¢ Battle of the Bulge, 4 attached ..	4.40

1995 WWII Anniversary Issues

SCOTT NO.	DESCRIPTION	UNUSED F/NH
504	32¢ Yalta Conference Begins	.75
505	55¢ Bombing of Dresden	1.20
506	$1 Iwo Jima Invaded by US Marines	2.25
507	32¢ Remagen Bridge Taken by US Forces	.75
508	55¢ Okinawa Invaded by US Forces	1.20
509	50¢ Death of F.D.R.	1.10
510	32¢ US/USSR troops meet at Elbe River	.75
511	60¢ Russian troops capture Berlin	1.40
512	55¢ Allies liberate concentration camps, 1945	1.25
513-16	75¢ VE Day, 4 attached	6.25
517	32¢ UN Charter signed	.75
518	55¢ Potsdam Conference convenes	1.25
519	60¢ Churchill resigns	1.40
520	$1 Enola Gay drops atomic bomb on Hiroshima, 1945	2.25
521-24	75¢ VJ Day, 4 attached	6.25

1994 WWII Anniversary Issues (continued)

SCOTT NO.	DESCRIPTION	UNUSED F/NH
562	$1 MacArthur returns to the Philippines, souvenir sheet	2.25
563	$1 Harry S. Truman/UN Charter souvenir sheet	2.25

Marshall Islands #567-580

SCOTT NO.	DESCRIPTION	UNUSED F/NH

567

1993 (continued)

567-70	29¢ New Capitol	2.60

571

571	50¢ Super Tanker "Eagle" souvenir sheet	1.10

572

572-75	29¢ Life in the 1800s, 4 attached	2.75

576

576	29¢ Christmas 1993	.70

577

577	$2.90 15th Anniversary Constitution souvenir sheet	6.25

578

578	29¢ 10th Anniversary Postal Service souvenir sheet	.70

579

579-80	50¢ World Cup Soccer, 2 attached	2.25

582a

Marshall Islands #582-597

SCOTT NO.	DESCRIPTION	UNUSED F/NH
582	50¢ Solar System, Planets, sheetlet of 12	13.00

583

587a

SCOTT NO.	DESCRIPTION	UNUSED F/NH
583-86	75¢ 25th Anniversary of First Moon Landing, 4 attached	6.25
586b	$3 25th Anniversary of First Moon Landing, souvenir sheet	6.25
587	"PHILAKOREA '94" souvenir sheet of 3	4.00

588

SCOTT NO.	DESCRIPTION	UNUSED F/NH
588	29¢ Christmas 1994	.70

589

1995

SCOTT NO.	DESCRIPTION	UNUSED F/NH
589	50¢ New Year 1995 (Year of the Boar)	2.50
590	55¢ Marine Life, 4 attached ...	4.75
591	55¢ John F. Kennedy, strip of 6	7.50
592	75¢ Marilyn Monroe, 4 attached	7.25
593	32¢ Cats, 4 attached	3.00

590a

591a

592a

593a

594a

595a

SCOTT NO.	DESCRIPTION	UNUSED F/NH
594	75¢ Space Shuttle 4 attached	6.25
595	60¢ Pacific Game Fish, 8 attached	13.75

596a

597a

SCOTT NO.	DESCRIPTION	UNUSED F/NH
596	32¢ Island Legends, 4 attached, plus 4 labels	3.00
597	32¢ Orchids (Singapore '95), miniature sheet of 4	3.00

Marshall Islands #598-605

SCOTT NO.	DESCRIPTION	UNUSED F/NH

598

598	50¢ Suzhou Gardens souvenir sheet	1.10

599

600a

599	32¢ Christmas 1995	.75
600	32¢ Jet Fighter Planes, sheetlet of 25	18.75

601

601	32¢ Yitzhak Rabin	.75

SCOTT NO.	DESCRIPTION	UNUSED F/NH

602

603a

604

605a

1996

602	50¢ New Year 1996 (Year of the Rat)	1.10
603	32¢ Native Birds, 4 attached ..	3.00
604	55¢ Wild Cats, 4 attached	4.75
605	32¢ Sailing Ships, sheetlet of 25	18.75

Marshall Islands #606-618

SCOTT NO.	DESCRIPTION	UNUSED F/NH
606	60¢ Olympic Games Centenary, 4 attached	5.50
607	55¢ History of the Marshall Islands, sheetlet of 12	15.00
608	32¢ Elvis Presley First #1 Hit 40th Anniversary	.75
609	50¢ The Palance Museum, Shenyang souvenir sheet	1.10
610	32¢ James Dean	.75
611	60¢ Automobiles, sheet of 8 ..	11.00
612	32¢ Island Legends 1996, 4 attached	3.00
613	55¢ Steam Locomotives, sheet of 12	14.50
614	32¢ Marine Life (Taipei '96), miniature sheet of 4	3.00
615	$3 Stick Chart, Canoe & Flag of the Republic	6.75
616	32¢ Christmas 1996	.75
617	32¢ World's Legendary Biplanes, sheet of 25	17.50
618	32¢ Native Crafts, 4 attached	3.00

606

607a

608

609

610

611a

612a

613a

614a

615

Marshall Islands #619-New Issues

SCOTT NO.	DESCRIPTION	UNUSED F/NH
	1997	
619	60¢ New Year 1997 (Year of the Ox)	1.35
620-21	32¢-60¢ Amata Kabua, President of Marshall Islands, set of 2	2.00
622	32¢ Elvis Presley, strip of 3 ...	2.25
623-24	32¢ Hong Kong '97, 2 sheets of 2	3.00
625	60¢ The Twelve Apostles, sheet of 12	16.00
626	$3 Rubens "The Last Supper", souvenir sheet	6.75
627	60¢ First Decade of the 20th Century, sheet of 15	19.50
628	60¢ Deng Xiaoping (1904-97), Chinese Leader	1.35
......	32¢ Native Crafts (1996), 4 attached, self-adhesive, Die-Cut	3.00
......	32¢ Native Crafts (1996), 4 attached, self-adhesive, perf.	3.00
......	16¢ Bristle-Thighed Curlew, strip of 4	1.45
......	50¢-$1 Anniv. 1st US & Marshall Islands Stamps, booklet of 7	8.75

616

617a

618a

619

620

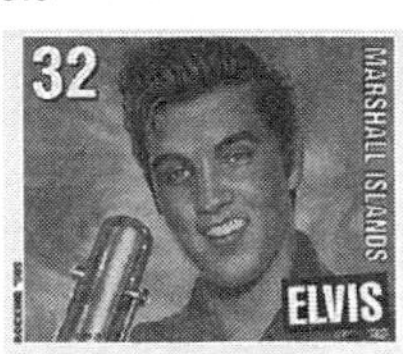

622a

623

625a

626

627a

Marshall Islands #B1; New Issue

SCOTT NO.	DESCRIPTION	UNUSED F/NH

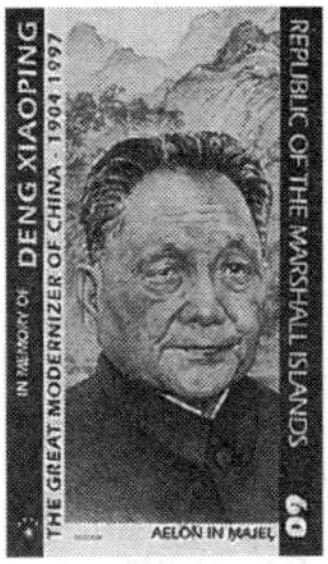

628

1996

SCOTT NO.	DESCRIPTION	UNUSED F/NH
B1	32¢+8¢ 50th Anniv. of Nuclear Testing, sheet of 6	5.50

Postal Stationery

SCOTT NO.	DESCRIPTION	UNUSED F/NH
......	20¢ Elvis Presley, postal card	.50

Marshall Islands #C1-C25b

SCOTT NO.	DESCRIPTION	UNUSED F/NH
	AIRMAIL	
	1985 AIR MAILS	
C1-2	44¢ Audubon Birds, attached	3.00

C8

C9

1986 AIR MAILS

SCOTT NO.	DESCRIPTION	UNUSED F/NH
C3-6	44¢ AMERIPEX '86, attached	3.75
C7	44¢ Operation Crossroads, souvenir sheet	5.00
C8	44¢ Statue of Liberty, Peace	1.25
C9-12	44¢ Girl Scouts, attached	3.75

C13

C17

1987 AIR MAILS

SCOTT NO.	DESCRIPTION	UNUSED F/NH
C13-16	44¢ Marine Birds, attached	3.75
C17-20	44¢ CAPEX '87, attached	3.75

C22

1988-89

SCOTT NO.	DESCRIPTION	UNUSED F/NH
C21	45¢ Space Shuttle	1.10
C22-25	12¢-45¢ Aircraft	2.75

Booklet Panes

SCOTT NO.	DESCRIPTION	UNUSED F/NH
C22a	12¢ Dornier DO288, pane (10)	4.00
C23a	36¢ Boeing 737, pane (10)	8.00
C24a	39¢ Hawker 748, pane (10)	8.50
C25a	45¢ Boeing 727, pane (10)	9.50
C25b	5 (36¢) & 5 (45¢), pane (10)	9.50

Micronesia #1-39; C4-C15

FEDERATED STATES OF MICRONESIA

Micronesia, formed from the major portion of the Caroline Islands, became postally autonomous in 1984. It forms part of the U.S. administered Trust Territories of the Pacific.

SCOTT NO.	DESCRIPTION	UNUSED F/NH

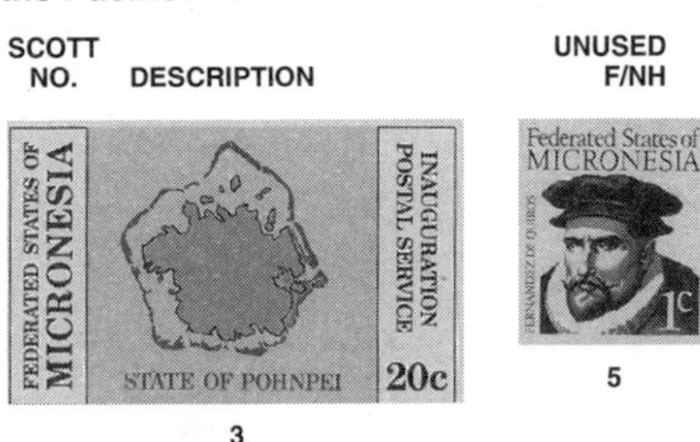

3 5

9

21

22

1984 COMMEMORATIVE

1-4	20¢ Postal Service, attached	2.50

1984 DEFINITIVES

5-20	**1¢-$5 16 varieties, singles, complete set**	**19.95**
5	1¢ Pedro de Quiros	
6	2¢ Louis Duperrey	
7	3¢ Fyedor Lutke	
8	4¢ Dumont d'Urville	
9	5¢ Men's House, Yap	
10	10¢ Sleeping Lady Hill	
11	13¢ Liduduhriab Waterfall	
12	17¢ Tonachau Peak	
13	19¢ Pedro de Quiros	
14	20¢ Louis Duperrey	
15	30¢ Fyedor Lutke	
16	37¢ Dumont d'Urville	
17	50¢ Devil Mask, Truk	
18	$1 Sokeh's Rock	
19	$2 Canoes	
20	$5 Stone Money	

1984 COMMEMORATIVES

21 & C4-6	20¢-40¢ AUSIPEX '84, 4 varieties	3.75
22 & C7-9	20¢-40¢ Christmas '84, 4 varieties	3.75

23

SCOTT NO.	DESCRIPTION	UNUSED F/NH

24

1985 COMMEMORATIVES

23 & C10-12	22¢-44¢ Ships, 4 varieties	4.00
24 & C13-14	22¢-44¢ Christmas '85, 3 varieties	4.00

25

25-28 & C15	22¢ Audubon, booklet of 4 attached, & 44¢ airmail	4.00

34 39

31

1985-88 DEFINITIVES

31-39 & C34-36	**12 varieties, singles, complete set ....**	**25.00**
31	3¢ Long-billed	
32	14¢ Truk Monarch	
33	15¢ Waterfall	
34	22¢ Tall Ship Senyavin	
35	22¢ Pohnpei Mountain starling	
36	25¢ Tonachau Peak	
37	36¢ Tall Ship	
38	45¢ Sleeping Lady	
39	$10 National Seal	
C34	33¢ Great truk white-eye	
C35	44¢ Blue-faced parrotfinch	
C36	$1 Yap monarch	

Booklet Panes 1988

33a	15¢ booklet pane of (10)	4.25
36a	25¢ booklet pane of (10)	7.00
36b	booklet pane of (10), 5—15¢ & 5—25¢	5.50

Micronesia #45-58; C16-C33

45

1985 COMMEMORATIVES & AIR MAILS

SCOTT NO.	DESCRIPTION	UNUSED F/NH
45 & C16-18	22¢-44¢ Nan Mandol Ruins, 4 varieties	4.00

46

C19

C20

52

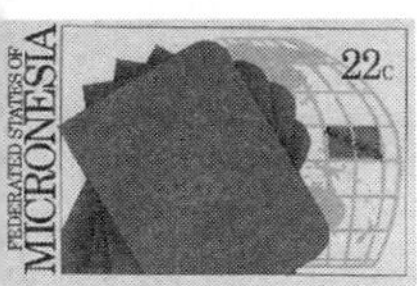

53

54

1986 COMMEMORATIVES & AIRMAILS

SCOTT NO.	DESCRIPTION	UNUSED F/NH
46 & C19-20	22¢, 44¢ Peace Year	4.50
48-51	22¢ on 20¢ Postal Service, block of 4 attached	2.50
52 & C21-24	22¢-44¢ AMERIPEX '86, 5 varieties	5.50
53	22¢ Passport	.80
54-55 & C26-27	5¢-44¢ Christmas, 4 varieties	4.00

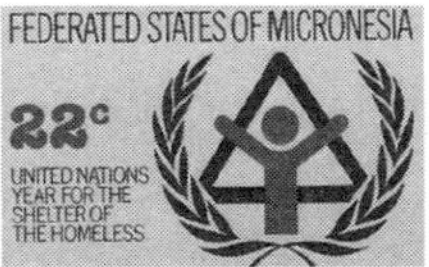

56

58

1987 COMMEMORATIVES & AIR MAILS

SCOTT NO.	DESCRIPTION	UNUSED F/NH
56 & C28-30	22¢-44¢ Shelter for Homeless, 4 varieties	4.25
57	$1 CAPEX '87 souvenir sheet .	3.25
58 & C31-33	22¢-44¢ Christmas, 4 varieties	3.75

59

63

67

Micronesia #59-105; C37-C38

SCOTT NO.	DESCRIPTION	UNUSED F/NH

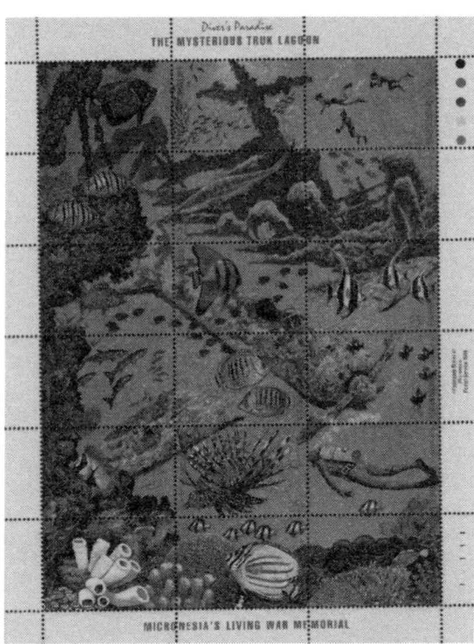

71

1988 COMMEMORATIVES & AIR MAILS

SCOTT NO.	DESCRIPTION	UNUSED F/NH
59-62 & C37-38	22¢, 44¢ Colonial Flags, 7 varieties	5.75
63-66	25¢ & 45¢ Summer Olympics, 2 pairs	3.00
67-70	25¢ Christmas, block of 4 attached	2.25
71	25¢ Truk Lagoon, souvenir sheet of 18 varieties	9.50

72

1989 COMMEMORATIVES

SCOTT NO.	DESCRIPTION	UNUSED F/NH
72-75	45¢ Flowers, block of 4 attached	3.75
76	$1 Japanese Art souvenir sheet	2.10
77-80	25¢, 45¢ Sharks, attached, 2 pairs	3.00
81	25¢ Space Achievements souvenir sheet of 9	4.50
82	$2.40 Priority Mail	4.75
83-102	1¢-$5 Seashells (12)	22.50
85a	15¢ Commercial trochus pane (10)	3.25
88a	25¢ Triton's trumpet pane (10)	5.50
88b	5 (15¢) + 5 (25¢) pane 10	4.50
103	25¢ Fruits & Flowers, sheet of 18	9.50
104-05	Christmas	1.50

76

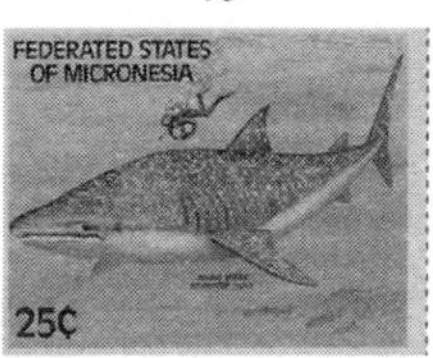

77

81

Micronesia

SCOTT NO.	DESCRIPTION	UNUSED F/NH

82

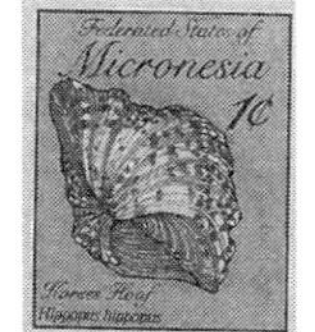

83

103a

104

106

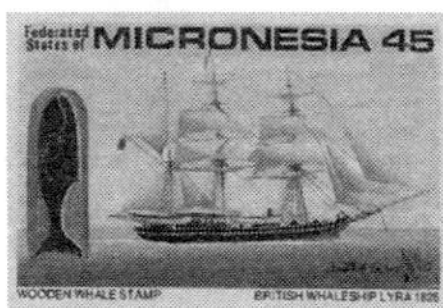

110

115

SCOTT NO.	DESCRIPTION	UNUSED F/NH

116

118

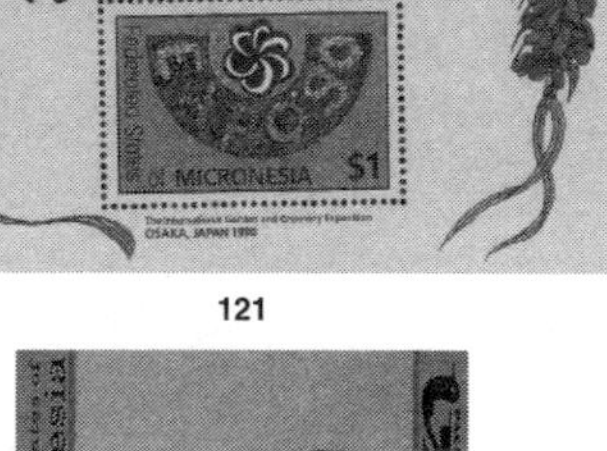

121

122

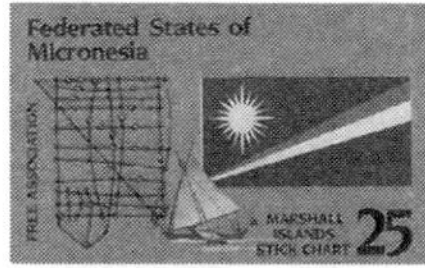

124

127

131a

Micronesia #106-149

SCOTT NO.	DESCRIPTION	UNUSED F/NH
	1990 COMMEMORATIVES	
106-09	World Wildlife Fund (4 varieties)	1.75
110-13	45¢ Whaling Ships & Artifacts, 4 attached	3.75
114	$1 Whaling Souvenir Sheet	2.50
115	$1 Penny Black Anniversary Souvenir Sheet	2.50
116-20	25¢ P.A.T.S. strip of 5	2.75
121	$1 Expo '90 Souvenir Sheet	2.50
122-23	25¢ & 45¢ Loading Mail	1.75
124-26	25¢ Joint Issue, 3 attached	2.00
127-30	45¢ Moths, 4 attached	3.75
131	25¢ Christmas, sheetlet of 9	5.00

132

134

138

143a

146

149a

1991

SCOTT NO.	DESCRIPTION	UNUSED F/NH
132	25¢+45¢ Government bldgs., Souvenir Sheet of 2	1.75
133	$1 New Capitol Souvenir Sheet	2.25
134-37	29¢+50¢ Turtles, 2 pairs	6.50
138-41	29¢ Operation Desert Storm, 4 attached	2.50
142	$2.90 Operation Desert Storm Priority Mail	6.00
142a	$2.90 Operation Desert Storm Souvenir Sheet	6.50
143	29¢ Phila Nippon Souvenir Sheet of 3	1.80
144	50¢ Phila Nippon Souvenir Sheet of 3	3.10
145	$1 Phila Nippon Souvenir Sheet	2.25
146-48	29¢ Christmas 1991 set of 3	2.75
149	29¢ Pohnpei Rain Forest, sheetlet of 18	12.00

150a

151a

152

Micronesia #150-186

SCOTT NO.	DESCRIPTION	UNUSED F/NH

154

1992

SCOTT NO.	DESCRIPTION	UNUSED F/NH
150	29¢ Peace Corps/Kennedy, strip of 5	3.25
151	29¢ Columbus, strip of 3	2.10
152-53	29¢, 50¢ UN Membership Anniversary	1.75
153a	same, Souvenir Sheet of 2	1.75
154	29¢ Christmas, 1992	.70

155a

1993

SCOTT NO.	DESCRIPTION	UNUSED F/NH
155	29¢ Pioneers of Flight I, 8 attached	5.00

168a

172

173

177a

179

182a

184

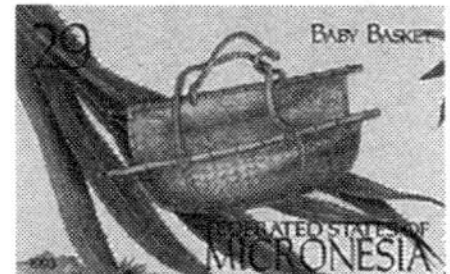

186a

1993-94

SCOTT NO.	DESCRIPTION	UNUSED F/NH
156-67	10¢-$2.90, Fish, 16 varieties	22.50

1993

SCOTT NO.	DESCRIPTION	UNUSED F/NH
168	29¢ Sailing Ships, sheetlet of 12	7.50
172	29¢ Thomas Jefferson	.70
173-76	29¢ Canoes, 4 attached	2.75
177	29¢ Local Leaders I, strip of 4	2.75
178	50¢ Pioneers of Flight II, 8 attached	8.75
179-80	29¢, 50¢ Tourist Attractions, Pohnpei	1.75
181	$1 Tourist Attractions, Souvenir Sheet	2.25
182-83	29¢, 50¢ Butterflies, 2 pairs	3.75
184-85	29¢-50¢ Christmas 1993	1.75
186	29¢ Micronesia Culture, sheetlet of 18	11.75

Micronesia #187-207

192a

193a

194

195a

196

198a

199a

201a

202

SCOTT NO.	DESCRIPTION	UNUSED F/NH
	1994	
187-89	29¢-50¢ Tourist Attractions, Kosrae	2.7
190	"Hong Kong '94" miniature sheet of 4 (#182a, 182b, 183a, 183b)	2.7
191	29¢ Pioneers of Flight III, 8 attached	5.0
192	29¢ 1994 Micronesian Games, 4 attached	2.7
193	29¢ Native Costumes, 4 attached ...	2.7
194	29¢ Constitution, 15th Anniversary .	.9
195	29¢ Flowers, strip of 4	2.7
196-97	50¢ World Cup Soccer, pair	2.2
198	29¢ 10th Anniv. Inauguration Postal Service, 4 attached	2.7
199	"PHILAKOREA '94" Dinosaur, miniature sheet of 3	4.2
200	50¢ Pioneers of Flight IV, 8 attached	8.7
201	29¢ Migratory Birds, 4 attached	3.9
202-03	29¢, 50¢ Christmas 1994	2.5
204-07	32¢ Local Leaders II, set of 4	3.9

208

209a

211a

228a

Micronesia #208-236

SCOTT NO.	DESCRIPTION	UNUSED F/NH

229

230a

231a

232

234

236

1995

SCOTT NO.	DESCRIPTION	UNUSED F/NH
208	50¢ New Year 1995 (Year of the Boar)	1.10
209	32¢ Chuuk Lagoon, 4 attached	3.50
210	32¢ Pioneers of Flight V, 8 attached	5.75
211	32¢ Dogs, 4 attached	3.00
213-26	32¢-$5.00 Fish, set of 7	24.50
227	32¢ Fish, sheetlet of 25 (1996)	18.75
228	32¢ Flowers II, strip of 4	3.00
229	$1 UN 50th Anniversary Souvenir Sheet	2.25
230	32¢ Orchids (Singapore '95), min. sheet of 4	3.00
231	60¢ US Warships, 4 attached	5.50
232	50¢ Temple of Heaven Souvenir Sheet	1.10
233	60¢ Pioneers of Flight VI, 8 attached	10.50
234-35	32¢-60¢ Christmas Poinsettias	2.00
236	32¢ Yitzhak Rabin	.75

Micronesia #237-253

SCOTT NO.	DESCRIPTION	UNUSED F/NH
	1996	
237	50¢ New Year 1996 (Year of the Rat)	1.10
238	32¢ Pioneers of Flight VII, 8 attached	5.75
239	32¢ Tourism in Yap, 4 attached	3.00
240	55¢ Sea Stars, 4 attached	6.00
241	60¢ Olympic Games Centenary, 4 attached	5.50
242	50¢ The Tarrying Garden, Suzhou Souvenir Sheet	1.10
243-44	32¢ Marine Vessels, 2 attached	1.50
245	55¢ Automobile, sheet of 8	10.50
247	32¢ Police Drug Enforcement Dog .	.75
248	32¢ Citrus Fruit, strip of 4	3.00
249	60¢ Pioneers of Flight VIII, 8 attached	10.50
250	32¢ Fish (Taipei '96), miniature sheet of 4	3.00
251-52	32¢-60¢ Christmas 1996, set of 2 ...	2.00
253	$3 Canoe & Flag of Micronesia	6.75

237

238a

239a

240

241

242

243

Micronesia #New Issues

245a

247

248a

249a

250a

251

253

SCOTT NO.	DESCRIPTION	UNUSED F/NH
	1997	
......	32¢ Happy Lunar New Year	.75
......	$2 Happy Lunar New Year, souvenir sheet	4.50
......	32¢ Sea Goddesses of the Pacific, sheet of 6	4.25
......	60¢ Deng Xiaoping, sheet of 4	5.25
......	$3 Deng Xiaoping, souvenir sheet ..	6.50
......	$2 Bridge to the Future, salute to Hong Kong, souvenir sheet	4.50
	Postal Stationery	
......	20¢ Views of Micronesia, set of 4 postal cards	1.80

Micronesia #C1/49; U1-U3

C1

C39

C43

C49

1984-94 AIR MAIL

SCOTT NO.	DESCRIPTION	UNUSED F/NH
C1-3	28¢-40¢ Aircraft, set of 3	2.50
C25	$1 Ameripex '86 Souvenir Sheet	4.25
C39-42	45¢ State Flags, block of 4 attached	3.75
C43-46	22¢-45¢ Aircraft Serving Micronesia (4 varieties)	3.10
C47-48	40¢, 50¢ Aircraft and Ships	1.95
C49	$2.90 25th Anniv. First Moon Landing, souvenir sheet	6.50

Postal Stationery

SCOTT NO.	DESCRIPTION	UNUSED F/NH
U1	20¢ National Flag	15.00
U2	22¢ Tail Ship Senyavin	9.00
U3	29¢ on 30¢ New Capitol	1.00

AFFORDABLE WORLDWIDE STAMP ALBUMS

TRAVELER ALBUM

This excellent loose-leaf album has space for 10,000 stamps from most countries. Headings feature the philatelic history of each stamp issuing country. Brightly colored loose-leaf binder. 272 pages (136 sheets) printed on both sides.

1HRS18 Traveler Album **$18.95**

2HRS9 Traveler (chipboard) expansion binder **$10.95**

NEW ADVENTURER III ALBUM

Start a child collecting with this inexpensive softbound version of the Traveler Album. Includes educational philatelic histories. 272 pages (136 sheets) printed on both sides.

1HRS17 Adventurer III Album **$10.95**

Palau #1-62

REPUBLIC OF PALAU

Palau is a Strategic Trust of the United States; a designation granted by the United Nations after World War II. It is the first Trust Territory to be granted postal independence, which became effective November 1, 1982. The first stamps were issued March 10, 1983.

1

5

1983 COMMEMORATIVES

SCOTT NO.	DESCRIPTION	UNUSED F/NH
1-4	20¢ Art and Preamble, attached .	3.25
5-8	20¢ Birds, attached	2.25

9

24

28

33

34

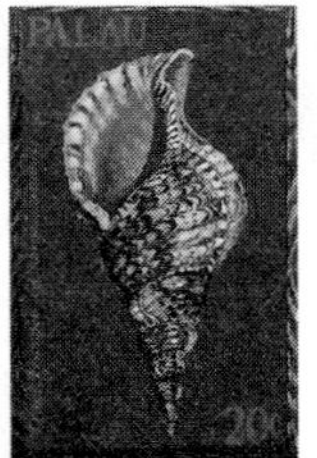

41

51

1983-84 DEFINITIVES

SCOTT NO.	DESCRIPTION	UNUSED F/NH
9-21	**1¢-$5, 13 varieties, singles, complete set**	**25.00**
9	1¢ Sea Fan	
10	3¢ Map Cowrie	
11	5¢ Jellyfish	
12	10¢ Hawksbill Turtle	
13	13¢ Giant Clam	
14	20¢ Parrotfish	
15	28¢ Chambered Nautilus	
16	30¢ Dappled Sea Cucumber	
17	37¢ Sea Urchin	
18	50¢ Starfish	
19	$1 Squid	
20	$2 Dugong (1984)	
21	$5 Pink Sponge (1984)	

1983-84 Booklet Panes

SCOTT NO.	DESCRIPTION	UNUSED F/NH
13a	13¢ Giant Clam (10)	11.00
13b	13¢ (5) & 20¢ (5)	13.50
14b	20¢ Parrotfish (10)	12.00

1983 COMMEMORATIVES

SCOTT NO.	DESCRIPTION	UNUSED F/NH
24-27	20¢ Whales, attached	2.50
28-32	20¢ Christmas, strip of 5	4.00
33-40	20¢ When Different Worlds Meet, attached........................	4.75

55

59

1984 COMMEMORATIVES

SCOTT NO.	DESCRIPTION	UNUSED F/NH
41-50	20¢ Seashells, attached	4.50
51-54	40¢ Explorer Ships, attached	4.00
55-58	20¢ Fishing, attached	2.25
59-62	20¢ Christmas, Flowers, attached	2.25

63

Palau #63-125; C17

67

86

90

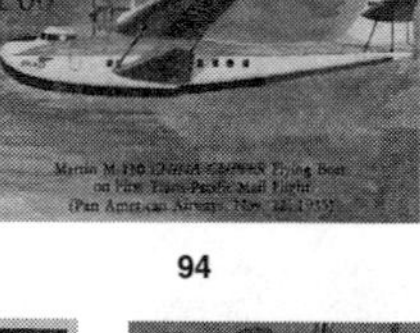

94

95

99

103a

104

109

113

117

SCOTT NO.	DESCRIPTION	UNUSED F/NH
	1985 COMMEMORATIVES	
63-66	22¢ Audubon—Birds, attached ...	2.75
67-70	22¢ Canoes, attached	2.50
	1985 DEFINITIVES	
75-85	**14¢-$10, 7 varieties, singles complete set ....**	**25.00**
75	14¢ Trumpet Triton	....
76	22¢ Parrotfish	....
77	25¢ Damsel Fish	....
79	33¢ Clownfish	....
80	39¢ Sea Turtle	....
81	44¢ Sailfish	....
85	$10 Spinner Dolphins	....
	1985 Booklet Panes	
75a	14¢ Trumpet Triton (10)	9.50
76a	22¢ Parrotfish (10)	11.50
76b	14¢ (5) & 22¢ (5)	13.50
	1985 COMMEMORATIVES	
86-89	44¢ Youth Year, attached	3.75
90-93	14¢-44¢ Christmas, 4 varieties	3.25
94	$1 Trans-Pacific, souvenir sheet .	3.50
95-98	44¢ Halley's Comet, attached	4.00
	1986 COMMEMORATIVES	
99-102	44¢ Songbirds, attached	4.00
103	14¢ World of Sea and Reef, Ameripex '86 sheet of 40	47.50
104-08	22¢ Seashells, strip of 5	3.25
109-12, C17	22¢ International Peace Year, 4 attached, 44¢ Airmail	4.00
113-16	22¢ Reptiles, attached	2.50
117-21	22¢ Christmas, attached	2.50

121B

122

SCOTT NO.	DESCRIPTION	UNUSED F/NH
	1987 COMMEMORATIVES	
121B-E	44¢ Butterflies, attached	4.50
122-25	44¢ Fruit Bats, attached	4.50

126

146

Palau #126-203

SCOTT NO.	DESCRIPTION	UNUSED F/NH
	1987-88 FLOWER DEFINITIVES	
126-42	**1¢-$5, 16 varieties, single complete set**	**42.50**
126	1¢ Kerdeu	......
127	3¢ Ngemoel	......
128	5¢ Uror	......
129	10¢ Woody Vine	......
130	14¢ Rur	......
131	15¢ Jaml (1988)	......
132	22¢ Denges	......
133	25¢ Ksid (1988)	......
134	36¢ Meldii (1988)	......
135	39¢ Emeridesh	......
136	44¢ Eskeam	......
137	45¢ Shrub (1988)	......
138	50¢ Rriu	......
139	$1 Koranges	......
140	$2 Meliin	......
141	$5 Orchid	......
142	$10 Flower Bouquet (1988)	19.00
	1987 Booklet Panes	
130a	14¢ Bikkia Palauensis (10)	4.50
132a	22¢ Bruguiera Gymnorhiza (10)	6.00
132b	14¢ (5) and 22¢ (5)	6.00
	1988 Booklet Panes	
131a	15¢ Limnophila (10)	3.50
133a	25¢ Ksid (10)	5.50
133b	15¢ (5) 25¢ (5)	5.50

155

164

173

178

SCOTT NO.	DESCRIPTION	UNUSED F/NH
	1987 COMMEMORATIVES (continued)	
146-49	22¢ Capex '87, attached	2.25
150-54	22¢ Seashells, strip of 5	3.00
155-63	14¢-44¢ U.S. Bicentennial 3 attached, strips of 3	5.50
164-67	12¢-44¢ Japan Links	2.75
168	$1 Japan souvenir sheet	2.50
173-77	22¢ Christmas, attached	3.10
178-82	22¢ Marine Species, attached	3.10

187

196a

197

198

SCOTT NO.	DESCRIPTION	UNUSED F/NH
	1988 COMMEMORATIVES	
183-86	44¢ Butterflies, attached	4.00
187-90	44¢ Birds, attached	4.00
191-95	25¢ Seashells, strip of 5	3.00
196	25¢ Finlandia sheetlet of 6	3.25
197	45¢ PRAGA '88, sheetlet of 6	6.00
198-202	25¢ Christmas, strip of 5	3.00
203	25¢ Chambered Nautilus, sheetlet of 5	3.50

Palau

SCOTT NO.	DESCRIPTION	UNUSED F/NH

SCOTT NO.	DESCRIPTION	UNUSED F/NH

203

204

208

217

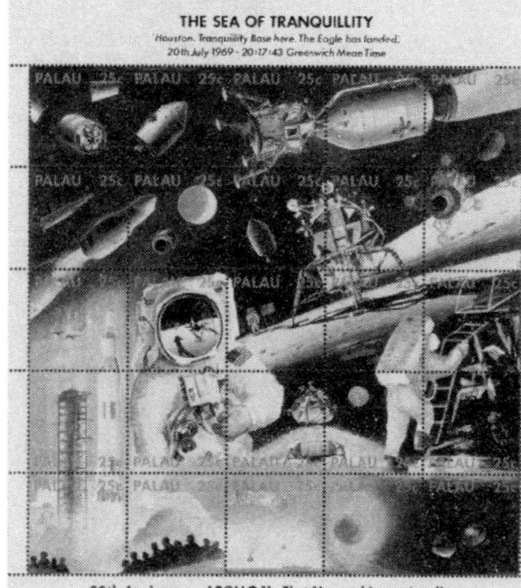

218

219

220a

221

Palau #204-258

1989 COMMEMORATIVES

SCOTT NO.	DESCRIPTION	UNUSED F/NH
204-07	45¢ Endangered Birds, attached	4.00
208-11	45¢ Mushrooms, attached	4.00
212-16	25¢ Seashells, strip of 5	3.50
217	$1 Japanese Art souvenir sheet	2.50
218	25¢ Apollo 11 mission, sheetlet of 25	13.50
219	$2.40 Priority Mail	5.00
220	25¢ Literacy (block of 10).......	6.25
221	25¢ Stilt Mangrove Fauna, sheetlet of 20	11.00
222-26	25¢ Christmas (strip of 5)	3.00

222

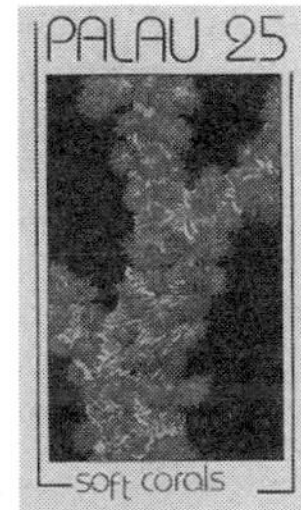

227

231

235a

236

237

242

246a

247

249

254

1990 COMMEMORATIVES

SCOTT NO.	DESCRIPTION	UNUSED F/NH
227-30	25¢ Soft Coral (4 attached).............	2.50
231-34	45¢ Forest Birds (4 attached)	4.00
235	Prince Boo Visit (sheet of 9)	5.00
236	$1 Penny Black Ann.	2.50
237-41	45¢ Tropical Orchids (strip of 5)	4.75
242-45	45¢ Butterflies II (4 attached)..........	3.75
246	25¢ Lagoon Life, sheet of 25	14.50
247-48	45¢ Pacifica, pair	2.75
249-53	25¢ Christmas, strip of 5	2.75
254-57	45¢ U.S. Forces in Palau, attached .	4.00
258	$1 U.S. Peleliu, souvenir sheet	2.35

Palau #259-299

259

263a

1991

SCOTT NO.	DESCRIPTION	UNUSED F/NH
259-62	30¢ Hard Corals, attached	2.75
263	30¢ Angaur—The Phosphate Island sheet of 16	10.50

267

288a

289a

290a

293a

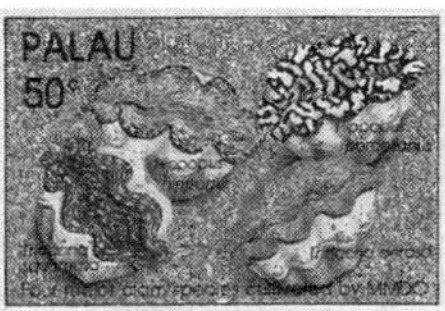

294a

295a

297a

298a

299a

1991-92

SCOTT NO.	DESCRIPTION	UNUSED F/NH
264-87	1¢-$10 Birds, 18 varieties	45.00

1991 Booklet Panes

SCOTT NO.	DESCRIPTION	UNUSED F/NH
270b	19¢ Palau fantail booklet pane (10)	4.00
272a	Booklet pane of 10, 19¢ (5) + 29¢ (5)	5.00
272b	29¢ Palau fruit dove booklet pane (10) ..	6.00

1991 (continued)

SCOTT NO.	DESCRIPTION	UNUSED F/NH
288	29¢ Christianity in Palau, sheetlet of 6 ...	3.50
289	29¢ Marine Life, sheetlet of 20	16.75
290	20¢ Operation Desert Storm, sheetlet of 9	4.50
291	$2.90 Operation Desert Storm Priority Mail	6.00
292	$2.90 Operation Desert Storm Souvenir Sheet	6.00
293	29¢ 10th Anniversary of Independence sheetlet of 8	5.50
294	50¢ Giant Clams, Souvenir Sheet of 5 ...	5.50
295	29¢ Japanese Heritage in Palau, sheet of 6	4.00
296	$1.00 Phila Nippon, Souvenir Sheet	2.10
297	29¢ Peace Corps, sheetlet of 6	4.00
298	29¢ Christmas, 1991, strip of 5	3.25
299	29¢ Pearl Harbor/WWII, sheetlet of 10 ...	6.75

Palau #300-312

SCOTT NO.	DESCRIPTION	UNUSED F/NH

300a

301a

302a

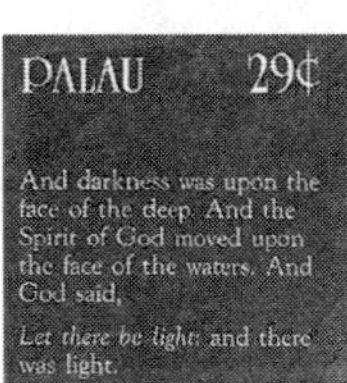

303a

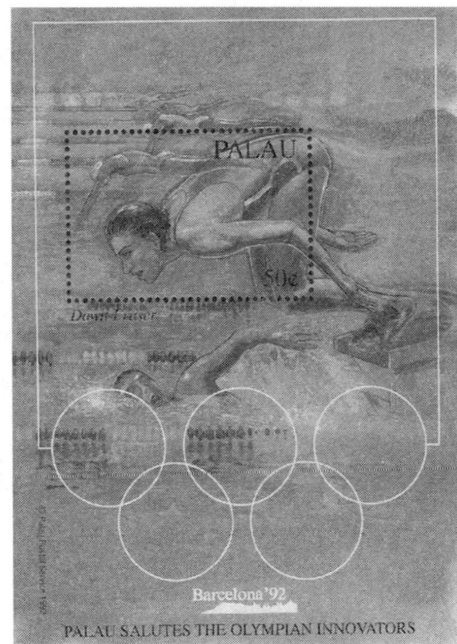

304

310e

312a

1992

SCOTT NO.	DESCRIPTION	UNUSED F/NH
300	50¢ Butterflies, attached	4.50
301	29¢ Shells, strip of 5	3.25
302	29¢ Columbus & Age of Discovery, sheetlet of 20	12.25
303	29¢ World Environment, sheetlet of 24	15.25
304-09	50¢ Olympians, set of 6 Souvenir Sheets	7.50
310	29¢ Elvis Presley, sheetlet of 9	6.50
311	50¢ WWII Aircraft, sheet of 10	10.00
312	29¢ Christmas, strip of 5	3.25

313a

314a

315a

316a

Palau #313-321

317a

318

319a

1993

SCOTT NO.	DESCRIPTION	UNUSED F/NH
313	50¢ Fauna, 4 attached	4.00
314	29¢ Seafood, 4 attached	2.25
315	50¢ Sharks, 4 attached	4.00
316	29¢ WWII in the Pacific, sheetlet of 10	6.50
317	29¢ Christmas 1993, strip of 5	3.75
318	29¢ Prehistoric Sea Creatures, sheet of 25	16.50
319	29¢ International Year of Indigeneous People, sheet of 2	2.75
320	$2.90 Quarrying of Stone Money, souvenir sheet	6.00
321	29¢ Jonah and the Whale, sheet of 25	16.50

321

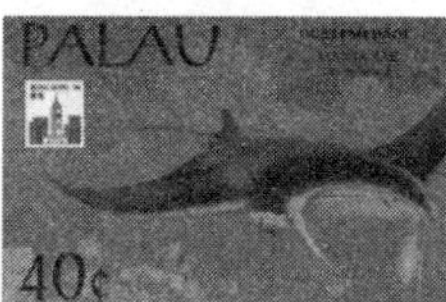

322a

323a

324a

327

334a

Palau #322-367b

SCOTT NO.	DESCRIPTION	UNUSED F/NH
	1994	
322	40¢ Rays "Hong Kong '94", 4 attached	3.50
323	20¢ Estuarine Crocodile, 4 attached	2.00
324	50¢ Large Seabirds, 4 attached	4.00
325	29¢ Action in the Pacific, 1944, sheet of 10	6.50
326	50¢ D-Day, sheet of 10	10.00
327	29¢ Pierre de Coubertin	.70
328-33	50¢-$2 Winter Olympic medalists, souvenir sheet of 1 (6)	12.50
334	29¢ PHILAKOREA '94 (Fish), sheetlet of 8	5.25
335	40¢ PHILAKOREA '94 (Mammals), sheetlet of 8	7.00
336	50¢ PHILAKOREA '94 (Birds), sheetlet of 8	8.00
337	29¢ 25th Anniversary First Manned Moon Landing, sheet of 20	13.00
338	29¢ Independence Day, strip of 5	3.25
339	$1 50th Anniv. of Invasion of Peleliu, souvenir sheet	2.50
340	29¢ Disney Characters Visit Palau, sheetlet of 9	5.75
341-42	$1 Mickey, Donald visiting Palau, souvenir sheet of 1 (2)	5.00
343	$2.90 Pluto, Mickey in Boat, souvenir sheet	6.00
344	20¢ Int. Year of the Family, sheetlet of 12	5.50
345	29¢ Christmas, strip of 5	3.25
346-48	29¢-50¢ World Cup '94, 3 sheetlets of 12	26.00
	1995	
350	32¢ Elvis Presley, sheetlet of 9	6.25
351-65	1¢-$10 Palau Fishes, set of 15	47.50
	1995 Booklet Panes	
366a	20¢ Magenta dottyback (10)	4.50
367a	32¢ Reef Lizardfish (10)	7.50
367b	same, 20¢ (5) & 32¢ (5)	6.00

337

338a

340a

344a

345a

346a

351

368a

Palau #368-384

369a

370a

372a

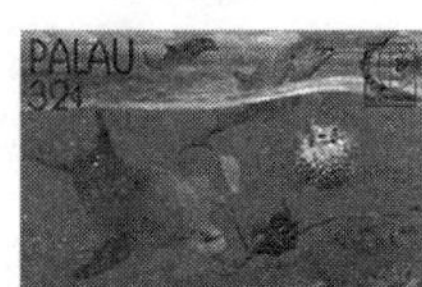

373a

374a

378

1995 (continued)

SCOTT NO.	DESCRIPTION	UNUSED F/NH
368	32¢ WWII Japanese Sunken Ships, sheetlet of 18	12.25
369	32¢ Flying Dinosaurs, sheetlet of 18	12.25
370	50¢ Experimental Aircraft (Jets), sheetlet of 12	12.50
371	$2 Experimental Aircraft (Concorde) souvenir sheet	4.50
372	32¢ Underwater Submersibles, sheetlet of 18	12.25
373	32¢ Marine Life (Singapore '95), 4 attached	3.00
374	60¢ UN, FAO, 50th Anniversary, 4 attached	5.50
375-76	$2 UN Emblem souvenir sheet (2)	9.00
377-78	20¢-32¢ Independence Anniversary, min. sheet of 4 & single	2.50
379-80	32¢-60¢ 50th End of WWII, sheetlets of 12 & 5	16.00
381	$3 B-29 Nose souvenir sheet	6.50
382	32¢ Christmas 1995, strip of 5	3.75
383	32¢ Life Cycle of the Sea Turtle, sheetlet of 12	9.00
384	32¢ John Lennon	.75

379a

381

382a

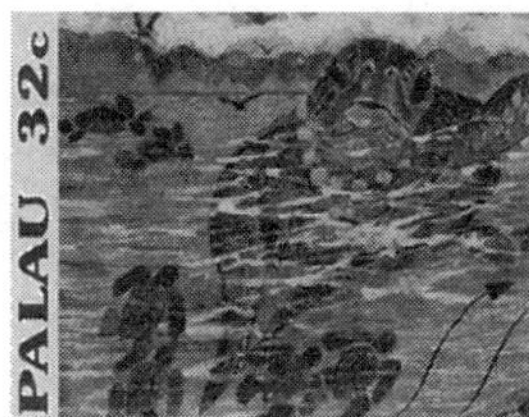

383a

384

385a

Palau #385-412

387

388a

389a

391

SCOTT NO.	DESCRIPTION	UNUSED F/NH
	1996	
385	10¢ New Year 1996 (Year of the Rat), strip of 4	1.00
386	60¢ New Year 1996 (Year of the Rat), min. sheet of 2	2.95
387	32¢ UNICEF, 50th Anniversary, 4 attached	3.00
388	32¢ Marine Life, strip of 5	3.75
389-90	32¢-60¢ The Circumnavigators, 2 sheetlets of 9	19.25
391-92	$3 The Circumnavigators, 2 souvenir sheets	13.00
392A-F	1¢-6¢ Disney Sweethearts, set of 6 ...	.55
393	60¢ Disney Sweethearts, sheetlet of 9	13.00
394-95	$2 Disney Sweethearts, 2 souvenir sheets	9.00
396	20¢ Jerusalem Bible Studies, sheetlet of 30	13.50
397-98	40¢ 1996 Summer Olympics, pair	1.80
399-400	60¢ 1996 Summer Olympics, pair	2.70
401	32¢ 1996 Summer Ollympics, sheet of 20	14.50
402	50¢ Birds over the Palau Lagoon, sheet of 20	21.50
403	40¢ Military Spy Aircraft, sheet of 12 .	10.50
404	60¢ Weird & Wonderful Aircraft, sheet of 12	16.00
405	$3 Stealth Bomber, souvenir sheet	6.75
406	$3 Martin Marietta X-24B, souvenir sheet	6.75
407-08	20¢ Independence, 2nd Anniversary, pair	.90
409	32¢ Christmas 1996, strip of 5	3.75
410	32¢ Voyage to Mars, sheet of 12	8.50
411-12	$3 Mars rover & Water probe, 2 souvenir sheets	13.50

392

Palau

SCOTT NO.	DESCRIPTION	UNUSED F/NH

393a

394

396a

397-98

399-400

401a

402a

403a

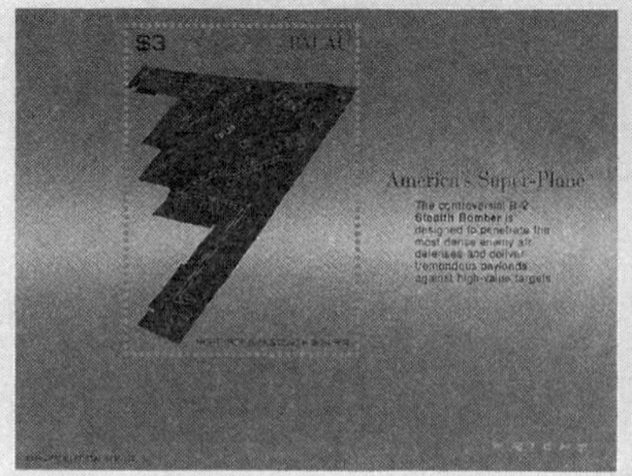

405

Palau

SCOTT NO.	DESCRIPTION	UNUSED F/NH	SCOTT NO.	DESCRIPTION	UNUSED F/NH

406

411

407-08

413

409a

415

410a

420

Palau #413-New Issues

SCOTT NO.	DESCRIPTION	UNUSED F/NH
	1997	
413	$1 50th Anniv. of South Pacific Commission, souvenir sheet	2.25
414-19	1¢-$3 Flowers (Hong Kong '97), set of 6	7.00
420	32¢ Shoreline Plants (Hong Kong '97), 4 attached	3.00
421	50¢ Shoreline Plants (Hong Kong '97), 4 attached	4.50
422	32¢ Bicentennial of the Parachute, sheet of 8	6.00
423	60¢ Bicentennial of the Parachute, sheet of 8	10.50
424-25	$2 Bicentennial of the Parachute, 2 souvenir sheets	9.00
426	20¢ Native Birds & Trees, sheet of 12	5.25
......	$2 Year of the Ox, souvenir sheet	4.50
......	32¢ 50th Anniv. of UNESCO, sheet of 8	5.50
......	60¢ 50th Anniv. of UNESCO, sheet of 5	6.50
......	$2 50th Anniv. of UNESCO, 2 souvenir sheets	9.00
......	32¢ Volcano Goddesses, sheet of 6 ..	4.25
......	32¢ Prints of Hiroshige, sheet of 5	3.50
......	$2 Prints of Hiroshige, 2 souvenir sheets	9.00

422a

424

426a

Palau #B1-B4; C1-C22; U1-U3; UC1; UX1

B1

1988 SEMI POSTAL

SCOTT NO.	DESCRIPTION	UNUSED F/NH
B1-B4	(25¢ + 5¢) + (45¢ + 5¢) Olympics, 2 pairs	4.50

AIR MAILS

C1

1984 AIR MAILS

SCOTT NO.	DESCRIPTION	UNUSED F/NH
C1-4	40¢ Seabirds, attached	3.75

C6

1985 AIR MAILS

SCOTT NO.	DESCRIPTION	UNUSED F/NH
C5	44¢ Audubon Birds	1.50
C6-9	44¢ German Links, attached	4.50
C10-13	44¢ Transpacific, attached	4.10

C14

C17

C18

1986 AIR MAILS

SCOTT NO.	DESCRIPTION	UNUSED F/NH
C14-16	44¢ Remeliik, strip of 3	4.00
C17	44¢ Statue of Liberty	1.25

1989 AIR MAILS

SCOTT NO.	DESCRIPTION	UNUSED F/NH
C18-20	36¢-45¢ Aircraft, complete set of 3	2.75

1991 AIR MAILS

SCOTT NO.	DESCRIPTION	UNUSED F/NH
C21	50¢ 10th Anniv. Airmail, self-adhesive	1.75

1989 BOOKLET PANES

SCOTT NO.	DESCRIPTION	UNUSED F/NH
C18a	36¢ Aircraft pane (10)	8.00
C19a	39¢ Aircraft pane (10)	8.50
C20a	45¢ Aircraft pane (10)	10.00
C20b	5 (36¢) + 5 (45¢) Aircraft pane (10)	8.50

C22a

1995

SCOTT NO.	DESCRIPTION	UNUSED F/NH
C22	50¢ Birds (Swallows), 4 attached	4.25

1985 ENVELOPE ENTIRES

SCOTT NO.	DESCRIPTION	UNUSED F/NH
U1	22¢ Marine Life	4.00
U2	22¢ Spear Fishing	7.00
U3	25¢ Chambered Nautilus	1.25
UC1	36¢ Bird, air letter sheet	6.00

1985 POSTAL CARDS

SCOTT NO.	DESCRIPTION	UNUSED F/NH
UX1	14¢ Marine Life	3.00

Philippines #212-240; E1; J1-J7

PHILIPPINES

U.S Stamps of various issues overprinted

PHILIPPINES

1899
On 260. Unwatermarked

SCOTT NO.	DESCRIPTION	UNUSED NH F	UNUSED NH AVG	UNUSED O.G. F	UNUSED O.G. AVG	USED F	USED AVG
212	50¢ orange	550.00	345.00	385.00	265.00	190.00	130.00

On 279, 279d, 267-68, 281, 282C, 283, 284, 275
Double Line Watermarked

SCOTT NO.	DESCRIPTION	UNUSED NH F	UNUSED NH AVG	UNUSED O.G. F	UNUSED O.G. AVG	USED F	USED AVG
213	1¢ yellow green	5.00	3.25	3.60	2.15	1.10	.65
214	2¢ orange red	2.25	1.35	1.40	.95	.85	.50
215	3¢ purple	9.00	6.25	5.75	3.75	2.10	1.30
216	5¢ blue	8.25	5.00	5.50	3.40	1.75	1.05
217	10¢ brown(Type I)	27.00	16.00	17.00	11.25	4.75	3.10
217A	10¢ orange brown(Type II)	295.00	205.00	195.00	115.00	45.00	27.50
218	15¢ olive green	48.00	29.50	35.00	21.50	8.75	5.25
219	50¢ orange	170.00	105.00	115.00	70.00	45.00	27.50

1901
On 280, 282, 272, 276-78

SCOTT NO.	DESCRIPTION	UNUSED NH F	UNUSED NH AVG	UNUSED O.G. F	UNUSED O.G. AVG	USED F	USED AVG
220	4¢ orange brown	32.50	23.00	22.50	14.00	6.00	3.75
221	6¢ lake	40.00	25.00	27.00	16.50	7.50	5.00
222	8¢ violet brown	45.00	27.50	30.00	18.50	8.00	4.75
223	$1 black (Type I)	565.00	375.00	375.00	230.00	240.00	150.00
223A	$1 black (Type II)	3200.00	2150.00	2200.00	1450.00	1100.00	695.00
224	$2 dark blue	810.00	495.00	550.00	360.00	330.00	215.00
225	$5 dark green	1895.00	1250.00	1295.00	850.00	910.00	595.00

1903-04
On 300-313

SCOTT NO.	DESCRIPTION	UNUSED NH F	UNUSED NH AVG	UNUSED O.G. F	UNUSED O.G. AVG	USED F	USED AVG
226	1¢ blue green	6.50	4.25	4.40	2.90	.50	.35
227	2¢ carmine	10.95	7.25	7.50	5.00	2.10	1.25
228	3¢ bright violet	105.00	70.00	72.00	46.50	17.50	11.50
229	4¢ brown	110.00	75.00	75.00	48.00	27.00	16.50
230	5¢ blue	18.00	11.00	12.00	7.75	1.50	.95
231	6¢ brownish lake	117.50	77.50	80.00	52.50	24.50	15.95
232	8¢ violet black	55.00	36.00	38.50	26.00	15.00	9.75
233	10¢ pale red brown	30.00	18.50	20.00	12.50	3.75	2.25
234	13¢ purple black	55.00	35.75	35.00	22.75	17.00	11.00
235	25¢ olive green	85.00	55.00	60.00	35.00	14.50	9.50
236	50¢ orange	215.00	140.00	140.00	90.00	42.50	27.50
237	$1 black	750.00	455.00	500.00	325.00	275.00	175.00
238	$2 dark blue	2150.00	1395.00	1425.00	950.00	900.00	585.00
239	$5 dark green	2300.00	1550.00	1625.00	1050.00	1100.00	715.00

On 319

SCOTT NO.	DESCRIPTION	UNUSED NH F	UNUSED NH AVG	UNUSED O.G. F	UNUSED O.G. AVG	USED F	USED AVG
240	2¢ carmine	8.25	5.35	5.50	3.65	2.75	1.75

SPECIAL DELIVERY STAMPS

PHILIPPINES

1901
U.S. E5 Surcharged

SCOTT NO.	DESCRIPTION	UNUSED NH F	UNUSED NH AVG	UNUSED O.G. F	UNUSED O.G. AVG	USED F	USED AVG
E1	10¢ dark blue	140.00	90.00	95.00	62.50	115.00	75.00

POSTAGE DUE STAMPS

PHILIPPINES

1899
U.S. J38-44
overprinted

SCOTT NO.	DESCRIPTION	UNUSED NH F	UNUSED NH AVG	UNUSED O.G. F	UNUSED O.G. AVG	USED F	USED AVG
J1	1¢ deep claret	7.50	4.75	4.75	3.10	1.95	1.25
J2	2¢ deep claret	7.10	4.50	4.50	2.95	2.00	1.35
J3	5¢ deep claret	17.50	11.50	11.50	7.50	3.50	2.25
J4	10¢ deep claret	22.50	14.50	14.00	9.00	6.75	4.40
J5	50¢ deep claret	215.00	140.00	145.00	95.00	97.50	63.50

1901

SCOTT NO.	DESCRIPTION	UNUSED NH F	UNUSED NH AVG	UNUSED O.G. F	UNUSED O.G. AVG	USED F	USED AVG
J6	3¢ deep claret	22.50	14.75	14.25	9.25	9.75	6.50
J7	30¢ deep claret	250.00	165.00	165.00	105.00	95.00	57.50

PUERTO RICO

1899

U.S. Stamps 279-79B, 281, 272, 282C overprinted

PORTO RICO

SCOTT NO.	DESCRIPTION	UNUSED O.G. F	UNUSED O.G. AVG	UNUSED F	UNUSED AVG	USED F	USED AVG
210	1¢ yellow green	9.50	5.85	6.50	4.10	1.75	1.15
211	2¢ carmine	8.75	5.75	6.00	3.95	1.65	1.05
212	5¢ blue	12.50	8.00	8.50	5.50	2.50	1.65
213	8¢ violet brown	45.00	28.50	27.50	18.00	17.50	11.50
214	10¢ brown (I)	30.00	19.25	19.00	12.25	6.00	3.95

1900

U.S. 279, 279B overprinted

PUERTO RICO

SCOTT NO.	DESCRIPTION	UNUSED O.G. F	UNUSED O.G. AVG	UNUSED F	UNUSED AVG	USED F	USED AVG
215	1¢ yellow green	8.50	5.65	6.00	4.25	1.95	1.15
216	2¢ carmine	7.95	5.15	5.50	3.60	1.50	.95

POSTAGE DUE STAMPS

1899

U.S. Postage Due Stamps J38 - 39, J41 overprinted

PORTO RICO

SCOTT NO.	DESCRIPTION	UNUSED O.G. F	UNUSED O.G. AVG	UNUSED F	UNUSED AVG	USED F	USED AVG
J1	1¢ deep claret	32.50	21.00	22.50	13.50	8.25	5.35
J2	2¢ deep claret	22.50	14.50	14.00	9.00	7.00	4.75
J3	10¢ deep claret	215.00	140.00	140.00	90.00	60.00	36.50

Ryukyu Islands #1-18

The Ryukyu Islands were under U.S. administration from April 1, 1945 until May 15, 1972. Prior to the General Issues of 1948, several Provisional Stamps were used.

RYUKYU ISLANDS

1, 1a, 3, 3a — 2, 2a, 5, 5a

4, 4a, 6, 6a — 7, 7a

1949 Second Printing

White gum & paper, sharp colors; clean perfs.

SCOTT NO.	DESCRIPTION	UNUSED F/NH	UNUSED F
1-7	**5s to 1y 7 varieties, complete**	**22.50**	**20.00**
1	5s Cycad	1.85	1.65
2	10s Lily	5.50	5.00
3	20s Cycad	3.75	3.35
4	30s Sailing Ship	2.25	2.00
5	40s Lily	1.95	1.75
6	50s Sailing Ship	4.25	3.75
7	1y Farmer	5.50	5.00

1948 First Printing

Thick yellow gum; gray paper; dull colors; rough perfs.

SCOTT NO.	DESCRIPTION	UNUSED F/NH	UNUSED F
1a-7a	**5s to 1y, 7 varieties, complete**	**425.00**	**375.00**
1a	5s Cycad	3.00	2.70
2a	10s Lily	1.75	1.60
3a	20s Cycad	1.75	1.60
4a	30s Sailing Ship	3.00	2.70
5a	40s Lily	45.00	40.00
6a	50s Sailing Ship	3.00	2.70
7a	1y Farmer	375.00	335.00

8

9

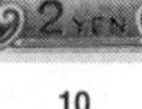

10

11

12

13

1950

SCOTT NO.	DESCRIPTION	UNUSED F/NH	UNUSED F
8-13	**50s to 5y, 6 varieties, complete**	**65.00**	**58.50**
8	50s Tile Roof	.25	.20
9	1y Ryukyu Girl	2.75	2.45
10	2y Shun Castle	13.00	11.75
11	3y Dragon Head	27.50	25.00
12	4y Women at Beach	16.75	15.00
13	5y Seashells	7.75	7.00

NOTE: The 1950 printing of #8 is on toned paper and has yellowish gum. A 1958 printing exhibits white paper and colorless gum.

14

15

1951

SCOTT NO.	DESCRIPTION	UNUSED F/NH	UNUSED F
14	3y Ryukyu University	52.50	47.50
15	3y Pine Tree	45.00	40.00

16, 16a-b, 17

18

SCOTT NO.	DESCRIPTION	UNUSED F/NH	UNUSED F
16	10y on 50s (no. 8) Type II	11.50	10.25
16a	same, Type I	28.50	25.00
16b	same, Type III	39.50	35.00
17	100y on 2y (no. 10)	1775.00	1600.00
18	3y Govt. of Ryukyu	125.00	100.00

Type I—Bars are narrow spaced; "10" normal
Type II—Bars are wide spaced; "10" normal
Type III—Bars are wide spaced; "10" wide spaced

Ryukyu Islands #19-42

19 20 21

1952-53

SCOTT NO.	DESCRIPTION	UNUSED F/NH
19-26	**1y to 100y, 8 varieties, complete ......**	**41.75**
19	1y Mandanbashi Bridge	.30
20	2y Main Hall of Shun Castle	.40
21	3y Shurei Gate	.50
22	6y Stone Gate, Sogenji Temple	2.00
23	10y Benzaiten-do Temple	3.00
24	30y Altar at Shuri Castle	10.00
25	50y Tamaudun Shuri	12.50
26	100y Stone Bridge, Hosho Pond	15.00

27 28

29 30

1953

SCOTT NO.	DESCRIPTION	UNUSED F/NH
27	3y Reception at Shuri Castle	12.25
28	6y Perry and Fleet	1.15
29	4y Chofu Ota and Pencil	10.75

1954

SCOTT NO.	DESCRIPTION	UNUSED F/NH
30	4y Shigo Toma & Pen	11.50

31 32 33

1954-55

SCOTT NO.	DESCRIPTION	UNUSED F/NH
31	4y Pottery	.90
32	15y Lacquerware (1955)	3.00
33	20y Textile Design (1955)	2.10

34 35

36 37 38

1955

SCOTT NO.	DESCRIPTION	UNUSED F/NH
34	4y Noguni Shrine & Sweet .... Potato Plant	12.00

1956

SCOTT NO.	DESCRIPTION	UNUSED F/NH
35	4y Stylized Trees	11.00
36	5y Willow Dance	.85
37	8y Straw Hat Dance	2.10
38	14y Group Dance	2.40

39 40

SCOTT NO.	DESCRIPTION	UNUSED F/NH
39	4y Dial Telephone	15.25
40	2y Garland, Bamboo & Plum	1.75

41 42

1957

SCOTT NO.	DESCRIPTION	UNUSED F/NH
41	4y Map & Pencil Rocket	.85
42	2y Phoenix	.25

43 44-53

Ryukyu Islands #43-80

SCOTT NO.	DESCRIPTION	UNUSED F/NH

1958

43	4y Ryukyu Stamps	1.00
44-53	**1/2¢ to $1.00, 10 varieties, complete, ungummed**	**50.00**
44	1/2¢ Yen, Symbol & Denom., orange	.80
45	1¢ same, yellow green	1.30
46	2¢ same, dark blue	1.60
47	3¢ same, deep carmine	1.60
48	4¢ same, bright green	2.25
49	same, orange	4.25
50	10¢ same, aquamarine	6.50
51	25¢ same, bright violet blue	7.50
51a	25¢ same, bright violet blue (with gum)	9.00
52	50¢ same, gray	16.75
52a	50¢ same, gray (with gum)	11.00
53	$1 same, rose lilac	13.00

54

55

54	3¢ Gate of Courtesy	1.40
55	1-1/2¢ Lion Dance	.30

56

57

1959

56	3¢ Mountains & Trees	.85
57	3¢ Yonaguni Moth	1.30

58, 76

63

58-62	**1/2¢ to 17¢, 5 varieties, complete**	**31.50**
58	1/2¢ Hibiscus	.30
59	3¢ Moorish Idol	.90
60	8¢ Seashell	9.50
61	13¢ Dead Leaf Butterfly	3.00
62	17¢ Jellyfish	19.50
63	1-1/2¢ Toy (Yakaji)	.70

SCOTT NO.	DESCRIPTION	UNUSED F/NH

64

65, 81

1960

64	3¢ University Badge	1.10

DANCES II

65-68	**1¢-10¢, 4 varieties, complete**	**5.50**
65	1¢ Munsunu	1.40
66	2-1/2¢ Nutwabushi	2.40
67	5¢ Hatomabushi	.90
68	10¢ Hanafubushi	.95

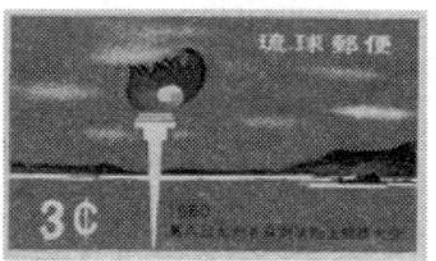

72

73

74

75

72	3¢ Torch & Nago Bay	7.50
73	8¢ Runners	1.10
74	3¢ Egret & Sun	6.00
75	1-1/2¢ Bull Fight	1.95

1960-61 REDRAWN INSCRIPTION

76-80	**1/2¢ to 17¢, 5 varieties, complete**	**14.50**
76	1/2¢ Hibiscus	.50
77	3¢ Moorish Idol	1.45
78	8¢ Seashell	1.45
79	13¢ Dead Leaf Butterfly	2.00
80	17¢ Jellyfish	9.50

Ryukyu Islands #81-105

SCOTT NO.	DESCRIPTION	UNUSED F/NH
	WITH "RYUKYUS" ADDED 1961-64	
81-87	**1¢ to $1.00, 8 varieties, Dancers, complete**	**11.25**
81	1¢ Munsuru	.20
82	2-1/2¢ Nutwabushi (1962)	.25
83	5¢ Hatomabushi (1962)	.45
84	10¢ Hanafubushi (1962)	.85
84A	20¢ Shundun (1964)	1.25
85	25¢ Hanagasabushi (1962)	1.50
86	50¢ Nubui Kuduchi	3.00
87	$1 Kutubushi	5.00

88

89

90

91

92

1961

SCOTT NO.	DESCRIPTION	UNUSED F/NH
88	3¢ Pine Tree	1.75
89	3¢ Naha, Steamer & Sailboat	2.25
90	3¢ White Silver Temple	2.25
91	3¢ Books & Bird	1.60
92	1-1/2¢ Eagles & Rising Sun	2.75

93

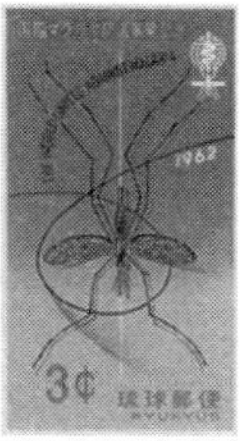

95

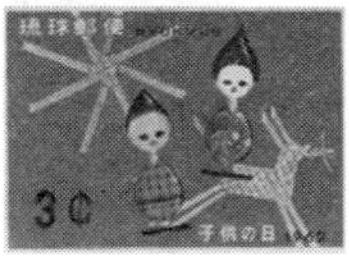

97

1962

SCOTT NO.	DESCRIPTION	UNUSED F/NH
93	1-1/2¢ Steps, Trees & Building	.75
94	3¢ GRI Building	1.25
95	3¢ Malaria Eradication	.70
96	8¢ Eradication Emblem	1.45
97	3¢ Children's Day	1.50

98

103

104

105

SCOTT NO.	DESCRIPTION	UNUSED F/NH
98-102	**1/2¢ to 17¢ varieties, Flowers, complete**	**2.95**
98	1/2¢ Sea Hibiscus	.18
99	3¢ Indian Coral Tree	.40
100	8¢ Iju	.50
101	13¢ Touch-Me-Not	.75
102	17¢ Shell Flower	1.25
103	3¢ Earthenware	4.00
104	3¢ Japanese Fencing	5.25
105	1-1/2¢ Bingata Cloth	1.25

106

107

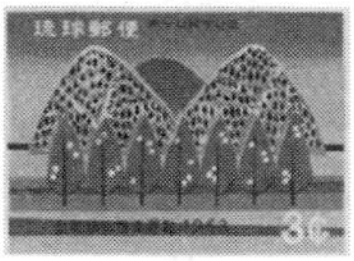

108

109

110

111

VERY FINE QUALITY: From 1935 to date, add 20% to the Fine price. Minimum of 3¢ per stamp.

Ryukyu Islands #106-129

112 113

114 115

116 117

1963

SCOTT NO.	DESCRIPTION	UNUSED F/NH
106	3¢ Stone Relief	1.20
107	1-1/2¢ Gooseneck Cactus	.20
108	3¢ Trees & Hills	1.20
109	3¢ Map of Okinawa	1.50
110	3¢ Hawks & Islands	1.25
111	3¢ Shioya Bridge	1.25
112	3¢ Lacquerware Bowl	3.00
113	3¢ Map of Far East	1.00
114	15¢ Mamaomoto	1.10
115	3¢ Nakagusuku Castle Site	.95
116	3¢ Human Rights	1.00
117	1-1/2¢ Dragon	.40

118 119

120, 120a 121

1964

SCOTT NO.	DESCRIPTION	UNUSED F/NH
118	3¢ Mothers' Day	.50
119	3¢ Agricultural Census	.50
120	3¢ Minsah Obi, rose pink	.65
120a	same, deep carmine	.90
121	3¢ Girl Scout & Emblem	.40
122	3¢ Shuri Relay Station	1.00
122a	3¢ same, inverted "1"	27.50
123	8¢ Antenna & map	1.50
124	3¢ Olympic Torch & Emblem	.40

122, 122a 123

124 125

126

127

1964-65

SCOTT NO.	DESCRIPTION	UNUSED F/NH
125	3¢ Karate, "Naihanchi"	.70
126	3¢ Karate, "Makiwara" (1965)	.60
127	3¢ Karate, "Kumite" (1965)	.60

128 129

1964

SCOTT NO.	DESCRIPTION	UNUSED F/NH
128	3¢ Miyara Dunchi	.40
129	1-1/2¢ Snake & Iris	.20

Ryukyu Islands #130-150

130  131 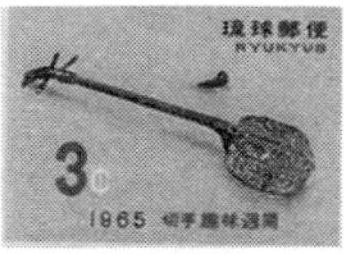 132  133  134  135

1965

SCOTT NO.	DESCRIPTION	UNUSED F/NH
130	3¢ Boy Scouts	.60
131	3¢ Onoyama Stadium	.30
132	3¢ Samisen of King Shoko	.60
133	3¢ Kin Power Plant	.30
134	3¢ ICY and United Nations	.25
135	3¢ Naha City Hall	.25

136  139

1965-66

SCOTT NO.	DESCRIPTION	UNUSED F/NH
136	3¢ Chinese Box Turtle	.40
137	3¢ Hawksbill Turtle (1966)	.30
138	3¢ Asian Terrapin (1966)	.30

1965

SCOTT NO.	DESCRIPTION	UNUSED F/NH
139	1-1/2¢ Horse	.20

140  141

143  144  145  146  147  148  149  150

1966

SCOTT NO.	DESCRIPTION	UNUSED F/NH
140	3¢ Woodpecker	.30
141	3¢ Sika Deer	.35
142	3¢ Dugong	.35
143	3¢ Swallow	.25
144	3¢ Memorial Day	.20
145	3¢ University of Ryukyus	.20
146	3¢ Lacquerware	.25
147	3¢ UNESCO	.25
148	3¢ Government Museum	.20
149	3¢ Nakasone T. Genga's Tomb	.20
150	1-1/2¢ Ram in Iris Wreath	.20

151  156

Ryukyu Islands #151-184

SCOTT NO.	DESCRIPTION	UNUSED F/NH
	1966-67	
151-55	**5 varieties, Fish, complete**	**1.60**
151	3¢ Clown Fish	.30
152	3¢ Young Boxfish (1967)	.30
153	3¢ Forceps Fish (1967)	.35
154	3¢ Spotted Triggerfish (1967)	.35
155	3¢ Saddleback Butterflyfish (1967)	.40
	1966	
156	3¢ Tsuboya Urn	.25

157

162

164

163

165

166

SCOTT NO.	DESCRIPTION	UNUSED F/NH
	1967-68	
157-61	**5 varieties, Seashells, complete**	**1.95**
157	3¢ Episcopal Miter	.30
158	3¢ Venus Comb Murex	.30
159	3¢ Chiragra Spider	.35
160	3¢ Green Turban	.35
161	3¢ Euprotomus Bulla	.75
162	3¢ Roofs & ITY Emblem	.25
163	3¢ Mobile TB Clinic	.25
164	3¢ Hojo Bridge, Enkaku Temple	.30
165	1-1/2¢ Monkey	.20
166	3¢ TV Tower & Map	.35

167

168

169

170

171

172

SCOTT NO.	DESCRIPTION	UNUSED F/NH
	1968	
167	3¢ Dr. Nakachi & Helper	.30
168	3¢ Pill Box	.45
169	3¢ Man, Library, Book & Map	.45
170	3¢ Mailmen's Uniforms & 1948 Stamp	.40
171	3¢ Main Gate, Enkaku Temple	.40
172	3¢ Old Man's Dance	.40

173

178

SCOTT NO.	DESCRIPTION	UNUSED F/NH
	1968-69	
173-77	**5 varieties, Crabs, complete**	**3.75**
173	3¢ Mictyris Longicarpus	.60
174	3¢ Uca Dubia Stimpson (1969)	.70
175	3¢ Baptozius Vinosus (1969)	.70
176	3¢ Cardisoma Carnifex (1969)	.95
177	3¢ Ocypode (1969)	.95

179

180

SCOTT NO.	DESCRIPTION	UNUSED F/NH
	1968	
178	3¢ Saraswati Pavilion	.40
179	3¢ Tennis Player	.40
180	1-1/2¢ Cock & Iris	.20
	1969	
181	3¢ Boxer	.40
182	3¢ Ink Slab Screen	.60
183	3¢ Antennas & Map	.30
184	3¢ Gate of Courtesy & Emblems	.30

Ryukyu Islands #185-194

181

182

183

184

185

186

187

188

189

SCOTT NO.	DESCRIPTION	UNUSED F/NH
	1969-70	
185-89	**5 varieties, Folklore, complete**	**3.45**
185	3¢ Tug of War Festival	.55
186	3¢ Hari Boat Race	.55
187	3¢ Izaiho Ceremony	.55
188	3¢ Mortardrum Dance (1970)	1.00
189	3¢ Sea God Dance	1.00

改訂 ½¢

(surcharge)
190

191

192

193

1969

SCOTT NO.	DESCRIPTION	UNUSED F/NH
190	1/2¢ on 3¢ (no. 99) Indian Coral Tree	.30
191	3¢ Nakamura-Ke Farm House ...	.30
192	3¢ Statue & Maps	.40
193	1-1/2¢ Dog & Flowers	.20
194	3¢ Sake Flask	.50

194

195

196

197

198

199

200

Ryukyu Islands #195-219

SCOTT NO.	DESCRIPTION	UNUSED F/NH
195-99	**5 varieties, Classic Opera, complete**	**3.50**
195	3¢ "The Bell"	.80
196	3¢ Child & Kidnapper	.80
197	3¢ Robe of Feathers	.80
198	3¢ Vengeance of Two Sons	.65
199	3¢ Virgin & the Dragon	.65
195-99a	**5 varieties, complete, sheets of 4**	**23.75**
195a	3¢ sheet of 4	5.50
196a	3¢ sheet of 4	5.00
197a	3¢ sheet of 4	4.75
198a	3¢ sheet of 4	4.75
199a	3¢ sheet of 4	4.75
200	3¢ Underwater Observatory	.40

201

204

205

206

207

208

212

210

1970-71 Portraits

SCOTT NO.	DESCRIPTION	UNUSED F/NH
201	3¢ Noboru Jahana	.55
202	3¢ Saion Gushichan Bunjaku	1.50
203	3¢ Choho Giwan (1971)	.65

1970

SCOTT NO.	DESCRIPTION	UNUSED F/NH
204	3¢ Map & People	.30
205	3¢ Great Cycad of Une	.35
206	3¢ Flag, Diet & Map	1.10
207	1-1/2¢ Boar & Cherry Blossoms	.20

1971

SCOTT NO.	DESCRIPTION	UNUSED F/NH
208-12	**5 varieties, Workers, complete**	**2.55**
208	3¢ Low Hand Loom	.45
209	3¢ Filature	.45
210	3¢ Farmer with Raincoat & Hat	.45
211	3¢ Rice Huller	.80
212	3¢ Fisherman's Box & Scoop	.55
213	3¢ Water Carrier	.55
214	3¢ Old & New Naha	.30
215	2¢ Caesalpinia Pulcherrima	.20
216	3¢ Madder	.20

213

214

215

217

218

219

1971-72 Government Parks

SCOTT NO.	DESCRIPTION	UNUSED F/NH
217	3¢ View from Mabuni Hill	.40
218	3¢ Mt. Arashi from Haneji Sea	.40
219	4¢ Yabuchi Is. from Yakena Port	.45

220

221

222

223

Ryukyu Islands #220-228; C1-C30

SCOTT NO.	DESCRIPTION	UNUSED F/NH
	1971	
220	4¢ Dancer	.20
221	4¢ Deva King	.25
222	2¢ Rat & Chrysanthemums	.20
223	4¢ Student Nurse	.35

224

225

227

226

228

SCOTT NO.	DESCRIPTION	UNUSED F/NH
	1972	
224	5¢ Birds & Seashore	.55
225	5¢ Coral Reef	.55
226	5¢ Sun Over Islands	.65
227	5¢ Dove & Flags	.95
228	5¢ Antique Sake Pot	.70

AIR MAIL STAMPS

C1-3

C4-8

SCOTT NO.	DESCRIPTION	UNUSED F/NH
	1950	
C1	8y Dove & Map, bright blue	87.50
C2	12y same, green	28.00
C3	16y same, rose carmine	19.50
	1951-54	
C4-8	**13y to 50y, 5 varieties, complete**	**27.00**
C4	13y Heavenly Maiden, blue	2.25
C5	18y same, green	3.00
C6	30y same, cerise	6.00
C7	40y same, red violet (1954)	8.00
C8	50y same, yellow orange (1954)	9.25

C9-13

改訂 9¢

C14-18

SCOTT NO.	DESCRIPTION	UNUSED F/NH
	1957	
C9-13	**15y to 60y, 5 varieties, complete**	**57.50**
C9	15y Maiden Playing Flute, blue green	4.50
C10	20y same, rose carmine	8.10
C11	35y same, yellow green	13.00
C12	45y same, reddish brown	15.00
C13	60y same, gray	20.00
	1959	
C14-18	**9¢ to 35¢, 5 varieties, complete**	**39.00**
C14	9¢ on 15y (no. C9)	2.75
C15	14¢ on 20y (no. C10)	4.00
C16	19¢ on 35y (no. C11)	6.00
C17	27¢ on 45y (no. C12)	11.50
C18	35¢ on 60y (no. C13)	16.75

改訂

9¢

(surcharge)
C19-23

C24

SCOTT NO.	DESCRIPTION	UNUSED F/NH
	1960	
C19-23	**9¢ to 35¢, 5 varieties, complete**	**18.25**
C19	9¢ on 4y (no. 31)	2.50
C20	14¢ on 5y (no. 36)	2.50
C21	19¢ on 15y (no. 32)	1.95
C22	27¢ on 14y (no. 38)	6.25
C23	35¢ on 20y (no. 33)	6.00
	1961	
C24-28	**9¢ to 35¢, 5 varieties, complete**	**7.10**
C24	9¢ Heavenly Maiden	.55
C25	14¢ Maiden Playing Flute	.70
C26	19¢ Wind God	.95
C27	27¢ Wind God	3.50
C28	35¢ Maiden Over Tree Tops	1.80

C29

C30

SCOTT NO.	DESCRIPTION	UNUSED F/NH
	1963	
C29	5-1/2¢ Jet & Gate of Courtesy	.25
C30	7¢ Jet Plane	.30

Ryukyu Islands #E1

SCOTT NO.	DESCRIPTION	UNUSED F/NH

E1

SPECIAL DELIVERY

1950

SCOTT NO.	DESCRIPTION	UNUSED F/NH
E1	5y Dragon & Map	27.50

SCOTT NO.	DESCRIPTION	UNUSED F/NH

U.N. Postage #1-28

UNITED NATIONS (NEW YORK)

1, 6

2, 10, UX1-2

3, 11

4, 7, 9

5

8

SCOTT NO.	DESCRIPTION	FIRST DAY COVERS SING	INSC. BLK	INSRIP BLK-4	UNUSED F/NH	USED F
	1951					
1-11	1¢ to $1 Definitives	85.00	150.00	40.00	8.00	7.00

12

13-14

15-16

17-18

SCOTT NO.	DESCRIPTION	FIRST DAY COVERS SING	INSC. BLK	INSRIP BLK-4	UNUSED F/NH	USED F
	1952-1953					
12-22	**1952-53 Issues, complete (11)**	......	......	......	**8.75**	......
	1952					
12	5¢ United Nations Day	1.20	2.50	1.40	.25	.20
13-14	3¢ & 5¢ Human Rights Day	2.00	5.00	3.00	.60	.50
	1953					
15-16	3¢ & 5¢ Refugee Issue	1.80	4.50	7.75	1.00	.80
17-18	3¢ & 5¢ U.P.U. Issue	3.00	7.50	11.50	2.30	1.20

19-20

21-22

23-24

25-26

27-28

SCOTT NO.	DESCRIPTION	FIRST DAY COVERS SING	INSC. BLK	INSRIP BLK-4	UNUSED F/NH	USED F
19-20	3¢ & 5¢ Technical Assistance	1.75	4.40	6.95	1.50	.95
21-22	3¢ & 5¢ Human Rights Day	7.75	18.50	12.75	2.50	1.25
	1954					
23-30	**1954 Issues, complete (8)**	......	......	......	**22.00**	......
23-24	3¢ & 8¢ Food & Agriculture	2.05	5.15	9.15	2.00	1.00
25-26	3¢ & 8¢ International Labor	2.75	6.85	18.50	4.00	1.50
27-28	3¢ & 8¢ Geneva	4.00	10.00	25.00	5.00	2.50

U.N. Postage #29-56

29 31  33  35

SCOTT NO.	DESCRIPTION	FIRST DAY COVERS SING	FIRST DAY COVERS INSC. BLK	INSRIP BLK-4	UNUSED F/NH	USED F
29-30	3¢ & 8¢ Human Rights Day	7.75	18.50	55.00	12.25	4.00
	1955					
31/40	**1955 Issues, (9) (No #38) .**	......	......	......	**12.25**	......
31-32	3¢ & 8¢ Int. Civil Aviation Org.	3.95	9.85	24.25	4.95	2.25
33-34	3¢ & 8¢ UNESCO	2.00	5.00	7.95	1.70	1.10
35-37	3¢ to 8¢ United Nations . . .	2.85	7.15	24.25	4.95	2.25
38	same, souvenir sheet	85.00	......	......	175.00	55.00
38 var	Second print, retouched . . .	......	......	......	180.00	65.00

39 41 43 45

SCOTT NO.	DESCRIPTION	FIRST DAY COVERS SING	FIRST DAY COVERS INSC. BLK	INSRIP BLK-4	UNUSED F/NH	USED F
39-40	3¢ & 8¢ Human Rights Day	2.00	5.00	6.25	1.30	.90
	1956					
41-48	**1956 Issues, complete (8) .**	......	......	......	**3.20**	......
41-42	3¢ & 8¢ International Telecommunications	2.00	5.00	6.25	1.30	.90
43-44	3¢ & 8¢ World Health Org. .	2.00	5.00	6.25	1.30	.90
45-46	3¢ & 8¢ United Nations Day	1.25	3.15	1.35	.35	.25

47 49 51 (No Halo) 53 (Halo) 55

SCOTT NO.	DESCRIPTION	FIRST DAY COVERS SING	FIRST DAY COVERS INSC. BLK	INSRIP BLK-4	UNUSED F/NH	USED F
47-48	3¢ & 8¢ Human Rights Day	1.25	3.15	1.25	.40	.30
	1957					
49-58	**1957 Issues, complete (10)**	......	......	......	**1.65**	......
49-50	3¢ & 8¢ Meteorological Org.	1.25	3.15	1.35	.35	.25
51-52	3¢ & 8¢ Emergency Force .	1.25	3.15	1.35	.35	.25
53-54	same, re-engraved	......	......	1.40	.35	.25
55-56	3¢ & 8¢ Security Council . .	1.25	3.15	1.35	.35	.25

SETS ONLY: Prices listed are for complete sets as indicated. We regrettably cannot supply individual stamps from sets.

U.N. Postage #57-87

57-58 59-60 61-62 63-64 65-66

SCOTT NO.	DESCRIPTION	FIRST DAY COVERS SING	INSC. BLK	INSRIP BLK-4	UNUSED F/NH	USED F
57-58	3¢ & 8¢ Human Rights Day	1.25	3.15	1.35	.35	.25
	1958					
59-68	**1958 Issues, complete (10) ....**	......	......	......	**1.65**	......
59-60	3¢ & 8¢ Atomic Energy Agency	1.25	3.15	1.35	.35	.25
61-62	3¢ & 8¢ Central Hall	1.25	3.15	1.35	.35	.25
63-64	4¢ & 8¢ U.N. Seal	1.25	3.15	1.35	.35	.25
65-66	4¢ & 8¢ Economic & Social Council	1.25	3.15	1.35	.35	.25

67-68 69-70 71-72 73-74 75-76

SCOTT NO.	DESCRIPTION	FIRST DAY COVERS SING	INSC. BLK	INSRIP BLK-4	UNUSED F/NH	USED F
67-68	4¢ & 8¢ Human Rights Day	1.21	3.15	1.35	.356	.21
	1959					
69-76	**1959 Issues, complete (8) ....**	......	......	......	**1.35**	......
69-70	4¢ & 8¢ Flushing Meadows	1.25	3.15	1.40	.35	.25
71-72	4¢ & 8¢ Economic Commission Europe	1.25	3.15	1.40	.35	.25
73-74	4¢ & 8¢ Trusteeship Council	1.25	3.15	1.40	.35	.25
75-76	4¢ & 8¢ World Refugee Year	1.25	3.15	1.40	.35	.25

77-78 79-80 81-82 83-85 86-87

SCOTT NO.	DESCRIPTION	FIRST DAY COVERS SING	INSC. BLK	INSRIP BLK-4	UNUSED F/NH	USED F
	1960					
77/87	**1960 Issues, (10) (No #85) ....**	......	......	......	**1.65**	......
77-78	4¢ & 8¢ Palais de Chaillot	1.25	3.15	1.40	.35	.25
79-80	4¢ & 8¢ Economic Commission Asia	1.25	3.15	1.40	.35	.25
81-82	4¢ & 8¢ 5th World Forestry Congress	1.25	3.15	1.40	.35	.25
83-84	4¢ & 8¢ 15th Anniversary	1.25	3.15	1.40	.35	.25
85	same, souvenir sheet	4.25	......	......	2.10	1.80
85 var	Broken "V" Variety	135.00	......	......	72.50	67.50
86-87	4¢ & 8¢ International Bank	1.25	3.15	1.40	.35	.25

FIRST DAY COVERS: Prices for United Nations First Day Covers are for cacheted, unaddressed covers with each variety in a set mounted on a separate cover. Complete sets mounted on one cover do exist and sell for a slightly lower price.

U.N. Postage #88-113

88-89 | 90-91 | 92 | 93-94

SCOTT NO.	DESCRIPTION	FIRST DAY COVERS SING	INSC. BLK	INSRIP BLK-4	UNUSED F/NH	USED F
	1961					
88-99	**1961 Issues, complete (12)**	......	......	......	**2.65**	......
88-89	4¢ & 8¢ International Court of Justice	1.25	3.15	1.35	.35	1.25
90-91	4¢ & 7¢ Int. Monetary Fund	1.25	3.15	1.35	.35	1.25
92	30¢ Abstract Flags	1.25	3.15	2.70	.60	.35
93-94	4¢ & 11¢ Economic Commission Latin America	1.25	3.15	2.70	.60	.35

95-96 | 97-99 | 100-101 | 102-103

SCOTT NO.	DESCRIPTION	FIRST DAY COVERS SING	INSC. BLK	INSRIP BLK-4	UNUSED F/NH	USED F
95-96	4¢ & 11¢ Economic Commission Africa	1.25	3.15	1.40	.35	.25
97-99	3¢, 4¢ & 13¢ Children's Fund	1.25	3.50	2.55	.55	.40
	1962					
100-13	**1962 Issues, complete (14)**	......	......	......	**2.95**	......
100-01	4¢ & 7¢ Housing & Community Development	1.25	3.15	1.40	.35	.25
102-03	4¢ & 11¢ Malaria Eradication	1.25	3.15	2.35	.50	.35

104 | 105 | 106 | 107

SCOTT NO.	DESCRIPTION	FIRST DAY COVERS SING	INSC. BLK	INSRIP BLK-4	UNUSED F/NH	USED F
104-07	1¢ to 11¢ Definitives	2.00	4.00	2.75	.55	.35

108-09 | 110-11 | 112-13 | 114-15 | 116-17

SCOTT NO.	DESCRIPTION	FIRST DAY COVERS SING	INSC. BLK	INSRIP BLK-4	UNUSED F/NH	USED F
108-09	5¢ & 15¢ Memorial Issue	1.25	3.15	3.40	.70	.55
110-11	4¢ & 11¢ Operation in the Congo	1.25	3.15	3.25	.65	.55
112-13	4¢ & 11¢ Peaceful Uses of Outer Space	1.25	3.15	1.70	.35	.30

U.N. Postage #114-145

SCOTT NO.	DESCRIPTION	FIRST DAY COVERS SING	INSC. BLK	INSRIP BLK-4	UNUSED F/NH	USED F
		1963				
114-22	**1963 Issues, complete (9)**	......	......	......	**2.10**	......
114-15	5¢ & 11¢ Science & Technology	1.25	3.15	1.85	.40	.35
116-17	5¢ & 11¢ Freedom From Hunger	1.25	3.15	1.85	.40	.35

118

119-20

121-22

123-24

SCOTT NO.	DESCRIPTION	FIRST DAY COVERS SING	INSC. BLK	INSRIP BLK-4	UNUSED F/NH	USED F
118	25¢ UNTEA	1.10	3.00	2.70	.60	.35
119-20	5¢ & 11¢ General Assem. Bldg.	1.25	3.15	1.85	.40	.35
121-22	5¢ & 11¢ Human Rights	1.25	3.15	1.85	.40	.35
		1964				
123-36	**1964 Issues, complete (14)**	......	......	......	**2.95**	......
123-24	5¢ & 11¢ Maritime Organization (IMCO)	1.25	3.15	1.85	.40	.35

125, UX3

126

127

128, U3-4

SCOTT NO.	DESCRIPTION	FIRST DAY COVERS SING	INSC. BLK	INSRIP BLK-4	UNUSED F/NH	USED F
125-28	2¢ to 50¢ Definitives	3.25	7.75	6.65	1.30	.85

129-30

131-32

133

134-36

SCOTT NO.	DESCRIPTION	FIRST DAY COVERS SING	INSC. BLK	INSRIP BLK-4	UNUSED F/NH	USED F
129-30	5¢ & 11¢ Trade & Development	1.25	3.15	1.85	.40	.35
131-32	5¢ & 11¢ Narcotics Control	1.25	3.45	1.85	.40	.35
133	5¢ Cessation of Nuclear Testing	.60	1.30	.65	.20	.15
134-36	4¢ to 11¢ Education for Progress	1.30	3.25	1.85	.40	.35

137-38

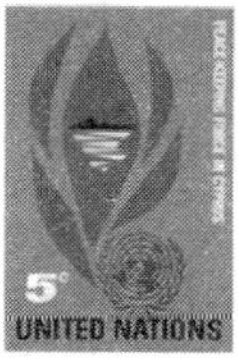

139-40

141-42

143-45

SCOTT NO.	DESCRIPTION	FIRST DAY COVERS SING	INSC. BLK	INSRIP BLK-4	UNUSED F/NH	USED F
137/53	**1965 Issues, (15) (No #145 or 150)**	......	......	......	**2.90**	......
137-38	5¢ & 11¢ United Nations Special Fund	1.25	3.15	1.45	.35	.30
139-40	5¢ & 11¢ United Nations Forces in Cyprus	1.25	3.15	1.45	.35	.30
141-42	5¢ & 11¢ I.T.U. Centenary	1.25	3.15	1.45	.35	.30
143-44	5¢ & 15¢ Int'l Cooperation Year	1.25	3.15	1.85	.40	.35
145	same, souvenir sheet	1.75	......	......	.60	.50

U.N. Postage #146-174

146  147  148  149  150

SCOTT NO.	DESCRIPTION	FIRST DAY COVERS SING	INSC. BLK	INSRIP BLK-4	UNUSED F/NH	USED F
146-49	1¢ to 25¢ Definitive	3.50	8.75	7.65	1.20	.95
	1966					
150	$1 Definitive	3.10	7.75	9.50	2.25	1.75

151-53  154-55  156-57  158-59  160

SCOTT NO.	DESCRIPTION	FIRST DAY COVERS SING	INSC. BLK	INSRIP BLK-4	UNUSED F/NH	USED F
	1965					
151-53	4¢ to 11¢ Population Trends	1.60	3.75	1.85	.40	.50
	1966					
154-63	**1966 Issues, complete (10)**	......	......	......	**1.70**	......
154-55	5¢ & 15¢ World Federation (WFUNA)	1.25	3.15	1.60	.35	.30
156-57	5¢ & 11¢ World Health Organization	1.25	3.15	1.60	.35	.30
158-59	5¢ & 11¢ Coffee Agreement	1.25	3.15	1.60	.35	.30
160	15¢ Peace Keeping Observers	.60	1.50	1.45	.35	.30

161-63  164-65  166  167  168-69

SCOTT NO.	DESCRIPTION	FIRST DAY COVERS SING	INSC. BLK	INSRIP BLK-4	UNUSED F/NH	USED F
161-63	4¢ to 11¢ UNICEF	1.60	3.75	1.85	.40	.35
	1967					
164/80	**1967 Issues, (16) (No #179)**	......	......	......	**3.20**	......
164-65	5¢ & 11¢ Development	1.25	3.15	1.45	.35	.30
166-67	1-1/2 ¢ & 5¢ Definitives	1.25	3.15	1.10	.35	.30
168-69	5¢ & 11¢ Independence	1.25	3.15	1.45	.35	.30

170  171  172  173  174

SCOTT NO.	DESCRIPTION	FIRST DAY COVERS SING	INSC. BLK	INSRIP BLK-4	UNUSED F/NH	USED F
170-74	4¢ to 15¢ Expo '67 Canada	3.00	7.50	4.20	.90	.85

U.N. Postage #175-198

175-76

177-78

179

180

SCOTT NO.	DESCRIPTION	FIRST DAY COVERS SING	FIRST DAY COVERS INSC. BLK	INSRIP BLK-4	UNUSED F/NH	USED F
175-76	5¢ & 15¢ International Tourist Year	1.25	3.15	1.65	.35	.25
177-78	6¢ & 13¢ Towards Disarmament	1.25	3.15	1.90	.40	.35
179	36¢ Chagall Window souvenir sheet	1.25	......	......	.65	.60
180	6¢ Kiss of Peace	.60	......	.65	.25	.15

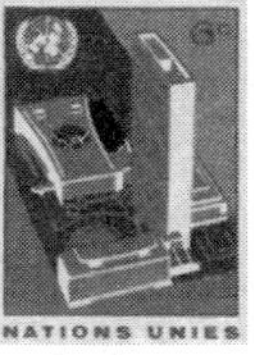

181-82 183-84 185-86 187, U5 188-89

1968

SCOTT NO.	DESCRIPTION	FIRST DAY COVERS SING	FIRST DAY COVERS INSC. BLK	INSRIP BLK-4	UNUSED F/NH	USED F
181-91	**1968 Issues, complete (11)**	......	......	......	**4.00**	......
181-82	6¢ & 13 ¢ Secretariat	1.25	3.15	1.80	.40	.35
183-84	6¢ & 75¢ H. Starcke	6.25	15.00	9.50	2.00	2.00
185-86	6¢ & 13¢ Industrial Development	1.25	3.15	1.65	.35	.30
187	6¢ Definitive	.60	1.50	.65	.25	.15
188-89	6¢ & 20¢ Weather Watch	1.25	3.15	2.30	.50	.40

190-91 192-93 194-95 196 197-98

SCOTT NO.	DESCRIPTION	FIRST DAY COVERS SING	FIRST DAY COVERS INSC. BLK	INSRIP BLK-4	UNUSED F/NH	USED F
190-91	6¢ & 13¢ International Year—Human Rights	1.25	3.15	2.30	.50	.40

1969

SCOTT NO.	DESCRIPTION	FIRST DAY COVERS SING	FIRST DAY COVERS INSC. BLK	INSRIP BLK-4	UNUSED F/NH	USED F
192-202	**1969 Issues (11)**	......	......	......	**2.35**	......
192-93	6¢ & 13¢ Institute Training Research	1.25	3.15	1.85	.40	.35
194-95	6¢ & 15¢ U.N. Building—Chile	1.25	3.15	2.15	.45	.40
196	13¢ Definitive	.60	1.50	1.40	.30	.25
197-98	6¢ & 13¢ Peace Through International Law	1.25	3.15	1.85	.40	.35

SETS ONLY: Prices listed are for complete sets as indicated. We regrettably cannot supply individual stamps from sets.

U.N. Postage #199-223

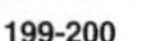
199-200

201-02

203-04

205-06

SCOTT NO.	DESCRIPTION	FIRST DAY COVERS SING	FIRST DAY COVERS INSC. BLK	INSRIP BLK-4	UNUSED F/NH	USED F
199-200	6¢ & 20¢ Labor & Development	1.25	3.15	2.35	.50	.45
201-02	6¢ & 13¢ Tunisian Mosaics	1.25	3.15	1.90	.40	.35

1970

SCOTT NO.	DESCRIPTION	FIRST DAY COVERS SING	FIRST DAY COVERS INSC. BLK	INSRIP BLK-4	UNUSED F/NH	USED F
203/14	**1970 Issues, (11) (No #212)**	......	......	......	**3.25**	......
203-04	6¢ & 25¢ Japanese Peace Bell	1.25	3.15	2.45	.55	.50
205-06	6¢ & 13¢ L. Mekong Delta Devel.	1.25	3.15	1.65	.35	.30

207-08

209-10

211-12

213-14

215

SCOTT NO.	DESCRIPTION	FIRST DAY COVERS SING	FIRST DAY COVERS INSC. BLK	INSRIP BLK-4	UNUSED F/NH	USED F
207-08	6¢ & 13¢ Fight Cancer	1.25	3.15	1.65	.35	.30
209-11	6¢ to 25¢ Peace & Progress	1.70	4.25	4.10	.90	.80
212	same, souvenir sheet	1.40	......	......	.90	.85
213-14	6¢ & 13¢ Peace, Justice & Prog.	1.25	3.15	1.65	.35	.30

1971

SCOTT NO.	DESCRIPTION	FIRST DAY COVERS SING	FIRST DAY COVERS INSC. BLK	INSRIP BLK-4	UNUSED F/NH	USED F
215-25	**1971 Issues (11)**	......	......	......	**3.25**	......
215	6¢ Peaceful Uses Sea-Bed	.60	1.50	.65	.20	.15

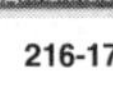
216-17

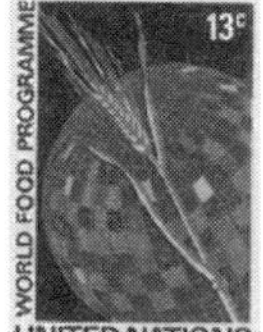

218

219

220

221

SCOTT NO.	DESCRIPTION	FIRST DAY COVERS SING	FIRST DAY COVERS INSC. BLK	INSRIP BLK-4	UNUSED F/NH	USED F
216-17	6¢ & 13¢ Support Refugees	1.25	3.15	1.65	.35	.30
218	13¢ World Food Programme	.60	1.50	1.20	.25	.20
219	20¢ Universal Postal Union Building	.70	1.75	1.65	.35	.35
220-21	8¢ & 13¢ Anti-Discrimination	1.25	3.15	1.85	.40	.35

222, UC12

223

SCOTT NO.	DESCRIPTION	FIRST DAY COVERS SING	FIRST DAY COVERS INSC. BLK	INSRIP BLK-4	UNUSED F/NH	USED F
222-23	8¢ & 60¢ Definitives	2.50	6.25	5.70	1.25	1.10

U.N. Postage #224-246

SCOTT NO.	DESCRIPTION	FIRST DAY COVERS SING	INSC. BLK	INSRIP BLK-4	UNUSED F/NH	USED F

224-25 226 227 228 229-30

SCOTT NO.	DESCRIPTION	FIRST DAY COVERS SING	INSC. BLK	INSRIP BLK-4	UNUSED F/NH	USED F
224-25	8¢ & 21¢ International School	1.25	3.15	2.75	.60	.55
	1972					
226-33	**1972 Issues, complete (8)**	......	......	......	**3.55**	......
226	95¢ Definitive	2.75	6.85	8.65	1.90	1.50
227	8¢ Non-Proliferation	.60	1.50	.80	.20	.15
228	15¢ World Health Org.	.60	1.50	1.40	.30	.25
229-30	8¢ & 15¢ Environment	1.25	3.15	2.15	.45	.40

231 232-33 234-35 236-37 238-39

SCOTT NO.	DESCRIPTION	FIRST DAY COVERS SING	INSC. BLK	INSRIP BLK-4	UNUSED F/NH	USED F
231	21¢ Economic Commission Europe	.75	1.85	2.10	.45	.40
232-33	8¢ & 15¢ Art—Sert Ceiling	1.25	3.15	2.15	.45	.40
	1973					
234-43	**1973 Issues, complete (10)**	......	......	......	**2.60**	......
234-35	8¢ & 15¢ Disarmament Decade	1.25	3.15	2.15	.45	.40
236-37	8¢ & 15¢ Drug Abuse	1.25	3.15	2.50	.55	.50
238-39	8¢ & 21¢ Volunteers Programme	1.25	3.15	2.75	.60	.55

240-41 242-43 244-45 246

SCOTT NO.	DESCRIPTION	FIRST DAY COVERS SING	INSC. BLK	INSRIP BLK-4	UNUSED F/NH	USED F
240-41	8¢ & 15¢ Namibia	1.25	3.15	2.55	.55	.50
242-43	8¢ & 21¢ Human Rights	1.25	3.15	2.75	.60	.55
	1974					
244-55	**1974 Issues, complete (12)**	......	......	......	**3.20**	......
244-45	10¢ & 21¢ ILO Headquarters	1.30	3.25	3.25	.70	.65
246	10¢ Universal Postal Union	.60	1.50	.95	.20	.15

INSCRIPTION BLOCKS: Each corner of United Nations complete sheets contains the U.N. Emblem plus the name of the issue in the selvage. These are offered as Inscription Blocks of Four.

U.N. Postage #247-271

247-48

249

251

252-53

250, U6

SCOTT NO.	DESCRIPTION	FIRST DAY COVERS SING	FIRST DAY COVERS INSC. BLK	INSRIP BLK-4	UNUSED F/NH	USED F
247-48	10¢ & 18¢ Brazil Peace Mural	1.25	3.15	2.55	.55	.50
249-51	2¢ to 18¢ Definitives	1.65	4.15	2.75	.60	.55
252-53	10¢ & 18¢ World Population Year	1.35	3.35	2.55	.55	.50

254-55

256-57

258-59

260-62

263-64

SCOTT NO.	DESCRIPTION	FIRST DAY COVERS SING	FIRST DAY COVERS INSC. BLK	INSRIP BLK-4	UNUSED F/NH	USED F
254-55	10¢ & 26¢ Law of the Sea	1.35	3.35	3.45	1.75	.70

1975

SCOTT NO.	DESCRIPTION	FIRST DAY COVERS SING	FIRST DAY COVERS INSC. BLK	INSRIP BLK-4	UNUSED F/NH	USED F
256/66	**1975 Issues, (10) (No #262) ....**	......	......	......	**4.05**	......
256-57	10¢ & 26¢ Peaceful Uses of Space	1.35	3.35	3.45	.75	.70
258-59	10¢ & 18¢ Int'l. Women's Year	1.25	3.15	2.55	.55	.50
260-61	10¢ & 26¢ Anniversary	1.30	3.35	3.00	.60	.60
262	same, souvenir sheet	1.55	......	......	1.00	.80
263-64	10¢ & 18¢ Namibia	1.25	3.15	2.55	.55	.50

265-66

267

268

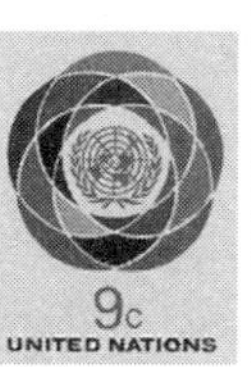

269

270

271

SCOTT NO.	DESCRIPTION	FIRST DAY COVERS SING	FIRST DAY COVERS INSC. BLK	INSRIP BLK-4	UNUSED F/NH	USED F
265-66	13¢ & 26¢ Peacekeeping	1.35	3.35	3.45	.75	.70

1976

SCOTT NO.	DESCRIPTION	FIRST DAY COVERS SING	FIRST DAY COVERS INSC. BLK	INSRIP BLK-4	UNUSED F/NH	USED F
267-80	**1976 Issues, complete (14) ....**	......	......	......	**7.90**	......
267-71	3¢ to 50¢ Definitives	3.10	7.75	7.45	1.60	1.35

272-73

274-75

276-77

278-79

280

U.N. Postage #272-301

SCOTT NO.	DESCRIPTION	FIRST DAY COVERS SING	INSC. BLK	INSRIP BLK-4	UNUSED F/NH	USED F
272-73	13¢ & 26¢ World Federation	1.50	3.75	3.25	.70	.65
274-75	13¢ & 31¢ Conf. on Trade & Dev.	1.45	3.65	4.70	.85	.75
276-77	13¢ & 25¢ Conference on Human Settlements	1.25	3.15	4.00	.85	.75
278-79	13¢ & 31¢ Postal Admin.	9.50	23.50	18.75	4.00	2.25
280	13¢ World Food Council	.60	1.50	1.40	.30	.25

281-82

283-84

285-86

287-88

1977

SCOTT NO.	DESCRIPTION	FIRST DAY COVERS SING	INSC. BLK	INSRIP BLK-4	UNUSED F/NH	USED F
281-90	**Issues, complete (10)**	......	......	......	**3.60**	......
281-82	13¢ & 31¢ WIPO	1.40	3.50	4.20	.90	.80
283-84	13¢ & 25¢ Water Conference	1.35	3.40	3.95	.85	.75
285-86	13¢ & 31¢ Security Council	1.50	3.75	4.05	.65	.60
287-88	13¢ & 25¢ Combat Racism	1.35	3.40	3.50	.75	.70

289-90

291

292

293

SCOTT NO.	DESCRIPTION	FIRST DAY COVERS SING	INSC. BLK	INSRIP BLK-4	UNUSED F/NH	USED F
289-90	13¢ & 18¢ Atomic Energy	1.25	3.15	3.00	.65	.60

1978

SCOTT NO.	DESCRIPTION	FIRST DAY COVERS SING	INSC. BLK	INSRIP BLK-4	UNUSED F/NH	USED F
291-303	**1978 Issues, complete (13)**	......	......	......	**5.65**	......
291-93	1¢, 25¢ & $1 Definitives	4.00	10.00	9.90	2.20	1.90

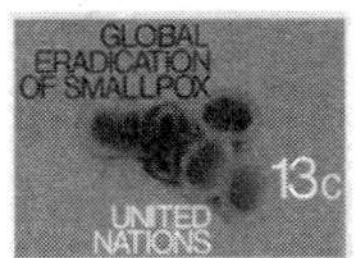

294-95

296-97

298-99

300-01

SCOTT NO.	DESCRIPTION	FIRST DAY COVERS SING	INSC. BLK	INSRIP BLK-4	UNUSED F/NH	USED F
294-95	13¢ & 31¢ Smallpox Eradication	1.40	3.50	4.40	.95	.85
296-97	13¢ & 18¢ Namibia	1.25	3.15	2.70	.60	.55
298-99	13¢ & 25¢ ICAO	1.30	3.25	3.50	.75	.70
300-01	13¢ & 18¢ General Assembly	1.25	3.15	2.70	.60	.55

302-03

304

305

306

307

U.N. Postage #302-342

SCOTT NO.	DESCRIPTION	FIRST DAY COVERS SING	INSC. BLK	INSRIP BLK-4	UNUSED F/NH	USED F
302-03	13¢ & 31¢ TCDC	1.50	3.75	4.00	.85	.75

1979

SCOTT NO.	DESCRIPTION	FIRST DAY COVERS SING	INSC. BLK	INSRIP BLK-4	UNUSED F/NH	USED F
304-15	**1979 Issues, complete (12)**	......	......	......	**4.15**	......
304-07	5¢, 14¢, 15¢ & 20¢ Definitives	2.00	5.00	4.40	.95	.85

308-09

310-11

312-13

314-15

SCOTT NO.	DESCRIPTION	FIRST DAY COVERS SING	INSC. BLK	INSRIP BLK-4	UNUSED F/NH	USED F
308-09	15¢ & 20¢ UNDRO	1.35	3.40	3.25	.70	.65
310-11	15¢ & 31¢ I.Y.C.	3.75	9.40	4.95	1.10	.95
312-13	15¢ & 31¢ Namibia	1.55	3.85	4.00	.85	.75
314-15	15¢ & 20¢ Court of Justice	1.40	3.50	3.50	.75	.60

316

317

318-19

320

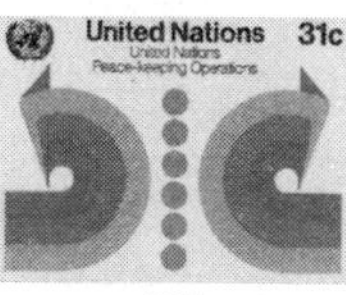

321

322

323

TURKEY
UNITED NATIONS 15¢

325

1980 World Flags

326 *Luxembourg*
327 *Fiji*
328 *Viet Nam*
329 *Guinea*
330 *Surinam*
331 *Bangladesh*
332 *Mali*
333 *Yugoslavia*
334 *France*
335 *Venezuela*
336 *El Salvador*
337 *Madagascar*
338 *Cameroon*
339 *Rwanda*
340 *Hungary*

UNITED NATIONS
15c
ECONOMIC AND SOCIAL COUNCIL

341

342

1980

SCOTT NO.	DESCRIPTION	FIRST DAY COVERS SING	INSC. BLK	INSRIP BLK-4	UNUSED F/NH	USED F
316/42	**1980 Issues, (26) (No #324)**	......	......	......	**8.10**	......
316-17	15¢ & 31¢ Economics	1.65	4.15	4.00	.85	.75
318-19	15¢ & 20¢ Decade for Women	1.35	3.40	3.50	.75	.60
320-21	15¢ & 31¢ Peacekeeping	1.60	4.00	4.20	.90	.80
322-23	15¢ & 31¢ Anniversary	1.55	3.90	4.00	.85	.75
324	same, souvenir sheet	1.45	......	......	.95	.90
325-40	15¢ 1980 World Flags, 16 varieties	10.00	......	16.50	3.50	4.50
341-42	15¢ & 20¢ Economic & Social Council	1.30	3.25	3.50	.75	.60

U.N. Postage #343-391

SCOTT NO.	DESCRIPTION	FIRST DAY COVERS SING	INSC. BLK	INSRIP BLK-4	UNUSED F/NH	USED F

343

United Nations International Year of Disabled Persons 20c

344

345

346-47

348

NEW AND RENEWABLE SOURCES OF ENERGY UNITED NATIONS 40c

349

1981 World Flags

350 *Djibouti*
351 *Sri Lanka*
352 *Bolivia*
353 *Equatorial Guinea*
354 *Malta*
355 *Czechoslovakia*
356 *Thailand*
357 *Trinidad*
358 *Ukraine*
359 *Kuwait*
360 *Sudan*
361 *Egypt*
362 *United States*
363 *Singapore*
364 *Panama*
365 *Costa Rica*

18c TENTH ANNIVERSARY OF THE UNITED NATIONS VOLUNTEERS PROGRAMME UNITED NATIONS

366

367

1981

SCOTT NO.	DESCRIPTION	FIRST DAY COVERS SING	INSC. BLK	INSRIP BLK-4	UNUSED F/NH	USED F
343-67	**1981 Issues, complete (25)**	......	......	......	**10.45**	......
343	15¢ Palestinian People	.75	1.85	1.60	.35	.30
344-45	20¢ & 35¢ Disabled Persons	1.70	4.25	4.75	1.00	.90
346-47	20¢ & 31¢ Fresco	1.60	4.00	4.75	1.00	.90
348-49	20¢ & 40¢ Sources of Energy	1.90	4.75	5.45	1.20	1.00
350-65	20¢ 1981 World Flags, 16 varieties	13.50	......	27.25	6.25	6.25
366-67	18¢ & 28¢ Volunteers Program	1.55	3.85	5.50	1.20	.85

368

369

370

20c UNITED NATIONS HUMAN ENVIRONMENT

371

372

373

1982 World Flags

374 *Austria*
375 *Malaysia*
376 *Seychelles*
377 *Ireland*
378 *Mozambique*
379 *Albania*
380 *Dominica*
381 *Solomon Islands*
382 *Philippines*
383 *Swaziland*
384 *Nicaragua*
385 *Burma*
386 *Cape Verde*
387 *Guyana*
388 *Belgium*
389 *Nigeria*

390-91

1982

SCOTT NO.	DESCRIPTION	FIRST DAY COVERS SING	INSC. BLK	INSRIP BLK-4	UNUSED F/NH	USED F
368-91	**1982 Issues, complete (24)**	......	......	......	**10.95**	......
368-70	17¢, 28¢ & 49¢ Definitives	2.50	6.25	9.25	2.00	1.55
371-72	20¢ & 40¢ Human Environment	1.95	4.85	7.00	1.40	1.15
373	20¢ Space Exploration	.90	2.25	3.25	.70	.40
374-89	20¢ World Flags, 16 varieties	13.00	......	28.00	6.25	6.00
390-91	20¢ & 28¢ Nature Conservation	1.75	4.35	5.75	1.20	1.00

U.N. Postage #392-416

392

393

394

395

396

397

398

1983 World Flags

399 *United Kingdom*
400 *Barbados*
401 *Nepal*
402 *Israel*
403 *Malawi*
404 *Byelorussian SSR*
405 *Jamaica*
406 *Kenya*
407 *China*
408 *Peru*
409 *Bulgaria*
410 *Canada*
411 *Somalia*
412 *Senegal*
413 *Brazil*
414 *Sweden*

415

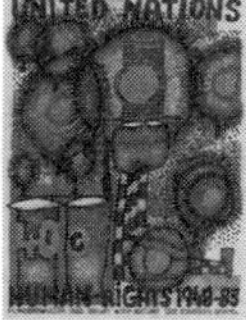
416

1983

SCOTT NO.	DESCRIPTION	FIRST DAY COVERS SING	INSC. BLK	INSRIP BLK-4	UNUSED F/NH	USED F
392-416	**1983 Issues, complete (25)**	......	......	......	**14.00**	......
392-93	20¢ & 40¢ World Communications Year	2.05	5.15	6.75	1.40	1.10
394-95	20¢ & 37¢ Safety at Sea	1.95	4.75	6.75	1.40	1.10
396	20¢ World Food Program	.85	2.10	3.95	.85	.50
397-98	20¢ & 28¢ Trade & Development	1.60	4.00	7.25	1.60	1.00
399-414	20¢ World Flags, 16 varieties	13.00	......	32.75	7.50	7.00
415-16	20¢ & 40¢ Human Rights	2.50	6.25	9.00	2.00	1.50

417-18

419

420

421

422

423

424

1984 World Flags

425 *Burundi*
426 *Pakistan*
427 *Benin*
428 *Italy*
429 *Tanzania*
430 *United Arab Emirates*
431 *Ecuador*
432 *Bahamas*
433 *Poland*
434 *Papua New Guinea*
435 *Uruguay*
436 *Chile*
437 *Paraguay*
438 *Bhutan*
439 *Central African Republic*
440 *Australia*

441

U.N. Postage #417-467

SCOTT NO.	DESCRIPTION	FIRST DAY COVERS SING	INSC. BLK	INSRIP BLK-4	UNUSED F/NH	USED F
		1984				
417-42	**1984 Issues, complete (25)**	......	......	......	**22.80**	......
417-18	20¢ & 40¢ Population	2.10	5.25	8.50	1.75	1.25
419-20	20¢ & 40¢ Food Day	2.10	5.25	9.50	2.00	1.25
421-22	20¢ & 50¢ Heritage	2.25	5.50	10.50	2.25	1.50
423-24	20¢ & 50¢ Future for Refugees	2.25	5.50	9.00	2.00	1.35
425-40	20¢ 1984 World Flags, 16 varieties	13.00	......	57.50	14.00	11.50
441-42	20¢ & 35¢ Youth Year	2.10	5.25	9.00	2.00	1.25

443

444

445

446

447

448

1985 World Flags

450 *Grenada*	**458** *Liberia*
451 *Germany-West*	**459** *Mauritius*
452 *Saudi Arabia*	**460** *Chad*
453 *Mexico*	**461** *Dominican Republic*
454 *Uganda*	**462** *Oman*
455 *Sao Tome & Principie*	**463** *Ghana*
456 *U.S.S.R.*	**464** *Sierra Leone*
457 *India*	**465** *Finland*

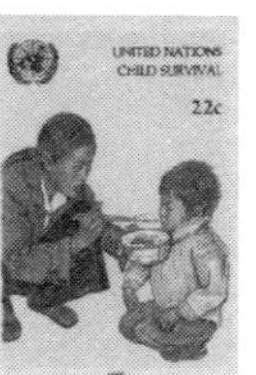
466

SCOTT NO.	DESCRIPTION	FIRST DAY COVERS SING	INSC. BLK	INSRIP BLK-4	UNUSED F/NH	USED F
		1985				
443/67	**1985 Issues, (24) (No #449)**	......	......	......	**25.65**	......
443	23¢ ILO—Turin Centre	1.00	2.50	3.70	.85	.50
444	50¢ United Nations University in Japan	1.65	4.15	7.75	1.65	1.10
445-46	22¢ & $3 Definitives	8.00	20.00	29.00	6.50	5.00
447-48	22¢ & 45¢ 40th Anniversary	2.30	5.75	8.75	1.75	1.50
449	same, souvenir sheet	2.50	......	......	2.50	1.50
450-65	22¢ 1985 World Flags, 16 varieties	14.00	......	60.00	14.50	11.00
466-67	22¢ & 33¢ Child Survival	2.25	5.65	7.95	1.75	1.10

468

469

473

475

476

1986 World Flags

477 *New Zealand*	**485** *Iceland*
478 *Lao PDR*	**486** *Antigua & Barbuda*
479 *Burkina Faso*	**487** *Angola*
480 *Gambia*	**488** *Botswana*
481 *Maldives*	**489** *Romania*
482 *Ethiopia*	**490** *Togo*
483 *Jordan*	**491** *Mauritania*
484 *Zambia*	**492** *Colombia*

U.N. Postage #468-518

SCOTT NO.	DESCRIPTION	FIRST DAY COVERS SING	INSC. BLK	INSRIP BLK-4	UNUSED F/NH	USED F
		1986				
468-92	**1986 Issues (25)**	......	......	......	**25.50**	......
468	22¢ African Crisis	1.05	2.60	3.25	.70	.40
469-72	22¢ Development, 4 varieties, attached	2.50	3.25	10.50	9.00	......
473-74	22¢ & 44¢ Philately	2.30	5.75	8.65	1.75	1.00
475-76	22¢ & 33¢ Peace Year	2.25	5.65	8.65	1.90	1.00
477-92	22¢ 1986 World Flags, 16 varieties	14.00	......	56.50	13.50	8.50

493a

494

495

497

1987 World Flags

499	*Comoros*	**507**	*Argentina*
500	*Democratic Yemen*	**508**	*Congo*
501	*Mongolia*	**509**	*Niger*
502	*Vanuatu*	**510**	*St. Lucia*
503	*Japan*	**511**	*Bahrain*
504	*Gabon*	**512**	*Haiti*
505	*Zimbabwe*	**513**	*Afghanistan*
506	*Iraq*	**514**	*Greece*

515

517

SCOTT NO.	DESCRIPTION	FIRST DAY COVERS SING	INSC. BLK	INSRIP BLK-4	UNUSED F/NH	USED F
		1986				
493	22¢ to 44¢ World Federation of United Nations Associations Souvenir sheet of 4 .	4.00	......	......	5.50	4.00
		1987				
494-518	**1987 Issues (25)**	......	......	......	**18.15**	......
494	22¢ Trygve Lie	1.05	2.60	5.00	1.00	.75
495-96	22¢ & 44¢ Shelter Homeless	2.25	5.65	8.50	1.75	1.75
497-98	22¢ & 33¢ Anti-Drug Campaign	2.25	5.65	8.25	1.65	1.65
499-514	22¢ 1987 World Flags, 16 varieties	14.00	......	52.50	12.50	10.00
515-16	22¢ & 39¢ United Nations Day	2.30	5.75	7.50	1.50	1.30
517-18	22¢ & 44¢ Child Immunization	2.35	5.70	9.00	2.10	2.00

519

521

522

524

526

1988 World Flags

528	*Spain*
529	*St. Vincent & Grenadines*
530	*Ivory Coast*
531	*Lebanon*
532	*Yemen*
533	*Cuba*
534	*Denmark*
535	*Libya*
536	*Qatar*
537	*Zaire*
538	*Norway*
539	*German Democratic Republic*
540	*Iran*
541	*Tunisia*
542	*Samoa*
543	*Belize*

544-45

U.N. Postage #519-578

SCOTT NO.	DESCRIPTION	FIRST DAY COVERS SING	FIRST DAY COVERS INSC. BLK	INSRIP BLK-4	UNUSED F/NH	USED F
	1988					
519/44	**1988 Issues (24) (No #522-23)**	......	......	......	**19.25**	......
519-20	22¢ & 33¢ World without Hunger	2.25	5.65	10.50	2.35	1.75
521	3¢ For a Better World	.90	2.25	.90	.20	.20
				Sheetlets		
522-23	25¢ & 44¢ Forest Conservation .... (set of 6, includes Geneva and Vienna)	15.00	40.00	130.00	27.50	25.00
524-25	25¢ & 50¢ Volunteer Day	2.60	6.50	10.50	2.25	2.00
526-27	25¢ & 38¢ Health in Sports	2.30	5.75	12.00	2.75	2.00
528-43	25¢ 1988 World Flags, 16 varieties	14.50	......	53.50	12.00	9.00
544	25¢ Human Rights	1.75	4.25	4.00	.75	.45
545	$1 Human Rights souvenir sheet	2.75	......	......	2.50	2.00

546

548

549

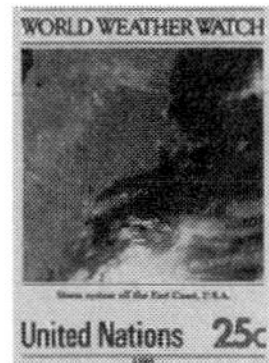

550

552 553

1989 World Flags

554 *Indonesia*
555 *Lesotho*
556 *Guatamala*
557 *Netherlands*
558 *South Africa*
559 *Portugal*
560 *Morocco*
561 *Syrian Arab Republic*
562 *Honduras*
563 *Kampuchea*
564 *Guinea-Bissau*
565 *Cyprus*
566 *Algeria*
567 *Brunei*
568 *St. Kitts & Nevis*
569 *United Nations*

570-71

SCOTT NO.	DESCRIPTION	FIRST DAY COVERS SING	FIRST DAY COVERS INSC. BLK	INSRIP BLK-4	UNUSED F/NH	USED F
	1989					
546-71	**1989 Issues (26)**	......	......	......	**30.00**	......
546-47	25¢ & 45¢ World Bank	2.60	6.50	12.00	2.75	2.00
548	25¢ Nobel Peace Prize	1.10	1.65	5.75	1.10	.95
549	45¢ United Nations Definitive	1.40	2.10	5.75	1.10	.95
550-51	25¢ & 36¢ Weather Watch	2.30	5.75	15.00	3.50	2.50
552-53	25¢ & 90¢ U.N. Offices in Vienna	3.75	9.25	23.50	5.50	5.00
554-69	25¢ 1989 World Flags, 16 varieties ...	14.50	......	57.50	13.50	10.00
				Sheetlets (12)		
570-71	25¢ & 45¢ Human Rights 40th Ann. .. (strips of 3 with tabs)	2.60	6.50	21.00	4.50	....

572

573-74

575-76

577-78

SCOTT NO.	DESCRIPTION	FIRST DAY COVERS SING	FIRST DAY COVERS INSC. BLK	INSRIP BLK-4	UNUSED F/NH	USED F
	1990					
572/83	**1990 Issues (11) (No #579)**	......	......	......	**25.50**	......
572	25¢ International Trade Center	1.75	2.95	10.50	2.10	1.80
573-74	25¢ & 40¢ AIDS	2.60	6.50	12.25	2.75	2.25
575-76	25¢ & 90¢ Medicinal Plants	3.75	9.25	16.00	3.50	2.50
577-78	25¢ & 45¢ United Nations 45th Anniversary	2.60	6.50	18.50	4.00	3.50

U.N. Postage #579-600

SCOTT NO.	DESCRIPTION	FIRST DAY COVERS SING	INSC. BLK	INSRIP BLK-4	UNUSED F/NH	USED F
579	25¢ & 45¢ United Nations 45th Anniversary Souvenir Sheet	2.10	......	......	5.50	4.50
580-81	25¢ & 36¢ Crime Prevention	2.30	5.75	18.00	4.00	3.00
				Sheetlets (12)		
582-83	25¢ & 45¢ Human Rights (strips of 3 with tabs)	2.60	6.50	23.00	5.00	....

580-81

584

588

590

591

592

593

595

597

1991

SCOTT NO.	DESCRIPTION	FIRST DAY COVERS SING	INSC. BLK	INSRIP BLK-4	UNUSED F/NH	USED F
584-600	**1991 Issues (17)**	......	......	......	27.50	......
584-87	30¢ Econ. Comm. for Europe, 4 varieties, attached	4.50	5.50	5.25	4.50	4.00
588-89	30¢ & 50¢ Namibia—A New Nation	3.50	8.75	10.50	2.35	2.00
590-91	30¢ & 50¢ Definitives	4.00	10.00	10.50	2.35	2.00
592	$2 Definitive	5.50	13.50	19.00	4.00	3.00
593-94	30¢ & 70¢ Children's Rights	4.00	10.00	12.50	3.00	2.75
595-96	30¢ & 90¢ Banning of Chemical	4.25	10.50	17.00	3.50	3.00
597-98	30¢ & 40¢ 40th Anniversary of UNPA	3.50	8.75	10.50	2.35	2.25
				Sheetlets (12)		
599-600	30¢ & 50¢ Human Rights (strips of 3 with tabs)	3.00	7.50	31.50	7.00	....

603

605

609

U.N. Postage #601-636

611

613

614

1992

SCOTT NO.	DESCRIPTION	FIRST DAY COVERS SING	INSC. BLK	INSRIP BLK-4	UNUSED F/NH	USED F
601-17	**1992 Issues (17) ....**	......	......	......	20.50	......
601-02	29¢-50¢ World Heritage—UNESCO	3.60	9.00	11.25	2.00	1.75
603-04	29¢ Clean Oceans, 2 varieties, attached ...	2.50	4.95	4.50	1.60	1.50
605-08	29¢ Earth Summit, 4 varieties, attached	3.50	4.25	3.50	2.75	2.50
609-10	29¢ Mission to Planet Earth, 2 varieties, attd	2.50	4.95	14.50	6.00	6.00
611-12	29¢-50¢ Science and Technology	3.60	9.00	8.75	1.95	1.75
613-15	4¢-40¢ Definitives	3.40	8.50	9.75	2.00	1.75
				Sheetlets (12)		
616-17	20¢-50¢ Human Rights (strips of 3 with tabs)	3.00	9.50	22.50	5.50	....

620

624

626

618

629

633

1993

SCOTT NO.	DESCRIPTION	FIRST DAY COVERS SING	INSC. BLK	INSRIP BLK-4	UNUSED F/NH	USED F
618-36	**1993 Issues (19) ....**	......	......	......	17.50	......
618-19	29¢-52¢ Aging	3.00	9.50	8.75	1.95	1.75
620-23	29¢ Endangered Species, 4 attached	3.50	4.25	3.50	2.75	2.50
624-25	29¢-50¢ Health Environment	3.60	9.00	8.75	1.95	1.75
626	5¢ Definitive	2.00	4.00	1.00	.20	.20
				Sheetlets (12)		
627-28	29¢-35¢ Human Rights (strips of 3 with tabs)	3.00	9.50	18.50	5.00	....
629-32	29¢ Peace, 4 attached	3.50	4.25	3.50	4.00	3.50
633-36	29¢ Environment—Climate, strip of 4	3.50	7.00	6.25(8)	2.75	2.50

637

643

644

645

646

U.N. Postage #637-670

647

651

653

655

1994

SCOTT NO.	DESCRIPTION	FIRST DAY COVERS SING	FIRST DAY COVERS INSC. BLK	INSRIP BLK-4	UNUSED F/NH	USED F
637-54	**1994 Issues (18)**	....	....	....	**13.60**	....
637-38	29¢-45¢ International Year of the Family ..	2.25	8.50	8.50	1.95	1.75
639-42	29¢ Endangered Species, 4 attached	3.00	4.25	3.50	2.50	2.25
643	50¢ Refugees	1.75	5.75	5.00	1.20	1.00
644-46	10¢-$1 Definitives (3)	3.50	12.50	12.00	2.75	2.25
647-50	29¢ International Decade for Natural Disaster Reduction, 4 attached	3.00	4.25	3.50	2.50	2.25
651-52	29¢-52¢ Population and Development	2.25	9.00	8.75	1.75	1.50
653-54	29¢-50¢ Development through Partnership	2.25	9.00	8.75	1.75	1.50

656

661

663

666

668

669a

671

1995

SCOTT NO.	DESCRIPTION	FIRST DAY COVERS SING	FIRST DAY COVERS INSC. BLK	INSRIP BLK-4	UNUSED F/NH	USED F
655/69	**1995 Issues (14) (No #665)**	....	....	....	**18.10**	....
655	32¢ 50th Anniversary of the UN	1.75	4.00	3.50	.75	.65
656	50¢ Social Summit	1.75	5.75	5.00	1.10	.85
657-60	29¢ Endangered Species, 4 attached	3.00	4.25	3.50	2.75	2.25
661-62	32¢-55¢ Youth: Our Future	2.50	9.00	8.00	1.80	1.50
663-64	32¢-50¢ 50th Anniversary of the UN	2.50	9.00	8.00	1.95	1.50
665	82¢ 50th Anniversary of the UN, Souvenir Sheet	2.50	....	....	2.10	1.95
666-67	32¢-40¢ 4th World Conference on Women	2.50	9.00	8.00	1.75	1.50
668	20¢ UN Headquarters	1.75	....	1.75	.40	.45
669	32¢ 50th Anniversary, Miniature Sheet of 12	....	....	....	8.50	....
669a-l	32¢ 50th Anniversary of the UN, booklet single	1.75	....	....	.75	.25
670	same, Souvenir booklet of 4 panes of 3	....	....	....	9.00	....

672

673

U.N. Postage #671-689

677A

682A

685

686

687

688

689

1996

SCOTT NO.	DESCRIPTION	FIRST DAY COVERS SING	FIRST DAY COVERS INSC. BLK	INSRIP BLK-4	UNUSED F/NH	USED F
671/89	**1996 Issues (18) (No 685)**	....	....	....	**14.20**	....
671	32¢ WFUNA 50th Anniversary	1.75	4.00	3.50	.75	.65
672-73	32¢-60¢ Definitives	2.50	9.00	8.00	2.00	1.60
674-77	32¢ Endangered Species, 4 attached	3.00	4.25	3.50	2.75	2.25
678-82	32¢ City Summit (Habitat II), strip of 5	3.75	5.00	9.00	3.50	3.00
683-84	32¢-50¢ Sport & the Environment	2.50	9.00	8.50	1.95	1.50
685	82¢ Sport & the Environment souvenir sheet	2.50	....	....	2.10	1.95
686-87	32¢-60¢ A Plea for Peace	2.50	9.00	9.00	2.00	1.75
688-89	32¢-60¢ UNICEF 50th Anniversary	2.50	9.00	9.00	2.00	1.75

1997 World Flags

690	*Tadjikistan*	**694**	*Liechtenstein*
691	*Georgia*	**695**	*South Korea*
692	*Armenia*	**696**	*Kazakhstan*
693	*Namibia*	**697**	*Latvia*

SCOTT NO.	DESCRIPTION	FIRST DAY COVERS SING	INSC. BLK	INSRIP BLK-4	UNUSED F/NH	USED F

700-03

1997

SCOTT NO.	DESCRIPTION	FIRST DAY COVERS SING	INSC. BLK	INSRIP BLK-4	UNUSED F/NH	USED F
690-97	1997 World Flags, 8 varieties	12.50	....	24.50	5.75	5.00
698-99	8¢-55¢ Flowers, UN Headquarters	2.25	8.00	8.00	1.85	1.50
700-03	32¢ Endangered Species, 4 attached	3.00	4.25	3.50	2.75	2.25
......	32¢ Earth Summit +5, 4 attached	3.00	4.25	3.50	2.75	2.25
......	$1 Earth Summit +5, souvenir sheet	2.50	....	....	2.25	1.75
......	32¢ Transportation, strip of 5	3.75	5.00	9.00	3.50	3.00
......	32¢-50¢ Tribute to Philately	2.50	9.00	8.50	1.95	1.50
......	32¢-60¢ Terracotta Warriors	2.50	9.00	9.00	2.00	1.75

U.N. Air Post #C1-C23

AIR MAIL ISSUE

C1-2, UC5 · C3-C4, UC1-2 · C5-6, UXC1, UXC3 · C7, UC4

SCOTT NO.	DESCRIPTION	FIRST DAY COVERS SING	FIRST DAY COVERS INSC. BLK	INSRIP BLK-4	UNUSED F/NH	USED F
	1951-77					
C1-C23	**AIR MAILS, complete (23)**	......	......	**38.50**	**7.85**	......
	1951-59					
C1-4	6¢, 10¢, 15¢ & 20¢	24.50	60.00	9.00	2.00	2.00
C5-7	4¢, 5¢ & 7¢ (1957-59)	1.65	4.15	2.25	.55	.45

C8, UXC4 · C9, UC6, UC8 · C10 · C11

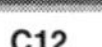

C12 · C13 · C14 · C15, UXC8

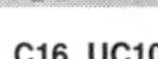

C16, UC10 · C17, UXC10 · C18 · C19, UC11

C20, UXC11 · C21 · C22 · C23

SCOTT NO.	DESCRIPTION	FIRST DAY COVERS SING	FIRST DAY COVERS INSC. BLK	INSRIP BLK-4	UNUSED F/NH	USED F
	1963-77					
C8-12	6¢, 8¢, 13¢, 15¢, & 25¢ (1963-64)	3.25	8.00	7.50	1.65	1.25
C13-14	10¢ & 20¢ (1968-69)	2.00	4.95	3.65	.75	.60
C15-18	9¢, 11¢, 17¢, & 21¢ (1972)	2.40	6.00	5.25	1.15	.95
C19-21	13¢, 18¢, & 26¢ (1974)	2.75	6.95	5.25	1.10	1.00
C22-23	25¢ & 31¢ (1977)	2.50	6.25	5.25	1.10	1.05

U.N. Postal Stationery #U1-U9; UC1-UC5

ENVELOPES AND AIR LETTER SHEETS

U1-U2

SCOTT NO.	DESCRIPTION	FIRST DAY COVER	UNUSED ENTIRE
	1953		
U1	3¢ blue	4.50	1.00
	1958		
U2	4¢ ultramarine	.95	.75

U3

SCOTT NO.	DESCRIPTION	FIRST DAY COVER	UNUSED ENTIRE
	1963		
U3	5¢ multicolored (design #128)	1.00	.30
	1969		
U4	6¢ multicolored (design #128)	.85	.25
	1973		
U5	8¢ multicolored (design #187)	.85	1.00
	1975		
U6	10¢ multicolored (design #250)	.95	.50

U7

SCOTT NO.	DESCRIPTION	FIRST DAY COVER	UNUSED ENTIRE
	1985		
U7	22¢ Strip Bouquet	2.00	9.50

U8

(Surcharge)
U9

SCOTT NO.	DESCRIPTION	FIRST DAY COVER	UNUSED ENTIRE
	1989		
U8	25¢ U.N. Headquarters	2.50	3.00
U9	25¢+4¢ surcharge (U8)	2.00	2.50
	1997		
U10	32¢ Cripticandina (79x38mm) .	1.35	.80
U11	32¢ Cripticandina (89x44mm) .	1.35	.80

AIRMAILS

SCOTT NO.	DESCRIPTION	FIRST DAY COVER	UNUSED ENTIRE
	1952		
UC1	10¢ blue, air letter (design #C3)		8.00
27.50			
	1954		
UC2	10¢ royal blue, white borders aerogramme (design of #C3) ..	......	8.00
	1958		
UC2a	10¢ royal blue, no border (design #C3)	......	7.50

UC3

SCOTT NO.	DESCRIPTION	FIRST DAY COVER	UNUSED ENTIRE
	1959		
UC3	7¢ blue	1.00	2.00
	1960		
UC4	10¢ ultramarine on bluish, letter sheet (design of #C7)	.95	.75
	1961		
UC5	11¢ ultramarine on bluish, letter sheet (design of #C1)	.85	1.00

U.N. Postal Stationery #UC5a-UC19

SCOTT NO.	DESCRIPTION	FIRST DAY COVER	UNUSED ENTIRE
	1965		
UC5a	11¢ dark blue on green, letter sheet (design of #C1)	......	2.25

UC6

SCOTT NO.	DESCRIPTION	FIRST DAY COVER	UNUSED ENTIRE
	1963		
UC6	8¢ multicolored (design #C9) ..	1.00	.75

UC7

SCOTT NO.	DESCRIPTION	FIRST DAY COVER	UNUSED ENTIRE
	1958		
UC7	13¢ shades-blue, letter sheet .	.95	.45
	1969		
UC8	10¢ multicolored (design #C9) ...	.95	.35

UC9

SCOTT NO.	DESCRIPTION	FIRST DAY COVER	UNUSED ENTIRE
	1972		
UC9	15¢ shades-blue, letter sheet ...	.95	.90
	1973		
UC10	11¢ multicolored (design #C16)	.95	.75
	1975		
UC11	13¢ multicolored (design #C19)	1.00	.45
UC12	18¢ multicolored, aerogramme (design of #222)	1.00	.55

UC13

SCOTT NO.	DESCRIPTION	FIRST DAY COVER	UNUSED ENTIRE
	1977		
UC13	22¢ multicolored, aerogramme ..	1.25	.90

UC14

UC16

SCOTT NO.	DESCRIPTION	FIRST DAY COVER	UNUSED ENTIRE
	1982		
UC14	30¢ black, aerogramme	3.00	1.80

(surcharge)
UC17

SCOTT NO.	DESCRIPTION	FIRST DAY COVER	UNUSED ENTIRE
	1988-89		
UC15	30¢ & 6¢ Surcharge on #UC14 .	11.50	35.00
UC16	39¢ U.N. Headquarters aerogramme	2.25	5.00
UC17	39¢+6¢ Surcharge on #UC16 ...	2.25	19.00

UC18

SCOTT NO.	DESCRIPTION	FIRST DAY COVER	UNUSED ENTIRE
	1982		
UC18	45¢ Winged Hand	1.95	2.00

(surcharge)
UC19

SCOTT NO.	DESCRIPTION	FIRST DAY COVER	UNUSED ENTIRE
	1995		
UC19	45¢+5¢ Surcharge on #UC18 .	5.00	7.00

U.N. Postal Stationery #UC20

SCOTT NO.	DESCRIPTION	FIRST DAY COVER	UNUSED ENTIRE

UC20

1997

SCOTT NO.	DESCRIPTION	FIRST DAY COVER	UNUSED ENTIRE
UC20	50¢ Cherry Blossoms	1.65	1.10

U.N. Postal Stationery #UX1-UX19; UXC1-UXC7

POSTAL CARDS

SCOTT NO.	DESCRIPTION	FIRST DAY COVER	UNUSED ENTIRE
	1952		
UX1	2¢ blue on buff (design of #2) .	1.65	.25
	1958		
UX2	3¢ gray olive on buff (design of #2)	.85	.25

UX3

SCOTT NO.	DESCRIPTION	FIRST DAY COVER	UNUSED ENTIRE
	1963		
UX3	4¢ multicolored (design of #125)	.85	.25

UX4

UX5-6

SCOTT NO.	DESCRIPTION	FIRST DAY COVER	UNUSED ENTIRE
	1969		
UX4	5¢ blue & black	.90	.25
	1973		
UX5	6¢ multicolored	.85	.25
	1975		
UX6	8¢ multicolored	1.00	.50

UX7

SCOTT NO.	DESCRIPTION	FIRST DAY COVER	UNUSED ENTIRE
	1977		
UX7	9¢ multicolored	1.00	.75

UX8

SCOTT NO.	DESCRIPTION	FIRST DAY COVER	UNUSED ENTIRE
	1982		
UX8	13¢ multicolored	1.10	.50

UX9

SCOTT NO.	DESCRIPTION	FIRST DAY COVER	UNUSED ENTIRE
	1989		
UX9	15¢ UN Complex	1.10	.85
UX10	15¢ UN Complex with trees	1.10	.85
UX11	15¢ Flags	1.10	.85
UX12	15¢ General Assembly	1.10	.85
UX13	15¢ UN Complex from East River	1.10	.85
UX14	36¢ UN Complex and Flags	1.50	1.20
UX15	36¢ Flags	1.50	1.20
UX16	36¢ UN Complex at Dusk	1.50	1.20
UX17	36¢ Security Council	1.50	1.20
UX18	36¢ UN Complex and Sculpture	1.50	1.20
UX19	40¢ UN Headquarters	1.60	1.35

AIR MAILS

SCOTT NO.	DESCRIPTION	FIRST DAY COVER	UNUSED ENTIRE
	1957		
UXC1	4¢ maroon on buff (design of #C5)	.60	.25

(surcharge)
UXC2

UXC4

SCOTT NO.	DESCRIPTION	FIRST DAY COVER	UNUSED ENTIRE
	1959		
UXC2	4¢ & 1¢ (on UXC1)	......	.75
UXC3	5¢ crimson on buff (design of #C6)	.70	1.00
UXC4	6¢ black & blue (design of #C8)	.85	.50

UXC5-6

SCOTT NO.	DESCRIPTION	FIRST DAY COVER	UNUSED ENTIRE
	1965		
UXC5	11¢ multicolored	1.00	.50
	1968		
UXC6	13¢ yellow & green	.95	.50

UXC7, UXC9

SCOTT NO.	DESCRIPTION	FIRST DAY COVER	UNUSED ENTIRE
	1969		
UXC7	8¢ multicolored	.90	.40

U.N. Postal Stationery #UXC8-UXC12

SCOTT NO.	DESCRIPTION	FIRST DAY COVER	UNUSED ENTIRE
	1972		
UXC8	9¢ multicolored (design of #C15)	1.00	.50
UXC9	15¢ multicolored	1.00	.55
	1975		
UXC10	11¢ shades—blue (design of #C17)	1.00	.40
UXC11	18¢ multicolored (design of #C20)	1.20	.55

UXC12

SCOTT NO.	DESCRIPTION	FIRST DAY COVER	UNUSED ENTIRE
	1982		
UXC12	28¢ multicolored	1.40	.70

U.N. Geneva #1-45

UNITED NATIONS; OFFICES IN GENEVA, SWITZERLAND

Denominations in Swiss Currency

NOTE: Unless illustrated, designs can be assumed to be similar to the equivalent New York or Vienna issues

4

SCOTT NO.	DESCRIPTION	FIRST DAY COVERS SING	FIRST DAY COVERS INSC. BLK	INSCRIP BLK-4	UNUSED F/NH	USED F
	1969-70					
1-14	5¢ to 10fr Definitives	45.00	110.00	50.00	11.00	10.00
	1971					
15-21	**1971 Issues, complete (7)**	......	......	......	**3.80**	......
15	30¢ Peaceful Uses Sea Bed	.95	2.40	1.40	.30	.25
16	50¢ Support for Refugees	1.10	2.75	1.95	.45	.40
17	50¢ World Food Programme	1.40	3.50	2.65	.55	.45
18	75¢ U.P.U. Building	2.75	6.85	4.00	.80	.80
19-20	30¢ & 50¢ Anti-Discrimination	2.25	5.65	4.25	.90	.60
21	1.10fr International School	3.65	9.00	4.75	1.00	1.15

22

SCOTT NO.	DESCRIPTION	FIRST DAY COVERS SING	FIRST DAY COVERS INSC. BLK	INSCRIP BLK-4	UNUSED F/NH	USED F
	1972					
22-29	**1972 Issues, complete (8)**	......	......	......	**5.95**	......
22	40¢ Definitive	1.10	2.75	1.90	.40	.35
23	40¢ Non Proliferation	2.15	5.40	3.50	.75	.75
24	80¢ World Health Day	2.15	5.40	3.75	.85	.85
25-26	40¢ & 80¢ Environment	3.75	9.50	7.95	1.75	1.40
27	1.10fr Economic Committee Europe	3.25	8.15	7.50	1.60	1.35
28-29	40¢ & 80¢ Art—Sert Ceiling	3.50	8.75	8.45	1.85	1.65
	1973					
30-36	**1973 Issues, complete (6)**	......	......	......	**4.60**	......
30-31	60¢ & 1.10fr Disarmament Decade	3.50	8.75	7.00	1.50	1.50
32	60¢ Drug Abuse	2.00	5.00	2.65	.60	.65
33	80¢ Volunteer	2.50	6.25	3.50	.75	.75
34	60¢ Namibia	2.05	5.15	2.75	.60	.75
35-36	40¢ & 80¢ Human Rights	2.65	6.65	6.50	1.40	1.00
	1974					
37-45	**1974 Issues, complete (9)**	......	......	......	**6.05**	......
37-38	60¢ & 80¢ ILO Headquarters	2.75	6.85	4.95	1.10	1.00
39-40	30¢ & 60¢ U.P.U. Centenary	2.25	5.65	4.95	1.10	.90
41-42	60¢ & 1fr Brazil Peace Mural	3.00	7.50	7.00	1.50	1.45
43-44	60¢ & 80¢ World Population Year	2.50	6.25	6.25	1.35	1.25
45	1.30fr Law of the Sea	2.25	5.65	5.95	1.30	1.15

U.N. Geneva #46-81

SCOTT NO.	DESCRIPTION	FIRST DAY COVERS SING	INSC. BLK	INSCRIP BLK-4	UNUSED F/NH	USED F
		1975				
46/56	**1975 Issues, (10) (No #52)**	......	......	......	**8.45**	......
46-47	60¢ & 90¢ Peaceful Use of Space ...	2.40	6.00	6.45	1.40	1.30
48-49	60¢ & 90¢ International Women's Year	2.75	6.85	7.50	1.60	1.40
50-51	60¢ & 90¢ 30th Anniversary	2.25	5.65	6.45	1.40	1.25
52	same, souvenir sheet	2.50	......	......	1.50	1.40
53-54	50¢ & 1.30fr Namibia	2.50	6.25	7.45	1.60	1.40
55-56	60¢ & 70¢ Peacekeeping	2.10	5.25	6.45	1.40	1.20

61 65 67 69 71

SCOTT NO.	DESCRIPTION	FIRST DAY COVERS SING	INSC. BLK	INSCRIP BLK-4	UNUSED F/NH	USED F
		1976				
57-63	**1976 Issues, (7)**	......	......	......	**8.95**	......
57	90¢ World Federation	1.80	4.50	4.45	1.00	.90
58	1.10fr Conference T.& D.	2.10	5.25	4.75	1.05	1.00
59-60	40¢ & 1.50fr Human Settlement	3.00	7.50	7.75	1.65	1.50
61-62	80¢ & 1.10fr Postal Administration ...	12.00	29.50	22.50	5.00	4.50
63	70¢ World Food Council	1.40	3.50	3.50	.75	.65
		1977				
64-72	**1977 Issues, complete (9)**	......	......	......	**6.95**	......
64	80¢ WIPO	1.40	3.50	3.75	.80	.70
65-66	80¢ & 1.10fr Water Conference	3.00	7.50	7.75	1.65	1.45
67-68	80¢ & 1.10fr Security Council	3.00	7.50	7.75	1.65	1.45
69-70	40¢ & 1.10fr Combat Racism	2.50	6.25	7.25	1.50	1.40
71-72	80¢ & 1.10fr Atomic Energy	3.00	7.50	7.75	1.65	1.45

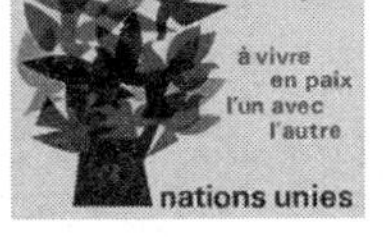

73

74

77

79

SCOTT NO.	DESCRIPTION	FIRST DAY COVERS SING	INSC. BLK	INSCRIP BLK-4	UNUSED F/NH	USED F
		1978				
73-81	**1978 Issues, complete (9)**	......	......	**30.95**	**6.50**	......
73	35¢ Definitive	.95	2.40	2.20	.45	.40
74-75	80¢ & 1.10fr Smallpox Eradication ...	2.95	7.50	7.70	1.65	1.45
76	80¢ Namibia	1.50	3.75	4.75	.90	.80
77-78	70¢ & 80¢ ICAO	2.25	5.65	6.25	1.35	1.20
79-80	70¢ & 1.10fr General Assembly	3.00	7.50	7.70	1.65	1.35
81	80¢ TCDC	1.40	3.50	3.95	.85	.75

U.N. Geneva #82-112

82

84

87

90

1979

SCOTT NO.	DESCRIPTION	FIRST DAY COVERS SING	FIRST DAY COVERS INSC. BLK	INSCRIP BLK-4	UNUSED F/NH	USED F
82-88	**1979 Issues, complete (7)**	......	......	......	**6.55**	......
82-83	80¢ & 1.50fr UNDRO	3.10	7.75	9.75	2.15	1.95
84-85	80¢ & 1.10fr I.Y.C.	4.75	11.85	9.50	2.00	1.40
86	1.10fr Namibia	1.90	4.75	4.75	1.05	.95
87-88	80¢ & 1.10fr Court of Justice	3.00	7.50	7.95	1.70	1.55

1980

SCOTT NO.	DESCRIPTION	FIRST DAY COVERS SING	FIRST DAY COVERS INSC. BLK	INSCRIP BLK-4	UNUSED F/NH	USED F
89/97	**1980 Issues, (8) (No #95)**	......	......	......	**5.15**	......
89	80¢ Economics	1.50	3.75	3.95	.85	.75
90-91	40¢ & 70¢ Decade for Women	1.95	4.95	5.25	1.15	1.00
92	1.10fr Peacekeeping	1.85	4.65	5.25	1.15	1.00

93

97

104

105

106

SCOTT NO.	DESCRIPTION	FIRST DAY COVERS SING	FIRST DAY COVERS INSC. BLK	INSCRIP BLK-4	UNUSED F/NH	USED F
93-94	40¢ & 70¢ 35th Anniversary	2.00	5.00	5.15	1.15	1.00
95	Same, Souvenir Sheet	2.75	......	......	1.40	1.25
96-97	40¢ & 70¢ Economic & Social Council	1.85	4.65	5.15	1.15	1.00

1981

SCOTT NO.	DESCRIPTION	FIRST DAY COVERS SING	FIRST DAY COVERS INSC. BLK	INSCRIP BLK-4	UNUSED F/NH	USED F
98-104	**1981 Issues, complete (7)**	......	......	......	**5.50**	......
98	80¢ Palestinian People	1.70	4.25	4.00	.85	.70
99-100	40¢ & 1.50fr Disabled People	2.75	6.85	7.65	1.70	1.45
101	80¢ Fresco	1.50	3.75	4.50	.95	.75
102	1.10fr Sources of Energy	1.50	3.75	5.25	1.15	1.00
103-04	40¢ & 70¢ Conservation	1.75	4.50	5.25	1.15	1.00

107

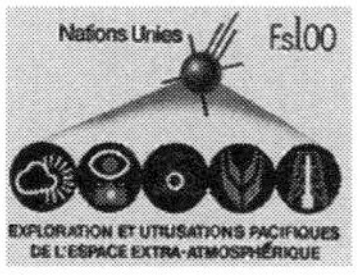

110

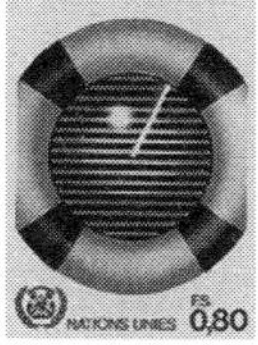

115

118

119

1982

SCOTT NO.	DESCRIPTION	FIRST DAY COVERS SING	FIRST DAY COVERS INSC. BLK	INSCRIP BLK-4	UNUSED F/NH	USED F
105-12	**1982 Issues, complete (8)**	......	......	......	**6.45**	......
105-06	30¢ & 1fr Definitives	2.10	5.25	6.50	1.40	1.40
107-08	40¢ & 1.20fr Human Environment	2.40	6.00	7.65	1.70	1.45
109-10	80¢ & 1fr Space Exploration	2.65	6.65	8.50	1.75	1.50
111-12	40¢ & 1.50fr Conservation	2.75	6.95	8.95	1.95	1.50

U.N. Geneva #113-145

SCOTT NO.	DESCRIPTION	FIRST DAY COVERS SING	FIRST DAY COVERS INSC. BLK	INSCRIP BLK-4	UNUSED F/NH	USED F
			1983			
113-20	**1983 Issues, complete (8)**	......	......	......	**8.35**	......
113	1.20fr World Communications	1.75	4.40	7.25	1.55	1.15
114-15	40¢ & 80¢ Safety at Sea	1.75	4.40	7.25	1.55	1.15
116	1.50fr World Food Program	2.25	5.65	8.00	1.70	1.45
117-18	80¢ & 1.10fr Trade & Development	2.75	6.95	8.95	1.95	1.70
119-20	40¢ & 1.20fr Human Rights	3.50	8.75	10.50	2.05	1.80

120

122

123

124

SCOTT NO.	DESCRIPTION	FIRST DAY COVERS SING	FIRST DAY COVERS INSC. BLK	INSCRIP BLK-4	UNUSED F/NH	USED F
			1984			
121-28	**1984 Issues, complete (8)**	......	......	......	**9.20**	......
121	1. 20fr Population	1.75	4.50	10.15	1.50	1.25
122-23	50¢ & 80¢ Food Day	1.75	4.50	8.50	1.75	1.25
124-25	50¢ & 70¢ Heritage	1.75	4.50	10.25	2.25	1.25

125

126

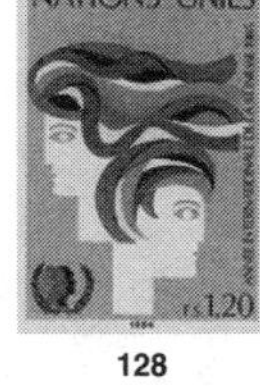

127

130

128

SCOTT NO.	DESCRIPTION	FIRST DAY COVERS SING	FIRST DAY COVERS INSC. BLK	INSCRIP BLK-4	UNUSED F/NH	USED F
126-27	35¢ & 1.50fr Future for Refugees	2.75	6.95	10.50	2.25	1.75
128	1.20fr Youth Year	1.75	4.50	8.95	1.95	1.25
			1985			
129/39	**1985 Issues, (10) (No #137)**	......	......	......	**11.50**	
129-30	80¢-1.20fr Turin Centre	2.75	6.95	12.95	2.75	1.75
131-32	50¢-80¢ U.N. University	2.00	5.00	8.95	1.95	1.25
133-34	20¢-1.20fr Definitives	2.25	5.65	9.75	2.10	1.25
135-36	50¢-70¢ 40th Anniversary	2.00	5.80	8.95	1.95	1.25
137	same, souvenir sheet	2.75	......	......	2.25	1.35
138-39	50¢-1.20fr Child Survival	5.75	14.50	15.25	3.40	2.50

133

134

145

148

SCOTT NO.	DESCRIPTION	FIRST DAY COVERS SING	FIRST DAY COVERS INSC. BLK	INSCRIP BLK-4	UNUSED F/NH	USED F
			1986			
140-49	**1986 Issues (10)**	......	......	......	**17.25**	......
140	1.40fr Africa in Crisis	2.00	5.00	11.00	2.50	1.25
141-44	35¢ Development, 4 varieties, attached	2.00	2.75	12.00	10.50	5.00
145	5¢ Definitive	1.10	2.75	.85	.20	.15

U.N. Geneva #146-192

149

152

153

164

178

SCOTT NO.	DESCRIPTION	FIRST DAY COVERS SING	INSC. BLK	INSCRIP BLK-4	UNUSED F/NH	USED F
146-47	50¢ & 80¢ Philately	1.85	4.65	9.50	2.00	.95
148-49	45¢ & 1.40fr Peace Year	2.75	6.95	13.50	3.00	1.50
150	35¢-70¢ WFUNA, souvenir sheet	2.75	......	......	5.50	2.75
	1987					
151-61	**1987 Issues (11)**	......	......	......	**12.75**	......
151	1.40fr Trygve Lie	2.00	5.00	10.15	2.00	1.75
152-53	90¢-1.40fr Definitive	3.50	8.75	13.00	2.00	1.75
154-55	50¢-90¢ Shelter Homeless	2.00	5.00	9.50	1.95	1.75
156-57	80¢-1.20fr Anti-Drug Campaign	2.75	6.95	13.00	2.00	1.75
158-59	35¢-50¢ United Nations Day	3.50	8.75	8.50	1.50	1.25
160-61	90¢-1.70fr Child Immunization	1.85	4.65	19.50	4.00	3.50
	1988					
162/172	**1988 Issues, (8) (No #165-66, 172)**	......	......	......	**9.00**	......
162-63	35¢-1.40fr World without Hunger	2.50	6.25	13.00	2.75	2.00
164	50¢ For a Better World	1.25	3.15	4.00	.85	.75
				Sheetlets		
165-66	50¢-1.10fr Forest Conservation (set of 6, includes NY and Vienna)	15.00	40.00	130.00	27.50	25.00
167-68	80¢-90¢ Volunteer Day	2.50	6.25	12.00	2.40	2.00
169-70	50¢-1.40fr Health in Sports	2.75	6.95	13.50	2.25	2.00
171	90¢ Human Rights 40th Anniversary	2.00	5.00	7.00	1.25	1.00
172	2fr Human Rights 40th Anniversary souvenir sheet	2.75	....	....	3.25	3.00

183

184

185

179

SCOTT NO.	DESCRIPTION	FIRST DAY COVERS SING	INSC. BLK	INSCRIP BLK-4	UNUSED F/NH	USED F
	1989					
173-81	**1989 Issues (9)**	......	......	....	**17.70**	....
173-74	80¢ & 1.40fr. World Bank	2.75	6.95	18.50	4.00	3.00
175	90¢ Nobel Peace Prize	1.50	3.75	8.00	1.40	1.10
176-77	90¢ & 1.10fr World Weather Watch	2.75	6.95	18.50	3.75	2.00
178-79	50¢ & 2fr UN Offices in Vienna	4.00	10.00	20.00	4.50	4.25
				Sheetlets (12)		
180-81	35¢ & 80¢ Human Rights 40th Ann. (strips of 3 w/tabs)	1.85	4.65	24.00	5.00	....
	1990					
182/94	**1990 Issues, No #190 (12)**	......	......	....	**27.50**	......
182	1.50fr International Trade	2.15	5.40	14.00	3.00	2.50
183	5fr Definitive	7.75	19.50	33.50	6.00	5.00
184-85	50¢ & 80¢ SIDA (AIDS)	2.15	5.50	14.00	3.25	2.75
186-87	90¢ & 1.40fr Medicinal Plants	3.60	9.00	18.00	3.50	3.00
188-89	90¢ & 1.10fr Anniversary of U.N	3.00	7.50	18.50	3.50	3.00
190	same, souvenir sheet	3.00	....	......	5.00	4.50
191-92	50¢ & 2fr Crime Prevention	4.15	10.50	19.50	3.75	3.25

U.N. Geneva #193-243

SCOTT NO.	DESCRIPTION	FIRST DAY COVERS SING	FIRST DAY COVERS INSC. BLK	INSCRIP BLK-4	UNUSED F/NH	USED F
				Sheetlets (12)		
193-94	35¢ & 90¢ Human Rights .... (strips of 3 w/tabs)	1.95	4.95	27.00	6.00	....

201 202 203 204

205 206 213

1991

SCOTT NO.	DESCRIPTION	FIRST DAY COVERS SING	FIRST DAY COVERS INSC. BLK	INSCRIP BLK-4	UNUSED F/NH	USED F
195-210	**1991 Issues (17) ....**	......	......	.....	**29.95**	......
195-98	90¢ Econ. Comm. for Europe, 4 varieties, attached	5.75	6.75	7.75	5.50	4.50
199-200	70¢ & 90¢ Namibia—A New Nation .	3.85	9.60	15.00	3.25	3.00
201-02	80¢ & 1.50fr Definitives	5.00	12.50	18.50	4.00	3.50
203-04	80¢ & 1.10fr Children's Rights	4.50	11.25	17.50	3.50	3.25
205-06	80¢ & 1.40fr Banning of Chemical Weapons	5.00	12.50	19.50	3.75	3.25
207-08	50¢ & 1.60fr 40th Anniv. of the UNPA	4.75	11.95	19.50	3.75	3.25
				Sheetlets (12)		
209-10	50¢ & 90¢ Human Rights (strips of 3 w/tabs)	2.75	7.50	32.50	7.00	....

1992

SCOTT NO.	DESCRIPTION	FIRST DAY COVERS SING	FIRST DAY COVERS INSC. BLK	INSCRIP BLK-4	UNUSED F/NH	USED F
211-25	**1992 Issues (15) ....**	......	......	......	**29.25**	......
211-12	50¢-1.10fr. World Heritage—UNESCO	3.60	9.00	18.75	3.75	3.50
213	3fr Definitive	6.00	15.00	21.25	3.75	3.50
214-15	80¢ Clean Oceans, 2 varieties, attached	2.75	5.35	7.50	2.50	2.00
216-19	75¢ Earth Summit, 4 varieties, attached	4.00	4.95	5.50	4.50	4.00
220-21	1.10fr Mission to Planet Earth, 2 varieties, attached	4.00	6.95	12.50	5.00	4.50
222-23	90¢-1.60fr Science and Technology	4.75	11.75	18.00	4.00	3.50
				Sheetlets (12)		
224-25	50¢-90¢ Human Rights (strips of 3 w/tabs	2.75	6.50	32.50	7.25	....

1993

SCOTT NO.	DESCRIPTION	FIRST DAY COVERS SING	FIRST DAY COVERS INSC. BLK	INSCRIP BLK-4	UNUSED F/NH	USED F
226-43	**1993 Issues (18) ....**	......	......	......	**27.00**	......
226-27	50¢-1.60fr Aging	3.60	9.00	23.50	4.00	3.50
228-31	80¢ Endangered Species, 4 attached	4.00	5.00	6.50	5.00	4.50
232-33	60¢-1fr Healthy Environment	3.00	8.00	11.00	2.50	2.00
				Sheetlets (12)		
234-35	50¢-90¢ Human Rights (strips of 3 w/tabs)	3.00	7.00	30.00	7.00	5.00
236-39	60¢ Peace, 4 attached	3.50	4.50	5.00	4.00	3.50
240-43	1.10fr Environment—Climate, strip of 4	3.50	8.00	14.00(8)	6.00	5.00

255

256

U.N. Geneva #244-276

SCOTT NO.	DESCRIPTION	FIRST DAY COVERS SING	FIRST DAY COVERS INSC. BLK	INSCRIP BLK-4	UNUSED F/NH	USED F
	1994					
244-61	**1994 Issues (18)**	....	....	....	**21.25**	....
244-45	80¢-1fr Intl. Year of the Family	3.50	12.50	12.50	3.25	3.00
246-49	80¢ Endangered Species, 4 attached	4.50	5.00	4.75	4.25	4.00
250	1.20fr Refugees	2.50	9.25	9.00	2.00	4.85
251-54	60¢ Intl. Decade for Natural Disaster Reduction, 4 attached	3.50	4.25	3.75	3.25	3.00
255-57	60¢-1.80fr Definitives (3)	5.00	17.50	17.50	4.50	4.00
258-59	60¢-80¢ Population and Development	2.75	10.00	10.00	2.35	2.00
260-61	80¢-1fr Development through Partnership	3.50	12.50	12.50	2.75	2.50
	1995					
262/75	**1995 Issues (13) (No #272)**	....	....	....	**25.00**	....
262	80¢ 50th Anniversary of the UN	1.75	6.50	6.00	1.25	1.00
263	1fr Social Summit	2.25	7.50	7.00	1.95	1.75
264-67	80¢ Endangered Species, 4 attached	4.50	5.00	7.00	6.50	6.00
268-69	80¢-1fr Youth: Our Future	3.50	12.50	13.50	3.25	3.00
270-71	60¢-1.80fr 50th Anniversary of the UN	4.75	12.50	15.50	4.00	3.50
272	2.40fr 50th Anniversary of the UN, souvenir sheet	4.50	....	....	4.25	4.00
273-74	60¢-1fr 4th Conference on Women ..	3.00	10.00	13.00	2.95	2.75
275	30¢ 50th Anniversary, min. sheet of 12	....	....	....	6.50	....
276	same, souvenir booklet of 4 panes of 3	....	....	....	7.00	....

277

278

279

280-83

284-88

291

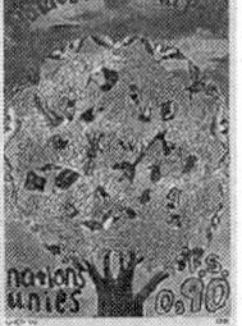

292

293

294

295

1996

SCOTT NO.	DESCRIPTION	FIRST DAY COVERS SING	FIRST DAY COVERS INSC. BLK	INSCRIP BLK-4	UNUSED F/NH	USED F
277/95	**1996 Issues (18) (No 291) ....**	....	....	....	**26.35**	....
277	80¢ WFUNA 50th Anniversary	1.75	6.50	6.00	1.25	1.00
278-79	40¢-70¢ Definitives	2.75	10.00	10.50	2.25	2.00
280-83	80¢ Endangered Species, 4 attached	4.50	5.00	7.00	6.50	6.00
284-88	80¢ City Summit (Habitat II), strip of 5	5.00	15.00	17.00	8.00	7.00
289-90	70¢-1.10fr Sport & the Environment	3.50	12.50	13.50	3.25	3.00
291	1.80fr Sport & the Environment souvenir sheet	3.50	....	....	3.75	3.00
292-93	80¢-1fr A Plea for Peace	3.50	12.50	13.50	3.25	3.00
294-95	80¢-1fr UNICEF 50th Anniversary ...	3.50	12.50	13.50	3.25	3.00

298-301

1997

SCOTT NO.	DESCRIPTION	FIRST DAY COVERS SING	FIRST DAY COVERS INSC. BLK	INSCRIP BLK-4	UNUSED F/NH	USED F
296-97	10¢-1.10fr Definitives	2.75	10.00	10.75	2.35	2.00
298-301	80¢ Endangered Speicies, 4 attached	4.50	5.00	7.00	6.50	6.00
......	45¢ Earth Summit +5, 4 attached	2.50	2.75	4.00	3.25	2.80
......	1.10fr Earth Summit, souvenir sheet	2.40	....	....	2.00	1.60
......	70¢ Transportation, strip of 5	4.50	13.50	15.50	7.00	6.00
......	70¢-1.10 fr Tribute to Philately	3.50	12.50	13.50	3.25	3.00
......	45¢-70¢ Terracotta Warriors	2.75	10.00	10.50	2.25	2.00

U.N. Geneva #UC1; UX1-UX10

AIR LETTER SHEETS & POSTAL CARDS

SCOTT NO.	DESCRIPTION	FIRST DAY COVERS	UNUSED ENTIRE
	1969		
UC1	65¢ ultramarine & light blue .	4.50	2.00
	1969		
UX1	20¢ olive green & black	1.65	.35
UX2	30¢ violet blue, blue, light & dark green	1.65	.35

UX3

UX4

SCOTT NO.	DESCRIPTION	FIRST DAY COVERS	UNUSED ENTIRE
	1977		
UX3	40¢ multicolored	1.25	.55
UX4	70¢ multicolored	1.65	1.75

UX5

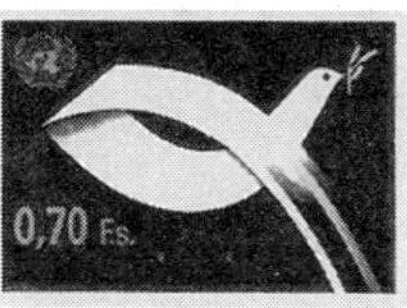

UX6

SCOTT NO.	DESCRIPTION	FIRST DAY COVERS	UNUSED ENTIRE
	1985		
UX5	50¢ Six Languages	1.25	1.00
UX6	70¢ Birds & Rainbow	1.65	4.75

UX7

SCOTT NO.	DESCRIPTION	FIRST DAY COVERS	UNUSED ENTIRE
	1986		
UX7	70¢+10¢ Surcharge on UX6	8.00	2.50
	1992		
UX8	90¢ U.N. Buildings	1.75	2.00

UX10

SCOTT NO.	DESCRIPTION	FIRST DAY COVERS	UNUSED ENTIRE
	1993		
UX9	50¢ + 10¢ Surcharge on UX5	2.00	1.60
UX10	80¢ Postal Card	1.75	3.00

U.N. Vienna #1-29
UNITED NATIONS: OFFICES IN VIENNA, AUSTRIA
Denominations in Austrian Currency

NOTE: Unless illustrated, designs can be assumed to be similar to the equivalent New York or Geneva issue

3 5 9 19 24

SCOTT NO.	DESCRIPTION	FIRST DAY COVERS SING	INSC. BLK	INSCRIP BLK-4	UNUSED F/NH	USED F
	1979					
1-6	50g to 10s Definitives	6.75	16.95	10.00	2.25	2.50
	1980					
7/16	**1980 Issues, (9) (No #14)**	......	......	......	**6.35**	.....
7	4s International Economic Order	3.75	9.50	11.50	1.25	1.20
8	2.50s International Economic Definitive	.85	2.15	(B)1.75	.40	.30
9-10	4s & 6s Decade for Women	3.10	7.75	6.50	1.25	1.40
11	6s Peacekeeping	1.95	4.85	5.25	1.15	1.05
12-13	4s & 6s 35th Anniversary	3.15	7.85	6.50	1.25	1.40
14	same, souvenir sheet	3.85	......	......	1.40	1.40
15-16	4s & 6s Economic and Social Council	2.35	5.85	6.50	1.40	1.20
	1981					
17-23	**1981 Issues, complete (7)**	......	......	......	**4.90**	......
17	4s Palestinian People	1.55	3.85	3.75	.85	.75
18-19	4s & 6s Disabled Persons	2.40	6.00	5.50	1.25	1.15
20	6s Fresco	1.45	3.65	3.45	.80	.75
21	7.50s Sources of Energy	1.95	4.85	3.95	.85	.70
22-23	5s & 7s Volunteers Program	2.75	6.85	6.75	1.40	1.25
	1982					
24-29	**1982 Issues, complete (6)**	......	......	......	**4.85**	......
24	3s Definitive	.85	2.15	3.00	.65	.45
25-26	5s & 7s Human Environment	2.50	6.25	9.00	1.95	1.40
27	5s Space Exploration	1.25	3.15	3.95	.85	.70
28-29	5s & 7s Nature Conservation	2.50	6.25	7.75	1.65	1.40

37

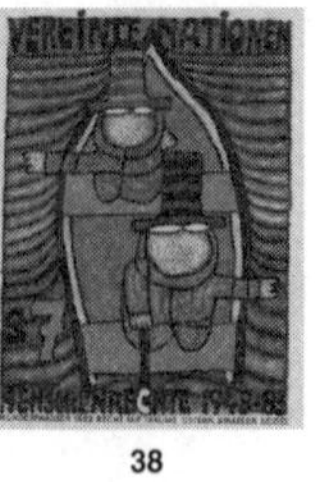
38

40

41

42

43

U.N. Vienna #30-77

SCOTT NO.	DESCRIPTION	FIRST DAY COVERS SING	INSC. BLK	INSCRIP BLK-4	UNUSED F/NH	USED F
	1983					
30-38	**1983 Issues, complete (9)**	......	......	......	**7.00**	......
30	4s World Communications	.85	2.15	3.95	.85	.55
31-32	4s & 6s Safety at Sea	2.15	5.35	6.15	1.40	1.25
33-34	5s & 7s World Food Program	2.60	6.50	4.45	1.65	1.40
35-36	4s & 8.50s Trade & Develop.	2.75	6.95	8.95	1.95	1.55
37-38	5s & 7s Human Rights	3.15	7.85	8.95	1.95	1.45

44 45 46 50 51

SCOTT NO.	DESCRIPTION	FIRST DAY COVERS SING	INSC. BLK	INSCRIP BLK-4	UNUSED F/NH	USED F
	1984					
39-47	**1984 Issues, complete (9)**	....	....	......	**8.55**	....
39	7s Population	1.40	3.50	4.50	1.00	.95
40-41	4.50s & 6s Food Day	1.85	4.65	7.25	1.50	1.50
42-43	3.50s & 15s Heritage	3.50	8.75	10.50	2.25	2.25
44-45	4.50s & 8.50s Future for Refugees	2.25	5.65	10.50	2.25	1.75
46-47	3.50s & 6.50s Youth Year	1.80	4.50	9.00	2.00	1.65
	1985					
48/56	**1985 Issues, (8) (No #54)**	......	......	......	**10.90**	......
48	7.50s I.L.O. Turin Centre	1.25	3.15	6.45	1.40	1.00
49	8.50s U.N. University	1.35	3.40	6.95	1.50	1.10
50-51	4.50s & 15s Definitives	3.15	7.95	13.75	3.25	2.35
52-53	6.50s & 8.50s 40th Anniversary	2.50	6.25	10.00	2.35	2.00
54	Same, Souvenir Sheet	3.25	......	......	3.00	2.50
55-56	4s-6s Child Survival	2.15	5.40	14.00	3.00	1.70

64 72 73

SCOTT NO.	DESCRIPTION	FIRST DAY COVERS SING	INSC. BLK	INSCRIP BLK-4	UNUSED F/NH	USED F
	1986					
57-65	**1986 Issues (9)**	......	......	......	**17.00**	......
57	8s Africa in Crisis	1.35	3.40	7.50	1.50	.90
58-61	4.50s Development, 4 varieties, attached	3.05	7.65	13.00	12.00	2.25
62-63	3.50s & 6.50s Philately	1.95	4.95	9.75	2.00	1.15
64-65	5s & 6s Peace Year	2.25	5.65	12.00	2.50	1.95
66	4s to 7s WFUNA, souvenir sheet	3.05	......	......	5.50	4.00
	1987					
67-77	**1987 Issues (11)**	......	......	......	**13.40**	......
67	8s Trygve Lie	1.35	3.40	7.50	1.10	1.00
68-69	4s & 9.50s Shelter Homeless	2.35	5.95	11.00	2.25	2.00
70-71	5s & 8s Anti-Drug Campaign	2.25	5.65	10.25	2.25	2.00
72-73	2s & 17s Definitives	3.45	8.65	16.00	2.75	2.25
74-75	5s & 6s United Nations Day	2.25	5.65	12.00	2.75	2.00
76-77	4s & 9.50s Child Immunization	2.35	5.95	14.00	3.00	2.50

U.N. Vienna #78-109

SCOTT NO.	DESCRIPTION	FIRST DAY COVERS SING	INSC. BLK	INSCRIP BLK-4	UNUSED F/NH	USED F
	1988					
78/86	**1988 Issues, (7) (No #80-81, 87) ....**	....	....	....	**8.30**	....
78-79	4s & 6s World Without Hunger	2.25	5.65	9.50	2.00	1.50
				Sheetlets		
80-81	4s & 5s Forest Conservation .... (set of 6, includes NY and Geneva)	22.50	65.00	130.00	27.50	25.00
82-83	6s & 7.50s Volunteer Day	2.35	5.95	14.00	2.75	2.00
84-85	6s & 8s Health in Sports	2.50	6.25	14.50	3.25	2.00
86	5s Human Rights 40th Anniversary	1.00	2.50	7.50	1.50	.60
87	11s Human Rights 40th Anniversary souvenir sheet	1.75	....	....	3.00	2.25

93

94

98

116

SCOTT NO.	DESCRIPTION	FIRST DAY COVERS SING	INSC. BLK	INSCRIP BLK-4	UNUSED F/NH	USED F
	1989					
88-96	**1989 Issues (9) ....**	....	....	....	**19.25**	....
88-89	5.50s & 8s World Bank.	2.35	5.95	16.50	3.50	3.00
90	6s Nobel Peace Prize	1.25	3.15	6.75	1.35	1.00
91-92	4s & 9.50s World Weather Watch	2.35	5.95	19.50	4.00	3.50
93-94	5s & 7.50s UN Office in Vienna	2.25	5.65	24.00	5.50	5.00
				Sheetlets(12)		
95-96	4s & 6s Human Rights, 40th Ann. (strips of 3 w/tabs)	2.25	5.65	28.00	6.00	....
	1990					
97/109	**1990 Issues, (12) (No #105) ....**	....	....	....	**23.00**	....
97	12s Int'l. Trade Center	2.15	5.40	10.50	2.00	1.50
98	1.50s Definitive	.85	2.15	1.80	.40	.30
99-100	5s & 11s AIDS	2.75	6.95	17.00	3.50	3.00
101-02	4.50s & 9.50s Medicinal Plants	2.50	6.25	18.00	3.50	3.00
103-04	7s & 9s 45th Anniv. of U.N.	2.75	6.95	18.00	4.00	3.50
105	same, souvenir sheet	2.75	......	......	4.50	4.00
106-07	6s & 8s Crime Prevention	2.50	6.25	18.00	4.00	3.25
				Sheetlets(12)		
108-09	4.50s & 7s Human Rights (strips of 3 w/tabs)	2.35	5.95	32.00	7.00	....

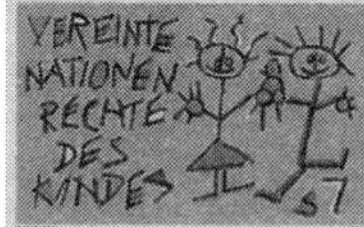

117

118

119

120

137

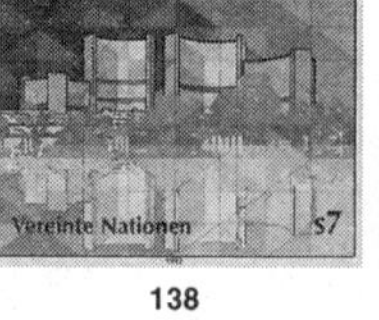

138

U.N. Vienna #110-177

1991

SCOTT NO.	DESCRIPTION	FIRST DAY COVERS SING	FIRST DAY COVERS INSC. BLK	INSCRIP BLK-4	UNUSED F/NH	USED F
110-24	**1991 Issues, (15)**	....	....	....	**28.95**	....
110-13	5s Econ. Comm. for Europe, 4 varieties, attached	5.50	13.75	6.50	5.00	4.50
114-15	6s & 9.50s Namibia—A New Nation	4.50	11.25	19.50	4.00	3.50
116	20s Definitive Issue	4.75	11.85	19.50	3.75	3.00
117-18	7s & 9s Children's Rights	4.50	11.25	14.50	3.25	3.00
119-20	5s & 10s Chemical Weapons	4.75	11.95	15.00	3.50	3.00
121-22	5s & 8s 40th Anniv. of U.N.P.A.	4.15	10.35	15.00	3.50	3.00
				Sheetlets(12)		
123-24	4.50s & 7s Human Rights (strips of 3 w/tabs)	2.50	6.25	34.50	7.50	....

1992

SCOTT NO.	DESCRIPTION	FIRST DAY COVERS SING	FIRST DAY COVERS INSC. BLK	INSCRIP BLK-4	UNUSED F/NH	USED F
125-40	**1992 Issues, (17)**	....	....	....	**30.00**	....
125-26	5s-9s World Heritage—UNESCO	4.25	10.75	15.00	3.25	3.00
127-28	7s Clean Oceans, 2 varieties, attached	4.25	5.50	7.50	3.00	2.50
129-32	5.50s Earth Summit, 4 varieties, attached	4.25	5.25	4.95	5.50	5.00
133-34	10s Mission to Planet Earth, 2 varieties, attached	4.25	5.50	13.00	6.00	5.50
135-36	5.50s-7s Science & Technology	4.00	10.25	13.00	2.75	2.25
137-38	5.50s-7s Definitives	4.00	10.25	13.00	2.75	2.50
				Sheetlets (12)		
139-40	6s-10s Human Rights (strips of 3 w/tabs)	2.75	6.95	36.00	8.50	....

149

167

168

169

1993

SCOTT NO.	DESCRIPTION	FIRST DAY COVERS SING	FIRST DAY COVERS INSC. BLK	INSCRIP BLK-4	UNUSED F/NH	USED F
141-59	**1993 Issues, (19)**	....	....	....	**30.75**	....
141-42	5.50s-7s Aging	4.00	10.25	11.00	2.50	2.25
143-46	7s Endangered Species, 4 attached	5.00	6.00	7.50	6.00	5.00
147-48	6s-10s Healthy Environment	4.00	11.50	13.00	3.00	2.50
149	13s Definitive	4.00	10.25	12.50	3.00	2.50
				Sheetlets (12)		
150-51	5s-6s Human Rights	3.00	7.00	34.00	7.50	....
152-55	5.50s Peace, 4 attached (strips of 3 w/tabs)	2.50	6.00	5.50	4.50	4.00
156-59	7s Environment—Climate, strip of 4	4.00	7.00	12.50(8)	6.00	5.50

1994

SCOTT NO.	DESCRIPTION	FIRST DAY COVERS SING	FIRST DAY COVERS INSC. BLK	INSCRIP BLK-4	UNUSED F/NH	USED F
160-77	**1994 Issues (18)**	....	....	....	**24.50**	....
160-61	5.50s-8s Intl. Year of the Family	3.00	10.75	10.50	2.75	2.50
162-65	7s Endangered Species, 4 attached	6.25	7.50	7.50	6.00	5.00
166	12s Refugees	3.50	12.00	11.75	2.25	1.75
167-69	50g-30s Definitives (3)	8.50	33.50	32.50	6.00	5.00
170-73	6s Intl. Decade for Natural Disaster Reduction, 4 attached	5.50	6.50	6.00	4.00	3.50
174-75	5.50s-7s Population and Development	3.00	10.25	10.00	2.50	2.25
176-77	6s-7s Development through Partnership	3.50	10.25	10.25	2.40	2.25

U.N. Vienna #178-192

SCOTT NO.	DESCRIPTION	FIRST DAY COVERS SING	INSC. BLK	INSCRIP BLK-4	UNUSED F/NH	USED F
		1995				
178/91	**1995 Issues (13) (No #188) ....**	....	....	....	**27.15**	....
178	7s 50th Anniversary of the UN	2.00	7.25	7.00	1.60	1.25
179	14s Social Summit	3.50	12.50	13.00	3.00	2.25
180-83	7s Endangered Species, 4 attached	6.25	7.50	8.00	7.00	6.00
184-85	6s-7s Youth: Our Future	3.50	10.25	11.50	2.75	2.50
186-87	7s-10s 50th Anniversary of the UN ..	4.00	11.50	13.50	3.25	3.00
188	17s 50th Anniversary of the UN, souvenir sheet	3.50	....	....	3.50	3.00
189-90	5.50s-6s 4th World Conference on Women	3.25	10.50	10.50	2.50	2.25
191	3s 50thAnniversary, min. sheet of 12	....	....	7.50	....	
192	same, souvenir booklet of 4 panes of 3	....	....	....	8.00	....

193

194

195

196-99

200-04

U.N. Vienna #193-217

207

208

209

210

211

1996

SCOTT NO.	DESCRIPTION	FIRST DAY COVERS SING	FIRST DAY COVERS INSC. BLK	INSCRIP BLK-4	UNUSED F/NH	USED F
193/211	**1996 Issues (18) (No 207)**	....	....	....	**27.15**	....
193	7s WFUNA 50th Anniversary	2.00	7.25	7..00	1.60	1.25
194-95	1s-10s Definitives	3.25	10.50	10.50	2.50	2.25
196-99	7s Endangered Species, 4 attached	6.25	7.50	8.00	7.00	6.00
200-04	6s City Summit (Habitat II), strip of 5	6.75	16.50	18.00	8.75	8.00
205-06	6s-7s Sport & the Environment	3.50	10.25	11.50	2.75	2.50
207	13s Sport & theEnvrinronment souvenir sheet	3.25	....	....	2.50	2.25
208-09	7s-10s A Plea for Peace	4.00	11.50	13.50	3.25	3.00
210-11	5.5s-8s UNICEF 50th Anniversary ...	3.50	10.25	11.50	2.75	2.50

214-17

1997

SCOTT NO.	DESCRIPTION	FIRST DAY COVERS SING	FIRST DAY COVERS INSC. BLK	INSCRIP BLK-4	UNUSED F/NH	USED F
212-13	5s-6s Definitives	3.25	10.50	10.50	2.50	2.25
214-17	7s Endangered Species, 4 attached	6.25	7.50	8.00	7.00	6.00

U.N. Vienna #U1-U2; UC1-UC5; UX1-UX8
AIR LETTER SHEETS & POSTAL CARDS

U1

1995

SCOTT NO.	DESCRIPTION	FIRST DAY COVER	UNUSED ENTIRE
U1	6s Vienna International Center	1.75	1.50
U2	7s Vienna Landscape	1.75	1.60

UC1

1962

SCOTT NO.	DESCRIPTION	FIRST DAY COVER	UNUSED ENTIRE
UC1	9s multicolored	4.00	4.00

UC3

UC5

1967

SCOTT NO.	DESCRIPTION	FIRST DAY COVER	UNUSED ENTIRE
UC2	9s+2s surcharge on UC1	18.50	37.50
UC3	11s Birds in Flight	3.50	3.50
UC4	11s+1s surcharged	3.50	35.00
UC5	12s Vienna Office	4.00	2.50

UX1 UX2

1982

SCOTT NO.	DESCRIPTION	FIRST DAY COVER	UNUSED ENTIRE
UX1	3s multicolored	.55	1.50
UX2	5s multicolored	1.75	1.00

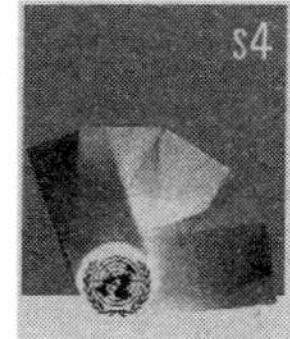

UX3

1985

SCOTT NO.	DESCRIPTION	FIRST DAY COVER	UNUSED ENTIRE
UX3	4s U.N. Emblem	.85	2.00

1992

SCOTT NO.	DESCRIPTION	FIRST DAY COVER	UNUSED ENTIRE
UX4	5s+1s surcharged	......	15.00
UX5	6s Reg Schek Painting	1.75	1.50

UX7

1993

SCOTT NO.	DESCRIPTION	FIRST DAY COVER	UNUSED ENTIRE
UX6	5s Postal Card	1.75	3.50
UX7	6s Postal Card	1.75	3.50

1994

SCOTT NO.	DESCRIPTION	FIRST DAY COVER	UNUSED ENTIRE
UX8	5s + 50g surcharge on UX6	1.75	2.00

Canada Postage #1-20

CANADA

1, 4, 12 *Beaver* — 2, 5, 10, 13 *Prince Albert* — 7 *Jacques Cartier* — 8, 11 — 9 *Queen Victoria*

SCOTT NO.	DESCRIPTION	UNUSED VF	UNUSED F	UNUSED AVG	USED VF	USED F	USED AVG
	1851 Laid paper, Imperforate (OG + 75%)						
1	3p red	15800.00	11300.00	6700.00	645.00	450.00	275.00
2	6p grayish purple	15800.00	11300.00	6700.00	855.00	600.00	425.00
	1852-55 Wove paper						
4	3p red	1050.00	800.00	600.00	200.00	140.00	95.00
4d	3p red (thin paper)	1050.00	800.00	600.00	245.00	170.00	115.00
5	6p slate gray	11200.00	8050.00	4825.00	715.00	500.00	335.00
	1855						
7	10p blue	6250.00	4750.00	3200.00	1040.00	725.00	450.00
	1857						
8	1/2p rose	595.00	450.00	300.00	470.00	325.00	210.00
9	7-1/2p green	8600.00	6150.00	3700.00	1790.00	1250.00	850.00
	Very thick soft wove paper						
10	6p reddish purple	16500.00	11900.00	7100.00	1955.00	1350.00	1050.00
	1858-59 Perf. 12						
11	1/2p rose	1250.00	950.00	725.00	800.00	550.00	350.00
12	3p red	2100.00	1575.00	1200.00	495.00	335.00	225.00
13	6p brown violet	8200.00	6250.00	4500.00	2970.00	2100.00	1600.00

14 *Queen Victoria* — 15 *Beaver* — 16, 17 *Prince Albert* — 18 *Queen Victoria* — 19 *Jacques Cartier* — 20 *Queen Victoria*

SCOTT NO.	DESCRIPTION	UNUSED VF	UNUSED F	UNUSED AVG	USED VF	USED F	USED AVG
	1859 (OG + 35%)						
14	1¢ rose	245.00	165.00	110.00	42.00	25.00	14.00
15	5¢ vermillion	225.00	150.00	100.00	19.50	11.50	8.00
16	10¢ black brown	9200.00	6600.00	3950.00	1650.00	1050.00	875.00
17	10¢ red lilac	595.00	395.00	260.00	74.50	45.00	27.50
18	12-1/2¢ yellow green	335.00	220.00	135.00	55.00	33.50	22.00
19	17¢ blue	575.00	385.00	250.00	99.00	60.00	37.50
	1864						
20	2¢ rose	350.00	230.00	160.00	240.00	145.00	95.00

21 — 22, 23, 31 — 24, 32 — 25, 33

ORIGINAL GUM: Prior to 1897, the Unused price is for stamps either without gum or with partial gum. If you require full original gum, use the OG premium. Never hinged quality is scarce on those issues. Please write for specific quotations for NH.

Canada Postage #21-40

26 27 28 29, 30

Queen Victoria

SCOTT NO.	DESCRIPTION	UNUSED VF	UNUSED F	UNUSED AVG	USED VF	USED F	USED AVG
	1868-75 Wove paper, Perf. 12, unwkd. (OG + 35%)						
21	1/2¢ black	45.00	30.00	21.00	41.50	25.00	16.00
22	1¢ brown red	395.00	260.00	175.00	66.00	40.00	28.00
23	1¢ yellow orange	745.00	495.00	325.00	86.00	52.50	35.00
24	2¢ green	410.00	275.00	170.00	44.00	26.50	16.00
25	3¢ red	675.00	450.00	300.00	17.00	10.00	6.50
26	5¢ olive gr. (pf. 11-1/2x12)	860.00	575.00	375.00	99.00	60.00	40.00
27	6¢ dark brown	700.00	475.00	300.00	58.50	35.00	25.00
28	12-1/2¢ blue	410.00	275.00	180.00	58.50	35.00	25.00
29	15¢ gray violet	52.50	35.00	23.00	27.00	16.00	11.00
29b	15¢ red lilac	650.00	435.00	300.00	91.00	55.00	28.00
30	15¢ gray	45.00	30.00	20.00	27.00	16.00	11.00
	1873-74 Wove paper. Perf. 11-1/2 x 12, unwatermarked						
21a	1/2¢ black	45.00	30.00	21.00	41.50	25.00	16.00
29a	15¢ gray violet	550.00	375.00	250.00	149.00	90.00	58.00
30a	15¢ gray	675.00	450.00	300.00	154.00	95.00	60.00
	1868 Wove paper. Perf. 12 watermarked						
22a	1¢ brown red	......	1450.00	800.00	......	175.00	115.00
24a	2¢ green	......	1450.00	800.00	......	165.00	115.00
25a	3¢ red	......	1600.00	950.00	......	145.00	95.00
27b	6¢ dark brown	......	1750.00	1150.00	......	575.00	375.00
28a	12-1/2¢ blue	......	1250.00	675.00	......	145.00	95.00
29c	15¢ gray violet	......	1950.00	1350.00	......	415.00	230.00
	1868 Laid Paper (OG + 20%)						
31	1¢ brown red	......	11000.00	6600.00	2255.00	1350.00	900.00
33	3¢ bright red	......	10000.00	6000.00	......	300.00	175.00

34 35 36 37, 41 38, 42

39, 43 44 40, 45 46, 47

Queen Victoria

SCOTT NO.	DESCRIPTION	UNUSED VF	UNUSED F	UNUSED AVG	USED VF	USED F	USED AVG
	1870-89 Perf. 12						
34	1/2¢ black	6.75	4.50	2.65	7.50	4.50	2.60
35	1¢ yellow	19.50	13.00	7.50	1.05	.65	.35
35a	1¢ orange	75.00	50.00	30.00	10.00	6.00	3.50
36	2¢ green	29.00	19.50	11.50	1.30	.75	.45
36d	2¢ blue green	55.00	37.50	21.00	4.25	2.50	1.50
37	3¢ dull red	60.00	40.00	25.00	2.85	1.75	.90
37c	3¢ orange red	67.50	45.00	25.00	2.05	1.25	.70
37d	3¢ copper red, pf. 12-1/2	......	4725.00	2800.00	594.00	360.00	250.00
38	5¢ slate green	300.00	200.00	110.00	20.00	12.00	8.25
39	6¢ yellow brown	240.00	160.00	110.00	20.00	12.00	8.25
40	10¢ dull rose lilac	335.00	220.00	135.00	55.00	33.50	22.00

Canada Postage #41-69

SCOTT NO.	DESCRIPTION	UNUSED VF	UNUSED F	UNUSED AVG	USED VF	USED F	USED AVG
	1873-79 Perf. 11-1/2 x 12 (OG + 20%)						
35d	1¢ orange	145.00	95.00	65.00	16.00	9.50	6.00
36e	2¢ green	180.00	120.00	82.50	22.00	13.50	9.00
37e	3¢ red	180.00	120.00	82.50	9.75	5.75	3.75
38a	5¢ slate green	345.00	230.00	155.00	37.00	22.00	15.00
39b	6¢ yellow brown	375.00	250.00	165.00	37.00	22.00	15.00
40c	10¢ pale milky rose lilac	675.00	450.00	295.00	250.00	150.00	105.00
	1888-93 Perf. 12						
41	3¢ bright vermillion	18.00	12.00	7.00	.50	.30	.15
41a	3¢ rose carmine	315.00	210.00	120.00	10.00	6.00	4.00
42	5¢ gray	40.00	27.50	15.00	5.00	3.00	1.60
43	6¢ red brown	45.00	30.00	17.00	14.25	8.50	4.50
43a	6¢ chocolate	55.00	37.50	22.00	16.00	9.50	6.00
44	8¢ gray	45.00	30.00	20.00	5.50	3.35	1.85
45	10¢ brown red	135.00	90.00	50.00	41.50	25.00	13.75
46	20¢ vermillion	215.00	145.00	95.00	60.00	36.00	25.00
47	50¢ deep blue	305.00	205.00	135.00	44.00	27.50	15.00

50-65
Queen Victoria in 1837 & 1897

SCOTT NO.	DESCRIPTION	UNUSED OG VF	UNUSED OG F	UNUSED OG AVG	USED VF	USED F	USED AVG
	1897 Jubilee Issue (NH + 100%)						
50	1/2¢ black	75.00	50.00	31.00	86.25	57.50	36.00
51	1¢ orange	7.75	5.25	3.00	7.50	5.00	2.75
52	2¢ green	12.25	8.25	4.50	12.25	8.25	4.50
53	3¢ bright rose	7.50	5.00	2.75	2.25	1.50	.90
54	5¢ deep blue	24.00	16.00	9.50	22.50	15.00	8.25
55	6¢ yellow brown	145.00	95.00	55.00	150.00	100.00	65.00
56	8¢ dark violet	29.50	19.50	11.00	24.50	16.50	10.00
57	10¢ brown violet	75.00	50.00	27.50	75.00	50.00	28.00
58	15¢ steel blue	145.00	95.00	55.00	135.00	90.00	50.00
59	20¢ vermillion	150.00	100.00	57.50	150.00	100.00	58.00
60	50¢ ultramarine	180.00	120.00	75.00	165.00	110.00	65.00
61	$1 lake	675.00	450.00	260.00	600.00	410.00	250.00
62	$2 dark purple	1125.00	750.00	475.00	540.00	360.00	220.00
63	$3 yellow bistre	1350.00	900.00	525.00	1025.00	695.00	450.00
64	$4 purple	1350.00	900.00	525.00	1025.00	695.00	450.00
65	$5 olive green	1400.00	950.00	550.00	995.00	650.00	425.00

66-73

74-84

Queen Victoria

85-86
Map Showing British Empire

77: 2¢ Die I. Frame of four thin lines
77a: 2¢ Die II. Frame of thick line between two thin lines

SCOTT NO.	DESCRIPTION	UNUSED OG VF	UNUSED OG F	UNUSED OG AVG	USED VF	USED F	USED AVG
	1897-98 Maple Leaves (NH + 100%)						
66	1/2¢ black	6.00	4.15	2.50	5.50	3.75	2.20
67	1¢ blue green	11.00	7.75	4.50	.90	.60	.40
68	2¢ purple	12.25	8.25	5.00	1.65	1.10	.65
69	3¢ carmine (1898)	12.25	8.25	5.00	.45	.30	.25

Canada Postage #70-95

SCOTT NO.	DESCRIPTION	UNUSED OG (NH + 100%) VF	F	AVG	USED VF	F	AVG
70	5¢ dark blue, bluish paper	55.00	37.50	25.00	5.75	3.75	2.20
71	6¢ brown..........................	52.50	35.00	22.00	24.00	16.00	11.00
72	8¢ orange.........................	82.00	55.00	33.50	9.00	6.00	3.75
73	10¢ brown violet (1898)	150.00	100.00	62.50	67.50	45.00	30.00
	1898-1902 Numerals (NH + 100%)						
74	1/2¢ black.........................	2.10	1.40	.85	1.60	1.10	.65
75	1¢ gray green....................	13.50	9.00	5.00	.30	.20	.15
76	2¢ purple (I).....................	14.00	9.50	5.50	.30	.20	.15
77	2¢ carmine (I) (1899)........	15.50	10.50	6.00	.30	.20	.15
77a	2¢ carmine (II).................	16.50	11.00	6.50	.45	.30	.20
78	3¢ carmine.......................	22.50	15.00	8.25	.45	.30	.20
79	5¢ blue, bluish paper	77.50	52.50	30.00	1.20	.80	.45
80	6¢ brown..........................	92.50	62.50	35.00	30.00	20.00	11.50
81	7¢ olive yellow (1902)........	45.00	30.00	18.00	11.50	7.75	4.50
82	8¢ orange.........................	105.00	71.50	40.00	16.50	11.00	6.25
83	10¢ brown violet...............	125.00	85.00	55.00	12.00	8.25	5.00
84	20¢ olive green (1900)......	270.00	180.00	110.00	69.50	46.50	30.00
	1898 IMPERIAL PENNY POSTAGE COMMEMORATIVE						
85	2¢ black, lavender & carmine	21.00	14.00	9.00	6.75	4.50	2.50
86	2¢ black, blue & carmine ..	21.00	14.00	9.00	6.75	4.50	2.50
	1899 69 & 78 surcharged						
87	2¢ on 3¢ carmine.............	7.75	5.25	3.00	4.95	3.35	2.00
88	2¢ on 3¢ carmine.............	8.00	5.75	3.35	3.75	2.50	1.40

89-95
King Edward VII

1903-08

SCOTT NO.	DESCRIPTION	UNUSED NH F	AVG	UNUSED O.G. F	AVG	USED F	AVG
89	1¢ green	13.50	9.50	8.00	5.50	.20	.15
90	2¢ carmine	13.50	9.50	8.00	5.50	.20	.15
90a	2¢ carmine, imperf. pair . . .	30.00	21.00	20.00	13.50	......	......
91	5¢ blue, blue paper	65.00	45.00	40.00	25.00	1.60	1.00
92	7¢ olive bistre	50.00	35.00	27.50	18.00	1.80	1.10
93	10¢ brown lilac	125.00	87.50	72.50	45.00	4.50	2.60
94	20¢ olive green	300.00	210.00	210.00	135.00	16.00	10.00
95	50¢ purple (1908)	525.00	365.00	300.00	200.00	50.00	30.00

96
Princess and Prince of Wales in 1908

97
Jacques Cartier and Samuel Champlain

98
Queen Alexandra and King Edward

99
Champlain's Home in Quebec

100
Generals Montcalm and Wolfe

101
View of Quebec in 1700

102
Champlain's Departure for the West

103
Arrival of Cartier at Quebec

NEVER HINGED: From 1897 to 1949, Unused OG is for stamps with original gum that have been higed. If you desire Never Hinged stamps, order from the NH listings.

Canada Postage #96-128a

SCOTT NO.	DESCRIPTION	UNUSED NH F	UNUSED NH AVG	UNUSED OG. F	UNUSED OG. AVG	USED F	USED AVG
	1908 QUEBEC TERCENTENARY ISSUE						
96-103	**1/2¢-20¢ complete, 8 varieties**	**460.00**	**290.00**	**240.00**	**147.50**	**255.00**	**155.00**
96	1/2¢ black brown	5.00	3.15	2.50	1.40	3.00	1.95
97	1¢ blue green	9.25	5.75	5.50	3.00	3.00	1.95
98	2¢ carmine	13.50	8.00	6.50	4.25	.95	1.55
99	5¢ dark blue	41.50	26.00	22.00	15.00	20.00	13.50
100	7¢ olive green	61.00	38.50	33.50	22.00	19.50	12.50
101	10¢ dark violet	83.00	52.50	40.00	25.00	45.00	27.50
102	15¢ red orange	121.00	75.00	60.00	39.50	72.50	45.00
103	20¢ yellow brown	149.00	94.50	85.00	45.00	105.00	62.50

104-34, 136-38, 184
King George V

SCOTT NO.	DESCRIPTION	UNUSED NH F	UNUSED NH AVG	UNUSED OG. F	UNUSED OG. AVG	USED F	USED AVG
	1912-25						
104-22	**1¢-$1 complete 18 varieties**	**555.00**	**450.00**	**315.00**	**240.00**	**31.75**	**19.25**
104	1¢ green	6.25	4.35	3.50	2.30	.20	.15
104a	same, booklet pane of 6	24.00	16.75	18.00	10.50	.....	.....
105	1¢ yellow (1922)	5.75	4.00	3.35	2.20	.20	.15
105a	same, booklet pane of 4	55.00	38.00	35.00	25.00	.....	.....
105b	same, booklet pane of 6	35.00	24.50	22.00	15.00	.....	.....
106	2¢ carmine	6.50	4.50	3.75	2.50	.20	.15
106a	same, booklet pane of 6	33.50	23.00	20.00	14.00	.....	.....
107	2¢ yellow green (1922)	5.50	4.25	3.00	1.95	.20	.15
107b	same, booklet pane of 4	45.00	31.50	28.00	19.50	.....	.....
107c	same, booklet pane of 6	240.00	165.00	160.00	110.00	.....	.....
108	3¢ brown (1918)	6.50	4.50	3.75	2.50	.20	.15
108a	same, booklet pane of 4	85.00	59.50	50.00	33.50	.....	.....
109	3¢ carmine (1923)	5.75	4.00	3.25	2.20	.20	.15
109a	same, booklet pane of 4	45.00	31.50	28.00	16.00	.....	.....
110	4¢ olive bistre (1922)	19.50	13.50	11.00	7.25	1.95	1.15
111	5¢ dark blue	70.00	49.00	40.00	25.00	.35	.20
112	5¢ violet (1922)	11.50	8.00	6.50	4.50	.35	.20
113	7¢ yellow ochre	25.00	17.50	15.00	10.00	1.40	.85
114	7¢ red brown (1924)	15.00	10.00	8.00	5.50	6.50	4.00
115	8¢ blue (1925)	25.00	17.50	15.00	9.50	7.75	4.50
116	10¢ plum	110.00	75.00	60.00	40.00	1.05	.60
117	10¢ blue (1922)	33.50	23.50	19.50	12.00	1.05	.60
118	10¢ bistre brown (1925)	26.00	18.00	15.00	10.00	.90	.55
119	20¢ olive green	52.00	36.00	30.00	19.50	.75	.45
120	50¢ black brown (1925)	57.50	40.00	33.00	22.00	1.95	1.15
120a	50¢ black	100.00	70.00	55.00	35.00	2.20	1.30
122	$1 orange (1923)	105.00	73.50	60.00	40.00	6.00	3.75
	1912 Coil Stamps; Perf. 8 Horizontally						
123	1¢ dark green	55.00	37.50	35.00	25.00	25.00	14.00
124	2¢ carmine	55.00	37.50	35.00	25.00	25.00	14.00
	1912-24 Perf. 8 Vertically						
125-30	**1¢-3¢ complete, 6 varieties**	**100.00**	**99.50**	**57.50**	**37.50**	**12.00**	**7.15**
125	1¢ green	11.00	7.50	6.00	3.75	.45	.30
126	1¢ yellow (1923)	7.00	4.75	4.50	2.75	5.00	3.00
126a	1¢ block of 4	41.50	29.00	23.00	14.00	.....	.....
127	2¢ carmine	19.50	13.50	11.00	6.50	.30	.20
128	2¢ green (1922)	7.00	4.75	4.50	2.75	.40	.25
128a	2¢ block of 4	41.50	29.00	23.00	14.00	.....	.....

SCOTT NO.	DESCRIPTION	UNUSED NH F	UNUSED NH AVG	UNUSED OG. F	UNUSED OG. AVG	USED F	USED AVG
129	3¢ brown (1918)	7.50	5.25	4.50	2.75	.45	.25
130	3¢ carmine (1924)	55.00	40.00	30.00	21.00	6.00	3.50
130a	3¢ block of 4	750.00	525.00	525.00	325.00	.....	.....
	1915-24 Perf. 12 Horizontally						
131	1¢ dark green	6.50	4.50	3.75	2.50	4.50	2.75
132	2¢ carmine	17.00	11.75	10.00	6.50	10.00	6.00
133	2¢ yellow green (1924)	82.50	57.00	50.00	30.00	45.00	28.00
134	3¢ brown (1921)	6.50	4.50	3.75	2.50	4.50	2.60

135
Quebec Conference of 1867

SCOTT NO.	DESCRIPTION	UNUSED NH F	UNUSED NH AVG	UNUSED OG. F	UNUSED OG. AVG	USED F	USED AVG
	1917 CONFEDERATE ISSUE						
135	3¢ brown	22.50	15.00	13.00	9.00	.40	.25
	1924 Imperforate						
136	1¢ yellow	45.00	30.00	31.00	22.00	31.00	22.00
137	2¢ green	45.00	30.00	31.00	22.00	31.00	22.00
138	3¢ carmine	22.00	14.50	15.00	10.00	16.00	12.00
	1926 109 Surcharged						
139	2¢ on 3¢ carmine	55.00	37.50	35.00	25.00	37.00	26.50
	109 Surcharged						
140	2¢ on 3¢ carmine	22.00	15.25	15.00	10.00	16.00	11.00

141
Sir John Macdonald

142
The Quebec Conference of 1867

143
The Parliament Building at Ottawa

144
Sir Wilfred Laurier

145
Map of Canada

1927 CONFEDERATION ISSUE

SCOTT NO.	DESCRIPTION	UNUSED NH F	UNUSED NH AVG	UNUSED OG. F	UNUSED OG. AVG	USED F	USED AVG
141-45	**1¢-12¢ complete, 5 varieties**	**34.50**	**21.50**	**21.75**	**15.25**	**8.25**	**5.10**
141	1¢ orange	2.70	1.90	1.95	1.30	.40	.25
142	2¢ green	1.60	1.15	1.10	.75	.20	.15
143	3¢ brown carmine	8.25	5.50	5.50	3.75	3.50	2.10
144	5¢ violet	5.00	3.25	3.35	2.20	1.60	1.00
145	12¢ dark blue	16.00	11.00	11.00	8.00	3.00	1.85

146
Thomas McGee

147
Sir Wilfred Laurier and Sir John Macdonald

148
Robert Baldwin and L.H. Lafontaine

1927 HISTORICAL ISSUE

SCOTT NO.	DESCRIPTION	UNUSED NH F	UNUSED NH AVG	UNUSED OG. F	UNUSED OG. AVG	USED F	USED AVG
146-48	**5¢-20¢ complete, 3 varieties**	**29.70**	**20.60**	**19.65**	**13.25**	**6.90**	**4.40**
146	5¢ violet	3.25	2.25	2.20	1.40	1.40	.85
147	12¢ green	8.00	5.50	5.50	3.50	2.50	1.60
148	20¢ brown carmine	20.00	14.00	13.00	9.00	3.35	2.20

149-154, 160, 161
King George V

155
Mt. Hurd

156
Quebec Bridge

157
Harvesting Wheat

158
Fishing Schooner "Bluenose"

159
The Parliament Building at Ottawa

1928-29

SCOTT NO.	DESCRIPTION	UNUSED NH F	UNUSED NH AVG	UNUSED OG. F	UNUSED OG. AVG	USED F	USED AVG
149-59	**1¢-$1 complete, 11 varieties**	**515.00**	**360.00**	**335.00**	**228.00**	**94.00**	**60.50**
149-55	**1¢-10¢, 7 varieties**	**43.95**	**30.50**	**28.95**	**18.15**	**17.15**	**10.15**
149	1¢ orange	2.20	1.50	1.40	1.00	.20	.15
149a	same, booklet pane of 6	15.00	10.00	10.00	6.50	.....	.....
150	2¢ green	.85	.55	.55	.40	.20	.15
150a	same, booklet pane of 6	22.00	15.00	15.00	10.00	.....	.....
151	3¢ dark carmine	11.50	8.00	8.50	5.00	8.00	4.50
152	4¢ bistre (1929)	11.50	8.00	7.50	4.50	3.50	2.10
153	5¢ deep violet	3.75	2.60	2.50	1.60	1.60	1.00
153a	same, booklet pane of 6	100.00	70.00	60.00	37.00	.....	.....
154	8¢ blue	8.25	5.75	5.00	3.30	3.75	2.30
155	10¢ green	8.25	5.75	5.00	3.30	.80	.45
156	12¢ gray (1929)	12.00	8.25	8.25	5.50	4.50	2.60
157	20¢ dark carmine (1929)	27.00	19.00	16.00	11.00	6.50	4.00
158	50¢ dark blue (1929)	210.00	145.00	140.00	95.00	33.00	22.00
159	$1 olive green (1929)	250.00	175.00	160.00	110.00	37.00	25.00
	1929 Coil Stamps. Perf. 8 Vertically						
160	1¢ orange	19.50	13.50	14.00	9.00	13.50	8.00
161	2¢ green	14.00	9.75	10.00	6.00	1.95	1.10

2¢ Die I. Above "POSTAGE" faint crescent in ball of ornament. Top letter "P" has tiny dot of color.

162-172, 178-183
King George V

173
Parliament Library at Ottawa

2¢ Die II. Stronger and clearer crescent, spot of color in "P" is larger.

174
The Old Citadel at Quebec

175
Harvesting Wheat on the Prairies

176
The Museum at Grand Pré, and Monument to Evangeline

177
Mt. Edith Cavell

VERY FINE QUALITY: To determine the Very Fine price, add the difference between the Fine and Average prices to the Fine quality price. For example: if the Fine price is $10.00 and the Average price is $6.00, the Very Fine price would be $14.00. From 1935 to date, add 20% to the Fine price to arrive at the Very Fine price.

Canada Postage #162-191a

SCOTT NO.	DESCRIPTION	UNUSED NH F	UNUSED NH AVG	UNUSED OG. F	UNUSED OG. AVG	USED F	USED AVG
			1930-31				
162-77	**1¢-$1 complete, 16 varieties**	**410.00**	**240.00**	**275.00**	**186.00**	**46.00**	**31.00**
162-72	**1¢-8¢, 11 varieties**	**45.00**	**26.50**	**29.25**	**19.75**	**14.00**	**9.30**
162	1¢ orange	.80	.50	.50	.35	.35	.25
163	1¢ deep green	1.00	.60	.65	.45	.20	.15
163a	same, booklet pane of 4	85.00	50.00	55.00	35.00	.....	.....
163c	same, booklet pane of 6	16.00	9.50	12.00	7.00	.....	.....
164	2¢ dull green	1.10	.65	.55	.40	.20	.15
164a	same, booklet pane of 6	25.00	15.00	16.50	11.00	.....	.....
165	2¢ deep red, die II	1.50	.90	1.00	.60	.20	.15
165a	2¢ deep red, die I	1.40	.85	.95	.55	.20	.15
165b	same, booklet pane of 6	22.00	13.00	15.00	9.50	.....	.....
166	2¢ dark brown, die II (1931)	1.15	.65	.65	.45	.20	.15
166a	same, booklet pane of 4	85.00	50.00	60.00	40.00	.....	.....
166b	2¢ dark brown, die I (1931)	4.00	2.50	2.75	1.75	2.60	1.75
166c	same, booklet pane of 6	27.50	16.50	19.50	12.50	.....	.....
167	3¢ deep red (1931)	1.55	.90	1.10	.65	.20	.15
167a	same, booklet pane of 4	27.00	16.00	19.50	12.50	.....	.....
168	4¢ yellow bistre	10.00	6.00	6.50	4.50	3.25	2.20
169	4¢ dull violet	5.50	3.25	3.35	2.20	2.50	1.60
170	5¢ dull blue	2.75	1.50	1.80	1.20	.20	.15
171	8¢ dark blue	16.00	9.50	11.00	7.50	5.00	3.25
172	8¢ red orange	6.00	3.50	3.70	2.50	2.50	1.60
173	10¢ olive green	7.00	4.25	5.00	3.30	.80	.45
174	12¢ gray black	13.00	7.75	9.50	5.50	4.00	2.50
175	20¢ brown red	25.00	15.00	16.00	11.00	.35	.20
176	50¢ dull blue	160.00	95.00	110.00	75.00	10.00	6.00
177	$1 dark olive green	175.00	105.00	120.00	82.00	19.50	12.00

Coil Pairs for Canada can be supplied at double the single price

1930-31 Coil Stamps. Perf. 8-1/2 Vertically

SCOTT NO.	DESCRIPTION	UNUSED NH F	UNUSED NH AVG	UNUSED OG. F	UNUSED OG. AVG	USED F	USED AVG
178-83	**1¢-3¢ complete, 6 varieties**	**59.00**	**32.00**	**33.00**	**22.00**	**13.60**	**8.30**
178	1¢ orange	12.00	6.00	6.50	4.50	6.00	3.60
179	1¢ deep green	7.00	3.50	4.00	2.50	3.25	1.95
180	2¢ dull green	6.00	3.00	3.50	2.20	2.75	1.60
181	2¢ deep red	14.00	7.25	7.50	5.00	1.60	1.10
182	2¢ dark brown (1931)	10.00	5.50	5.00	3.50	.45	.30
183	3¢ deep red (1931)	16.00	8.50	8.25	5.50	.30	.20

1931 Design of 1912-25. Perf. 12x8

SCOTT NO.	DESCRIPTION	UNUSED NH F	UNUSED NH AVG	UNUSED OG. F	UNUSED OG. AVG	USED F	USED AVG
184	3¢ carmine	3.00	1.75	2.25	1.50	1.75	1.00

190
Sir George Etienne Cartier

192
King George V

193
Prince of Wales

194
Allegorical Figure of Britannia Surveying the British Empire

1931

SCOTT NO.	DESCRIPTION	UNUSED NH F	UNUSED NH AVG	UNUSED OG. F	UNUSED OG. AVG	USED F	USED AVG
190	10¢ dark green	7.00	5.00	5.00	3.30	.20	.15

1932
165 & 165a surcharged

SCOTT NO.	DESCRIPTION	UNUSED NH F	UNUSED NH AVG	UNUSED OG. F	UNUSED OG. AVG	USED F	USED AVG
191	3¢ on 2¢ deep red, die II	1.00	.70	.75	.40	.20	.15
191a	3¢ on 2¢ deep red, die I	2.25	1.55	1.60	.95	1.10	.95

SCOTT NO.	DESCRIPTION	UNUSED NH F	UNUSED NH AVG	UNUSED OG. F	UNUSED OG. AVG	USED F	USED AVG
	1932 OTTAWA CONFERENCE ISSUE						
192-94	**3¢-13¢ complete, 3 varieties . . .**	**14.00**	**9.50**	**10.00**	**6.00**	**5.50**	**3.75**
192	3¢ deep red	.80	.55	.55	.35	.20	.15
193	5¢ dull blue	6.00	4.25	4.00	2.70	1.60	1.10
194	13¢ deep green	8.00	5.25	6.00	3.25	4.00	2.70

195-200, 205-207
King George V

201
The Old Citadel at Quebec

SCOTT NO.	DESCRIPTION	UNUSED NH F	UNUSED NH AVG	UNUSED OG. F	UNUSED OG. AVG	USED F	USED AVG
	1932						
195-201	**1¢-31¢ complete, 7 varieties . . .**	**83.00**	**52.00**	**56.00**	**35.90**	**8.65**	**5.70**
195	1¢ dark green	.80	.60	.60	.35	.20	.15
195a	same, booklet pane of 4	80.00	55.00	60.00	35.00	.....	.....
195b	same, booklet pane of 6	25.00	17.50	20.00	12.00	.....	.....
196	2¢ black brown	.95	.55	.65	.40	.20	.15
196a	same, booklet pane of 4	80.00	50.00	60.00	37.50	.....	.....
196b	same, booklet pane of 6	16.00	9.50	12.50	10.00	.....	.....
197	3¢ deep red	1.10	.65	.85	.50	.20	.15
197a	same, booklet pane of 4	25.00	15.00	17.50	13.00	.....	.....
198	4¢ ochre	30.00	18.00	20.00	13.00	3.60	2.40
199	5¢ dark blue	6.00	3.50	4.00	2.80	.20	.15
200	8¢ red orange	16.00	9.50	11.00	7.25	2.75	1.80
201	13¢ dull violet	32.50	19.50	22.00	13.50	1.95	1.20

202
Parliament Buildings at Ottawa

203

204
S.S. Royal William

SCOTT NO.	DESCRIPTION	UNUSED NH F	UNUSED NH AVG	UNUSED OG. F	UNUSED OG. AVG	USED F	USED AVG
	1933-34 COMMEMORATIVES						
202/10	**(202-04, 208-10), 6 varieties . . . . .**	**73.00**	**43.50**	**50.65**	**34.20**	**21.25**	**12.95**
	1933						
202	5¢ Postal Union	8.00	4.75	5.50	4.00	2.20	1.45
203	20¢ Grain Exhibition	35.00	21.00	25.00	16.00	10.00	5.50
204	5¢ Trans-Atlantic Crossing	9.00	5.25	5.75	4.00	2.20	1.45
	1933 Coil Stamps Perf. 8-1/2 Vertically						
205	1¢ dark green	16.00	9.50	11.00	7.00	1.60	1.10
206	2¢ black brown	18.00	10.50	12.50	8.00	.50	.35
207	3¢ deep red	12.50	7.00	8.00	5.50	.25	.15

208

209

210

SCOTT NO.	DESCRIPTION	UNUSED NH F	UNUSED NH AVG	UNUSED OG. F	UNUSED OG. AVG	USED F	USED AVG
	1934						
208	3¢ Jacques Cartier	3.00	1.75	2.20	1.60	1.00	.60
209	10¢ Loyalists Monument	20.00	12.00	13.50	9.50	5.50	3.75
210	2¢ New Brunswick	1.95	1.20	1.40	.90	1.50	.90

Canada Postage #211-230

211 212 213

214

215

216

1935 SILVER JUBILEE ISSUE

SCOTT NO.	DESCRIPTION	PLATE BLOCKS F/NH	PLATE BLOCKS AVG	UNUSED F/NH	UNUSED F	USED F
211-16	**1¢-13¢ complete, 6 varieties**	.....	.....	**20.50**	**15.00**	**8.25**
211	1¢ Princess Elizabeth	4.00	3.00	.40	.30	.20
212	2¢ Duke of York	8.25	6.95	.70	.60	.15
213	3¢ George & Mary	16.00	12.50	1.90	1.40	.15
214	5¢ Prince of Wales	41.00	30.00	5.00	3.60	2.25
215	10¢ Windsor Castle	50.00	36.00	6.00	4.50	1.95
216	13¢ Royal Yacht	62.50	42.50	7.75	5.50	4.00

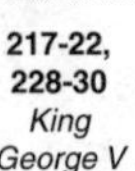

217-22,
228-30
King George V

223

224

225

226

227

1935

SCOTT NO.	DESCRIPTION	PLATE BLOCKS F/NH	PLATE BLOCKS AVG	UNUSED F/NH	UNUSED F	USED F
217-27	**1¢-$1 complete, 11 varieties**	.....	.....	**147.00**	**96.50**	**13.95**
217	1¢ green	2.75	2.20	.30	.25	.15
217a	same, booklet pane of 4	.....	.....	50.00	33.00	.....
217b	same, booklet pane of 4	.....	.....	25.00	16.50	.....
218	2¢ brown	4.00	3.00	.40	.30	.15
218a	same, booklet pane of 4	.....	.....	50.00	33.00	.....
219	3¢ dark carmine	5.50	4.50	.55	.45	.15
219a	same, booklet pane of 4	.....	.....	16.50	11.00	.....
220	4¢ yellow	23.00	17.50	2.95	2.20	.35
221	5¢ blue	20.00	15.50	2.50	1.95	.15
222	8¢ deep orange	22.00	16.50	2.95	2.20	1.45
223	10¢ Mounted Policeman	53.00	37.00	7.25	5.25	.15
224	13¢ Conference of 1864	55.00	38.50	7.25	5.25	.55
225	20¢ Niagara Falls	195.00	145.00	25.00	16.50	.40
226	50¢ Parliament Building	260.00	175.00	33.00	22.00	3.60
227	$1 Champlain Monument	500.00	325.00	72.50	45.00	7.75

1935 Coil Stamps Perf. 8 Vertically

SCOTT NO.	DESCRIPTION	PLATE BLOCKS F/NH	PLATE BLOCKS AVG	UNUSED F/NH	UNUSED F	USED F
228-30	**1¢-3¢ coils, complete, 3 varieties**	.....	.....	**30.95**	**22.50**	**2.30**
228	1¢ green	.....	.....	12.00	9.00	1.55
229	2¢ brown	.....	.....	10.00	7.25	.60
230	3¢ dark carmine	.....	.....	10.50	7.50	.30

231-236,
238-240
*King
George VI*

237

1937

SCOTT NO.	DESCRIPTION	PLATE BLOCKS F/NH	PLATE BLOCKS AVG	UNUSED F/NH	UNUSED F	USED F
231-36	**1¢-8¢ complete, 6 varieties**	.....	.....	**8.30**	**6.40**	**.80**
231	1¢ green	2.50	2.05	.40	.35	.15
231a	same, booklet pane of 4	.....	.....	10.00	6.50	.....
231b	same, booklet pane of 6	.....	.....	1.65	1.10	.....
232	2¢ brown	3.00	2.50	.55	.40	.15
232a	same, booklet pane of 4	.....	.....	10.00	6.50	.....
232b	same, booklet pane of 6	.....	.....	5.00	3.30	.....
233	3¢ carmine	2.75	2.25	.55	.45	.15
233a	same, booklet pane of 4	.....	.....	2.25	1.65	.....
234	4¢ yellow	12.50	11.00	2.50	1.95	.15
235	5¢ blue	12.00	9.50	2.25	1.65	.15
236	8¢ orange	12.00	9.00	2.50	1.95	.25
237	3¢ Coronation	1.90	1.55	.25	.20	.15

Coil Stamps Perf. 8 Vertically

SCOTT NO.	DESCRIPTION	PLATE BLOCKS F/NH	PLATE BLOCKS AVG	UNUSED F/NH	UNUSED F	USED F
238-40	**1¢-3¢ coils, complete, 3 varieties**	......	.....	**6.85**	**5.25**	**1.25**
238	1¢ green	.....	.....	1.10	.85	.85
239	2¢ brown	......	.....	1.95	1.40	.30
240	3¢ carmine	.....	.....	4.15	3.30	.15

242

243

244

241

245

246

247

248

1938

SCOTT NO.	DESCRIPTION	PLATE BLOCKS F/NH	PLATE BLOCKS AVG	UNUSED F/NH	UNUSED F	USED F
241-45	**10¢-$1 complete, 5 varieties**	.....	.....	**120.00**	**77.50**	**9.10**
241	10¢ Memorial Hall	23.50	16.50	5.00	3.60	.15
242	13¢ Halifax Harbor	41.50	27.50	8.25	5.50	.35
243	20¢ Fort Garry Gate	82.50	52.50	16.50	11.00	.25
244	50¢ Vancouver Harbor	125.00	77.00	22.00	14.00	3.35
245	$1 Chateau de Ramezay	350.00	230.00	75.00	47.50	5.50

1939 Royal Visit

SCOTT NO.	DESCRIPTION	PLATE BLOCKS F/NH	PLATE BLOCKS AVG	UNUSED F/NH	UNUSED F	USED F
246-48	**1¢-3¢ complete, 3 varieties**	**4.00**	**3.15**	**.70**	**.55**	**.40**
246	1¢ Princess Elizabeth & Margaret	1.40	1.10	.25	.20	.15
247	2¢ War Memorial	1.40	1.10	.25	.20	.15
248	3¢ King George VI & Queen Elizabeth	1.40	1.10	.25	.20	.15

SCOTT NO.	DESCRIPTION	PLATE BLOCKS F/NH	PLATE BLOCKS AVG	UNUSED F/NH	UNUSED F	USED F

249, 255, 263, 278

250, 254, 264, 267, 279, 281

251, 252, 265, 266, 280

King George VI

257

258, 259

260

261

262

253

256

1942-43 WAR ISSUE

SCOTT NO.	DESCRIPTION	PLATE BLOCKS F/NH	PLATE BLOCKS AVG	UNUSED F/NH	UNUSED F	USED F
249-62	**1¢-$1 complete, 14 varieties**	.....	.....	**120.00**	**79.50**	**13.75**
249	1¢ green	.95	.75	.25	.20	.15
249a	same, booklet pane of 4	.....	.....	4.50	3.05	.....
249b	same, booklet pane of 6	.....	.....	1.65	1.40	.....
249c	same, booklet pane of 3	.....	.....	1.65	1.10	.....
250	2¢ brown	1.95	1.40	.40	.30	.15
250a	same, booklet pane of 4	.....	.....	4.50	3.05	.....
250b	same, booklet pane of 6	.....	.....	4.50	3.05	.....
251	3¢ dark carmine	2.35	1.85	.40	.30	.15
251a	same, booklet pane of 4	.....	.....	1.95	1.40	.....
252	3¢ rose violet (1943)	1.95	1.40	.40	.30	.15
252a	same, booklet pane of 4	.....	.....	1.65	1.10	.....
252b	same, booklet pane of 3	.....	.....	2.25	1.80	.....
252c	same, booklet pane of 6	.....	.....	4.50	3.05	.....
253	4¢ Grain Elevators	11.00	8.00	1.40	.90	.45
254	4¢ dark carmine (1943)	2.05	1.50	.40	.30	.15
254a	same, booklet pane of 6	.....	.....	1.95	1.40	.....
254b	same, booklet pane of 3	.....	.....	1.95	1.40	.....
255	5¢ deep blue	5.00	3.30	1.00	.65	.15
256	8¢ Farm Scene	10.50	7.25	1.95	1.40	.35
257	10¢ Parliament Buildings	17.50	13.00	3.85	2.75	.15
258	13¢ "Ram" Tank	25.00	18.25	5.00	3.60	3.05
259	14¢ "Ram" Tank (1943)	36.00	27.00	7.75	5.50	.20
260	20¢ Corvette	27..50	21.00	6.50	4.50	.20
261	50¢ Munitions Factory	125.00	80.00	25.00	16.50	1.65
262	$1 Destroyer	345..00	235.00	72.50	46.50	7.50

Coil Stamps Perf. 8 Vertically

SCOTT NO.	DESCRIPTION	PLATE BLOCKS F/NH	PLATE BLOCKS AVG	UNUSED F/NH	UNUSED F	USED F
263-67	**1¢-4¢ complete, 5 varieties**	.....	.....	**9.00**	**6.00**	**1.75**
263	1¢ green	.....	.....	.90	.65	.30
264	2¢ brown	.....	.....	1.30	.95	.55
265	3¢ dark carmine	.....	.....	1.30	.95	.55
266	3¢ rose violet (1943)	.....	.....	2.50	1.65	.25
267	4¢ dark carmine (1943)	.....	.....	3.50	2.20	.20

268

269

270

VERY FINE QUALITY: From 1935 to date, add 20% to the Fine price. Minimum of 3¢ per stamp.

Canada Postage #268-283

271

272

273

1946 PEACE ISSUE

SCOTT NO.	DESCRIPTION	PLATEBLOCK F/NH	PLATEBLOCK F	UNUSED F/NH	UNUSED F	USED F
268-73	**8¢-$1 complete, 6 varieties ....**	**......**	**......**	**60.50**	**41.25**	**5.15**
268	8¢ Farm Scene	5.80	4.40	1.10	.95	.55
269	10¢ Great Bear Lake	6.35	5.50	1.25	1.05	.15
270	14¢ Hydro-Electric Power Station	13.75	11.00	2.75	2.20	.20
271	20¢ Reaper & Harvester	17.60	13.75	3.30	2.75	.15
272	50¢ Lumber Industry	84.15	61.60	16.50	12.10	1.65
273	$1 New Train Ferry	181.50	129.25	38.50	27.50	2.75

274

275

276

277

1947-49 COMMEMORATIVES

SCOTT NO.	DESCRIPTION	PLATEBLOCK F/NH	PLATEBLOCK F	UNUSED F/NH	UNUSED F	USED F
274/83	**274-77, 282-83, complete, 6 varieties ..**	**4.00**	**3.40**	**1.25**	**.85**	**.95**
274	4¢ Alexander G. Bell	.70	.60	.20	.15	.15
275	4¢ Canadian Citizen	.70	.60	.20	.15	.15

1948

SCOTT NO.	DESCRIPTION	PLATEBLOCK F/NH	PLATEBLOCK F	UNUSED F/NH	UNUSED F	USED F
276	4¢ Princess Elizabeth	.70	.60	.20	.15	.15
277	4¢ Parliament Building	.70	.60	.20	.15	.15

Designs of 1942-43
Coil Stamps Perf. 9-1/2 Vertically

SCOTT NO.	DESCRIPTION	PLATEBLOCK F/NH	PLATEBLOCK F	UNUSED F/NH	UNUSED F	USED F
278-81	**1¢-4¢ complete, 4 varieties ....**		**......**	**25.00**	**22.50**	**10.50**
278	1¢ green			2.90	2.50	1.65
279	2¢ brown			9.90	9.00	5.50
280	3¢ rose violet			5.25	4.75	1.95
281	4¢ dark carmine			8.25	7.50	2.15

282

283

1949

SCOTT NO.	DESCRIPTION	PLATEBLOCK F/NH	PLATEBLOCK F	UNUSED F/NH	UNUSED F	USED F
282	4¢ Cabot's "Matthew"	.70	.60	.20	.15	.15
283	4¢ Founding of Halifax	.70	.60	.20	.15	.15

COMMEMORATIVES: Commemorative stamps are special issues released to honor or recognize persons, organizations, historical events or landmarks. They are usually issued in the current first class denomination to supplement regular issues.

Canada Postage #284-319

284, 289, 295, 297 — 285, 290, 298, 305, 309 — 286, 291, 296, 299

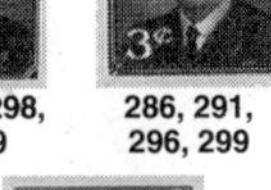

287, 292, 300, 306, 310 — 288, 293

King George VI

1949 (with "Postes-Postage")

SCOTT NO.	DESCRIPTION	PLATE BLOCK F/NH	UNUSED F/NH	USED F
284-88	**1¢-5¢ complete, 5 varieties ....**	**8.30**	**1.80**	**.70**
284	1¢ green	.65	.20	.15
284a	same, booklet pane of 3	......	.55	......
285	2¢ sepia	.95	.20	.15
286	3¢ rose violet	1.10	.25	.15
286a	same, booklet pane of 3	......	1.10	......
286b	same, booklet pane of 4	......	1.40	......
287	4 dark carmine	1.65	.35	.15
287a	same, booklet pane of 3	......	7.70	......
287b	same, booklet pane of 6	......	9.90	......
288	5¢ deep blue	4.40	.90	.15

1950 Type of 1949 (without "Postes-Postage")

SCOTT NO.	DESCRIPTION	PLATE BLOCK F/NH	UNUSED F/NH	USED F
289-93	**1¢-5¢ complete, 5 varieties ....**	**9.50**	**1.65**	**2.05**
289	1¢ green	.65	.20	.15
290	2¢ sepia	1.95	.25	.20
291	3¢ rose violet	.85	.20	.15
292	4¢ dark carmine	1.10	.25	.15
293	5¢ deep blue	5.50	1.05	1.50

294

301

SCOTT NO.	DESCRIPTION	PLATE BLOCK F/NH	UNUSED F/NH	USED F
294	50¢ Oil Wells, Alberta	60.50	12.65	1.05

Coil Stamps Perf. 9-1/2 Vertically

SCOTT NO.	DESCRIPTION	PLATE BLOCK F/NH	UNUSED F/NH	USED F
295-300	**1¢-4¢ complete, 6 vars.......**		**16.80**	**3.30**

(without "Postes-Postage")

SCOTT NO.	DESCRIPTION	PLATE BLOCK F/NH	UNUSED F/NH	USED F
295	1¢ green	......	.35	.30
296	3¢ rose violet	......	.65	.55

(with "Postes-Postage")

SCOTT NO.	DESCRIPTION	PLATE BLOCK F/NH	UNUSED F/NH	USED F
297	1¢ green	......	.35	.25
298	2¢ sepia	......	1.95	1.40
299	3¢ rose violet	......	1.10	.20
300	4¢ dark carmine	......	12.65	.75
301	10¢ Fur Resources	3.30	.65	.15

302 — 303 — 304

1951

SCOTT NO.	DESCRIPTION	PLATE BLOCK F/NH	UNUSED F/NH	USED F
302	$1 Fishing	300.00	65.00	12.00

1951-52 COMMEMORATIVES

SCOTT NO.	DESCRIPTION	PLATE BLOCK F/NH	UNUSED F/NH	USED F
303/19	**(303-04, 311-15, 317-19) complete, 10 vars. ..**	**25.10**	**5.25**	**2.90**
303	3¢ Sir Robert L. Borden	.80	.20	.15
304	4¢ William L.M. King .	1.00	.25	.15

(with "Postes-Postage")

SCOTT NO.	DESCRIPTION	PLATE BLOCK F/NH	UNUSED F/NH	USED F
305	2¢ olive green	.80	.20	.15
306	4¢ orange vermillion .	1.00	.20	.15
306a	same, booklet pane of 3......		1.65	......
306b	same, booklet pane of 6......		2.00	......

Coil Stamps Perf. 9-1/2 Vertically

SCOTT NO.	DESCRIPTION	PLATE BLOCK F/NH	UNUSED F/NH	USED F
309	2¢ olive green	......	1.00	.65
310	4¢ orange vermillion .	......	2.05	.80

311

314

1951 "CAPEX" Exhibition

SCOTT NO.	DESCRIPTION	PLATE BLOCK F/NH	UNUSED F/NH	USED F
311	4¢ Trains of 1851 & 1951	2.50	.55	.15
312	5¢ Steamships	8.25	1.65	1.35
313	7¢ Stagecoach & Plane .	4.95	1.00	.35
314	15¢ "Three Pence Beaver"	4.95	1.00	.30
315	4¢ Royal Visit	.95	.20	.15

315

316

317

318

319

1952

SCOTT NO.	DESCRIPTION	PLATE BLOCK F/NH	UNUSED F/NH	USED F
316	20¢ Paper Production	6.60	1.35	.15
317	4¢ Red Cross	.95	.20	.15
318	3¢ J.J.C. Abbott	.95	.20	.15
319	4¢ A. Mackenzie	1.10	.25	.10

Canada Postage #320-351

320

321

1952-53

SCOTT NO.	DESCRIPTION	PLATE BLOCK F/NH	UNUSED F/NH	USED F
320	7¢ Canada Goose	1.80	.35	.15
321	$1 Indian House & Totem Pole (1953)	55.00	12.10	.80

322

323

324

1953-54 COMMEMORATIVES

SCOTT NO.	DESCRIPTION	PLATE BLOCK F/NH	UNUSED F/NH	USED F
322/50	**(322-24, 330, 335-36, 349-50) complete, 8 varieties**	**8.95**	**1.90**	**1.15**
322	2¢ Polar Bear	.80	.20	.15
323	3¢ Moose	.90	.20	.15
324	4¢ Bighorn Sheep	1.10	.25	.15

325-29, 331-33

330

1953

SCOTT NO.	DESCRIPTION	PLATE BLOCK F/NH	UNUSED F/NH	USED F
325-29	**1¢-5¢ complete, 5 vars.**	**4.50**	**1.10**	**.70**
325	1¢ violet brown	.70	.20	.15
325a	same, booklet pane of 3		.60	......
326	2¢ green	.70	.20	.15
327	3¢ carmine rose	.85	.20	.15
327a	same, booklet pane of 3	......	1.40	......
327b	same, booklet pane of 4	......	1.40	......
328	4¢ violet	1.10	.25	.15
328a	same, bklt. pane of 3 .	......	1.65	......
328b	same, bklt. pane of 6 .	......	1.95	......
329	5¢ ultramarine	1.40	.30	.15
330	4¢ Queen Elizabeth II	.95	.20	.15

Coil Stamps Perf. 9-1/2 Vertically

SCOTT NO.	DESCRIPTION	PLATE BLOCK F/NH	UNUSED F/NH	USED F
331-33	**2¢-4¢ complete, 3 vars. ......**		**4.90**	**3.45**
331	2¢ green	......	1.20	1.00
332	3¢ carmine rose	......	1.20	1.00
333	4¢ violet	......	2.75	1.65

334

335

336

337-342, 345-348

343

SCOTT NO.	DESCRIPTION	PLATE BLOCK F/NH	UNUSED F/NH	USED F
334	50¢ Textile Industry ...	21.00	4.70	.20

1954

SCOTT NO.	DESCRIPTION	PLATE BLOCK F/NH	UNUSED F/NH	USED F
335	4¢ Walrus	1.40	.30	.15
336	5¢ Beaver	1.65	.35	.15
336a	same, booklet pane of 5	......	1.95	......
337-43	**1¢-15¢ cpl., 7 vars. ...**	**10.65**	**2.35**	**1.00**
337	1¢ violet brown	.70	.20	.15
337a	same, booklet pane of 5	......	.75	......
338	2¢ green	.70	.20	.15
338a	mini pane of 25	......	4.40	......
338a	sealed pack of 2	......	8.80	......
339	3¢ carmine rose	.70	.20	.15
340	4¢ violet	.85	.20	.15
340a	same, booklet pane of 5	......	1.65	......
340b	same, booklet pane of 6	......	5.50	......
341	5¢ bright blue	1.10	.20	.15
341a	same, booklet pane of 5	......	1.65	......
341b	mini sheet of 20	......	8.25	......
342	6¢ orange	1.65	.35	.15
343	15¢ Gannet	5.50	1.10	.15

Coil Stamps Perf. 9-1/2 Vertically

SCOTT NO.	DESCRIPTION	PLATE BLOCK F/NH	UNUSED F/NH	USED F
345-48	**2¢-4¢ complete, 3 vars. ......**		**3.30**	**.60**
345	2¢ green	......	.35	.20
347	4¢ violet	......	1.25	.25
348	5¢ bright blue	......	1.85	.20

349

350

351

SCOTT NO.	DESCRIPTION	PLATE BLOCK F/NH	UNUSED F/NH	USED F
349	4¢ J.S.D. Thompson ..	1.30	.25	.15
350	5¢ M. Bowell	1.30	.25	.15

1955

SCOTT NO.	DESCRIPTION	PLATE BLOCK F/NH	UNUSED F/NH	USED F
351	10¢ Eskimo in Kayak .	1.65	.35	.15

352

353

Canada Postage #352-378

SCOTT NO.	DESCRIPTION	PLATE BLOCK F/NH	UNUSED F/NH	USED F
	1955-56 COMMEMORATIVES			
352/64	**(352-61, 364 (complete, 11 varieties ....**	**14.00**	**3.25**	**1.60**
352	4¢ Musk Ox	1.30	.30	.15
353	5¢ Whooping Cranes	1.30	.30	.15

355

357

354

356

358

1955

SCOTT NO.	DESCRIPTION	PLATE BLOCK F/NH	UNUSED F/NH	USED F
354	5¢ Intl. Civil Aviation Org.	1.30	.30	.15
355	5¢ Alberta-Saskatchewan	1.30	.30	.15
356	5¢ Boy Scout Jamboree .	1.30	.30	.15
357	4¢ R.B. Bennett	1.30	.30	.15
358	5¢ C. Tupper	1.30	.30	.15

359

360

361

362

364

363

1956

SCOTT NO.	DESCRIPTION	PLATE BLOCK F/NH	UNUSED F/NH	USED F
359	5¢ Hockey Players	1.30	.30	.15
360	4¢ Caribou	1.50	.35	.15
361	5¢ Mountain Goat	1.50	.35	.15
362	20¢ Paper Industry ...	6.60	1.35	.15
363	25¢ Chemical Industry	8.25	1.65	.15
364	5¢ Fire Prevention	1.30	.30	.15

365

SCOTT NO.	DESCRIPTION	PLATE BLOCK F/NH	UNUSED F/NH	USED F
	1957 COMMEMORATIVES			
365-74	**complete, 10 varieties**	**17.50(7)**	**4.80**	**3.15**
365-68	Recreation, attached .	1.90	1.45	1.60
365	5¢ Fishing	......	.40	.20
366	5¢ Swimming	......	.40	.20
367	5¢ Hunting	......	.40	.20
368	5¢ Skiing	......	.40	.20

369

370

371

372

373

374

SCOTT NO.	DESCRIPTION	PLATE BLOCK F/NH	UNUSED F/NH	USED F
369	5¢ Loon	1.20	.30	.15
370	5¢ D. Thompson, Explorer	1.20	.30	.15
371	5¢ Parliament Building	1.20	.30	.15
372	15¢ Posthorn & Globe	11.00	2.20	1.75
373	5¢ Coal Miner	1.00	.25	.15
374	5¢ Royal Visit	1.00	.25	.15

375

376

377

378

SCOTT NO.	DESCRIPTION	PLATE BLOCK F/NH	UNUSED F/NH	USED F
	1958 COMMEMORATIVES			
375-82	**complete, 8 varieties**	**9.50(6)**	**1.95**	**1.15**
375	5¢ Newspaper	......	.30	.15
376	5¢ Int'l. Geophysical Year	......	.25	.15
377	5¢ Miner Panning Gold ...	1.75	.25	.15
378	5¢ La Verendrye, Explorer	1.30	.25	.15

379

380

Canada Postage #379-400

381

382

SCOTT NO.	DESCRIPTION	PLATE BLOCK F/NH	UNUSED F/NH	USED F
79	5¢ S. deChamplain	3.10	.25	.15
80	5¢ National Health	1.30	.25	.15
81	5¢ Petroleum Industry	1.30	.25	.15
82	5¢ Speaker's Chair & Mace	1.30	.25	.15

383

384

385

386

389

387

388

1959 COMMEMORATIVES

SCOTT NO.	DESCRIPTION	PLATE BLOCK F/NH	UNUSED F/NH	USED F
33-88	**complete, 6 varieties**	**9.00**	**1.45**	**.85**
33	5¢ Old & Modern Planes	1.35	.25	.15
34	5¢ NATO Anniversary ..	1.20	.25	.15
35	5¢ Woman Tending Tree	1.10	.25	.15
36	5¢ Royal Tour	1.10	.25	.15
37	5¢ St. Lawrence Seaway	3.60	.25	.15
37a	same, center inverted ...	...	9250.00	8500.00
38	5¢ Plains of Abraham ...	1.10	.25	.15

1960-62 COMMEMORATIVES

SCOTT NO.	DESCRIPTION	PLATE BLOCK F/NH	UNUSED F/NH	USED F
39-400	**complete, 12 varieties ....**	**12.50**	**2.85**	**1.70**
39	5¢ Girl Guides Emblem	1.10	.25	.15

390

391

392

SCOTT NO.	DESCRIPTION	PLATE BLOCK F/NH	UNUSED F/NH	USED F
390	5¢ Battle of Long Sault ..	1.10	.25	.15

1961

SCOTT NO.	DESCRIPTION	PLATE BLOCK F/NH	UNUSED F/NH	USED F
391	5¢ Earth Mover	1.10	.25	.15
392	5¢ E.P. Johnson	1.10	.25	.15

393

395

396

394

397

SCOTT NO.	DESCRIPTION	PLATE BLOCK F/NH	UNUSED F/NH	USED F
393	5¢ A. Meighen	1.10	.25	.15
394	5¢ Colombo Plan	1.10	.25	.15
395	5¢ Natural Resources ...	1.10	.25	.15

1962

SCOTT NO.	DESCRIPTION	PLATE BLOCK F/NH	UNUSED F/NH	USED F
396	5¢ Education	1.10	.25	.15
397	5¢ Red River Settlement	1.10	.25	.15

398

399

400

401-09

SCOTT NO.	DESCRIPTION	PLATE BLOCK F/NH	UNUSED F/NH	USED F
398	5¢ Jean Talon	1.10	.25	.15
399	5¢ Victoria, B.C.	1.10	.25	.15
400	5¢ Trans-Canada	1.10	.25	.15

Canada Postage #401-430

SCOTT NO.	DESCRIPTION	PLATE BLOCK F/NH	UNUSED F/NH	USED F
	1962-63			
401-05	**1¢-5¢ complete, 5 varieties**	**6.50**	**1.00**	**.70**
401	1¢ deep brown (1963)	.45	.20	.15
401a	same, booklet pane of 5	......	3.30	......
402	2¢ green (1963)	3.60	.20	.15
402a	mini pane of 25	......	4.70	......
402a	same, sealed pack of 2	......	10.50	......
403	3¢ purple (1963)	.70	.20	.15
404	4¢ carmine (1963)	1.00	.20	.15
404a	same, booklet pane of 5	......	3.30	......
404b	mini pane of 25	......	6.60	......
405	5¢ violet blue	1.20	.25	.15
405a	same, booklet pane of 5	......	3.85	......
405b	mini pane of 20	......	7.15	......
	1963-64 Coil Stamps, Perf. 9-1/2 Horiz.			
406-09	**2¢-5¢ complete, 4 varieties**	**......**	**11.40**	**3.65**
406	2¢ green	......	3.30	1.55
407	3¢ purple (1964)	......	2.30	.95
408	4¢ carmine	......	3.30	.95
409	5¢ violet blue	......	3.10	.40

410

411

412

413

SCOTT NO.	DESCRIPTION	PLATE BLOCK F/NH	UNUSED F/NH	USED F
	1963-64 COMMEMORATIVES			
410/35	**(410, 412-13, 416-17, 431-35) 10 varieties.**	**10.20**	**2.35**	**1.45**
410	5¢ Sir Casimir S. Gzowski	1.10	.25	.15
411	$1 Export Trade	74.25	15.00	2.50
412	5¢ Sir M. Frobisher, Explorer	1.10	.25	.15
413	5¢ First Mail Routes ..	1.10	.25	.15

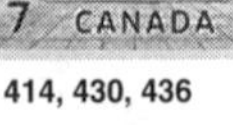

414, 430, 436

415

416

417

SCOTT NO.	DESCRIPTION	PLATE BLOCK F/NH	UNUSED F/NH	USED F
	1963-64			
414	7¢ Jet Takeoff (1964)	1.50	.35	.55
415	15¢ Canada Geese	11.00	2.20	.20
	1964			
416	5¢ World Peace	1.10	.25	.15
417	5¢ Canadian Unity	1.10	.25	.15

418
Ontario & White Trillium

429A
Canada & Maple Leaf

COATS OF ARMS & FLORAL EMBLEMS

419 *Quebec & White Garden Lily*
420 *Nova Scotia & Mayflower*
421 *New Brunswick & Purple Violet (1965)*
422 *Manitoba & Prairie Crocus (1965)*
423 *British Columbia & Dogwood (1965)*
424 *Prince Edward Island & Lady's Slipper (1965)*
425 *Saskatchewan & Prairie Lily (1966)*
426 *Alberta & Wild Rose (1966)*
427 *Newfoundland & Pitcher Plant (1966)*
428 *Yukon & Fireweed (1966)*
429 *Northwest Territories & Mountain Avens (1966)*

SCOTT NO.	DESCRIPTION	PLATE BLOCK F/NH	UNUSED F/NH	USED F
	1964-66			
418-29A	**complete, 13 varieties**	**13.60**	**3.10**	**2.00**
418	5¢ red brown, buff & green	1.10	.25	.15
419	5¢ green, yellow & orange	1.10	.25	.20
420	5¢ blue, pink & green	1.10	.25	.15
421	5¢ carmine, green & violet	1.10	.25	.15
422	5¢ red brown, lilac & green	1.10	.25	.15
423	5¢ lilac, green & bistre	1.10	.25	.15
424	5¢ violet, green & deep rose	1.10	.25	.15
425	5¢ sepia, orange & green	1.10	.25	.20
426	5¢ green, yellow & carmine	1.10	.25	.15
427	5¢ black, green & carmine	1.10	.25	.15
428	5¢ dark blue, rose & green	1.10	.25	.15
429	5¢ olive, yellow & green	1.10	.25	.20
429A	5¢ dark blue & red (1966)	1.10	.25	.15
	1964 Surcharged on 414			
430	8¢ on 7¢ Jet Takeoff	1.65	.35	.35

431

432

433

434, 435

437

Canada Postage #431-453

SCOTT NO.	DESCRIPTION	PLATE BLOCK F/NH	UNUSED F/NH	USED F
431	5¢ Charlottetown Conference	1.10	.25	.15
432	5¢ Quebec Conference	1.10	.20	.15
433	5¢ Queen Elizabeth's Visit	1.10	.25	.15
434	3¢ Christmas	.85	.20	.15
434a	mini sheet of 25	......	7.50	......
434a	same, sealed pack of 2	......	15.50	......
435	5¢ Christmas	1.10	.25	.15

Jet Type of 1964

436	8¢ Jet Takeoff	1.65	.35	.25

1965 COMMEMORATIVES

437-44	**8 varieties ....**	**7.80**	**1.85**	**1.15**
437	5¢ I.C.Y.	1.00	.25	.15

438

439

440

441

442

438	5¢ Sir Wilfred Grenfell	1.00	.25	.15
439	5¢ National Flag	1.00	.25	.15
440	5¢ Winston Churchill .	1.00	.25	.15
441	5¢ Inter-Parliamentary	1.00	.25	.15
442	5¢ Ottawa, National Capital	1.00	.25	.15

443-44

445

446

443	3¢ Christmas	.80	.20	.15
443a	mini pane of 25	......	6.50	......
443a	same, sealed pack of 2	......	13.00	......
444	5¢ Christmas	1.40	.25	.15

1966 COMMEMORATIVES

445-52	**8 varieties ....**	**7.75**	**1.80**	**1.15**
445	5¢ Alouette II Satellite	1.10	.25	.15
446	5¢ La Salle Arrival	1.10	.25	.15

447

448

SCOTT NO.	DESCRIPTION	PLATE BLOCK F/NH	UNUSED F/NH	USED F
447	5¢ Highway Safety ..	1.10	.25	.15
448	5¢ London Conference	1.10	.25	.15

449

450

451, 452

453

449	5¢ Atomic Reactor ..	1.10	.25	.15
450	5¢ Parliamentary Library	1.10	.25	.15
451	3¢ Christmas	.70	.20	.15
451a	mini pane of 25	......	4.50	......
451a	same, sealed pack of 2	......	9.00	......
452	5¢ Christmas	.85	.20	.15

1967 COMMEMORATIVES

453/77	**(453, 469-77) complete, 10 varieties ....**	**10.00**	**2.30**	**.45**
453	5¢ National Centennial	1.10	.25	.15

454

455

456, 466

457, 467

458, 468

459-460F, 468A-B, 543-49

461

465B

Canada Postage #454-477

SCOTT NO.	DESCRIPTION	PLATE BLOCK F/NH	UNUSED F/NH	USED F

Regional Views & Art Designs
1967-72 Perf.12 except as noted

SCOTT NO.	DESCRIPTION	PLATE BLOCK F/NH	UNUSED F/NH	USED F
454-65B	**1¢-$1 complete, 14 varieties ....**	**95.50**	**18.25**	**2.50**
454-64	**1¢-20¢, 11 varieties**	**21.00**	**3.35**	**1.45**
454	1¢ brown	.90	.20	.15
454a	same, booklet pane of 5	......	.45	......
454b	booklet pane, 1¢(1), 6¢(4)	......	1.65	......
454c	booklet pane, 1¢(5), 3¢(5)	......	3.85	......

NOTE—#454d, 454e, 456a, 457d, 458d, 460g, and 460h are Booklet Singles

SCOTT NO.	DESCRIPTION	PLATE BLOCK F/NH	UNUSED F/NH	USED F
454d	1¢ perf. 10 (1968) ...	......	.25	.20
454e	1¢ 12-1/2 x 12 (1969)	......	.45	.15
455	2¢ green	1.40	.20	.15
455a	booklet pane 2¢(4), 3¢(4)	......	1.65	......
456	3¢ dull purple	1.20	.20	.15
456a	3¢ 12-1/2 x 12 (1971)	......	1.10	.45
457	4¢ carmine rose	1.65	.20	.15
457a	same, booklet pane 5	......	1.20	......
457b	miniature pane of 25	......	16.50	......
457c	same, booklet pane of 25	......	7.70	......
457d	4¢ perf.10 (1968)	......	.70	.30
458	5¢ blue	.85	.20	.15
458a	same, booklet pane of 5	......	5.50	......
458b	miniature pane of 20	......	24.75	......
458c	booklet pane of 20, perf.10	.....	6.05	......
458d	5¢ perf. 10 (1968) ...	......	.70	.30
459	6¢ orange, perf. 10 (1968)	3.85	.35	.15
459a	same, booklet pane of 25	......	7.70	......
459b	6¢ orange 12-1/2x12 (1969)	3.30	.35	.15
460	6¢ black, 12-1/2x12 (1970)	1.95	.25	.15
460a	booklet pane of 25, perf.10	......	15.40	......
460b	booklet pane of 25, 12-1/2x12......		13.60	......
460c	6¢ black, 12-1/2x12 (1970)	2.20	.30	.15
460d	booklet pane of 4, 12-1/2x12	.....	5.50	......
460e	booklet pane of 4, perf.10	......	7.70	......
460f	6¢ black, perf. 12 (1972)	2.50	.40	.15
460g	6¢ black, perf. 10 (I)	......	1.40	.40
460h	6¢ black, perf. 10 (II)	......	1.95	.85

460, 460a, b,& g: Original Die. Weak shading lines around 6.
460 c, d, e, & h: Reworked plate lines strengthened, darker.
460f: Original Die. Strong shading lines, similar to 468B, but Perf 12x12 .

SCOTT NO.	DESCRIPTION	PLATE BLOCK F/NH	UNUSED F/NH	USED F
461	8¢ "Alaska Highway"	2.00	.35	.20
462	10¢ "The Jack Pine"	1.80	.35	.15
463	15¢ "Bylot Island"	3.30	.55	.15
464	20¢ "The Ferry, Quebec"	3.30	.70	.15
465	25¢ "The Solemn Land"	6.90	1.40	.15
465A	50¢ "Summer Stores"	22.00	4.40	.15
465B	$1 "Imp. Wildcat No. 3"	49.50	9.90	.80

1967-70 Coil Stamps

SCOTT NO.	DESCRIPTION	PLATE BLOCK F/NH	UNUSED F/NH	USED F
466-68B	**3¢-6¢ complete, 5 varieties**	**......**	**4.50**	**3.35**

Perf. 9-1/2 Horizontally

SCOTT NO.	DESCRIPTION	PLATE BLOCK F/NH	UNUSED F/NH	USED F
466	3¢ dull purple	......	1.55	.95
467	4¢ carmine rose	......	.90	1.55
468	5¢ blue	......	1.65	.70

Perf. 10 Horizontally

SCOTT NO.	DESCRIPTION	PLATE BLOCK F/NH	UNUSED F/NH	USED F
468A	6¢ orange (1969)	......	.35	.15
468B	6¢ black (1970)	......	.35	.15

NOTE : See #543-50 for similar issues

469

470

471

472

473

1967

SCOTT NO.	DESCRIPTION	PLATE BLOCK F/NH	UNUSED F/NH	USED F
469	5¢ Expo '67	1.10	.25	.15
470	5¢ Women's Franchise .	1.10	.25	.15
471	5¢ Royal Visit	1.10	.25	.15
472	5¢ Pan-American Games	1.10	.25	.15
473	5¢ Canadian Press........	1.10	.25	.15

474

475

476, 477

SCOTT NO.	DESCRIPTION	PLATE BLOCK F/NH	UNUSED F/NH	USED F
474	5¢ George P. Vanier	1.10	.25	.15
475	5¢ View of Toronto	1.10	.25	.15
476	3¢ Christmas	.90	.20	.15
476a	miniature pane of 25	......	4.25	......
476a	same, sealed pack of 2 .	......	8.50	......
477	5¢ Christmas	.85	.20	.15

CANADA
5
478

479

Canada Postage #478-493

SCOTT NO.	DESCRIPTION	PLATE BLOCK F/NH	UNUSED F/NH	USED F

480

481

482

1968 COMMEMORATIVES

SCOTT NO.	DESCRIPTION	PLATE BLOCK F/NH	UNUSED F/NH	USED F
478-89	**complete, 12 varieties**	**22.00**	**4.30**	**2.70**
478	5¢ Gray Jays	4.15	.45	.15
479	5¢ Weather Map & Inst .	1.10	.25	.15
480	5¢ Narwhal	1.10	.25	.15
481	5¢ Int'l Hydro. Decade	1.10	.25	.15
482	5¢ Voyage of "Nonsuch"	1.40	.25	.15

483

484

485

486

SCOTT NO.	DESCRIPTION	PLATE BLOCK F/NH	UNUSED F/NH	USED F
483	5¢ Lacrosse Players	1.10	.25	.15
484	5¢ G. Brown, Politician ...	1.10	.25	.15
485	5¢ H. Bourassa, Journalist	1.10	.25	.15
486	15¢ W.W.I Armistice	8.25	1.65	1.20

NOTE: Beginning with #478, some issues show a printer's inscription with no actual plate number.

487

488

490

491

492

493

SCOTT NO.	DESCRIPTION	PLATE BLOCK F/NH	UNUSED F/NH	USED F
487	5¢ J. McCrae	1.10	.25	.15
488	5¢ Eskimo Family ...	.85	.20	.15
488a	same, booklet pane of 10	.....	3.15	.....
489	6¢ Mother & Child ...	1.10	.25	.15

1969 COMMEMORATIVES

SCOTT NO.	DESCRIPTION	PLATE BLOCK F/NH	UNUSED F/NH	USED F
490-504	**complete, 15 varieties**	**48.25**	**11.25**	**7.15**
490	6¢ Game of Curling .	1.10	.25	.15
491	6¢ V. Massey	1.10	.25	.15
492	50¢ A. deSuzor-Cote, Artist	17.60	3.85	2.20
493	6¢ I.L.O.	1.10	.25	.15

494

495

496

499

500

501

Canada Postage #494-530

502, 503   504

SCOTT NO.	DESCRIPTION	PLATE BLOCK F/NH	UNUSED F/NH	USED F
494	15¢ Vickers Vimy Over Atlantic	8.80	2.85	1.65
495	6¢ Sir W. Osler	1.10	.25	.15
496	6¢ White Throated Sparrows	1.65	.35	.15
497	10¢ Ipswich Sparrow	3.85	.75	.50
498	25¢ Hermit Thrush ..	8.25	1.65	1.55
499	6¢ Map of Prince Edward Island	1.10	.25	.15
500	6¢ Canada Games ..	1.10	.25	.15
501	6¢ Sir Isaac Brock ...	1.10	.25	.15
502	5¢ Children of Various Races	.85	.20	.15
502a	booklet pane of 10 ..	......	2.75	......
503	6¢ Children Various Races	.85	.20	.15
504	6¢ Stephen Leacock	1.20	.25	.15

505

506

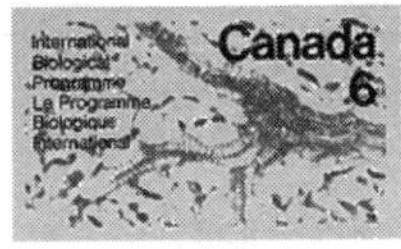

507

1970 COMMEMORATIVES

SCOTT NO.	DESCRIPTION	PLATE BLOCK F/NH	UNUSED F/NH	USED F
505/31	**(505-18, 531) 15 varieties**	**24.50**	**11.75**	**11.00**
505	6¢ Manitoba Cent. ..	.85	.20	.15
506	6¢ N.W. Territory Centenary	.85	.20	.15
507	6¢ International Biological	.85	.20	.15

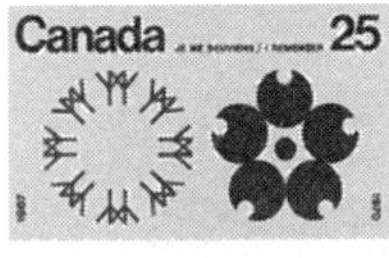

508

509

SCOTT NO.	DESCRIPTION	PLATE BLOCK F/NH	UNUSED F/NH	USED F
508-11	Expo '70 attached ...	9.90	8.80	8.80
508	25¢ Emblems	......	2.15	2.15
509	25¢ Dogwood	......	2.15	2.15
510	25¢ Lily	......	2.15	2.15
511	25¢ Trilium	......	2.15	2.15

512

513-514

515   516

517

518

SCOTT NO.	DESCRIPTION	PLATE BLOCK F/NH	UNUSED F/NH	USED F
512	6¢ H. Kelsey—Explorer	.85	.20	.15
513	10¢ 25th U.N. Anniversary	3.30	.70	.45
514	15¢ 25th U.N. Anniversary	4.95	1.00	1.10
515	6¢ L. Riel—Metis Leader	.85	.20	.15
516	6¢ Sir A. Mackenzie-Explorer	.85	.20	.15
517	6¢ Sir O. Mowat Confederation Father	.85	.20	.15
518	6¢ Isle of Spruce	.85	.20	.15

519   524

529

530

SCOTT NO.	DESCRIPTION	PLATE BLOCK F/NH	UNUSED F/NH	USED F
519-30	**5¢-15¢ complete, 12 varieties ....**	**16.75**	**5.50**	**2.4**
519-23	5¢ Christmas, attached	4.95(10)	2.25	2.0
519	5¢ Santa Claus	......	.40	
520	5¢ Sleigh	......	.40	
521	5¢ Nativity	......	.40	
522	5¢ Skiing	......	.40	
523	5¢ Snowman & Tree	......	.40	
524-28	6¢ Christmas, attached	6.00(10)	2.50	2.
524	6¢ Christ Child	......	.45	
525	6¢ Tree & Children ..	......	.45	
526	6¢ Toy Store	......	.45	
527	6¢ Santa Claus	......	.45	
528	6¢ Church	......	.45	

NOTE: We cannot supply blocks or pairs of the 5¢ & 6¢ Christmas designs in varying combinations of designs.

SCOTT NO.	DESCRIPTION	PLATE BLOCK F/NH	UNUSED F/NH	USED F
529	10¢ Christ Child	2.20	.40	
530	15¢ Snowmobile & Trees	4.50	.85	

Canada Postage #531-558

531

532

SCOTT NO.	DESCRIPTION	PLATE BLOCK F/NH	UNUSED F/NH	USED F
31	6¢ Sir Donald A. Smith	.85	.20	.15

1971 COMMEMORATIVES

SCOTT NO.	DESCRIPTION	PLATE BLOCK F/NH	UNUSED F/NH	USED F
32/58	**(532-42, 552-58) complete, 18 varieties**	**29.75**	**6.10**	**7.00**
32	6¢ E. Carr—Painter & Writer	.85	.20	.15

533

534

535

539

SCOTT NO.	DESCRIPTION	PLATE BLOCK F/NH	UNUSED F/NH	USED F
33	6¢ Discovery of Insulin	.85	.20	.15
34	6¢ Sir E. Rutherford—Physicist	.85	.20	.15
35-38	6¢-7¢ Maple Leaves ..	4.00	.90	.50
35	6¢ Maple Seeds	1.10	.25	.15
36	6¢ Summer Leaf	1.10	.25	.15
37	Autumn Leaf	1.10	.25	.15
38	7¢ Winter Leaf	1.10	.25	.15
39	6¢ L. Papineau—Polit. Reform	.85	.20	.15

540

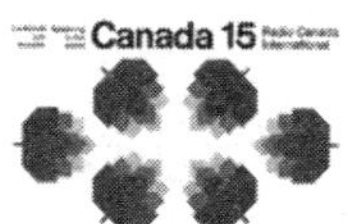

541

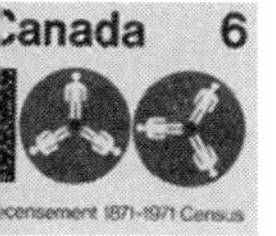

542

543, 549

544, 550

SCOTT NO.	DESCRIPTION	PLATE BLOCK F/NH	UNUSED F/NH	USED F
540	6¢ Copper Mine Expedition	.85	.20	.15
541	15¢ Radio Canada Int'l	7.70	1.65	1.40
542	6¢ Census Centennial	.85	.20	.15

1971

SCOTT NO.	DESCRIPTION	PLATE BLOCK F/NH	UNUSED F/NH	USED F
543	7¢ Trans. & Communication	3.30	.30	.15
543a	bklt. pane, 7¢(3), 3¢(1), 1¢(1)		3.05	......
543b	bklt. pane 7¢(12), 3¢(4), 1¢(4)......		7.70	......
544	8¢ Parliamentary Library	3.30	.30	.15
544a	bklt. pane 8¢(2), 6¢(1), 1¢(3)		1.95	......
544b	bklt. pane 8¢(11), 6¢(1), 1¢(6)......		5.80	......
544c	bklt. pane 8¢(5), 6¢(1), 1¢(4)		2.50	......

1971 Coil Stamps Perf.10 Horizontally

SCOTT NO.	DESCRIPTION	PLATE BLOCK F/NH	UNUSED F/NH	USED F
549	7¢ Trans. & Communication	......	.40	.15
550	8¢ Parliamentary Library	......	.35	.15

552

553

SCOTT NO.	DESCRIPTION	PLATE BLOCK F/NH	UNUSED F/NH	USED F
552	7¢ B.C. Centennial ..	.85	.20	.15
553	7¢ Paul Kane	2.50	.35	.15

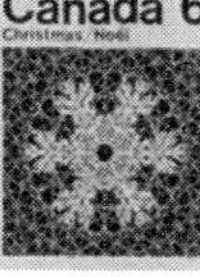

554-55

556-57

SCOTT NO.	DESCRIPTION	PLATE BLOCK F/NH	UNUSED F/NH	USED F
554-57	6¢-15¢ Christmas ...	8.00	1.65	1.50
554	6¢ Snowflake, dark blue	.85	.20	.15
555	7¢ same, bright green	1.10	.25	.15
556	10¢ same, deep carmine & silver	2.20	.45	.40
557	15¢ same, light ultramarine, deep carmine & silver	4.00	.85	.85

558

559

560

561

SCOTT NO.	DESCRIPTION	PLATE BLOCK F/NH	UNUSED F/NH	USED F
558	7¢ P. Laporte	2.65	.25	.15

Canada Postage #559-599a

SCOTT NO.	DESCRIPTION	PLATE BLOCK F/NH	UNUSED F/NH	USED F
	1972 COMMEMORATIVES			
559/610	**(559-61, 582-85, 606-10) 12 varieties**	**47.85(9)**	**9.75**	**7.55**
559	8¢ Figure Skating	1.10	.25	.15
560	8¢ W.H.O. Heart Disease	1.40	.30	.15
561	8¢ Frontenac & Ft. St. Louis	1.10	.25	.15

VERY FINE QUALITY: From 1935 to date, add 20% to the Fine price. Minimum of 3¢ per stamp.

562

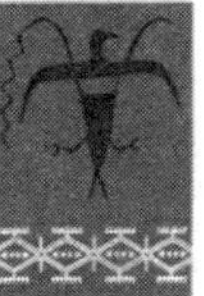

564

SCOTT NO.	DESCRIPTION	PLATE BLOCK F/NH	UNUSED F/NH	USED F
	1972-76 INDIAN PEOPLES OF CANADA			
562-81	**complete, 20 varieties**	**14.00**	**5.90**	**2.85**
562-63	Plains, attached	1.65	.70	.60
562	8¢ Buffalo Chase	......	.30	.15
563	8¢ Indian Artifacts ...	......	.30	.15
564-65	Plains, attached	1.65	.70	.60
564	8¢ Thunderbird Symbolism	......	.30	.15
565	8¢ Sun Dance Costume	......	.30	.15
566-67	Algonkians, attached (1973)	1.65	.70	.60
566	8¢ Algonkian Artifacts	......	.30	.15
567	8¢ Micmac Indians ..	......	.30	.15
568-69	Algonkians, attached (1973)	1.65	.70	.60
568	8¢ Thunderbird Symbolism	......	.30	.15
569	8¢ Costume	......	.30	.15
570-71	Pacific, attached (1974)	1.65	.70	.50
570	8¢ Nootka Sound House	......	.30	.15
571	8¢ Artifacts	......	.30	.15
572-73	Pacific, attached (1974)	1.65	.70	.50
572	8¢ Chief in Chilkat Blanket	......	.30	.15
573	8¢ Thunderbird—Kwakiutl	......	.30	.15
574-75	Subarctic, attached (1975)	1.20	.50	.45
574	8¢ Canoe & Artifacts	......	.25	.15
575	8¢ Dance—Kutcha-Kutchin	......	.25	.15
576-77	Subarctic, attached (1975)	1.20	.50	.45
576	8¢ Kutchin Costume	......	.25	.15
577	8¢ Ojibwa Thunderbird	......	.25	.15
578-79	Iroquois, attached (1976)	1.20	.50	.45
578	10¢ Masks	......	.25	.15
579	10¢ Camp	......	.25	.15
580-81	Iroquois, attached (1976)	1.20	.50	.45
580	10¢ Iroquois Thunderbird	......	.25	.15
581	10¢ Man & Woman .	......	.25	.15

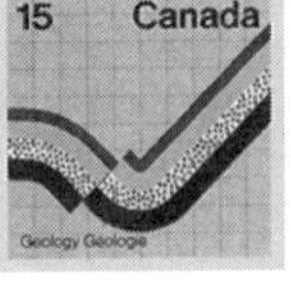

582

SCOTT NO.	DESCRIPTION	PLATE BLOCK F/NH	UNUSED F/NH	USED F
	1972 EARTH SCIENCES			
582-85	Sciences, attached .	38.50(16)	7.50	7.50
582	15¢ Geology	......	1.80	1.50
583	15¢ Geography	......	1.80	1.50
584	15¢ Photogrammetry	......	1.80	1.50
585	15¢ Cartography	......	1.80	1.50

NOTE: Plate Block Price is for a miniature pane of 16 Stamps.

586

593, 593b, 593A, 604-605

SCOTT NO.	DESCRIPTION	PLATE BLOCK F/NH	UNUSED F/NH	USED F
	1973-76 DEFINITIVE ISSUE PERF. 12 x 12-1/2			
586-93A	**1¢-10¢, 9 varieties .**	**6.85**	**1.75**	**1.3**
586	1¢ Sir J. Macdonald	.70	.20	.1
586a	bklt. pane 1¢(3), 6¢(1), 8¢(2)	......	.40	.....
586b	bklt. pane 1¢(6), 6¢(1), 8¢(11)	......	1.65	.....
586c	bklt. pane 1¢(2), 2¢(4), 8¢(4)	......	1.30	.....
587	2¢ Sir W. Laurier	.70	.20	.1
588	3¢ Sir R.L. Borden ..	.70	.20	.1
589	4¢ W.L. Mackenzie King	.70	.20	.1
590	5¢ R.B. Bennett	.80	.20	.1
591	6¢ L.B. Pearson	.80	.20	.1
592	7¢ L. St. Laurent (1974)	.85	.20	.1
593	8¢ Queen Elizabeth	.85	.20	.1
593b	same (pf. 13x13-1/2) (1976)	4.95	.80	.4
593A	10¢ Queen Elizabeth (perf 13x13-1/2) (1976)	1.10	.25	.1
593c	10¢ same, perf 12x12-1/2 booklet single	......	.35	.2

594, 594a, 594B

599, 599a, 600

SCOTT NO.	DESCRIPTION	PLATE BLOCK F/NH	UNUSED F/NH	USED F
	1972-73 Photogravure & Engraved Perf. 12-1/2x12			
594-99	**10¢-$1, 6 varieties .**	**23.60**	**5.00**	**1.2**
594	10¢ Forests	1.10	.25	.1
595	15¢ Mountain Sheep	1.55	.35	.1
596	20¢ Prairie Mosaic ..	2.30	.50	.1
597	25¢ Polar Bears	2.55	.55	.1
598	50¢ Seashore	5.25	1.10	.1
599	$1 Vancouver Skyline(1973)	12.10	2.50	.5

NOTE: #594-97 exist with 2 types of phosphor tagging. Prices are for Ottawa tagged. Winnipeg tagged are listed on page 320.

SCOTT NO.	DESCRIPTION	PLATE BLOCK F/NH	UNUSED F/NH	USED F
	1976-77 Perf. 13			
594a	10¢ Forests	1.40	.30	.1
595a	15¢ Mountain Sheep	1.85	.40	.2
596a	20¢ Prairie Mosaic ..	2.65	.55	.1
597a	25¢ Polar Bears	2.50	.75	.1
598a	50¢ Seashore	8.00	1.65	.1
599a	$1 Vancouver Skyline(1977)	12.10	2.50	.4

Canada Postage #600-624

SCOTT NO.	DESCRIPTION	PLATE BLOCK F/NH	UNUSED F/NH	USED F
	1972 Lithographed & Engraved Perf. 11			
600	$1 Vancouver Skyline	22.00	4.95	1.95
601	$2 Quebec Buildings	19.80	4.15	2.50
	1974-76 Coil Stamps			
604	8¢ Queen Elizabeth	......	.25	.15
605	10¢ Queen Elizabeth (1976)	......	.30	.15

606, 607

608, 609

1972

SCOTT NO.	DESCRIPTION	PLATE BLOCK F/NH	UNUSED F/NH	USED F
606-09	6¢-15¢ Christmas ...	7.00	1.45	1.25
606	6¢ Five candles	.85	.20	.15
607	8¢ same	1.10	.25	.15
608	10¢ Six candles	1.95	.40	.25
609	15¢ same	3.30	.70	.80

610

611

SCOTT NO.	DESCRIPTION	PLATE BLOCK F/NH	UNUSED F/NH	USED F
610	8¢ C.Krieghoff—Painter	1.10	.25	.15
	1973 COMMEMORATIVES			
611-28	**18 varieties, complete**	**27.40**	**6.15**	**4.95**
611	8¢ Monseignor De Laval	1.00	.25	.15

612

SCOTT NO.	DESCRIPTION	PLATE BLOCK F/NH	UNUSED F/NH	USED F
612	8¢ G.A. French & Map	1.35	.30	.15
613	10¢ Spectrograph ...	1.65	.35	.35
614	15¢ "Musical Ride" ..	3.30	.70	.60

615

616

617

618

SCOTT NO.	DESCRIPTION	PLATE BLOCK F/NH	UNUSED F/NH	USED F
615	8¢ J. Mance—Nurse	1.00	.25	.15
616	8¢ J. Howe	1.00	.25	.15
617	15¢ "Mist Fantasy" Painting	2.75	.55	.50
618	8¢ P.E.I. Confederation	1.00	.25	.15

619

620, 621

SCOTT NO.	DESCRIPTION	PLATE BLOCK F/NH	UNUSED F/NH	USED F
619	8¢ Scottish Settlers .	1.00	.25	.15
620	8¢ Royal Visit	1.00	.25	.15
621	15¢ same	3.10	.70	.60

622

623, 624

SCOTT NO.	DESCRIPTION	PLATE BLOCK F/NH	UNUSED F/NH	USED F
622	8¢ Nellie McClung ...	1.00	.25	.15
623	8¢ 21st Olympic Games	1.00	.25	.15
624	15¢ same	2.75	.55	.60

Canada Postage #625-655

625

627

SCOTT NO.	DESCRIPTION	PLATE BLOCK F/NH	UNUSED F/NH	USED F
625-28	6¢ to 15¢ Christmas	5.75	1.20	1.10
625	6¢ Skate	.80	.20	.15
626	8¢ Bird Ornament ...	1.00	.25	.15
627	10¢ Santa Claus	1.40	.30	.30
628	15¢ Shepherd	2.75	.55	.60

629

633

1974 COMMEMORATIVES

SCOTT NO.	DESCRIPTION	PLATE BLOCK F/NH	UNUSED F/NH	USED F
629-55	**complete, 27 varieties**	**22.40(16)**	**9.15**	**6.25**
629-32	Summer Olympics, attached	1.65	1.40	1.35
629	8¢ Children Diving ..	......	.35	.20
630	8¢ Jogging	......	.35	.20
631	8¢ Bicycling	......	.35	.20
632	8¢ Hiking	......	.35	.20
633	8¢ Winnipeg Centenary	1.00	.25	.15

634

SCOTT NO.	DESCRIPTION	PLATE BLOCK F/NH	UNUSED F/NH	USED F
634-39	Postal Carriers, attached	3.60(6)	3.00	2.75
634	8¢ Postal Clerk & Client	......	.40	.35
635	8¢ Mail Pick-up	......	.40	.35
636	8¢ Mail Handler	......	.40	.35
637	8¢ Sorting Mail	......	.40	.35
638	8¢ Letter Carrier	......	.40	.35
639	8¢ Rural Delivery	......	.40	.35

640

641

642

643

644

648, 649

SCOTT NO.	DESCRIPTION	PLATE BLOCK F/NH	UNUSED F/NH	USED F
640	8¢ Agriculture Symbol	1.00	.25	.15
641	8¢ Antique to Modern Phones	1.00	.25	.15
642	8¢ World Cycling Championship	1.00	.25	.15
643	8¢ Mennonite Settlers	1.00	.25	.15
644-47	Winter Olympics, attached	1.65	1.40	1.20
644	8¢ Snowshoeing	......	.35	.20
645	8¢ Skiing	....	.35	.20
646	8¢ Skating	.....	.35	.20
647	8¢ Curling	.....	.35	.20
648	8¢ U.P.U. Cent.	1.00	.25	.15
649	15¢ same	2.75	.55	.5

650

651

SCOTT NO.	DESCRIPTION	PLATE BLOCK F/NH	UNUSED F/NH	USED F
650-53	6¢ to 15¢ Christmas	5.65	1.25	1.1
650	6¢ Nativity	.80	.20	.15
651	8¢ Skaters in Hull	.80	.20	.15
652	10¢ The Ice Cone ...	1.60	.35	.3
653	15¢ Laurentian Village	2.75	.55	.5

654

655

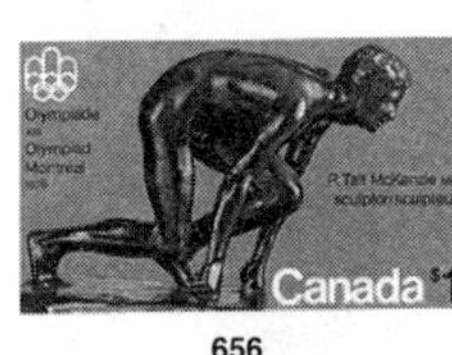

656

657

SCOTT NO.	DESCRIPTION	PLATE BLOCK F/NH	UNUSED F/NH	USED F
654	8¢ G. Marconi—Radio Inventor	1.00	.25	.1
655	8¢ W.H. Merritt & Welland Canal	1.00	.25	.1

Canada Postage #656-680

SCOTT NO.	DESCRIPTION	PLATE BLOCK F/NH	UNUSED F/NH	USED F
	1975 COMMEMORATIVES			
656-80	**complete, 25 varieties**	**67.50(18)**	**16.40**	**12.00**
656	$1 "The Sprinter"	11.00	2.50	1.95
657	$2 "The Plunger"	25.35	5.75	4.40

658 **659**

SCOTT NO.	DESCRIPTION	PLATE BLOCK F/NH	UNUSED F/NH	USED F
658-59	Writers, attached	1.05	.45	.40
658	8¢ L.M. Montgomery—Author		.20	.15
659	8¢ L. Hemon—Author	....	.20	.15

660 **661**

SCOTT NO.	DESCRIPTION	PLATE BLOCK F/NH	UNUSED F/NH	USED F
660	8¢ M. Bourgeoys—Educator	1.00	.25	.15
661	8¢ A. Desjardins—Credit Union	1.00	.25	.15

662-63

664 **666**

SCOTT NO.	DESCRIPTION	PLATE BLOCK F/NH	UNUSED F/NH	USED F
662-63	Religious, attached .	1.05	.45	.45
662	8¢ S Chown & Church	......	.20	.20
663	8¢ J. Cook & Church	......	.20	.20
664	20¢ Pole Vaulter	3.30	.75	.50
665	25¢ Marathon Runner	3.85	.85	.55
666	50¢ Hurdler	6.60	1.50	1.10

667 **668**

669

670

SCOTT NO.	DESCRIPTION	PLATE BLOCK F/NH	UNUSED F/NH	USED F
667	8¢ Calgary Centenary	1.10	.25	.15
668	8¢ Int'l. Women's Year	1.10	.25	.15
669	8¢ "Justice"	1.10	.25	.15
670-73	Ships, attached	2.75	2.20	1.85
670	8¢ W.D. Lawrence ..	......	.55	.35
671	8¢ Beaver	......	.55	.35
672	8¢ Neptune	......	.55	.35
673	8¢ Quadra	......	.55	.35

674

676

679

680

SCOTT NO.	DESCRIPTION	PLATE BLOCK F/NH	UNUSED F/NH	USED F
674-79	6¢ to 15¢ Christmas	4.50(4)	1.35	1.25
674-75	Christmas, attached	.85	.40	.35
674	6¢ Santa Claus	......	.20	.15
675	6¢ Skater	......	.20	.15
676-77	Christmas, attached	1.05	.40	.35
676	8¢ Child	......	.20	.15
677	8¢ Family & Tree	......	.20	.15
678	10¢ Gift	1.10	.25	.25
679	15¢ Trees	1.65	.35	.35
680	8¢ Horn & Crest	1.10	.25	.15

681

Canada Postage #681-703

SCOTT NO.	DESCRIPTION	PLATE BLOCK F/NH	UNUSED F/NH	USED F
	1976 COMMEMORATIVES			
681-703	**complete, 23 varieties ....**	**75.00(18)**	**18.15**	**14.25**
681	8¢ Olympic Flame ...	1.05	.25	.15
682	20¢ Opening Ceremony	2.60	.55	.55
683	25¢ Receiving Medals	3.30	.75	.75

684

687

SCOTT NO.	DESCRIPTION	PLATE BLOCK F/NH	UNUSED F/NH	USED F
684	20¢ Communication Arts	4.40	1.00	.60
685	25¢ Handicraft Tools	4.95	1.10	.75
686	50¢ Performing Arts	8.25	1.85	1.30
687	$1 Notre Dame & Tower	11.00	2.50	1.95
688	$2 Olympic Stadium	25.85	5.80	4.40

689

690

691

SCOTT NO.	DESCRIPTION	PLATE BLOCK F/NH	UNUSED F/NH	USED F
689	20¢ Olympic Winter Games	3.30	.75	.70
690	20¢ "Habitat"	2.20	.50	.45
691	10¢ Benjamin Franklin	1.20	.30	.25

692

693

SCOTT NO.	DESCRIPTION	PLATE BLOCK F/NH	UNUSED F/NH	USED F
692-93	Military College, attached	1.05	.40	.35
692	8¢ Color Parade	.20	.15	
693	8¢ Wing Parade	......	.20	.15

694

695

696

697

SCOTT NO.	DESCRIPTION	PLATE BLOCK F/NH	UNUSED F/NH	USED F
694	20¢ Olympiad—Phys. Disabled	3.00	.65	.60
695-96	Authors, attached	1.05	.40	.35
695	8¢ R.W. Service—Author	......	.20	.15
696	8¢ G. Guevremont—Author	......	.20	.15
697	8¢ Nativity Window .	.85	.20	.15
698	10¢ same	1.05	.25	.15
699	20¢ same	2.15	.45	.45

700

704

SCOTT NO.	DESCRIPTION	PLATE BLOCK F/NH	UNUSED F/NH	USED F
700-03	Inland Vessels, attached	1.75	1.40	1.30
700	10¢ Northcote	......	.35	.30
701	10¢ Passport	......	.35	.30
702	10¢ Chicora	......	.35	.30
703	10¢ Athabasca	......	.35	.30

Canada Postage #704-737

SCOTT NO.	DESCRIPTION	PLATE BLOCK F/NH	UNUSED F/NH	USED F
	1977 COMMEMORATIVES			
704/51 (704, 732-51) complete, 21 varieties		**20.85(14)**	**6.10**	**4.65**
704	25¢ Silver Jubilee	3.05	.65	.55

705, 781, 781a

713, 713a, 716, 716a, 789, 789a, 791, 792

714, 715, 729, 730, 790, 797, 800, 806

1977-79 Definitives
Perf. 12x12-1/2

SCOTT NO.	DESCRIPTION	PLATE BLOCK F/NH	UNUSED F/NH	USED F
705-27	**1¢ to $2 complete, 22 varieties**	**66.50**	**14.85**	**5.75**
705	1¢ Bottle Gentian	.65	.20	.15
707	2¢ Western Columbine	.65	.20	.15
708	3¢ Canada Lily	.65	.20	.15
709	4¢ Hepatica	.65	.20	.15
710	5¢ Shooting Star	.65	.20	.15
711	10¢ Lady's Slipper	.80	.20	.15
711a	same, perf.13 (1978)	1.10	.25	.15
712	12¢ Jewelweed, perf 13x13-1/2 (1978)	1.45	.30	.15
713	12¢ Queen Elizabeth II, perf.13x13-1/2	1.30	.30	.15
713a	same, perf.12x12-1/2	......	.35	.20
714	12¢ Parliament, perf.13	1.20	.25	.15
715	14¢ same, perf.13 (1978)	1.35	.30	.15
716	14¢ Queen Elizabeth II perf. 13x13-1/2	1.35	.30	.15
716a	14¢ same, perf 12x12-1/2	......	.30	.20
716b	same, booklet pane of 25	......	5.80	......

NOTE: 713a and 716a are from booklet panes. 713a will have one or more straight edges, 716a may or may not have straight edges.

717

723, 723A

726

Perforated 13-1/2

SCOTT NO.	DESCRIPTION	PLATE BLOCK F/NH	UNUSED F/NH	USED F
717	15¢ Trembling Aspen	1.80	.40	.15
718	20¢ Douglas Fir	1.55	.35	.15
719	25¢ Sugar Maple	2.00	.45	.15
720	30¢ Oak Leaf	2.50	.55	.25
721	35¢ White Pine (1979)	2.75	.60	.35
723	50¢ Main Street (1978)	4.25	.95	.30
723A	50¢ same, 1978 Lic. Plate	4.70	1.00	.25
724	75¢ Row Houses (1978)	6.35	1.40	.50
725	80¢ Maritime (1978)	7.15	1.50	.55
726	$1 Fundy Park (1979)	8.80	1.95	.45
727	$2 Kluane Park (1979)	17.60	3.85	1.30

1977-78 Coil Stamps Perf. 10 Vert.

SCOTT NO.	DESCRIPTION	PLATE BLOCK F/NH	UNUSED F/NH	USED F
729	12¢ Parliament	....	.25	.15
730	14¢ same (1978)	....	.30	.15

732

733

735

1977 COMMEMORATIVES

SCOTT NO.	DESCRIPTION	PLATE BLOCK F/NH	UNUSED F/NH	USED F
732	12¢ Cougar	1.20	.25	.15
733-34	Thomson, attached	1.20	.50	.45
733	12¢ Algonquin Park	......	.25	.15
734	12¢ Autumn Birches	......	.25	.15
735	12¢ Crown & Lion	1.20	.25	.15

736

737

SCOTT NO.	DESCRIPTION	PLATE BLOCK F/NH	UNUSED F/NH	USED F
736	12¢ Badge & Ribbon	1.20	.25	.15
737	12¢ Peace Bridge	1.20	.25	.15

738-39

740

741

Canada Postage #738-772

SCOTT NO.	DESCRIPTION	PLATE BLOCK F/NH	UNUSED F/NH	USED F
738-39	Pioneers, attached	1.20	.50	.45
738	12¢ Bernier & CGS Arctic	......	.25	.15
739	12¢ Fleming & RR Bridge	......	.25	.15
740	25¢ Peace Tower	3.30	.75	.75

744

SCOTT NO.	DESCRIPTION	PLATE BLOCK F/NH	UNUSED F/NH	USED F
741	10¢ Braves & Star	1.05	.25	.15
742	12¢ Angelic Choir	1.20	.25	.10
743	25¢ Christ Child	2.45	.50	.50
744-47	Sailing Ships	1.30	1.00	.95
744	12¢ Pinky	......	.25	.20
745	12¢ Tern	......	.25	.20
746	12¢ Five Masted	......	.25	.20
747	12¢ Mackinaw	......	.25	.20

748-49

SCOTT NO.	DESCRIPTION	PLATE BLOCK F/NH	UNUSED F/NH	USED F
748-49	Inuit, attached	1.20	.50	.45
748	12¢ Hunting Seal	......	.25	.20
749	12¢ Fishing	......	.25	.20
750-51	Inuit, attached	1.20	.50	.45
750	12¢ Disguised Archer	......	.25	.20
751	12¢ Hunters of Old	......	.25	.20

752

753

1978 COMMEMORATIVES

SCOTT NO.	DESCRIPTION	PLATE BLOCK F/NH	UNUSED F/NH	USED F
752/79	**(No #756a)28 varieties**	**33.00(19)**	**9.15**	**6.30**
752	12¢ Peregrine Falcon	1.20	.25	.15
753	12¢ CAPEX Victoria	1.10	.25	.15
754	14¢ CAPEX Cartier	1.35	.25	.15
755	30¢ CAPEX Victoria	2.65	.55	.55
756	$1.25 CAPEX Albert	8.25	1.85	1.40
756a	$1.69 CAPEX sheet of 3	......	2.15	2.15

757

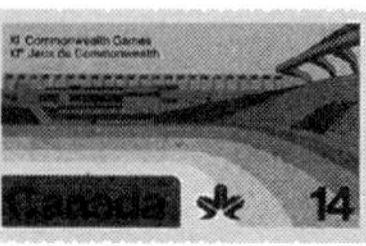

759

SCOTT NO.	DESCRIPTION	PLATE BLOCK F/NH	UNUSED F/NH	USED F
757	14¢ Games Symbol	1.15	.25	.15
758	30¢ Badminton Players	2.50	.55	.35
759-60	Comm. Games, attached	1.20	.50	.45
759	14¢ Stadium	......	.25	.15
760	14¢ Runners	......	.25	.15
761-62	Comm. Games, attached	2.45	1.05	.95
761	30¢ Edmonton	......	.45	.35
762	30¢ Bowls	......	.45	.35

763

764

SCOTT NO.	DESCRIPTION	PLATE BLOCK F/NH	UNUSED F/NH	USED F
763-64	Captain Cook, attached	1.15	.50	.45
763	14¢ Captain Cook ...	......	.25	.15
764	14¢ Nootka Sound ..	......	.25	.15

765-66

767

768

769

770

SCOTT NO.	DESCRIPTION	PLATE BLOCK F/NH	UNUSED F/NH	USED F
765-66	Resources, attached	1.20	.50	.45
765	14¢ Miners	......	.25	.15
766	14¢ Tar Sands	......	.25	.15
767	14¢ CNE 100th Anniversary	1.15	.25	.15
768	14¢ Mere d'Youville	1.15	.25	.15
769-70	Inuit, attached	1.20	.50	.45
769	14¢ Woman Walking	......	.25	.15
770	14¢ Migration	......	.25	.15
771-72	Inuit, attached	1.20	.50	.45
771	14¢ Plane over Village	......	.25	.15
772	14¢ Dog Team & Sled	......	.25	.15

Canada Postage #773-820

773

SCOTT NO.	DESCRIPTION	PLATE BLOCK F/NH	UNUSED F/NH	USED F
773	12¢ Mary & Child w/pea	1.05	.25	.15
774	14¢ Mary & Child w/apple	1.15	.25	.15
775	30¢ Mary & Child w/goldfinch	2.50	.55	.35
776-79	Ice Vessels, attached	1.20	1.00	.95
776	14¢ Robinson	......	.25	.15
777	14¢ St. Roch	......	.25	.15
778	14¢ Northern Light ..	......	.25	.15
779	14¢ Labrador	......	.25	.15

1979 COMMEMORATIVES

SCOTT NO.	DESCRIPTION	PLATE BLOCK F/NH	UNUSED F/NH	USED F
780/846	**(780, 813-20, 833-46) complete, 23 varieties ....**	**27.10(16)**	**8.20**	**4.55**

780

SCOTT NO.	DESCRIPTION	PLATE BLOCK F/NH	UNUSED F/NH	USED F
780	14¢ Quebec Winter Carnival	1.15	.25	.15

1977-83 Definitives Perf 13x131/2

SCOTT NO.	DESCRIPTION	PLATE BLOCK F/NH	UNUSED F/NH	USED F
781-92	**1¢-32¢ complete, 11 varieties ....**	**13.00**	**3.15**	**1.60**
781	1¢ Gentian (1979) ...	.65	.20	.15
781a	1¢ same, perf 12x12-1/2	......	.20	.15
781b	booklet pane, 1¢ (2—781a), 12¢ (4—713a)	......	.85	......
782	2¢ Western Columbine (1979)	.65	.20	.15
782a	booklet pane, 2¢ (4—782b), 12¢ (3—716a)	......	.80	......
782b	2¢ same, perf 12x121/2 (1978).	.....	.20	.15
783	3¢ Canada Lily (1979)	.65	.20	.15
784	4¢ Hepatica (1979) .	.65	.20	.15
785	5¢ Shooting Star (1979)	.65	.20	.15
786	10¢ Lady's-Slipper (1979)	.90	.20	.15
787	15¢ Violet (1979)	1.35	.30	.15
789	17¢ Queen Elizabeth II (1979)	1.50	.35	.15
789a	17¢ same, 12x12-1/2 (1979)	.....	.35	.15
789b	booklet pane of 25 ..	.....	7.45	.....
790	17¢ Parliament Bldg. (1979)	1.50	.30	.15
791	30¢ Queen Elizabeth II (1982)	2.50	.55	.15
792	32¢ Queen Elizabeth II (1983)	2.75	.60	.15

NOTE: 781a, 782b, 797 & 800 are from booklet panes and will have one or more straight edges. 789a may or may not have straight edges.

1979 Perf 12x12-1/2

SCOTT NO.	DESCRIPTION	PLATE BLOCK F/NH	UNUSED F/NH	USED F
797	1¢ Parliament Building	.....	.35	.30
797a	booklet pane 1¢ (1—797), 5¢ (3—800), 17¢ (2—789a)	.....	.90	.....
800	5¢ Parliament Building	.....	.20	.15

1979 Coil Stamps Perf 10 Vertical

SCOTT NO.	DESCRIPTION	PLATE BLOCK F/NH	UNUSED F/NH	USED F
806	17¢ Parliament Building, slate green	.....	.50	.15

813

815

817

818

819-20

1979

SCOTT NO.	DESCRIPTION	PLATE BLOCK F/NH	UNUSED F/NH	USED F
813	17¢ Turtle	1.50	.30	.15
814	35¢ Whale	3.05	.65	.35
815-16	Postal Code, attached	1.65	.65	.45
815	17¢ Woman's Finger	......	.30	.15
816	17¢ Man's Finger	......	.30	.15
817-18	Writers, attached	1.65	.65	.45
817	17¢ "Fruits of the Earth"	......	.30	.15
818	17¢ "The Golden Vessel"	......	.30	.15
819-20	Colonels, attached ..	1.65	.65	.45
819	17¢ Charles de Salaberry	......	.30	.15
820	17¢ John By	......	.30	.15

821 *Ontario*

SCOTT NO.	DESCRIPTION	PLATE BLOCK F/NH	UNUSED F/NH	USED F

PROVINCIAL FLAGS

822 *Quebec*	**827** *Prince Edward Island*
823 *Nova Scotia*	**828** *Saskatchewan*
824 *New Brunswick*	**829** *Alberta*
825 *Manitoba*	**830** *Newfoundland*
826 *British Columbia*	**831** *Northern Teritories*

SCOTT NO.	DESCRIPTION	PLATE BLOCK F/NH	UNUSED F/NH	USED F
832a	17¢ Sheet of 12 varieties, attached	......	4.00	......
821-32	set of singles	......	......	2.00
Any	17¢ single	......	.30	.20

833

834

SCOTT NO.	DESCRIPTION	PLATE BLOCK F/NH	UNUSED F/NH	USED F
833	17¢ Canoe—kayak .	1.50	.30	.15
834	17¢ Field Hockey	1.50	.30	.15

835-36

SCOTT NO.	DESCRIPTION	PLATE BLOCK F/NH	UNUSED F/NH	USED F
835-36	Inuit, attached	1.60	.65	.60
835	17¢ Summer Tent ...	......	.30	.20
836	17¢ Igloo	......	.30	.20
837-38	Inuit, attached	1.60	.65	.60
837	17¢ The Dance	......	.30	.20
838	17¢ Soapstone Figures	......	.30	.20

839

842

SCOTT NO.	DESCRIPTION	PLATE BLOCK F/NH	UNUSED F/NH	USED F
839	15¢ Wooden Train ..	1.00	.25	.15
840	17¢ Horse Pull Toy .	1.30	.30	.15
841	35¢ Knitted Doll	2.75	.60	.30
842	17¢ I.Y.C.	1.50	.30	.15

843

SCOTT NO.	DESCRIPTION	PLATE BLOCK F/NH	UNUSED F/NH	USED F
843-44	Flying Boats, attached	1.60	.65	.50
843	17¢ Curtiss, HS2L ...	......	.30	.20
844	17¢ Canadair CL215	......	.30	.20
845-46	Flying Boats, attached	3.55	1.50	1.40
845	35¢ Vichers Vedette	......	.70	.50
846	35¢ Consolidated Canso	......	.70	.50

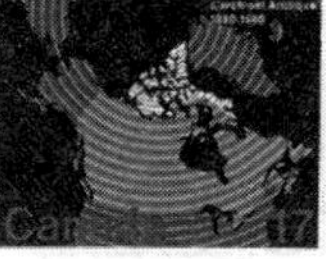

847 848

1980 COMMEMORATIVES

SCOTT NO.	DESCRIPTION	PLATE BLOCK F/NH	UNUSED F/NH	USED F
847-77	**complete, 31 varieties**	**42.25(23)**	**12.35**	**6.30**
847	17¢ Arctic Islands Map	1.50	.30	.15
848	35¢ Olympic Skiing	2.90	.60	.55

853

849

SCOTT NO.	DESCRIPTION	PLATE BLOCK F/NH	UNUSED F/NH	USED F
849-50	Artists, attached	1.60	.65	.50
849	17¢ School Trustees	......	.30	.15
850	17¢ Inspiration	......	.30	.15
851-52	Artists, attached	3.05	1.30	1.10
851	35¢ Parliament Bldgs.	......	.60	.35
852	35¢ Sunrise on the Saguenay......		.60	.35
853	17¢ Atlantic Whitefish	1.55	.35	.15
854	17¢ Greater Prairie Chicken	1.55	.35	.15

855 856

857-58

Canada Postage #855-884

859

SCOTT NO.	DESCRIPTION	PLATE BLOCK F/NH	UNUSED F/NH	USED F
55	17¢ Gardening	1.50	.30	.15
56	17¢ Rehabilitation ...	1.50	.30	.15
57-58	"O Canada", attached	1.60	.65	.50
57	17¢ Bars of Music ...	......	.30	.15
58	17¢ Three Musicians	......	.30	.15
59	17¢ John Diefenbaker	1.50	.30	.15

860

862

863

SCOTT NO.	DESCRIPTION	PLATE BLOCK F/NH	UNUSED F/NH	USED F
860-61	Musicians, attached	1.60	.65	.50
860	17¢ Emma Albani ...	......	.30	.15
861	17¢ Healy Willan	......	.30	.15
862	17¢ Ned Hanlan	1.50	.30	.15
863	17¢ Saskatchewan .	1.50	.30	.15
864	17¢ Alberta	1.50	.30	.15

865

866-67

SCOTT NO.	DESCRIPTION	PLATE BLOCK F/NH	UNUSED F/NH	USED F
865	35¢ Uranium Resources	2.95	.60	.35
866-67	Inuit, attached	1.75	.70	.50
866	17¢ Sedna	......	.35	.15
867	17¢ Sun	......	.35	.15

870

SCOTT NO.	DESCRIPTION	PLATE BLOCK F/NH	UNUSED F/NH	USED F
868-69	Inuit, attached	3.05	1.30	1.10
868	35¢ Bird Spirit	......	.60	.35
869	35¢ Shaman	......	.60	.35
870	15¢ Christmas	1.35	.30	.15
871	17¢ Christmas	1.50	.30	.15
872	35¢ Christmas	2.95	.60	.35

873

877

878

SCOTT NO.	DESCRIPTION	PLATE BLOCK F/NH	UNUSED F/NH	USED F
873-74	Aircraft	1.65	.75	.65
873	17¢ Avro Canada CF-100	......	.35	.15
874	17¢ Avro Lancaster .	......	.35	.15
875-76	Aircraft, attached	3.25	1.40	1.20
875	35¢ Curtiss JN-4	......	.65	.35
876	35¢ Hawker Hurricane	......	.65	.35
877	17¢ Dr. Lachapelle .	1.50	.30	.15

1981 COMMEMORATIVES

SCOTT NO.	DESCRIPTION	PLATE BLOCK F/NH	UNUSED F/NH	USED F
878-906	**complete, 29 varieties**	**32.45(19)**	**10.35**	**5.45**
878	17¢ Antique Instrument	1.50	.30	.15

879

883

SCOTT NO.	DESCRIPTION	PLATE BLOCK F/NH	UNUSED F/NH	USED F
879-82	Feminists, attached .	1.65	1.40	1.10
879	17¢ Emily Stowe	......	.35	.20
880	17¢ Louise McKinney	......	.35	.20
881	17¢ Idola Saint-Jean	......	.35	.20
882	17¢ Henrietta Edwards	......	.35	.20
883	17¢ Marmot	1.50	.30	.15
884	35¢ Bison	3.30	.75	.40

Canada Postage #885-913a

885 887

SCOTT NO.	DESCRIPTION	PLATE BLOCK F/NH	UNUSED F/NH	USED F
885-86	Women, attached	1.60	.65	.50
885	17¢ Kateri Tekakwitha	......	.30	.15
886	17¢ Marie de L'Incarnation	......	.30	.15
887	17¢ "At Baie Saint-Paul"	1.50	.30	.15
888	17¢ Self-Portrait	1.50	.30	.15
889	35¢ Untitled No. 6 ...	2.95	.60	.40

890

894

SCOTT NO.	DESCRIPTION	PLATE BLOCK F/NH	UNUSED F/NH	USED F
890-93	Canada Day, attached	1.65(8)	1.40	1.30
890	17¢ Canada in 1867	......	.35	.20
891	17¢ Canada in 1873	......	.35	.20
892	17¢ Canada in 1905	......	.35	.20
893	17¢ Canada in 1949	......	.35	.20
894-95	Botanists, attached .	1.60	.65	.35
894	17¢ Frere Marie Victorin	......	.30	.15
895	17¢ John Macoun ...	......	.30	.15

896

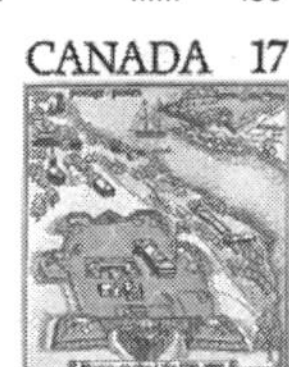

897

898

899

SCOTT NO.	DESCRIPTION	PLATE BLOCK F/NH	UNUSED F/NH	USED F
896	17¢ Montreal Rose .	1.65	.30	.15
897	17¢ Niagara-on-the-Lake	1.65	.30	.15
898	17¢ Acadians	1.65	.30	.15
899	17¢ Aaron Mosher ..	1.65	.30	.15

900

SCOTT NO.	DESCRIPTION	PLATE BLOCK F/NH	UNUSED F/NH	USED F
900	15¢ Christmas Tree in 1781	1.30	.30	.15
901	15¢ Christmas Tree in 1881	1.30	.30	.15
902	15¢ Christmas Tree in 1981	1.30	.30	.15

903

SCOTT NO.	DESCRIPTION	PLATE BLOCK F/NH	UNUSED F/NH	USED F
903-04	Aircraft, attached	1.65	.75	.50
903	17¢ Canadair CL-41 Tutor	......	.35	.15
904	17¢ de Havilland Tiger Moth	......	.35	.15
905-06	Aircraft, attached	3.25	1.40	1.20
905	35¢ Avro Canada C-102	......	.65	.40
906	35¢ de Havilland Canada Dash-7	......	.65	.40

907, 908

909

SCOTT NO.	DESCRIPTION	PLATE BLOCK F/NH	UNUSED F/NH	USED F
907	(30¢) "A" Maple Leaf	2.60	1.55	.15
908	(30¢) "A" Maple Leaf, Coil	......	1.90	.15

1982 COMMEMORATIVES

SCOTT NO.	DESCRIPTION	PLATE BLOCK F/NH	UNUSED F/NH	USED F
909/75	**(909-16, 954, 967-75) 18 varieties, complete**	**51.25(16)**	**11.95**	**4.35**
909	30¢ 1851 Beaver	2.65	.55	.15
910	30¢ 1908 Champlain	2.65	.55	.15
911	35¢ 1935 Mountie ...	3.15	.65	.35
912	35¢ 1928 Mt. Hurd ..	3.15	.65	.35
913	60¢ 1929 Bluenose .	6.35	1.30	.55
913a	$1.90 Phil. Exhib. sheet of 5	......	3.60	......

914

915

Canada Postage #914-953

916

SCOTT NO.	DESCRIPTION	PLATE BLOCK F/NH	UNUSED F/NH	USED F
914	30¢ Jules Leger	2.65	.55	.15
915	30¢ Terry Fox	2.65	.55	.15
916	30¢ Constitution	2.65	.55	.15

917

925/952, 1194, 1194A

938

939

926

1982-87 DEFINITIVES

SCOTT NO.	DESCRIPTION	PLATE BLOCK F/NH	UNUSED F/NH	USED F
917-37	**1¢-$5 complete, 23 varieties ....**	**135.00**	**27.50**	**9.00**
917a-21a	**1¢-10¢, 5 varieties**	**4.10**	**1.00**	**.70**
917	1¢ Decoy	.80	.20	.15
917a	1¢ perf.13x13-1/2 (1985)	.80	.20	.15
918	2¢ Fishing Spear ...	.80	.20	.15
918a	2¢ perf.13x13-1/2 (1985)	.80	.20	.15
919	3¢ Stable Lantern ..	.80	.20	.15
919a	3¢ perf.13x13-1/2 (1985)	.80	.20	.15
920	5¢ Bucket	.80	.20	.15
920a	5¢ perf.13x13-1/2 (1984)	.80	.20	.15
921	10¢ Weathercock ..	1.10	.25	.15
921a	10¢ perf.13x13-1/2 (1985)	1.10	.25	.15
922	20¢ Ice Skates	2.25	.45	.15
923	30¢ Maple Leaf, blue & red, perf.13x13-1/2	2.55	.55	.15
923a	30¢ booklet pane (20) perf 12x12-1/2	......	9.90	......
923b	as above, single	......	.20	.20
924	32¢ Maple Leaf, red & brown, perf.13x13-1/2 (1983)	2.55	.55	.15
924a	32¢ booklet pane (25), perf. 12x12-1/2	......	13.75	......
924b	as above, single	......	.60	.20
925	34¢ Parliament (multicolored, perf.13x13-1/2 (1985)	2.75	.60	.15
925a	34¢ booklet pane (25) perf.13x13-1/2	......	13.71	......
925b	34¢ single, perf 13-1/2x14	.....	.60	....
926	34¢ Elizabeth II (1985), perf.13x13-1/2	2.75	.60	.15
926A	36¢ Elizabeth II (1987) perf. 13-1/2x14	20.00	4.00	.55
926B	36¢ Parliament Library (1987)	3.05	.65	.25
926Bc	as above, booklet pane (10)		6.05	......
926Bd	as above, booklet pane (25)		14.81	....
926Be	Booklet single (perf. 13-1/2x14)	......	.60	......

SCOTT NO.	DESCRIPTION	PLATE BLOCK F/NH	UNUSED F/NH	USED F
927	37¢ Plow (1983)	3.15	.21	.25
928	39¢ Settle bed (1985)	3.30	.75	.25
929	48¢ Cradle (1983) .	4.15	.80	.30
930	50¢ Sleigh (1985) ..	4.40	.85	.30
931	60¢ Ontario Street .	4.95	.95	.35
932	64¢ Stove (1983) ...	5.80	1.00	.40
933	68¢ Spinning Wheel (1985)	1.80	1.10	.40
934	$1 Glacier Park (1984)	8.80	1.75	.25
935	$1.50 Waterton Lakes	12.25	2.50	.80
936	$2 Banff Park (1985)	17.20	3.50	1.10
937	$5 Point Pelee (1983)	41.25	8.50	2.50

1982-87 BOOKLET SINGLES

SCOTT NO.	DESCRIPTION	PLATE BLOCK F/NH	UNUSED F/NH	USED F
938-948	**1¢-36¢ complete, 11 varieties ....**	**......**	**3.85**	**1.65**
938	1¢ East Block (1987)	......	.20	.15
939	2¢ West Block (1985)	......	.20	.15
940	5¢ Maple Leaf (1982)	......	.20	.15
941	5¢ East Block (1985)	......	.20	.15
942	6¢ West Block (1987)	......	.20	.15
943	8¢ Maple Leaf (1983)	......	.20	.15
944	10¢ Maple Leaf (1982)	......	.25	.15
945	30¢ Maple Leaf, red perf. 12x12-1/2 (1982)	......	.61	.15
945a	booklet pane 2# 940, 1 #944, 1 #945	......	1.20	......
946	32¢ Maple Leaf, brown on white, perf.12x12-1/2 (1983)		.65	.15
946b	booklet pane 2 #941, 1 #943, 1 #946	......	1.10	......
947	34¢ Library, slate blue, perf.12x12-1/2 (1985)	......	.60	.15
947a	booklet pane, 3 #939, 2 #941, 1 #947	......	1.40	......
948	36¢ Parliament Library (1987)	......	.65	.25
948a	booklet pane, 2 #938, 2 #942, #948	......	1.00	......

1982-1987 COILS

SCOTT NO.	DESCRIPTION	PLATE BLOCK F/NH	UNUSED F/NH	USED F
950-53	30¢-36¢ complete, 4 varieties		2.65	.55
950	30¢ Maple Leaf (1982)	......	.95	.15
951	32¢ Maple Leaf (1983)	......	.60	.15
952	34¢ Parliament (1985)	......	.60	.15
953	36¢ Parliament (1987)	......	.65	.15

954

Paintings

955 *Yukon Territories*

956 *Quebec*
957 *Newfoundland*
958 *Northwest Territories*
959 *Prince Edward Island*
960 *Nova Scotia*
961 *Saskatchewan*
962 *Ontario*
963 *New Brunswick*
964 *Alberta*
965 *British Columbia*
966 *Manitoba*

Canada Postage #954-998

1982 COMMEMORATIVES

SCOTT NO.	DESCRIPTION	PLATE BLOCK F/NH	UNUSED F/NH	USED F
954	30¢ Salvation Army	2.65	.55	.15
955-66	set of singles	......	6.00	4.50
......	same, any 30¢ single	......	.75	.40
966a	sheet of 12 varieties, attached	......	5.50	......

967

968

969

SCOTT NO.	DESCRIPTION	PLATE BLOCK F/NH	UNUSED F/NH	USED F
967	30¢ Regina	2.65	.55	.15
968	30¢ Henley Regatta	2.21	.55	.15
969-70	30¢ Aircraft, attached	2.65	1.00	.90
969	30¢ Fairchild FC-2W1	....	.45	.15
970	30¢ De Havilland Canada Beaver	....	.45	.15
971-72	Aircraft, attached	6.20	2.20	2.10
971	60¢ Noorduyn Norseman.....	....	1.00	.50
972	60¢ Fokker Super Universal	....	1.00	.50

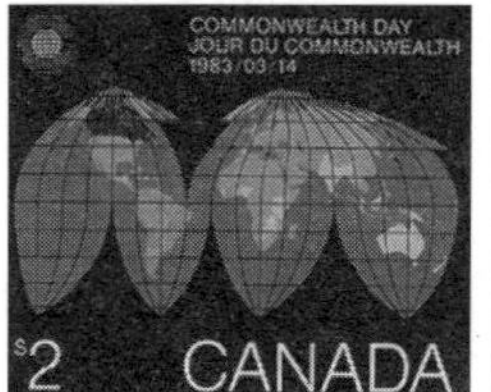

977

CANADA 32

976

978

SCOTT NO.	DESCRIPTION	PLATE BLOCK F/NH	UNUSED F/NH	USED F
973	30¢ Joseph, Mary & Infant	2.65	.55	.15
974	35¢ Shepherds	3.05	.65	.25
975	60¢ Wise Men	....5.25	1.10	.45

1983 COMMEMORATIVES

SCOTT NO.	DESCRIPTION	PLATE BLOCK F/NH	UNUSED F/NH	USED F
976/1008 (976-82, 993-1008)	**complete, 23 varieties**	**73.25(20)**	**22.25**	**9.30**
976	32¢ World Comm. Year	2.85	.60	.25
977	$2 Commonwealth Day	27.50	10.00	4.00
978-79	Poet/Author, attached	2.85	1.20	1.10
978	32¢ Laure Conan	......	.55	.25
979	32¢ E.J. Pratt	......	.55	.25

980

981

SCOTT NO.	DESCRIPTION	PLATE BLOCK F/NH	UNUSED F/NH	USED F
980	32¢ St.John Ambulance	3.10	.60	.25
981	32¢ University Games	3.10	.60	.25
982	64¢ University Games	3.10	1.20	.45

983 *Ft. Henry*

Forts

984 *Ft. William*
985 *Ft. Rodd Hill*
986 *Ft. Wellington*
987 *Fort Prince of Wales*
988 *Halifax Citadel*
989 *Ft. Chambly*
990 *Ft. No. 1 Pt. Levis*
991 *Ft. at Coteau-du-Lac*
992 *Fort Beausejour*

SCOTT NO.	DESCRIPTION	PLATE BLOCK F/NH	UNUSED F/NH	USED F
992a	32¢ Forts, pane of 10	......	7.00	6.50
983-92	set of singles	......	6.50	2.75
......	Any 32¢ single Fort	......	.75	.30

993

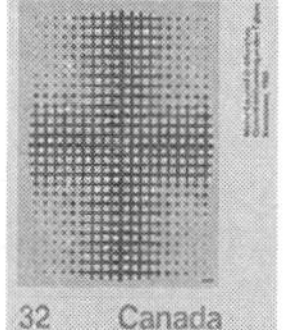

994

CANADA 32

995

997

Canada 32

996

998

SCOTT NO.	DESCRIPTION	PLATE BLOCK F/NH	UNUSED F/NH	USED F
993	32¢ Boy Scouts	2.75	.60	.25
994	32¢ Council of Churches	2.75	.60	.25
995	32¢ Humphrey Gilbert	2.75	.60	.25
996	32¢ Nickel	2.75	.60	.25
997	32¢ Josiah Henson	2.75	.60	.25
998	32¢ Fr. Antoine Labelle	2.75	.60	.25

Canada Postage #999-1031

999

1003

1004

1007

SCOTT NO.	DESCRIPTION	PLATE BLOCK F/NH	UNUSED F/NH	USED F
999-1000	Steam Trains, attached	2.75	1.10	1.20
999	32¢ Toronto 4-4-0	......	.55	.25
1000	32¢ Dorchester 0-4-0	......	.55	.25
1001	37¢ Samson 0-6-0	3.10	.65	.30
1002	64¢ Adam Brown 4-4-0	5.50	1.10	.52
1003	32¢ Law School	2.75	.60	.25
1004	32¢ City Church	2.75	.60	.25
1005	37¢ Family	3.05	.65	.30
1006	64¢ County Chapel	5.50	1.10	.52
1007-08	Army Regiment, attached	2.75	1.10	1.00
1007	32¢ Canada & Br.Reg.	......	.55	.25
1008	32¢ Winn. & Dragoons	......	.55	.25

1009

1010

1011

1012

1984 COMMEMORATIVES

SCOTT NO.	DESCRIPTION	PLATE BLOCK F/NH	UNUSED F/NH	USED F
1009/44	**(1009-15, 1028-39, 1040-44) complete, 24 varieties**	**60.15(20)**	**14.25**	**6.25**
1009	32¢ Yellowknife	2.75	.60	.25
1010	32¢ Year of the Arts	2.75	.60	.25
1011	32¢ Cartier	2.75	.60	.25
1012	32¢ Tall Ships	2.75	.60	.25

1013

1014

1015

SCOTT NO.	DESCRIPTION	PLATE BLOCK F/NH	UNUSED F/NH	USED F
1013	32¢ Canadian Red Cross	2.75	.60	.25
1014	32¢ New Brunswick	2.75	.60	.25
1015	32¢ St. Lawrence Seaway	2.75	.60	.25

PROVINCIAL LANDSCAPES BY JEAN PAUL LEMIEUX

1016 *New Brunswick*

1017 *British Columbia*
1018 *Yukon Territory*
1019 *Quebec*
1020 *Manitoba*
1021 *Alberta*
1022 *Prince Edward Island*
1023 *Saskatchewan*
1024 *Nova Scotia*
1025 *Northwest Territories*
1026 *Newfoundland*
1027 *Ontario*

1027a	sheet of 12 varieties attached	......	6.50	6.00
1016-27	set of singles	......	7.00	3.50
.....	Any 32¢ single Provinces	......	.75	.30

1028

1029

1030

SCOTT NO.	DESCRIPTION	PLATE BLOCK F/NH	UNUSED F/NH	USED F
1028	32¢ Loyalists	2.75	.60	.25
1029	32¢ Catholicism	2.75	.60	.25
1030	32¢ Papal Visit	2.75	.60	.25
1031	64¢ Papal Visit	5.25	1.10	.52

1032

Canada Postage #1032-1062

1036

1040

1043

1044

1045

1046

SCOTT NO.	DESCRIPTION	PLATE BLOCK F/NH	UNUSED F/NH	USED F
1032-35	Lighthouses, attached	2.75	2.25	1.75
1032	32¢ Louisbourg	......	.60	.25
1033	32¢ Fisgard	......	.60	.25
1034	32¢ Ile Verte	......	.60	.25
1035	32¢ Gilbraltar Point .	......	.60	.25
1036-37	Locomotives, attached	2.75	1.20	1.00
1036	32¢ Scotia 0-6-0	......	.60	.15
1037	32¢ Countess of Dufferin 4-4-0	....	.60	.15
1038	37¢ Grand Trunk 2-6-0	3.15	.65	.30
1039	64¢ Canadian Pacific 4-6-0	5.25	1.10	.52
1039a	Locomotive Souvenir Sheet	......	2.75	2.75
1040	32¢ Christmas	2.75	.60	.25
1041	37¢ Christmas	3.15	.60	.30
1042	64¢ Christmas	5.25	1.10	.52
1043	32¢ Royal Air Force	2.75	1.00	.25
1044	32¢ Newspaper	2.75	1.00	.25

1985 COMMEMORATIVES

SCOTT NO.	DESCRIPTION	PLATE BLOCK F/NH	UNUSED F/NH	USED F
1045/76	**(1045-49, 1060-66, 1067-76) complete, 24 varieties**	**49.40(16)**	**13.75**	**6.00**
1045	32¢ Youth Year	2.75	.60	.25
1046	32¢ Canadian Astronaut	2.75	.60	.25

1047-48

1049

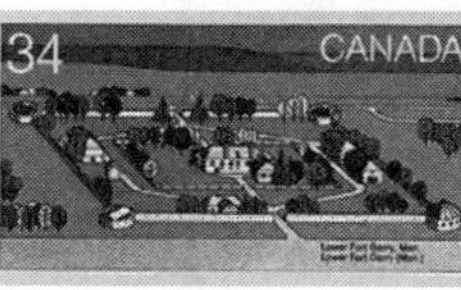

1050

FORTS

1050 *Lower Ft. Gar*
1051 *Fort Anne*
1052 *Fort York*
1053 *Castle Hill*
1054 *Fort Whoop U*
1055 *Fort Erie*
1056 *Fort Walsh*
1057 *Fort Lennox*
1058 *York Redoubt*
1059 *Fort Frederick*

1060

1061

1062

1063

1067

SCOTT NO.	DESCRIPTION	PLATE BLOCK F/NH	UNUSED F/NH	USED F
1047-48	Women, attached	2.75	1.20	1.00
1047	32¢ T. Casgrain	......	.60	.25
1048	32¢ E. Murphy	......	.60	.25
1049	32¢ G. Dumont	2.75	.60	.25
1059a	34¢ Forts pane of 10	......	7.50	6.00
1050-59	set of singles	......	7.00	3.00
......	any Fort single	......	.70	.30
1060	34¢ Louis Hebert	2.75	.60	.27
1061	34¢ Inter-Parliamentary	2.75	.60	.27
1062	34¢ Girl Guides	2.75	.60	.27

Canada Postage #1063-1107b

SCOTT NO.	DESCRIPTION	PLATE BLOCK F/NH	UNUSED F/NH	USED F
1063-66	Lighthouses, attached	2.75	2.50	2.00
1063	34¢ Sisters Islets	......	.60	.27
1064	34¢ Pelee Passage	......	.60	.27
1065	34¢ Haut-fond Prince	......	.60	.27
1066	34¢ Rose Blanche	......	.60	.27
1066b	Lighthouse Souvenir Sheet	......	2.95	2.50
1067	34¢ Christmas	2.75	.60	.27
1068	39¢ Christmas	3.60	.75	.40
1069	68¢ Christmas	6.05	1.35	.60
1070	32¢ Christmas, booklet single	......	.80	......
1070a	same, booklet pane of 10	......	7.70	......
1071-72	Locomotives, attached	2.75	1.25	.75
1071	34¢ GT Class K2	....	.60	.27
1072	34¢ CP Class P2a	....	.60	.27
1073	39¢ CMoR Class 010a	3.30	.75	.40
1074	68¢ CGR Class H4D	6.05	.35	.75
1075	34¢ Royal Navy	2.75	.60	.27
1076	34¢ Montreal Museum	2.75	.60	.27

1075

1076

1077

1078

1986 COMMEMORATIVES

SCOTT NO.	DESCRIPTION	PLATE BLOCK F/NH	UNUSED F/NH	USED F
1077/1121	(1077-79, 1090-1107,1108-16, 1117-21) complete, 35 varieties	69.75	21.25	9.60
1077	34¢ Computer Map	2.75	.60	.27
1078	34¢ Expo '86	2.75	.60	.27
1079	39¢ Expo '86	3.30	.75	.32

1987 HERITAGE ARTIFACTS

SCOTT NO.	DESCRIPTION	PLATE BLOCK F/NH	UNUSED F/NH	USED F
1080	25¢ Butter Stamp	1.95	.60	.20
1081	42¢ Linen Chest	3.30	1.00	.35
1082	55¢ Iron Kettle	4.40	1.20	.45
1083	72¢ Hand-drawn Cart	6.35	1.50	.60

1986-87 Definitive

SCOTT NO.	DESCRIPTION	PLATE BLOCK F/NH	UNUSED F/NH	USED F
1084	$5 La Mauricie	37.50	8.50	3.50

1090

1091

1092

1094

1986 COMMEMORATIVES

SCOTT NO.	DESCRIPTION	PLATE BLOCK F/NH	UNUSED F/NH	USED F
1090	34¢ Philippe Aubert de Gaspe	2.75	.60	.27
1091	34¢ Molly Brant	2.75	.60	.27
1092	34¢ Expo '86	2.75	.60	.27
1093	68¢ Expo '86	6.05	1.30	.55
1094	34¢ Canadian Forces Postal Service	2.75	.60	.27

1095

1099

SCOTT NO.	DESCRIPTION	PLATE BLOCK F/NH	UNUSED F/NH	USED F
1095-98	Birds, attached	2.50	2.25	2.00
1095	34¢ Great Blue Heron	......	.60	.27
1096	34¢ Snow Goose	......	.60	.27
1097	34¢ Great Horned Owl	......	.60	.27
1098	34¢ Spruce Grouse	......	.60	.27
1099-1102	Science & Technology, attached	2.75	2.50	2.00
1099	34¢ Rotary Snowplow	......	.60	.27
1100	34¢ Canadarm	......	.60	.27
1101	34¢ Anti-gravity Flight Suit.......		.60	.27
1102	34¢ Variable-pitch Propeller......		.60	.27

1103

1104

SCOTT NO.	DESCRIPTION	PLATE BLOCK F/NH	UNUSED F/NH	USED F
1103	34¢ CBC	2.75	.60	.27
1104-07	Exploration, attached	2.75	2.50	2.00
1104	34¢ Continent	......	.60	.27
1105	34¢ Vikings	....	.60	.27
1106	34¢ John Cabot ..	....	.60	.27
1107	34¢ Hudson Bay .	......	.60	.27
1107b	CAPEX souvenir sheet	......	2.20	2.00

Canada Postage #1108-1145

1108

1110

SCOTT NO.	DESCRIPTION	PLATE BLOCK F/NH	UNUSED F/NH	USED F
1108-09	Frontier Peacemakers, attached	2.75	1.25	1.00
1108	34¢ Crowfoot	......	.60	.27
1109	34¢ J.F. Macleod	......	.60	.27
1110	34¢ Peace Year ..	2.75	.60	.27

1111

1113

SCOTT NO.	DESCRIPTION	PLATE BLOCK F/NH	UNUSED F/NH	USED F
1111-12	Calgary, attached	2.75	1.25	1.00
1111	34¢ Ice Hockey ...	......	.60	.27
1112	34¢ Biathlon	......	.60	.27
1113	34¢ Christmas Angels	2.75	.60	.27
1114	39¢ Christmas Angels	3.30	.75	.32
1115	68¢ Christmas Angels	6.05	1.30	.55
1116	29¢ Christmas Angels, booklet singles	......	.60	.25
1116a	same, booklet pane of 10	......	6.10	......

1117

SCOTT NO.	DESCRIPTION	PLATE BLOCK F/NH	UNUSED F/NH	USED F
1117	34¢ John Molson	2.75	.60	.27
1118-19	Locomotive, attached	2.75	1.25	1.00
1118	34¢ CN V1a	......	.60	.27
1119	34¢ CP T1a	......	.60	.27
1120	39¢ CN U2a	3.30	.75	.32
1121	68¢ CP H1c	5.25	1.10	.55

1122

1987 COMMEMORATIVES

SCOTT NO.	DESCRIPTION	PLATE BLOCK F/NH	UNUSED F/NH	USED F
1122/54	**(1122-25, 1126-54) complete, 33 varieties**	**65.50**	**19.50**	**9.60**
1122	34¢ Toronto P.O.	2.75	.60	.27

1987 CAPEX EXHIBITION

SCOTT NO.	DESCRIPTION	PLATE BLOCK F/NH	UNUSED F/NH	USED F
1123	36¢ Nelson-Miramichi: Post Office	2.85	.60	.30
1124	42¢ Saint Ours P.O.	3.30	.75	.40
1125	72¢ Battleford P.O.	6.00	1.25	.65
1125A	CAPEX Souvenir Sheet	......	3.00	2.50
1126-29	Exploration, attached	2.75	2.20	2.00
1126	34¢ Brule	......	.60	.27
1127	34¢ Radisson	......	.60	.27
1128	34¢ Jolliet	......	.60	.27
1129	34¢ Wilderness	......	.60	.27
1130	36¢ Calgary Olympics	2.85	.60	.30
1131	42¢ Calgary Olympics	3.30	.75	.40

1132

1133

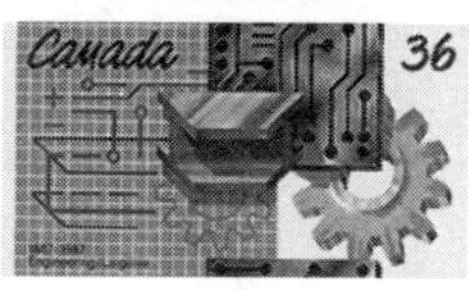

1134

SCOTT NO.	DESCRIPTION	PLATE BLOCK F/NH	UNUSED F/NH	USED F
1132	36¢ Volunteers	4.15	.60	.30
1133	36¢ Charter of Freedom	2.85	.60	.30
1134	36¢ Engineering	2.85	.60	.30

1135

1139

1141

1145

1987 COMMEMORATIVES (continued)

SCOTT NO.	DESCRIPTION	PLATE BLOCK F/NH	UNUSED F/NH	USED F
1135-38	Science & Tech., attached	2.85	2.45	2.20
1135	36¢ Reginald A. Fessenden	......	.60	.30
1136	36¢ Charles Fenerty	......	.60	.30
1137	36¢ Desbarats & Leggo	......	.60	.30
1138	36¢ Frederick N. Gisborne	......	.60	.30
1139-40	Steamships, attached	2.85	1.20	1.10
1139	36¢ Segwun	......	.60	.30
1140	36¢ Princess Marguerite	......	.60	.30
1141-44	Historic Shipwrecks, att'd.	2.85	2.45	2.20
1141	36¢ Hamilton & Scourge	......	.60	.30
1142	36¢ San Juan	......	.60	.30
1143	36¢ Breadalbane	......	.60	.30
1144	36¢ Ericsson	......	.60	.30
1145	36¢ Air Canada	2.85	.60	.30

Canada Postage #1146-1188a

1146

1147

1148

1154

SCOTT NO.	DESCRIPTION	PLATE BLOCK F/NH	UNUSED F/NH	USED F
1146	36¢ Quebec Summit	2.85	.60	.30
1147	36¢ Commonwealth Mtg.	2.85	.60	.30
1148	36¢ Christmas	2.85	.60	.30
1149	42¢ Christmas	3.30	.75	.40
1150	72¢ Christmas	6.35	1.40	.65
1151	31¢ Christmas booklet single	......	.55	.25
1151a	same, booklet pane of 10	......	5.25	......
1152-53	Calgary Olympics, attached	2.85	1.35	1.10
1152	36¢ Cross-Country Skiing	......	.60	.30
1153	36¢ Ski Jumping	......	.60	.30
1154	36¢ Grey Cup	2.85	.60	.30

1155 1162 1163

1165 1166 1169

1987-91 DEFINITIVE ISSUES

SCOTT NO.	DESCRIPTION	PLATE BLOCK F/NH	UNUSED F/NH	USED F
1155	1¢ Flying Squirrel	.80	.20	.15
1156	2¢ Porcupine	.80	.20	.15
1157	3¢ Muskrat	.80	.20	.15
1158	5¢ Hare	.80	.20	.15
1159	6¢ Red Fox	.80	.20	.15
1160	10¢ Skunk	1.00	.25	.15
1160a	same, perf. 13x12-1/2	18.75	3.75	.50
1161	25¢ Beaver	2.00	.50	.20
1162	37¢ Elizabeth II	3.05	.75	.30
1163	37¢ Parliament	3.05	.75	.30
1163a	same, bklt. pane of 10 (1988)	......	7.50	7.50
1163b	same, bklt. pane of 25 (1988)	......	18.80	15.00
1163c	37¢, perf. 13-1/2x14 (1988)	......	1.20	......
1164	38¢ Elizabeth II (1988)	3.30	.75	.30
1164a	38¢, perf. 13x13-1/2	......	1.50	.75
1164b	same, booklet pane of 10	......	6.00	6.00
1165	38¢ Clock Tower (1988)	3.30	.65	.15
1165a	same, booklet pane of 10	......	6.00	6.00
1165b	same, booklet pane of 25	......	18.75	18.75
1166	39¢ Flag & Clouds ..	3.30	.75	.15
1166a	same, booklet pane of 10	......	7.50	6.75
1166b	same, booklet pane of 25	......	22.50	18.75
1166c	same, perf. 12-1/2x13		5.50	.40
1167	39¢ Elizabeth II	3.30	.75	.15
1167a	same, booklet pane of 10	......	6.75	6.00
1167b	39¢, perf. 13 (1990)	40.00	7.50	.50
1168	40¢ Elizabeth II (1990)	3.30	.75	.15
1168a	same, booklet pane of 10	......	7.50	6.75
1169	40¢ Flag and Mountains (1990)	3.30	.70	.15
1169a	same, booklet pane of 25	......	26.25	18.75
1169b	same, booklet pane of 10	......	7.50	6.75
1170	43¢ Lynx	4.50	1.00	.30
1171	44¢ Walrus (1989) ..	4.50	1.00	.20
1171a	44¢, perf. 12-1/2x13	......	1.25	.30
1171b	same, booklet pane of 5	....	6.25	....
1172	45¢ Pronghorn (1990)	4.50	.95	.30
1172b	same, booklet pane of 5	7.50	1.50	.30
1172d	45¢, perf. 13	56.25	11.25	1.20
1172A	46¢, Wolverine (1990)	3.85	1.00	.30
1172Ac	46¢, perf. 12-1/2x13	......	.85	.30
1172Ae	same, booklet pane of 5	......	1.15	.30
1172Ag	same, perf. 14-1/2x14		1.90	.40
1173	57¢ Killer Whale	4.90	1.15	.35
1174	59¢ Musk-ox (1989)	4.90	1.15	.35
1174a	same, perf. 13	22.50	4.90	.60
1175	61¢ Timber Wolf (1990)	5.65	1.15	.40
1175a	61¢, perf. 13	225.00	50.00	.50
1176	63¢ Harbor Porpoise	6.00	1.35	.40
1176a	63¢, perf. 13	22.50	4.90	.60
1177	74¢ Wapiti (1988) ...	7.50	1.50	.60
1178	76¢ Grizzly Bear (1989)	6.00	1.35	.40
1178a	76¢, perf. 12-1/2x13	......	2.25	.35
1178b	same, booklet pane of 5	....	12.00	....
1178c	same, perf. 13	112.50	26.25	2.75
1179	78¢ Beluga (1990) ..	7.50	1.50	.55
1179a	same, booklet pane of 5	......	8.00	......
1179b	78¢, perf. 13	90.00	18.75	2.65
1179c	same, perf. 12-1/2x13	13.15	2.25	.60
1180	80¢ Peary caribou (1990)	7.15	1.50	.60
1180a	80¢, perf. 12-1/2x13	6.60	2.00	.55
1180b	same, booklet pane of 5	....	10.50	....
1180c	80¢, perf. 14-1/2x14	16.90	3.75	.60

1181

SCOTT NO.	DESCRIPTION	PLATE BLOCK F/NH	UNUSED F/NH	USED F
1181	$1 Runnymede Library	7.50	1.50	.80
1182	$2 McAdam Train Station	15.00	3.00	1.50
1183	$5 Bonsecours Market	40.00	8.50	4.00

1184

BOOKLET STAMPS

SCOTT NO.	DESCRIPTION	PLATE BLOCK F/NH	UNUSED F/NH	USED F
1184	1¢ Flag, booklet single (1990)		.20	.15
1185	5¢ Flag, booklet single (1990)		.20	.15
1186	6¢ Parliament East (1989)	......	.25	.15
1187	37¢ Parliament booklet single		.65	.25
1187a	booklet pane (4), 1 #938, 2 #942, 1 #1187	......	.90	......
1188	38¢ Parliament Library booklet single (1989)	......	.65	.25
1188a	booklet pane (5), 3 #939a, 1 #1186, 1 #1188	......	1.05	......

Canada Postage #1189-1228

SCOTT NO.	DESCRIPTION	PLATE BLOCK F/NH	UNUSED F/NH	USED F
1189	39¢ Flag booklet single (1990)		.75	.30
1189a	booklet pane (4), 1 #1184, 2 #1185, 1 #1189	......	1.05	......
1190	40¢ Flag booklet single (1990)		.85	.25
1190a	booklet pane (4) 2 #1184, 1 #1185, 1 #1190	......	.95	......

1191, 1192, 1193

SELF-ADHESIVE BOOKLET STAMPS

SCOTT NO.	DESCRIPTION	PLATE BLOCK F/NH	UNUSED F/NH	USED F
1191	38¢ Flag, forest (1989)	......	1.15	.60
1191a	same, booklet pane of 12	......	13.75	......
1192	39¢ Flag field (1990)	......	1.15	.60
1192a	same, booklet pane of 12	......	13.75	......
1193	40¢ Flag, seacoast (1991)	......	1.15	.60
1193a	same, booklet pane of 12	......	13.75	......

COIL STAMPS

SCOTT NO.	DESCRIPTION	PLATE BLOCK F/NH	UNUSED F/NH	USED F
1194	37¢ Parliament Library (1988)		.65	.25
1194A	38¢ Parliament Library (1989)......		.65	.25
1194B	39¢ Flag (1990)	......	.75	.25
1194C	40¢ Flag (1990)	......	.75	.25

1988 COMMEMORATIVES

SCOTT NO.	DESCRIPTION	PLATE BLOCK F/NH	UNUSED F/NH	USED F
1195/1236	**(1195-1225, 1226-36) complete, 39 varieties**	**68.75**	**28.50**	**12.75**
1195-96	Calgary Olympics, att'd.	3.05	1.50	1.15
1195	37¢ Alpine Skiing	......	.65	.30
1196	37¢ Curling	......	.65	.30
1197	43¢ Figure Skating	3.30	.75	.60
1198	74¢ Luge	5.80	1.50	.95
1199-1202	Explorers, attached	3.05	3.00	2.25
1199	37¢ Anthony Henday	......	.65	.30
1200	37¢ George Vancouver	......	.65	.30
1201	37¢ Simon Fraser	......	.65	.30
1202	37¢ John Palliser	......	.65	.30

1203

1204

SCOTT NO.	DESCRIPTION	PLATE BLOCK F/NH	UNUSED F/NH	USED F
1203	50¢ Canadian Art	5.00	1.10	.95
1204-05	Wildlife Conservation, att'd.	3.30	1.40	.95
1204	37¢ Ducks Unlimited	......	.65	.30
1205	37¢ Moose	......	.65	.30

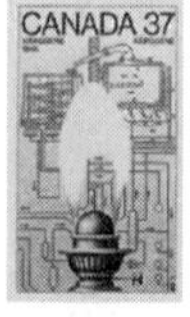

1206

1210

1216

SCOTT NO.	DESCRIPTION	PLATE BLOCK F/NH	UNUSED F/NH	USED F
1206-09	Science & Technology, att'd.	3.05	2.50	2.00
1206	37¢ Kerosene	......	.65	.30
1207	37¢ Marquis Wheat .	......	.65	.30
1208	37¢ Electron Microscope	......	.65	.30
1209	37¢ Cancer Therapy	......	.65	.30
1210-13	Butterflies, attached	3.05	3.00	2.25
1210	37¢ Short-tailed Swallowtail	......	.65	.30
1211	37¢ Northern Blue ...	......	.65	.30
1212	37¢ Macoun's Arctic	......	.65	.30
1213	37¢ Tiger Swallowtail	......	.65	.30

1214

1215

1217-20

1221

SCOTT NO.	DESCRIPTION	PLATE BLOCK F/NH	UNUSED F/NH	USED F
1214	37¢ Harbor Entrance	3.05	.65	.25
1215	37¢ 4-H Club Anniv.	3.05	.65	.25
1216	37¢ Les Forges Du St. Maurice	3.05	.65	.25
1217-20	Dogs, attached	3.05	3.00	2.25
1217	37¢ Tahltan Bear Dog	......	.65	.25
1218	37¢ Nova Scotia Retriever	......	.65	.25
1219	37¢ Canadian Eskimo Dog	......	.65	.25
1220	37¢ Newfoundland Dog	......	.65	.25
1221	37¢ Baseball	4.15	.65	.25

1222

1226

1227

1228

SCOTT NO.	DESCRIPTION	PLATE BLOCK F/NH	UNUSED F/NH	USED F
1222	37¢ Christmas Nativity	3.50	.75	.25
1223	43¢ Virgin & Child ...	4.00	.90	.75
1224	74¢ Virgin & Child ...	6.00	1.15	.95
1225	32¢ Christmas Icons booklet single	......	.75	.30
1225a	same, booklet pane of 10	......	7.00	5.25
1226	37¢ Charles Inglis ...	3.05	.65	.25
1227	37¢ Ann Hopkins	3.05	.65	.25
1228	37¢ Angus Walters .	3.05	.65	.25

1229-32

Canada Postage #1229-1273b

SCOTT NO.	DESCRIPTION	PLATE BLOCK F/NH	UNUSED F/NH	USED F
1229-32	Small Craft Series, attached	3.30	2.70	2.25
1229	37¢ Chipewyan Canoe	......	.65	.25
1230	37¢ Haida Canoe	......	.65	.25
1231	37¢ Inuit Kayak	......	.65	.25
1232	37¢ Micmac Canoe	......	.65	.25
1233-36	Explorers, attached	3.30	3.00	2.25
1233	38¢ Matonabbee	......	.65	.25
1234	38¢ Sir John Franklin	......	.65	.25
1235	38¢ J.B.Tyrrell	......	.65	.25
1236	38¢ V. Stefansson	......	.65	.25

1237

1989 COMMEMORATIVES

1237/63	**(1237-56, 1257, 1258, 1259, 1260-63) complete, 26 varieties**	**39.45**	**17.75**	**7.25**

1237-40	Canadian Photography, att'd.	3.30	3.00	2.25
1237	38¢ W. Notman	......	.65	.25
1238	38¢ W.H. Boorne	......	.65	.25
1239	38¢ A. Henderson	......	.65	.25
1240	38¢ J.E. Livernois	......	.65	.25
1241	50¢ Canadian Art	5.00	1.10	.95

1243

1245

1243-44	19th Century Poets, att'd.	3.30	1.40	.95
1243	38¢ L.H.Frechette	......	.65	.25
1244	38¢ A. Lampman	......	.65	.25
1245-48	Mushrooms, attached	3.30	2.70	2.25
1245	38¢ Cinnabar Chanterelle	......	.65	.25
1246	38¢ Common Morel	......	.65	.25
1247	38¢ Spindell Coral	......	.65	.25
1248	38¢ Admirable Boletus	......	.65	.25

1249

1251

1252

1249-50	Canadian Infantry, attached	3.50	1.50	1.15
1249	38¢ Light Infantry	.....	.65	.25
1250	38¢ Royal 22nd Regiment	......	.65	.25
1251	38¢ International Trade	3.30	.65	.25

SCOTT NO.	DESCRIPTION	PLATE BLOCK F/NH	UNUSED F/NH	USED F
1252-55	Performing Arts, attached	3.30	2.70	2.25
1252	38¢ Dance	......	.65	.25
1253	38¢ Music	......	.65	.25
1254	38¢ Film	......	.65	.25
1255	38¢ Theatre	......	.65	.25

1256, 1256a

1259, 1259a

1260

1256	38¢ Christmas 1989	3.30	.65	.25
1256a	same, booklet single	....	3.75	.75
1256a	same, booklet pane of 10	45.00	....	....
1257	44¢ Christmas 1989	4.60	.85	.40
1257a	same, booklet single	....	4.50	.75
1257a	same, booklet pane of 5	22.50	....	....
1258	76¢ Christmas 1989	6.35	1.40	.70
1258a	same, booklet single	....	5.50	.75
1258a	same, booklet pane of 5	26.25	....	....
1259	33¢ Christmas, booklet single	......	.70	.25
1259a	same, booklet pane of 10	......	6.75	5.25
1260-63	WWII 50th Anniversary, att'd.	3.30	3.00	2.25
1260	38¢ Declaration of War	......	.65	.25
1261	38¢ Army Mobilization	......	.65	.25
1262	38¢ Navy Convoy System	......	.65	.25
1263	38¢ Commonwealth Training	......	.65	.25

1264

1270

1990 COMMEMORATIVES

1264/1301	**(1264-73, 1274-94, 1295, 1296, 1297, 1298-1301) complete, 38 vars.**	**54.85**	**25.50**	**9.90**

1264-65	Norman Bethune, attached	3.30	1.50	1.15
1264	39¢ Bethune in Canada	.....	.70	.25
1265	39¢ Bethune in China	.....	.70	.25
1266-69	Small Craft Series, att'd.	3.30	2.70	2.25
1266	39¢ Dory	.....	.70	.25
1267	39¢ Pointer	.....	.70	.25
1268	39¢ York Boat	.....	.70	.25
1269	39¢ North Canoe	.....	.70	.25
1270	39¢ Multiculturalism	3.30	.70	.25
1271	50¢ Canadian Art, "The West Wind"	4.40	.95	.75

1272

1273

1274

1272-73	Canada Postal System 39¢ booklet pair	.....	1.50	1.00
1273a	same, booklet pane of 8	.....	6.00	.....
1273b	same, booklet pane of 9	.....	6.50	.....

Canada Postage #1274-1320

SCOTT NO.	DESCRIPTION	PLATE BLOCK F/NH	UNUSED F/NH	USED F
1274-77	Dolls of Canada, attached	3.30	2.70	2.25
1274	39¢ Native Dolls	.....	.70	.25
1275	39¢ Settlers' Dolls	.....	.70	.25
1276	39¢ Four Commercial Dolls	.....	.70	.25
1277	39¢ Five Commercial Dolls	.....	.70	.25

1278

1279

SCOTT NO.	DESCRIPTION	PLATE BLOCK F/NH	UNUSED F/NH	USED F
1278	39¢ Canada/Flag Day	3.30	.75	.25
1279-82	Prehistoric Life, attached	3.30	2.70	2.25
1279	39¢ Trilobite	......	.70	.25
1280	39¢ Sea Scorpion	......	.70	.25
1281	39¢ Fossil Algae	......	.70	.25
1282	39¢ Soft Invertebrate	......	.70	.25

1283

1287

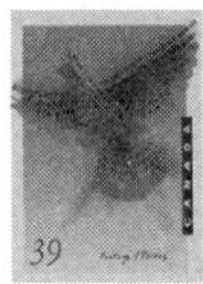
1288

1289

1293

SCOTT NO.	DESCRIPTION	PLATE BLOCK F/NH	UNUSED F/NH	USED F
1283-86	Canadian Forests, attached	3.30	3.00	2.25
1283	39¢ Acadian	......	.70	.25
1284	39¢ Great Lakes—St.Lawrence.....		.70	.25
1285	39¢ Coast	......	.70	.25
1286	39¢ Boreal	......	.70	.25
1287	39¢ Climate Observations	3.30	.70	.25
1288	39¢ Int'l. Literacy Year	3.30	.70	.25
1289-92	Can. Lore & Legend, attached	3.30	3.00	2.25
1289	39¢ Sasquatch	......	.70	.25
1290	39¢ Kraken	......	.70	.25
1291	39¢ Werewolf	......	.70	.25
1292	39¢ Ogopogo	......	.70	.25
1293	39¢ Agnes Macphail	3.30	.70	.25

1294

1297

SCOTT NO.	DESCRIPTION	PLATE BLOCK F/NH	UNUSED F/NH	USED F
1294	39¢ Native Mary & Child	3.20	.75	.25
1294a	same, booklet pane of 10	......	7.25	......
1295	45¢ Inuit, Mother & Child	3.86	.85	.40
1295a	same, booklet pane of 5	......	4.40	......
1296	78¢ Raven Children	6.60	1.50	.60
1296a	same, booklet pane of 5	......	7.45	......
1297	34¢ Christmas, booklet sgl.	......	.65	.25
1297a	same, booklet pane of 10	......	7.00	......

SCOTT NO.	DESCRIPTION	PLATE BLOCK F/NH	UNUSED F/NH	USED F
1298-1301	World War II—1940, att'd.	3.30	3.00	2.25
1298	39¢ Home Front ..	......	.70	.25
1299	39¢ Communal War Efforts	......	.70	.25
1300	39¢ Food Production	......	.70	.25
1301	39¢ Science and War	......	.70	.25

1302

1311

1991 COMMEMORATIVES

SCOTT NO.	DESCRIPTION	PLATE BLOCK F/NH	UNUSED F/NH	USED F
1302-43, 1345-48, 46 varieties		**30.55**	**29.75**	**11.25**
1302-05	Canadian Doctors, att'd.	3.50	2.70	2.25
1302	40¢ Jennie Trout	......	.75	.25
1303	40¢ Wilder Penfield......	.35	.75	
1304	40¢ Sir Frederick Banting	......	.75	.25
1305	40¢ Harold Griffith ...	......	.75	.25
1306-09	Prehistoric Life, attached	3.50	2.70	1.50
1306	40¢ Microfossils	......	.75	.25
1307	40¢ Early tree	......	.75	.25
1308	40¢ Early fish	......	.75	.25
1309	40¢ Land reptile	......	.75	.25
1310	50¢ Canadian Art, "Forest, British Columbia"	4.50	.95	.75
1311	40¢ The Butchart Gardens, attached booklet single	......	.75	.25
1312	40¢ International Peace Garden, booklet single	......	.75	.25
1313	40¢ Royal Botanical Garden, booklet single	......	.75	.25
1314	40¢ Montreal Botanical Garden, booklet single	......	.75	.25
1315	40¢ Halifax Public Gardens, booklet single	......	.75	.25
1315a	Public Gardens, strip of 5	......	3.50	1.75
1315b	Public Gardens, attached booklet pane of 10 ..	......	6.95	....

1316

1321

SCOTT NO.	DESCRIPTION	PLATE BLOCK F/NH	UNUSED F/NH	USED F
1316	40¢ Canada Day	3.50	.75	.25
1317-20	Small Craft Series, attached	3.50	2.70	2.25
1317	40¢ Verchere Rowboat	......	.75	.25
1318	40¢ Touring Kayak ..	......	.75	.25
1319	40¢ Sailing Dinghy ..	......	.75	.25
1320	40¢ Cedar Strip Canoe	......	.75	.25

Canada Postage #1321-1362b

SCOTT NO.	DESCRIPTION	PLATE BLOCK F/NH	UNUSED F/NH	USED F
1321	40¢ South Nahanni River	......	.75	.25
1322	40¢ Athabasca River	......	.75	.25
1323	40¢ Voyageur Waterway	......	.75	.25
1324	40¢ Jacques Cartier River	......	.75	.25
1325	40¢ Main River	......	.75	.25
1325a	Canadian Rivers, strip of 5	......	3.50	1.75
1325b	Canadian Rivers, attached booklet pane of 10 ..	......	6.95	......

1326

1330

SCOTT NO.	DESCRIPTION	PLATE BLOCK F/NH	UNUSED F/NH	USED F
1326-29	Arrival of the Ukrainians, attached	3.50	2.70	1.50
1326	40¢ Leaving	....	.75	.25
1327	40¢ Winter in Canada	....	.75	.25
1328	40¢ Clearing Land ..	....	.75	.25
1329	40¢ Growing Wheat	....	.75	.25
1330-33	Dangerous Public Service Occupations, attached	3.50	2.70	2.25
1330	40¢ Ski Patrol	....	.75	.25
1331	40¢ Police	....	.75	.25
1332	40¢ Firefighters	....	.75	.25
1333	40¢ Search & Rescue	....	.75	.25

1334

1338

1339

1342

SCOTT NO.	DESCRIPTION	PLATE BLOCK F/NH	UNUSED F/NH	USED F
1334-37	Folktales, attached ..	3.50	2.70	2.25
1334	40¢ Witched Canoe	....	.75	.25
1335	40¢ Orphan Boy	....	.75	.25
1336	40¢ Chinook Wind ..	....	.75	.25
1337	40¢ Buried Treasure	....	.75	.25
1338	40¢ Queen's University, booklet, single	....	.75	.25
1338a	Same booklet pane of 10	....	6.95	....
1339	40¢ Santa at Fireplace	3.60	.75	.25
1339a	Same, booklet pane of 10	....	6.95	....
1340	46¢ Santa with White horse, tree	4.10	.85	.40
1340a	Same, booklet pane of 5	....	4.40	....
1341	80¢ Sinterklaas, girl	7.00	1.50	.70
1341a	Same, booklet pane of 5	....	7.75	....
1342	35¢ Santa with Punchbowl, booklet, single	....	.70	.25
1342a	Same, booklet pane of 10	....	6.95	....

1343

1349

SCOTT NO.	DESCRIPTION	PLATE BLOCK F/NH	UNUSED F/NH	USED F
1343	40¢ Basketball Centennial	3.60	.75	.25
1344	40¢-80¢ Basketball Souvenir Sheet of 3	....	3.00	....
1345-48	World War II—1941, att'd.	3.50	3.00	2.25
1345	40¢ Women's Armed Forces	....	.80	.25
1346	40¢ War Industry	....	.80	.25
1347	40¢ Cadets and Veterans	....	.80	.25
1348	40¢ Defense of Hong Kong	....	.80	.25

1991-96 Regular Issue

SCOTT NO.	DESCRIPTION	PLATE BLOCK F/NH	UNUSED F/NH	USED F
1349	1¢ Blueberry (1992)	.80	.20	.15
1350	2¢ Wild Strawberry (1992)	.80	.20	.15
1351	3¢ Black Crowberry (1992)	.80	.20	.15
1352	5¢ Rose Hip (1992) .	.80	.20	.15
1353	6¢ Black Raspberry (1992)	.80	.20	.15
1354	10¢ Kinnikinnick (1992)	1.00	.25	.15
1355	25¢ Saskatoon berry (1992)	2.00	.50	.15
1358	42¢ Flag + Rolling Hills	3.20	.75	.20
1358a	Same, booklet pane of 10	....	7.50	6.00
1358b	Same, booklet pane of 50	....	37.50	33.75
1358c	Same, booklet pane of 25	....	18.75	15.00
1359	42¢ Queen Elizabeth II (Karsh)	3.20	.75	.20
1359a	Same, booklet pane of 10	....	7.50	6.00
1360	43¢ Queen Elizabeth II (Karsh) (1992)	4.15	.95	.20
1360a	Same, booklet pane of 10	....	9.40	7.50
1360B	43¢ Flag + Prairie (1992)	4.15	.95	.20
1360Bc	Same, booklet pane of 10	....	7.50	6.00
1360Bd	Same, booklet pane of 25	....	22.50	18.75
1360H	45¢ Queen Elizabeth II (Karsh) (1995)	3.20	.75	.20
1360Hi	Same, booklet pane of 10	....	7.50	6.00
1360J	45¢ Flag & Building (1995)	3.20	.75	.20
1360Jk	Same, booklet pane of 10	....	9.40	7.50
1360Jl	Same, booklet pane of 25	....	28.15	22.50
1360m	45¢ Flag & Building, perf. 13½ x 13	3.20	.75	.20
1360mn	Same, booklet pane of 10	....	7.50	6.00
1360mo	Same, booklet pane of 25	....	18.75	15.00

1361

SCOTT NO.	DESCRIPTION	PLATE BLOCK F/NH	UNUSED F/NH	USED F
1361	48¢ McIntosh Apple Tree, perf. 13	4.15	.95	.25
1361a	Same, perf. 14½ x 14	....	1.15	.30
1361b	Same, booklet pane of 5	....	5.65	4.50
1362	49¢ Delicious Apple perf.13 (1992)	4.15	.95	.25
1362a	Same, perf. 14½ x 14	3.95	1.15	.30
1362b	Same, booklet pane of 5	....	5.65	4.50

Canada Postage #1363-1440b

SCOTT NO.	DESCRIPTION	PLATE BLOCK F/NH	UNUSED F/NH	USED F
1363	50¢ Snow Apple (1994)	3.95	.95	.30
1363b	Same, perf. 14½ x 14	3.95	.90	.25
1363bc	Same, booklet pane of 5	....	4.50	....
1364	52¢ Gravenstein apple (1995)	3.95	.95	.25
1364a	Same, booklet pane of 5	....	5.65	4.50
1364b	52¢ Gravenstein apple, perf. 14½ x 14	3.95	1.15	.30
1364bc	Same, booklet pane of 5	....	4.50	....
1366	65¢ Black Walnut Tree	4.90	1.15	.35
1367	67¢ Beaked Hazelnut (1992)	4.90	1.15	.35
1368	69¢ Shagbark Hickory (1994)	4.90	1.15	.35
1369	71¢ American Chestnut (1995)	4.90	1.10	.35
1371	84¢ Stanley Plum Tree, perf. 13	5.65	1.35	.40
1371a	Same, perf. 14½ x 14	....	1.50	.50
1371b	Same, booklet pane of 5	....	7.50	....
1372	86¢ Bartlett Pear, perf. 13 (1992)	9.00	2.65	.60
1372a	Same, perf. 14½ x 14	13.15	1.50	.60
1372b	Same, booklet pane of 5	....	7.50	....
1373	88¢ Westcot Apricot (1994)	6.40	1.50	.50
1373b	Same, perf. 14½ x 14	6.75	1.50	.60
1363bc	Same, booklet pane of 5	....	7.50	....
1374	90¢ Elberta Peach (1995)	6.00	1.45	.45
1374a	Same, booklet pane of 5	7.50	1.50	.45
1374b	Same, booklet pane of 5, perf. 14½ x 14	....	9.40	7.50
1375	$1 Yorkton Court House (1994)	6.75	1.50	.55
1376	$2 Provincial Normal School, Nova Scotia (1994) .	13.15	3.00	1.05
1378	$5 Carnegie Public Library, Victoria	33.75	7.50	2.25
1388	42¢ Flag and Mountains, quick-stick (1992)	....	.80	.30
1388a	Same, booklet pane of 12	....	10.00	....
1389	43¢ Flag, estuary shore (1993)	....	.80	.30
1394	42¢ Canadian Flag + Rolling Hills, coil	....	.80	.30
1395	43¢ Canadian Flag, coil (1992)	....	.80	.30
1396	45¢ Canadian Flag, coil (1995)	....	.80	.20

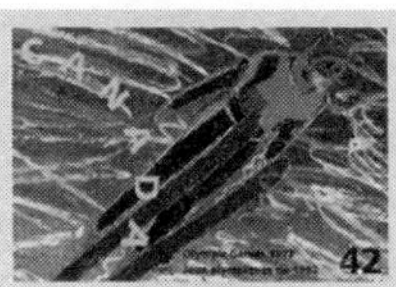

1399

1404

1992 COMMEMORATIVES

SCOTT NO.	DESCRIPTION	PLATE BLOCK F/NH	UNUSED F/NH	USED F
1399-1455, 57 varieties		**44.15**	**49.00**	**19.40**
1399	42¢ Ski Jumping	....	.95	.25
1400	42¢ Figure Skating ..	....	.95	.25
1401	42¢ Hockey	....	.95	.25
1402	42¢ Bobsledding	....	.95	.25
1403	42¢ Alpine Skiing	....	.95	.25
1403a	Olympic Winter Games, Strips of 5	....	4.50	3.00
1403b	Olympic Winter Games, booklet pane of 10 ..	....	8.00	5.00
1404-05	350th Anniversary of Montreal, attached ..	3.60	1.50	1.00
1404	42¢ Modern Montreal	....	.80	.25
1405	42¢ Early Montreal ..	....	.80	.25
1406	48¢ Jaques Cartier .	3.95	.90	.40
1407	84¢ Columbus	7.65	1.65	.60
1407a	42¢-84¢ Canada '92, Souvenir Sheet of 4	....	4.00	....
1408	42¢ The Margaree River	....	.85	.25
1409	42¢ Eliot or West River	....	.85	.25
1410	42¢ Ottowa River	....	.85	.25
1411	42¢ Niagara River ...	....	.85	.25
1412	42¢ South Saskatchewan River	....	.85	.25
1412a	Canadian Rivers II, Strip of 5	....	4.00	3.00
1412b	Canadian Rivers II, booklet pane of 10 ..	....	8.00	5.00

1413

1420

SCOTT NO.	DESCRIPTION	PLATE BLOCK F/NH	UNUSED F/NH	USED F
1413	42¢ 50th Anniversary of the Alaska Highway	3.60	.80	.25
1414	42¢ Gymnastics	....	.95	.25
1415	42¢ Track and Field	....	.95	.25
1416	42¢ Diving	....	.95	.25
1417	42¢ Cycling	....	.95	.25
1418	42¢ Swimming	....	.95	.25
1418a	Olympic Summer Games, Strip of 5, attached ..	....	4.50	3.00
1418b	Olympic Summer Games, booklet pane of 10 ..	....	8.00	5.00
1419	50¢ Canadian Art "Red Nasturtiums"	4.40	.95	.75
1420	Nova Scotia	....	1.50	.75
1421	Ontario	....	1.50	.75
1422	Prince Edward Island	....	1.50	.75
1423	New Brunswick	....	1.50	.75
1424	Quebec	....	1.50	.75
1425	Saskatchewan	....	1.50	.75
1426	Manitoba	....	1.50	.75
1427	Northwest Territories	....	1.50	.75
1428	Alberta	....	1.50	.75
1429	British Columbia	....	1.50	.75
1430	Yukon	....	1.50	.75
1431	Newfoundland	....	1.50	.75
1431a	42¢ 125th Anniversary of Canada, 12 various attached	......	16.50	8.50

1432

1436

SCOTT NO.	DESCRIPTION	PLATE BLOCK F/NH	UNUSED F/NH	USED F
1432-35	Canadian Folk Heroes, attached	3.60	3.00	2.25
1432	42¢ Jerry Potts	....	.80	.25
1433	42¢ Capt. William Jackman	....	.80	.25
1434	42¢ Laura Secord	....	.80	.25
1435	42¢ Joseph Montferrand	....	.80	.25
1436	42¢ Copper	....	.85	.25
1437	42¢ Sodalite	....	.85	.25
1438	42¢ Gold	....	.85	.25
1439	42¢ Galena	....	.85	.25
1440	42¢ Grossular	....	.85	.25
1440a	Minerals, Strip of 5	....	4.00	3.00
1440b	Minerals, booklet pane of 10	....	8.00	5.00

Canada Postage #1441-1471b

1443a

1441

SCOTT NO.	DESCRIPTION	PLATE BLOCK F/NH	UNUSED F/NH	USED F
1441-42	Canadian Space Exploration, attached	3.60	1.50	1.15
1441	42¢ Anik E2 Satellite	....	.80	.25
1442	42¢ Earth, Space Shuttle	....	.80	.25
1443-45	National Hockey League, booklet singles	....	2.40	.75
1443a	Skates, Stick, booklet pane of 8	....	6.40	....
1444a	Team Emblems, booklet pane of 8	....	6.40	....
1445a	Goalie's Mask, booklet pane of 9	....	7.20	....

1446-47

SCOTT NO.	DESCRIPTION	PLATE BLOCK F/NH	UNUSED F/NH	USED F
1446-47	Order of Canada + D. Michener, attached	3.60	1.50	1.15
1446	42¢ Order of Canada	....	.80	.25
1447	42¢ Daniel Roland Michener	....	.80	.25
1448-51	World War II—1942, att'd.	3.60	3.00	2.25
1448	42¢ War Reporting	....	.80	.25
1449	42¢ Newfoundland Air Bases	....	.80	.25
1450	42¢ Raid on Dieppe	....	.80	.25
1451	42¢ U-boats offshore	....	.80	.25

1452

1455

SCOTT NO.	DESCRIPTION	PLATE BLOCK F/NH	UNUSED F/NH	USED F
1452	42¢ Jouluvana—Christmas	3.90	.80	.25
1452a	Same, perf. 13½	3.90	.80	.25
1452b	Same, booklet pane of 10	....	7.75	....
1453	48¢ La Befana—Christmas	3.95	.90	.30
1453a	Same, booklet pane of 5	....	4.50	....
1454	84¢ Weihnachtsmann	6.75	1.50	.50
1454a	Same, booklet pane of 5	....	7.50	....
1455	37¢ Santa Claus	....	.70	.25
1455a	Same, booklet pane of 10	....	6.75	....

1456

1460

1993 COMMEMORATIVES

SCOTT NO.	DESCRIPTION	PLATE BLOCK F/NH	UNUSED F/NH	USED F
1456-89, 1491-1506, 50 varieties		37.55	35.95	12.35
1456-59	Canadian Women, attached....	3.60	3.00	2.25
1456	43¢ Adelaide Sophia Hoodless....		.80	.25
1457	43¢ Marie-Josephine Gerin-Lajoie	...	.80	.25
1458	43¢ Pitseolak Ashoona	....	.80	.25
1459	43¢ Helen Kinnear	....	.80	.25
1460	43¢ Stanley Cup Centennial	3.60	.80	.25

1461

1467

SCOTT NO.	DESCRIPTION	PLATE BLOCK F/NH	UNUSED F/NH	USED F
1461	43¢ Coverlet "Bed Rugg", New Brunswick	....	.85	.25
1462	43¢ Pieced Quilt, Ontario	....	.85	.25
1463	43¢ Doukhobor Bedcover, Saskatchewan	....	.85	.25
1464	43¢ Kwakwaka'wakw ceremonial robe, British Columbia	....	.85	.25
1465	43¢ Boutonne coverlet, Quebec	....	.85	.25
1465a	Handcrafted Textiles, Strip of 5....		4.00	3.00
1465b	Handcrafted Textiles, booklet pane of 10 ..	....	8.00	5.00
1461-65	Same, set of 5 singles	....	3.90	....
1466	86¢ Canadian Art—"Drawing for the Owl"	6.75	1.50	.95
1467	43¢ Empress Hotel, Victoria, B.C.	....	.85	.25
1468	43¢ Banff Springs Hotel, Banff, Alberta	....	.85	.25
1469	43¢ Royal York Hotel, Toronto, Ontario	....	.85	.25
1470	43¢ Chateau Frontenac, Quebec City, Quebec	....	.85	.25
1471	43¢ Algonquin Hotel, St. Andrews, N.B. ...	....	.85	.25
1471a	Canadian Pacific Hotels, strip of 5	....	4.00	3.00
1471b	Canadian Pacific Hotels, booklet pane of 10 ..	....	8.00	5.00

1472

1484

Canada Postage #1472-1508

SCOTT NO.	DESCRIPTION	PLATE BLOCK F/NH	UNUSED F/NH	USED F
1472	43¢ Algonquin Park, Ontario	....	.85	.35
1473	43¢ De la Gaspesie Park, Quebec	....	.85	.35
1474	43¢ Cedar Dunes Park, P.E.I.	....	.85	.35
1475	43¢ Cape St. Mary's Reserve, Newfoundland	....	.85	.35
1476	43¢ Mount Robson Park, B.C..	....	.85	.35
1477	43¢ Writing-On-Stone Park, Alberta.	....	.85	.35
1478	43¢ Spruce Woods Park, Manitoba	....	.85	.35
1479	43¢ Herschel Island Park, Yukon	....	.85	.35
1480	43¢ Cypress Hills Park, Saskatchewan	....	.85	.35
1481	43¢ The Rocks Park, New Brunswick	....	.85	.35
1482	43¢ Blomidon Park, Nova Scotia	....	.85	.35
1483	43¢ Katannilik Park, Northwest Territories	....	.85	.35
1483a	100th Anniversary of Territorial Parks, 12 varieties attached	...	9.75	4.50
1484	43¢ Toronto Bicentennial	3.60	.80	.25
1485	43¢ Fraser River	...	.85	.25
1486	43¢ Yukon River	...	.85	.25
1487	43¢ Red River	...	.85	.25
1488	43¢ St. Lawrence River	...	.85	.25
1489	43¢ St. John River ..	...	.85	.25
1489a	Canadian Rivers III, strip of 5	...	4.00	3.00
1489b	Canadian Rivers III, booklet pane of 10	...	8.00	5.00

1490a

SCOTT NO.	DESCRIPTION	PLATE BLOCK F/NH	UNUSED F/NH	USED F
1490	43¢-86¢ Canadian Motor Vehicles souvenir sheet of 6	...	7.50	6.00

1491

SCOTT NO.	DESCRIPTION	PLATE BLOCK F/NH	UNUSED F/NH	USED F
1491-94	Canadian Folklore—Folk Songs, attached....	3.60	3.00	2.25
1491	43¢ The Alberta Homesteader	...	.80	.25
1492	43¢ Les Raftmans	...	.80	.25
1493	43¢ I'se the B'y that Builds the Boat	...	.80	.25
1494	43¢ Bear Song	...	.80	.25

1495

SCOTT NO.	DESCRIPTION	PLATE BLOCK F/NH	UNUSED F/NH	USED F
1495-98	Dinosaurs, attached	3.60	3.00	2.25
1495	43¢ Massospondylus (Jurassic period)	...	.80	.25
1496	43¢ Styracosaurus (Cretaceous period)	...	.80	.25
1497	43¢ Albertosaurus (Cretaceous period)	...	.80	.25
1498	43¢ Platecarpus (Cretaceous period)	...	.80	.25

1499

1502

SCOTT NO.	DESCRIPTION	PLATE BLOCK F/NH	UNUSED F/NH	USED F
1499	43¢ Santa Claus—Poland	3.60	.80	.25
1499a	same, booklet pane of 10	...	7.75	...
1500	49¢ Santa Claus—Russia	3.90	.90	.30
1500a	same, booklet pane of 5	...	4.50	...
1501	86¢ Father Christmas, Australia	6.75	1.50	.50
1501a	same, booklet pane of 5	...	7.50	...
1502	38¢ Santa Claus	...	.70	.25
1502a	same, booklet pane of 10	...	6.75	...
1503-06	World War II—1943	3.60	3.00	2.25
1503	43¢ Aid to Allies	...	.80	.25
1504	43¢ Canada's Bomber Force	...	.80	.25
1505	43¢ Battle of the Atlantic	...	.80	.25
1506	43¢ Invasion of Italy	...	.80	.25

1507

1994

SCOTT NO.	DESCRIPTION	PLATE BLOCK F/NH	UNUSED F/NH	USED F
1507-08	43¢ Greeting booklet (10 stamps w/35 stickers)	...	8.00	...

Canada Postage #1509-1540

1509

1510

1994 COMMEMORATIVES

SCOTT NO.	DESCRIPTION	PLATE BLOCK F/NH	UNUSED F/NH	USED F
1509-22, 1524-26, 1528-40,	**41 varieties**	**31.45**	**30.25**	**13.40**
1509	43¢ Jeanne Sauve	3.60	.80	.25
1510	43¢ T. Eaton Prestige	3.60	.80	.25
1510a	43¢ T. Eaton Prestige, booklet of 10	...	8.00	...
1511	43¢ Saguenay River	...	.85	.25
1512	43¢ French River	...	.85	.25
1513	43¢ Mackenzie River	...	.85	.25
1514	43¢ Churchill River	...	.85	.25
1515	43¢ Columbia River	...	.85	.25
1515a	Canadian Rivers IV, strip of 5	...	4.00	3.00
1515b	Canadian Rivers IV, booklet pane of 10	...	8.00	5.00
1516	88¢ Canadian Art "Vera"	6.75	1.50	.75

1517

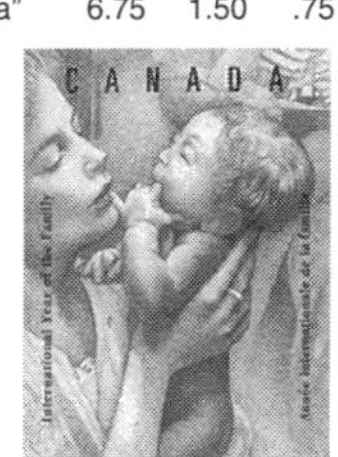

1523a

SCOTT NO.	DESCRIPTION	PLATE BLOCK F/NH	UNUSED F/NH	USED F
1517-18	Commonwealth Games, attached	3.60	1.50	.60
1517	43¢ Lawn Bowls	...	.80	.25
1518	43¢ Lacrosse	...	.80	.25
1519-20	Commonwealth Games, attached	3.60	1.50	.60
1519	43¢ Wheelchair Marathon	...	.80	.25
1520	43¢ High Jump	...	.80	.25
1521	50¢ Commonwealth Games (Diving)	4.00	.90	.35
1522	88¢ Commonwealth Games (Cycling)	6.75	1.50	.75
1523	43¢ Intl. Year of the Family, souvenir sheet of 5	...	3.75	3.00

1524a

1525

SCOTT NO.	DESCRIPTION	PLATE BLOCK F/NH	UNUSED F/NH	USED F
1524	Canada Day—Maple Trees, 12 varieties, attached	...	9.00	6.00
1525-26	Famous Canadians, attached	3.60	1.50	1.15
1525	43¢ Billy Bishop, Fighter Ace	...	.80	.25
1526	43¢ Mary Travers, Folk Singer	...	.80	.25
1527	43¢-88¢ Historic Motor Vehicles, souvenir sheet of 6	...	6.00	5.75

1528

SCOTT NO.	DESCRIPTION	PLATE BLOCK F/NH	UNUSED F/NH	USED F
1528	43¢ 50th Anniversary of ICAO	3.60	.80	.25
1529-32	Dinosaurs, attached	3.60	3.00	2.25
1529	43¢ Coryphodon	...	.80	.25
1530	43¢ Megacerops	...	.80	.25
1531	43¢ Short-Faced Bear	...	.80	.25
1532	43¢ Woolly Mammoth	...	.80	.25

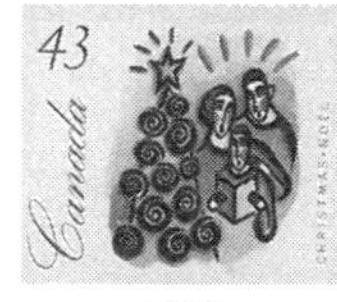

1533

1536

SCOTT NO.	DESCRIPTION	PLATE BLOCK F/NH	UNUSED F/NH	USED F
1533	43¢ Family Singing Carols	3.60	.80	.25
1533a	same, booklet pane of 10	...	7.75	...
1534	50¢ Choir	3.95	.90	.30
1534a	same, booklet pane of 5	...	4.50	...
1535	88¢ Caroling	6.75	1.50	.75
1535a	same, booklet pane of 5	...	7.50	...
1536	38¢ Caroling Soloist, booklet single	...	.70	.25
1536a	same, booklet pane of 10	...	6.75	...
1537-40	World War II—1944, attached	3.60	3.00	2.25
1537	43¢ D-Day Beachhead	...	.80	.25
1538	43¢ Artillery—Normandy	...	.80	.25
1539	43¢ Tactical Air Forces	...	.80	.25
1540	43¢ Walcheren and Scheldt	...	.80	.25

Canada Postage #1541-1573

SCOTT NO.	DESCRIPTION	PLATE BLOCK F/NH	UNUSED F/NH	USED F
	1995 Commemoratives			
1541-51, 1552-58, 1562-67, 1570-90,	**47 varieties**	**51.50**	**33.85**	**10.40**
1541-44	World War II—1945, attached	3.60	3.00	2.25
1541	43¢ Veterans Return Home	....	.80	.25
1542	43¢ Freeing the POW	....	.80	.25
1543	43¢ Libertation of Civilians	....	.80	.25
1544	43¢ Crossing the Rhine	....	.80	.25
1545	88¢ Canadian Art "Floraison"	6.75	1.50	.75
1546	(43¢) Canada Flag over Lake	3.60	.85	.25
1547	(43¢) Louisbourg Harbor, ships near Dauphin Gate	....	.85	.25
1548	(43¢) Walls, streets & buildings of Louisbourg	....	.85	.25
1549	(43¢) Museum behind King's Bastion	....	.85	.25
1550	(43¢) Drawing of King's Garden, Convent, Hospital & barracks	....	.85	.25
1551	(43¢) Partially eroded fortifications	....	.85	.25
1551a	(43¢) Fortress of Louisbourg, strip of 5	....	4.00	3.00
1551b	(43¢) Fortress of Louisbourg, booklet pane of 10	....	8.00	5.00
1552	43¢-88¢ Historic Land Vehicles/Farm and Frontier souvenir sheet of 6	....	6.00	5.75
1553	43¢ Banff Springs Golf Club	....	.85	.25
1554	43¢ Riverside Country Club	....	.85	.25
1555	43¢ Glen Abbey Golf Club	....	.85	.25
1556	43¢ Victoria Golf Club	....	.85	.25
1557	43¢ Royal Montreal Golf Club	....	.85	.25
1557a	43¢ Royal Canadian Golf Assoc., strip of 5	....	4.00	3.00
1557b	43¢ Royal Canadian Golf Assoc., booklet pane of 10	....	8.00	5.00
1558	43¢ Lunenberg Academy Centennial	3.60	.80	.25
1559-61	43¢ Group of Seven 75th Anniv. 3 souv. sheets (2 w/3 stamps and 1 w/4 stamps)	....	8.00	7.50
1562	43¢ Winnipeg, Manitoba 125th Anniversary	3.60	.80	.25
1563-66	Migratory Wildlife, attached	3.60	3.00	2.25
1563, 65-67	Migratory Wildlife, attached (revised inscription)	3.60	3.00	2.25
1563	45¢ Monarch Butterfly	....	.80	.25
1564	45¢ Belted Kingfisher	....	.80	.25
1565	45¢ Northern Pintail	....	.80	.25
1566	45¢ Hoary Bat	....	.80	.25
1568-69	45¢ Canadian Memorial College, Toronto, Greetings Booklet (10 stamps w/15 stickers)	....	8.25	....
1570-73	45¢ Canadian Bridges, attached	3.60	3.00	2.25
1570	45¢ Quebec Bridge, Quebec	....	.80	.25
1571	45¢ Highway 403-401-410 interchange, Ontario	....	.80	.25
1572	45¢ Hartland Covered Wooden Bridge, New Brunswick	....	.80	.25
1573	45¢ Alex Fraser Bridger, British Columbia	....	.80	.25

1546

1547

1553

1558

1559a

1562

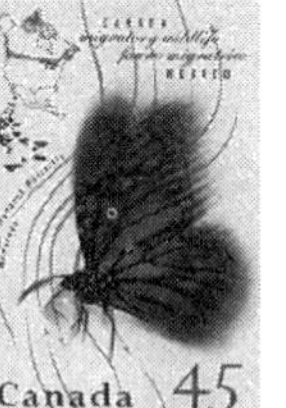

1563

1570

1574

Canada Postage #1574-1590

SCOTT NO.	DESCRIPTION	PLATE BLOCK F/NH	UNUSED F/NH	USED F
1574	45¢ Polar bear, caribou	....	.80	.25
1575	45¢ Arctic poppy, cargo canoe	....	.80	.25
1576	45¢ Inuk man, igloo, sled dogs	....	.80	.25
1577	45¢ Dog-sled team, ski plane	....	.80	.25
1578	45¢ Children	....	.80	.25
1578a	45¢ Canadian Arctic, strip of 5	....	4.00	3.00
1578b	45¢ Canadian Arctic, booklet pane of 10	....	8.00	5.00
1579	45¢ Superman	....	.80	.25
1580	45¢ Johnny Canuck	....	.80	.25
1581	45¢ Nelvana	....	.80	.25
1582	45¢ Captain Canuck	....	.80	.25
1583	45¢ Fleur de Lys	....	.80	.25
1583a	45¢ Comic Book Characters, strip of 5	....	4.00	3.00
1583b	45¢ Comic Book Characters, booklet pane of 10	....	8.00	5.00
1584	45¢ United Nations, 50th Anniversary	3.60	.80	.25
1585	45¢ The Nativity	3.60	.80	.25
1585a	same, booklet pane of 10	....	8.00	....
1586	52¢ The Annunciation	4.10	.95	.30
1586a	same, booklet pane of 5	....	4.75	....
1587	90¢ Flight to Egypt	6.95	1.55	.50
1587a	same, booklet pane of 5	....	7.75	....
1588	40¢ Holly, booklet single	....	.80	.25
1588a	same, booklet pane of 10	....	7.50	....
1589	45¢ La Francophonie's Agency, 25th Anniversary	3.60	.80	.25
1590	45¢ End of the Holocaust, 50th Anniversary	3.60	.80	.25

1579

1584

1585

1588

1589

1590

1591

1595

1600

1602

Canada Postage #1591-1615e

SCOTT NO.	DESCRIPTION	PLATE BLOCK F/NH	UNUSED F/NH	USED F
	1996			
1591-94	Birds, attached	3.60	2.70	1.50
1591	45¢ American Kestrel	....	.80	.25
1592	45¢ Atlantic Puffin	....	.80	.25
1593	45¢ Pileated Woodpecker	....	.80	.25
1594	45¢ Ruby-throated Hummingbird	....	.80	.25
1595-98	High Technology Industries, attached	3.60	2.70	1.50
1595	45¢ Ocean technology	....	.80	.25
1596	45¢ Aerospace technology	....	.80	.25
1597	45¢ Information technology	....	.80	.25
1598	45¢ Biotechnology	....	.80	.25
1600-01	45¢ Special Occasions, Greetings Booklet (10 stamps w/15 stickers)	....	8.25	....
1602	90¢ Canadian Art—"The Spirit of Haida Gwaii"	6.95	1.55	.50
1603	45¢ AIDS Awareness	3.60	.80	.25
1604	45¢-90¢ Historic Canadian Industrial & Commercial Vehicles souvenir sheet of 6	....	6.50	5.00
1605	5¢-45¢ CAPEX '96 souvenir pane of 25 vehicle stamps	....	6.50	5.00
1606	45¢ Yukon Gold Rush centennial, strip of 5	....	3.75	2.50
1606a	45¢ Jim Mason's discovery on Rabbit Creek, 1896	....	.80	.25
1606b	45¢ Miners trekking to gold fields, boats on Lake Laberge	....	.80	.25
1606c	45¢ Supr. Sam Steele, North West Mounted Police	....	.80	.25
1606d	45¢ Dawson, boom town, city of entertainment	....	.80	.25
1606e	45¢ Klondike gold fields	....	.80	.25
1607	45¢ Canada Day (Maple Leaf), self-adhesive	3.60	.80	.25
1607a	same, pane of 12	....	9.50	....
1608	45¢ Ethel Catherwood, high jump, 1928	....	.80	.25
1609	45¢ Etienne Desmarteau, 56 lb. weight throw, 1904	....	.80	.25
1610	45¢ Fanny Rosenfeld, 100m, 400m relay, 1928	....	.80	.25
1611	45¢ Gerald Ouellette, smallbore, fifle, prone, 1956	....	.80	.25
1612	45¢ Percy Williams, 100m, 200m, 1928	....	.80	.25
1612a	45¢ Canadian Gold Medalists, strip of 5	....	3.75	2.00
1612b	45¢ Canadian Gold Medalists, booklet pane of 10	....	7.50	4.00
1613	45¢ 125th Anniv. of British Columbia's Entry into Confederation	3.60	.80	.25
1614	45¢ Canadian Heraldy	3.60	.80	.25
1615	45¢ Motion Pictures Centennial, self-adhesive, sheet of 5	....	3.75	2.00
1615a	45¢ L'arrivee d'un train en gate, Lumiere cinematography, 1896	....	.80	.25
1615b	45¢ Back to God's Country, Nell & Ernest Shipman, 1919	....	.80	.25
1615c	45¢ Hen Hop, Norman McLaren, 1942	....	.80	.25
1615d	45¢ Pour la suite du monde, Pierre Perrault, Michel Brault, 1963	....	.80	.25
1615e	45¢ Goin' Down the Road, Don Shebib, 1970	....	.80	.25

1603

1604a

1606a

1607

1608

1613

1614

1615a

1617

Canada Postage #1616-1637

SCOTT NO.	DESCRIPTION	PLATE BLOCK F/NH	UNUSED F/NH	USED F
616	45¢ Motion Pictures Centennial, self-adhesive, sheet of 5	....	3.75	2.00
616a	45¢ Mon oncle Antoine, Claude Jutra, 1971	....	.80	.25
616b	45¢ The Apprenticeship of Duddy Kravitz, Ted Kotcheff, 1974	....	.80	.25
616c	45¢ Les Ordres, Michel Brault, 1974	....	.80	.25
616d	45¢ Les Bons Debarras, Francis Mankiewicz, 1980	....	.80	.25
616e	45¢ The Grey Fox, Phillip Borsos, 1982	....	.80	.25
617	45¢ Edouard Montpetit, Educator	3.60	.80	.25
618-21	Winnie the Pooh, attached	3.60	2.70	1.50
618	45¢ Winnie, Lt. Colebourne, 1914	....	.80	.25
619	45¢ Winnie, Christopher Robin, 1925	....	.80	.25
620	45¢ Milne and Shepard's Winnie the Pooh, 1926	....	.80	.25
621	45¢ Winnie the Pooh at Walt Disney World, 1996	....	.80	.25
621b	same, souvenir sheet of 4 (#1618-21)	....	3.00	2.50
......	same, booklet pane of 8 (2 blocks, #1618-21)	....	5.50	4.50
.....	same, 2 booklet panes plus souvenir book	....	10.75	....
622	45¢ Margaret Laurence (1926-1987)	....	.80	.25
623	45¢ Donald G. Creighton (1902-1979)	....	.80	.25
624	45¢ Gabrielle Roy (1909-1983)	....	.80	.25
625	45¢ Felix-Antoine Savard (1896-1982)	....	.80	.25
626	45¢ Thomas C. Halliburton (1796-1865)	....	.80	.25
626a	45¢ Canadian Authors, strip of 5	....	3.75	2.00
626b	45¢ Canadian Authors, booklet pane of 10	....	7.50	4.00
627	45¢ Children on snowshoes, sled	3.60	.80	.25
627a	same, booklet pane of 10	....	7.50	....
628	52¢ Santa Claus skiing	4.10	.95	.30
628a	same, booklet pane of 10	....	4.75	....
629	90¢ Children skating	6.95	1.55	.50
629a	same, booklet pane of 10	....	7.75	....

1618

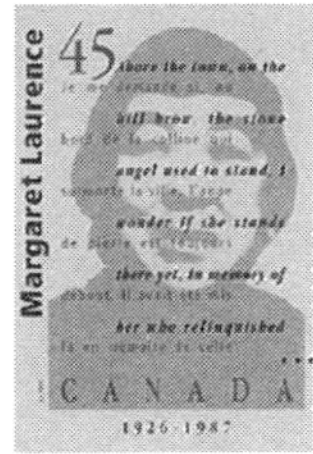

1622

1627

1630

1631

1635

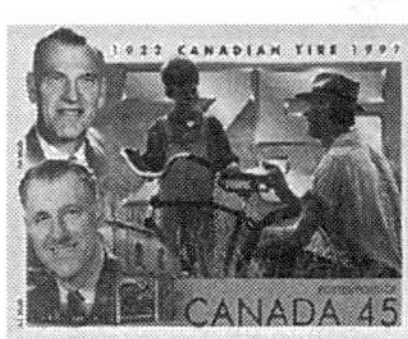

1636

1637

1997

SCOTT NO.	DESCRIPTION	PLATE BLOCK F/NH	UNUSED F/NH	USED F
1630	45¢ New Year 1997 (Year of the Ox)	....	1.40	1.00
1630a	same, souvenir sheet of 2	....	3.00	2.25
......	same, souvenir sheet of 2, with Hong Kong '97 overprint	....	5.00	3.50
1631-34	Birds of Canada, attached	3.60	2.70	1.50
1631	45¢ Mountain bluebird	....	.80	.25
1632	45¢ Western grebe	....	.80	.25
1633	45¢ Northern gannet	....	.80	.25
1634	45¢ Scarlet tanager	....	.80	.25
1635	90¢ Canadian Art "York Boat on Lake Winnipeg"	6.95	1.55	.50
1636	45¢ Canadian Tire, 75th Anniv.	3.60	.80	.25
1637	45¢ Father Charles-Emile Gadbois (1906-1981)	3.60	.80	.25

Canada Postage #1638-New Issues

1638

SCOTT NO.	DESCRIPTION	PLATE BLOCK F/NH	UNUSED F/NH	USED F
1638	45¢ Blue poppy	....	.80	.25
1638a	same, booklet pane of 12	....	9.50	....
......	45¢ Victorian Order of Nurses	3.60	.80	.25
......	45¢ Law Society of Upper Canada	3.60	.80	.25
......	45¢ Ocean Fish, attached	3.60	2.70	1.50
......	45¢ Confederation Bridge, attached	3.60	1.45	.80
......	45¢-90¢ Gilles Villeneuve, Formula 1 driver, set of 2	10.55	2.35	.75
......	same, souvenir sheet of 8	....	6.75	....
......	45¢ John Cabot	3.60	.80	.25
......	45¢ Canada's scenic highways (Canada Day), attached	3.60	2.70	1.50
......	45¢ Industrial Design	3.60	.80	.25
......	45¢ Highland Games	3.60	.80	.25
......	45¢ Knights of Columbus in Canada	3.60	.80	.25
......	45¢ World Congress of the PTT	3.60	.80	.25
......	45¢ Canada's Year of Asia Pacific	3.60	.80	.25

SCOTT NO.	DESCRIPTION	PLATE BLOCK F/NH	UNUSED F/NH	USED F

CANADA PHOSPHOR TAGGED ISSUES

Overprinted with barely visible phosphorescent ink

TYPES OF TAGGING

I = Wide Side Bars
II = Wide Bar in Middle
III = Bar at Right or Left
IV = Narrow Bar in Middle
V = Narrow Side Bars

SCOTT NO.	DESCRIPTION	PLATE CORNER BLOCKS F/NH	UNUSED F/NH
	1962-63 Queen Elizabeth II		
337-41p	1¢-5¢ Elizabeth .... (5)	52.50	10.60
401-5p	1¢-5¢ Elizabeth .... (5)	10.75	1.75
404pIV	4¢ Carmine—IV	6.00	1.25
404pII	4¢ Carmine—II	17.50	4.00
405q	5¢ Elizabeth, mini. pane of 25	......	41.25
	1964-67		
434-35p	3¢-5¢ 1964 Christmas .. (2)	13.00	2.25
434q	3¢ mini. pane of 25	......	12.10
434q	same, sealed pack of 2	......	25.00
443-44p	3¢-5¢ 1965 Christmas .. (2)	3.50	.65
443q	3¢ mini. pane of 25	......	7.70
443q	same, sealed pack of 2	......	15.75
451-52p	3¢-5¢ 1966 Christmas .. (2)	3.50	.80
451q	3¢ mini. pane of 25	......	5.15
451q	same, sealed pack of 2	......	10.50
453p	5¢ Centennial	2.25	.45
	1967-72 Queen Elizabeth II		
454-58pI	1¢-5¢—I .... (4)	12.50	1.75
454-58pII	1¢-5¢—II .... (4)	12.50	1.65
454-57pV	1¢-5¢—V .... (4)	7.75	.95
454ep	1¢ booklet single—V	......	.25
457p	4¢ carmine—III	2.75	.35
458q	5¢ mini. pane of 20	......	65.00
459p	6¢ orange, perf.10—I	4.50	.65
459bp	6¢ orange, perf.12-1/2x12—I	4.50	.65
460p	6¢ black, perf 12-1/2x12—I	5.50	.40
460cp	6¢ black, perf 12-1/2x12—II	4.25	.50
460gp	6¢ black, booklet single, perf.10—V	......	.75
460pII	6¢ black, perf. 12—II	4.00	.55
460pV	6¢ black, perf. 12—V	4.00	.50
	1967 Views		
462-65pI	10¢-25¢—I .... (4)	45.00	9.00
462-63pV	10¢-15¢—V .... (2)	12.50	2.00
	1967-69		
476-77p	3¢-5¢ 1967 Christmas .. (2)	3.50	.65
476q	3¢ mini. pane of 25	......	3.30
476q	same, sealed pack of 2	......	7.00
488-89p	5¢-6¢ 1968 Christmas .. (2)	3.75	.70
488q	5¢ booklet pane of 10	......	4.15
502-3p	5¢-6¢ 1969 Christmas .. (2)	3.50	.60
502q	5¢ booklet pane of 10	......	3.85
	1970-71		
505p	6¢ Manitoba	1.75	.35
508-11p	25¢ Expo '70 .... (4)	12.50	11.00
513-14p	10¢-15¢ U.N. .... (2)	20.00	3.15
519-30p	5¢-15¢ Christmas .... (12)	23.50	6.05
541p	15¢ Radio Canada	17.25	3.05
	1971 Queen Elizabeth II		
543-44p	7¢-8¢—I .... (2)	9.25	1.05
544q	booklet pane, ... 8¢(2), 6¢(1), 1¢(3)	......	2.20
544r	booklet pane, ... 8¢(11), 6¢(1), 1¢(6)	......	6.05
544s	booklet pane, ... 8¢(5), 6¢(1), 1¢(4)	......	2.75
544pV	8¢ slate—V	4.25	.60
550p	8¢ slate, coil	......	.30
	1971-72		
554-57p	6¢-15¢ Christmas .... (4)	11.00	2.50
560p	8¢ World Health Day	3.25	.65
561p	8¢ Frontenac	5.75	.95
562-63p	8¢ Indians .... (2)	3.75	1.20
564-65p	8¢ Indians .... (2)	3.75	1.20
582-85p	15¢ Sciences .... (4)	16.00	13.20
	1972 Pictorials		
594-97	10¢-25¢—V .... (4)	10.50	2.25
594-97p I	10¢-25¢—I .... (4)	35.00	7.50
	1972		
606-09p	6¢-15¢ Christmas—V ... (4)	12.75	2.65
606-09pI	6¢-15¢ Christmas—I ..... (4)	15.00	3.50
610p	8¢ Krieghoff	3.50	.40

Canada Postage #B1-B13a; C1-C4

SEMI-POSTAL STAMPS

B4

B7

SCOTT NO.	DESCRIPTION	PLATE BLOCKS F/NH	UNUSED F/NH	USED F
	1974-76			
B1-12	**Olympics, 12 varieties .**	**28.50**	**5.95**	**5.95**
	1974			
B1-3	Emblems, 3 varieties	7.50	1.75	1.75
B1	8¢ + 2¢ Olympic Emblem	1.75	.55	.55
B2	10¢ + 5¢ same	2.65	.55	.55
B3	15¢ + 5¢ same	3.40	.75	.75
	1975			
B4-6	Water Sports, 3 varieties	7.25	1.50	1.50
B4	8¢ + 2¢ Swimming	1.75	.35	.50
B5	10¢ + 5¢ Rowing	2.65	.55	.55
B6	15¢ + 5¢ Sailing	3.40	.75	.75
B7-9	Combat Sports, 3 varieties	7.25	1.50	1.50
B7	8¢ + 2¢ Fencing	1.75	.35	.35
B8	10¢ + 5¢ Boxing	2.65	.55	.55
B9	15¢ + 5¢ Judo	3.40	.75	.75
	1976			
B10-12	Team Sports, 3 varieties	8.00	1.50	1.50
B10	8¢ + 2¢ Basketball	1.75	.35	.35
B11	10¢ + 5¢ Gymnastics	2.65	.50	.55
B12	20¢ + 5¢ Soccer	3.85	.85	.85

B13

SCOTT NO.	DESCRIPTION	PLATE BLOCKS F/NH	UNUSED F/NH	USED F
	1997			
B13	45¢ + 5¢ Literacy	....	.90	.40
B13a	same, booklet pane of 10	....	8.75	....

AIR POST STAMPS

C1

C2

C5

SCOTT NO.	DESCRIPTION	UNUSED NH VF	UNUSED NH F	UNUSED NH AVG	UNUSED O.G. VF	UNUSED O.G. F	UNUSED O.G. AVG	USED VF	USED F	USED AVG
	1928									
C1	5¢ brown olive	9.75	7.45	5.75	6.45	4.95	3.30	2.85	2.20	1.35
	1930									
C2	5¢ olive brown	46.50	35.75	26.50	32.15	24.75	16.50	23.50	18.15	11.00
	1932									
C3	6¢ on 5¢ brown olive ..	7.50	5.80	4.00	4.75	3.60	2.40	2.55	1.95	1.10
C4	6¢ on 5¢ olive brown ..	14.25	11.00	8.50	10.00	7.70	4.95	8.60	6.60	4.15

Canada #C5-C9a; CE1-CE4

C6 C7 C9

SCOTT NO.	DESCRIPTION	PLATE BLOCK F / NH	PLATE BLOCK F / OG	UNUSED F / NH	UNUSED F / OG	USED F
	1935					
C5	6¢ red brown	11.55	9.35	1.95	1.45	.85
	1938					
C6	6¢ blue	12.10	9.65	2.20	1.65	.20
	1942-43					
C7	6¢ deep blue	13.75	11.00	2.75	2.05	.75
C8	7¢ deep blue (1943)	2.75	2.20	.55	.45	.15
	1946					
C9	7¢ deep blue	2.65	2.20	.55	.45	.15
C9a	same, booklet pane of 4	......	......	2.20	1.80	.....

AIR POST SPECIAL DELIVERY

CE1

CE3

SCOTT NO.	DESCRIPTION	PLATE BLOCK F / NH	PLATE BLOCK F / OG	UNUSED F / NH	UNUSED F / OG	USED F
	1942-43					
CE1	16¢ bright ultramarine	10.75	8.25	2.20	1.65	1.50
CE2	17¢ bright ultramarine (1943)	12.10	10.00	2.75	2.10	1.95
	1946					
CE3	17¢ bright ultramarine (circumflex "E")	23.10	17.60	5.50	3.75	3.60
	1947					
CE4	17¢ bright ultramarine (grave "E")	23.10	17.60	5.50	3.75	3.60

Canada #E1-E10

SCOTT NO.	DESCRIPTION	UNUSED NH VF	F	AVG	UNUSED O.G. VF	F	AVG	USED VF	F	AVG

SPECIAL DELIVERY STAMPS

E1

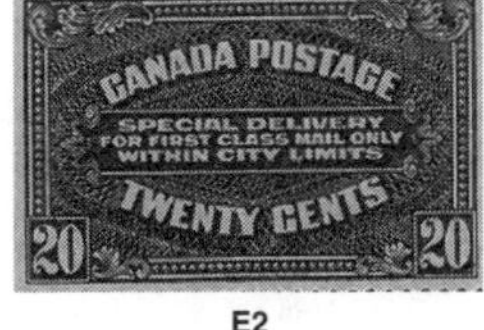

E2

E3

SCOTT NO.	DESCRIPTION	UNUSED NH VF	F	AVG	UNUSED O.G. VF	F	AVG	USED VF	F	AVG
	1898									
E1	10¢ blue green	70.00	49.50	38.50	39.50	30.25	20.35	7.85	6.05	3.60
	1922									
E2	20¢ carmine	78.50	55.00	44.00	42.95	33.00	22.00	7.85	6.05	3.60
	1927									
E3	20¢ orange	14.50	9.90	7.50	8.25	6.35	3.85	8.25	6.35	3.85

E4

E5

E6

SCOTT NO.	DESCRIPTION	UNUSED NH VF	F	AVG	UNUSED O.G. VF	F	AVG	USED VF	F	AVG
	1930									
E4	20¢ henna brown	62.50	44.00	35.00	35.75	27.50	19.25	18.50	12.65	7.70
	1933									
E5	20¢ henna brown	**50.00**	**38.50**	**30.00**	**32.50**	**24.75**	**16.50**	**21.50**	**16.50**	**10.45**

E7

E10

E11

SCOTT NO.	DESCRIPTION	PLATE BLOCK F / NH	PLATE BLOCK F / OG	UNUSED F / NH	UNUSED F / OG	USED F
	1935					
E6	20¢ dark carmine	72.50	46.50	10.00	6.10	4.50
	1938-39					
E7	10¢ dark green(1939)	24.75	19.25	5.00	3.85	2.75
E8	20¢ dark carmine	215.00	155.00	27.50	19.25	22.50
E9	10¢ on 20¢ dark carmine (#E8) (1939)	36.95	26.50	5.50	3.85	3.85
	1942					
E10	10¢ green	11.50	9.00	2.50	1.95	1.15

Canada #E11; MR1-MR7a

SCOTT NO.	DESCRIPTION	PLATE BLOCK F / NH	PLATE BLOCK F / OG	UNUSED F / NH	UNUSED F / OG	USED F
		1946				
E11	10¢ green	8.00	6.75	1.65	1.40	.75

SCOTT NO.	DESCRIPTION	UNUSED NH F	UNUSED NH AVG	UNUSED F	UNUSED AVG	USED F	USED AVG

WAR TAX STAMPS

MR1

2¢ + 1¢ Die I. Below large letter "T" there is a clear horizontal line of color. Die II. Right side of line is replaced by two short lines and five dots.

MR3

SCOTT NO.	DESCRIPTION	UNUSED NH F	UNUSED NH AVG	UNUSED F	UNUSED AVG	USED F	USED AVG
	1915						
MR1	1¢ green	7.70	4.50	4.40	2.50	.20	.15
MR2	2¢ carmine	7.70	4.50	4.40	2.50	.20	.15
	1916 Perf 12						
MR3	2¢ + 1¢ carmine (I)	12.00	6.00	6.05	3.60	.20	.15
MR3a	2¢ + 1¢ carmine(II)	100.00	55.00	60.50	36.30	1.95	1.15
MR4	2¢ + 1¢ brown (II)	6.75	3.65	3.50	2.15	.20	.15
MR4a	2¢ + 1¢ brown (I)	265.00	160.00	154.00	88.00	5.50	3.30
	Perf 12 x 8						
MR5	2¢ + 1¢ carmine	37.50	21.00	19.25	11.00	14.30	8.25
	Coil Stamps Perf. 8 Vertically						
MR6	2¢ + 1¢ carmine (I)	105.00	50.00	60.50	36.30	3.30	2.00
MR7	2¢ + 1¢ brown (II)	13.50	7.35	8.00	4.70	.55	.35
MR7a	2¢ + 1¢ brown (I)	115.00	55.00	71.50	38.50	4.15	2.50

Canada #F1-F3; J1-J20

REGISTRATION STAMPS

F1

1875-88 Perf. 12 (NH+50%)

SCOTT NO.	DESCRIPTION	UNUSED O.G. VF	F	AVG	UNUSED VF	F	AVG	USED VF	F	AVG
F1	2¢ orange	85.00	56.00	34.00	70.00	46.75	28.50	4.15	2.75	1.55
F1a	2¢ vermillion	100.00	66.00	39.50	82.50	55.00	33.00	9.50	6.35	3.40
F1b	2¢ rose carmine	195.00	130.00	79.50	165.00	110.00	66.00	110.00	72.50	40.00
F1d	2¢ orange, perf 12x11-1/2 .	365.00	245.00	158.00	305.00	203.50	132.50	88.00	58.85	32.50
F2	5¢ dark green	100.00	66.00	41.50	82.50	55.00	34.50	4.15	2.75	1.55
F2d	5¢ dark green, perf 12x11-1/2	645.00	430.00	265.00	535.00	355.00	220.00	185.00	125.00	67.50
F3	8¢ blue	550.00	365.00	245.00	455.00	305.00	205.00	410.00	275.00	148.50

POSTAGE DUE STAMPS

J1

J6

J11

J15

J21

SCOTT NO.	DESCRIPTION	UNUSED NH F	AVG	UNUSED F	AVG	USED F	AVG
	1906-28						
J1	1¢ violet	7.00	4.25	4.40	3.05	1.95	1.20
J2	2¢ violet	11.00	6.00	4.95	3.30	.45	.30
J3	4¢ violet (1928)	50.00	28.50	31.35	20.35	9.90	6.60
J4	5¢ violet	9.00	5.45	5.50	3.30	.85	.50
J5	10¢ violet (1928)	32.50	18.50	19.25	11.50	5.50	3.30
	1930-32						
J6	1¢ dark violet	8.50	5.10	4.95	3.30	2.20	1.40
J7	2¢ dark violet	5.00	2.95	3.05	2.20	.55	.35
J8	4¢ dark violet	10.00	5.80	6.05	4.15	1.95	1.20
J9	5¢ dark violet	10.00	5.80	6.05	4.15	2.75	1.65
J10	10¢ dark violet (1932)	60.00	36.30	35.75	24.75	5.00	3.30
	1933-34						
J11	1¢ dark violet (1934)	8.50	5.10	4.95	3.30	3.30	2.20
J12	2¢ dark violet	3.75	2.20	2.20	1.40	.65	.40
J13	4¢ dark violet	9.00	5.45	5.50	3.85	3.60	2.20
J14	10¢ dark violet	14.50	8.75	8.80	6.05	3.05	1.75

SCOTT NO.	DESCRIPTION	PLATE BLOCK F / NH	F / OG	UNUSED F / NH	F / OG	USED F
	1935-65					
J15-20	**1¢-10¢ complete, 7 varieties .....**	**40.00**	**36.50**	**5.50**	**4.95**	**3.35**
J15	1¢ dark violet	.80	.55	.20	.15	.15
J16	2¢ dark violet	.80	.55	.20	.15	.15
J16B	3¢ dark violet (1965)	13.75	9.60	1.95	1.35	.85
J17	4¢ dark violet	1.35	.95	.20	.15	.15
J18	5¢ dark violet (1948)	2.20	1.55	.35	.25	.20
J19	6¢ dark violet (1957)	13.75	9.60	1.95	1.35	1.00
J20	10¢ dark violet	1.55	1.10	.25	.20	.15

Canada #J21-J40; O1-O49; CO1-CO2; EO1-EO2

SCOTT NO.	DESCRIPTION	PLATE BLOCKS F/NH	UNUSED F/NH	USED F

POSTAGE DUES

1967 Perf. 12
Regular Size Design 20mm X 17mm

SCOTT NO.	DESCRIPTION	PLATE BLOCKS F/NH	UNUSED F/NH	USED F
J21-27	**1¢-10¢ cpl., 7 vars.**	**18.00**	**3.50**	**3.40**
J21	1¢ carmine rose	1.40	.25	.25
J22	2¢ carmine rose	1.40	.25	.25
J23	3¢ carmine rose	1.40	.25	.25
J24	4¢ carmine rose	2.20	.45	.45
J25	5¢ carmine rose	8.25	1.65	1.55
J26	6¢ carmine rose	2.15	.40	.40
J27	10¢ carmine rose	2.15	.40	.40

1969-78 Perf. 12 (White or Yellow Gum)
Modular Size Design 20mm x 15-3/4 mm

SCOTT NO.	DESCRIPTION	PLATE BLOCKS F/NH	UNUSED F/NH	USED F
J28/37	**(J28-31, J33-37) 9 vars.**	**6.50**	**1.95**	**1.60**
J28	1¢ carmine rose (1970)	.65	.20	.15
J29	2¢ carmine rose (1972)	.65	.20	.15
J30	3¢ carmine rose (1974)	.65	.20	.15
J31	4¢ carmine rose (1969)	.65	.20	.15
J32a	5¢ carmine rose (1977)	125.00	24.75	24.75
J33	6¢ carmine rose (1972)	.65	.20	.15
J34	8¢ carmine rose	.80	.20	.15
J35	10¢ carmine rose (1969)	1.00	.20	.20
J36	12¢ carmine rose (1969)	1.10	.25	.25
J37	16¢ carmine rose (1974)	1.65	.40	.35

1977-78
Perf. 12-1/2 X 12

SCOTT NO.	DESCRIPTION	PLATE BLOCKS F/NH	UNUSED F/NH	USED F
J28a-40	**1¢-50¢ cpl., 9 vars.**	**24.00**	**5.05**	**4.75**
J28a	1¢ carmine rose	.65	.20	.15
J31a	4¢ carmine rose	.65	.20	.15
J32	5¢ carmine rose	.65	.20	.15
J34a	8¢ carmine rose (1978)	1.95	.40	.25
J35a	10¢ carmine rose	.90	.20	.15
J36a	12¢ carmine rose	11.00	2.25	1.40
J38	20¢ carmine rose	1.95	.40	.35
J39	24¢ carmine rose	2.55	.50	.45
J40	50¢ carmine rose	4.95	1.00	1.95

OFFICIAL STAMPS

1949-50
#249, 250, 252, 254, 269-73
overprinted O.H.M.S.

SCOTT NO.	DESCRIPTION	PLATE BLOCKS F/NH	UNUSED F/NH	USED F
O1-10	**1¢-$1 complete, 9 vars.**		**290.00**	**165.00**
O1-8	**1¢-20¢, 7 varieties**		**47.50**	**18.50**
O1	1¢ green	10.45	2.15	1.65
O2	2¢ brown	110.00	15.40	11.00
O3	3¢ rose violet	10.75	2.20	1.10
O4	4¢ dark carmine	14.85	3.30	.85
O6	10¢ olive	18.70	4.05	.55
O7	14¢ black brown	29.45	6.45	1.85
O8	20¢ slate black	79.75	16.50	2.50
O9	50¢ dark blue green	962.50	203.50	121.00
O10	$1 red violet	247.50	52.25	35.75

1950 #294 overprinted O.H.M.S.

SCOTT NO.	DESCRIPTION	PLATE BLOCKS F/NH	UNUSED F/NH	USED F
O11	50¢ dull green	148.50	30.75	16.50

1950 #284-88 overprinted O.H.M.S.

SCOTT NO.	DESCRIPTION	PLATE BLOCKS F/NH	UNUSED F/NH	USED F
O12-15A	**1¢-5¢ cpl., 5 vars.**	**26.75**	**4.90**	**2..50**
O12	1¢ green	3.50	.30	.30
O13	2¢ sepia	3.80	.80	.75
O14	3¢ rose violet	4.95	1.00	.40
O15	4¢ dark carmine	4.95	1.00	.15
O15A	5¢ deep blue	11.00	2.05	1.10

1950 #284-88, 269-71, 294, 273 overprinted G

SCOTT NO.	DESCRIPTION	PLATE BLOCKS F/NH	UNUSED F/NH	USED F
O16-25	**1¢-$1 complete, 10 vars.**		**115.00**	**60.00**
O16-24	**1¢-50¢, 9 varieties**		**37.00**	**8.00**
O16	1¢ green	1.75	.25	.15
O17	2¢ sepia	5.50	1.00	.65
O18	3¢ rose violet	4.95	1.00	.15
O19	4¢ dark carmine	5.25	1.10	.15
O20	5¢ deep blue	11.00	1.20	.75
O21	10¢ olive	12.10	2.60	.40
O22	14¢ black brown	31.35	7.15	1.65
O23	20¢ slate black	74.25	14.85	.90
O24	50¢ dull green	49.50	9.90	3.60
O25	$1 red violet	368.50	82.50	55.00

1950-51 #301, 302 overprinted G

SCOTT NO.	DESCRIPTION	PLATE BLOCKS F/NH	UNUSED F/NH	USED F
O26	10¢ black brown	6.05	1.30	.20
O27	$1 bright ultramarine	395.00	74.25	55.00

1951-53 #305-06, 316, 320-21 overprinted G

SCOTT NO.	DESCRIPTION	PLATE BLOCKS F/NH	UNUSED F/NH	USED F
O28	2¢ olive green	1.85	.40	.15
O29	4¢ orange vermillion ('52)	3.60	.65	.15
O30	20¢ gray (1952)	9.35	2.10	.15
O31	7¢ blue (1952)	14.60	3.15	.80
O32	$1 gray (1953)	60.50	12.65	7.45

1953 #325-29, 334 overprinted G

SCOTT NO.	DESCRIPTION	PLATE BLOCKS F/NH	UNUSED F/NH	USED F
O33-37	**1¢-5¢ complete, 5vars.**	**8.40**	**1.90**	**.70**
O33	1¢ violet brown	1.35	.30	.15
O34	2¢ green	1.55	.35	.15
O35	3¢ carmine	1.55	.35	.15
O36	4¢ violet	2.20	.50	.15
O37	5¢ ultramarine	2.20	.50	.15
O38	50¢ lightgreen	24.20	5.25	1.00

1955 #351 overprinted G

SCOTT NO.	DESCRIPTION	PLATE BLOCKS F/NH	UNUSED F/NH	USED F
O39	10¢ violet brown	3.55	.80	.15

1955-56 #337, 338, 340, 341, 362 overprinted G

SCOTT NO.	DESCRIPTION	PLATE BLOCKS F/NH	UNUSED F/NH	USED F
O40-45	**1¢-20¢ cpl., 5vars.**	**17.00**	**3.55**	**.80**
O40	1¢ violet brown(1956)	1.30	.30	.25
O41	2¢ green (1956)	1.65	.35	.15
O43	4¢ violet(1956)	5.35	1.00	.15
O44	5¢ bright blue	2.05	.45	.15
O45	20¢ green(1956)	7.70	1.65	.15

1963 #401, 402, 404, 405 overprinted G

SCOTT NO.	DESCRIPTION	PLATE BLOCKS F/NH	UNUSED F/NH	USED F
O46-49	**1¢-5¢ cpl., 4 vars.**	**14.60**	**2.30**	**2.30**
O46	1¢ deep brown	2.75	.60	.60
O47	2¢ green	2.75	.60	.60
O48	4¢ carmine	7.15	.75	.75
O49	5¢ violet blue	2.75	.45	.45

1949-50 AIR POST OFFICIAL STAMPS

SCOTT NO.	DESCRIPTION	PLATE BLOCKS F/NH	UNUSED F/NH	USED F
CO1	7¢ deep blue, O.H.M.S.(C9)	38.50	8.25	2.65
CO2	7¢ deep blue, G (C9)	88.00	18.15	13.75

1950 SPECIAL DELIVERY OFFICIAL STAMPS

SCOTT NO.	DESCRIPTION	PLATE BLOCKS F/NH	UNUSED F/NH	USED F
EO1	10¢ green, O.H.M.S.(E11)	99.00	20.35	12.10
EO2	10¢ green, G (E11)	130.00	30.00	25.00

British Columbia & Vancouver Island #1-18

1

3

Queen Victoria

4

7

Seal

SCOTT NO.	DESCRIPTION	UNUSED O.G. VF	F	AVG	UNUSED VF	F	AVG	USED VF	F	AV
	1860 Imperforate									
1	2-1/2p dull rose	5000.00	3350.00	2650.00	4000.00	2675.00	2150.00	...	...	.
	1860 Perforated 14									
2	2-1/2p dull rose	410.00	315.00	150.00	275.00	210.00	100.00	180.00	137.50	66.0
	VANCOUVER ISLAND									
	1865 Imperforate									
3	5¢ rose	29500.00	23500.00	18500.00	24500.00	19500.00	15850.00	8250.00	6500.00	5750.0
4	10¢ blue	2300.00	1770.00	1175.00	1535.00	1180.00	785.00	1225.00	935.00	605.0
	Perforated 14									
5	5¢ rose	375.00	285.00	155.00	250.00	192.50	101.75	170.00	132.00	66.0
6	10¢ blue	375.00	285.00	155.00	250.00	192.50	101.75	170.00	132.00	66.0
	BRITISH COLUMBIA									
	1865									
7	3p blue	112.50	85.00	57.75	75.00	57.75	38.50	71.50	55.00	35.7
	New Values surcharged on 1865 design									
	1867-69 Perforated 14									
8	2¢ brown	112.50	85.00	57.75	75.00	57.75	38.50	64.50	49.50	33.0
9	5¢ bright red	155.00	120.00	78.50	105.00	79.75	52.25	105.00	79.75	52.2
10	10¢ lilac rose ...	1340.00	1030.00	675.00	895.00	687.50	450.00	...	...	..
11	25¢ orange	185.00	148.50	99.00	125.00	99.00	66.00	125.00	99.00	66.0
12	50¢ violet	850.00	650.00	435.00	565.00	434.50	291.50	...	...	..
13	$1 green	1125.00	865.00	575.00	750.00	577.50	385.00	...	...	..
	1869 Perforated 12-1/2									
14	5¢ bright red	750.00	575.00	475.00	535.00	412.50	341.00	900.00	412.50	341.5
15	10¢ lilac rose ...	700.00	540.00	360.00	500.00	385.00	258.50	575.00	302.50	200.0
16	25¢ orange	700.00	540.00	310.00	500.00	385.00	220.00	500.00	275.00	192.5
17	50¢ violet	750.00	575.00	370.00	535.00	412.50	264.00	550.00	330.00	220.0
18	$1 green	1195.00	925.00	600.00	855.00	660.00	434.50	1200.00	715.00	456.5

Newfoundland #1-23

1, 15A, 16

2, 11, 17

3, 11A

4, 12, 18

6, 13, 20

7, 21

8, 22

9, 15, 23

24, 38
Codfish

25, 26, 40
Seal

1857 Imperforate, Thick Paper

SCOTT NO.	DESCRIPTION	UNUSED O.G. VF	UNUSED O.G. F	UNUSED O.G. AVG	UNUSED VF	UNUSED F	UNUSED AVG	USED VF	USED F	USED AVG
1	1p brown violet	107.50	82.50	57.75	72.50	55.00	38.50	140.00	100.00	70.00
2	2p scarlet vermillion ..	13000.00	9000.00	6750.00	10000.00	1200.00	5400.00	5500.00	3950.00	2825.00
3	3p green	540.00	410.00	260.00	360.00	275.00	175.00	425.00	300.00	225.00
4	4p scarlet vermillion ..	6500.00	4250.00	2975.00	4750.00	2875.00	2150.00	3200.00	2000.00	1500.00
5	5p brown violet	395.00	305.00	195.00	265.00	205.00	130.00	355.00	275.00	180.00
6	6p scarlet vermillion ..	12800.00	9175.00	6500.00	9450.00	7300.00	5175.00	3450.00	2475.00	1750.00
7	6-1/2p scarlet vermillion	2700.00	19350.00	1395.00	1925.00	1375.00	990.00	2475.00	1775.00	1240.00
8	8p scarlet vermillion ..	415.00	320.00	295.00	275.00	215.00	195.00	395.00	300.00	205.00
9	1sh scarlet vermillion	15100.00	10750.00	7550.00	11925.00	8500.00	6150.00	5400.00	3800.00	2700.00

1860 Thin Paper

SCOTT NO.	DESCRIPTION	UNUSED O.G. VF	UNUSED O.G. F	UNUSED O.G. AVG	UNUSED VF	UNUSED F	UNUSED AVG	USED VF	USED F	USED AVG
11	2p orange	475.00	370.00	245.00	325.00	247.50	165.00	285.00	220.00	148.50
11A	3p green	80.00	62.00	39.50	53.50	41.25	26.40	100.00	83.00	55.00
12	4p orange	3600.00	2775.00	1875.00	2400.00	1800.00	1250.00	850.00	660.00	440.00
12A	5p violet brown	127.50	100.00	49.50	85.00	66.00	33.00	180.00	138.00	88.00
13	6p orange	3900.00	3000.00	2250.00	2600.00	2000.00	1500.00	715.00	550.00	385.00

1861-62 Thin Paper

SCOTT NO.	DESCRIPTION	UNUSED O.G. VF	UNUSED O.G. F	UNUSED O.G. AVG	UNUSED VF	UNUSED F	UNUSED AVG	USED VF	USED F	USED AVG
15	1sh orange	27000.00	19250.00	12500.00	21500.00	15450.00	10900.00	8050.00	5750.00	4600.00
15A	1p violet brown	195.00	150.00	100.00	130.00	100.00	66.00	175.00	138.00	105.00
16	1p reddish brown ..	4725.00	3375.00	2375.00	3775.00	2700.00	1950.00	...	...	...
17	2p rose	195.00	150.00	100.00	130.00	100.00	66.00	175.00	138.00	83.00
18	4p rose	58.75	45.00	25.50	39.25	30.25	17.00	65.00	50.00	24.00
19	5p reddish brown ..	64.50	44.50	33.00	43.00	33.00	22.00	71.50	55.00	34.65
20	6p rose	32.25	24.75	13.20	21.50	16.50	8.80	69.00	53.00	35.75
21	6-1/2p rose	96.75	74.25	39.60	64.50	49.50	26.40	145.00	110.00	63.25
22	8p rose	82.50	63.50	33.00	55.00	42.35	22.00	215.00	165.00	110.00
23	1sh rose	48.50	37.00	19.75	32.00	24.75	13.20	145.00	110.00	71.50

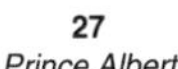

27
Prince Albert

28, 29
Queen Victoria

30
Fishing Ship

31
Queen Victoria

32, 32A, 37
Prince of Wales

35, 36
Queen Victoria

Newfoundland #24-55

SCOTT NO.	DESCRIPTION	UNUSED O.G. VF	UNUSED O.G. F	UNUSED O.G. AVG	UNUSED VF	UNUSED F	UNUSED AVG	USED VF	USED F	USED AVG
	1865-94 Perforate 12 Yellow Paper									
24	2¢ green	74.50	57.25	39.25	57.25	44.00	30.25	32.00	24.75	13.75
24a	2¢ green (white paper)	56.00	43.00	26.50	43.00	33.00	20.35	22.75	17.60	9.90
25	5¢ brown	560.00	430.00	300.00	430.00	330.00	230.00	285.00	220.00	148.00
26	5¢ black (1868)	280.00	215.00	143.00	215.00	165.00	110.00	120.00	93.00	60.50
27	10¢ black	280.00	215.00	143.00	215.00	165.00	110.00	71.50	55.00	38.50
27a	10¢ black (white paper)	130.00	100.00	64.50	100.00	77.00	49.50	43.00	33.00	18.15
28	12¢ pale red brown	345.00	265.00	175.00	265.00	204.00	137.50	165.00	126.50	87.50
28a	12¢ pale red brown (white paper)	45.50	35.00	18.50	35.00	26.95	14.30	35.00	26.95	14.30
29	12¢ brown (1894) ..	45.50	35.00	18.50	35.00	26.95	14.30	32.00	24.75	13.20
30	13¢ orange	110.00	85.00	57.25	85.75	66.00	44.00	57.25	44.00	30.25
31	24¢ blue	37.50	28.50	20.00	28.75	22.00	15.40	26.50	20.35	13.75
	1868-94									
32	1¢ violet	37.00	28.50	18.50	28.50	22.00	14.30	28.50	22.00	11.00
32A	1¢ brown lilac, re-engraved (1871)	56.00	43.00	23.00	43.00	33.00	17.60	43.00	33.00	17.60
33	3¢ vermillion (1870)	345.00	265.00	180.00	265.00	203.50	137.50	165.00	26.50	71.50
34	3¢ blue (1873)	280.00	215.00	143.00	215.00	165.00	110.00	23.00	17.60	9.90
35	6¢ dull rose (1870)	16.00	12.15	7.15	12.15	9.35	5.50	12.25	9.35	5.50
36	6¢ carmine lake (1894)	18.50	14.25	10.00	14.25	11.00	7.70	14.25	11.00	7.70
	1876-79 Rouletted									
37	1¢ brown lilac (1877)	52.00	40.00	40.00	40.00	30.25	30.75	21.50	16.50	11.00
38	2¢ green (1879)	63.00	48.50	48.50	48.50	37.40	37.40	35.75	27.50	17.60
39	3¢ blue (1877)	170.00	130.00	100.00	130.00	99.00	99.00	10.00	770	5.25
40	5¢ blue	110.00	85.75	85.75	85.75	66.00	66.00	10.00	7.70	5.25

41-45
Prince of Wales

46-48
Codfish

53-55
Seal

56-58
Newfoundland Dog

59
Schooner

SCOTT NO.	DESCRIPTION	UNUSED O.G. VF	UNUSED O.G. F	UNUSED O.G. AVG	UNUSED VF	UNUSED F	UNUSED AVG	USED VF	USED F	USED AVG
	1880-96 Perforate 12									
41	1¢ violet brown	15.50	10.50	5.65	13.00	8.80	4.70	9.25	7.15	3.60
42	1¢ gray brown	15.50	10.50	5.65	13.00	8.80	4.70	9.25	7.15	3.60
43	1¢ brown (Reissue) (1896)	35.00	23.75	13.25	29.50	19.80	11.00	23.50	18.15	10.20
44	1¢ deep green (1887)	9.90	6.60	3.95	8.25	5.50	3.30	3.60	2.75	1.65
45	1¢ green (Reissue) (1897)	10.75	7.25	4.50	9.00	6.05	3.85	6.50	4.95	2.75
46	2¢ yellow green	19.75	13.25	7.95	16.50	11.00	6.60	13.50	10.45	5.50
47	2¢ green (Reissue) (1896)	44.50	29.50	15.85	37.00	24.75	13.20	19.25	14.85	8.25
48	2¢ red orange (1887)	16.75	11.25	5.95	14.00	9.35	4.95	7.50	5.80	3.30
49	3¢ blue	24.00	16.50	9.95	20.00	13.75	8.25	4.25	3.30	1.85
51	3¢ umber brown (1887)	19.75	13.25	8.50	16.50	11.00	7.15	4.25	3.30	1.85
52	3¢ violet brown (Reissue) (1896) ...	52.50	35.00	18.50	43.75	29.15	15.40	38.00	29.15	15.40
53	5¢ pale blue	290.00	198.00	120.00	245.00	165.00	99.00	11.25	8.80	4.95
54	5¢ dark blue (1887)	120.00	79.00	46.25	100.00	66.00	38.50	8.50	6.60	3.60
55	5¢ bright blue (1894)	24.50	76.50	9.95	20.50	13.75	8.25	6.50	4.95	2.50

60
Queen Victoria

ONE CENT
ONE CENT
ONE CENT
1897
60a surcharged in black

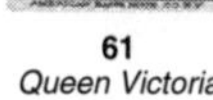

61
Queen Victoria

62
John Cabot

63
Cape Bonavista

Newfoundland #56-77

COTT NO.	DESCRIPTION	UNUSED O.G. VF	F	AVG	UNUSED VF	F	AVG	USED VF	F	AVG
	1887-96									
5	1/2¢ rose red	7.25	5.65	3.30	6.10	4.70	2.75	5.75	4.40	2.50
7	1/2¢ orange red (1896)	38.50	29.75	15.85	32.00	24.75	13.20	34.00	26.40	15.40
3	1/2¢ black (1894) ..	6.00	4.60	2.45	5.00	3.85	2.05	5.00	3.85	2.05
9	10¢ black	55.75	43.00	26.50	46.50	35.75	22.00	43.00	33.00	17.60
	1890									
)	3¢ slate	9.40	7.25	3.95	7.85	6.05	3.30	.85	.65	.40

64
Caribou Hunting

65
Mining

66
Logging

67
Fishing

68
Cabot's Ship

69
Ptarmigan

70
Seals

71
Salmon Fishing

72
Seal of Colony

73
Coast Scene

74
King Henry VII

1897 CABOT ISSUE

COTT NO.	DESCRIPTION	UNUSED O.G. VF	F	AVG	UNUSED VF	F	AVG	USED VF	F	AVG
1-74	**1¢-60¢ complete, 14 varieties ....**	**360.00**	**275.00**	**170.00**	**206.00**	**149.00**	**97.50**	**153.50**	**118.00**	**64.75**
1	1¢ deep green	2.70	2.10	1.40	1.55	1.20	.80	1.55	1.20	.65
2	2¢ carmine lake ..	3.40	2.60	1.75	1.95	1.50	1.00	1.55	1.20	.65
3	3¢ ultramarine	5.00	3.85	2.50	2.85	2.20	1.45	1.45	1.10	.60
4	4¢ olive green	8.15	6.30	4.00	4.65	3.60	2.30	3.55	2.75	1.65
5	5¢ violet	8.15	6.30	4.00	4.65	3.60	2.30	3.55	2.75	1.65
6	6¢ red brown	7.45	5.75	3.85	4.25	3.30	2.20	4.30	3.30	2.00
7	8¢ red orange	16.20	12.50	7.70	9.25	7.15	4.40	6.45	4.95	2.75
3	10¢ black brown .	22.50	17.25	10.50	12.85	9.90	6.05	6.10	4.70	2.60
9	12¢ dark blue	23.50	18.25	11.50	13.50	10.45	6.60	7.50	5.80	3.15
0	15¢ scarlet	23.50	18.25	11.50	13.50	10.45	6.60	8.25	6.35	3.50
1	24¢ gray violet	23.50	18.25	11.50	13.50	10.45	6.60	8.50	6.60	3.60
2	30¢ slate	68.25	53.00	31.75	39.00	30.25	18.15	35.75	27.50	15.40
3	35¢ red	150.00	115.00	70.00	85.75	66.00	40.15	64.75	49.50	26.40
4	60¢ black	16.85	12.50	7.70	9.65	7.15	4.40	8.50	6.60	3.60
	1897									
5	1¢ on 3¢ gray lilac, Type a	21.35	16.50	10.75	14.25	11.00	7.15	12.85	9.90	5.25
6	1¢ on 3¢ gray lilac, Type b	128.50	100.00	66.00	85.75	66.00	44.00	100.00	77.00	38.50
7	1¢ on 3¢ gray lilac, Type c	645.00	495.00	345.00	429.00	330.00	231.00	479.00	468.50	203.50

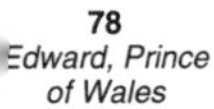
78
Edward, Prince of Wales

79, 80
Queen Victoria

81, 82
King Edward VII

83
Queen Alexandria

84
Queen Mary

85
King George V

Newfoundland #78-97

SCOTT NO.	DESCRIPTION	UNUSED O.G. VF	F	AVG	UNUSED VF	F	AVG	USED VF	F	AVG
	1897-1901 ROYAL FAMILY ISSUE									
78-85	**1/2¢-5¢ complete, 8 varieties ....**	**105.00**	**80.50**	**52.50**	**58.00**	**44.75**	**29.00**	**18.40**	**14.00**	**8.10**
78	1/2¢ olive green ..	3.85	3.00	2.00	2.15	1.65	1.10	2.65	2.05	1.10
79	1¢ carmine rose .	5.40	4.10	2.80	3.00	2.30	1.55	3.55	2.75	1.55
80	1¢ yellow green (1898)	3.25	2.50	1.70	1.80	1.40	.95	.25	.20	.15
81	2¢ orange	6.40	4.95	3.15	3.55	2.75	1.75	4.30	3.30	2.00
82	2¢ vermillion (1898)	11.60	8.90	5.95	6.45	4.95	3.30	.75	.55	.35
83	3¢ orange (1898)	20.60	15.85	10.00	11.45	8.80	5.60	.75	.55	.35
84	4¢ violet (1901) ..	27.00	20.75	13.85	15.00	11.55	7.70	4.30	3.30	1.85
85	5¢ blue (1899)	32.00	24.75	15.85	17.85	13.75	8.60	2.85	2.20	1.20

86
Map of Newfoundland

87
King James I

88
Arms of the London & Bristol Company

89
John Guy

90
Guy's Ship the "Endeavour"

91
View of the Town of Cupids

92, 92A, 98
Lord Bacon

93, 99
View of Mosquito Bay

94, 100
Logging Camp

95, 101
Paper Mills

96, 102
King Edward VII

SCOTT NO.	DESCRIPTION	UNUSED O.G. VF	F	AVG	UNUSED VF	F	AVG	USED VF	F	AVG
	1908									
86	2¢ rose carmine .	25.75	19.75	13.85	14.30	11.00	7.70	1.45	1.10	.70
	1910 JOHN GUY ISSUE—Lithographed Perf.12									
87/97	**(87-92, 92A, 93-97) 12 varieties ....**	**475.00**	**350.00**	**195.00**	**285.00**	**219.00**	**145.00**	**320.00**	**245.00**	**129.00**
87	1¢ deep green, perf. 12x11	2.30	1.75	1.25	1.45	1.10	.80	1.10	.85	.50
87a	1¢ deep green	5.25	4.00	2.65	6.80	2.50	1.65	2.15	1.65	1.00
87b	1¢ deep green, perf. 12x14	4.00	3.10	1.90	2.55	1.95	1.20	1.95	1.50	.95
88	2¢ carmine	8.00	6.15	4.25	5.00	3.85	2.65	.85	.65	.40
88a	2¢ carmine, perf. 12x14	5.75	4.40	2.95	3.55	2.75	1.85	.85	.65	.40
88c	2¢ carmine, perf. 12x11-1/2 ...	210.00	160.00	105.00	129.00	99.00	66.00	85.00	66.00	35.75
89	3¢ brown olive	13.65	10.50	7.00	8.55	6.60	4.40	10.75	8.25	4.40
90	4¢ dull violet	22.75	17.60	11.45	14.25	11.00	7.15	9.30	7.15	3.60
91	5¢ ultramarine, perf. 14x12	9.00	7.00	4.75	5.75	4.40	2.95	3.50	2.75	1.50
91a	5¢ ultramarine	20.50	15.85	11.45	12.85	9.90	7.15	4.30	3.30	1.85
92	6¢ claret (I)	91.00	70.00	46.50	57.25	44.00	29.15	57.25	44.00	23.60
92A	6¢ claret (II)	34.50	26.50	17.60	21.45	16.50	11.00	25.75	19.80	11.00
93	8¢ pale brown	57.25	44.00	29.00	35.75	27.50	18.15	45.00	34.65	17.60
94	9¢ olive green	57.25	44.00	29.00	35.75	27.50	18.15	45.00	34.65	17.60
95	10¢ violet black ..	57.25	44.00	29.00	35.75	27.50	18.15	40.00	30.25	15.95
96	12¢ lilac brown ...	57.25	44.00	29.00	35.75	27.50	18.15	45.00	34.65	17.60
97	15¢ gray black	68.50	52.75	35.00	43.00	33.00	22.00	55.75	42.90	22.00

#92 Type I. "Z" of "COLONIZATION" is reversed. #92A Type II. "Z" is normal

Newfoundland #98-114

97, 103 King George V — 104 Queen Mary — 105 King George — 106 Prince of Wales — 107 Prince Albert — 108 Princess Mary — 109 Prince Henry

1911 Engraved. Perf. 14

COTT NO.	DESCRIPTION	UNUSED O.G. VF	UNUSED O.G. F	UNUSED O.G. AVG	UNUSED VF	UNUSED F	UNUSED AVG	USED VF	USED F	USED AVG
8-103	**6¢-15¢ complete, 6 varieties ....**	450.00	345.00	310.00	285.00	216.00	132.00	280.00	216.00	117.50
8	6¢ brown violet .	27.95	21.50	14.95	21.50	13.45	9.35	17.15	13.20	8.80
9	8¢ bistre brown .	68.50	52.75	34.25	43.00	33.00	21.45	43.00	33.00	21.45
00	9¢ olive green ...	57.25	44.00	28.00	35.75	27.50	17.60	35.25	27.50	17.60
01	10¢ violet black .	115.00	88.00	52.00	71.50	55.00	32.50	71.50	55.00	17.60
02	12¢ red brown ..	103.00	79.25	46.50	64.50	49.50	29.15	64.50	49.50	29.15
03	15¢ slate brown	103.00	79.25	46.50	64.50	49.50	29.15	64.50	49.50	29.15

110 Prince George — 111 Prince John — 112 Queen Alexandria — 113 Duke of Connaught — 114 Seal of Colony — 115

1911 ROYAL FAMILY ISSUE

COTT NO.	DESCRIPTION	UNUSED O.G. VF	UNUSED O.G. F	UNUSED O.G. AVG	UNUSED VF	UNUSED F	UNUSED AVG	USED VF	USED F	USED AVG
04-14	**1¢-15¢ complete, 11 varieties ......**	347.00	268.00	175.00	178.00	137.00	91.25	170.00	130.00	85.00
04	1¢ yellow green	2.95	2.25	1.60	1.45	1.10	.80	.25	.20	.15
05	2¢ carmine	3.60	2.75	1.75	1.80	1.40	.90	.25	.20	.15
06	3¢ red brown	33.75	26.00	16.50	17.15	13.20	8.80	17.15	13.20	8.80
07	4¢ violet	25.00	19.50	13.50	12.85	9.90	7.15	11.45	8.80	6.05
08	5¢ ultramarine ..	14.25	11.00	7.50	7.15	5.50	3.60	1.80	1.40	.75
09	6¢ black	25.00	19.50	13.50	12.85	9.90	7.15	12.85	9.90	7.15
10	8¢ blue (paper colored) .	94.25	72.50	44.00	47.95	36.85	23.65	47.95	36.85	23.65
10a	8¢ peacock blue (white paper)	99.50	76.50	48.00	50.00	38.50	24.75	50.00	38.50	24.75
11	9¢ blue violet	35.00	27.00	18.00	17.85	13.75	8.80	17.85	13.75	8.80
12	10¢ dark green .	45.00	35.00	24.00	23.50	18.15	12.10	23.50	18.15	12.10
13	12¢ plum	45.00	35.00	24.00	23.50	18.15	12.10	23.50	18.15	12.10
14	50¢ magenta	41.50	32.00	21.50	21.45	16.50	11.00	21.45	16.50	11.00

116

72 surcharged

THREE CENTS

70 & 73 surcharged

131 — 132 — 133 — 134

135 — 136 — 137 — 138 — 139 — 140

Newfoundland #115-144

SCOTT NO.	DESCRIPTION	UNUSED O.G. VF	UNUSED O.G. F	UNUSED O.G. AVG	UNUSED VF	UNUSED F	UNUSED AVG	USED VF	USED F	USED AVG
	1919 TRAIL OF THE CARIBOU ISSUE									
115-26	**1¢ -36¢ complete, 12 varieties ......**	**240.00**	**186.00**	**120.00**	**138.00**	**106.50**	**69.50**	**123.50**	**94.50**	**61.35**
115	1¢ green	2.30	1. 75	1.15	1.30	1.00	.65	.40	.30	.20
116	2¢ scarlet	2.55	1.95	1.45	1.45	1.10	.80	.55	.40	.25
117	3¢ red brown	3.20	2.45	1.65	1.80	1.40	.90	.35	.25	.15
118	4¢ violet	5.00	3.85	2.50	2.85	2.20	1.45	1.45	1.10	.65
119	5¢ ultramarine ..	5.75	4.40	2.70	3.25	2.50	1.55	1.45	1.10	.65
120	6¢ gray	26.00	20.25	13.50	15.00	11.55	7.70	15.00	11.55	7.70
121	8¢ magenta	20.00	15.50	10.50	11.45	8.80	6.05	10.75	8.25	5.50
122	10¢ dark green .	15.00	11.55	6.75	8.50	6.60	3.85	3.50	2.75	1.65
123	12¢ orange	50.00	38.50	25.00	28.50	22.00	14.30	25.00	19.25	12.65
124	15¢ dark blue	41.25	31.75	20.25	23.50	18.15	11.55	23.50	18.15	11.00
125	24¢ bistre	46.00	35.50	23.00	26.50	20.35	13.20	26.50	20.35	13.20
126	36¢ olive green .	37.35	28.75	19.25	21.45	16.50	11.00	21.50	16.50	11.00

SCOTT NO.	DESCRIPTION	UNUSED O.G. F	UNUSED O.G. AVG	UNUSED F	UNUSED AVG	USED F	USED AVG
	1920						
127	2¢ on 30¢ slate	6.90	4.25	4.95	3.05	4.95	3.05
	Bars 10-1/2mm apart						
128	3¢ on 15¢ scarlet	247.50	150.00	165.00	104.50	181.50	104.50
	Bars 13-1/2mm apart						
129	3¢ on 15¢ scarlet	11.55	6.95	8.25	6.05	8.25	6.05
130	3¢ on 35¢ red	11.55	6.95	8.25	6.05	8.25	6.05

141

142

143

144

145, 163, 172
Map of Newfoundland

146, 164, 173
S.S. Caribou

SCOTT NO.	DESCRIPTION	UNUSED O.G. F	UNUSED O.G. AVG	UNUSED F	UNUSED AVG	USED F	USED AVG
	1923-24 PICTORIAL ISSUE						
131-44	**1¢-24¢ complete, 14 varieties ....**	**121.00**	**73.00**	**85.00**	**50.95**	**77.00**	**47.00**
131	1¢ gray green	2.65	1.60	1.95	1.05	.25	.15
132	2¢ carmine	1.75	1.05	1.30	.65	.20	.15
133	3¢ brown	2.65	1.60	1.95	1.05	.20	.15
134	4¢ brown violet	2.20	1.35	1.65	.90	1.55	.95
135	5¢ ultramarine	3.85	2.30	2.75	1.50	1.75	1.10
136	6¢ gray black	4.80	2.85	3.30	1.75	3.30	1.75
137	8¢ dull violet	3.85	2.30	2.75	1.50	2.60	1.40
138	9¢ slate green	24.75	14.85	16.50	10.45	16.50	10.45
139	10¢ dark violet	4.25	2.55	3.05	1.65	1.75	1.10
140	11¢ olive green	7.70	4.60	5.50	3.05	5.50	3.05
141	12¢ lake	8.00	4.80	5.80	3.15	5.80	3.15
142	15¢ deep blue	9.10	5.45	6.60	3.85	6.35	3.60
143	20¢ red brown (1924)	8.80	5.25	6.35	3.30	4.95	2.75
144	24¢ black brown (1924)	44.00	26.50	30.25	19.80	30.25	19.80

147, 165, 174
Queen Mary and King George

148, 166, 175
Prince of Wales

149, 167, 176
Express Train

150, 168, 177
Newfoundland Hotel, St. John's

151, 178
Town of Heart's Content

Newfoundland #145-182

152
Cabot Tower, St. John's

153, 169, 179
War Memorial, St. John's

154
Post Office, St. John's

156, 170, 180
First Airplane to Cross Atlantic Non-Stop

157, 171, 181
House of Parliament, St. John's

159, 182
Grand Falls, Labrador

1928 Tourist Publicity Issue
Unwatermarked. Thin paper, dull colors

COTT NO.	DESCRIPTION	UNUSED O.G. F	UNUSED O.G. AVG	UNUSED F	UNUSED AVG	USED F	USED AVG
5-59	**1¢-30¢ complete, 15 varieties**	**97.85**	**58.75**	**67.25**	**38.25**	**51.00**	**30.25**
5	1¢ deep green	1.65	1.00	1.05	.55	.55	.35
46	2¢ deep carmine	2.15	1.30	1.50	.85	.55	.35
7	3¢ brown	2.75	1.65	1.85	1.00	.35	.20
8	4¢ lilac rose	3.30	2.00	2.10	1.40	1.65	1.00
9	5¢ slate green	6.35	3.80	4.40	2.50	3.05	1.85
0	6¢ ultramarine	4.70	2.80	3.30	1.95	2.75	1.50
1	8¢ light red brown	6.35	3.80	4.40	2.50	3.60	1.95
2	9¢ myrtle green	7.45	4.50	5.50	2.75	4.40	2.50
3	10¢ dark violet	7.45	4.50	5.50	2.75	3.85	2.20
4	12¢ brown carmine	5.50	3.30	3.85	2.20	3.05	1.65
5	14¢ red brown	7.45	4.50	5.50	2.75	3.05	2.20
6	15¢ dark blue	8.00	4.80	6.05	3.05	4.95	2.65
7	20¢ gray black	7.45	4.50	5.50	3.05	3.30	1.85
8	28¢ gray green	24.75	14.85	14.85	9.90	13.75	8.80
9	30¢ olive brown	7.70	4.50	5.50	3.05	4.95	2.65

1929

COTT NO.	DESCRIPTION	UNUSED O.G. F	UNUSED O.G. AVG	UNUSED F	UNUSED AVG	USED F	USED AVG
0	3¢ on 6¢ gray black	3.50	2.10	2.95	1.75	2.95	1.75

1929-31 Tourist Publicity Issue
Types of 1928 re-engraved
Unwatermarked. Thicker paper, brighter colors

COTT NO.	DESCRIPTION	UNUSED O.G. F	UNUSED O.G. AVG	UNUSED F	UNUSED AVG	USED F	USED AVG
3-71	**1¢-20¢ complete, 9 varieties**	**123.00**	**73.95**	**78.00**	**44.00**	**50.25**	**27.00**
3	1¢ green	1.75	1.05	1.30	.65	.45	.30
4	2¢ deep carmine	1.75	1.05	1.30	.65	.20	.15
5	3¢ deep red brown	2.00	1.20	1.45	.80	.20	.15
6	4¢ magenta	2.95	1.75	2.10	1.10	1.00	.60
7	5¢ slate green	4.40	2.65	3.15	1.75	1.00	.60
8	6¢ ultramarine	11.55	6.95	8.25	4.40	6.60	3.60
9	10¢ dark violet	6.05	3.65	4.40	2.50	1.65	1.00
0	15¢ deep blue (1930)	41.25	24.95	24.75	14.30	23.10	12.10
1	20¢ gray black (1931)	57.75	34.75	35.75	20.35	18.70	9.90

1931 Tourist Publicity Issue
Types of 1928 re-engraved, watermarked, coat of arms
Thicker paper, brighter colors

COTT NO.	DESCRIPTION	UNUSED O.G. F	UNUSED O.G. AVG	UNUSED F	UNUSED AVG	USED F	USED AVG
2-82	**1¢-30¢ complete, 11 varieties**	**195.00**	**114.00**	**130.00**	**71.50**	**93.50**	**50.50**
2	1¢ green	2.50	1.40	1.65	.95	.90	.55
3	2¢ red	3.85	2.30	2.50	1.40	1.20	.75
4	3¢ red brown	3.85	2.30	2.50	1.40	.90	.55
5	4¢ rose	4.95	3.00	3.35	1.85	1.35	.85
6	5¢ greenish gray	9.90	5.95	7.15	3.85	6.05	3.30
7	6¢ ultramarine	22.00	13.25	15.40	8.80	13.75	7.70
8	8¢ light red brown	22.00	13.25	15.40	8.80	13.75	7.70
9	10¢ dark violet	11.55	6.95	8.25	4.40	6.05	3.30
30	15¢ deep blue	41.25	24.75	27.50	14.85	24.75	13.20
31	20¢ gray black	44.00	26.00	29.15	15.40	8.80	4.40
32	30¢ olive brown	38.50	21.00	24.75	13.20	20.90	11.00

Newfoundland #183-211

SCOTT NO.	DESCRIPTION	UNUSED O.G. F	UNUSED O.G. AVG	UNUSED F	UNUSED AVG	USED F	USED AV

THREE CENTS

160
136 surcharged in red

183, 253
Codfish

185, 186
King George

187
Queen Mary

188, 189
Prince of Wales

190, 191, 25
Caribou

192
Princess Elizabeth

193, 260
Salmon

194, 261
Newfoundland Dog

195, 262
Northern Seal

196, 263
Trans-Atlantic Beacon

1932-37 RESOURCES ISSUE Perf. 13-1/2

SCOTT NO.	DESCRIPTION	UNUSED O.G. F	UNUSED O.G. AVG	UNUSED F	UNUSED AVG	USED F	USED AV
183-99	**1¢-48¢ complete, 17 varieties**	**93.50**	**56.00**	**57.00**	**36.50**	**37.95**	**25.7**
183	1¢ green	1.50	.95	1.05	.65	.35	.2
184	1¢ gray black	.35	.20	.25	.20	.20	.1
185	2¢ rose	1.50	.90	1.05	.65	.20	.1
186	2¢ green	1.50	.90	1.00	.65	.20	.1
187	3¢ orange brown	1.20	.75	.85	.55	.20	.1
188	4¢ deep violet	4.95	2.90	3.60	2.30	1.40	.9
189	4¢ rose lake	.55	.35	.40	.30	.20	.1
190	5¢ violet brown (I)	6.60	3.95	4.40	2.75	.90	.5
191	5¢ deep violet (II)	1.00	.60	.65	.50	.20	.1
191a	5¢ deep violet (I)	10.45	6.25	7.00	5.25	.60	.4
192	6¢ dull blue	11.00	6.60	7.15	5.35	7.15	5.3
193	10¢ olive black	1.40	.85	.95	.60	.60	.4
194	14¢ black	2.75	1.65	1.95	1.30	1.65	1.1
195	15¢ magenta	2.75	1.65	1.95	1.30	1.65	1.1
196	20¢ gray green	2.75	1.65	2.95	1.30	.85	.5
197	25¢ gray	3.05	1.85	2.10	1.40	1.75	1.1
198	30¢ ultramarine	30.25	18.15	20.35	12.10	18.15	12.1
199	48¢ red brown (1937)	14.85	8.95	10.45	6.60	4.25	2.7

197, 265
Sealing Fleet

198
Fishing Fleet

208
The Duchess of York

209, 259
Corner Brook Paper Mills

210, 264
Loading Iron Ore, B Island

1932 Perf. 13-1/2

SCOTT NO.	DESCRIPTION	UNUSED O.G. F	UNUSED O.G. AVG	UNUSED F	UNUSED AVG	USED F	USED AV
208-10	**7¢-24¢ complete, 3 varieties**	**6.60**	**4.00**	**4.70**	**3.15**	**4.50**	**3.1**
208	7¢ red brown	1.55	.95	1.10	.75	1.10	.7
209	8¢ orange red	1.55	.95	1.10	.75	1.00	.6
210	24¢ light blue	3.85	2.30	2.75	1.85	2.65	1.8

1933 LAND & SEA OVERPRINT

SCOTT NO.	DESCRIPTION	UNUSED O.G. F	UNUSED O.G. AVG	UNUSED F	UNUSED AVG	USED F	USED AV
211	15¢ brown	10.00	6.00	7.15	4.40	5.75	3.5

Newfoundland #212-232

COTT NO.	DESCRIPTION	UNUSED O.G. F	AVG	UNUSED F	AVG	USED F	AVG

L. & S. Post.

211
o. C9 with Overprint and Bars

212
Sir Humphrey Gilbert

213
Compton Castle, Devon

214
The Gilbert Arms

215
Eton College

216
Token to Gilbert from Queen Elizabeth

217
ilbert Commissioned by Queen Elizabeth

218
Gilbert's Fleet Leaving Plymouth

219
The Fleet Arriving at St. John's

220
Annexation of Newfoundland

221
Coat of Arms of England

1933 SIR HUMPHREY GILBERT ISSUE

COTT NO.	DESCRIPTION	UNUSED O.G. F	AVG	UNUSED F	AVG	USED F	AVG
12-25	**1¢-32¢ complete, 14 varieties**	**144.00**	**86.75**	**98.75**	**65.95**	**94.75**	**67.50**
12	1¢ gray black	.95	.60	.75	.50	.55	.40
13	2¢ green	1.20	.75	.95	.60	.55	.40
14	3¢ yellow brown	1.65	1.00	1.30	.85	.95	.65
15	4¢ carmine	1.65	1.00	1.30	.85	.40	.30
16	5¢ dull violet	2.10	1.30	1.65	1.10	.95	.65
17	7¢ blue	15.95	9.50	10.45	6.60	12.65	8.25
18	8¢ orange red	8.25	5.00	5.80	3.85	5.80	4.15
19	9¢ ultramarine	9.35	5.60	6.35	4.15	6.30	4.40
20	10¢ red brown	8.25	5.00	5.80	3.85	4.95	3.60
21	14¢ black	18.15	10.95	12.65	8.25	11.55	8.25
22	15¢ claret	18.15	10.95	12.40	8.00	11.00	8.25
23	20¢ deep green	11.00	6.60	8.25	5.50	7.70	5.25
24	24¢ violet brown	27.50	16.50	18.15	12.65	18.15	13.20
25	32¢ gray	27.50	16.50	18.15	12.65	18.15	13.20

222
Gilbert on the "Squirrel"

223
1624 Map of Newfoundland

224
Queen Elizabeth I

225
Gilbert Statue at Truro

226
Windsor Castle and King George

1935 SILVER JUBILEE

COTT NO.	DESCRIPTION	UNUSED F/NH	UNUSED F	USED F
26-29	**4¢-24¢ complete, 4 varieties**	**11.00**	**8.40**	**8.00**
26	4¢ bright rose	1.10	.85	.60
27	5¢ violet	1.10	.85	.75
28	7¢ dark blue	2.75	2.20	2.20
29	24¢ olive green	6.60	4.95	4.95

1937 CORONATION ISSUE

SCOTT NO.	DESCRIPTION	UNUSED F/NH	UNUSED F	USED F
230-32	**2¢-5¢ complete, 3 varieties**	**1.90**	**1.55**	**1.40**
230	2¢ deep green	.55	.45	.40
231	4¢ carmine rose	.55	.45	.35
232	5¢ dark violet	.90	.75	.75

Newfoundland #233-243

230
King George VI and Queen Elizabeth

233

234
Die I: Fine Impression
Die II: Coarse Impression

235

236

237

238

239

240

241

242

243

245, 254
King George VI

1937 LONG CORONATION ISSUE

SCOTT NO.	DESCRIPTION	UNUSED F/NH	UNUSED F	USED F
233-43	**1¢-48¢ complete, 11 varieties ......**	**30.25**	**20.95**	**17.85**
233	1¢ Codfish	.50	.35	.25
234	3¢ Map, die I	2.05	1.40	.60
234a	3¢ same, die II ..	1.85	1.20	.45
235	7¢ Caribou	2.20	1.55	1.35
236	8¢ Paper Mills ...	2.20	1.55	1.50
237	10¢ Salmon	4.15	2.75	2.50
238	14¢ Newfoundland Dog	3.30	2.30	2.05
239	15¢ Northern Seal	3.30	2.30	2.05
240	20¢ Cape Race	2.75	1.95	1.65
241	24¢ Bell Island ..	3.60	2.55	2.30
242	25¢ Sealing Fleet	3.60	2.55	2.20
243	48¢ Fishing Fleet	4.15	2.75	2.50

249

2

250
249 surcharged

Newfoundland #245-270

OTT O.	DESCRIPTION	UNUSED F/NH	UNUSED F	USED F
	1938 ROYAL FAMILY Perf. 13-1/2			
48	**2¢-7¢ complete, 4 varieties ....**	**6.55**	**4.45**	**1.65**
	2¢ green	1.65	1.10	.15
	3¢ dark carmine	1.85	1.10	.15
	4¢ light blue	1.95	1.40	.15
	7¢ dark ultramarine	1.65	1.10	1.20
	5¢ violet blue	.85	.60	.60
	249 SURCHARGED			
	2¢ on 5¢ violet blue	1.30	.95	.95
	4¢ on 5¢ violet blue	1.00	.75	.75

252

267

OTT O.	DESCRIPTION	UNUSED F/NH	UNUSED F	USED F
	1941 GRENFELL ISSUE			
	5¢ dull blue	.45	.35	.35
	1941-44 RESOURCES ISSUE Designs of 1931-38. Perf. 12-1/2			
-66	**1¢-48¢ complete, 14 varieties ......**	**16.25**	**10.25**	**10.30**
	1¢ dark gray	.30	.20	.15
	2¢ deep green ..	.30	.20	.15
	3¢ rose carmine	.30	.25	.15
	4¢ blue	.65	.45	.15
	5¢ violet	.65	.50	.15
	7¢ violet blue (1942)	1.00	.65	.85
	8¢ red	.85	.65	.60
	10¢ brownish black	.85	.55	.55
	14¢ black	1.65	1.10	1.20
	15¢ pale rose violet	1.65	1.10	1.20
	20¢ green	1.65	1.10	1.20
	24¢ deep blue ...	1.95	1.35	1.55
	25¢ slate	1.95	1.35	1.55
	48¢ red brown (1944)	3.30	2.20	1.40

TWO

CENTS

268
267 surcharged

269

270

SCOTT NO.	DESCRIPTION	UNUSED F/NH	UNUSED F	USED F
	1943-47			
267	30¢ Memorial University	1.45	1.05	.95
268	2¢ on 30¢ University (1946)	.35	.30	.30
269	4¢ Princess Elizabeth (1947)	.35	.30	.15
270	5¢ Cabot (1947)	.35	.30	.15

Newfoundland #C2-C12

AIR POST STAMPS

Trans-Atlantic
AIR POST,
1919.
ONE DOLLAR.

C2
70 surcharged

AIR MAIL
to Halifax, N.S.
1921

C3
73 overprinted

Air Mail
DE PINEDO
1927

C4
74 overprinted

Trans-Atlantic
AIR MAIL
By B. M.
"Columbia"
September
1930
Fifty Cents

C5
126 surcharged

C6, C9
Airplane and Dog Team

SCOTT NO.	DESCRIPTION	UNUSED N.H. VF	UNUSED N.H. F	UNUSED N.H. AVG	UNUSED VF	UNUSED F	UNUSED AVG	USED VF	USED F	USED AV
	1919									
C2	$1 on 15¢ scarlet	320.00	247.50	150.00	214.50	165.00	107.25	235.00	181.50	107.2
C2a	same without comma after "POST"	400.00	308.00	185.00	285.00	220.00	128.50	285.00	220.00	126.5
	1921									
C3	35¢ red	250.00	192.50	115.00	170.00	132.00	77.00	170.00	132.00	77.0
C3a	same with period after "1921"	265.00	203.50	122.50	195.00	148.50	88.00	195.00	148.50	88.0

C7, C10
First Trans-atlantic Airmail

C8, C11
Routes of Historic Trans-atlantic Flights

SCOTT NO.	DESCRIPTION	UNUSED N.H. VF	UNUSED N.H. F	UNUSED N.H. AVG	UNUSED VF	UNUSED F	UNUSED AVG	USED VF	USED F	USED AV
	1931 Unwatermarked									
C6	15¢ brown	12.85	9.90	5.95	8.50	6.60	4.40	8.50	6.60	4.4
C7	50¢ green	32.15	24.75	15.00	21.50	16.50	11.00	23.50	18.15	12.6
C8	$1 blue	85.75	66.00	39.50	57.25	44.00	30.25	60.00	46.75	31.3
	Watermarked Coat of Arms									
C9	15¢ brown	10.00	7.70	4.56	7.15	5.50	3.30	7.15	5.50	3.3
C10	50¢ green	50.00	38.50	23.00	32.15	24.75	16.50	30.75	23.65	15.9
C11	$1 blue	120.00	93.50	56.00	78.50	60.50	42.35	75.00	57.75	38.5

TRANS-ATLANTIC
WEST TO EAST
Per Dornier DO-X
May, 1932.
One Dollar and Fifty Cents

C12
C11 surcharged

C13

SCOTT NO.	DESCRIPTION	UNUSED N.H. VF	UNUSED N.H. F	UNUSED N.H. AVG	UNUSED VF	UNUSED F	UNUSED AVG	USED VF	USED F	USED AV
	1932 TRANS-ATLANTIC FLIGHT									
C12	$1.50 on $1 blue	470.00	360.00	225.00	360.00	275.00	181.50	360.00	275.00	181.5

Newfoundland #C13-C19

C14

C15

1933 LABRADOR ISSUE

SCOTT NO.	DESCRIPTION	UNUSED N.H. VF	F	AVG	UNUSED VF	F	AVG	USED VF	F	AVG
C13-17	**5¢-75¢ complete, 5 varieties ....**	**206.00**	**172.50**	**103.50**	**135.00**	**112.50**	**75.00**	**135.00**	**112.50**	**75.00**
C13	5¢ "Put to Flight"	15.85	13.20	7.95	9.90	8.25	5.75	9.90	8.25	5.80
C14	10¢ "Land of Heart's Delight" .	23.75	19.80	11.85	13.75	11.55	8.00	13.75	11.55	8.00
C15	30¢ "Spotting the Herd"	39.50	33.00	19.75	26.50	22.00	14.85	26.50	22.00	14.85
C16	60¢ "News from Home"	69.25	57.75	34.75	46.25	38.50	24.75	46.25	38.50	24.75
C17	75¢ "Labrador, The Land of Gold"	69.25	57.75	34.75	46.25	38.00	25.85	46.25	38.00	25.85

C16

C17

1933
GEN. BALBO
FLIGHT.
$4.50

C18
C17 Surcharged

1933 BALBOA FLIGHT ISSUE

SCOTT NO.	DESCRIPTION	UNUSED N.H. VF	F	AVG	UNUSED VF	F	AVG	USED VF	F	AVG
C18	$4.50 on 75¢ bistre	650.00	545.00	330.00	460.00	385.00	302.50	460.00	385.00	302.50

C19

1943

SCOTT NO.	DESCRIPTION	UNUSED N.H. VF	F	AVG	UNUSED VF	F	AVG	USED VF	F	AVG
C19	7¢ St. John's	.55	.45	.40	.50	.40	.35	.30	.25	.15

POSTAGE DUE STAMPS

J1

1939 Unwatermarked, Perf. 10-1/2x10

SCOTT NO.	DESCRIPTION	UNUSED F/NH	UNUSED F	USED F
J1	1¢ yellow green	2.50	1.65	1.65
J2	2¢ vermillion	3.85	2.50	2.50
J3	3¢ ultramarine ..	4.95	3.30	3.30
J4	4¢ yellow orange	6.05	4.15	4.15
J5	5¢ pale brown ...	4.15	2.75	2.75
J6	10¢ dark violet ..	3.85	2.65	2.65

1946-49
Unwatermarked, Perf. 11

SCOTT NO.	DESCRIPTION	UNUSED F/NH	UNUSED F	USED F
J1a	1¢ yellow green	4.95	3.30	3.30
	Unwatermarked, Perf. 11x9			
J2a	2¢ vermillion	4.95	3.30	3.30
J3a	3¢ ultramarine ..	5.50	3.85	3.85
J4a	4¢ yellow orange	7.15	4.95	4.95
	Watermarked, Perf. 11			
J7	10¢ dark violet ..	9.35	6.35	6.35

NEW BRUNSWICK

1
Crown of Great Britain surrounded by Heraldic Flowers of the United Kingdom

6

7

8

9

10

1851 PENCE ISSUE. Imperforate

SCOTT NO.	DESCRIPTION	UNUSED O.G. VF	UNUSED O.G. F	UNUSED O.G. AVG	UNUSED VF	UNUSED F	UNUSED AVG	USED VF	USED F	USED AVG
1	3p red	2025.00	1565.00	865.00	1350.00	1045.00	577.50	285.00	220.00	137.50
2	6p olive yellow	4800.00	3700.00	2250.00	3200.00	2475.00	1495.00	715.00	550.00	275.00
3	1sh bright red violet .	16750.00	11200.00	8000.00	10000.00	8000.00	5000.00	3350.00	2400.00	1210.00
4	1sh dull violet	14000.00	10500.00	7700.00	10000.00	7700.00	4800.00	4200.00	3000.00	1595.00

11

1860-63 CENTS ISSUE
(NH + 50%)

SCOTT NO.	DESCRIPTION	UNUSED O.G. VF	UNUSED O.G. F	UNUSED O.G. AVG	UNUSED VF	UNUSED F	UNUSED AVG	USED VF	USED F	USED AVG
6	1¢ Locomotive	18.85	14.30	9.25	14.50	11.00	7.15	14.50	11.00	7.15
7	2¢ Queen Victoria, orange (1863)	10.25	7.85	4.70	7.85	6.05	3.60	7.85	6.05	3.60
8	5¢ same, yellow green	8.45	6.45	4.25	6.50	4.95	3.30	6.50	4.95	3.30
9	10¢ same, vermillion	34.45	26.45	17.15	26.50	20.35	13.20	26.50	20.35	11.00
10	12-1/2¢ Ships	41.95	33.50	22.85	32.25	25.85	17.60	32.25	24.75	16.50
11	17¢ Prince of Wales	37.00	28.50	19.30	28.50	22.00	14.85	28.50	22.00	14.85

Nova Scotia #1-13

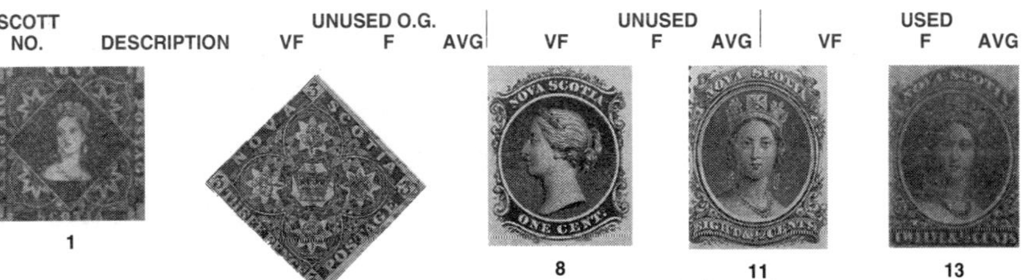

1

8

11
Queen Victoria

13

2, 3
Royal Crown and Heraldic Flowers of the United Kingdom

SCOTT NO.	DESCRIPTION	UNUSED O.G. VF	UNUSED O.G. F	UNUSED O.G. AVG	UNUSED VF	UNUSED F	UNUSED AVG	USED VF	USED F	USED AVG
	1851-53 PENCE ISSUE Imperf. Blue Paper									
1	1p Queen Victoria ...	2250.00	1725.00	925.00	1500.00	1155.00	616.00	285.00	220.00	148.50
2	3p blue	895.00	685.00	385.00	595.00	457.00	242.00	105.00	82.50	55.00
3	3p dark blue	1295.00	990.00	545.00	860.00	660.00	363.00	92.50	71.50	49.50
4	6p yellow green	3485.00	2675.00	2050.00	2325.00	1785.00	1375.00	430.00	330.00	220.00
5	6p dark green	7650.00	5885.00	4535.00	5100.00	3925.00	3025.00	775.00	577.50	385.00
6	1sh reddish violet	22500.00	14750.00	12500.00	16500.00	12500.00	8000.00	2800.00	2150.00	1650.00
7	1sh dull violet	22500.00	14750.00	12500.00	16500.00	12500.00	8000.00	42800.00	2150.00	1650.00
	1860-63 CENTS ISSUE White or Yellowish Paper, Perf. 12 (NH + 50%)									
8	1¢ black	6.50	4.30	2.65	5.40	3.60	2.20	4.95	3.30	2.20
9	2¢ lilac	8.85	5.95	3.95	7.40	4.95	3.30	7.40	4.95	3.30
10	5¢ blue	340.00	230.00	150.00	285.00	192.50	126.50	11.50	7.70	4.25
11	8-1/2¢ green	5.95	3.95	2.65	4.95	3.30	2.20	19.75	13.20	8.25
12	10¢ vermillion	8.85	5.95	3.95	7.40	4.95	3.30	7.40	4.95	3.30
13	12-1/2¢ black	29.75	19.75	15.00	24.75	16.50	12.65	24.75	16.50	11.55

Prince Edward Island #1-16

1, 5 2, 6 3, 7 4 8 9

Queen Victoria

1861 PENCE ISSUE, Perf. 9

SCOTT NO.	DESCRIPTION	UNUSED O.G. VF	UNUSED O.G. F	UNUSED O.G. AVG	UNUSED VF	UNUSED F	UNUSED AVG	USED VF	USED F	USED AVG
1	2p dull rose	480.00	370.00	230.00	320.00	247.50	154.00	145.00	110.00	77.00
2	3p blue	855.00	660.00	130.00	570.00	440.00	286.00	320.00	247.50	165.00
3	6p yellow green	1290.00	990.00	660.00	860.00	660.00	440.00	430.00	330.00	220.00

1862-65 PENCE ISSUE, Perf. 11 to 12
(NH + 50%)

SCOTT NO.	DESCRIPTION	UNUSED O.G. VF	UNUSED O.G. F	UNUSED O.G. AVG	UNUSED VF	UNUSED F	UNUSED AVG	USED VF	USED F	USED AVG
4	1p yellow orange	25.00	19.25	13.50	19.25	14.85	10.45	19.25	14.85	10.45
5	2p rose	7.50	5.75	3.60	5.75	4.40	2.75	5.75	4.40	2.75
6	3p blue	12.00	7.85	4.30	9.30	6.05	3.30	7.15	5.50	3.30
7	6p yellow green	90.00	53.50	35.75	69.50	41.25	27.50	53.50	41.25	27.50
8	9p violet	60.50	35.75	23.50	46.50	27.50	18.15	35.75	27.50	18.15

1868-70 PENCE ISSUE
(NH + 50%)

SCOTT NO.	DESCRIPTION	UNUSED O.G. VF	UNUSED O.G. F	UNUSED O.G. AVG	UNUSED VF	UNUSED F	UNUSED AVG	USED VF	USED F	USED AVG
9	4p black	10.25	7.85	5.40	7.85	6.05	4.15	19.25	14.85	9.35
10	4-1/2p brown (1870)	46.50	35.75	25.00	35.75	27.50	19.25	43.00	33.00	22.00

10 11 12 13 14 15

Queen Victoria

16

Queen Victoria

1872 CENTS ISSUE
(NH + 40%)

SCOTT NO.	DESCRIPTION	UNUSED O.G. VF	UNUSED O.G. F	UNUSED O.G. AVG	UNUSED VF	UNUSED F	UNUSED AVG	USED VF	USED F	USED AVG
11	1¢ brown orange	6.00	4.60	3.00	5.00	3.85	2.50	9.30	7.15	4.70
12	2¢ ultramarine	12.90	9.90	6.60	10.75	8.25	5.50	23.50	18.15	12.10
13	3¢ rose	20.75	15.85	10.55	17.25	13.20	8.80	15.00	11.55	7.70
14	4¢ green	6.90	5.25	3.65	5.75	4.40	3.05	26.50	20.35	13.75
15	6¢ black	5.75	4.30	3.30	4.75	3.60	2.75	23.50	18.15	12.10
16	12¢ violet	6.50	5.00	3.30	5.40	4.15	2.75	35.75	27.50	20.35

Economically priced

UNITED STATES ALBUMS

INDEPENDENCE U.S. ALBUM

Contains the same information as the popular U.S. Liberty Album. Pages are printed both sides to make an excellent, economical album. Colorful illustrated binder. Expandable; loose-leaf. Over 200 pages.

1HRS28—Independence Album
$18.95

2HRS2—Independence expansion binder, 1-3/4" size
$10.95

NEW FREEDOM U.S. ALBUM

Ideal for the beginning collector—an economical album with the same basic contents as the Independence Album. Over 200 pages.Colorful, softbound cover.

1HRS29—Freedom III Album
$10.95

Continuing the Harris Tradition for quality... and now more affordable than ever!

U.S. BINDERS

(pages not included)

(#2HRS1)	Liberty 2" Traditional binder.	**$11.95**
(#2HRS13)	Liberty 2-1/2" Traditional binder	**$12.95**
(#2HRS2)	Independence 1-3/4" chipboard binder)	**$10.95**

Order from your local dealer or direct from H.E. Harris.

FIRST DAY COVER ALBUM

Handsome and durable loose-leaf album to protect and display all your covers

Luxurious leather-look album with gold-stamped title displays first day covers in clear vinyl pages. Two pockets per page; each 20-page album holds 80 covers back-to-back. Durable two-post loose-leaf binder makes it simple to add extra pages as your collection grows.

1HRS30—Harris First Day Cover Album **$16.95**

Round out your collection

WORLDWIDE STAMP ALBUMS

(All albums include pages for U.S. stamps)

STATESMAN ALBUM

Our most popular loose-leaf album! Covers all stamp-issuing countries, with space for more than 25,000 stamps. Includes interesting historical and geographical information. Vinyl loose-leaf binder. 660 pages (330 sheets) printed on both sides.

1HRS15—Statesman Album **$37.95**
2HRS6—Statesman Expansion Binder, 2" size **$11.95**

STATESMAN HEIRLOOM ALBUM

Same pages as the new Statesman Traditional Album (1HRS15) and housed in the Worldwide Edition Heirloom Binder in your choice of 2-1/2" or 3-1/2" capacity.

1HRS25—Statesman Heirloom (2-1/2) **$39.95**
1HRS26—Statesman Heirloom (3-1/2) **$42.95**
2HRS7—Heirloom Expansion Binder (2-1/2) **$16.95**
2HRS8—Heirloom Expansion Binder (3-1/2) **$18.95**

ALL PURPOSE VINYL BINDER

Durable vinyl screw-post binder accommodates extra pages, Speed-rille® pages and all Harris supplements.

2HRS10—All Purpose Binder (Maroon) **$10.95**

Order from your local dealer or direct from H.E. Harris.

HEIRLOOM

U.S., Worldwide & Canada Edition
Loose-leaf Binders
Distinctive quality that lasts for generations

Made for distinction and quality in elegant leather grain vinyl. Each is embossed in rich gold tone—the U.S. edition with the Great Seal of the United States, the Worldwide edition with a stylized world map and the Canada edition with a maple leaf motif. A built-in label holder on the spine gives the option of organizing a collection however the collector wishes. Available in 2-1/2" and 3-1/2" spine widths to meet your collection needs.

2HRS3—U.S. Heirloom (2-1/2") **$16.95**
2HRS4—U.S. Heirloom (3-1/2") **$18.95**
2HRS7—Worldwide Heirloom (2-1/2") **$16.95**
2HRS8—Worldwide Heirloom (3-1/2") **$18.95**
2HRS11—Canada Heirloom (2-1/2") **$15.95**

Order from your local dealer or direct from H.E. Harris.

HOW TO WRITE YOUR ORDER

Please use order form

1. Print all requested information (name, address, etc.)
2. Indicate quantity, country (U.S, UN, CAN or province), catalog number, item description (sgle., pt. block, F.D. cover, etc.)
3. Specify condition (F, VF, NH etc.) and check whether used or unused.
4. Enter price as listed in this catalog.
5. Total all purchases, adding shipping/handling charge from table below. Alabama residents (only) also add sales tax.
6. Payment may be made by check, money order, or credit card (VISA, Discover or MasterCard accepted). ORDERS FROM OUTSIDE THE U.S. MUST BE PAID BY CREDIT CARD, and all payment must be in U.S. funds.

SHIPPING AND HANDLING CHARGES

Safe delivery by mail or U.P.S. is guaranteed. We assume all losses. The following charges cover only part of actual postage or freight, insurance and handling cost.

If "TOTAL ALL PAGES" AMOUNT IS:

$50.00 or less .... add $3.50
$51.00 to $250.00 .... add $5.00
OVER $250.00 .... add $7.50

The H.E. HARRIS PERFORMANCE PLEDGE

- All stamps are genuine, exactly as described, and have been inspected by our staff experts.
- H.E. Harris & Co. upholds the standards set forth by the American Philatelic Society and the American Stamp Dealers Association.
- If you have any problem with your order, phone us at 1-800-528-3992. We will handle it to your complete satisfaction.
- 30 day return privilege on all merchandise.

P.O. Box 817, Florence, AL 35631

Please print.

Name ______________________________

Address ______________________________

City/State/Zip ______________________________

Phone (in case of question about your order) ______________________________

FOR CREDIT CARD ORDERS

CARD # ☐☐☐☐☐☐☐☐☐☐☐☐☐☐☐☐

EXPIRATION DATE: MONTH ☐ YEAR ☐

❑ VISA ❑ DISCOVER ❑ MASTERCARD

Cardholder Signature ______________________________

Qty.	Country, Catalog and Description	Cond.	Unused	Used	Price	Office Use

If necessary, continue order on reverse side. Total both sides here.		
	Total all merchandise	
	Shipping/Handling (see table, facing page)	
	AL residents add sales tax	
	TOTAL PURCHASE	

Quantity	Country, Catalog and Description	Condition	Unused	Used	Price	Office Use

Quantity	Country, Catalog and Description	Condition	Unused	Used	Price	Office Use

Quantity	Country, Catalog and Description	Condition	Unused	Used	Price	Office Use

H.E. Harris & Co.®

P.O. Box 817, Florence, AL 35631

Please print.

Name ______________________________

Address ______________________________

City/State/Zip ______________________________

Phone (in case of question about your order) ______________________________

FOR CREDIT CARD ORDERS

CARD # | | | | | | | | | | | | | | | | |

EXPIRATION DATE: MONTH [ ] YEAR [ ]

❑ VISA ❑ DISCOVER ❑ MASTERCARD

Cardholder Signature ______________________________

Qty.	Country, Catalog and Description	Cond.	Unused	Used	Price	Office Use

If necessary, continue order on reverse side. Total both sides here.		
	Total all merchandise	
	Shipping/Handling (see table, facing page)	
	AL residents add sales tax	
	TOTAL PURCHASE	

Quantity	Country, Catalog and Description	Condition	Unused	Used	Price	Office Use

Quantity	Country, Catalog and Description	Condition	Unused	Used	Price	Office Use

Quantity	Country, Catalog and Description	Condition	Unused	Used	Price	Office Use

P.O. Box 817, Florence, AL 35631

Please print.

Name ___

Address ___

City/State/Zip ___

Phone (in case of question about your order) ___

FOR CREDIT CARD ORDERS

CARD # [ ][ ][ ][ ][ ][ ][ ][ ][ ][ ][ ][ ][ ][ ][ ][ ]

EXPIRATION DATE: MONTH [ ] YEAR [ ]

❑ VISA ❑ DISCOVER ❑ MASTERCARD

Cardholder Signature ___

Qty.	Country, Catalog and Description	Cond.	Unused	Used	Price	Office Use

If necessary, continue order on reverse side. Total both sides here.	
Total all merchandise	
Shipping/Handling (see table, facing page)	
AL residents add sales tax	
TOTAL PURCHASE	

Quantity	Country, Catalog and Description	Condition	Unused	Used	Price	Office Use

Quantity	Country, Catalog and Description	Condition	Unused	Used	Price	Office Use

Quantity	Country, Catalog and Description	Condition	Unused	Used	Price	Office Use

P.O. Box 817, Florence, AL 35631

Please print.

Name ______________________________

Address ______________________________

City/State/Zip ______________________________

Phone (in case of question about your order) ______________________________

FOR CREDIT CARD ORDERS

CARD # | | | | | | | | | | | | | | | | |

EXPIRATION DATE: MONTH ______ YEAR ______

❑ VISA ❑ DISCOVER ❑ MASTERCARD

Cardholder Signature ______________________________

Qty.	Country, Catalog and Description	Cond.	Unused	Used	Price	Office Use

If necessary, continue order on reverse side. Total both sides here.		
	Total all merchandise	
	Shipping/Handling (see table, facing page)	
	AL residents add sales tax	
	TOTAL PURCHASE	

Quantity	Country, Catalog and Description	Condition	Unused	Used	Price	Office Use

Quantity	Country, Catalog and Description	Condition	Unused	Used	Price	Office Use

Quantity	Country, Catalog and Description	Condition	Unused	Used	Price	Office Use

P.O. Box 817, Florence, AL 35631

Please print.

Name ____________________

Address ____________________

City/State/Zip ____________________

Phone (in case of question about your order) ____________________

FOR CREDIT CARD ORDERS

CARD # [| | | | | | | | | | | | | | |]

EXPIRATION DATE: MONTH [ ] YEAR [ ]

❏ VISA ❏ DISCOVER ❏ MASTERCARD

Cardholder Signature ____________________

Qty.	Country, Catalog and Description	Cond.	Unused	Used	Price	Office Use

If necessary, continue order on reverse side. Total both sides here.		
	Total all merchandise	
	Shipping/Handling (see table, facing page)	
	AL residents add sales tax	
	TOTAL PURCHASE	

Quantity	Country, Catalog and Description	Condition	Unused	Used	Price	Office Use

Quantity	Country, Catalog and Description	Condition	Unused	Used	Price	Office Use